FUNDAMENTALS OF SCOTS LAW

AUSTRALIA
Law Book Co.
Sydney

CANADA and USA
Carswell
Toronto

HONG KONG
Sweet & Maxwell Asia

NEW ZEALAND
Brookers
Wellington

SINGAPORE and MALAYSIA
Sweet & Maxwell Asia
Singapore and Kuala Lumpur

FUNDAMENTALS OF SCOTS LAW

By

Christina Ashton
David Brand
Dr Douglas Brodie
James Chalmers
Professor Vic Craig
Stuart R. Cross
Valerie Finch
Alasdair Gordon
Dr Anne Griffiths
Professor Hector MacQueen

Published in 2003 by

W. Green & Son Ltd
21 Alva Street
Edinburgh EH2 4PS

www.wgreen.co.uk

Printed in Great Britain by
Ashford Colour Press, Gosport, Hants

No natural forests were destroyed to make this product;
Only farmed timber was used and replanted

A CIP catalogue record for this book is available from the British Library

ISBN 0 414 01451 0

Preface

The original concept for this book was to build upon the great success that Enid Marshall achieved with her textbook *General Principles on Scots Law* (all seven editions). As many readers shall be aware, Enid wrote a number of our most successful student texts over a great number of years and we are extremely proud to have been associated with her books which have helped generations of students. Indeed, it is not an exaggeration to say that they also changed the face of Scottish textbooks and many of the books which followed owe much to these works which married accessibility with extremely high standards of scholarship.

What better way to take Marshall's traditional multi-subject concept to a new level than to make a fresh start by bringing together an expert multi-contributor team of current scholars and lecturers, spanning both the "old" and "new" law schools, from across the whole of Scotland?

From the outset it was felt that we had a great opportunity to develop a new type of legal textbook. Textbooks for other professional subjects were making good use of new typesetting methods to benefit the reader, so why should a legal textbook not follow suit? Thus, a great deal of research was undertaken to analyse how textbooks in other professional areas were developing and which new features we could, and more importantly should, employ. We hope we have achieved a reader-friendly method which not only provides an up-to-date, clear and concise account of a broad range of legal topics but contributes towards a genuine understanding of the diverse aspects of Scots law for students who are studying Scots law as their main degree or as a part of another course in Scotland.

We have also grasped the opportunity to add revision appendices to assist students to apply their understanding gained through reading this book in an exam environment.

Of course, there are a great number of people whom our contributors wish to acknowledge, including Professor Eric Clive, Martin Hogg, Dr David Nichols, David Sellar, Professor Niall Whitty, and, of course, all of the contributors' respective families.

Finally, I would like to thank all of the contributors for being so open-minded and dedicated to the project. Also special mention must go to Stephen Chubb, Head of Editorial Operations, and Alan Bett, Marketing Executive, at W. Green for following us on this quest to bring a genuine understanding of the fundamentals of Scots Law to students.

Neil M. McKinlay
Senior Commissioning Editor, W. Green
July 2003

CONTENTS

TABLE OF CASES

TABLE OF STATUTES

1424 Act of 1424 2–03
Royal Mines Act (c.12) 0–33, 10–34
1449 Leases Act (c.12) 10–59, 10–60, 10–64, 12–65
1469 Prescription Act (c.28) 2–03
1567 Incest Act (c.15) 14–34
1594 Patricide Act 12–08
1573 Act of 1573 (c.55) 2–03
1592 Compensation Act (c.143) 5–92
1617 Prescription Act (c.12) 10–31
Registration Act (c.16) 10–29, 10–30
1662 Act of Sederunt 11–43
1696 Blank Bonds and Trusts Act (c.25) 13–77
1700 Act of Settlement (12 and 13 Will. 3, c.2) 3–06, 3–24, 3–56
s.11(3) 3–15
1706 Protestant Religion and Presbyterian Church Act 3–56
1707 Union with England Act (c.7) 3–06, 3–29, 4–03, 4–21
Union with Scotland Act (6 Ann. c.11) 2–02, 2–14, 3–06, 3–29, 4–03, 4–21
1746 Tenures Abolition Act (20 Geo. 2 (1746–7) c.50) 10–29
1801 Union with Ireland Act 3–29
1849 Judicial Factors Act (12 and 13 Vict. c.51)
s.11 11–51
1853 Universities (Scotland) Act 3–29
1857 Registration of Leases (Scotland) Act (20 and 21 Vict. c.26) 10–59
1862 Moveable Property (Scotland) Act 10–20
1874 Conveyancing (Scotland) Act (37 and 38 Vict. c.94)
s.39 12–29
1880 Married Women's Policies of Assurance (Scotland) Act (43 and 44 Vict. c.26) 12–45
s.2 13–34
1881 Presumption of Life Limitation (Scotland) Act 12–04
1882 Bills of Exchange Act (45 and 46 Vict. c.61)
s.60 8–23
1887 Criminal Procedure (Scotland) Act (50 and 51 Vict. c.35)
s.56 14–49
s.61 14–45
1889 Herring Fishery (Scotland) Act (52 and 53 Vict. c.23) 3–30
1890 Factors (Scotland) Act
s.1(1) 7–08
Partnership Act (53 and 54 Vict. c.39) 6–45
s.4(2) 6–45
s.5 .... 7–01, 7–06, 7–13, 7–21, 7–24
s.8 7–24
s.36(1) 7–43
(2) 7–43
1907 Sheriff Courts (Scotland) Act (7 Edw. 7 c.51) 1–05, 10–64
1911 Parliament Act (1 and 2 Geo. 5 c.13) 2–10, 3–06, 3–12, 3–22, 3–36, 3–42 3–46
Official Secrets Act (1 and 2 Geo. 5 c.28) 1–27
1914 Entail (Scotland) Act (4 and 5 Geo. 5 c.43) 11–22
1919 Acquisition of Land (Assessment of Compensation) Act (9 and 10 Geo. 5 c.57)
s.7 3–27
1920 Government of Ireland Act (10 and 11 Geo. 5 c.67) 3–29
Official Secrets Act (10 and 11 Geo. 5 c.75) 1–27
1921 Trusts (Scotland) Act (11 and 12 Geo. 5 c.58) 11–60
s.3 .... 11–30, 11–31
(a) 11–31
(c) 11–35, 12–64
s.4 .... 11–50, 11–51, 11–65
(1)(a)–(ee) 11–65
(f) 11–38

TABLE OF STATUTORY INSTRUMENTS

Chapter 1

STRUCTURE OF THE LEGAL SYSTEM

Christina Ashton[1]

INTRODUCTION

In this Chapter we will consider how the legal system operates as a broad concept, examining the courts and tribunals as well as the people who work in the legal profession. **1–01**

The Scottish courts are divided into two distinct and separate systems, each with its own jurisdiction, and indeed as will be seen, its own language.

CIVIL LEGAL SYSTEM

The civil courts in Scotland are the sheriff court, the Court of Session and the House of Lords. The Court of Session is divided into two distinct parts—the Inner House and the Outer House. **1–02**

Civil cases are adversarial, meaning that the judge will hear legal argument and evidence from all of the parties and then make a judgment based on the "balance of probabilities". This standard of proof is not as high as is required in criminal cases. Where a case involves the interpretation or validity of EU law, the court in Scotland will suspend the case until a ruling on the matter has been sought from the European Court of Justice. Once that ruling has been made, the domestic court will apply it to the facts of the case and make a decision.

---

[1] Lecturer in Law, Napier University.

Sheriff court

1–03 This is the busiest court in Scotland because it deals with both civil and criminal matters. It is essentially a local court. Since 1975, Scotland has been divided up into six sheriffdoms.

Key Concepts

The Sheriffdoms:

- Grampian, Highland and Islands;
- Tayside, Central and Fife;
- Lothian and Borders;
- Glasgow and Strathkelvin;
- North Strathclyde; and
- South Strathclyde, Dumfries and Galloway.

Each sheriffdom is headed by a Sheriff Principal, who is a full-time judge and administers the work of the sheriffdom. He is assisted by a number of sheriffs, around 15 in each sheriffdom, except Glasgow and Strathkelvin where the number is greater. Both sheriffs and the Sheriff Principal are required to be solicitors or advocates of at least ten years standing and they now retire at age 70.[2] They are appointed by the monarch on the recommendation of the First Minister after consultation with the Lord President. The Sheriff Principal may act as an appeal judge in certain types of action.

Each sheriffdom (except Glasgow and Strathkelvin) is divided into districts; there are 49 currently throughout Scotland. One or more sheriffs will be appointed to sit in the sheriff court in one of these districts, but each sheriff has jurisdiction over all matters occurring anywhere within the sheriffdom. The sheriff court is a "court of first instance", *i.e.* cases will start and be determined there.

The boundaries of the sheriffdoms can be altered by The Scottish Ministers at any time under the terms of the Sheriff Courts (Scotland) Act 1971.

In late 1999, a crisis hit the legal system as a result of the incorporation of the European Convention on Human Rights into Scots Law.

Starrs v Ruxton

2000 J.C. 208

In this case an accused man was able to plead that he did not have a fair trial as required by the Convention because the temporary sheriff who heard his case was not impartial. He was able to argue this because temporary sheriffs were appointed by the Secretary of State for Scotland on the advice of the Lord Advocate,[3] held office for short periods of time and could be dismissed at short notice. They did not have security of tenure of office because they depended on the Lord Advocate's "good will" to have their contracts renewed. This was held to be contrary to Article 6(1) of the Convention.

---

[2] Judicial Pensions and Retirement Act 1993. Note that those appointed prior to 1995 are required to retire at 72.

[3] Sheriff Courts (Scotland) Act 1971, s.11.

As a result of this case, all 126 temporary sheriffs had to be dismissed and a new system put into place. They have now been replaced by part-time sheriffs who hold office for a fixed term and cannot be dismissed without good cause.[4]

Jurisdiction of the sheriff court

The civil jurisdiction of the sheriff court is considerable. There are two aspects to the jurisdiction: **1–04**

(a) jurisdiction over persons; and
(b) jurisdiction because of the subject-matter.

Jurisdiction over persons

The general principle is that a case will be heard by the court which has jurisdiction over the **1–05** defender. The legal maxim is *actor sequitur forum rei*—the pursuer follows the court of the defender. The defender must normally either live in the sheriffdom or have a place of business there.

The Civil Jurisdiction and Judgments Act 1982 controls jurisdiction in a number of areas. This Act was passed primarily to give effect to the Brussels Convention of 1968 but it has wider scope than the Convention. Its provisions give effect to judgments made by a court in one part of the UK, as well as courts outside the EU area. A new set of rules for jurisdiction in Scotland was also introduced.

Key Concepts

The main rules under the **1982 Act** are:

- a person may be sued in the court where s/he is domiciled, *i.e.* where s/he has a usual residence;
- if the person has no fixed address, the court with jurisdiction will be where s/he is personally cited, *i.e.* handed the summons to appear in court;
- if the matter concerns a contract, the jurisdiction will lie with the court where the contract is to be performed;
- if the matter concerns a delict, the jurisdiction will lie with the court where the wrongful act occurred;
- if the matter involves a consumer contract, the consumer may sue the other party in the court where he is domiciled. This is a special rule to protect consumers and ensure that their legal expenses are kept to the minimum.

If the rules of the 1982 Act do not apply to the matter, the jurisdiction rules are as in the Sheriff Courts (Scotland) Act 1907, as amended.

[4] Bail, Judicial Appointments etc. (Scotland) Act 2000.

> **Key Concepts**
>
> **Jurisdiction rules** under the Sheriff Courts (Scotland) Act 1907:
>
> - the defender resides in the sheriffdom, or has recently done so (within the last 40 days) but has now moved and has no known address in Scotland;
> - the defender has a business in the sheriffdom and is personally cited or cited at his place of business;
> - the defender is the owner or tenant of heritable property situated in the sheriffdom and the case involves that property;
> - the action is concerned with a contract performed in the sheriffdom and the defender is personally cited there.

Subject-matter of the jurisdiction

1–06 Generally, a sheriff court has unlimited jurisdiction. However, some cases must be sent to a particular court for disposal. For instance, judicial review cases can only be heard in the Court of Session. Actions involving the status of a person, *e.g.* a declarator of marriage, may also only be heard in the Court of Session.

The sheriff court has privative jurisdiction, *i.e.* exclusive jurisdiction over certain matters and an action involving these must be raised in the sheriff court. Examples include actions involving sums of money less than £5,000.

Cases before the sheriff court

1–07 Sheriff courts deal with three types of cases:

Ordinary cause

1–08 These are cases involving sums of money over £5,000, or where another remedy is sought, *e.g.* recovery of heritable property, divorce, or aliment of children. A record of proceedings is kept so that an appeal can be made. The action is commenced by means of an "initial writ". It is possible for the sheriff to remit an ordinary cause to the Court of Session if the case is of sufficient importance or difficulty and any of the parties has requested this.

Summary cause

1–09 These mainly involve actions for sums of money between £1,500 and £5,000. Since June 2002,[5] an action of damages for personal injury must be brought as a summary cause, even though the sum sued for is less than £1,500. Actions of damages for defamation and actions of aliment are not competent as small claims actions and must be brought as a summary cause. No record is made of the proceedings, other than the notes taken by the sheriff. This will make an appeal more difficult.

---

[5] Act of Sederunt (Summary Cause Rules) 2002 (SSI 2002/132).

Small claims

This procedure was introduced as a new form of summary cause by the Law Reform (Miscellaneous Provisions) (Scotland) Act 1985. It is relatively informal and was devised to help individual citizens to resolve minor disputes where the amount claimed is less than £1,500 (for many years this was £750). The pursuer does not require to be legally represented and no record of the proceedings is made. As a result of the changes made in June 2002,[6] maximum expenses of £100 can be awarded where the sum claimed is between £200 and £1,000, and 10 per cent of the value of the claim for sums over £1,000. A claim of less than £200 will not attract expenses. **1–10**

Appeals from the sheriff court

Ordinary cause

An appeal from the sheriff may be made to the Sheriff Principal, and thence to the Inner House of the Court of Session. A further appeal to the House of Lords will be on a point of law only. **1–11**

Alternatively, an appeal can be made directly to the Inner House from the decision of the sheriff. This is more likely to happen when both parties are determined that they will appeal whatever the decision of the Sheriff Principal, or where the issue is one of importance and therefore requires a decision from a senior court.

A party will appeal to the Sheriff Principal where he is trying to keep costs down: an appeal to the Inner House will require representation by an advocate or solicitor-advocate, as well as the local solicitor. There is therefore considerable cost.

Summary cause

An appeal from the sheriff to the Sheriff Principal is allowed on a point of law only. A further appeal will lie on a point of law to the Inner House, and thence to the House of Lords. **1–12**

Small claims

An appeal from the sheriff will be to the Sheriff Principal on a point of law only. **1–13**

Court of Session

Established in 1532, the Court of Session sits in Parliament House, Edinburgh. Unless the matter is privative to the Court of Session, a pursuer may start his case in the sheriff court or the Court of Session. The pursuer will decide which court after asking himself certain questions, such as: **1–14**

- Is the claim for a large sum of money, say £100,000?
- Is there an important or difficult point of law involved? Do I therefore need an authoritative judgment?
- Do I have enough money to pay the legal fees?

The Court of Session is divided into two Houses—the Inner House and the Outer House. The terms come from when the court was being set up: a group of eminent judges would meet together in an inner room of Parliament House. Individual judges who were less experienced would meet with parties in other rooms of Parliament House—outer rooms. If a party did not like the judgment

---

6 Act of Sederunt (Small Claims Rules) 2002 (SSI 2002/133).

of the individual judge, he would go to the inner room and ask the group to look again at the matter. Thus, the appellate court known as the Inner House was created.

The main statute which covers the procedures and composition of the Court is the Court of Session Act 1988. Currently there is a maximum of 32 judges.[7] The retirement age for Senators of the College of Justice, as they are officially known, is 70 years.[8] Two of the judges are permanently seconded to other bodies: one to the Scottish Law Commission as its Chairman and the other to the Scottish Land Court. The most senior judge in the Court of Session is the Lord President, who, along with the second most senior judge, the Lord Justice Clerk, is appointed by the monarch on the nomination of the Prime Minister. The Prime Minister may only consider candidates recommended to him by the First Minister of the Scottish Executive. The judges in the Court of Session are appointed by the monarch on the recommendation of the First Minister after consultation with the Lord President. The judges will be sheriffs or sheriffs principal of five years' standing, or advocates or solicitors with five years' right of audience in the Court of Session. All of the judges in the Court of Session are also judges in the High Court of Justiciary. The Lord President takes the title of Lord Justice General when sitting in the High Court.

Outer House

1–15 This is a court of first instance, staffed by 20 judges. Cases are heard by a single judge, known as a Lord Ordinary.

Jurisdiction extends to all civil matters, except those which are privative to another court, or when the matter is specifically excluded by statute. Jurisdiction also extends to the whole of Scotland. Under the Civil Jurisdiction and Judgments Act 1982, jurisdiction will be over persons who are domiciled in Scotland.

Certain issues are privative to the Outer House, for instance, a petition seeking judicial review of an administrative decision must be commenced in the Outer House.

It is still possible to seek a jury trial in the Outer House although it is uncommon and is confined to a narrow range of uncomplicated cases, *e.g.* defamation or action for damages for personal injury. The jury would consist of 12 persons.

The normal method of raising an action is to issue a "summons" to the defender; this is essentially a statement of claim and summons the defender to appear in court to answer the claim. If the defender wishes to defend the claim, he will lodge written defences, answering the issues raised in the summons. These will form the basis of the "open record" and the two parties will then agree certain facts and each will answer the allegations made by the other. This process of agreement and answers will result in a "closed record" which is the final document presented to the Court. The closed record will have the pursuer's statement of the remedies he seeks (the conclusions), the agreed facts and those facts the pursuer avers (the condescendence), the facts as the defender sees them, the pursuer's pleas-in-law followed by the defender's pleas-in-law. If the case turns only on a question of fact, there will be a proof (trial) before the Lord Ordinary.

The decision of the court on a question of fact is called a "decree"—this may either grant the pursuer's request for remedy, or it may "assoilzie" the defender, *i.e.* state that he is not liable.

If the case requires a decision on a question of law, then the question of law must first be settled by the Lord Ordinary. The pleas-in-law are considered by the court and an interlocutor will be issued. This will "sustain" the pleas-in-law of one party and "repel" those of the other. If necessary, the interlocutor on the question of law will be applied to the questions of fact. On occasion, the Lord Ordinary will not be able to decide the question of law without knowing the facts of the case. The evidence will be heard first before the question of law is decided. This is called "proof before answer".

---

[7] Maximum Number of Judges (Scotland) Order 1999 (SSI 1999/158).
[8] Judicial Pensions and Retirement Act 1993.

The other main method of seeking the judgment of the court is to petition the court, *e.g.* to appoint new trustees or wind up a company. If the petition is opposed, the statement of opposition is called the "answers" and the party opposing is called the respondent.

Inner House

This is basically the appeal court, but it can be a court of first instance in limited circumstances, *e.g.* appeals against the decision of some tribunals and a petition to the *nobile officium*. **1–16**

The Inner House is divided into two Divisions, simply called the First Division and the Second Division. Each division has five judges. The First Division is headed by the Lord President, the most senior judge in Scotland. The Second Division is headed by the Lord Justice Clerk, the second most senior judge. If there is a heavy workload, an extra Division of five judges from the Outer House may be convened; currently there is an Extra Division sitting.

For most appeals, only three judges, called Lords of Session, will sit, but if the matter is particularly important or difficult, a bench of five or seven judges may be convened. An appeal will take the form of a "reclaiming motion" or a statutory "appeal". It is unusual for additional evidence to be heard in an appeal; the normal procedure is for the court to consider the legal arguments of the parties. The court may give a decision immediately, with one judge stating the decision and the reasons in an "opinion". If the issue is more difficult, the judges will make "avizandum" meaning that they will retire to consider their decision and give written opinions at a later date. A judge who does not agree with the majority of the bench will give a "dissenting" opinion. The decision of the Inner House will either take the form of "adhering" to the interlocutor of the Lord Ordinary (*i.e.* dismissing the appeal) or "recalling" the interlocutor of the Lord Ordinary and giving a different one.

House of Lords

The House of Lords is an appellate court and is the final court of appeal for civil cases from Scotland. There are relatively few appeals from Scotland: in 2001, there were only four appeals while in 2000 there were five. **1–17**

There are 12 Law Lords (Lords of Appeal in Ordinary) of whom normally two will be Scottish trained judges.[9] Although it is not a rule that a Scottish judge sits to hear an appeal from Scotland, it is usual for at least one of the five judges to be Scottish.

In an appeal from a decision of the Inner House, the appellant will petition the House "praying" that the interlocutor of the Inner House be altered. Once the House of Lords has given its judgment, the matter is returned to the Inner House to apply that judgment. The House of Lords will normally only hear appeals on important or difficult questions of law, or questions of fact and law.

After the Union of the Parliaments in 1707, there was doubt whether an appeal might be heard by the Lords. However, in *Greenshields v Magistrates of Edinburgh*,[10] the right to appeal to the House of Lords was established and has not been seriously challenged since.

European Court of Justice

Although not an appeal court within the Scottish legal system, the European Court of Justice is part of the system for any issues relating to matters covered by the European Treaties. It is a requirement that where such an issue arises in the case before the domestic court, the direction of **1–18**

[9] At the time of writing, these are Lord Hope and Lord Clyde.

[10] (1710–1711) Rob. 12.

the ECJ must either be sought, or if a decision already exists on the same issue, that decision must be followed by the domestic court.

There are four main types of cases which may be brought to the ECJ.

(1) *Proceedings brought by the Commission against a Member State (Art.226)*: This type of case may occur where the Commission considers that the Member State has failed to fulfil its obligations under the Treaties. The Commission must first ask the Member State for its observations and then the Commission will deliver a reasoned opinion on the matter if it still considers there is a failure. The Member State will be given an opportunity to fulfil its obligations, failing which the Commission will refer the matter to the ECJ. For instance, in *Commission v UK*,[11] the UK was held to be in default of its Community obligations because it had not complied with an EC Directive on sex equality. In *EC Commission v Belgium*,[12] the Belgian Government was unable to obtain parliamentary approval for a Treaty obligation because the Belgian Parliament had been dissolved. The ECJ found that the Member State was in default.

(2) *Proceedings by one Member State against another Member State (Art.228)*: The aggrieved Member State must first refer the matter to the Commission which is required to deliver a reasoned opinion on the issue. If the ECJ then finds that the Member State has failed to comply with a Treaty obligation, the Member State is obliged to take the necessary measures to comply. Continued failure will allow the Commission to bring an action to impose financial penalties on the Member State.

(3) *Proceedings by a Member State or Community institution against the Council or Commission (Art.230)*: It is open to a Member State or an institution of the Community to initiate proceedings against the Council or Commission on the ground that they have failed to act in accordance with the Treaty.

(4) *Preliminary rulings (Art.234)*: These are proceedings where a national court or tribunal seeks the judgment of the ECJ on an interpretation of the Treaty or the validity and interpretation of acts of the institutions. The ruling will be sought on specific questions asked by the domestic court: the ECJ does not resolve the dispute. Instead, the domestic court will apply the ruling to the facts of the case. In the UK, in *R. v International Stock Exchange Ex p. Else*,[13] Lord Bingham gave guidance on the circumstances when a preliminary ruling should be sought from the ECJ. The facts must first be established and then the court must find that the Community law issue is critical to the court's final decision. If the point is reasonably clear and free from doubt, the court may decline to make a reference.

In addition to these types of cases, the ECJ may give an Opinion on whether a particular legal measure or administrative action would conform with Community law. Such Opinions may be requested by the Council, Commission or any Member State. In 1994, the Council asked the Court whether the EC had the necessary competence to accede to the European Convention on Human Rights. In its Opinion 2/94, the ECJ argued that the Treaties would need to be amended by the Member States to enable the Community to accede to the Convention.[14]

CRIMINAL LEGAL SYSTEM

1–19 The criminal courts in Scotland are the district court, the sheriff court, the High Court of Justiciary as a trial court, and the High Court of Justiciary as an appeal court. In addition, cases may be sent to the European Court of Justice for interpretation of European Community law. Prosecutions are brought by the Crown "in the public interest". Reports of offences are made by the police and

---

[11] Case 165/82 [1984] 1 All E.R. 353.
[12] Case 77/69 [1970] E.C.R. 237.
[13] [1993] Q.B. 534.
[14] Opinion 2/94 [1996] E.C.R. I–1759.

other bodies to the procurator fiscal and the Crown Office. The number of these reports has now reached 285,000 each year.[15] Each report has to be considered and a decision made as to whether prosecution "in the public interest" is warranted. Around 118,000 cases are disposed of annually in the Scottish criminal courts.

Since the Scotland Act 1998 came into force, any cases involving devolution issues may be sent to the Judicial Committee of the Privy Council for decision.[16]

The criminal jurisdiction of the courts is split into two types of procedure—summary and solemn. Summary jurisdiction falls to the District and the Sheriff Summary court, where cases are heard "on complaint" by a judge sitting alone. In solemn jurisdiction, the accused appears "on indictment" and faces a judge sitting with a jury of 15 people. Although there are certain crimes and offences which must be heard in a particular court using either the summary or solemn procedure, it is generally at the discretion of the prosecutor to which court the accused will be directed. In most cases, the procurator fiscal decides whether or not to prosecute an accused person and will decide the venue of the prosecution. In serious cases, the procurator fiscal will consult with the Crown Office in Edinburgh, which is the office of the Lord Advocate, and an advocate-depute will decide whether the prosecution should proceed in the High Court of Justiciary. The procurator fiscal usually handles summary complaints while prosecutions on indictment, particularly those before the High Court of Justiciary, will be handled by an advocate-depute appointed by the Lord Advocate. In December 2002, the Justice Minister announced a new system for prosecutions of serious crimes. There will be three categories of prosecutor: senior advocates-depute who will handle the most serious crimes and decide which cases will be heard in the High Court; advocates-depute to handle the majority of the High Court cases; and *ad hoc* advocates-depute who will assist as required. For the first time, solicitor advocates and procurators fiscal will be included in the pool for advocates-depute.

The procedure for bringing and conducting prosecutions is covered by the Criminal Procedure (Scotland) Act 1995.

District court

The district court was created by the District Courts (Scotland) Act 1975 after the reorganisation **1–20**
of local authority areas and replaced the Justice of the Peace Courts and the Burgh Police Courts. The district court deals with minor crimes and offences and is mainly presided over by lay justices of the peace. In Glasgow District Court, the work is shared between lay justices and legally qualified stipendiary magistrates.

The district court is a local court, to be found in all local authority areas, except Orkney Council, where the work is done by the sheriff court. The area covered by the court is called the commission area and the justices are appointed to hold a commission for that area alone.

Each commission area has to have a Justices' Committee which decides on the court duty rota, arranges training for justices and oversees the administrative arrangements for the court. The frequency of the court's sitting will be decided according to the number of cases referred to it by the local procurator fiscal and it is up to the Justices' Committee in consultation with the Clerk of the Court to ensure that the court is staffed. The court may sit daily, or two or three times a week, or even only two or three times a month.

The Clerk of the Court is employed and appointed by the local authority and must be a solicitor or advocate. The council must also appoint a Clerk of the Peace (usually the same person as the Clerk of Court) and his statutory function is to advise the justices on their duties and perform administrative duties for the Justices' Committee (*e.g.* ensuring that an annual meeting of justices is held). The council is also responsible for providing suitable premises for the court and for ensuring that sufficient administrative and clerical staff and resources are available to service the court properly.

---

15 The number of recorded crimes was 427,000 in 2002.

16 See para. 1–33 below.

The Clerk of the Court, or a depute clerk, will act as legal assessor in the court, advising the justice on the law. The clerk is not however involved in making judicial decisions, such as guilt or innocence, or how far mitigating circumstances should affect a sentence. In August 2000, the position of the clerk as a legal adviser was challenged under the Scotland Act 1998 on the grounds that discussions between the justice and the clerk were not held in open court and therefore were contrary to Art.6 of the European Convention of Human Rights (right to a fair and impartial tribunal). The case was eventually heard by the Privy Council[17] which held that although part of the tribunal, the clerk is sufficiently independent in relation to his function to ensure the court's independence and impartiality.

The work of the district court is scrutinised by the Scottish Executive and by the Scottish Parliament. The First Minister is responsible for appointing most justices; he receives recommendations from the local Advisory Committee and appoints justices in the name of the Queen.

Some justices are councillors nominated for appointment by their councils. Up to one quarter of the council's membership may be so appointed. Until recently, many councillor J.P.s were active members of the bench but after a challenge to their position under the Scotland Act, the Scottish Executive advised that councillors should no longer serve on the bench. They are still available for signing duties.

There are few requirements for appointment as a justice, although it is required that a justice lives in the commission area or within 15 miles of it. Most justices are male, over 50 and white. Attempts have been made over the years to try to have a bench which is more representative of the community in which it works. Thus the number of younger people and women has increased, but the number of justices from ethnic communities is still too low.

Once a J.P. reaches the age of 70 s/he will be placed on the "supplemental list" and will no longer be able to sit on the bench. Currently, there are around 4,000 justices, but only 800 or so participate in court work. A justice may also be placed on the supplemental list if they become infirm or are negligent of their duties. The Bail, Judicial Appointments, etc. (Scotland) Act 2000[18] amended the District Courts (Scotland) Act 1975 so that a justice may be removed from office for "neglect of duty", which includes failure to undergo training.

Stipendiary magistrates are appointed by the local authority and are solicitors or advocates of at least five years' standing. They do not sit with a legal assessor, and they have the same powers of disposal as a sheriff sitting in a summary case.

Jurisdiction of the district court

1–21 The court has jurisdiction over any summary case which occurs in its commission area and which has been declared by statute to be within its competency. The main statute covering the jurisdiction of the district court is the Criminal Procedure (Scotland) Act 1995.

The kinds of cases heard by the court are common law offences, *e.g.* minor assault, breach of the peace, theft, and statutory offences such as parking offences, litter, and minor road offences. The district courts disposed of 42,000 cases in 2000–01, while the sheriff courts disposed of 72,000.

The district court and the sheriff court both hear cases using the summary procedure and the decision as to whether the case is heard in the District or sheriff court is for the procurator fiscal to make.

[17] *Clark v Kelly*, 2003 S.L.T. 308.
[18] s.8(1).

Key Concepts

District court or **sheriff court**? The decision is taken on the basis of:

- the seriousness of the offence;
- the sentence which can be imposed;
- whether the sheriff court is very busy; and
- perhaps also on the basis of the proficiency of the justices.

The justice has the power to impose up to 60 days' imprisonment and/or a fine up to £2,500. However, it should be noted that some statutes impose a different maximum penalty and the court cannot exceed such penalty. The court also has other types of sentence that can be imposed and these are discussed below.

A stipendiary magistrate has the same sentencing powers as the sheriff, that is, up to three months' imprisonment and up to £5,000 fine.

Sheriff court

You will recall that the sheriff court is a local court which deals with both civil and criminal cases **1–22** and as such it is the busiest of the courts.

Jurisdiction of the sheriff court

The jurisdiction is over most criminal offences committed within the sheriffdom. However, there **1–23** are certain types of cases which are privative (*i.e.* exclusive) to other courts. For instance, parking and litter offences are privative to the district court while murder and rape cases may only be heard in the High Court of Justiciary. Thus, many of the cases which come before the sheriff court could have been heard by one of the other courts. The decision to prosecute a case in the sheriff court, or elsewhere, is taken by the procurator fiscal.

Criminal cases are prosecuted using either the summary procedure or solemn procedure. Both the court procedures and the sentencing powers available are different, depending on the type of prosecution procedure used.

The Sheriff Court at Hamilton is the venue for a pilot Youth Court. This introduces a fast-track court procedure for repeat offenders aged 16 and 17 years old. The procedure aims to bring these young offenders to court within 10 days of the date of charge.

Summary procedure

This is used for more minor crimes and offences. The case is heard by a sheriff sitting without a **1–24** jury. A sheriff's powers of disposal are limited by the Criminal Procedure (Scotland) Act 1995 to three months' imprisonment and/or a fine up to £5,000.[19] If a person has committed a second or subsequent offence of dishonest appropriation or personal violence, he may be sentenced to up to six months' imprisonment.

[19] This was amended by the Crime and Punishment (Scotland) Act 1997, s.13, to six months for first offence, 12 months for a second or subsequent offence. The section has not, at the time of writing, been brought into force.

Solemn procedure

1–25 Here the sheriff will sit with a jury of 15 persons. The accused appears on indictment, charged with a serious offence, such as robbery, serious assault, or a serious motoring offence, and can be sentenced to up to three years' imprisonment[20] and/or an unlimited fine. However, some statutory offences, such as motoring offences, specify a range of sentencing options, and the sheriff is required to implement those. If an accused is found guilty, the sheriff may remit the accused to the High Court for sentence if he believes that his sentencing powers are inadequate for the gravity of the crime. The sheriff courts disposed of around 3,000 solemn cases each year, while the High Court disposed of just under 1,000 cases in the year 2000–2001.

High Court of Justiciary

1–26 The High Court of Justiciary is the senior criminal court and handles both appeal cases and trials. It is the last court of appeal for criminal appeals in Scotland, unless the matter of the appeal refers to a devolution issue under the Scotland Act 1998: in this case, the last court of appeal is the Judicial Committee of the Privy Council.[21]

In December 2002, a report compiled by a committee under Lord Bonomy, a judge in the Supreme Courts, concluded that changes needed to be made to the way in which the High Court operates. One of his recommendations was increased sentencing powers for the Sheriff Solemn Court to ease pressure on the High Court.

Trial Court

1–27 The High Court is a circuit court, sitting in various locations in Scotland, using the local sheriff court as its base. This allows the criminal justice system to operate at all levels within a locality, instead of the most serious cases being sent to the court in Edinburgh where all serious civil matters are heard. It further allows the accused to be tried by "his peers" since the jury will be drawn from people on the local electoral register.

Section 2(1) of the Criminal Procedure (Scotland) Act 1995 allows the High Court to sit at such times and in such places as the Lord Justice General may determine. Currently seven principal locations are used: Edinburgh, Glasgow, Inverness, Aberdeen, Kilmarnock, Paisley and one or other of Perth, Forfar or Dundee. Occasional sittings are held in other towns such as Peterhead, Stirling and Dunfermline.

There is a permanent sitting of the court in Glasgow because of the large number of cases (50 per cent of the total cases of the High Court) emanating from that area. In a very exceptional case, the trial of the two men, accused of bombing Pan-Am Flight 203 over Lockerbie in 1988, causing the deaths of 270 people, was held in the Netherlands before three judges sitting without a jury.[22] A fourth judge was available in case one of the judges became ill or died. This trial was enabled by an Order in Council made under the United Nations Act 1946.[23]

As a trial court, the High Court is presided over by a Lord Commissioner of Justiciary, who sits with a jury of 15. In a case of particular difficulty or importance, two or more judges may sit with the jury, but this is unusual, having occurred in only a few cases in the last century, *e.g. H.M. Advocate v McKenzie*.[24] Currently there are 32 judges available to sit in the High Court either on trials or appeals: of these three are women.

---

20 The 1997 Act again amended this sentence, increasing it to five years but the section is not yet implemented.
21 *Follen v H.M. Advocate*, 2001 S.C. (P.C.) 105; 2001 S.L.T. 774.
22 *H.M. Advocate v Megrahi (No.4)*, 2001 G.W.D. 5–177.
23 High Court of Justiciary (Proceedings in the Netherlands) (United Nations) Order 1998 (SI 1998/2251).
24 1970 S.L.T. 81.

The territorial jurisdiction of the High Court as a trial court is the whole of Scotland together with the territorial waters of Scotland. Certain crimes committed outside Scotland may also be heard, *e.g.* hi-jacking by a Scottish national anywhere in the world.

The case jurisdiction of the High Court is only limited by statute. Thus, the High Court could hear a breach of the peace case normally heard in the sheriff or district court, but this would be unusual and wasteful of the court's time. In practice the court will hear the more serious crimes such as armed robbery and serious assault. Certain crimes are privative to the High Court, *i.e.* the High Court has exclusive jurisdiction. These are murder, rape and treason. Certain statutory offences must be tried in the High Court, such as offences under the Official Secrets Acts 1911 and 1920.

Cases within the High Court are taken on solemn procedure. The accused is indicted to appear before the court to answer the charge and will often appear from custody. The powers of sentencing available to the High Court are unlimited imprisonment and unlimited fine, although these are of course subject to the provisions of a statute. Thus the court may impose only a sentence of life imprisonment on a person convicted of murder.

Appeal Court

The High Court of Justiciary is the highest criminal appeal court in Scotland and all appeals must be heard there, whether coming from the district court or the High Court itself. The territorial jurisdiction is the whole of Scotland. There is no right of appeal to the House of Lords.[25] In 2001, there were 3,495 appeals, a 10 per cent increase on the number in 2000. **1–28**

In criminal cases, the accused may appeal against conviction, and/or against sentence, except where the sentence imposed is prescribed by statute, *e.g.* the mandatory sentence for murder is life imprisonment and a person so convicted may not appeal against that sentence, but may appeal against the conviction. Most appeals are against sentence only (88 per cent).

The system of appeals changed as a result of the Criminal Procedure (Scotland) Act 1995. Originally, any person convicted could appeal and their appeal would be heard by a bench of three judges at the High Court in Edinburgh, sitting as a court of appeal. This meant that there were many appeals made which had no foundation and were unreasonable. Accordingly, the High Court was unable to cope with the volume of appeals and delays in the appeal procedure became extensive.

The new system is a two-stage one whereby the accused states the reasons for appeal, *e.g.* the sentence is too severe, and these are considered by a single High Court judge who "sifts" the appeals. If he decides that there are no grounds for appeal, the appellant may appeal that decision to a bench of three judges. If the "sifting" judge decides that there are grounds for appeal, the matter goes before the appeal court. It is possible for the sifting judge to decide that the grounds of appeal stated by the appellant are irrelevant or incompetent, but that there are other grounds for appeal not stated by the appellant. Such a decision would go to the appeal court.

A convicted person may always seek leave to appeal, whether the case has been heard by solemn or summary procedure. In certain circumstances it is possible for the prosecution to appeal against the level of sentence where it appears to be too lenient.

There are a number of different methods of appeal.

(1) *Stated case*: This is the method used after summary conviction to appeal against that conviction and/or sentence. The judge will prepare a statement of the facts found proved and will request the High Court to answer questions of law which the accused or prosecutor wants answered. This kind of appeal is known as a Justiciary Appeal and there are around 3,000 each year.
(2) *Appeal by Bill of Suspension or Advocation*: After summary conviction, a bill of suspension is used by the accused where appeal by stated case is inappropriate or incompetent. It is most often used if there have been irregularities in the trial procedures. A bill of advocation

[25] *Macintosh v Lord Advocate* (1876) 3 R. (HL) 34.

is used by the prosecutor to appeal against the acquittal of the accused on the ground of an alleged miscarriage of justice. These bills are very rare.

(3) *Note of appeal*: This is a faster method of appeal, used when the offender wishes to appeal against sentence only. The sentence may be increased or decreased by the High Court.

(4) *Solemn appeals*: There is one ground of appeal for solemn cases—miscarriage of justice. This ground of appeal, called a Criminal Appeal, was clarified by the Criminal Procedure (Scotland) Act 1995, s.106 as amended by the Crime and Punishment (Scotland) Act 1997. The statute allows review by the High Court against a conviction and/or sentence and allows the court to take into account evidence which was not heard at the original trial and where the jury returned a verdict "no reasonable jury properly directed could have returned". There are around 800 Criminal Appeals each year. The Lord Advocate may appeal against sentences he considers unduly lenient.[26] Leave to appeal by the trial judge is now required for solemn appeals. The High Court may authorise a re-trial to take place, although it is up to the Crown to decide whether a re-trial should take place. This power is rarely used by the High Court.

(5) *Lord Advocate's Reference*: This applies where an indictment has led to an acquittal or conviction but has raised a point of law which requires clarification by the court. The decision of the court has no effect on an acquittal. Such references are infrequent, there having been only six from 1983 to 1996.

Miscarriages of justice

1–29 In recent years there have been a number of prominent miscarriages of justice in England and Wales. These resulted in a Royal Commission on Criminal Justice in 1991. One of its recommendations was that an independent review authority should be set up to decide whether or not a case should be referred to the Court of Appeal. This decision had previously been taken by the Home Secretary once all of the normal appeals process had been exhausted. In Scotland, the Secretary of State undertook to consider whether a similar body was needed and a Committee on Appeals Criteria and Alleged Miscarriages of Justice was set up in 1994 under the chairmanship of Sir Stewart Sutherland.

The position on allegations of miscarriage of justice in Scotland was that the Secretary of State had power to refer the case back to the High Court to be heard as if it were an appeal. The Sutherland Committee reported in 1996 and recommended that an independent body be set up to consider and refer miscarriages of justice. This was rejected by the Conservative Government but a change was forced on the Government during the passage of the Crime and Punishment (Scotland) Act 1997.

The Scottish Criminal Cases Review Committee was set up in 1998 with its first chairperson being Professor Sheila McLean. The Commission is independent of government: its members are appointed by the Queen on the recommendation of the Scottish Ministers. At least one-third of the members must be advocates or solicitors of 10 years' standing and at least two-thirds must have experience of the criminal justice system, including the investigation of offences and treatment of offenders.

Verdicts

1–30 In Scotland, an accused person may be convicted, or acquitted, or found "not proven". This last verdict has the same effect as an acquittal in that the accused is set free and there is no criminal record kept. However in some ways it is unsatisfactory since it indicates that the court felt the accused was not wholly innocent but there was not enough evidence to meet the requirement of "beyond reasonable doubt" which is the standard of proof required in criminal cases. The verdict

[26] *H.M. Advocate v McPhee*, 1994 S.L.T. 1292.

does not, contrary to popular misconception, allow the prosecution of the person to be reopened if further evidence comes to light in the future. Once a verdict of "not proven" is given, the rule of double jeopardy comes into play, this says that a person cannot be tried twice for the same crime.

Sentencing powers

The broad sentencing powers at common law have been described above. However, courts have more sentencing options open to them other than a fine or imprisonment. The courts may also be given statutory sentencing powers for specific offences, such as disqualification from driving where the offender has twelve or more penalty points on his driving licence. **1–31**

Options available to the courts include:

- Absolute discharge—under summary procedure, no conviction is recorded. This verdict is especially useful in minor cases where the offender hopes to join the armed forces and a criminal conviction might preclude that.
- Admonition.
- Caution (pronounced "cayshun")—this requires the offender to pay a sum of money to the court as security for his/her good behaviour for a specified period of time. This will be up to six months in the district court, and up to one year in the sheriff court. The money can be repaid at the end of the period if the offender has been of good behaviour.
- Probation under the supervision of a social worker for 1–3 years. Under summary procedure, no conviction is recorded.
- Community service order—this requires the offender to undertake unpaid work for a period of between 80 and 300 hours. This work will be under the supervision of a social worker and is a direct alternative to imprisonment.
- Deferral of sentence, subject to conditions.
- Hospital or guardianship order—if the offender suffers from a mental disorder, or detention in hospital if the accused is insane or unfit for trial.
- Compensation order—this can be made in addition to another penalty such as a fine. The offender is required to pay a sum of money to the victim of his crime.
- Drug treatment and testing order—this is only available where the offender is over 16, is dependent on drugs or substance abuse, and is suitable and willing to be made subject to the order. The order lasts for between six months and three years.
- Restriction of liberty order—which is imposed for up to 12 months on an offender aged over 16 years. The order restricts the offender's movements requiring them to be in a specified place at a specified time, or not to be in a specified place at a specified time. An example would be a football hooligan required to attend at a police station when his team is playing.
- Forfeiture order—this can be imposed on the property of the offender which has been used in committing a crime, *e.g.* a motor car used as a getaway vehicle, or for the transport of drugs. The order allows the sale of the property.
- Supervised attendance order—where an offender has been sentenced to a fine, but has defaulted on payment, the sheriff or justice may decide to imprison him. The SAO takes the place of the term of imprisonment. The offender must consent to the order being imposed on him and he will then be required to undertake 10 to 100 hours in a supervised activity, either attending relevant courses or doing community service work. The Criminal Justice (Scotland) Act 2003, s.50 amends the 1995 Act to allow supervised attendance orders to be used as a first instance of disposal for adult offenders.
- Young offenders, *i.e.* those between 16 and 21 may be sent to a detention centre for a period of four weeks to four months, or a young offender's institution for a period not exceeding that which would have been imposed on an adult.

The vast majority of sentences imposed are fines, particularly in the district court where these account for 90 per cent of the penalties imposed.

The Crime and Punishment (Scotland) Act 1997 provides for an automatic life sentence to be imposed on offenders over 21 who have previously committed a qualifying offence (such as culpable homicide, attempted murder, rape, robbery with a firearm) and who have been again convicted of a qualifying offence. However, the mandatory nature of this provision is mitigated by a provision whereby the court need not impose the automatic life sentence if it is not in the interests of justice to do so. This appears to give the court discretion in sentencing. The Lord Advocate is given the right to appeal against a decision not to impose the automatic life sentence.

Before sentence is passed on a person who has been found guilty, the court will give that person an opportunity to have his/her say, in particular to explain why they committed the crime and to put forward any relevant information about their circumstances.

The court will then take certain circumstances into account before passing sentence.

Key Concepts

Factors affecting **sentence**:

- the accused's personal circumstances;
- any criminal record;
- the circumstances of the offence;
- the accused's age if s/he is under 21;
- whether the accused has served any previous custodial sentence;
- time spent by the accused in custody awaiting trial;
- a plea of guilty;
- any minimum sentence required by law;
- racial aggravation; and
- any guidance or guidelines provided by the High Court.

Alternatives to prosecution

1–32 The business of the courts has increased markedly over the years and cases take longer to come to court after the decision to prosecute has been taken. In the early 1990s it was obvious that action would have to be taken before the whole system ground to a halt. The Criminal Justice (Scotland) Act 1987 had introduced the concept of "fiscal fines" whereby cases which could be brought before the district court could be diverted out of the court system by allowing the accused to pay a fine. The idea was that if the fine was paid, there would be no prosecution and the acceptance of the "offer" of the fiscal fine was not recorded as a conviction. This was introduced in 1988 with the fine being set at £25.

In the Criminal Justice (Scotland) Act 1995, all summary statutory offences were made triable in the district court, thus opening the way to introduce fiscal fines for a larger number of offences. The scale of penalties was also increased up to £100. As a result of this and as expected, there has been an increase in the number of fiscal fines and thus a decrease in the number of cases before the district court.

A recent development has been the introduction of a Drugs Court in Glasgow as a pilot scheme. The remit of the Drugs Court is to act as an alternative method of dealing with prosecutions for drug-related offences. Offenders must agree to accept medical and rehabilitative treatment for their drug problem. Section 42 of the Criminal Justice (Scotland) Act 2003 gives additional sentencing powers to the Drugs Court where an offender has failed to comply with a drug treatment and testing order or probation order.

"Devolution issues"

As the result of the Scotland Act 1998, the Scottish Executive is required to ensure that any subordinate legislation or any other actions undertaken by them are compatible with Convention rights and with Community law.[27] This section of the Act does not apply to the Lord Advocate when his act is done to prosecute an offence, or is done in his capacity as head of the systems of criminal prosecution and investigation of deaths in Scotland, where such an act would not be unlawful under s.6 of the Human Rights Act 1998. The section protects the prosecuting authorities when they are found to be prosecuting a violation of a statutory provision which is held to be incompatible with Convention rights. The section also ensures that the Lord Advocate is able to bring a prosecution under UK legislation where the prosecuting authorities in England have been able to do so under the same legislation. This ensures that UK legislation is applied the same way across the UK. **1–33**

A person seeking a remedy after being adversely affected by an Act of the Scottish Executive or an Act of the Scottish Parliament will bring a "devolution issue" before the courts. The concept of the devolution issue is raised in s.98, which refers the reader to Sch.6 where the devolution issue is defined.

Any alleged breach of the Convention under the Scotland Act will become a devolution issue for the purposes of Sch.6. The validity of an Act of the Scottish Parliament cannot however be challenged on the grounds that the proceedings leading to its enactment were invalid.[28]

In terms of human rights issues, para.1 of Sch.6 defines a devolution issue as:

> "(a) a question whether an Act of the Scottish Parliament or any provision of an Act of the Scottish Parliament is within the legislative competence of the Parliament...
> (d) a question whether a purported or proposed exercise of a function by a member of the Scottish Executive is, or would be, incompatible with any of the Convention rights or with Community law.
> (e) a question whether a failure to act by a member of the Scottish Executive is incompatible with any of the Convention rights or with Community law."

Proceedings for the determination of a devolution issue may be instituted by the Advocate General or the Lord Advocate, or by a person, who is a "victim" in terms of Art.34 of the European Convention on Human Rights, during the course of existing legal proceedings.[29] A devolution issue may therefore be raised in any court or tribunal proceedings but para.5 of the Schedule requires that the Advocate General and the Lord Advocate are given intimation that the devolution issue has arisen. Either Law Officer may then become a party to the proceedings as far as it relates to the devolution issue.

In criminal cases it is possible to raise a devolution issue but this is subject to time limits. In a case brought on indictment the devolution issue must be raised within seven days of the indictment being served. In summary cases the devolution issue must be stated before the accused has been asked to plead.

When a devolution issue is raised in a tribunal from which there is no appeal, the tribunal must refer the devolution issue to the Inner House of the Court of Session; any other tribunal may choose to do this.[30] Any civil court (except the House of Lords or the Court of Session sitting with three or more judges) may refer the devolution issue to the Inner House.[31] Any criminal court (except the High Court of Justiciary sitting with two or more judges) may refer the devolution issue to the High Court of Justiciary.[32] These provisions are designed to ensure that where necessary a lower court may refer a devolution issue to a superior court and it will be dealt with by the superior court, not just passed upwards to another court. The superior court may itself refer the

---

[27] s.57(2).
[28] s.28(5).
[29] s.100(1).
[30] Sch.6, para.8.
[31] Sch.6, para.7.
[32] Sch.6, para.9.

devolution issue to a higher court. This applies to the Court of Session convened as a court with at least three judges and the High Court of Justiciary convened with at least two judges. The court to which the reference will be made, in both civil and criminal cases, is the Judicial Committee of the Privy Council. This requirement creates the first time an appeal route from the High Court of Justiciary acting in its appellant capacity.

Once the decision on the reference has been given, the right of appeal against that decision will come into operation. Where the reference has been made under paras 7 or 8 to the Inner House, appeal is to the Judicial Committee. Where the reference has arisen under para.9 or the devolution issue has arisen in the ordinary course of proceedings before the High Court of Justiciary as an appeal court, then any appeal requires leave to appeal from the High Court or the Judicial Committee and is made to the Judicial Committee.[33] Where there is a reference to the Inner House in a case from which there is no appeal to the House of Lords[34] then appeal may be made to the Judicial Committee with the leave of the Inner House or the Judicial Committee.[35] The routes for reference and appeal are set out in the table below.

Court in which devolution issue is raised	**Court for reference**	**Appeal**
Any tribunal (except those where there is no appeal)	Inner House of Court of Session (para.8)	Judicial Committee of Privy Council (para.12)
Civil court, *i.e.* sheriff court, Outer House of Court of Session	Inner House of Court of Session (para.7)	Judicial Committee of Privy Council (para.12)
Criminal court, *i.e.* district court, sheriff court, High Court of Justiciary as trial court	High Court of Justiciary as appeal court (para.9)	Judicial Committee of Privy Council but only with leave to appeal (para.13(a))
Court of Session with at least three judges, but not if devolution issue raised under paras 7 or 8	Judicial Committee of Privy Council (para.10)	Judicial Committee of Privy Council but only with leave to appeal and if not right of appeal to House of Lords (para.13 (b))
High Court of Justiciary with at least two judges, but not if the devolution issue was raised under para.9	Judicial Committee of Privy Council (para.11)	Judicial Committee of Privy Council but only with leave to appeal (para.13 (a))

Where the devolution issue concerns the proposed exercise of a function by a member of the Scottish Executive, then the person making the reference must notify a member of the Scottish Executive that the issue has been raised. The devolution issue may not have arisen in judicial proceedings but any of the Law Officers may refer the issue of the proposed exercise. Thereafter, no member of the Executive may exercise the function until the matter is disposed of. If a member of the Scottish Executive does exercise the function, the Advocate General or any other person may bring proceedings against the Scottish Executive.

Normally, when a legal provision or action is found to be *ultra vires* the provision or action is treated as null and void. A court action to challenge the validity of a provision of an action made under the Scotland Act will take time to be heard and decided. It is likely therefore that the provision may have been implemented before the action is raised, and individuals may have relied upon the provision or action. Any decision of invalidity will be retrospective and may cause difficulty for those who have relied upon it. The Act allows the court to limit the effect of such a

[33] Sch.6, para.13(a).
[34] For instance, from the Lands Valuation Appeal Court.
[35] Sch.6, para.13(b).

decision by removing or limiting any retrospective effect of the decision or suspending the effect of the decision, pending its being corrected.[36] The court is required to have regard to the effect the making of an order would have on persons who are not parties to the proceedings and the court must order intimation to the Lord Advocate, and if the matter is a devolution issue, to the appropriate Law Officer.

TRIBUNALS

The State is involved in more and more areas of our lives and so disputes will inevitably arise from the application of the numerous rules and regulations made by the Executive. These disputes could be settled in the courts but they would clog up an already overcrowded legal system. Alternatively, they could be settled by the government department or body which has responsibility for the regulations. The problem envisaged here was that the body would in effect be policing itself. Neither of these options was considered satisfactory, hence the creation of a new machinery to handle these disputes—tribunals. **1–34**

Key Concepts

Reasons why tribunals are **necessary in modern society**:

- ordinary courts could not cope with the volume of cases likely to arise;
- there is often no necessity for the formality encountered in a court;
- there may be a need for expert and specialised knowledge which a judge may not have;
- tribunals are cheap to set up and operate;
- judges are required to interpret legislation and are often unable to take into account social principles and policies behind the legislation; and
- the subject-matter of the disputes may be comparatively trifling.

Tribunals are independent adjudicatory bodies set up under statute and occasionally by prerogative. The term "tribunal" is not defined in legislation but it appears to cover any person or body of persons who have judicial or quasi-judicial functions. Lord Denning described a tribunal hearing as "more in the nature of an inquiry before an investigating body charged with the task of finding out what happened".[37]

Tribunals are the primary mechanism provided by Parliament for the resolution of certain grievances between the citizen and State but a few tribunals also cover disputes between citizen and citizen, for instance employment tribunals. There are around 2,000 different tribunals in the UK today covering a wide range of topics such as benefit appeals, value added tax tribunals, immigration adjudicators, child support appeals, the children's hearing. Many of the tribunals come under the supervisory control of the Council on Tribunals.

From the end of the Second World War, tribunals proliferated mainly because of the setting up of the welfare state. Tribunals were seen as necessary for the benefit of the public and to ensure fair treatment by officials.

In 1958 the Franks Committee[38] reported on the working of tribunals clarifying the place of tribunals within the justice system. The recommendations contained in the Franks Report were largely implemented by the Tribunals and Inquiries Act 1958 now consolidated into the Tribunals

[36] s.102(2).
[37] *R. v National Insurance Commissioner Ex p. Viscusi* [1974] 1 W.L.R. 646.
[38] Report of the Committee on Administrative Tribunals and Inquiries, Cmnd.218 (1957).

and Inquiries Act 1992. Other parts of the report were implemented by means of changes in administrative procedures.

A constant theme of the Franks Report was that there were three characteristics of a tribunal: openness, fairness and impartiality. Openness includes knowledge of the essential reasoning behind decisions and publicity of proceedings. Impartiality refers to the freedom of the tribunal from the interference of the government department. Fairness refers to the adoption of a clear procedure so that parties know their rights and the case they have to meet.

Key Concepts

A tribunal will have some, but not all, of these **properties**:

- it will make final, legally enforceable decisions;
- it will be independent of any department;
- it will hold a public hearing which is judicial in nature;
- its members will possess the relevant expertise;
- it will give reasoned decisions; and
- it will allow an appeal to the Court of Session or High Court of Justice on a point of law.

Those tribunals which are under the direct supervision of the Council on Tribunals are specified in Sch.1 of the Tribunals and Inquiries Act 1992. Tribunals can be added to the list in Sch.1 by means of an order made by the Lord Advocate or Lord Chancellor. Around 60 tribunals are named at present. Many more are not scheduled and so remain outside the jurisdiction of the Council.

Most tribunals are set up by statute and the powers and duties are regulated either in the statute itself or in regulations made under the statute.

Recommendations of the Franks Report

1–35 The report was the first systematic examination of the work of tribunals and is remarkable for its clarity.

The report made a number of recommendations, most of which were either enacted in the 1958 Act or were implemented by changing administrative procedures. One of its main recommendations was that there should be two Councils on Tribunals, one for England and Wales and one for Scotland. These Councils would have a general co-ordinating role regarding existing tribunals and an advisory role in respect of new ones. In the event, one Council on Tribunals was created with provision for a Scottish Committee to oversee tribunals with a Scottish dimension.

Some of the other important recommendations and the Government's reactions are:

(1) Chairmen of tribunals should be appointed by the Lord Chancellor and wing members by the Council. The 1992 Act, s.5 provided for the chairman to be appointed by the Lord Chancellor directly or by the Minister concerned. Wing members are normally appointed by the Minister.
(2) Chairmen should normally have a legal qualification, particularly in appellate tribunals. This has become the norm for most tribunals.
(3) The procedure in tribunals should be formulated by the Council to ensure an orderly procedure in an informal atmosphere. Although the Council must be consulted by departments, it has an advisory role only in the formulation of tribunal procedure.
(4) The citizen should be informed of any right to apply to a tribunal and be given information on the case he will have to meet. This recommendation is now followed by all tribunals.

(5) Tribunal hearings should be public except where public security or intimate personal or financial details are to be discussed. Most tribunals are heard in public although the public are unlikely to know of their existence. Employment tribunals are often reported in the press. Some tribunals are always held in private, for instance, children's hearings.
(6) Legal representation should normally be allowed. One of the difficulties in allowing legal representation is that legal aid is not generally available. As a result of the Human Rights Act 1998, legal aid is now available for some tribunals.
(7) Decisions should be fully reasoned and written notice of the decisions sent to parties as soon as possible.
(8) Appeals to the Court of Session or High Court of Justice should be allowed on questions of fact, or law and fact. Section 11 limits appeals to questions of law only but the appellant may require the tribunal to state a case to the Court of Session or the High Court of Justice.

Children's hearing system

The children's hearing system was introduced in 1971 as a result of the Social Work (Scotland) Act 1968, itself the result of the report of the Kilbrandon Committee of 1964. The Committee's remit was to consider the functioning of Scottish juvenile courts in dealing with children who were in trouble for various reasons such as criminal behaviour, care and protection and being beyond parental control. The report recommended a new and radical approach to how children in trouble were considered. Their approach was that children in need of care and juvenile offenders had similar characteristics and therefore "a unified welfare-based system which responded to their needs rather than their deeds was required." **1–36**

Children should not normally be brought before the courts but referred to a new local official, the Reporter to the Children's Panel, to see if there are sufficient grounds for referral and whether compulsory care is necessary. The report emphasised the need for care, and in fact the report referred to the juvenile panel as a "locally based treatment authority". The needs of the child were to be paramount, with the existing concept of punishment being discarded.

Key Concepts

Why the **Children's Hearing** is a distinctive tribunal:

- It seeks to find a resolution of problems outwith the court system.
- It works in a fairly informal way by discussion between the child, the parents and the panel.
- The panel comprises three lay members from the local community and by law must include both a man and a woman on the panel.
- If there is a dispute regarding the reasons for referral, this is dealt with away from the panel by the sheriff.

The system has continued to work, largely unchanged, and attracts much international interest. In 1995, the Children (Scotland) Act reaffirmed the Children's Hearing system, but made some procedural changes. The Scottish Children's Reporter Administration was established in 1996, taking over the organisation of the service on a national rather than regional basis and taking the service out of local authority control. However, there are still local offices with local reporters. Reporters are often legally qualified, but some will have a social work qualification.

It is the duty of the reporter to assess the evidence relating to an allegation made involving a child. That evidence has to meet the criminal standard of "beyond reasonable doubt" if an allegation of criminal activity has been made, or meet the civil standard of "on the balance of probabilities" in all other allegations.

Constanda v M
1997 S.L.T. 1396

The child was referred to the children's hearing on the grounds that he had been exposed to moral danger. The statement of facts included an allegation that the boy had exposed himself and committed lewd practices in front of another child. There was lack of corroboration and the grounds of referral were discharged. On appeal, the court held that where a child was alleged to have committed criminal acts, the normal standard of criminal evidence must be applied. If there is sufficient evidence, the reporter will investigate the child's case further.

A child can be referred to the children's reporter by anyone who considers the child needs compulsory measures of supervision, *e.g.* police officer, health visitor, teacher or social worker. The 1995 Act changed the wording from "care" to "supervision".

A child may have committed an offence or be the victim of a criminal offence.

G v Templeton
1998 S.C.L.R. 180

The father of a girl struck her face, causing bruising. The reporter referred the girl and her sister to the children's hearing on the grounds that she had been the victim of a criminal assault and the father was a member of the same household. The father argued that he had been exercising his parental right to punish his daughter and therefore there had been no assault. He lost his appeal on the grounds that a parent had the right to use reasonable chastisement but when excessive force was used his motive of chastisement was immaterial.

Where a child under the age of 16 is alleged to have committed a crime, prosecution in the courts can only take place on the instructions of the Lord Advocate.[39] The child must be aged at least eight-years-old[40] since below that age the child is considered not to have the mental capacity to commit a crime.

Before the hearing, the children's panel will receive reports from social work, school and any other professional involved in the case. In this instance, the child may have to be kept in a place of safety; the panel will issue a warrant for this and it will have effect for 22 days. The reporter may issue additional warrants on the panel's authority for up to 66 days. It is also possible for the reporter to apply to the sheriff for a warrant without limit.

If the children's hearing decides that compulsory supervision is necessary, the child will be placed on a supervision requirement. This will require: supervision by a social worker in the child's home, or foster care for the child, or residential care, including residence in secure accommodation. Supervision lasts for one year but must be reviewed by the panel before the end of the year. Review can be requested by a social worker at any time, and by the child or parents after three months have elapsed.

Compulsory measures of supervision are necessary under the Children (Scotland) Act 1995, s.52 if one or more conditions arise in relation to the child.

---

[39] Criminal Procedure (Scotland) Act 1995, s.42(1).

[40] Criminal Procedure (Scotland) Act 1995, s.41.

Key Concepts

Conditions for referral

- The child is beyond the control of the relevant person.
- The child is falling into bad associations or is exposed to moral danger.
- The child is likely to suffer unnecessarily or be seriously impaired in health or development due to lack of parental care.
- The child is a victim of a Sch.1 offence under the Criminal Procedure (Scotland) Act 1995.
- The child is, or is likely to become, a member of the same household as a child in respect of whom a scheduled offence has been committed.
- The child is, or is likely to become, a member of the same household as a person who has committed a scheduled offence.
- The child is, or is about to become, a member of a household where a member has committed the offence of incest.
- The child has failed to attend school regularly without reasonable excuse.
- The child has committed an offence.
- The child has misused alcohol or drugs.
- The child has misused a volatile substance by deliberately inhaling its vapours.
- The child is being accommodated by the local authority, or is subject to a parental responsibility order and his/her behaviour requires special measures of adequate supervision in the child's interest or the interests of others.

The procedure at the children's hearing is informal and all of the parties are encouraged to enter into the discussion. The three panel members will try to involve the child in seeking solutions to the problems s/he is facing.

Legal representation for the children involved in children's hearing is now available as a result of a recent case. In *S v Principal Reporter (No.2)*[41] the children's hearing was held to be an independent and impartial tribunal and the provisions of Art.6 of the European Convention on Human Rights was held to apply to it. This means that particularly where there is any prospect of a child being detained in secure accommodation, legal representation is now a requirement.

On occasion, there will appear to be a conflict of interest between the child and the parent or guardian. Section 41 of the 1995 Act requires the children's hearing to consider whether to appoint a safeguarder to support children and help them express their views.

Appeal against the children's hearing decision may be made to the sheriff and a private hearing will be heard. Evidence may be heard from both sides. Further appeal is available to the sheriff principal or Court of Session, and against the sheriff principal's decision on a point of law to the Court of Session.[42]

---

[41] 2001 S.L.T. 1304.
[42] 1995 Act, s.51(11).

OMBUDSMEN IN SCOTLAND

1–37 Devolution has led to considerable changes in the Ombudsman system in Scotland. In the early days of the Scottish Parliament, complaints of injustice caused by maladministration were directed to the Scottish Parliamentary Commissioner for Administration.[43] Maladministration is not defined by statute but generally it appears to consist of issues such as poor administrative practices, or the wrong application of rules, or giving misleading or inadequate advice, or failing to inform a person of a right of appeal. A person making a complaint that he has suffered "injustice caused by maladministration" must normally have exhausted the internal complaints procedure of the department or body concerned before the relevant Ombudsman will investigate the matter.

The SPCA was also the holder of the office of Parliamentary Commissioner for Administration in the UK Parliament. Section 91 of the 1998 Act required the Scottish Parliament to establish provision for the investigation of complaints and this has now been implemented by the Scottish Public Services Ombudsman Act 2002. This Act establishes a "one-stop shop" to streamline the public sector complaints system by creating a single Ombudsman to replace the SPCA, the Health Commissioner for Scotland, Local Government Ombudsman and the Housing Association Ombudsman for Scotland. The new Ombudsman, Professor Alice Brown, was appointed on September 30, 2002. Her new post will include the complaints handling system of Scottish Enterprise, Highland and Islands Enterprise and the Mental Welfare Commission.

The SPSO is appointed by the Queen on the nomination of the Scottish Parliament and will be able to accept complaints directly from members of the public. The PCA and SPCA were unable to investigate complaints unless an M.P. or M.S.P. referred the matter to them. This "M.P./M.S.P. filter" was an unnecessary complication to the complaints system but Members of the two Parliaments had wanted to ensure that they were kept informed of events in their constituencies.

The new system is intended to simplify the complaints procedure in Scotland by creating just one Ombudsman to oversee a number of different subject areas. Schedule 2 to the 2002 Act lists the bodies which fall within the remit of the SPSO. The list includes the Scottish Parliament and Scottish Administration, the health service bodies in Scotland, local authorities, registered social landlords, a substantial number of Scottish public authorities and a number of cross-border public authorities.[44]

The Ombudsman has power to conduct an investigation[45] after receiving a complaint from a member of the public, or a request from a listed authority.

(1) *Complaint from a member of the public*: The person must have suffered injustice or hardship in consequence of maladministration or a "service failure" although the latter will not lead to an investigation involving a family health service provider or a registered social landlord.[46] The person aggrieved may make the complaint or may instruct another to act on his behalf.[47] This provision is intended to improve accessibility to the Ombudsman by allowing the person himself or perhaps his M.S.P. or local councillor to make the complaint. The legal representatives of a deceased person may make a complaint if that person suffered maladministration before his death.

The complaint must normally be made within 12 months of the aggrieved person being made aware of the maladministration. However, the Ombudsman has discretion to extend this time limit of she deems it appropriate to do so. The complaint may be made in writing, or by electronic means, or, at the discretion of the Ombudsman, orally.[48]

(2) *Request by listed authority*: This is an interesting development in Ombudsman services. Previously an Ombudsman such as the PCA could only investigate a public body where a complaint had been received. Sometimes a public body would be criticised but if no

---

[43] The Scotland Act 1998 (Trans...ory and Transitional Provisions) (Complaints of Maladministration) Order 1999.
[44] *e.g.* Criminal Injuries Compensation Authority, Forestry Commissioners, Sea Fish Industry Authority.
[45] 2002 Act, s.2.
[46] 2002 Act, s.5(2).
[47] 2002 Act, s.9(1).
[48] 2002 Act, s.10(3).

complaint had been received there could be no investigation. The Scottish Executive has indicated that this request for an investigation should only be made where the authority has taken all reasonable steps to resolve the problem.

Investigations

The Ombudsman cannot investigate a number of issues such as any actions taken by the police or prosecution authorities in the investigation or prevention of crime, the commencement or conduct of civil or criminal proceedings, contractual or commercial transactions of any listed authority (except certain NHS contracts), any issues relating to personnel matters, or the determination of the amount of any rent or service charge.[49] **1–38**

The Ombudsman has power under s.13 to require any member, officer of any other person to supply information and produce documents relevant to the investigation. She has the same powers as the Court of Session to require the attendance and examination of witnesses and the production of documents.[50] She may not however require the production of papers from the Scottish Cabinet or the UK Cabinet. Any person who obstructs the Ombudsman in her investigation or commits an act (or fails to do so) which would constitute contempt of court in the Court of Session, may be liable to be sent to the Court of Session to be dealt with. Investigations are to be held in private.

Reports

The Ombudsman may make a number of reports about her activities. **1–39**

(1) *Report on a decision not to investigate*: The Ombudsman has discretion as to whether she should investigate a complaint[51] and may not be compelled to do so. However, if she declines to investigate, she must send a statement of her decision and the reasons for it to the aggrieved person or their representative and the listed authority or person alleged to have committed the maladministration.[52]

(2) *Investigation report*: This report must be sent to the persons listed in s.11 and also to the Scottish Ministers.[53] In addition, a copy of the report has to be laid before Parliament. Normally no individuals will be identified in the report unless the Ombudsman decides that disclosure is in the public interest and the interests of the person in question. The listed authority must make the report available for inspection or purchase and publicise these arrangements.

(3) *Special reports*: A special report may be made where the Ombudsman considers that the aggrieved person has suffered injustice or hardship and this has not been, nor is likely to be, remedied. This report is laid before Parliament and copied to those who were sent the original investigation report. The provision allowing a special report to be made is intended to encourage compliance with the decision in the Ombudsman original report.

(4) *Annual reports*: The Ombudsman is required to lay a general report before the Parliament on the performance of her functions. She may also lay other reports before Parliament if she thinks these are necessary to publicise an issue.[54]

[49] 2002 Act, s.8 and Sch.4.
[50] 2002 Act, s.13(4).
[51] 2002 Act, s.2(3).
[52] 2002 Act, s.11(2).
[53] 2002 Act, s.15.
[54] 2002 Act, s.17.

LEGAL PROFESSION

1–40 In Scotland, there are two branches of the legal profession—solicitors and advocates. Members of these branches must be legally qualified and also be a member of the relevant regulatory body. Solicitors may now become solicitor-advocates and these are considered separately below.

Advocates

1–41 An advocate is a specialist court practitioner who practices "at the Bar", *i.e.* the bar of the court. Each advocate is a member of the Faculty of Advocates. Unlike solicitors, advocates may not practise in a partnership; each advocate practises on "his own account". However, they all subscribe to Faculty Services Ltd, a company set up by the Faculty to assist advocates in collecting their fees and receiving instructions from clients. There are around 420 practising advocates.

Although advocates work mainly in the Edinburgh courts, they appear in other courts in Scotland, particularly the High Court in Glasgow. Until the Law Reform (Miscellaneous Provisions) (Scotland) Act 1990, only advocates had the right to appear before the Superior Courts: now solicitors may apply for this privilege and these are known as solicitor-advocates.

A newly-qualified advocate is referred to as "junior counsel" and after a period of some years' practice, may then apply to become a Queen's Counsel. Not every advocate will apply to "take silk" as it called; many will be content to continue with their practice as a junior counsel to retirement. Junior counsel may be instructed in a case on his/her own, but if the matter is particularly important, the client may be advised that both senior and junior counsel be retained.

Counsel must be instructed through a solicitor: it is not possible for a client to approach an advocate directly. If there is a meeting between the client and counsel, the solicitor must also be present. This is important since the solicitor is responsible for making the formal instructions to counsel and for paying the advocate's fees from money obtained from the client.

An advocate need not accept instructions from a client, although there is a rule—the cab rank rule—which states that an advocate should take a case unless there are good reasons for not doing so, *e.g.* the advocate is employed on another case at the same time, or there is a conflict of interest with another client. The cab rank rule is an ancient principle devised to ensure that a client will always have someone to plead for him in court.

As well as appearing in court, advocates are consulted about matters where the client is uncertain as to his legal grounds. These are called "opinions" and the advocate will draw up his or her opinion of the legal merits of the case. This will often be used as a method of settling a dispute without going to court. The solicitor will draw up a "Memorial for Opinion of Counsel" stating the facts, asking for the counsel's opinion of the legal principles and enclosing various supporting documents.

Solicitors

1–42 Formerly called "writers" or "law agents" the correct term for these legally qualified persons is solicitor. The profession is regulated by statute and it is currently under review by the Scottish Parliament. The consolidating statute, Solicitors (Scotland) Act 1980, has been amended by various other statutes—Law Reform (Miscellaneous Provisions) (Scotland) Acts of 1980, 1985 and 1990 and the Solicitors (Scotland) Act 1988. These Acts set out the requirements for entry to the profession as well as regulating how solicitors may carry out their practice.

Although many solicitors will work either in a sole person practice or in partnership, many more are employed by large companies and public authorities. Each solicitor must have a practising certificate and this must be renewed each year. In addition, solicitors must contribute to the Guarantee Fund and be covered by the master policy of professional indemnity, which exists to protect clients from the negligence of a solicitor.

The regulatory body is the Law Society of Scotland and all practising solicitors must be included on the Roll of Solicitors administered by the Society. The Law Society has a number of functions including setting the education, training and admission requirements for the profession. The Society ensures that professional standards and discipline are upheld. As mentioned above, it has set up and administers a guarantee fund, which is available to compensate clients if they suffer loss as a result of the dishonesty of their solicitor.

If a client makes a complaint about a solicitor, it will be investigated by the Law Society, who may then refer the matter to the Scottish Solicitors' Discipline Tribunal. Complaints may also be referred to the tribunal by judges, the Lord Advocate, the Scottish Legal Aid Board and other bodies. The tribunal has the power to discipline a solicitor by fining him, or suspending his practising certificate or requiring him to practice for a period of time as an assistant, or striking his name from the Roll of Solicitors. There is a right of appeal from the tribunal to the Court of Session.

Solicitor-advocates

These were created by the Solicitors (Scotland) Act 1980, as amended by the Law Reform (Miscellaneous Provisions) (Scotland) Act 1990. A qualified solicitor may be given the right of audience in the Supreme Courts. The solicitor has to satisfy the Council of the Law Society of Scotland that he has completed the necessary training in pleading for the court in which he seeks audience, has the necessary knowledge and the necessary experience of proceedings in the sheriff court and that he is a fit and proper person to have the right of audience in the court. By 2000, there were around 120 solicitor-advocates in practice. **1–43**

Basically, the intending solicitor-advocate must have court practice of at least five years, have undertaken the necessary training, passed written examinations and sat in the court for a minimum number of days. A panel of five solicitors will then consider the application and make a recommendation to the Council of the Law Society.

A solicitor-advocate has the same rights of audience as an advocate but may not work as a junior to a Queen's Counsel. The Faculty of Advocates took a decision some years ago not to work with solicitor-advocates to try to preserve their monopoly. Clients who retain a solicitor-advocate do not need to retain a solicitor and an advocate, thus saving themselves some legal fees.

LAW OFFICERS FOR SCOTLAND

The Law Officers for Scotland are the Lord Advocate and the Solicitor General for Scotland. Additionally, the Scotland Act 1998 created the post of Advocate-General for Scotland, who is the Scottish Law Officer in the UK government and is responsible for advising the UK Government on matters of Scots law. **1–44**

The Law Officers (L.A. and S.G.) are political appointments made by the Queen on the recommendation of the First Minister and with the approval of the Scottish Parliament. Initially, the Lord Advocate was a member of the Scottish Cabinet but this is no longer the case. Both Law Officers are members of the Scottish Executive. They need not be members of the Scottish Parliament, but may be called upon by the Parliament to give statements and answer questions.

The L.A. is head of the systems of criminal prosecution and investigation of deaths in Scotland, and as such he exercises his powers independently of the Scottish Executive. He alone decides whether a prosecution will take place and he has control over the procurator fiscal service. Although the L.A. and S.G. may themselves prosecute a major crime, it is now unusual for them to do so, instead advocates are appointed by the L.A. to act as "advocates-depute" to prosecute solemn crimes in the High Court.

PUBLIC DEFENCE SOLICITOR'S OFFICE (PDSO)

1–45 A recent innovation in Scotland was the introduction of the PDSO. On October 1, 1998, a pilot scheme was set up covering the summary courts of Edinburgh District Court and Edinburgh Sheriff Court. The scheme was to test the feasibility of providing criminal assistance through solicitors employed directly by the Scottish Legal Aid Board.[55] The PDSO would comprise no more than six solicitors for a period of five years, working in the summary courts. To ensure a steady flow of clients, the Scottish Legal Aid Board directed that defendants seeking legal aid and whose birthdays fell within the months of January and February, would be represented by the PDSO, unless they were granted a waiver to use a private solicitor. This system ran until July 2000 when the PDSO took over 60 per cent of the sheriff court summary duty solicitor scheme.

The Minister of Justice was required to lay a report before the Scottish Parliament within three years of the start of the office, giving the results of the pilot scheme. After independent research was carried out on the pilot scheme, the Minister announced that it would be extended and it will be "rolled" out in various areas of Scotland.

---

[55] Legal Aid (Scotland) Act 1986, s.28A, inserted by the Crime and Punishment (Scotland) Act 1997, s.50.

Quick Quiz

Civil legal system

- Describe the kinds of cases heard in the sheriff court.
- What qualifications must a person have to become a judge in the Court of Session?
- What are the main differences between the Inner House and the Outer House?
- In what circumstances would a court refer an issue to the European Court of Justice?

Criminal legal system

- Who takes the decision to prosecute a person?
- In summary cases, what factors will a prosecutor take into account when deciding to send a case to the district court?
- Describe the procedure for appealing against the sentence imposed by the sheriff solemn court.
- What is the difference between a not guilty verdict and a not proven verdict?
- Explain what is meant by the term "devolution issue".

Tribunals

- Why are tribunals necessary in modern society?
- How does the Council on Tribunals supervise tribunals?
- What were the reasons for setting up children's hearings?
- In what circumstances will a child be referred to a children's hearing?

Ombudsmen, the legal profession and law officers

- What is the role of the Scottish Public Services Ombudsman?
- Are there any differences between the SPSO's powers and those of the PCA?
- Differentiate between an advocate and a solicitor.
- Who are the Law Officers for Scotland and what is their role in the legal system?

Further Reading

Professor Walker's text, *The Scottish Legal System* (8th ed., 2001) gives a fine account of the development of the courts in Scotland. Many cases and materials of relevance are included in ***The Legal System of Scotland: Cases and Materials*, by A. Paterson, T. Bates and M. Poustie** (4th ed., 1998) as well as interesting discussion. ***The Scottish Criminal Courts in Action*, by Sheriff A. Stewart** (1997) is entertaining as well as instructive and is particularly useful for students.

Readers may be interested in studying the previous system of Ombudsman in Scotland and a good account of this and of tribunals in general, can be found in ***Administrative Law in Scotland*, by Valerie Finch and Christina Ashton** (1997). The children's hearing system is comprehensively discussed by **A. Lockyer and F. Stone in *Juvenile Justice in Scotland*** (1998).

Chapter 2

SOURCES OF SCOTS LAW

Christina Ashton[1]

INTRODUCTION

There are many definitions of what laws are and why society needs them. One view is that law is a system of rules and regulations by which we regulate our lives so that we have the most freedom for ourselves while not harming or restricting the freedoms of others. Laws will try to strike a balance between these two competing needs, since "one man's freedom is another man's prison." **2–01**

Laws are also the ways by which a government controls the population of the country. Violent or dishonest behaviour is controlled by the criminal law and the state, in the form of the government, administers that law. But the government also controls many other areas of law, such as in housing law where the standard of house building is quality controlled, and a landlord can only evict a tenant if the correct legal procedure had been carried out. In company law, a new company has to be registered and fulfill certain requirements, and some people are prohibited from being directors. In employment law, there are regulations regarding the amount of redundancy awarded to a worker and employers cannot discriminate against employees on the grounds of race, sex, marital status or disability.

Laws therefore affect every aspect of our lives. Each activity is subject to control by the civil or criminal laws, and sometimes by both. Thus, if you travel by public transport, you are conveyed under a contract of carriage. If you buy a newspaper, you enter into a contract of sale with the shopkeeper. At all times you are subject to the criminal law, so you do not leave a bus or train without paying for your ticket and you obey the road traffic laws. Each of us is also subject to the civil law of delict which says that we must not harm anyone else by our actions. For instance, if

---

[1] Lecturer in Law, Napier University.

you jump off the bus without looking and knock an elderly woman over, then you may be liable in damages for negligence if you have caused her injury.

Types of legal system

2–02 There are two main types of legal system in the world. The continental or civilian system is based on Roman law and found in European countries. The Anglo-American system is based on English common law, and as the name suggests, is found in England, the US and other countries which were part of the British Empire, such as Australia and Canada.

Scotland has a mixed legal system derived from both Roman law and the common law. It is said to have more empathy with the civilian systems of law. There is no doubt that the strongest influence for several centuries has been the law of England. Nevertheless, the Scots system retains elements of difference which have been protected by the Act of Union 1707 and jealously guarded by the courts since that time.

Why is the Scots system so different from the English system?

2–03 The two systems evolved differently because there were different historical influences upon them.

In Scotland, the feudal period (1018–1296) was a time of significant English influence, first because of the marriage of the Saxon princess Margaret to King Malcolm Canmore. During the reign of Malcolm and Margaret, the lowland people of Scotland adopted English as their first language and their customs became more Anglo-Saxon. The Norman Conquest of England in 1066 did not affect Scotland immediately, but Norman noblemen and clergy came north by the end of the eleventh century and settled here, taking up important positions in the Church and the Government. The reign of King David I (1124–53) saw an increase in Anglo-Norman influence. David I had spent many years in England and he was responsible for the introduction of much of the feudal system of land tenure, along with other English institutions, particularly the office of Sheriff.

The feudal system was a "protective" system whereby the vassal (or farmer) was allowed to work the land to support himself and his family and in return he pledged his support if the superior (or lord) required military help to settle some dispute. The superior protected the vassal from robbers and raiders. The superior himself was likely to be a vassal of a greater lord or baron, or indeed of the King, from whom the land was ultimately acquired. Thus, there was a hierarchy of land tenure. Much later the emphasis changed from military help to paying a rent with crops or money. The feudal system also introduced the concept that the King was lord of all the land in Scotland and the "fountain of all justice". In David I's reign, a king's court was set up to settle disputes between the barons or to hear appeals from lower courts.

Another great influence at this time was the Church of Rome and its canon law. Under David's patronage, the Church became a rich, powerful body with the jurisdiction and right to hold both civil and criminal courts. It is thought that the canon law introduced elements of Roman law into the Scots law and procedure which were then becoming established. The idea of the king as "fountain of justice" helped to establish a more uniform system of law; cases were commenced by the issue of a writ or "brieve" in the king's name. This would require an official to carry out an action or investigation.

From 1296 to 1603, Scots legal history went through a "Dark Age". Scotland and England were frequently at war and Scotland formed an alliance with France. Thus, influences upon the Scots legal system, such as were possible, came from the Continent. However, there were a few glimmers of light during this turbulent time. Regular meetings of Parliament were held from around 1346 when David II was captured by the English and held for ransom. By 1366, the burgesses from the burghs were participating in the Parliament and the levying of taxation was made with their agreement. At first however, the Parliament's main role was as a court of first instance and for appeals. It was not until the reign of James I (1406–37) that Parliament became primarily a legislature.

In the fifteenth and sixteenth centuries, a number of statutes were passed which had effect for centuries. For instance, the Prescription Act 1469 established the long negative prescription while the Act of 1573, c.55, regulated the law of divorce for desertion. An Act of 1424 ensured that the poor had access to legal aid.

The Court of Session was set up in 1532 and from its proceedings, legal writings in the form of "Practicks" were produced and notes of legal directions. These helped to set up a more unified system of law. The court was given power to make Acts of Sederunt to regulate the way in which the court operated. The judges were known as Senators of the College of Justice (as they still are today) and initially they sat as a collegiate body. By the beginning of the seventeenth century however, it appears that the modern form of the court was starting to take shape, with a small number of judges sitting in the Outer House hearing witnesses.

From the Union of the Crowns in 1603 up until 1800, there was a great interest in Roman law and many young Scotsmen studied in France and Holland, bringing back with them the principles of Roman law and using them when they became practitioners and judges in Scotland. Roman law became a major factor in forming Scots law, particularly in the law of obligations and moveable property. In 1617, the General Register of Sasines was set up to record transactions relating to land. The creation of a record of land transactions has helped to ensure that buyers of land in Scotland receive secure title to that land.

From 1655, there was much movement in the legal system with the publication of "institutional writings". These became important sources of law and are discussed in more detail later in this Chapter.

The High Court of Justiciary was established in 1672, consisting of five judges from the Court of Session and the Justice-General and Justice-Clerk. The judges were known as Commissioners of Justiciary (now Lords Commissioners of Justiciary) and they dealt with criminal cases in Edinburgh. The office of Lord Justice General was hereditary until 1837 when the then holder, the Duke of Montrose, died. The office was then merged with that of the Lord President.

The Union of the Parliaments of Scotland and England on May 1, 1707 dissolved the two Parliaments and created a new Parliament of Great Britain. The Union was created by means of a treaty negotiated by the two states; each Parliament then ratified the treaty. Article XIX of the Union Treaty specified that the Scots Law and the Scottish Courts should continue. Although the Treaty stated that no causes in Scotland should be heard in the Courts of Chancery, Queen's Bench, Common Pleas, "or any other court in Westminster Hall", this was held not to include the House of Lords. The practice of sending civil appeals to the House of Lords began within a short time of the Union coming into effect.[2]

From 1800, there began what we now call the modern period of Scots law. Scots students no longer went to the Continent to study; the Napoleonic Wars prevented such travel. English law now became the major influence on Scots law, mainly because of two factors:

- the House of Lords now heard all Scottish civil appeals; and
- the Westminster Parliament passed all laws.

Both of these institutions were based on English models and were peopled by mainly English-trained lawyers and judges. Concepts of English law were used to decide Scots law, thus changing the Scots principles and causing confusion. There was growing concern with the decisions made by the House of Lords during the eighteenth and early nineteenth centuries. In 1876, the Appellate Jurisdiction Act was passed and this ensured that at least one of the judges in the House of Lords was Scottish-trained.

The office of Secretary for Scotland was created in 1885 to administer matters such as law and order and education in Scotland and this office became a Cabinet post in 1892. The powers of the Scottish Office gradually increased over the years so that the Secretary of State for Scotland, as the office was now termed, had responsibility for the wide range of matters seen in modern times. The

[2] *Greenshields v Magistrates of Edinburgh* (1710–1711) Rob. 12.

presence of a Scottish Minister in the Cabinet brought benefits for Scotland but it is difficult to gauge the extent of benefit since Cabinet discussions remain secret. The Scottish Office was not autonomous; it operated within the Whitehall system of government and its funding came from the UK Treasury.

On a number of occasions since the 1960s, the Secretary of State for Scotland has belonged to a party which did not have a majority of Scottish seats in the UK Parliament; thus it could be said that the Government as represented by the Secretary of State did not represent the majority of the electors. This "democratic deficit" was particularly acute during the 1980s Governments of Margaret Thatcher. The Conservative Government implemented policies which were not supported by the majority of Scottish electors, *e.g.* the replacement of household rates with the community charge or "poll tax". There was an impression that the needs of Scotland were not being given due consideration by a government which drew its support from other parts of the UK.

In 1988, the Campaign for a Scottish Assembly published *A Claim of Right for Scotland* in which they declared that Scotland had a right to decide her own constitution and called for a convention to be set up to devise a scheme for a Parliament or Assembly.[3] The next year the Constitutional Convention was set up drawing support from a wide range of people and groups. In 1995 the Convention published its final report *Scotland's Parliament. Scotland's Right* and this formed the basis of the Labour Government's proposals in 1997. After a referendum in September 1997 affirmed the support of the Scottish electorate for devolution, the UK Parliament passed the Scotland Act in 1998 and a new system of government came into being in Scotland in May 1999.

CATEGORISING LAW

Distinction between public/private law

2–04 What does the phrase "public/private law" mean? In practical terms, very little. It is a simple method of categorising the various "branches" of law and keeping like subjects together. For instance, Scots private law comprises a number of different areas of law, such as succession, family law, delict and so on. In all of these areas, the involvement of the state is minimal and the cases may involve the breakdown of relationships between individuals or legal persons, such as companies and partnerships.

Where the law relates to the government of the country or to the relationship between the State and an individual citizen, the law will be termed "Public Law". It regulates the activities of public authorities such as the courts, Scottish Executive and Scottish Parliament, and local government. Examples of Public Law topics include Constitutional Law, Criminal Law and EU Law.

Distinction between civil law and criminal law

2–05 The main difference between civil law and criminal law is that there is a different court system for each. A criminal case will be heard in courts which have different procedures, rules of evidence and remedies from a case heard in a civil court. The distinction is therefore very important since it affects the outcome of the case for the people concerned.

Many people think of criminal courts when asked to describe what they think a court is. Most people will talk about "prosecuting" someone for damaging their property instead of "suing" them. Many of these misconceptions arise because the media expose us to the criminal legal procedure more often than civil courts. Discussion of the technicalities of a clause in a contract would not make good TV or cinema, but the very human stories of a criminal court can make for riveting viewing.

---

3 O. Edwards (ed.), *A Claim of Right for Scotland* (1989).

The criminal law has a separate structure of courts, which deal with issues affecting the liberty of individuals, the punishment of persons found guilty and to a limited extent, the compensation of victims of criminal behaviour. The standard of proof required in a criminal case is very high—"beyond reasonable doubt". This means that if there is some doubt and that doubt is reasonably held, the accused must be acquitted. In Scotland, an accused can only be found guilty if the evidence is corroborated, that is, there are at least two independent sources or witnesses that the accused committed the crime.

It is now very rare for a private prosecution by a victim of a crime. In one of only two in the twentieth century, a woman who had been raped and slashed with a razor was granted a Bill for Criminal Letters. The Lord Advocate then took on the case and the culprits were successfully prosecuted and punished.[4]

A civil case will occur where the relationship between two or more parties breaks down or where the conduct of one party has caused loss to another. Examples of civil actions would occur when a builder fails to complete a house extension, or a dry cleaning firm ruins an item of clothing, or a van driver hits another vehicle. In all of these cases, the person aggrieved may take these people to court if they do not otherwise fulfil the contract or pay compensation for the damage they have caused. In these examples, the criminal law is not involved. However, if the van driver drives off without leaving his name and other details, he will be guilty of an offence and thus it can be seen that an action which otherwise would be only a civil matter can escalate to involve the criminal law.

Distinction between common law and statute law

Another distinction which has to be noted is between common law and statute law. **2–06**

Common law was originally the body of law common to the whole country based on ancient customs and worked out and built up in the courts by the process of declaration of rules and their application to cases. Much of the common law has now been superseded by statute law, but it is still very important in Scotland in many areas. For instance, it controls the operation of contract, delict and much of the criminal law.

Statute law is the most important form of law. It is enacted by the UK and the Scottish Parliaments and it will usually overturn any other type of law except EU law, where special rules and problems exist.

SOURCES OF LAW

Rules and principles of law must have a source, and it is this source which will give the rule its **2–07**
authority and binding force. In the Scottish legal system, as in England and Wales, there is in effect a hierarchy of sources of law, whereby legislation takes precedence over case law, which takes precedence over authoritative writings, and so on. If one source is incorporated into a higher source, the original will lose its authority. Thus, many instances of custom are now incorporated into legislation, and custom is rarely relied upon as a source of law. Similarly, if a decision in a case is subsequently confirmed, or negated, by an Act of Parliament, the legislative provision becomes the legal and binding principle. There are now a myriad of different sources of the law in Scotland. Legislation is passed by the UK Parliament, by the Scottish Parliament, and by the European Union, while case law and other common law sources still play an important part.

---

[4] *H v Sweeney*, 1983 S.L.T. 48.

Key Concepts

Sources of law:

- Legislation;
- Judicial precedent;
- Authoritative writings;
- Custom;
- Equity.

LEGISLATION

2–08 Legislation is the most important source of law and arguably the legislation created by the UK is the highest source of law affecting Scotland. Although with the advent of the Scottish Parliament there is less UK legislation having effect on the Scottish legal system, this form of law is still the most authoritative because of the doctrine of supremacy of Parliament. As you will see below, laws made by the Scottish Parliament are subject to certain requirements and the Scotland Act 1998, s.28(7) clearly states that the UK Parliament retains the power to make laws for Scotland. As regards the laws made by the European Union, the doctrine of supremacy of Parliament is also relevant and the UK Parliament retains the right to make laws for the UK while allowing the European institutions to make laws within the context of those areas covered by the various European treaties.

Legislation made by the UK Parliament

2–09 Every autumn, or after a General Election, the Queen opens Parliament and announces in the Queen's Speech the Government's legislative plans for the coming parliamentary session. Around 20 pieces of legislation will be announced at this time, but many more Bills will be introduced and passed during the course of the year.

Key Concepts

Generally speaking there are three types of **Bills**:

- a **Private Bill**, which applies to a particular area or person or persons;
- a **Hybrid Bill**, which is a combination of the other two; and
- a **Public Bill**, which has general application.

Private Bills concern particular bodies, for instance a local authority or public corporation. The procedure for passing these Bills is slightly different from that for a Public Bill. There is often very little discussion of the contents of the Bill within Parliament. The Committee Stage will consist of hearings, during which the proposers and opponents of the Bill will be given the opportunity to put forward their evidence.

Hybrid Bills are those which on the whole have general application but they appear to contain particular provisions affecting the interests of particular persons or organisations. For instance, the building of the Channel Tunnel rail link required an Act which involved a private company being given compulsory purchase powers to buy the land to build the northern end of the tunnel.[5] A Bill which appears to affect private interests must be considered by the Examiners of Petitions for Private Bills to decide whether aspects of the Private Business Standing Orders apply. If they do, the Bill is treated as a hybrid Bill. This entails the committee stage of the Bill being considered by a Select Committee, rather than a Standing Committee. Anyone who opposes the Bill may submit a petition to the Select Committee, using the same format as for a Private Bill. The Select Committee will consider evidence put forward by the promoters of the Bill and by their opponents. The Committee then considers the Bill and reports to the House. The Bill will be recommitted to a Committee of the Whole House or a Standing Committee, and thereafter proceeds as a Public Bill. The same process is used in the House of Lords.

Public Bills are of course the most important of the three types and they take up the greater part of the legislative programme of Parliament. There are two types of Public Bills—Government Bills and Private Members' Bills.

The proposal for a *Private Member's Bill* may come from an M.P. him or herself, from a pressure group or indeed from the Government. M.P.s lucky in the ballot for Private Members' Bills will find themselves inundated with ideas for a Bill. Increasingly, the Government will suggest to M.P.s that they might present Bills on matters which the Government would like to see promoted but to which the Government is unable to devote time, or with which they do not wish to be too closely associated because of the controversial nature of the Bill. Such a Bill will receive preferential treatment compared to Bills put forward without the blessing of the government, for instance, the Hunting with Dogs Bill put forward in the 1997–1998 session did not have the blessing of Government and ran out of time, although the vast majority of M.P.s voted in its favour at second reading.

There are three methods of initiating a Private Member's Bill.

(1) *Ballot*: At the start of each session of Parliament a ballot of backbench M.P.s is held. The first 20 M.P.s whose names are drawn out are allowed time to present a Bill. The debates take place on 13 Fridays and the proposer is able to choose which date they wish to present their Bill for its second reading. Those M.P.s who have a low number in the ballot will be able to choose to present their Bill first on one of the seven Fridays set aside for the second reading debates. The rest of the Fridays are used for later stages of Private Members' Bills. The chances of Bills completing the process are very small; to have a chance the Bill has to be one of the first seven in the ballot, non-controversial and have cross-party support. On average six Bills presented through the ballot will become law. In the 1996–97 session, no less than 14 of the 20 were successful.

If the Bill is uncontroversial, it will often pass the second reading with minimum debate. However, if the Bill next on the order paper for the day is controversial or opposed, the opponents may decide to debate the uncontroversial Bill in the hope of "talking out" the second Bill. Many Private Members' Bills will fail because the requisite number of M.P.s are not present to support a closure motion. A closure motion is used to bring the debate to a close, thus preventing the Bill from being "talked out". If 100 M.P.s support the closure motion, the Bills following after will be rescheduled and not lost. If the Bill does not pass its second reading, it will fall.

(2) *Ten minute rule Bill*: This is introduced on a Tuesday or Wednesday afternoon after ministerial question time. It is a popular way of introducing a Bill to Parliament because of the high profile nature of its timing. In many respects, however, the proposer is not seriously trying to create new law but is trying to highlight the need for change in some aspect of the law. The proposer of the Bill speaks for 10 minutes, then anyone opposed to it speaks for 10 minutes, and then there is a vote. Even if it passes this stage, it is unlikely to become law because no government time will be given to it. Generally, only one ten minute rule Bill will become law each session.

(3) *Ordinary presentation Bill*: Here a Bill is introduced to Parliament during the course of the day; there is no particular time given over to it. The Bill is presented formally but the M.P.

[5] Channel Tunnel Rail Link Act 1996.

does not make a speech when presenting it. Normally, only one or two Bills will pass into law, although in the session 1990–91, eight such Bills were passed, including two specifically for Scotland.[6] Of the other six, three related to the welfare of animals.

Private Members' Bills serve a useful function. They ensure that backbench M.P.s are more fully involved in the legislative process. They may change the law when the Government is unwilling to do so but there is support in the House for such a change. In recent years, however, the success rate for Private Members' Bills has dropped. In 1990–91, 19 out of 119 Bills passed were Private Members' Bills, while in 1995–96 17 out of 89 Bills were from private members. In 1999–2000, this number had dropped to 6 out of 104 Bills, a marked decrease.

A Government Bill is prepared by legal draftsmen in the Parliamentary Counsel Office after consultation with the department proposing the Bill. It will have been considered by a Cabinet Committee and then the Cabinet will approve it. Often the Bill will have been the subject of extensive consultation with pressure and interest groups before it reached the draft stage. There may have been a Green Paper (consultation document) or a White Paper (statement of policy) on the subject before the Bill is introduced to Parliament. The Labour Government elected in 1997 announced that it would publish more draft Bills to enable wider consultation and pre-legislative scrutiny.

A Bill may be introduced in either House but certain Bills will always be introduced first to the House of Commons; these include Money Bills (*i.e.* those which seek to raise taxation or involve expenditure), controversial Bills, and Bills of constitutional significance. A Bill which starts in the House of Lords will progress through the same stages as in the House of Commons.

Stages of a Bill

2–10

First Reading	A Bill is taken as read for the first time if certain formalities are gone through. At the start of business the Speaker calls upon the minister in charge of the Bill—he stands up and nods, the clerk reads out the short title of the Bill and the minister names a date for the second reading. This allows the Bill to be printed.
Second Reading	This is a general debate about the principles of the Bill—no amendments are allowed at this stage. At the end of the debate the motion is put to the vote. A Bill can be lost at this stage although it is uncommon, for instance the Shops Bill in April 1986 was lost at second reading. After a Bill has been given a second reading, the House considers any clauses which require a Money Resolution (which will authorise expenditure) or Ways and Means Resolution (which authorises the levying of taxes or other charges). The Standing Committee cannot consider these clauses of the Bill until the resolutions have been agreed.
Committee Stage	At committee stage, the Bill is considered clause by clause and amendments are made. There are two types of committee: the Standing Committee and the Committee of the Whole House: (1) A Standing Committee consists of between 18 and 50 M.P.s chosen to reflect the political composition of the House. The committee will include the minister in charge of the Bill and usually a front-bench spokesperson from the opposition parties. A new standing committee is appointed for each Bill and it will disband once it has reported to the House. It is possible for the House to commit the Bill initially to a Special Standing Committee which spends time considering the issues raised by

6 Age of Capacity (Scotland) Act 1991 and Mental Health Detention (Scotland) Act 1991.

	the Bill before proceeding to consider the Bill in the normal way. This procedure was used for the recent Immigration and Asylum Act 1999. (2) In a Committee of the Whole House all of the M.P.s consider the Bill clause by clause on the floor of the House. This is set up for Bills of constitutional importance, such as the Scotland Bill during 1998 and the House of Lords Bill during 1999. It is also used for Bills which need to be passed quickly, such as the annual Finance Bill. Amendments are voted on as they occur. The Government usually opposes amendments but may support some.
Report Stage (also called the **Consideration Stage**)	If the Bill has been before a Committee of the Whole House this stage is a formality. Otherwise, this stage informs M.P.s who were not on the Standing Committee of any amendments. The new clauses will be debated and the government may make further amendments if it had agreed to do so in committee. There is no vote.
Third Reading	The Bill is debated in principle and a vote taken. No amendments may be taken. It is unusual for a Bill to be lost here.

Once these stages have been completed, the Bill is sent to the other House where the whole procedure is gone through again. The process in the House of Lords is the same, except for three differences. First, the committee stage is a Committee of the Whole House. Second, there is no guillotine motion and debate is therefore unrestricted. Finally, it is possible to make an amendment at third reading.

After both Houses have agreed the Bill, it is sent for Royal Assent and comes into effect, either immediately, or on a date specified in the Act, or on a date to be decided by the minister. The Act will state which of these dates is to be followed. It is not unusual for an Act to be brought into effect in stages.

One of the problems with this legislative procedure is the amount of time it takes. This allows opponents of a Bill to lengthen the process further by putting down many amendments. In November 2000, the House of Commons adopted a new system to try to timetable Bills more effectively. The programme motion sets out the amount of time allocated to any stage of a Bill. The motion is agreed by the Government and the opposition parties before it is submitted to the House. If the Government and Opposition do not agree the programme motion, the Government may feel compelled to put an allocation of time motion, commonly and colourfully called a "guillotine" motion. This formalises the timetable for the Bill and allows proceedings to be brought to a conclusion once the time allocated has been exhausted. It curtails debate but also prevents consideration of those parts of the Bill not yet reached by the Standing Committee or the House.

On occasion, the two Houses will not agree a Bill. If the House of Lords amends a Commons Bill and the Commons does not agree with the amendment, the House of Lords has a stark choice: it may either accept the Commons wording, or it may refuse to change its amendment. In the latter case, the Bill will fall. The Government is at liberty to bring back an identical Bill in the next session of Parliament. If the House of Lords still refuses to accept the Bill without amending it, the Speaker of the House of Commons may sign a declaration and the Bill will proceed to Royal Assent without the consent of the House of Lords. This procedure is controlled by the Parliament Act 1911, as amended by the Parliament Act 1949. One year must have elapsed between the Bill's Second Reading in the Commons in the first session and the Bill being passed by the Commons in the second session. In this way, the power of the House of Lords to block legislation is curtailed.

Normally, if a Bill does not receive the Royal Assent by the time Parliament is prorogued at the end of a parliamentary session, it will fall. In 1998, the House agreed that it may be possible for a government Bill to be carried forward into the next parliamentary session. The first Bill to be carried forward was the Financial Services and Markets Bill 1998–99 which was taken forward to the 1999–2000 session after a debate on October 25, 1999.

Subordinate legislation

2–11 The considerable detail of how legislation is to work cannot be set out comfortably in a statute; it is therefore included in subordinate or delegated legislation. This kind of legislation will take the form of statutory instruments or Orders in Council.

> **Key Concept**
>
> **Subordinate legislation** derives its authority from a parent or enabling Act and it must only seek to do what the parent Act allows. If an instrument goes beyond the authority given in the parent Act, it will be *ultra vires*, literally beyond the powers. Subordinate legislation may therefore be challenged in the courts; an Act of Parliament may not be challenged for lack or excess of power.

Advantages and uses of subordinate legislation:

(1) Subordinate legislation saves parliamentary time. There has been a marked increase in the amount of primary legislation passed by Parliament each year and there is always difficulty in finding enough time to pass all of the legislation that the Government and backbench M.P.s want. The general practice is to enact the policy, and leave it to the Government to fill in the details of how the policy will be implemented.

(2) Subordinate legislation allows the Government to seek advice from experts in the area under consideration, *e.g.* road traffic laws, food hygiene standards.

(3) This type of legislation is useful in times of emergency when there is no time to enact primary legislation. An example occurred in the late 1980s when radioactive fallout from the Chernobyl nuclear power station in the USSR affected animals grazing on upland pastures in southern Scotland and the Lake District.

(4) Subordinate legislation is used to bring a statute, or part of statute, into operation. The parent Act will state whether it is to come into effect on a particular day or whether the Secretary of State is to make a commencement order. This is one of the most common uses of statutory instruments. There may be more than one commencement order for a statute, bringing in different sections at different times.

(5) If an amendment needs to be made in the future, it is the regulation which is being amended not the Act itself. Thus it is easier and quicker to react to changing or unforeseen circumstances.

Disadvantages of subordinate legislation:

(1) Lack of consultation. There is relatively little consultation regarding the content or implementation of statutory instruments, except where technical issues are being implemented.

(2) Inadequate controls. Parliament does not exercise strict control over the implementation of statutory instruments. When a statutory instrument is laid in Parliament, it cannot be amended by an M.P., although an M.P. may ask questions of the minister regarding the effect of the instrument. If there is dissent, the Government will withdraw the instrument, redraft it and re-introduce it. The Joint Committee on Statutory Instruments, which is a joint committee of members of both Houses and is sometimes called the Scrutiny Committee, scrutinises statutory instruments, but only after they have come into effect. The Joint Committee is not able to comment on the merits of the instrument, only whether it was correctly drafted. The Committee will report to the House any instance where the authority

of the Act has been exceeded, or there has been an "unexpected or unusual" use of the powers. If there is a defect in the instrument, damage may already have been done since it will have been put into effect. Similarly, although it is possible to challenge a regulation in court as being *ultra vires*, this can only happen after the regulation has been brought into effect and the damage has been done. In any event, the regulation may have been drafted very widely, making it impossible for any action to be *ultra vires*.

(3) Lack of publicity. There is little publicity that a statutory instrument has been brought into force. The Statutory Instruments Act 1946 sets out rules for numbering, printing and publication of statutory instruments but many rules and regulations will not come within the terms of the 1946 Act.

(4) Use of skeleton statutes. A skeleton statute is one which gives the briefest detail of policy and leaves the minister to flesh out the detail. This may speed up the process of passing the statute but it has little to do with democracy, since the implementation of detail of the policy is left to ministers and officials.

(5) "Henry VIII" clauses. These clauses give power to a minister to amend a statute by means of an order or regulation. Note that this power can apply to any statute, not just the parent Act. Such clauses are very powerful weapons; they are supposed to be used sparingly but have been used increasingly over the last two or three decades. An example of a Henry VIII clause is found in s.2(2) of the European Communities Act 1972.

Example of a "Henry VIII" Clause

European Communities Act 1972, s.2(2)

"2. General implementation of Treaties

(2) Subject to Schedule 2 to this Act, at any time after its passing Her Majesty may by Order in Council, and any designated Minister or department may by regulations, make provision—

(a) for the purpose of implementing any Community obligation of the UK, or enabling any such obligation to be implemented, or of enabling any rights enjoyed or to be enjoyed by the UK under or by virtue of the Treaties to be exercised; or

(b) for the purpose of dealing with matters arising out of or related to any such obligation or rights or the coming into force, or the operation from time to time, of subsection(1) above:

and in the exercise of any statutory power or duty, including any power to give directions or to legislate by means of orders, rules, regulations or other subordinate instrument, the person entrusted with the power or duty may have regard to the objects of the Communities and to any such obligation or rights as aforesaid."

Statutory Instruments

Statutory Instruments are often known as Regulations or Rules. The power to make Instruments will be delegated to a minister. Many Statutory Instruments must be laid before Parliament. However, they are not scrutinised to any extent; they are laid on the table of the House (literally) for a period of time. If the parent Act has declared that the Instrument is to be passed using the *negative resolution* procedure, it will come into effect in 40 days unless either House resolves that it should be annulled. Note that the regulation cannot be amended. **2–12**

The other main method of laying the Instrument is the *affirmative resolution* procedure. Here the Instrument requires the approval of Parliament during a debate in the House which will last for up to 90 minutes. Again no amendment of the Instrument is allowed. If the resolution is not passed, the Instrument will be taken back by the department concerned for amendment and resubmission.

Orders in Council

2–13 The "Council" referred to here is the Privy Council which advises the Queen on matters of national importance and constitutional significance. There are two types of Order in Council. The first is an Order which is made with the authority of the royal prerogative. This kind of Order does not require the approval of Parliament and is usually reserved for matters of some importance, such as the order to dissolve Parliament. This type is made by the Privy Council with the authority of the Queen. The Privy Council is involved in the regulation of professional bodies such as the General Medical Council. Parliament is not involved in creating the Order. The second type is used by the Government, but does not bypass Parliament. The parent Act will authorise the use of an Order in Council to legislate in some area. Orders in Council were used to transfer powers from Ministers of the UK Government to those of the devolved assemblies.[7]

Legislation of the Scottish Parliament

2–14 The Labour Party elected to government in May 1997 included a commitment to creating a Scottish Parliament in its manifesto, but this was qualified by a requirement for the Scottish people to agree to devolution in a referendum. The Government published a White Paper called *Scotland's Parliament* in July 1997, setting out the proposals.[8] The referendum contained two questions, one to confirm support for a Scottish Parliament and the other to consent to the Parliament having tax-varying powers.

The referendum was held on September 11, 1997[9] and both questions were answered in the affirmative. The first question had 74.3 per cent in favour, 25.7 per cent against. The second question, on tax-varying powers, had 63.5 per cent in favour, 36.5 per cent against.

The Scotland Bill was introduced to the UK Parliament in December 1997 and became law in November 1998. Elections to the new Parliament were held on May 6, 1999 and the new Parliament had its first sitting on May 12. The Queen officially opened the Parliament on July 1, 1999, signalling the transfer of powers from Westminster to the new Parliament and the Scottish Executive.

The Scotland Act 1998 created the Scottish Parliament by devolving certain powers from the UK Parliament to the Scottish Parliament and the Scottish Administration.

> **Key Concept**
>
> **Devolution** may be defined as a delegation of power from a central body to local bodies. The idea is to allow decisions to be made closer to the people who will be affected.

The UK Parliament retains a number of powers, known as "reserved powers". These are mainly concerned with issues with international impact, for instance defence and foreign affairs, and issues which need to be the same throughout the UK such as social security and other benefits and employment laws. The UK Parliament retains the right to legislate for Scotland on any matter. Section 28(7) of the Act clearly states: "This section does not affect the power of the Parliament of the UK to make laws for Scotland." This section reiterates the doctrine of supremacy of the UK Parliament, a doctrine which could not in any case be abandoned by them.[10] A convention, called the Sewel Convention, has evolved to ensure that the consent of the Scottish Parliament is sought before the UK Parliament legislates on a matter which is otherwise devolved.

---

[7] See for instance, Scotland Act 1998 (Transfer of Functions to the Scottish Ministers etc.) Order 1999 (SI 1999/1750).

[8] Cmnd.3658 (1997).

[9] This date had particular historical significance—700 years before in 1297, William Wallace led the Scots army against the English army and defeated them at the Battle of Stirling Bridge!

[10] According to Lord Hope of Craighead in House of Lords debates on the Bill—*Hansard*, HL Vol.592, col.796 (1998).

The Scotland Act does not state which powers have been devolved to the Scottish Parliament and Scottish Executive. Rather, the devolved bodies have the power to legislate on any topic not specifically excluded in the Scotland Act. This is called the retaining model of devolution, where everything is devolved except a limited number of exceptions.

The other model of devolution is called the transferring model and this involves stating the specific areas in which devolved powers may be exercised; anything which is not specified will be retained by the central body. This is not a satisfactory method of devolution; it was used in the Scotland Act 1978 which was repealed after the 1979 referendum did not reach the required minimum vote. Its main drawback is that it must constantly be updated. As each statute was passed by the UK Parliament an amendment would need to be made to specify whether the powers in the statute were devolved or retained.

The power to make laws is contained in s.28, which is read in conjunction with s.29. The latter section sets out the Parliament's legislative competence.

Key Concepts

Limits on the **legislative competence** of the Scottish Parliament:

- The Scottish Parliament may not legislate for another country or territory.
- The Scottish Parliament may not legislate on a matter which is reserved to the UK Parliament as detailed in Schedule 5.
- The Scottish Parliament may not legislate in breach of the restrictions in Schedule 4. This schedule states that certain UK statutes may not be amended or repealed by the Scottish Parliament, *e.g.* the Act of Union 1707; European Communities Act 1972; Human Rights Act 1998; Scotland Act 1998.
- Legislation of the Scottish Parliament must not be incompatible with Convention rights or EC law.
- The Scottish Parliament may not remove the Lord Advocate from his position as head of the systems of criminal prosecution and investigation of deaths in Scotland.

Reserved matters

Reserved matters are detailed in Sch.5 to the Act. Part I contains general reservations under the headings of the constitution: political parties; foreign affairs; public service; defence and treason. Each reservation has a number of examples. For instance, under the Constitution, the matters specifically reserved are the succession to the Crown, the Union of the Kingdoms of Scotland and England, the Parliament of the UK, and the continued existence of the Supreme Courts of Scotland. **2–15**

In Part II, specific reservations are set out. This section is highly detailed in places, but more general in others. There are 11 "Heads" each with sections detailing certain areas of activity. These sections give the reservations followed by any exceptions to the reservations or interpretations of these.

Head A: Financial and Economic Matters

General fiscal, economic and monetary policy; issue of money; taxes and excise duties; government borrowing and lending; exchange rate; Bank of England.

Exceptions: local taxes.

Head B: Home Affairs
Drugs offences; Data Protection Act 1998; elections for all elections except local authority elections; firearms; immigration and nationality; scientific experiments on live animals; national security; betting, gaming and lotteries; emergency powers; extradition.

Head C: Trade and Industry
Business associations; insolvency (except where Scots law is different); competition; intellectual property; consumer protection; weights and measures; telecommunications and wireless telegraphy; postal services; research councils.

Head D: Energy
Provision and supply of all forms of energy.
Exceptions: pollution control for electricity; manufacture and shipping of gas otherwise than through pipes; some coal environmental issues.

Head E: Transport
Rail, road, marine and air transport.
Exceptions: Each of these sections contains exceptions, *e.g.* rail travel—provision and regulation of railways is reserved but grants to provide rail services is not.

Head F: Social Security
This reservation covers all forms of social security and benefits to ensure that all citizens of the UK have access to the same level of benefits wherever they live.
Child support; occupational and personal pensions, war pensions.
Exceptions: promotion of social welfare by local authorities.

Head G: Regulation of Professions
Examples: Architects, auditors, doctors, nurses, vets, and dentists.

Head H: Employment
Employment and industrial relations; health and safety; job search and support.
Exceptions: food safety; careers services.

Head J: Health and Medicines
Xenotransplantation; embryology; surrogacy; genetics; abortion; medicines and poisons.

Head K: Media and Culture
Broadcasting.

Head L: Miscellaneous
Power to determine salaries of judiciary; equal opportunities; designation of timescales, time zones, British Summer Time.
Exceptions: computation of legal periods of time; Scottish bank and public holidays.

Scrutiny of proposed legislation in Scottish Parliament

2–16 Section 28(1) of the Act states: "The Parliament may make laws, to be known as the Acts of the Scottish Parliament." A proposed statute is a Bill and this will become an Act of the Scottish Parliament (ASP) when it is passed by the Parliament and receives the Royal Assent. The validity of an ASP is not affected by any invalidity in the proceedings and ASPs are to be judicially noticed. This means that the Act does not require that evidence of its existence and contents have to be led in court proceedings.[11]

A Bill may be presented by:

- a member of the Scottish Executive;
- a committee of the Parliament; or
- an individual member.

Before a Bill is presented to the Parliament, a member of the Scottish Executive must make a statement that the provisions of the Bill are, in their view, within the legislative competence of the Parliament.[12] The Presiding Officer must also consider the Bill before it is submitted to Parliament and make a similar statement as to the legislative competence.[13]

Executive Bills (s.36)

Generally, there is considerable consultation on a Bill before it is presented to the Parliament. There are five stages in the legislative process: **2–17**

(1) Introduction of the Bill and consideration by the relevant committee. The Executive makes a statement of legislative competence and a memorandum detailing the consultation that took place and the effect of the changes to be enacted. A financial memorandum is also included. The Presiding Officer will make his statement regarding the legislative competence. The Bill is then authorised to be printed and published.
(2) Stage 1 of the Legislative process. The Bill is sent to the relevant committee where the principles are considered. A report is prepared for the Parliament and a debate and vote is held in the Parliament on the principles.
(3) Stage 2 of the Bill. This is a detailed consideration of each clause. The Bill may be sent to one or more committees for consideration, but one committee will act as the "Lead Committee" drawing all of the comments together. If the Bill confers powers to make subordinate legislation, the Subordinate Legislation Committee must consider and report on these aspects of the Bill. There must be a period of at least two weeks between Stage 1 and Stage 2. The committees will consider any amendments made by any M.S.P.
(4) After a further lapse of two weeks, the Bill moves to Stage 3, where the amended Bill is returned to the Parliament for final discussion and vote.
(5) The fifth and final stage is the submission for Royal Assent.[14] However this cannot take place immediately. There must be a period of four weeks from the final vote in the Parliament to the presentation for Royal Assent. This four-week moratorium allows any Law Officer of the UK or any Minister of the UK to consider the Bill and its implications. If any of them feel that the Parliament has legislated beyond its competence, then they may refer the matter to the Judicial Committee of the Privy Council under s.33 (Law Officers) or s.35 (Ministers). If the JCPC finds that the Bill is outwith the legislative competence, the Bill must be changed. It will be returned to the Parliament to amend. If the amendment is made and there is no further challenge, the Bill is sent by the Presiding Officer to the Queen for Royal Assent. It is possible for this four-week period to be curtailed if the Law Officers and Secretaries of State indicate that they do not intend to refer the Bill.

---

[11] There is an equivalent rule for UK statutes in the Interpretation Act 1978, s.3.
[12] Scotland Act 1998, s.31(1).
[13] Scotland Act 1998, s.31(2).
[14] Scotland Act 1998, s.32.

Committee Bill

2–18 This is a new development in UK Parliamentary affairs and its inclusion indicated the view of the Government that M.S.P.s should be more involved in the making of legislation than their counterparts in the UK Parliament.

If a committee has conducted inquiries into an area of law and decided that changes in the law should be made, the committee may report on this to the Parliament. If the Parliament agrees, the Scottish Executive then has five "sitting days" to decide whether or not to propose legislation. If the Scottish Executive declines to bring forward a Bill, the Parliament may decide to authorise the drafting of a Bill by adopting the committee's report. The Bill is then introduced to the Parliament with a general debate (Stage 1) and, if approved, it proceeds to committee stage (Stage 2) and then final debate in Parliament (Stage 3). There is no need for the general principles to be considered by a committee at Stage 1. The requirements for legislative competence still apply.

The first Committee Bill was introduced by the Justice 1 Committee in 2001 and was passed as the Protection from Abuse (Scotland) Act 2001. In December 2002, the Education, Culture and Sport Committee introduced the Commissioner for Children and Young People (Scotland) Bill which received the Royal Assent on May 1, 2003.

Member's Bill

2–19 There are two methods for an individual M.S.P. to propose legislation. In the first method, an M.S.P. submits a written proposal to a committee, which may proceed by holding an inquiry into whether such legislation is required. If the committee decides to do so, the Bill proceeds as if it were a committee Bill. The second method requires the M.S.P. to obtain the support of at least 11 other M.S.P.s. The proposer lodges the Bill with the Parliamentary Clerk. If 11 signatures are received within a month, the Bill will proceed as if it were an Executive Bill. The Presiding Officer gives the usual statement on legislative competence. One of the first member's Bills was introduced by Tommy Sheridan M.S.P. to abolish poindings and warrant sales in 2001.[15] At the time of writing, there are seven member's Bills being discussed by the Parliament.

Special Bills

2–20 (1) *Budget Bills*: A budget Bill is an executive Bill to authorise payments to be made from the Scottish Consolidated Fund. It may only be introduced by a member of the Scottish Executive. No financial memorandum, explanatory note or policy memorandum is required.

The Bill has a slightly different procedure from an executive Bill. Stage 1 of the Bill does not include consideration of the general principles by a committee. Stage 2 is taken by the Finance Committee. Stage 3 may not begin earlier than 20 days after the introduction of the Bill and it must be completed within 30 days of its introduction. No amendments may be made except on the proposal of a member of the Scottish Executive.

(2) *Private Bill*: This is a Bill introduced by an individual, or a body corporate, or an unincorporated association for the purpose of obtaining powers which are in conflict with the general law. The original Standing Orders for the Parliament stated that a Private Bill had to be introduced on March 27 or November 27 each year, but this has been revised and a Private Bill may be introduced on any sitting day. At Stage 1 the committee may require additional reports and information, may ask the proposer to advertise the Bill and invite objections. The committee must prepare a report on the need for the provisions and detail any objections to the Bill. The first Private Bill was introduced in June 2002.[16]

---

15 Abolition of Poindings and Warrant Sales Act 2001.

16 Robin Rigg, Offshore Wind Farm (Navigation and Fishing) Bill. This Bill ran out of time at the end of the first session of the Parliament and was reintroduced in the second session. At the time of writing it was awaiting the Royal Assent.

(3) *Emergency Bill*: The first measure to be considered by the Parliament was an emergency Bill, the Mental Health (Public Safety and Appeals) (Scotland) Act 1999. The procedure is an accelerated one but the Scottish Parliament must first agree to allow the Bill to be treated as an emergency measure. There is no Stage 1 committee scrutiny and Stage 2 committee scrutiny is taken by a Committee of the Whole House. There are no time limits, indeed Standing Orders state that the Bill should complete its parliamentary stages on the same day it is introduced to the Parliament. The Executive may however propose that a longer period be given for consideration and this occurred with the 1999 Act.

Subordinate legislation in the Scottish Parliament

The Scotland Act 1998 gives power to Her Majesty in Council, Ministers of the Crown and Scottish Ministers to make subordinate legislation. Schedule 7 of the Act states the procedure to be used when enacting subordinate legislation under specific sections of the Act. For instance, subordinate legislation made under s.30 (legislative competence of the Parliament) has to be passed using Type A procedure. This requires an Order in Council to be laid before each House of Parliament and the Scottish Parliament and approved by resolution of each House and the Scottish Parliament. **2–21**

Where the power to create subordinate legislation is given in a UK statute passed before devolution, and this power has been transferred to the Scottish Ministers, the procedure for scrutiny must be the same in the Scottish Parliament. Thus, if the pre-devolution statute required that subordinate legislation should be passed using the affirmative resolution procedure, the Scottish Parliament must use the same procedure to enact post-devolution subordinate legislation.

The Scotland Act also allows the transfer of functions from a UK Minister to the Scottish Ministers, where those functions relate to Scotland.[17] This is done by an Order in Council made with the approval of both Houses of Parliament and the Scottish Parliament.

The Scottish Parliament's role is to scrutinise subordinate legislation, not make it. The content and purpose of subordinate legislation must be within the Parliament's legal powers.

Statutory Instruments made under the authority of the provisions of the Scotland Act are known as Scottish Statutory Instruments (SSIs). An instrument is laid before Parliament by lodging it with the Clerk of Parliament at least 21 days before it is due to come into force. The instrument is then referred for consideration to the relevant lead committee and to the Subordinate Legislation Committee. The Subordinate Legislation Committee will decide whether Parliament's attention should be drawn to the instrument because of some procedural or technical irregularity. This committee reports to the lead committee and Parliament within 20 days of the instrument being laid. The lead committee will consider the merits of the instrument.

If an instrument is subject to annulment any member may propose its annulment within 40 days of the instrument being laid. A debate is held by the lead committee on the annulment motion lasting up to 90 minutes. The lead committee will report to Parliament and make its recommendation within 40 days of the instrument being laid. A debate may be held by Parliament on the annulment if the committee so recommends.

Byelaws

In addition to Statutory Instruments made by the Scottish Parliament, another form of subordinate legislation is found in Scotland. This is made by local authorities and certain other public bodies, such as railway authorities. Byelaws are made under the authority of statute; the Local Government (Scotland) Act 1973 as amended is the statute which governs byelaws for local authorities in Scotland. Byelaws made before the reorganisation of local government in 1996 were to cease to have effect on December 31, 1999[18] although the minister could grant exemption or **2–22**

[17] 1998 Act, s.63.
[18] Local Government etc. (Scotland) Act 1994, s.59(6).

postpone that date. Generally, byelaws are required to be reviewed every 10 years to ensure they are still needed and up to date.

Byelaws must satisfy a number of conditions. They must be within the terms of the authorising statute, reasonable and certain. In addition, they must not exercise power for an improper purpose, or make lawful something declared unlawful by general law, or take away any rights specifically given, or be manifestly unjust.

Many offences made by byelaws were superseded by offences created by the Civic Government (Scotland) Act 1982 and local authorities were required to ensure that byelaws did not duplicate those contained in the Act. One of the most common byelaws related to dog fouling: s.48 of the 1982 Act clarified the offence.

The effect of a byelaw is the same as any other piece of legislation; there is a strong presumption in favour of validity if it has been passed and confirmed.[19] Before seeking confirmation by the relevant Minister, the local authority must publish a notice in local newspapers stating its intention to legislate and saying where a copy of the draft byelaw may be inspected. The notice must also state that objections should be sent to the minister.

The Minister may confirm, modify or refuse the byelaw. He must take objections into consideration and may order a local inquiry to be held by a sheriff. Once confirmed, the byelaw must be publicised in the area affected. This is important because different councils will have different byelaws for the same activity.

Each council is required to keep a register of byelaws which must be open for public inspection. Once a byelaw is confirmed, it has the status of subordinate legislation. It can therefore be challenged as *ultra vires*.[20]

LEGISLATION CREATED BY THE EUROPEAN UNION

2–23 The European Community is an international organisation, created by various treaties. It has its own institutions and law-making powers and these powers can give individuals rights which are enforceable in domestic courts or in the European Court of Justice (ECJ). Duties may be imposed on Member States either by the treaties themselves or by legislation created under the authority of the treaties. The law of the EU is known as the *acquis communitaire* or "Community patrimony". The effect of this is to bind all new Member States to all of the law pertaining at the time of their accession.[21] Normally, under international law, a new state signatory to a treaty will not be bound by any acts done under the treaty before that state became a signatory. All EU Member States, new or existing, have to ensure that their domestic law is in conformity with the provisions of the treaties.

The UK became a member of the European Economic Community (EEC) on January 1, 1973 by signing the Treaty of Rome and ratifying this through the European Communities Act 1972. At that time, there were six founding Member States[22] of the three Communities set up by various treaties. The European Coal and Steel Community (ECSC) was created by the Treaty of Paris in 1951, while the EEC and the European Atomic Energy Community (Euratom) were created by the Treaty of Rome in 1957. In 1973, three states acceded to the EEC: the UK, Ireland and Denmark, followed in 1979 by Greece and in 1986 by Spain and Portugal. Austria, Finland and Sweden joined in 1995 and in December 2002, negotiations were completed to allow a further ten states to join in 2004. The current membership of the EU is 15 Member States.

The three original Communities became known as the European Union under the Treaty on European Union in 1992.[23] This treaty was ratified by the UK Parliament in the European

[19] *MacCallum v Brown*, 1999 S.C.C.R. 806.
[20] See G. Junor "Byelaws—By Law", 2002 S.L.T. 131.
[21] C. Ashton and V. Finch, *Constitutional Law in Scotland* (2000).
[22] France, Germany, Italy, Belgium, Luxembourg, Netherlands.
[23] Sometimes referred to as the Maastricht Treaty.

Communities (Amendment) Act 1993. The Treaty on European Union 1997 (TEU)[24] provided a number of objectives of the EU at Art.2.

Key Concepts

Objectives of the EU: These referred to a number of goals:

- strengthening of economic and social cohesion;
- establishment of economic and monetary union, including a single currency;
- implementation of a common foreign and security policy, including a possible common defence;
- introduction of a citizenship of the EU;
- control of borders, asylum and immigration; and
- prevention of and combating crime.

The TEU 1997 made other changes in the organisation of Community institutions. The use of the majority or qualified majority voting by the Council was increased to try to improve its law-making power and there was an increase in the involvement of the European Parliament in making laws. As a result of these changes, the articles of the EC Treaty were re-numbered and you should be aware of these changes when referring to cases and materials produced before the TEU.

Institutions of the EC

The EU consists of three "pillars". The first pillar is the EC or the community pillar of the EU. The second pillar is the common foreign and security policy while the third is police and judicial co-operation in criminal matters. **2–24**

Key Concepts

The five principal institutions of the EC:

- The European Parliament
- The Council
- The Commission
- The European Court of Justice
- The Court of Auditors

The Court of Auditors ensures that the accounts of the EU are properly monitored. In addition, there are other "institutions" such as the Economic and Social Committee and the Committee of the Regions, but these do not have the same status or importance as the major institutions.

European Parliament

Although listed first in Art.7 of the EC Treaty, the Parliament's powers and influence are limited. When the UK joined in 1973, the members of the Parliament were delegates appointed by the **2–25**

[24] The Amsterdam Treaty.

parliaments of the individual Member States. In 1976, the Council decided that the Parliament should be directly elected by the electors of the Member States.[25] The first directly-elected Parliament took office in 1979. Members are elected for a term of five years. Each Member State is allocated a number of seats, the number depending on the state's population size. The smaller countries have a larger number of seats than their population would merit, but this is to ensure that the voices of all Member States have a chance to be heard. There are 626 seats in the Parliament, which is a unicameral or single chamber. The numbers allocated to each Member State will change after 2004 to allow for the accession of new Member States.

Allocation of seats in the European Parliament

Austria	21	Belgium	25
Denmark	16	Finland	16
France	87	Germany	99
Greece	25	Ireland	15
Italy	87	Luxembourg	6
Netherlands	31	Portugal	25
Spain	64	Sweden	22
UK	87		

Since there are no European political parties, the parties from the Member States are grouped together into nine political affiliations.

Although Art.196 of the EC Treaty requires the Parliament to meet at least once each year, in practice it meets in plenary session 12 to 15 times each year, roughly every four weeks. Before 1986, the role of the Parliament was to approve the annual Community budget. These proposals were submitted by the Commission to the Council which then submitted a draft budget to the Parliament to accept, amend or reject.

The legislative role of the Parliament has been developed over the years. The Council is the principal law-making body but generally the Council is required to consult with the Parliament on the laws it makes. The ECJ held in *Re Road Taxes* case that a failure to consult by the Council could lead to annulment of the instrument.[26] The Maastricht and Amsterdam Treaties extended the power of the Parliament. The co-decision procedure under Art.251 requires decisions of the Council to be submitted to the Council and the Parliament. The Parliament's agreement is required for the decision to be implemented. These procedures are discussed in more detail below.

The European Parliament was stated by the European Court of Human Rights to be "the principal form of democratic, political accountability in the Community system"[27] and it has an important role to fulfil in bringing the Commission to account. The Parliament may censure the Commission as a whole, but not individual Commissioners.

Council

2–26 The Council should not be confused with the European Council which is a twice-yearly meeting of the heads of state and government to discuss the future policy and development of the EU. The Council comprises ministers from each Member State "authorised to commit the government of that Member State."[28] The membership of the Council will change depending on the matter being discussed; for instance a matter involving agriculture will require the attendance of the agriculture ministers from each Member State. The Council meetings are chaired by a minister from the Member State that currently holds the Presidency of the Council. Each Member State holds the

---

[25] Ratified in the UK by the European Assembly Elections Act 1978.
[26] Case C–21/94 *Re Road Taxes: European Parliament v European Union Council* [1996] 1 C.M.L.R. 94.
[27] *Matthews v UK* (1999) 28 E.H.R.R. 361.
[28] EC Treaty, Art.203.

Presidency for six months and the European Council will normally meet in that Member State towards the end of the term of the Presidency.

The Council has a lead role in the making of legislation since it must approve those instruments proposed by the Commission. The Commission makes proposals to the Committee of Permanent Representatives (COREPER) which will consider these and make recommendations to the Council. COREPER comprises senior civil servants and diplomats from each Member State, their task being to consider the implications of each proposal for their respective Member State and to try to resolve differences. All meetings of the Council are held in private, thus allowing the representatives of each Member State to argue for their own interests, without the glare of public scrutiny and the disapproval that might bring. Each representative has of course to persuade their own government and parliament of the value of the Council's decisions. The Council will reach agreement in three different ways, and different issues will require a different voting mechanism. An Article of the Treaty may specify which voting mechanism is to be used.

Unanimous vote

This is usually required for a new policy, or where a Commission proposal is being amended without the agreement of the Commission. Unanimity is required in areas of social policy, *e.g.* the social protection of workers. This allows one Member State to have a power of "veto". Article 11 provides that if a Member State objects to a proposal because of important national interests, the Council should refer the matter to the European Council for unanimous decision. **2–27**

Qualified majority voting (QMV)

QMV is required for various issues, such as employment and social matters, equal opportunities, foreign and security policy, and public health. Each Member State has a number of votes. **2–28**

Qualified majority voting

France, Germany, Italy and UK	10 votes each
Spain	8 votes
Belgium, Greece, Netherlands, Portugal	5 votes each
Austria, Sweden	4 votes each
Denmark, Finland and Ireland	3 votes each
Luxembourg	2 votes

An act of the Council will require 62 votes in favour out of a total of 87. In some matters, there is a requirement for at least 62 votes from at least 10 Member States voting in favour.

Majority voting

This is the normal method of voting in the Council except where the Treaty Article requires unanimity or QMV. **2–29**

Commission

The Commission—"the guardian of the Treaties"—is the administrative body of the EU and is responsible for all aspects of Community decision-making. The Commission has 20 members, appointed for a fixed term of five years, which may be renewed. The governments of the Member States will agree the appointments of the various Commissioners. The governments however cannot dismiss a Commissioner, although political pressure could be brought to force their **2–30** resignation. The European Parliament may pass a censure motion to remove all Commissioners, but there is nothing to prevent the governments reappointing the same Commissioners and seeking to have them approved by the Parliament.

A Commissioner must be a national of a Member State and no Member State may have more than two Commissioners. The "Big Four" and Spain have two Commissioners each and the other 10 Member States have one each. Once appointed, a Commissioner becomes a servant of the EU, and is required "in the general interests of the Community, (to) be completely independent in the performance of their duties. In the performance of these duties they shall neither seek nor take instructions from any government or from any other body."[29]

Each Commissioner is responsible for one or more of the 24 Directorates-General of the Commission. These cover the policy responsibilities of the Commission, such as agriculture, environment, industry and employment. A President is nominated by "common accord" of the Member States to lead the Commission. The Parliament will also be consulted on the nomination. Both the President and the Commissioners have to be formally approved by the Parliament and again by the governments of the Member States.

The role of the Commission is to initiate and implement Community policy. The proposals for legislation are considered by the Council and the Parliament. The Commission will consult widely on its policy proposals before any initiatives are put forward. The Commission's second role is to ensure that all Member States and organisations affected by Community laws implement the legislation in the manner prescribed. Enforcement proceedings may be commenced against a Member State which is in breach of a Community obligation or has failed to implement Community legislation. If the Commission believes that a Member State is in breach of its obligations it will ask the Member State for its observations and thereafter may deliver a reasoned opinion to the Member State. If the Member State still fails to comply with the opinion, the Commission may refer the matter to the ECJ.[30] The Member State will be required to pay a financial penalty if the ECJ rules against it.

Once the Council has made policy, the Commission has to ensure that the policy is implemented. This permanent administration of the EU is centred in Brussels.

European Court of Justice

2–31 The European Court of Justice (ECJ) is the sole arbiter of the interpretation and application of Community law. The Court is presided over by a President, who holds office for three years and is elected by his fellow judges. Each Member State appoints a judge from the ranks of people who are eligible for the highest judicial offices in the respective state. The appointments are made "by common accord of the governments of the Member States for a term of six years."[31] The judges sit in chambers of three or five, or in a Grand Chamber comprising 11 judges. The judges are assisted by eight Advocates-General, who are appointed in the same way as judges and are drawn from the same group of highly qualified people. The Advocate-General will make reasoned submissions to the Court as to the interpretation of the law in cases before the Court.[32] These submissions will often be the basis of the Court's final decision.

By the early the 1980s it was becoming obvious that the ECJ was unable to cope with the number of cases being brought and in 1989 the Court of First Instance (CFI) was created to reduce pressure on the main court. It is intended that the jurisdiction of the CFI will be extended by the Treaty of Nice 2000. The CFI consists of 12 members, who sit in chambers of three or five judges. Currently its jurisdiction covers disputes between the Community and its servants, cases involving competition law and applications for judicial review. Decisions of the CFI may be appealed on a question of law to the ECJ.

---

[29] EC Treaty, Art.213(2).
[30] EC Treaty, Art.226.
[31] EC Treaty, Art.223.
[32] EC Treaty, Art.222.

The law of the EC

EC law has two sources: primary legislation, that is the various treaties creating the European Union, and secondary legislation which is passed under the authority of the Treaties. Some of the most important treaties have already been mentioned above but they are: **2–32**

Treaty	Effect
Treaty of Paris 1951	Created European Coal and Steel Community
Treaties of Rome 1957	Created European Economic Community and European Atomic Energy Authority
Treaty of Accession 1972	Enlarged EEC by allowing entry of UK, Ireland and Denmark.
Treaty of European Union 1992 (Maastricht)	Created European Union
Treaty on European Union 1997 (Amsterdam)	Set new objectives for the EU
Treaty of Nice 2000	Agreed EU Charter of Fundamental Rights

Some Articles of the Treaties give rise to rights which are "directly effective" in the domestic courts.

Key Concepts

The term "**direct effect**" means that individuals in Member States may claim rights which have been conferred by the treaties and the domestic courts are required to uphold these rights.[33]

The doctrine of direct effect requires that the Article (or Regulation or Directive, as discussed below) must be clear, precise and unconditional, and there must be no discretion in implementation left to a Member State or Community institution.[34]

The secondary legislation made by the EC is very important and each type has different implications for Member States. Article 249 empowers the "European Parliament, acting jointly with the Council, the Council and the Commission" to "make regulations and issue directives, take decisions, make recommendations or deliver opinions."

Regulations

Regulations are proposed by the Commission to the Council and the Parliament. A regulation passed by the EC will become law in all of the Member States automatically. The legislatures of the Member States do not have to enact the regulation. Regulations are therefore said to have direct applicability and they are binding in their entirety.[35] A regulation may also have direct effect. **2–33**

[33] Case 26/62 *Van Gend en Loos v Nederlandse Administratie der Belastingen* [1963] E.C.R. 3; [1963] C.M.L.R. 105.
[34] Case 41/74 *van Duyn v Home Office* [1974] E.C.R. 1337.
[35] Case 128/78 *Commission v UK, Re Tachographs* [1979] E.C.R. 419.

Directives

2–34 A directive will be proposed by the Commission and passed by the Parliament and the Council. It is binding upon the Member States to which it is addressed and as regards the result to be achieved but it requires each Member State to take appropriate action to bring the directive into effect. A directive does not therefore have direct applicability. There is normally a time limit within which the directive must be implemented.

A directive may however have direct effect, creating rights for individual citizens in the Member State. The time limit for implementation of the directive must have expired before an individual may invoke it in a court action.[36] One problem that had to be addressed by the ECJ was whether a directive could be enforced by an individual against a government or public body, or by an individual against another individual. In the former, the ECJ held that this was vertical direct effect and was available in certain circumstances. The latter is called horizontal direct effect and this has caused more difficult problems.

The meaning of *vertical direct effect* was illustrated in the following case.

Marshall v South West Hampshire Area Health Authority
[1986] 2 All E.R. 584

A woman employee was required to retire at the age of 62 years. The employer operated a system whereby female employees retired at 60 and males at 65, although a woman could continue to work until age 65 if the employer still required her services. M had been asked to stay on when she reached 60 and she then intended to work until she reached 65.

She claimed that the health authority had discriminated against her on the grounds of her sex and this was contrary to Art.119 of the EC Treaty and the Equal Treatment Directive 76/207. On a referral to the ECJ, the Health Authority was found to be a public authority within the terms of the Directive and was liable for the failure to follow the terms of the Directive.

The application of direct effect vertically, but not horizontally, may lead to different outcomes for people depending on whether they work in the public or private sectors. For instance, a dental nurse working in an NHS hospital may sue the health authority for non-compliance with a directive, but a dental nurse working in a private dental practice may not sue her employer for the same non-compliance.[37] The ECJ recognised this problem and stated in *Marleasing S.A. v La Comercial International de Alimentacion S.A.*[38] that national courts were required by Art.5 of the EC Treaty to do everything possible to reconcile domestic law with a directive's provisions. They should also interpret and apply domestic law so as to be in conformity with EC law.

Francovich and Bonfaci v Italy
Cases C–6/90 & 9/90 [1991] E.C.R. I–5357

The applicants were able to claim compensation from the Italian Government for its failure to implement a Directive. The ECJ recognised that the Directive, which protected employees where their employer became insolvent, could not be enforced directly against private employers but stated that it could be enforced by way of "a right of reparation" against the Member State.

[36] Case 148/78 *Pubblico Ministero v Ratti* [1979] E.C.R. 1629.
[37] Case C–91/92 *Faccini Dori v Recreb Srl* [1995] 1 C.M.L.R. 665.
[38] [1992] 1 C.M.L.R. 305.

If an individual suffers loss caused by a failure or breach of Community law by the Member State, he may claim compensation for that loss.[39] The breach must be sufficiently serious and there must be a causal link between the breach and the loss suffered.

Decisions

These are issued by the Commission and are binding in their entirety on those to whom they are addressed. A decision may be issued to a Member State, a public body, a private company or an individual. A decision is directly applicable. Decisions are used particularly in the area of competition law. **2–35**

How legislation is made in the EU

All legislation made by the EU institutions derives its authority from the treaties. The preamble to the legislation must state which Article has authorised the making of the measure. The Article will also specify which legislative procedure is to be used, for instance the voting requirements in the Council. Each measure must specify the reasons for its creation[40] as well as detailing any proposals or opinions required by the Treaty Article. Failure to include the reasoning and information may lead to annulment of the legislative measure. **2–36**

There are six separate methods of enacting legislation in the EC:

(1) *Commission acting alone*: This is a limited power granted by a few articles of the EC Treaty. One example is Art.86(3) which allows the Commission to address directives or decisions to Member States in respect of financial relations between Member States and public undertakings, such as privatised utilities.

(2) *Council and Commission acting alone*: The treaties do allow the Council to adopt a Commission proposal without the involvement of the European Parliament, but it is common for the Parliament to be consulted on the measure. The Treaty Article will specify which voting procedure is to be used in the Council. Examples of the areas covered by this procedure include measures relating to the free movement of capital (Arts 57 and 60), measures to effect economic sanctions against a third country (Art.301) and measures relating to Economic and Monetary Policy (Arts 99 and 104).

(3) *Council, Commission and Consultation with Parliament*: Originally this was the only procedure to involve the Parliament in making Community laws. Later treaties, particularly the TEU, have enhanced the Parliament's role in law-making. This procedure requires the Commission to propose measures and submit them to the Parliament for its opinion. The final decision is made by the Council. The Parliament must be given the opportunity to consider the measure and produce an opinion, but the Council does not have to accept that opinion. If no genuine consultation takes place, the measure may be declared void by the ECJ.[41] If the Council subsequently changes the measure on which Parliament has already given an opinion, a fresh consultation has to be made. Examples of the policy areas in which this consultation procedure is required include measures to harmonise indirect taxes (Art.93), measures to increase the rights of an EU citizen (Art.22), and measures concerning employment (Art.128).

(4) *Council, Commission and Parliament—co-operation procedure under Article 252*: The Commission makes a proposal for legislation and sends it to the Council and Parliament. The Parliament will give its opinion to the Council, which will then adopt a common position, using a qualified majority vote. If the common position amends the Commission's proposal, the Council must adopt unanimously. The common position is forwarded to the

---

[39] Case C–48/93 *R. v Secretary of State for Trade Ex p Factortame Ltd. (No.4)* [1996] 2 W.L.R. 506.

[40] Art.253, formerly Art.190.

[41] Case 138/79 *Roquette Freres v Council* [1980] E.C.R. 3333.

Parliament with the Council's reasons for taking that position. The Commission will also give its opinion on the common position to the Parliament. The Parliament then has three months to make its deliberations and it may take one of three courses of action:

(a) Parliament may approve the common position or do nothing. The Council can then adopt the measure but has to do so within three months. Failure to do so means that the measure will fall.
(b) Parliament may reject the common position by an absolute majority of its membership, *i.e.* 314 M.E.P.s out of 626. The Council can only adopt the measure after this by voting unanimously.
(c) Parliament may propose amendments by an absolute majority of its membership. The Commission then has one month to consider these and forward a re-examined proposal to the Council, with its reasons for not accepting any of the Parliament's amendments. Council can adopt the proposal by qualified majority vote, or using a unanimous vote, amend the proposal or adopt any of the Parliament's amendments rejected by the Commission.

The co-operation procedure now applies in limited areas of policy, such as those of Arts 102, 103 and 106 on aspects of economic and monetary policy.

(5) *Council, Commission and Parliament—co-decision procedure under Article 251*: This complex procedure was introduced by the Maastricht Treaty and was further amended by the Amsterdam Treaty. The procedure is the same as the co-operation procedure until the Council has approved a common position and sent it to the Parliament. If the Parliament does not decide on the common position or approves it within the three month period, the Council is deemed to have adopted the measure. Note that the Council does not have to adopt the measure as in the co-operation procedure. If the Parliament rejects the common position by an absolute majority of its membership, the measure is deemed not to have been adopted. This in effect gives the Parliament a right of veto. Parliament may make amendments and if these are passed by absolute majority of the membership, they will be sent to the Council and Commission. The Commission will give its opinion, accepting or rejecting all or some of the amendments. The Council may adopt the amended proposal, using qualified majority voting if the Commission has also agreed, or unanimity for each amendment rejected by the Commission. The Council may also fail to adopt the measure. In this case, a conciliation committee is convened, comprising equal numbers of members from the Council and Parliament. The committee will try to agree a joint text within a period of six weeks. If one institution does not approve the joint text, the measure is deemed not adopted. Examples of policy areas where the procedure is used include the free movement of workers (Art.40), completion of the internal market (Art.95) and provisions regarding the European Social Fund (Art.148).

(6) *Council, Commission and assent of Parliament*: Here an Act is adopted by the Council after Parliament has assented to a proposal of the Commission. Parliament's assent will be achieved by a simple majority of the votes cast. Examples of policy areas where this is used include uniform election procedures for M.E.P.s (Art.190(4)) and enlarging the membership of the Communities (Art.49, TEU).

JUDICIAL PRECEDENT

2–37 After legislation, judicial precedent, or case-law, is the most authoritative source of law. It is judge-made law, created in the course of deciding cases and as such it has to be extracted from the written judgment. This can make its exact meaning more problematic; some judges will be very precise and clear in their written judgments, others will be less explicit. Judicial precedent is sometimes also called *stare decisis*, literally, to stand by decisions. The principle of *stare decisis* means that a court is bound to follow the law set down in a previous case by a higher court.

Generally, in Scotland it was considered that a single precedent could not bind a court, that there needed to be a series of decisions. The influence of the House of Lords and the increased availability of law reports affected that position, and the principle of judicial precedent, certainly in civil cases, is now more often followed. The doctrine of judicial precedent is not followed slavishly; the previous decision must fulfill two requirements if it is to be binding upon the current case.

Key Concepts

The **precedent** must:

- be "in point"; and
- have been made by a higher court.

In addition to these two requirements, there is also a practical issue: it must be possible to extract the *ratio decidendi* of the precedent.

The precedent must be in point

This means that the question of law in the previous case must be the same as the one to be decided now. If the case is in point, then the relationship of the courts is considered to find out whether the precedent is to be considered as binding or not. Although the facts of the two cases will be broadly similar, it is the question of law which is pertinent. **2–38**

If the precedent is not exactly in point, then the precedent will have persuasive, not binding, force. Persuasive means that the judge may accept the reasoning or not; very often the standing of the judge in the preceding case will affect whether the ratio is followed.

If the precedent is not in point, the judge will distinguish the two cases, by pointing out where the two cases differ.

The position of the court

There is a hierarchy of courts in Scotland and the question of whether a precedent is binding or not will depend upon the position of the court which made the previous decision in relation to the one now deciding the question of law. The basic rule is that a court is only bound by another court of higher standing. The decision of a court of equal or lower standing is only persuasive. The Scottish courts will consider the precedents of courts elsewhere in the UK, but with the exception of decisions of the House of Lords as discussed below, will not be bound by these precedents. **2–39**

Civil courts

- *European Court of Justice*: The ECJ does not itself operate a system of judicial precedent but in all questions of the interpretation of European Community law, all UK courts must follow the decisions of the ECJ. **2–40**
- *House of Lords*: Decisions of the House of Lords are binding on all Scottish civil courts. Formerly, the House itself was bound by its previous decisions[42] but in 1966, the Lord Chancellor issued a Practice Direction which stated that the Law Lords would be willing to depart from precedents of the House when circumstances warranted that it do so.[43] A decision of the House of Lords made in an English appeal is likely to be binding on the

[42] *London Street Tramways v London County Council* [1898] A.C. 375.

[43] Practice Direction is stated at [1966] 1 W.L.R. 1234; [1966] 3 All E.R. 77.

Scottish courts where the issue involves a statute with UK application. However, the Inner House declined to follow such a decision in *McDonald v Secretary of State for Scotland*[44] where the meaning of s.21 of the Crown Proceedings Act 1947 was in issue. The Lord Justice Clerk, Lord Ross, declared that a decision of the English court had "great weight" but was not binding in Scotland.

- *Privy Council*: Normally decisions of the Privy Council only have persuasive effect. However, a decision of the Privy Council on a "devolution issue" will be binding in all legal proceedings, other than those of the Privy Council itself.[45]
- *Inner House of the Court of Session*: One Division will normally regard itself as bound by the decision of the other or its own previous decision. If there is a conflict of precedent, then a Full Bench will be convened to decide the matter and this court may overrule any precedent of either Division, or itself.
- *Outer House of the Court of Session*: A Lord Ordinary is bound to apply the precedents of the Inner House but is not bound by the previous decisions of another Lord Ordinary.[46]
- *Sheriff court*: A sheriff is bound by the same precedents as a Lord Ordinary.

Criminal courts

2–41 The doctrine of judicial precedent is less rigid in the criminal courts. Although the point of law may be the same, there may be differing facts which affect that point of law.

- *High Court of Justiciary as a Court of Appeal*: Basically, it will not be bound by its own decisions. If there is any doubt regarding the precedent, a Full Bench would be convened.
- *High Court of Justiciary (trial court)*: The High Court sitting as a trial court will be bound by the precedents of the Appeal Court, but not the decision of another Lord of Justiciary.
- *Sheriff court*: Until 1987, it was thought that sheriffs were not bound by the decisions of the High Court sitting as a trial court. However, the Appeal Court held in *Jessop v Stevenson*[47] that the sheriff was bound by the decision of the High Court sitting as a trial court. Sheriffs are therefore bound by the High Court decisions, whether these are from the trial court or the appeal court.
- *District court*: As you would expect, a district court is bound by the decisions of the High Court of Justiciary sitting as an appeal court or a trial court.

Key Concept

The ***ratio decidendi*** (reason for a decision) is the point of law on which the previous decision was based.

It can be difficult to find the *ratio decidendi* of a case and indeed sometimes there will be no useful *ratio* at all. In an appeal court, several judges may have given their opinions but may have arrived at the same conclusion by a different line of reasoning. Thus, finding the *ratio* of that judicial precedent may be difficult.

Key Concept

Obiter dicta—these are remarks of the judge, which are not essential for the disposal of the case. They tend to be hypotheses indicating what his preferred decision would have been if the facts had been slightly different.

---

44 1994 S.L.T. 692.
45 Scotland Act 1998, s.103.
46 *McFarlane v Tayside Health Board*, 1997 S.L.T. 211.
47 1987 S.C.C.R. 655; 1988 S.L.T. 223.

Such remarks are only persuasive; they are never binding. Nevertheless, they can be useful illustrations of how different scenarios would have led to a different decision. Their usefulness will depend on the authority and standing of the judge, for instance an *obiter* remark by the Lord President will be carefully considered by judges in later cases.

As with all such doctrines, judicial precedent has its advantages and disadvantages. Among the advantages are:

(1) *Certainty*: Lawyers can consult the law reports and determine what the law is on a particular issue and thus be better able to advise their clients on the likely outcome of litigation.
(2) *Consistency*: It is important that there is equality of treatment in the courts, and the use of precedents can assist in ensuring consistency.
(3) *Orderly development*: Judges will extend, or limit, a principle of law established in an earlier case, thus developing that principle in an orderly way. Again, it assists lawyers to advise their clients on the likelihood of a successful outcome.

The disadvantages of the application of the doctrine include:

(1) *Rigidity*: The lack of flexibility may lead to the law failing to keep up with changes of attitude in society.
(2) *Artificial distinctions*: The precedent applicable to a current case may not be appropriate in the circumstances and the judge may therefore feel that it would be unjust to apply it. The judge may then seek to distinguish elements of the two cases in such a way as to draw fine or artificial distinctions between them.
(3) *Difficult to find*: As noted above, it may be difficult to decide what the precedent is, but it may also be difficult to find a precedent among the many thousands of reported cases. The introduction of legal databases will make this task easier and faster.

AUTHORITATIVE WRITERS

Authoritative writers are the writers who first brought the principles of Scots law together into one **2–42** document. They mostly lived in the seventeenth and eighteenth centuries but their work and their influence upon the law of Scotland cannot be underestimated. Although the scope of their authority has dwindled they are still referred to on occasions when there is no statute or precedent covering the issue of law in question. They are sometimes also referred to as institutional writers because of the way they compiled their works, following the order of the textbooks of Roman law, such as Justinian's Institutes. A statement in an institutional writing may be given the same authority as one of the Inner House. There are eight writers whose influence is considered to have been extensive.

(1) **Sir Thomas Craig of Riccarton** (1538–1608): His work *Ius Feudale* (Feudal Law) is the earliest of the institutional writings, although it was not published until 1655 after his death.
(2) **Sir George Mackenzie of Rosehaugh** (1636–91): Mackenzie was a criminal prosecutor of some notoriety and is credited as the founder of the Advocates' Library, now the National Library of Scotland. He published the *Laws and Customs of Scotland in Matters Criminal* in 1678.
(3) **James Dalrymple, Viscount Stair** (1619–95): Viscount Stair is the most prominent of all the institutional writers. He lived in troubled political times and his law career reflects this. He was Lord President of the Court of Session from 1671 to 1681 before falling out of favour and fleeing to Holland. He returned to Scotland when William of Orange and Mary took the throne in 1688 and he was reappointed Lord President in 1689. His institutional work was first published in 1681 and the *Institutions of the Law of Scotland* began the systematic development of Scots law. Stair based his work on the broad principles found in the customary law, feudal law, Roman law and the law of the Bible.

(4) **Lord Bankton** (1685–1760): Bankton's work *An Institute of the Laws of Scotland* published between 1751 and 1753 compares the Scots law with the English law of the time.
(5) **Professor John Erskine** (1695–1768): Erskine's work *An Institute of the Law of Scotland* is regarded as second to Stair's work in terms of influence upon the Scots legal system. Published after his death, Erskine's *Institute* is the most authoritative statement of Scots law in the eighteenth century, setting out the rules of Scots common law before the impact of legislation and judicial precedent.
(6) **Baron David Hume** (1757–1838): Hume's work deals with the criminal law. The *Commentaries on the Law of Scotland respecting the Description and Punishment of Crimes* was published in 1797.
(7) **Professor George Bell** (1770–1843): Bell published two works of institutional status. The *Commentaries on the law of Scotland and on the Principles of Mercantile Jurisprudence* was published in 1810 and set out the principles of the mercantile law and bankruptcy. The second work *Principles of the Law of Scotland* published in 1829 was originally a student textbook which was reworked and enlarged.

CUSTOM

2–43 It is less common now for custom to act as a source of new law. Many of the customs which were part of the common law were incorporated into the authoritative writings. For instance, Stair recognised that the udal law of Orkney and Shetland, which regulated the system of land tenure, was enforceable in the Scottish courts. Custom is recognised as occurring in three instances.

The first instance is the custom or common law described by Stair as "our ancient and immemorial customs". Such customs do not require to be proved in court, since they are part of the common law and are thus known to the court. Most customs have now been enacted as legislation, *e.g.* the legal rights of a widow and her children to share in a deceased man's estate were recognised at common law and now by the Succession (Scotland) Act 1964.

The second instance is where the custom has been put forward as an authoritative source of new law. Such customs will be hard to prove before the courts and certain conditions must be fulfilled. There must have been a long acquiescence of the custom so that it is believed to be the law. It must be definite and certain, and fair and reasonable. It must also be an exception to the general rule of law, but no inconsistent with it.

The third instance involves the customary practice of a trade or profession. In some commercial contracts the parties will include, or leave out, terms which are recognised in the trade or profession as having a particular meaning. The court will seek evidence that the terms are recognised generally throughout the trade or profession.

Wilkie v Scottish Aviation Ltd

1956 S.C. 198

The contract between the parties made no reference to remuneration for the pursuer. He presented an account for his services based on a schedule of charges issued by his professional body but the defenders refused to pay. W. claimed that the remuneration was based on the custom of his profession and was therefore an implied condition of the contract. The court held that the custom had to be shown to be reasonable, certain and notorious. In this case, the method of remuneration was well recognised and the defenders should have known of it.

EQUITY

The term "equity" is used in two senses in Scots law. 2–44

Equity meaning "fairness" or "reasonableness" or "natural justice"

The broad meaning of equity in Scotland has allowed Scottish judges to deal with cases in a fair and just manner. It is seen in the remedies available to parties in the courts and in the way the court will give a remedy it deems appropriate, although the party has not asked for it. If a person is in breach of contract, the court may give the remedy of damages to the aggrieved party and require the party in breach to perform the contract. If a contract states that excessive penalties are imposed if the contract is breached, the court may intervene if it appears that these penalties are unjustified. 2–45

It can be argued that equity as a source of new law is not exhausted. The common law may require a judge to exercise his discretion in interpreting the law. Similarly, a statutory provision may allow a judge to exercise discretion within certain limitation.

Equity referring to the *nobile officium*

The equitable power of the Court of Session and the High Court of Justiciary, known as the *nobile officium* is a power whereby the court, as a last resort, may declare certain actions to be unlawful or give a remedy where none is otherwise available. 2–46

The *nobile officium* of the Court of Session is important for the law of trusts. It may be that a trust condition is so restrictive that the trust is unable to operate. The Court may remove the condition.[48] The essence of the *nobile officium* is that the law is allowed to operate in circumstances where a technicality would otherwise prevent it.

Roberts, Petitioner

(1901) 3 F. 779

The petitioner was a bankrupt who had completed all of the requirements needed to discharge his bankruptcy, except for making a certain statutory declaration. He was prevented from doing so because he had become insane. The Court dispensed with the declaration to allow him to be discharged.

The equitable power may be used to give effect to rights Parliament has obviously intended to give, but the statutory provision is defective.

Wan Ping Nam v German Federal Republic Minister of Justice

1972 J.C. 43

Statutory provisions provided relief for individuals who had been imprisoned pending an extradition hearing. The provision stated that an application could be made to a Sheriff Court for a writ of *habeas corpus*, a remedy unknown to Scots law. The Court used its declaratory power to give effect to the intention of Parliament.

The High Court of Justiciary has a declaratory power whereby it can declare acts to be criminal. This power is used sparingly.

---

[48] *Gibson's Trustees, Petitioners*, 1933 S.C. 19.

Khaliq v H.M. Advocate

1984 J.C. 23

A shop-keeper was found guilty of selling "glue-sniffing" kits to children; the offence was not recognized in Scots law but the High Court decided that it was the type of behaviour considered by the common law to be harmful.

The Court also exercised the *nobile officium* to allow an appeal to be heard where this had previously been abandoned. The petitioner's legal adviser had given him inaccurate advice.[49] It is however unusual for the High Court to allow a petition to the *nobile officium* to correct errors made by the legal profession.

[49] *McIntosh, Petitioner*, 1995 S.L.T. 796.

Quick Quiz

Legislation

- What are the differences between a Private Bill and a Private Member's Bill in the UK Parliament?
- Describe the stages of a UK Bill.
- What are the advantages of using subordinate legislation?
- Define what is meant by the retaining model of devolution.
- Why is there a period of four weeks between the Scottish Parliament passing a Bill and it receiving the Royal Assent?

European Union

- What is the Council of Ministers?
- Describe the method of voting used in the Council.
- Define the doctrine of direct effect.
- What is the co-decision procedure for making law in the EU?

Judicial precedent, authoritative writers and equity

- When will a precedent be binding on a current case?
- Define *ratio decidendi* and *obiter dicta.* What is the main difference between the two?
- How important are institutional works to the law today?
- In what circumstances may the *nobile officium* be invoked?

Further Reading

The historical development of Scots law is given detailed treatment by **Professor David Walker** in his text ***The Scottish Legal System*** (8th ed., 2001).

An account of the legislative powers of the UK Parliament and the Scottish Parliament is contained in **C. Ashton and V. Finch, *Constitutional Law in Scotland*** (2000), while a more detailed account is found in **Profs Bradley and Ewing, *Constitutional and Administrative Law*** (13th ed., 2003).

The legal system of the European Union is discussed in more detail in **C. Vincenzi and J. Fairhurst, *Law of the European Communities*** (3rd ed., 2002).

Judicial precedent and the other sources of Scots law are discussed by **R. White and I. Willock, *Scottish Legal System*** (1999).

Chapter 3

CONSTITUTIONAL LAW I — UNITED KINGDOM

Valerie Finch[1]

GENERAL NATURE OF THE UNITED KINGDOM CONSTITUTION

Every country requires a system of law and government so that the affairs of the state can be administered. This system of law and government is generally described as a constitution. The word constitution is often taken to denote a formal legal document which sets out the framework for the government of the state. The UK, unlike most other modern democracies, does not have a formal constitution embodied in a single legal document. This does not mean that the UK has no constitution. The wider definition of a constitution is that it encompasses the whole system of government of a country and will include all of the rules which establish and regulate the government. **3–01**

A select committee of the House of Lords was appointed in 2001 to review the workings of the constitution. This committee has defined the constitution as

> "the set of laws, rules and practices that create the basic institutions of the state, and its component and related parts, and stipulate the powers of those institutions and the relationship between the different institutions and between those institutions and the individual."[2]

---

[1] Lecturer in Law, Paisley University.
[2] H.L. 11 (2001–2002).

Key Concepts

The **constitution** of the UK relates to such matters as:

- the rules of government of the state;
- who will be a citizen of the state;
- how the government will be elected; and
- how the rules can be changed.

Three characteristics of the UK constitution are that is an unwritten constitution, it is flexible and it is parliamentary rather than presidential.

Written/unwritten constitutions

3–02 Most civilised states now have written constitutions. These constitutions have often been the result of political upheaval in the state, *e.g.* a civil war or the attainment of independence. The UK has had no such radical change in the nature of its government in modern times and so the need for a written constitution has never arisen. The constitution of the UK is described as "unwritten" because there is no single constitutional document. This is misleading because the UK constitution is more written than most. Although there is not a single constitutional document, many of our constitutional rules are found in statutes and cases. In theory it would be possible to extract all of the principles of constitutional significance from legislation and cases and combine them together in one document and call it the constitution.

There are some advantages in having a written constitution:

(1) The existence of a written constitution would mean that constitutional law could be more easily distinguished from other laws. However, the lack of a written constitution does not mean that the government of the country is unregulated. A country does not need a written constitution to ensure that the rights of its citizens are protected.

(2) Written constitutions generally allow the courts to declare laws as unconstitutional. The courts in the UK do not have power to declare an Act of Parliament unconstitutional. As such a power is not given to the courts, their role is limited to interpreting legislation in order to ensure that the Executive (the government) does not have too much power.

In reality *all* constitutions have both written and unwritten elements. This means that the classification of constitutions into written and unwritten is largely unsatisfactory. No one document can contain all of the rules and procedures necessary for a government to operate. All constitutions are comprised of written rules and procedures *and* the unwritten habits and practices. The written elements give stability and continuity; the unwritten elements allow for flexibility.

Rigid/flexible constitutions

3–03 To be of use to a nation, the constitution has to be amenable to change to meet the different aspirations of a changing society. A flexible constitution is one which can be changed by the same process as any other law. A rigid constitution is one which can only be changed by means of a special process. Most written constitutions fall into this category. However, the processes used for amending the constitution vary from easy to difficult and thus the degree of rigidity also varies. The constitution may require the consent of other bodies (*e.g.* the individual states of the USA) or of the people themselves in a referendum, as in the Republic of Ireland.

Some constitutions can be changed by the Legislature alone and others require the involvement of the Legislature and another body. A constitution which requires amendment by both Legislature and another body is called a supreme constitution. Examples of supreme constitutions occur in Australia, Ireland and Denmark. A supreme constitution means that all the organs of state are subordinate to the constitution. Amendments cannot be made without the use of the special process stated in the constitution and no one organ has the power to make these amendments. While a supreme constitution has much to commend it, it does make for difficulties if the amending process is too complex.

The UK constitution is flexible as in theory any part of it can be changed by an ordinary Act of Parliament. No matter how radical the change in the law the courts would be unable to declare the legislation invalid on the ground that it was unconstitutional. The courts must give effect to the will of Parliament where it is expressed in clear and unambiguous terms.

A flexible constitution has certain advantages:

- it can be adapted to suit political and cultural changes and so is less likely to fall out of date; and
- it can be temporarily set aside in times of national emergency.

There are also obvious dangers in having a flexible constitution:

- individual rights which have been developed through ordinary legal processes can be taken away with equal ease; and
- without political restraint a government with a large majority could push constitutional amendments through Parliament in order to undermine democracy and entrench its position of power.

Presidential and parliamentary constitutions

The distinction between a Presidential and a parliamentary government is that a President will be **3–04**
merely the Head of State and will not sit in the Legislature. In a parliamentary constitution, there will be a Prime Minister who will invariably sit in the Legislature and a separate Head of State, such as a monarch. Presidential Executives are found mainly in those countries where the USA has had influence. The great majority of members of a parliamentary Executive such as the UK government do not sit in the Parliament—they are civil servants and other officials. Only the heads of government departments sit in the Parliament. Other members of the Executive and the Judiciary are precluded from sitting as members of the Parliament.

Key Concepts

A **constitution** is the system of government of a country. It will include all of the rules which establish and regulate the government.

A constitution may be contained in a **formal document** or derived from a variety of legal sources.

The Constitution of the UK can be described as an **unwritten** and **flexible parliamentary constitution**.

SOURCES OF CONSTITUTIONAL LAW

The rules relating to the UK Constitution can be found mainly in the ordinary sources of law, *i.e.* **3–05**
legislation, judicial precedent, custom and authoritative writings. Acts of Parliament which have constitutional significance have no special legal status, they are ordinary Acts of Parliament subject to the same rules of interpretation and potentially subject to future repeal in the same way

as any other Act of Parliament. Judicial precedent as a source of law is less important in constitutional law than in many other branches of law. This is because important questions of constitutional law seldom come before the courts. Textbooks are given more respect as a source of law in the field of constitutional law as there are a number of influential writers. Custom also plays a greater role as many of the rules of constitutional law are not based on any of the more formal sources of law but are merely based on convention.

Legislation

3–06 Although there is not a single document which comprises a constitution of the UK, there are a substantial number of statutes which relate to the system of government. Some important examples are:

- *The Bill of Rights and Claim of Right 1689*: The Bill of Rights by the English Parliament and the equivalent Claim of Right by the Scottish Parliament curbed the powers of the monarch to rule by prerogative right. The two instruments both declared that the monarch could not make laws or raise taxes without the consent of Parliament.
- *Act of Settlement 1700*: This Act of the English Parliament was incorporated into the Acts of Union 1707. The 1700 Act settled that on the death of Queen Anne the protestant heirs of Sophia, Electress of Hanover should succeed to the throne rather than the heir according to the constitution who was the deposed Catholic King James VII and II. The parliament enacted the statute with Anne's consent to ensure that the "Auld Pretender" could not succeed on her death. The Act also contained some restrictions on the power of the monarch which were complementary to the earlier Bill of Rights and Claim of Right of 1689.
- *Acts of Union 1707*: There were two Acts of Union, one passed by the Scottish Parliament and one by the English Parliament. The two Legislatures ceased to exist on April 30, 1707 and the new Parliament of Great Britain came into being on May 1, 1707.

Other statutes of constitutional importance include:

- the European Communities Act 1972, which ratified the treaty obligations signed by the government for the UK to become a member of the European Communities on January 1, 1973;
- the Parliament Acts 1911 and 1949, which curtailed the power of the House of Lords to prevent the passage of a Government Bill;
- the Human Rights Act 1998 which incorporated the European Convention on Human Rights into the domestic law of the UK; and
- the Scotland Act 1998, which created the Scottish Parliament and devolved to it the power to legislate over certain matters.

Although there are a significant number of statutes which relate to the form and functions of the government of the UK they do not cover all matters of importance. If they were collected together they would not give a clear account of the constitution. The legislation must be considered in conjunction with the other sources.

Case law

3–07 The decisions of the superior courts may declare the law in relation to constitutional matters. Notable decisions include the case of *Entick v Carrington*,[3] in which it was held that a government Minister had no power to issue search warrants and warrants for the arrest of those publishing

[3] (1765) 19 St. Tr. 1030.

seditious papers, and *Burmah Oil Co. v Lord Advocate*,[4] in which it was held that the Government was obliged to pay compensation where property of a subject had been destroyed.

The courts have no power to question the validity of an Act of Parliament although there is a duty under the European Communities Act 1972 to disapply an Act of Parliament which clashes with Community Law.[5] The courts can however mitigate the effect of changes in the law by interpreting Acts where the meaning is unclear or is disputed. Important principles of Constitutional Law may arise out of the interpretation of statutes.

Common law presumptions of legislative intent

These are established principles used by the courts when interpreting legislation. These principles are guides to interpretation rather than conclusive rules. One presumption is that an Act is not intended to have retrospective effect unless there is a clear and unqualified indication that Parliament intended it to have such effect. This principle was applied in the case of *R. v Lambert*. **3–08**

R. v Lambert

[2001] 3 All E.R. 577

A person who had been convicted at trial before the Human Rights Act 1998 came into force claimed on appeal that his rights under the Human Rights Act had been infringed. The House of Lords held that the provisions of the Human Rights Act did not create any rights before the date when it came into force.

Another presumption is that statutes do not bind the Crown unless it is expressly stated or there is a necessary implication. This principle was considered in the case of *Lord Advocate v Strathclyde Regional Council*.

Lord Advocate v Strathclyde Regional Council

1990 S.L.T. 158

The Property Services Agency was carrying out work on the perimeter fence at Faslane nuclear base which caused some obstruction of the highway. No permission had been sought from either the roads authority, Strathclyde Regional Council, or the planning authority, Dumbarton District Council. Both authorities took action to have the road cleared. In an appeal to the House of Lords, Strathclyde Regional Council and Dumbarton District Council argued, unsuccessfully, that the rule that statutes do not apply to the Crown, unless there was express provision to that effect, was limited to provisions which would affect prejudicially the property rights, interests and privileges of the Crown. The House of Lords held that the Crown was not bound by any statutory provision unless an intention to be bound was included in the Act by express words or necessary implication.

The principles of interpretation may change and develop over time. There used to be a principle that the courts could not look at *Hansard* (the record of parliamentary debates) in order to discover the intention behind the legislation. It was made clear in the case of *Pepper v Hart*[6] that the courts may now look at *Hansard* in order to ascertain the intention of the person who proposed the legislation.

---

[4] [1965] A.C. 75.
[5] European Communities Act 1972, s.3.
[6] [1993] A.C. 593.

Royal prerogative

3–09 This has been described as the "inherent legal attributes unique to the Crown". Prerogative powers originate from before the Union of the Crowns in 1603. The sovereign then held all executive power and was able to do what he or she wished. Parliament met only when the sovereign called it, and that could be infrequently. During the seventeenth century, the power of Parliament gradually increased and the sovereign's powers were transferred to his ministers and to Parliament itself. Today, most prerogative powers are exercised by the Queen, on the advice of her ministers.

Prerogative power is a legal source of law and as such is recognised and enforced by the courts. The exercise of the power is controlled by convention and so for example, although the appointment of ministers is made by the Queen, she does not choose them but is given their names by the Prime Minister. The Queen signs the formal proclamation that Parliament is to be dissolved and a General Election held but the Prime Minister advises the Queen that he wishes to call an election and the date on which he wishes to be held. Technically, the Queen could refuse his request, but she is unlikely to do so unless she felt the Prime Minister was acting capriciously or that the country was in danger.

In the seventeenth century, the courts and Parliament laid down the limitations of today's prerogative powers. It was held that the king could not act as a judge, he had to dispense justice through his judges.[7] The king could only make laws through Parliament.[8] During this century there were many disputes between the king and Parliament, culminating of course in the Civil War, the beheading of Charles I and expulsion of Charles II. When the monarchy was restored, there was relative calm until Charles II died and his brother James came to the throne. James VII and II was a Roman Catholic and wanted his religion to be the official religion of the country. Parliament resisted this and James was forced to abdicate in 1688 and his sister Mary and her husband, William of Orange, were invited to take the throne. The offer of the throne was made by Parliament in the Bill of Rights 1689, which set out the powers of Parliament and declared that certain uses of the prerogative were illegal. In Scotland, the invitation to take the throne was passed by the Scottish Parliament and called the Claim of Right. Gradually over the coming years, the right to use the prerogative was transformed from the king to his ministers and Parliament.

Key Concepts

Examples of the **Royal prerogative** include:

- appointment of ministers;
- dissolution of Parliament; and
- power of pardon.

The term "Royal prerogative" denotes attributes of the Crown, which do not apply to ordinary people. It is important to note that, although the prerogative can be abolished or changed by statute, no new prerogative powers can be created. This was established by the decision in *BBC v Johns*,[9] where Lord Diplock gave the leading judgment:

> "It is 350 years and a civil war too late for the Queen's courts to broaden the prerogative. The limits within which the executive government may impose obligations or restraints on citizens of the UK without any statutory authority are now well settled and incapable of extension."

A prerogative power may however be applied to new circumstances.

[7] *Prohibitions del Roy* (1607) 12 Co. Rep. 63.
[8] *The Case of Proclamations* (1611) 12 Co. Rep. 74.
[9] [1965] Ch. 32.

R. v Home Secretary Ex p. Northumbria Police Authority
[1989] Q.B. 26

The Home Secretary issued CS gas and baton rounds to all police forces in England and Wales. The local police authority objected to this and sought a declaration that the Home Secretary did not have the power to issue such equipment without their consent. The court held that the Home Secretary did have such power, this being derived from the Police Act 1964 and the royal prerogative of keeping the Queen's peace. The Home Secretary could "supply equipment reasonably required by police forces to discharge their functions".

Authoritative works

When no other source of law is available the courts may turn to the works of eminent authors who have collected the law into one place. The works of Dicey are of particular importance.[10] Such works however never have binding force, they are persuasive only and will only be consulted when no other authority such as statute or case law is available. **3–10**

Conventions

Conventions are non-legal "rules" of the constitution, which exist because they allow the administration of government to run more smoothly. Conventions usually evolve over a long period of time. They are not entrenched rules. They can develop and change as the habits and practices of Parliament change. They are obeyed because of the implications if they are not. For instance, the convention may relate to a constitutional principle: if the convention is ignored the principle may be put at risk. One example of such a convention is the convention is that the sovereign will not refuse Royal Assent to a Bill. Technically, she may refuse but this would cause a major constitutional crisis since she would then be going against her Government and Parliament. Queen Anne was the last sovereign to refuse to give a Bill of the Royal Assent, in 1708, when she refused to sign the Scottish Militia Bill. **3–11**

The office of Prime Minister is based on convention. No statute states that there must be a Prime Minister, yet it is taken for granted that there will be a Prime Minister at the head of the Government. It is now also taken as convention that the Prime Minister will be a member of the House of Commons, not the Lords. The last peer to act as Prime Minister was Lord Salisbury in 1902. In 1962, the Earl of Home (Alex Douglas-Home) disclaimed his peerage and sought a seat in the Commons to continue as Prime Minister.

There is also a convention that each government Minister should be a member of the Commons or a peer in the House of Lords. This is to ensure that government policies can be questioned by members of the two Houses. Where a Minister is appointed and does not have a seat in Parliament, he must either fight a by-election to enter the Commons or be granted a peerage. In the summer of 1998, Gus McDonald was appointed as a Minister in the Scottish Office. He was not an M.P. and so it was announced that he would be made a life peer later in the year.

When a General Election is held, and the outcome is that the Prime Minister who called the election has lost it, the convention is that he and his government immediately resign unless he or she believes that a coalition government may be formed. John Major resigned as Prime Minister on the day after the 1997 election. In 1974, Edward Heath waited three days before resigning, since he had been seeking the support of the Liberal M.P.s to allow him to carry on.

---

[10] A. V. Dicey, *The Law of the Consitution* (E. C. S. Wade ed., 10th ed., Macmillan, 1959).

Consequences of a breach of a convention

3–12 Although the breach of a conventional rule does not have legal consequences, there may be political or constitutional implications. For instance, there is a convention that Ministers do not make statements that are contrary to government policy. Should a Minister do so, he is expected to resign from the government. In 1982, Nicholas Fairbairn, the Solicitor-General for Scotland, resigned after making comments to the press on a case known as the Glasgow Rape case, the day before the Lord Advocate was due to give a statement on the matter to Parliament.

Occasionally, a convention will be deliberately disregarded and lead to drastic consequences. In 1909 and 1910, the House of Lords disregarded the convention that the House of Commons, as the elected chamber, should have the final say in the passing of Bills, particularly Money or Finance Bills. The Parliament Act 1911 was forced through Parliament restating the convention and redefining the relationship between the two Houses.

It can be argued that the rules under which the Government in the UK operates would be more transparent if conventions were formally written down. However, that would destroy their great usefulness, the ability to adapt and change. New conventions can be created to meet changing circumstances, for example there is a convention known as the Sewell convention by which the Westminster Parliament will refrain from legislating in relation to Scotland on matters which have been devolved to the Scottish Parliament. Under the convention, the Westminster Parliament will only extend legislation on such matters to Scotland on the request of the Scottish Parliament.

Key Concepts

In the absence of a formal written constitution, the **sources of constitutional law** are the same as those of law in general, namely legislation, judicial precedent and custom.

Although there are **Acts of Parliament** which have constitutional significance they are nevertheless ordinary Acts of Parliament.

Custom, in the form of conventions, is an important source of operational rules.

DOCTRINES OF THE CONSTITUTION

Separation of powers

3–13 A system of government is normally divided into three branches: the Legislature, the Executive and Judiciary. In the UK, these are represented by Parliament, the political government and civil service, and the courts. The doctrine of separation of powers states that the functions carried out by each of the branches should be separate and there should be no overlapping or mixing of these functions. The doctrine was stated by the French jurist, Montesquieu in 1748, who proposed that there should be a separation of the powers of government to ensure that one branch would not become so powerful that it could override the other two.

In the UK, the doctrine has not been developed to give such defined boundaries as in the countries such as the USA where the constitutions clearly define the role of each branch of government and establish the extent to which each branch is influenced and controlled by the others. Indeed, in the UK there is no significant separation of powers between the Legislature and the Executive, and the main importance of the doctrine is in relation to the independence of the judiciary.

Relationship between the Legislature and the Executive

In the UK the Legislature and the Executive have common members. For instance, by convention, all members of the government are also members of either the House of Commons or the House of Lords, so that they may be questioned on their policies and actions. There is a limit of 95 on the number of government Ministers who may sit in the House of Commons. Since there are between 110 and 120 ministerial posts, it is obvious that some Ministers must of necessity sit in the Lords. This ensures that the government must include the House of Lords in its work. **3–14**

There are also rules which prevent members of the executive forming too great a portion of the membership of the legislature. Civil servants, members of the non-departmental public bodies, members of the armed forces and other government agencies are prevented from sitting in the House of Commons by means of the House of Commons Disqualification Act 1975. This is recognition of the importance of keeping the lawmakers separate from those who implement the law.

Until June 2003 the Lord Chancellor was a prominent member of all three branches. In the Legislature he acted as the Speaker of the House of Lords. In the Executive, he was a member of the Cabinet and had his own government department. He was also head of the Judiciary in England and Wales, as well as a Lord of Appeal in Ordinary in the House of Lords. By convention, however, he did not hear cases in the High Court and did not normally sit to hear appeals in the House of Lords. The Prime Minister announced the abolition of the Office of Lord Chancellor as part of a Cabinet reshuffle on June 13, 2003. The House of Lords will now choose its own Speaker by a process determined by the House itself. The Speaker will not be a member of the Cabinet and so will have the same independence from the Executive as the Speaker of the House of Commons. The Lord Chancellor's Department has been replaced by the Department of Constitutional Affairs.

One of the functions of Parliament is to pass legislation, but this function is shared with the Executive as government departments may pass subordinate legislation. The Executive controls the Legislature by establishing policy and controlling the Parliamentary schedule; but the Legislature also controls the Executive by exerting its power to prevent legislation being passed and ultimately it can bring about the downfall of a government by passing a vote of no confidence in it. This last occurred in 1979 when James Callaghan's Labour Government was forced to call a General Election. Members of the government owe their position to the support of their party in Parliament and thus the governing party can exert influence over the government.

Independence of the Judiciary

The independence of the Judiciary is arguably the most important part of the doctrine. **3–15**

Recent constitutional changes have increased the independence of the Judiciary. Following the incorporation of the European Charter on Human Rights into domestic law by the Scotland Act 1998 and the Human Rights Act 1998, it became apparent that changes would have to be made in order to ensure that the right under Article 6 to a trial before an independent and unbiased tribunal could be sustained. The level of political control over appointment of judges has been reduced by the introduction of a Judicial Appointments Board in Scotland. The Board has 10 members, half from the legal profession and half from commerce and academia. In England the office of the Lord Chancellor has been abolished and it is proposed that a Judicial Appointments Commission be established by 2004. As part of the same reforms, the Lord Chancellor will cease to sit as a judge and the Appellate Committee of the House of Lords will become a fully independent Supreme Court.

Judges in the superior courts cannot be removed easily; the Act of Settlement 1700 gives judges security of tenure of office *ad vitam aut culpam* (during good behaviour). Judges of the superior courts in England and Wales may only be removed by Her Majesty on an address presented to her by both Houses of Parliament.[11] In Scotland there is no similar statutory provision of removal and it is therefore uncertain as to how a judge might be removed. Judges need not fear that their salaries may be reduced because they have displeased either the Legislature or the Executive. Judges' salaries are a charge on the Consolidated Fund and do not require the annual authorisation of Parliament; they are not therefore debated in the House. The judges fulfil an important role in ensuring that the rights of the individual citizen are not infringed by an Executive exceeding its powers. The independence of the Judiciary is thus a check on the power if the Executive.

The functions of the Executive and Judiciary do, however, mingle in some respects. For instance, the Executive may make decisions, which have a judicial element; for example the reporter in a public inquiry has to weigh the competing arguments and come to a decision. Tribunals are administrative authorities but they fulfil a judicial function and are regarded as part of the machinery of justice. In Scotland, the sheriff has administrative duties as well as extensive judicial functions.

The Judiciary and the Legislature are less intermingled. Members of the Judiciary are disqualified from membership of the House of Commons by the 1975 Act, although there are, of course, judges who sit in the House of Lords to hear appeals from the lower courts. These Lords of Appeal in Ordinary may participate in debates on legislation but they are careful not to intervene in matters which are political in nature. By convention, lay peers do not participate in the work of the Appellate Committee.

Judges may not review the validity of an Act of Parliament, although this convention has now been modified by the UK's membership of the European Community where it is possible for a British Court to declare that an Act of the UK Parliament is incompatible with EC law.[12] Under the Human Rights Act 1998 the courts may declare that an Act of Parliament is incompatible with the European Convention on Human Rights, but such a declaration does not mean that they may disapply the Act in question.

On occasions, the Judiciary exercises legislative functions. In Scotland, the Court of Session and the High Court of Justiciary have certain equitable powers, which enable them to declare certain actions to be unlawful or to give a remedy where none is otherwise available. The exercise of the *nobile officium* (equitable power) of the Court of Session allows the law to be implemented in circumstances where a technicality would otherwise have prevented it. The power may also be used, albeit very sparingly, to insert a provision into a statute or document where this provision was accidentally omitted or was unforeseen.

Wang Ping Nam v German Federal Republic Minister of Justice

1972 S.L.T. 220

A member of a ship's crew was accused of a murder which had been committed while the ship was at sea. When the ship docked at Greenock, the crewman was taken into custody and held pending extradition to Germany where the ship was registered. The relevant extradition statute gave relief to persons so imprisoned by stating that they could apply to the Sheriff Court for a writ of *habeas corpus.* This writ however is unknown in Scots law and the court therefore invoked the *nobile officium* to give effect to the rights Parliament obviously intended to give.

The High Court of Justiciary has a similar equitable power whereby it can declare acts to be criminal. Again, the power is used sparingly although it was seen in *Khaliq v H.M. Advocate.*

[11] Supreme Court Act 1981, s.11(3).
[12] European Communities Act 1972, s.3.

Khaliq v H.M. Advocate

1984 J.C. 23

A shop-keeper was found guilty of selling "glue-sniffing kits" to children. This offence had not been previously recognised in Scots law but the High Court of Justiciary decided that it was the type of behaviour considered by the common law to be harmful.

Key Concepts

The concept of **separation of powers** states that each branch of government, the Legislature, the Executive and Judiciary, should be separate and have independent status, and no individual should serve in more than one branch.

Separation of powers is a device to control and prevent the **abuse of power**.

Rule of law

The rule of law is not easy to define but it could be said to mean that the government must obey the law and should not act beyond the powers granted to it or without lawful authority. The idea of rule of law was formulated by A.V. Dicey in *The Law of the Constitution* in 1885. He identified three aspects of the British Constitution at that time which he felt embodied the rule of law: **3–16**

(1) Absence of arbitrary power.
(2) Equality before the law.
(3) The constitution is the result of the ordinary law of the land.

Absence of arbitrary power

Dicey defined the rule of law as the "absolute supremacy or predominance of regular law as opposed to the influence of arbitrary power". It is unclear exactly what he meant by "regular law". Lawful authority normally means authority derived from a statute and it is possible that Parliament will legislate in such a way that the Executive is given very wide discretionary powers so that virtually any exercise of the power is capable of being considered within the law. The rule of law means that discretionary powers need to be controlled by ensuring that government business is carried on using rules and principles, which restrict the use of discretionary power. An example of abuse of power by the Executive arose in the case of *Congreve v Home Office*. **3–17**

Congreve v Home Office

[1976] Q.B. 629

In anticipation of a large rise in the cost of television licences many people renewed their licences one month early so that they would obtain their licences at the previous price. The minister decided to revoke any licences which had been prematurely renewed, thus forcing payment of the higher fee. Lord Denning stated that if the minister revoked a licence "without giving reasons, or for no good reason, the courts can set aside his revocation and restore the licence. It would be a misuse of the power conferred on him by Parliament: and these courts have authority—and, I would add, the duty—to correct a misuse of power by a minister of his department."

The classic case on rule of law is the English case of *Entick v Carrington*[13]:

Entick v Carrington

(1765) 19 State T.R. 1030

The King's messengers executed a warrant from the Secretary of State to arrest Entick and to seize his books and papers. However, to do so, they broke and entered his house and took away papers. Entick sued for trespass to his house and goods. The defendants said that the warrant was commonly used and had been executed before without challenge and that the power of seizure was essential to the government. The court held that since there was no statute or judicial precedent upholding the legality of the warrant, the practice was illegal.

The act of a public authority may be upheld if it was in accordance with the law in the sense that it did not infringe any law. This was seen in *Malone v Metropolitan Police Commissioner*[14]:

Malone v Metropolitan Police Commissioner

[1979] Ch. 344

The tapping of a suspect's telephone was held to be lawful since it was carried out on the authority of the Home Secretary using the normal procedure. Malone subsequently successfully complained to the European Court of Human Rights that the telephone tapping was a violation of Art.8 of the European Convention on Human Rights, the right to respect for private life and correspondence. Legislation was subsequently passed providing legal authority for the interception of communications.[15]

The rule of law will of course be undermined if the government indulges in breaches of the law. One breach of the doctrine occurred where it appeared that the ill treatment of terrorist suspects in Northern Ireland was officially but unlawfully authorised. The issue was raised in the ECHR, which held that the procedures contravened Art.3 of the European Convention on Human Rights in that they amounted to inhuman and degrading treatment but they did not amount to torture.[16]

It is also important that the government should comply with judgments of the courts and, in this regard, it is contrary to the principle of the rule of law that the government should introduce retrospective legislation to mitigate the effects of a decision made against it.

Burmah Oil Co. Ltd v Lord Advocate

[1965] A.C. 75

The House of Lords held that compensation should be awarded to the Burmah Oil Co. for property which had been destroyed by the British military authorities during wartime to prevent it falling into enemy hands. The company's success in this case meant that others in a similar position would have a claim against the government; these claims would have amounted to many millions of pounds, which the government was reluctant to pay. The War Damages Act 1965 was passed to prevent such compensation being payable. The Act was retrospective in that actions instituted before the Act was passed were to be dismissed by the courts.

---

13 *Entick v Carrington* (1765) 19 State T.R. 1030 (Court of Common Pleas).
14 *Malone v Metropolitan Police Commissioner* [1979] Ch. 344.
15 Interception of Communications Act 1985.
16 *Ireland v UK* (1978) E.H.R.R. 25.

The government has used its legislative powers to pass other statutes which have retrospective effect. One example is the War Crimes Act 1991, which allows charges to be brought for murder, manslaughter or culpable homicide, against a person in the UK, who was not necessarily a UK citizen at the time of the alleged offence, who committed the offence during the Second World War in Germany or in territory occupied by Germany and where the offence constituted a violation of the laws and customs of war. Retrospective penal legislation of this type may contravene Art.7 of the European Convention on Human Rights.

Equality before the law

According to Dicey the rule of law means: "equality before the law, or the equal subjection of all classes to the ordinary law of the land administered by the ordinary law courts..." **3–18**

His idea was that officials should not be exempt from the obedience to the law and should comply with the decisions of the courts. Dicey's ideas have been criticised as lacking foresight and indeed accuracy. Even at the time he was writing, certain people had immunity from suit and prosecution, for instance, the monarch, diplomats, M.P.s and judges. The immunity of the Crown, as opposed to the monarch in her personal capacity, has been changed by the Crown Proceedings Act 1947 and the Crown is now in normal circumstances as liable to suit for contract or delict as any ordinary citizen. However, some immunities still exist. Section 10 of the 1947 Act prevents an action for delict were a member of the armed forces has been killed or injured by another and the Secretary of State has certified that the injury was one attributable to service for the purposes of pension entitlement. This section threw up many injustices and it was put into suspense by the Crown Proceedings (Armed Forces) Act 1987, but it can be revived by the Secretary of State if he thinks it expedient to do so where there are warlike conditions. The immunities of the Crown have largely disappeared, including in England and Wales the immunity of a minister from the effects of an injunction.

M v Home Office

[1994] 1 A.C. 377

The Home Secretary was found to be in contempt of court by ignoring an injunction preventing the deportation of a Zairian national who had claimed political asylum. This case however has not been followed in Scotland where the Court of Session considered that interdicts against the Crown were prohibited by the Crown Proceedings Act 1947, s.21.[17]

There must be open access to the courts or tribunals so that a citizen may obtain redress of his grievance. In a civilised society, this also means that access to this redress should not depend on your wealth; a state will assist a complainant who has only modest, or less than modest, wealth to bring their action to court. If this does not happen, then only those with financial resources will have access to justice.

The constitution is the result of the ordinary law of the land

Dicey placed a lot of emphasis on the fact that the main source of the individual's rights and freedoms was decisions of the courts. Statute law has steadily encroached on the common law in this area and the citizen now has many more explicit rights than Dicey had in mind. The incorporation of the European Convention on Human Rights and Fundamental Freedoms into the domestic law of the UK by the Human Rights Act 1998 is an important milestone in the **3–19**

---

[17] *McDonald v Secretary of State for Scotland*, 1994 S.L.T. 692.

development of civil rights in the UK as it provides a set of principles by which to test whether the actions of government are according to law.

Other theories of the rule of law

3–20 In 1959, the International Commission of Jurists compiled the Declaration of Delhi. This declared that the purpose of all law was respect for "the supreme value of human personality". The Declaration set out minimum standards, which included representative government, basic human freedoms, the right to a fair trial and an independent Judiciary. This is a wider description of the rule of law than Dicey's and it probably represents what most people think of as the rule of law.

Laws should be open and made known by proper and sufficient publication and publicity. In the UK it is generally held that "ignorance of the law is no excuse" and that everyone has access to the law. This of course is somewhat unreasonable; there are so many laws, rules and regulations being created by the Executive that it is impossible for the ordinary citizen to know them all. It should also be remembered that many guidelines and rules are not published at all and so the citizen cannot find out to which rules he is subject.

The rule of law and the European Convention on Human Rights

3–21 The European Convention on Human Rights and Fundamental Freedoms was incorporated into the domestic law of the UK by the Human Rights Act 1998. One effect of this incorporation is that the jurisprudence of the ECHR is now taken into account by the UK courts. The tests which have been applied by the ECHR and which are now applied by domestic courts include a test based on the rule of law.

> **Key Concepts**
>
> **Restrictions on human rights** are deemed to be justified if they meet the following four criteria:
>
> (1) they must be lawful;
>
> (2) they must be intended to pursue a legitimate purpose;
>
> (3) they must be "necessary in a democratic society"; and
>
> (4) they must not be discriminatory.

The test of lawfulness is based on a premise that interference with Convention rights is *prima facie* unlawful, therefore any interference must be specifically authorised. In giving specific authorisation for an infringement of a right "the law must indicate the scope of any such discretion conferred on the competent authorities and the manner of its exercise with sufficient clarity, having regard to the legitimate aim of the measure in question, to give the individual adequate protection against arbitrary interference".[18] This is a restatement of Dicey's first principle of the rule of law as "the absolute supremacy or predominance of regular law as opposed to the influence of arbitrary power".[19]

---

[18] *Malone v UK* (1985) 7 E.H.R.R. 14, para.68.

[19] A. V. Dicey, *The Law of the Constitution* (E. C. S. Wade ed., 10th ed., Macmillan, 1959), p.202.

Key Concepts

The **rule of law** means that government must be conducted according to law.

Dicey identified three aspects of the British Constitution which were indicative of the rule of law:

(1) absence of arbitrary power;

(2) equality before the law; and

(3) the constitution is the result of the ordinary law of the land.

Supremacy of Parliament

The doctrine of supremacy of Parliament is also called "sovereignty of Parliament". This idea refers to the supreme legal and political authority of Parliament to make laws for the UK. The doctrine, of course, has been modified by the effect of the UK's membership of the European Community. Devolution of legislative power within the UK also has implications for the doctrine of supremacy of Parliament. An Act of Parliament has to be passed by the House of Lords, the House of Commons and receive the Royal Assent. Although an Act may be passed without the consent of the House of Lords, the power to do so derives from the Parliament Acts 1911 and 1949. The House of Commons and the House of Lords acting alone may not pass statutes; the three elements of the "Queen in Parliament" are required for a statute to claim its legitimacy. A resolution of one of the Houses, or a proclamation by the Crown, does not have force of law unless a statute or subordinate legislation is enacted to bring it into law. **3–22**

Traditional doctrine

The traditional doctrine of supremacy of Parliament has three aspects: **3–23**

(1) Parliament can make or unmake any law it pleases;
(2) no other body may question the validity of an Act of Parliament; and
(3) no Parliament can bind its successors.

Parliament can make or unmake any law it pleases

This aspect of the doctrine states that Parliament is the supreme lawmaker and that there is no matter which cannot be legislated for. However, the proposition is limited by the realities of what Parliament can and cannot do. It is, for instance, possible for Parliament to legislate to ban smoking on the streets of Paris. The reality is that such a law would be neither practicable nor possible. Such a law would be absurd and could not be enforced. Parliament is thus restricted by its territorial jurisdiction, in that it can only make effective laws for those areas it controls. However, Parliament can pass laws so that a person abroad committing a particular offence under UK law may be tried in this country. So in recent years, legislation has been passed making it illegal for a British citizen to engage in procuring children for sexual purposes. The War Crimes Act 1991 is a further example of this type of legislation. **3–24**

Parliament may extend the boundaries of the state by legislation. So in 1965 the Continental Shelf Act was passed to give the UK sovereignty over the continental shelf out to 200 miles from the coast or to a half-way mark where the coastal waters of another state intervened. In 1972, the Island of Rockall Act was passed to extend British sovereignty to that small island in the Atlantic Ocean and thus ensure control over any mineral wealth on the surrounding seabed.

Parliament may legislate to extend its own life. During both of the World Wars, Parliament extended its life so as to prevent the holding of a General Election during the war. Parliament has altered the succession to the throne by the Act of Settlement 1700 and again by His Majesty's Declaration of Abdication Act 1936.

No other body may question the validity of an Act of Parliament

3–25 This has been interpreted as meaning that the courts may not question an Act's validity and the courts have indeed shown considerable reluctance to interfere in how a statute has been passed.

British Railways Board v Pickin
[1974] A.C. 765

In this case it was alleged that there had been procedural errors made during the passage of a private Act of Parliament. The courts however would not challenge the Act on the basis that it was *prima facie* valid. The House of Lords held that the respondent was not entitled to examine proceedings in Parliament to show that fraud had occurred and that any question as to the validity of the statute would require to be investigated by "the High Court of Parliament" in other words by the internal procedures of the two Houses.

The courts will, however, now look at the proceedings in Parliament where they are considering the interpretation of a statute and there is some ambiguity in the terms of the statute and the intention of its proposers. The courts will then look at the Official Record of proceedings in the House, *Hansard*, to determine the words used and their meaning. However, only the words of the proposers of the Bill, whether minister or private member, may be considered.[20]

No Parliament can bind its successors

3–26 This element of the doctrine has itself a number of aspects flowing from the supposition that the ultimate lawmaker cannot bind itself or its successors, or it will then be subject to some higher law and thus not be the ultimate lawmaker.

Doctrine of implied repeal

3–27 A later Act of Parliament will repeal an earlier contradictory statute by implication. The courts recognise the principle of implied repeal in *Ellen Street Estates Ltd v Minister of Health*.

Ellen Street Estates Ltd v Minister of Health
[1934] 1 K.B. 590

The case involved the assessment of compensation for property which had been acquired under a compulsory purchase scheme. The wording of the Acquisition of Land (Assessment of Compensation) Act 1919, s.7 said that the provisions of any Act authorising compulsory acquisition: "shall ... have effect subject to this Act, and so far as inconsistent with this Act those provisions shall cease to have or shall not have effect."

[20] *Pepper v Hart* [1992] 3 W.L.R. 1032.

It was argued that this Act applied to later Acts, in particular to the Housing Act 1925. The Court of Appeal however rejected this argument and held that the 1919 Act had been overridden by the provisions of the later Acts since the terms of the 1919 Act could not control future Parliaments. This meant that the higher rate of compensation authorised by the 1925 Act had to be paid.

Independence statutes

There must be some limitations to the exercise of this element of the doctrine. For instance, from the 1940s to 1960s, Parliament granted many previous colonies their independence by passing a statute for that purpose. It would be ludicrous to suppose that Parliament now could repeal any of those independence statutes. Parliament had itself acknowledged the reality of this situation. The Statute of Westminster 1931, s.4 enacted that Parliament would not legislate for a dominion unless the dominion so requested and then consented to such legislation. Under the Scotland Act 1998 powers to legislate over certain matters have been devolved to the Scottish Parliament while other powers have been reserved to the UK Parliament. It is unclear whether the Scotland Act has the same status as the independence statutes. **3–28**

Statutes with "special status"

In the past, the Union Acts have apparently attempted to prevent their repeal by their wording. The Act of Union with Ireland 1801 established the United Kingdom of Great Britain and Ireland and its wording implied that the Union was intended to be permanent. However, after a century of conflict, the Government of Ireland Act 1920 was passed to establish two Parliaments for Ireland, one for Northern Ireland and one for the South. The Irish Free State was subsequently established in 1922, thus finally breaking the terms of the Act of Union 1801. Independence was granted to the southern part of the island by the Ireland Act 1949. This Act also made provision for the future governance and status of Northern Ireland. **3–29**

Unlike the Irish Union, the Union between Scotland and England still subsists and in Scotland at least is the subject of a belief that the Act of Union 1707 has a special status not found in other statutes. The Treaty of Union set up a new Parliament of Great Britain and appears to state that this Parliament could freely legislate in most areas of law, but acknowledged there would be some areas, which were declared to be fundamental and unalterable. The Treaty was ratified by an Act of each Parliament, first in Scotland, then in England; the English Parliament recognised and agreed the terms of the Treaty and the contents of the Scottish Act. It could therefore be said that it agreed that certain parts of the Treaty were accepted as being unalterable. However, one of the unalterable provisions was repealed by the Universities (Scotland) Act 1853, which abolished the requirement that University professors should be Presbyterians. Article 19 of the Treaty retained the Court of Session and the High Court Justiciary as the supreme court of Scotland: "... subject nevertheless to such regulations for the better administration of justice as shall be made by the Parliament of Great Britain." The courts in Scotland have reserved their judgment on the hypothetical case of Parliament trying to pass legislation, which would seek to abolish the Scottish Supreme Courts.

McCormick v Lord Advocate

1953 S.C. 396

This case arose out of the use of the royal title "Queen Elizabeth II" in Scotland when there had not been a Queen Elizabeth I. The challenge failed on the ground that a title is no more than that. It carries no great legal significance. However, Lord President Cooper took the opportunity to consider the doctrine of supremacy of

Parliament. He described the doctrine as a "distinctively English principle which has no counterpart in Scottish constitutional law." He went on to say:

"Considering that the Union legislation extinguished the Parliaments of Scotland and England and replaced them by a new Parliament, I have difficulty in seeing why it should have been supposed that the new Parliament of Great Britain must inherit all the peculiar characteristics of the English Parliament but none of the Scottish Parliament, as if that happened in 1707 was that Scottish representatives were admitted to the Parliament of England. That is not what was done. Further, the Treaty and associated legislation, by which the Parliament of Great Britain was brought into being as the successor of the expressly reserve to the Parliament of Great Britain powers of subsequent modification, and other clauses which either contain no such power or emphatically exclude subsequent alteration by declarations that the provision shall be fundamental and unalterable in all time coming, or declarations of a like effect."

"I have not found in the Union legislation any provision that the Parliament of Great Britain should be 'absolutely sovereign' in the sense that Parliament should be free to alter the Treaty at will."

The Scottish Courts have tended to be reluctant to enter into debate regarding the status of the Treaty of Union.[21]

Robbie the Pict v Hingston (No.2)
1998 S.L.T. 1201

Robbie was charged with failing to pay the toll to cross the Skye bridge. He maintained that the toll was a tax or excise within the meaning of Art.XVIII of the Treaty of Union. There was a contravention of the Treaty because the tax was being imposed in Scotland in a different way from similar provisions in England where bridge tolls were only imposed where there was an alternative route which could be taken. On appeal to the High Court of Justiciary, it was held that a road toll was not an excise within the meaning of Art.XVIII. However, Lord Coulsfield, giving the Opinion of the Court said that Art.XVIII might prohibit a different application of identical legislation between England and Scotland.

International law

3–30 British courts do not recognise international laws as limiting the supremacy of Parliament. International law and domestic law are two separate systems and international law has no status within the UK unless and until it is incorporated into UK law by means of legislation. This is called a dualist approach and is contrasted with the monist approach whereby international law is automatically incorporated into domestic law, with no requirements for domestic legislation to be passed. Such international law then takes precedence over the domestic legislation. The monist approach is used in France and Italy.

Ratification of a treaty by the government will not incorporate a treaty into UK law. Legislation is also required. The European Convention on Human Rights is a good example of this. For many years, persons claiming a breach of the Convention in the British courts had no case because the Convention was not part of UK law. The British Government ratified the Convention in 1966 and British citizens could then take a complaint against the UK government to the ECHR. However, it was not until the European Convention on Human Rights was incorporated into domestic law, by

---

[21] See, *e.g. Gibson v Lord Advocate*, 1975 S.L.T. 134; *Sillars v Smith*, 1982 S.L.T. 539.

the Scotland Act 1998 and the Human Rights Act 1998 that actions could based on rights under the European Convention in Human Rights could be brought before the UK courts.

If a treaty is to be ratified by the government but does not require to be brought into UK law, the text of it is laid before Parliament before the ratification takes place. This ensures that the Legislature is aware of what the Executive is doing. The courts will not interfere in the ratification process since it is seen as a prerogative of the Crown and not justiciable.

Blackburn v Attorney General

[1971] 1 W.L.R. 1037

The court did not recognise the contents of the EEC Treaty, which was about to be ratified by the Crown, that is the British government. Lord Denning remarked famously that the courts could not look at the treaty until it was embodied in a statute.

Where domestic law conflicts with international law, the courts will always implement the domestic law.

Mortensen v Peters

(1906) 8 F. (J.) 93

The Scandinavian captain of a fishing vessel was caught fishing in the Moray Firth and charged with and convicted of fishing illegally contrary to bylaws made under the Herring Fishery (Scotland) Act 1889. At the time of the offence, the boat was outside the three-mile limit, in international waters. However the byelaw prohibited fishing in the whole of the Moray Firth, most of which was in international waters. On appeal, the High Court of Justiciary upheld the conviction; the terms of the legislation were unambiguous and affected everyone including foreigners. This decision has been upheld in other cases, including *Croft v Dunphy PC*[22] where Lord MacMillan said:

"Legislation of Parliament, even in contravention of generally acknowledged principles of international law, is binding upon, and must be enforced by, the courts of this country."

Although the courts try to interpret domestic law as not being in conflict with international law if there is a conflict the court will uphold the domestic law even if this results in the UK breaching a Treaty obligation.

Parliamentary supremacy and EC law

The UK became a member of the EC on January 1, 1973, having ratified the Accession Treaty in 1972 and having implemented it by means of the European Communities Act 1972. Parliament recognised the special status of the EC Treaties in the Act and in particular recognised the common requirements and objectives of EC law. **3–31**

The European Communities Act 1972, section 2(1) incorporates all existing EC law into UK law and states:

"(1) All such rights, powers, liabilities, obligations and restrictions from time to time created or arising by or under the Treaties. And all such remedies and procedures from time to time provided for by or under the Treaties, as in accordance with the Treaties are without further enactment to be given legal effect or used in the UK, shall be recognized and available in law, and be enforced, allowed and followed accordingly; and the expression 'enforceable

---

[22] [1933] A.C.C. 156.

Community right' and similar expressions shall be read as referring to one to which this subsection applies."

Future EC law is given effect by virtue of section 2(4):

"(4) The provision that may be under subsection (2) above includes subject to Schedule 2 to this Act, any such provision (of any such extent) might be made by Act of Parliament, and any enactment passed or to be passed, other than one contained in this Part of this Act, shall be construed and have effect subject to the foregoing provisions of this section …"

The Act gives power to the government to amend existing legislation or create new legislation by means of statutory instruments (s.2(2)). This has the beneficial effect of allowing changes to be made quickly. However, some matters may require to be enacted by statute rather than subordinate legislation; for instance, where an EC directive has to be implemented with retrospective effect, this could only be achieved by passing a statute. Section 3(1) of the Act states that questions of the interpretation of EC law are to be determined: "in accordance with the principles laid down by any relevant decision of the European Court." Thus acknowledging the primacy of the European Court of Justice.

Section 2(1) clearly provides that EC law in existence on January 1, 1973 is to be given effect; this therefore provides that if a rule of EC law conflicts with a domestic law made before January 1, 1973, the EC law will prevail. There is no difficulty with this; the principle in fact occurs with the traditional doctrine of implied repeal that a later Act, in this case the European Communities Act 1972, will prevail over a conflicting earlier Act.

The problem occurs when a provision of EC law is inconsistent with a post-1972 Act. The ECJ has always made it clear that it views EC law as supreme over domestic law. This has given rise to difficulties in reconciling the doctrine of supremacy of Parliament with the idea of supremacy of EC law. Where a statute is passed after January 1, 1973 and conflicts with EC law, the British courts endeavour to interpret the statute so as to conform with the EC law. The words in UK statutes are interpreted as widely as possible to achieve consistency.

Where a UK statute cannot be construed in conformity with EC Law, EC law must be applied in preference to the UK statute. This principle was asserted by the House of Lords in *R. v Secretary of State for Transport Ex p. Factortame*.

R. v Secretary of State for Transport Ex p. Factortame

[1990] 2 A.C. 85

The EC common fishing policy required that fishing vessels from all member states should have equal access to the fishing grounds. When fishing conservation measures were introduced a number of Spanish vessels were counted as part of the British quota because their owners had registered as British Companies. The Government introduced the Merchant Shipping Act 1988 to restrict registration so that only those with a genuine connection with the UK could register as British boats. Factortame challenged the regulations as being incompatible with EC law.

The House of Lords held unanimously that: "By virtue of section 2(4) of the European Communities Act 1972, Part II of the Act of 1988 is to be construed and take effect subject to directly enforceable Community rights and those rights are, by section 2(1) of the Act of 1972 to be 'recognised and available in law …' "

The case then went to the ECJ for a preliminary ruling and on its return to the House of Lords, Lord Bridge declared: "Whatever the limitation of its sovereignty Parliament accepted when it enacted the European Communities Act 1972 was entirely voluntary. Under… the Act of 1972 it has always been clear that it was the duty of a UK court, when delivering final judgement, to override any rule of national law found to be in conflict with any directly enforceable rule of community law."

The principle of the supremacy of EC law was further reinforced in *R. v Secretary of State for Employment Ex p. Equal Opportunities Commission*[23] where the provisions of the Employment Protection (Consolidation) Act 1978 were held to be incompatible with Art.119 EC and with Council directives. In this case, there was no reference to the ECJ; the British courts decided for the first time without prompting from the ECJ that British statutory provisions were unenforceable.

The political realities of EC membership dictate that so long as the UK wishes to remain in the EC, the supremacy of Parliament must if necessary give way to the greater authority of Community law. However, the UK's continued membership of the EC is dependent on Parliament not passing another statute to take the UK out of the EC. As such then the doctrine is intact although it depends for its validity not on its legality, but on the political views of the government of the day.

Key Concepts

The **Westminster Parliament** has supreme political and legal authority to make laws for the UK.

The traditional doctrine of **supremacy of Parliament** has a number of elements:

- Parliament is the supreme lawmaker in the UK.
- An Act of Parliament is the highest source of law in the UK.
- No Parliament can bind it successors.

UNITED KINGDOM PARLIAMENT

Key Concepts 3–32

Parliament consists of:

- the Sovereign;
- the House of Lords; and
- the House of Commons.

The Monarch

The Queen is a part of Parliament in a formal sense. All Acts of Parliament require the approval of 3–33 the "Queen in Parliament", *i.e.* they must be passed by both Houses of Parliament and receive the Royal Assent before they can become law. The Queen also summons Parliament, prorogues it at the end of each annual session and dissolves Parliament at the end of its five-year term.

House of Lords

The House of Lords consists of unelected members. They are members either because they hold a 3–34 hereditary peerage or because they have been appointed by the Crown. There are four main categories of members and, until 1999 the total membership was around 1200.

The numbers in March 1998 were:

---

[23] [1995] 1 A.C. 1.

- 759 hereditary peers;
- 26 spiritual peers, *e.g.* Archbishop of Canterbury, Bishop of London;
- 464 life peers; and
- 26 Law Lords (serving and retired).

Life peers are created under the Life Peerages Act 1958. These are conferred on the recipient for the duration of their life and do not pass to their heir on their death. The objective of the Act was to increase the number of Labour peers in the Upper House.

Life peers tend to be working members of the House and participate in its work. Hereditary peers, on the other hand, do not attend in large numbers except when there is a vote which is of importance to them, for example during debates on measures to ban hunting with hounds, or to reduce the age of consent for homosexuals.

Reform of the House of Lords

3–35 Reform of the House of Lords is now under way. The first stage was achieved by the House of Lords Act 1999 which removed the automatic right of a hereditary peer to take a seat in the House of Lords. Hereditary peers have not all been banished from the House. In addition to the Earl Marshal and the Lord Great Chamberlain, 90 hereditary peers continue to participate as active members of the House until the reforms are complete. Fifteen of the 90 places are taken by hereditary peers who are office holders and 75 were elected by a ballot under which places were allocated to reflect the balance of political parties.

Lord Gray's Motion

2000 S.C. (H.L.) 46

The Treaty of Union included a provision that there would be 16 Scottish peers in the House of Lords. The removal of the right of hereditary peers to participate in the business of the House was therefore challenged as being contrary to the terms of the Treaty of Union. The House of Lords Committee of Privileges held, however, that the Treaty of Union did not provide an unalterable restraint on the powers of Parliament.

Hereditary peers who are not members of the House of Lords may stand for election to the House of Commons.

Powers of the House of Lords

3–36 The House of Lords is one element of the supreme lawmaker and as such its members do have the power to introduce legislation. However, this is not done often except where the government is introducing a Bill first into the Lords rather than the Commons. This often occurs for legislation that is less contentious. A Bill that purports to raise or spend revenue must always start its parliamentary life in the Commons. This is because the Commons is the elected chamber and is subject to the will of the people.

The Parliament Acts of 1911 and 1949 had a marked effect on the powers of the House of Lords. In 1906 a Liberal government was elected on a mandate to bring about social reform. The Lords was, as it always has been, dominated by the Conservative party and conflict between the two Houses was inevitable. In 1909 the Lords voted against the Finance Bill. This Bill had proposed increases in taxes on income and property to finance old-age pensions and unemployment insurance. The increases would affect members of the Lords particularly. The Government called a General Election which they won, although with a reduced majority. The Finance Bill was then enacted. The Government decided that the powers of the Lords should be curtailed so that a similar situation could not arise. However it was obvious that the Lords would not willingly vote to curtail their own powers and so the Prime Minister, Asquith, asked the new King George V to create new Liberal peers so that there would be a Liberal majority. Around 400 new peers would be required. The king agreed provided there was direct electoral support for the proposals. Another General Election was called and the Liberals were returned with their mandate. The Lords then realised that they could not win and did not oppose the Parliament Bill.

The Parliament Act 1949 was proposed by the Labour Government elected in the post-war landslide of 1945. The Government had a huge nationalisation programme and decided to extend it to other areas, in particular to the shipbuilding industry. The Lords had indicated that they would be unwilling to allow any such Nationalisation Bill to be passed. The Government then decided to curtail the delaying power further by reducing the two-year period to one year.

Bills which are not subject to the Parliament Acts are:

- Bills prolonging the length of a Parliament beyond five years;
- Private Bills;
- Bills sent up to the Lords less than a month before the end of a session;
- Bills which start in the Lords.

The Parliament Acts had three main consequences:

- The House of Lords no longer has the power of veto over a Public Bill, except one which tries to extend the life of Parliament beyond five years. The power of veto remains for Private Bills and subordinate legislation.
- The House of Lords was given a delaying power on Public Bills. Where a Bill is passed by the House of Commons but rejected by the House of Lords in two successive sessions it may be presented for Royal Assent provided one year has elapsed between its Commons second reading in the first session and its third reading in the same House in the following session.
- Money Bills certified as such by the Speaker may be presented for the Royal Assent if not passed by the Lords within one month of being sent there by the Commons.

Functions of the House of Lords

(1) *Scrutinising the work of the House of Commons*: The Lords is regarded by many as the "Protector of the Constitution". If the government has a very large majority in the Commons, it can pass any legislation it pleases since there will be no opposition in the Commons to stop it. The Lords however have traditionally taken a more "conservative" view and thus might try to stop legislation which was very radical, *e.g.* legislation to abolish the monarchy. The Lords also have the power to prevent the government introducing legislation to extend the life of Parliament; if this were not so, then a government could pass a Bill which would mean it could stay in office indefinitely. **3–37**

(2) *Revision of legislation*: The House spends about two thirds of its time on legislation. This is one of the most important roles of the Lords, particularly where a Bill has been "guillotined" in the Commons. This occurs when the government curtails debate on a Bill to ensure it is not talked out by opponents. There is no guillotine or closure motion in the Lords and so there can be a full debate on the implications of the Bill. The Lords may make amendments to the Bill to clarify it or change its meaning entirely.

(3) *Debates*: Members of the Lords have a wide range of experience and provide a source of independent expertise. The working peers include many former ministers, former M.P.s, business people, who have achieved much and are thus able to make worthwhile contributions to debates. There is no guillotine, are no closure motions, and no votes of confidence which if lost would cause the government to resign. The debates therefore can be more open and wide-ranging and less political. Most Wednesdays are for general debates. Once a month, time is set aside for two short debates on topics are suggested by

backbench or crossbench peers and chosen by ballot. Other debates are agreed between the business managers (*e.g.* whips) of the political parties.

(4) *Select committees*: Members of the House of Lords are also involved in joint committees with the Commons, the most important being the Joint Committee on Subordinate Legislation and European Communities legislation. It also has a number of Select Committees which include the Science and Technology Select Committee and the Economic Affairs Committee. A Constitution Select Committee was set up in 2001 "to examine the constitutional implications of all Public Bills coming before the House; and to keep under review the operation of the constitution". The Constitutional Committee began its work with an enquiry into the working of devolution. Adhoc committees are also set up from time to time to examine issues which are outside the remits of the main investigative committees.

(5) *Final court of appeal*: The House of Lords is the final court of appeal in all civil actions in the UK and final court for criminal cases in England and Wales (not Scotland). Only the legally-qualified judges sit on appeals; by convention, no non-legally qualified peer may do so. However the Appellate Committee of the House of Lords is expected to be replaced by a fully independent Supreme Court in 2004.

House of Commons

3–38 At least every five years the membership of the House of Commons changes after a General Election. The right to vote, called the franchise, is given to every British citizen, who is at least 18 years old, is resident in the UK, is not subject to a disqualification and whose name appears on the Electoral Register.

Generally, those entitled to vote are residents of the UK who are either:

- British citizens; or
- citizens of British dependent territories; or
- British overseas citizens; or
- Commonwealth citizens; or
- citizens of the Irish Republic.

A citizen of the EU may vote in European Parliamentary elections and local elections, but not General Elections. Those who are disqualified from voting include:

- aliens;
- minors (under 18);
- hereditary peers and peeresses who have seats in the House of Lords;
- prisoners;
- patients in mental hospitals (the insane are regarded as not having the capacity to understand why they are voting and so they do not have the vote—a voluntary mental patient might not have lost the capacity of understanding and may be able to vote by post if they are so registered); and
- overseas voters (a British citizen who resides abroad and has done so for more than 20 years may not vote in UK elections).

Disqualification from membership of the House of Commons

3–39 A person may be elected to sit in the Commons but be unable to take that seat because of a disqualification. These are stated in the House of Commons (Disqualification) Act 1975 as:

- minors (a candidate must be 21 before he or she can take their seat);
- aliens;
- peers who have seats in the House of Lords;

- clerics (members of the established churches of England, Wales, Scotland and Northern Ireland and Roman Catholic priests are disqualified but the clergy of other religions are not disqualified);
- psychiatric patients (if a member becomes mentally ill, this has to be reported to the Speaker and after six months, the seat may be declared vacant if the member is still certified as ill);
- bankrupts (a bankrupt may not be elected to the Commons—if a member subsequently becomes bankrupt he or she will have to resign their seat unless the bankruptcy is cleared within six months);
- prisoners (a person who is sentenced to imprisonment of more than one year or an indefinite sentence (as for murder) is disqualified—no such person may now be nominated as a candidate);
- holders of public office (people who hold certain public offices may not sit, *e.g.* judges, police, members of the armed forces, civil servants, members of certain boards and tribunals);
- persons convicted of corrupt or illegal practices (these are electoral offences such as bribery, personation); and
- The Advocate-General for Scotland.

Functions of Members of Parliament

The current electoral system in the UK means that an M.P. is elected to represent a constituency. However, most M.P.s are also elected because they represent a particular political party. **3–40**

The functions of M.P.s are to:

- Check on the activities and power of government. The Government's own backbench M.P.s may have more power than those of the Opposition.
- Act for constituents in grievances they may have against central or local government. The M.P. may ask questions of Ministers, or lobby for the constituent, or refer the matter to the Parliamentary Ombudsman.
- Represent pressure groups. Many M.P.s have links with pressure groups such as the trade unions, professional bodies or charities.
- Represent and support the party.
- Work in committees of the House of Commons.

Functions of the House of Commons

The House of Commons does not govern the country. This is done by the central government departments, local authorities and other bodies which are charged by legislation to perform these functions. **3–41**

The House of Commons is a body which:

- scrutinises proposed legislation brought to it by the Government, individual members and other private bodies;
- questions the actions of government Ministers and departments;
- debates various issues and ensures different opinions are heard; and
- checks the financial probity of the Government.

Scrutinising legislation

There are three types of Bills: **3–42**

- Private Bills—which apply to particular areas or persons;

- Hybrid Bills—which apply to particular persons but which also contain sections which alter the general law of the land;
- Public Bills—which have general application.

Private Bills concern particular bodies, *e.g.* a local authority or public corporation. The procedure for passing these Bills is slightly different from that for a Public Bill. There is often no or very little discussion of the contents of the Bill within Parliament. Hybrid Bills are those which on the whole have general application but also contain particular provisions applying specifically to particular persons. For instance, the building of the Channel Tunnel required an Act which involved a private company being given compulsory purchase powers to buy the land to build the northern end of the tunnel. Public Bills are the most important of the three types and they take up the greater part of the legislative programme of Parliament. There are two types of Public Bills: Government Bills and Private Members' Bills. The proposal for a Private Member's Bill may come from the M.P. him/herself, from a pressure group or indeed from the Government.

The methods of initiating a Private Members' Bill are:

- *Ballot*—at the start of each session of Parliament a ballot of backbench M.P.s is held. The first 20 names drawn out are allowed time to present a Bill. The debates take place on 10 Friday mornings; if there is no vote in favour of the Bill progressing it will fall. The chances of Bills completing the process are very small—to have a chance the Bill has to be one of the first six in the ballot, non-controversial and have cross-party support.
- *Ten minute rule Bill*—this is introduced on a Tuesday or Wednesday afternoon before ministerial question time. It is a popular way of introducing a Bill to Parliament because of its timing but a Bill introduced in this way is highly unlikely to become law. The proposer of the Bill speaks for 10 minutes, then anyone opposed to it speaks for 10 minutes, and then there is a vote. Even if it passes this stage, it is unlikely to become law because no government time will be given to it.
- *Standing Order 58*—here a Bill is introduced to Parliament during the course of the day—there is no particular time given over to it and the chances of it becoming law are very small.

A Government Bill is prepared by Parliamentary draftsmen in consultation with the department proposing the Bill. It will have been considered by a Cabinet Committee and the Cabinet and will have their approval. Also, very often it will have been the subject of extensive consultation with pressure and interest groups before it reached the draft stage.

A Bill may be introduced in either House but certain Bills will always be introduced first to the House of Commons. These include Money Bills, controversial Bills, Bills of constitutional significance.

Stages of a Bill

First Reading	Standing Order 35. This is a formal stage. At the start of business the Speaker calls upon the minister in charge of the Bill—he stands up and nods; the clerk reads out the short title of the Bill and Minister names a second reading date. There is no debate. The first reading merely allows the Bill to be printed.
Second Reading	This is a general debate about the principles of the Bill. No amendments are allowed at this stage. At the end of the debate the motion is put and voted on. A Bill can be lost at this stage although it is uncommon.

Committee Stage	The Bill is considered clause by clause and amendments made. There are two types of committee, the standing committee and a committee of the whole house. The standing committee has about 30 M.P.s chosen to reflect the political make-up of the House. A committee of the whole house consists of all M.P.s. They consider the Bill clause by clause on the floor of the House. A committee of the whole house will be set up for Bills of constitutional importance such as the Scotland Bill 1998. Amendments are voted on as they occur. The government usually opposes amendments but may support some.
Report Stage	If the Bill has been before a committee of the whole house this stage is a formality. Otherwise this stage informs M.P.s who were not on the standing committee of any amendments. The new clauses will be debated and the government may make further amendments if it had agreed to do so in committee. There is no vote.
Third Reading	This is similar to the Second Reading except for amendments made in committee. The Bill is debated in principle and a vote taken. It is unusual for a Bill to be lost here.

Once this procedure has been carried out, the Bill is sent to the other House where the whole procedure is gone through again.

After both Houses have agreed the Bill, it is sent for Royal Assent and comes into effect, either immediately, or on a date specified in the Act, or on a date to be decided by the Minister. The Act will state which of these dates is to be followed. It is not unusual for an Act to be brought into effect in stages. For instance, the Consumer Credit Act 1974 was not fully implemented for more than 10 years.

If a Bill is rejected by the other House or is amended by them, a different procedure comes into play. A Bill from the House of Lords rejected by the Commons will fall. A Bill from the Commons rejected or amended by the Lords returns to the Commons where the amendment is considered. If the Commons rejects the Lords amendment, it goes back to the Lords for them to re-consider. If the Lords still oppose the Bill as passed by the Commons, then there are discussions among the party managers to try to come to a consensus. If this fails, the Bill is withdrawn. If the government reintroduces the Bill in the next session of Parliament and the same happens again, the Parliament Acts 1911 and 1949 may be brought into play and the Bill will be passed without the consent of the House of Lords.

Questions

At the beginning of business on Monday to Thursday each week ministers are required to answer **3–43** questions which have been laid down in advance by backbench M.P.s. The Ministers take it in turn to answer questions; usually they will appear every three or four weeks and will answer questions for about an hour. The Prime Minister is the exception to this: he will answer questions for 30 minutes every Wednesday.

Ministers may only be questioned on matters for which they have responsibility. This has caused much confusion in recent years. During the late 1980s, the Thatcher Government introduced reforms of the civil servants, implementing the "Next Steps Initiative" which set up agencies to carry out functions which were previously carried out by central government departments. These were under the leadership of Agency Chief Executives who had day-to-day control of the agency's functions. The Government decided that any parliamentary questions which involved the work of an agency would be passed for answer to the Chief Executive and would no longer be answered on the floor of the House by the minister. This outraged many opposition M.P.s but the practice persisted and is still in place. Thus a question on a matter which is within the remit of an agency will be sent to the Chief Executive who will reply directly to the M.P. The minister will not be involved and the M.P. will not be able to ask supplementary questions on the floor of the House. The answers are now published in *Hansard* at the end of the day's debate.

The Scott Inquiry into the Arms for Iraq affair in 1992 highlighted that Ministers were answering some questions in a dubious manner. Answers are usually prepared for Ministers by their civil servants and they are now instructed to be as open and truthful as possible. In particular, an answer should not be given which is literally true but likely to give rise to misleading inferences.

Key Concepts

A minister should try to answer **questions** where possible, but there are instances when he may decline to do so:

- The question does not relate to the Minster's departmental responsibilities.
- They are statements not questions.
- The matter is currently *sub judice*.
- The matter was asked in the previous three months.
- The cost of finding the answer would be too costly.
- The answer might damage national security.
- The matter involves confidential exchanges between governments.
- The question relates to commercial or contractual confidentiality.

Debates

3–44 M.P.s participate in debates on the second readings of Bills, motions to approve some aspect of government policy, motions set down by the opposition parties to challenge government policies, the budget proposals and many other matters. Each day there is an adjournment debate, taking place at the end of the day for 30 minutes. The topic is chosen by a backbench M.P. who has competed successfully in a ballot to bring the matter to the attention of a minister and the House.

Select Committees

3–45 There are some 33 Select Committees set up for the whole parliamentary session. There are 17 departmental Select Committees which "shadow" a government department and investigate the workings of the department and its associated public bodies and agencies. Other committees are concerned with the internal workings of the House, *e.g.* select committees on services and standing orders. Some select committees are very important to the work of the House of Commons. Arguably the most important one is the Public Accounts Committee.

Financial proceedings

A government cannot function if it is unable to raise and spend revenue. This principle was seen at work in the conflict between the House of Commons and House of Lords in 1909–1911 which led to the passage of the Parliament Act 1911, curtailing, *inter alia*, the power of the House of Lords to delay Financial Bills of the Government. 3–46

Key Concepts

The basic rules for **spending and taxing**:

- Legislative approval is required for taxation and expenditure proposals.
- Only the Crown (*i.e.* a minister) may move such proposals.
- Proposals must originate in the Commons.
- Spending and taxing proposals in a Bill must be approved separately. They are usually voted on after the second reading of the Bill.

The timetable for expenditure proposals has been modified recently. The Chancellor of the Exchequer announced in 1998 that the departmental estimates would be for three years rather than the previous one. The Treasury receives all of the departmental "bids" for funding and allocates the available funds according to government policy. Negotiations for funds go on for several months. Eventually the proposals are set before the House for debate, usually around March of each year. Three days are set aside for the debates, which must be concluded before August 5. Once the estimates are approved, an annual Appropriation Bill is enacted; this usually occurs in late July.

The Budget

The Chancellor of the Exchequer presents his spending plans in March of each year together with his plans for raising the money needed to pay for these plans. This is known as the Budget statement and is one of the highlights of the parliamentary year. As soon as the statement is made, the House passes a series of financial resolutions which authorise the immediate alteration of taxation amounts. These are given interim legitimacy by the Provisional Collection of Taxes Act 1968 until the Budget proposals are passed in the Finance Act. 3–47

POWERS AND PRIVILEGES OF PARLIAMENT

Parliamentary privilege is the sum of the rights enjoyed by each House of Parliament, and by Members of each House individually. Parliamentary privilege confers rights which exceed those possessed by other bodies or individuals. The exercise of the rights of privilege is justified by the fact that they are necessary so that both Houses of Parliament can discharge their functions. 3–48

Powers of the House of Commons

Powers of the Speaker

3–49 In order to ensure that debates can be conducted in a reasonably orderly manner the Speaker has various powers. These powers may also be exercised by a Deputy Speaker when he is presiding in the House.

- *Calls to Order.* The Speaker will call a Member to order if he or she deviates from the topic under discussion or if he or she persistently interrupts a Member who is speaking or if he or she uses unparliamentary language. Should a Member disregard this call to order, the Speaker may instruct that Member to resume his/her seat. If this order is disobeyed, the Speaker may request the Member to leave the Chamber for the remainder of that day's sitting. If the Member does not leave, the Speaker may invoke Standing Order No.43, which requires the Member to leave the House and its precincts for the remainder of that day's sitting. If a Member refuses to leave, then he or she may be named under Standing Order No.44.
- *Naming and Suspension.* The Speaker may name a Member who has abused the rules of the House. The most senior government Minister present then moves that the Member be removed. If the motion is agreed to the Member is suspended for a number of days. Short periods of suspension are not accompanied by a forfeiture of salary but for more serious abuses of parliamentary rules a specific period of suspension with suspension of salary may be imposed. Apart from continuing to serve on committees for the consideration of Private Bills, the Member may not enter the Parliament buildings for the duration of the suspension.
- *Suspension of sitting.* If a situation of grave disorder arises in the House, the Speaker may, under Standing Order No.46, adjourn the House without question or suspend the sitting until a time of his or her choosing. These suspensions are usually only for a short period of time (up to 30 minutes).
- *Expulsion.* Expulsion is the ultimate power available to the House. Members in the past have been expelled for such crimes as perjury, forgery, fraud and corruption. An expelled Member may seek re-election to the House, even by standing in a by-election of the same Parliament that elected him. Expulsions are rare. The most recent was in 1954.
- *Censure.* Members may be admonished by the Speaker standing in their places for unparliamentary conduct. The last Member to be admonished was Mr Tam Dalyell in 1968.

Powers of the Committee on Standards and Privileges

3–50 The Select Committee on Standards and Privileges was established in 1995. At the same time the office of Parliamentary Commissioner for Standards was created. His responsibilities include that of maintaining the Register of Members' Interests. The Committee drew up a Code of Conduct on Standards and Privileges in 1996[24] The Code is based on the "Seven Principles of Public Life" set out by the Committee on Standards in Public Life (the Nolan Committee).[25] The principles are as follows.

Key Concept

Seven principles of public life: selflessness, integrity, objectivity, accountability, openness, honesty, and leadership.

[24] House of Commons, *The Code of Conduct together with the Guide to the Rules Relating to the Conduct of Members*, H.C. 688 (1995–6).

[25] Select Committee on Standards in Public Life, First Report, H.C. 637 (1994–95).

The 1996 Code of Conduct also includes some new principles, including that M.P.s should avoid conflicts of interest, maintain the integrity of Parliament, register their interests, act openly with ministers, other Members and public officials and not misuse confidential information. The Select Committee on Standards and Privileges considers the conduct of Members and makes reports on its findings.

Powers over non-members

The powers which may be exercised over non-Members are usually only invoked if there has been **3–51** conduct amounting to contempt. Contempt may be disorderly or disrespectful conduct, words which impugn the character of proceedings of the House, premature publication of Committee proceedings, or obstructing Members or officials in the discharge of their duty.

Power to detain

When there is unruly conduct within the Parliament buildings offenders are removed and escorted **3–52** from the premises by the Serjeant at Arms and his staff of doorkeepers. If the disruption was serious, the offenders may be detained in a police custody room on the premises until the House rises at the end of the day. Where the conduct amounted to a criminal offence the offenders may be transferred to police custody.

Power to compel committee witnesses to attend

If a select committee witness is unwilling to attend, the committee can order the attendance of a **3–53** witness at a specified date and time. If the witness does not respond the House may order the Serjeant at Arms to serve a warrant on the witness. The Serjeant or his appointee may call on the full assistance of the civil authorities, including the police. The last use of the warrant was in January 1992 when the Maxwell brothers were obliged to attend the Social Security Select Committee which was investigating the operation of pension funds.

Imprisonment

The House still retains the power to imprison for a period not exceeding the length of the **3–54** Parliamentary session. This power has not been exercised for over 120 years. Offenders are ordered to be detained either in one of H.M. Prisons, or in the custody of the Serjeant at Arms.

THE GOVERNMENT

Key Concepts **3–55**

Central Government consists of:

- The sovereign.
- The Privy Council.
- The ministers of the Crown.
- Central Government departments.
- The civil service.

The sovereign

3–56 Succession to the throne is governed by the Act of Settlement 1700. The main principle of succession is that on the death of the monarch, the right to succeed to the throne descends to the heirs of her body.

There are three rules which are applied:

(1) *Preference for males*. Sons of the monarch rank before daughters regardless of age.
(2) *Primogeniture*. The oldest son ranks before younger sons.
(3) *Representation*. A child or other descendant of a person who would have succeeded if he had survived may succeed in his or her place, for example the children of the oldest son will rank ahead of the younger sons.

The person who succeeds to the throne must take the coronation oath, declare that he is a faithful protestant and promise to uphold the Church of England and the Church of Scotland. When a monarch dies his heir succeeds automatically and immediately. Where the heir to the throne is under the age of 18, is ill and incapable or is absent from the UK and unable to return when he succeeds to the throne the royal functions must, according to the Regency Act 1937, be carried out by a regent. A regent can exercise all of the royal powers except that he must not assent to a Bill altering the succession to the throne. He is also not permitted to assent to a Bill repealing the Scots Act, which protects the status of the Church of Scotland.[26] The regent is usually the next person in line to succeed to the throne who is over the age of eighteen.

Royal functions can be delegated to Counsellors of State if the monarch is to be outside the UK or is suffering from a mental or physical disability which is not sufficiently serious or permanent to justify the appointment of a regent. The Counsellor's of State are the monarch's spouse and the next four persons in line of succession over the age of eighteen. Counsellors of State may not dissolve Parliament or confer honours.

Privy Council

3–57 Privy Councillors are appointed for life by letters patent issued by the Queen on the advice of the government. They adopt the title "Right Honourable". They take an oath which binds them to secrecy on Privy Council business.

Key Concepts

Membership of the **Privy Council**:

- Lord President of the Council, a member of the Government.
- All past and present Cabinet Ministers.
- The Speaker of the House of Commons.
- The Lords of Appeal in Ordinary and the holders of other high judicial offices.
- The Archbishops of Canterbury and York.
- Leading statesmen from Commonwealth countries.

The quorum of the Privy Council is three members and usually four are summoned to attend. They are selected as being suitable for the business to be dealt with. A larger meeting may be convened for business of state importance, for example approval of the marriage of the heir to the throne. The majority of the business of the Privy Council consists of giving formal effect to acts of the Crown done under the authority of the royal prerogative or of statute. The Council issues

[26] Protestant Religion and Presbyterian Church Act 1706.

proclamations for summoning, proroguing and dissolving Parliament and may issue Orders in Council for a wide range of purposes, including, making delegated legislation, declaring states of emergency and giving effect to a decision of the Judicial Committee of the Privy Council.

The Judicial Committee of the Privy Council consists of Privy Councillors who hold or have held high judicial office. It hears appeals from ecclesiastical courts of the Church of England, from certain professional regulatory bodies and from courts in some Commonwealth Countries. It now has a new role as the final court of appeal for cases in Scotland where a devolution issue has been raised.

Ministers of the crown

Prime Minister and the Cabinet

The Cabinet is composed of around 20 senior M.P.s and peers, each holding some important **3–58** government office or responsibility. There are no set rules for who must be included in a Cabinet but the Chancellor of the Exchequer, Home Secretary, Defence Secretary and Foreign Secretary are invariably included. The Prime Minister is chosen as a result of either a successful general Election, in which his party is returned as the largest party, or on the resignation of a former Prime Minister, such as occurred in 1990 when Margaret Thatcher was forced to resign by her Parliamentary party. In either event, the party leader must be invited by the Queen to form a government.

The Prime Minister has huge powers.

Patronage

The Prime Minister appoints his Cabinet and all of the other ministerial posts. However, his power **3–59** is not unlimited; he has to try to reconcile the various "wings" of the party and there may be people who have helped him attain his position and therefore need to be rewarded. Thatcher's first Government contained Ministers who were to the left of the Conservative Party, and she needed to keep the left happy for the sake of party unity.

Dissolution of Parliament

The Prime Minister decides when he will call a General Election, unless he is unlucky enough to **3–60** have lost a motion of no confidence in his government when he will be obliged to call an election. The Prime Minster will decide the date of an election after consulting close colleagues. He does not have to consult the Cabinet.

Powers relating to the Cabinet

The size and composition of the Cabinet is decided by the Prime Minister alone, as are the sizes **3–61** and composition of Cabinet Committees which discuss proposed legislation and other matters. The Prime Minister decides when the cabinet will meet, what will be discussed and what will be written in the minutes. Votes are not often taken in Cabinet; rather the Prime Minister "senses the mood of the meeting" and sums up for the minutes.

Ministerial responsibility

3–62

Key Concepts

The term "**ministerial responsibility**" applies in two circumstances:

(1) Collective responsibility; the obligation to adhere publicly to government policies.

(2) Individual responsibility; the responsibility of a Minister for the actions of his department.

Collective responsibility is the responsibility of the government as a whole for the decisions it has made and the policies it has carried out. It is particularly important in the Cabinet where decisions are taken in secret and where the discussions leading to a decision remain confidential.

There are some good reasons for this secrecy:

- It preserves an image of a united government. Nothing damages a government more than the impression that it is split on a certain issue. The Major Government was an example of this.
- It suggests a stability, which reassures the money markets.
- It presents a united front in policies for both friends and enemies of the country so that they know where the government stands on particular issues.
- It helps government ministers who are under attack for a particular policy. As the policy has been decided by the Cabinet, all members of the Cabinet must stand by it and the minister who has to implement it.
- It helps to hide mistakes inefficiency and deceit.

If a minister is unable to accept a decision, he must resign office. Examples of such resignations include Michael Heseltine over the Westland affair and Geoffrey Howe in 1990 over Thatcher's European policy. This latter resignation was devastating to Mrs Thatcher. Howe's resignation speech in the House of Commons signalled the end of her leadership of the Conservative Party. Most ministers however make their protest in Cabinet and then accept the final decision, thus keeping their cabinet post. In recent years it has become more common for ministers unhappy with decisions to "leak" their dissent to the media.

Individual ministerial responsibility is a more complex principle. It refers to the Minister's responsibility for the actions of himself as a government Minister, those of any junior ministers and those of his civil servants. It does not refer to the actions of a Minister in his or her personal capacity. So a Minister who has indulged in misconduct which does not amount to a crime will not necessarily have to resign, although pressure may be brought by his party to do so because of the embarrassment being caused to the party.

Historically, a Minister was responsible for the actions, or inaction, of civil servants and this was feasible because government departments were small and manageable and ministers could keep a watch on what was happening. The idea was that the civil servants were carrying out the instructions and policies of the minister and therefore should be protected from public criticism by them being named as the "culprits". Civil servants are required to work for any government and every government in an impartial manner so that the administration of government will flow smoothly from Conservative government to Labour government, and so on.

By the end of the Second World War, however, government departments were larger and their work more diverse. It was impossible for a Minister to know the day-to-day operational details within the department. The question of a Minister's responsibility was brought up in the Crichel Down Affair in the early 1950s. The Air Ministry acquired farmland in 1938 by compulsory purchase. When it no longer required the land as a bombing range the minister transferred it to the Ministry of Agriculture, who transferred it to the Commissioners for Crown Lands, who let it to a tenant. The original owner was prevented from buying the land back (the normal procedure in such cases) or leasing it. Other landowners were similarly affected. An inquiry published in 1954 concluded that civil servants in the Ministry of Agriculture had acted in a high-handed and deceitful manner. There was considerable criticism and the Agriculture Minister, Sir Thomas Dugdale, resigned taking full responsibility for the mistakes of his officials. Although this appears to be the doctrine working properly, in fact Dugdale had been involved in the decisions and the civil servants had been named in the inquiry report.

After this affair, the Home Secretary stated how the doctrine should work:

Key Concepts

A Minister should **protect a civil servant** where the civil servant:

- has carried out an explicit order; or
- has acted in accordance with the Minister's policy.

A Minister is under **no obligation** to protect a civil servant:

- if he has acted contrary to the minister's orders and without the Minister's knowledge.

The Home Secretary, however, stated that the minister would remain "constitutionally responsible to Parliament for the fact that something has gone wrong".

Departments

Each government department (with the exception of non-political departments such as the Inland Revenue) is headed by a member of the Government. The most important have the title Secretary of State. All Secretaries of State are members of the Cabinet. Other departments are headed by other ministers, not all of whom are in the Cabinet. In recent years departments have tended to become larger as functions are amalgamated to form departments with wide portfolios. These departments have a Secretary of State or other senior minister at their head and other junior ministers responsible for specific functions. **3–63**

Scottish business at Westminster

The Scottish Office was replaced by the Scotland Office on July 1, 1999, following devolution and the establishment of a Scottish Executive. Many of the responsibilities of the former Scottish Office were transferred to the Scottish Executive. In June 2003 the Scotland Office was abolished and responsibility for its business was taken over by the new Department of Constitutional Affairs. There is a Memorandum of Understanding and a set of Concordats dealing with the division of functions between the Scottish and UK administrations. There are also more detailed bilateral Concordats between the Scottish Executive and individual UK government departments. The UK Government retains responsibility for a range of issues including employment, fiscal and economic policy, taxation, social security, benefits and pensions. The Secretary of State for Scotland and the Scotland Office represented Scottish interests in matters reserved to the UK Parliament until June 2003 when it became apparent that the volume of business no longer justified a separate Cabinet post of a separate department for Scottish Affairs. The title of Secretary of State for Scotland is now held by the Minster of Transport who represents Scottish interests on a part-time basis. **3–64**

> **Key Concepts**
>
> The **Secretary of State**:
>
> - represents Scottish interests within the UK Government in matters that are reserved to the UK Parliament under the terms of the Scotland Act 1998;
> - encourages co-operation between the Parliaments and between the UK Government and Scottish Executive;
> - intervenes in relations between UK and Scottish Administrations if required by the Scotland Act;
> - pays grant to the Scottish Consolidated Fund;
> - manages other financial transactions; and
> - exercises certain residual functions in reserved matters, such as the conduct and funding of elections.

Under s.35 of the Scotland Act the Secretary of State may make an Order prohibiting the Scottish Parliament's Presiding Officer from submitting a Bill for Royal Assent, which he or she has reasonable grounds to believe would be incompatible with:

- any international obligations;
- the interests of defence; or
- the interests of national security.

The Secretary of State may also make an Order under s.35 if he or she reasonably believes that the Scottish Parliament Bill makes modifications to, and would have an adverse effect on, the operation of the law as it applies to reserved matters. These powers have not yet been exercised.

The Advocate-General for Scotland is the principal legal adviser to the Government as regards Scots law. Following devolution, the Lord Advocate and the Solicitor General for Scotland transferred to the Scottish Executive and a new office of Advocate-General was created. The Advocate General for Scotland is a Minister of the Crown and is responsible to Parliament. The Advocate General sits on a number of Cabinet Committees. She is also responsible for the Office of the Solicitor to the Advocate-General for Scotland, which provides legal advice to most UK departments in relation to Scotland. She also exercises statutory functions under the Scotland Act.

> **Key Concepts**
>
> Functions of the **Advocate-General**:
>
> - advising the UK Government on Scots Law;
> - referring Bills of the Scottish Parliament to the Judicial Committee of the Privy Council for decisions on their competence; and
> - raising proceedings in the courts or the Judicial Committee on devolution issues. She receives notice of all devolution issues raised in court cases and can intervene in the courts or the Judicial Committee.

Civil Service

3–65 The civil service is part of the Executive arm of government. Its traditional role is to advise ministers on policy matters and, once the policy has been decided, implement that policy. The civil servant is a Crown servant and may enjoy certain of the immunities afforded to the Crown.

However, it is now considered that civil servants are responsible to the government of the day rather that the state and it is to the government that they owe their loyalty. They are not answerable to Parliament and if required to give evidence before a Select Committee their answers must reflect the government's policy because they are deemed to speak on behalf of their Minister. If a civil servant were able to speak freely they might give a view that conflicted with government policy, and this would undermine their professional political impartiality.

In 1968 a report on the working of the civil service was released. The recommendations of the Fulton report were wide-ranging but the government did not implement them all. Changes did occur in the way civil servants were recruited and promoted and a new Civil Services Department was set up to deal with these. The report also recommended that certain functions carried out by civil servants in government departments should be devolved to bodies, which would exist outside the departmental framework while still being subject to ministerial guidance. The Civil Aviation Authority and the Healthy and Safety Commission were created as a result. Another recommendation was that semi-autonomous boards should be created, with a small core of civil servants in the department making policy for boards and agencies to implement. This part of the report was not implemented but it became the starting point for the Thatcher reforms in the 1980s.

The Thatcher Government of 1979 embarked on changes in the civil service, which have altered it considerably. They privatised public utilities and amenities, introduced Executive agencies, new management practices and contracting out of services. The new structure of government has been called "the new public management" and it consists of a number of components:

Key Concepts

New public management

- professional management;
- goals and targets identified and set;
- greater competition;
- decentralisation to smaller units.

Change did not happen immediately on the Thatcher Government coming to office, it took some years before the really radical reforms could be pushed through. One of the most notable features of the reforms was the split between service delivery and the making of policy which resulted from the Next Steps Initiative by which many of the functions previously carried out by government departments are now carried out by executive agencies.

Executive agencies and civil servants

Civil servants who are transferred to an Executive agency remain as civil servants, but their conditions of service will not necessarily remain the same. The civil service used to have the image of being a uniform service, where staff could move from one department to another on being promoted. Pay grades were universal: a higher executive officer in the Ministry of Defence would be on the same scale as a higher executive officer in the Scottish Office. Conditions of service were also uniform. Now, an Agency Chief Executive can implement pay scales and conditions of service which he or she considers appropriate. This means that civil servants wishing to transfer back into the mainstream service, so as to become involved in policy making, may have difficulty in doing so without losing seniority or pay. In 1979, there were around 750,000 civil servants. By the end of 1996, 365,000 civil servants had been transferred to 129 executive agencies, while around 100,000 civil service posts had disappeared. **3–66**

Quick Quiz

- List three characteristics of the UK constitution.
- Can an Act of Parliament be declared invalid by the courts?
- Give three examples of prerogative powers.
- What are the three branches of government?
- What three meanings did Dicey ascribe to the principle of the rule of law?
- List the four criteria by which the legality of restrictions on human rights are measured.
- List three categories of people who are disqualified from voting in parliamentary elections.
- When may a Minister decline to answer questions in Parliament?
- List the "Seven Principles of Public Life" set out by the Committee on Standards in Public Life.
- What are the functions of the Advocate-General?
- Are the following statements True or False?
  - (a) New prerogative powers can be created to suit changing circumstances.
  - (b) It is not possible to create new conventions.
  - (c) The office of Prime Minister is created by statute.
  - (d) The rule of law means that the government must obey the law.
  - (e) The UK Parliament may repeal the Scotland Act 1998.
  - (f) A subsequent Act of Parliament automatically repeals any inconsistent provisions in earlier statutes.
  - (g) Hereditary peers are all disqualified from sitting in the House of Commons.
  - (h) The minimum age required to sit as a Member of Parliament is 18 years.
  - (i) A Bill may be introduced first into the House of Lords.
  - (j) The House of Commons has power to imprison a person who disrupts its proceedings.

Further Reading

Books

There are two books which give comprehensive and up-to-date accounts of United Kingdom Constitutional Law: **A. Bradley and K. Ewing, *Constitutional and Administrative Law*** (Addison Wesley Longman, 2002) and **H. Barnett, *Constitutional and Administrative Law*** (Cavendish, London, 2002).

Another up to date book which concentrates more on practice and less on theories and concepts is: **C. Turpin, *British Government and the Constitution*** (Butterworths, London, 2002).

A Scottish perspective is provided by: **C. Ashton and V. Finch, *Constitutional Law in Scotland*** (W. Green, 2000).

Internet sources

Internet sources are very useful as they provide up to date information from the institutions themselves. Two particularly useful sites are:

- Houses of Parliament Home page: *www.parliament.uk*
- UK Online Government Gateway site: *www.open.gov.uk*

Chapter 4

CONSTITUTIONAL LAW II — SCOTLAND

Valerie Finch[1]

SCOTTISH GOVERNMENT

The opening sentence of the first section of the Scotland Act 1998 is: "*There shall be a Scottish Parliament.*" This Act marks the culmination of a long campaign for major constitutional reform in the UK. Within some political parties there has always been a desire for an independent Scotland whereas others are content with the level of devolution provided by the Scotland Act. Devolution is the delegation of power from a central government to local bodies without the relinquishment of sovereignty. The scheme of devolution means that although there is now a Scottish Parliament it operates subject to statutory authority from the Westminster Parliament and the extent of it powers is limited. **4–01**

History of devolution

The concept of a Scottish Parliament is not new. Scotland had its own Parliament until the union of the Scottish and English Parliaments in 1707. A number of Acts of the original Scottish Parliament are still in force today. The 1707 Treaty of Union merged the existing Parliaments of Scotland and England. The Treaty provisions included safeguards for the Scottish church and the separate Scottish legal system. The combined Parliament was supposed to be a new Parliament **4–02**

[1] Lecturer in Law, Paisley University.

rather than a continuation of the former English Parliament, however the new Parliament consisted of all existing English M.P.s and peers. Seats for 45 M.P.s from Scotland were created in the House of Commons and 16 peers of Scotland became hereditary peers in the House of Lords. The new British Parliament continued to follow the procedures and practices of the English Parliament. A post of Secretary for Scotland was created to look after Scottish interests but it lapsed in 1746 and was not revived until 1855. The post became a Secretary of State post in 1926 with responsibility for a government department known as the Scottish Office.

During the twentieth century there were a number of campaigns for Scottish independence. In 1973 the Royal Commission on the Constitution recommended a form of legislative devolution for Scotland. Subsequently the Government put forward legislation to establish a Scottish Assembly. The resulting Act, the Scotland Act 1978, required that 40 per cent of the Scottish electorate had to vote support the Act for it to come into force. A referendum was held in 1979 and the devolution scheme was supported by 52 per cent of those voting. As this was not equal to 40 per cent of those entitled to vote the scheme was not implemented and shortly afterwards there was a change of political party in government.

The new Conservative Government of 1979 did not support devolution but preferred instead to further devolve the administrative government of Scotland and to allow special treatment of Scottish business in Parliament itself. However, it was not always possible to devote an appropriate amount of Parliamentary time to Scottish business. Scottish legislative changes were often included in UK statutes when separate legislation would have been more suitable. The political pressure for reform continued to grow and a body called the Scottish Constitutional Convention came together in the late 1980s to campaign for devolution. The Scottish Constitutional Convention included some of the political parties in Scotland, local authorities, the churches and many other organisations. Over the next few years several reports were published. Its main demand was for a Scottish Parliament with law-making powers. A devolution policy was included in the Labour Party manifesto for the May 1997 General Election. After election, the Labour Government arranged for a referendum on its proposals, which were set out in a White Paper of July 1997, "*Scotland's Parliament*". The referendum was held on September 11, 1997 and produced clear majorities for the two propositions about the creation of a Scottish Parliament and its having certain tax-varying powers. Following this result, the Scotland Act was passed in Parliament in 1998.

Key Concepts

Under the devolved framework of government in the UK, there is now a **Scottish Parliament**. There are also Regional Assemblies in Wales and Northern Ireland.

Devolution is the delegation of power from a central government to local bodies without the relinquishment of sovereignty.

Relations between UK Parliament and Scottish Parliament

4–03 It is important to remember that the constitutional change that has occurred in the UK through the process of devolution has not created a federal structure but remains unitary. The Scottish Parliament operates as a self-contained and fully functioning Parliament in its own right. Legislation can be passed by the Scottish Parliament without going through the Westminster Parliament. However, the UK Parliament at Westminster retains power to legislate on all matters, both reserved and devolved.[2] There is however a convention of devolution that the UK Parliament will not normally legislate on devolved matters without the consent of the Scottish Parliament. It may sometimes be more convenient for Westminster to legislate for the whole UK even where

[2] Scotland Act 1998, s.28(7).

some of the subject-matter falls within the Parliament's legislative competence and this Sewel Convention (named after Lord Sewel) provides a means for this to happen.

Any powers which remain with the UK Parliament at Westminster are known as reserved powers.

Key Concepts

Reserved matters include:

- Constitutional matters
- UK foreign policy
- UK defence and national security
- The fiscal, economic and monetary system
- Immigration and nationality
- Energy: electricity, coal, gas and nuclear energy
- Common markets
- Trade and industry, including competition and customer protection
- Some aspects of transport, including railways, transport safety and regulation
- Employment legislation
- Social security
- Gambling and the National Lottery
- Data protection
- Abortion, human fertilisation and embryology, genetics and vivisection
- Equal opportunities

The powers which are not designated by the Scotland Act as reserved are known as residual powers. There is no explicit indication of the extent of the devolved powers but they include the following matters:

Key Concepts

Devolved powers

- Health
- Education and training
- Local government
- Social work
- Housing
- Planning
- Tourism
- Economic development and financial assistance to industry
- Some aspects of transport, including the Scottish road network, bus policy and ports and harbours

- Law and home affairs, including most aspects of criminal and civil law, the prosecution system and the courts
- Police and fire services
- Prisons
- Environment
- Natural heritage
- Agriculture, forestry and fishing
- Sport and the arts
- Statistics, public registers and records

Since the Scottish Parliament is a subordinate body, created by a UK statute, the laws which it enacts are also subordinate. This means that, unlike Acts of the UK Parliament, the Acts of the Scottish Parliament are subject to the scrutiny of the courts and can be declared invalid. There is also the possibility that, in the future, the UK Parliament may legislate to reduce or even remove the powers of the Scottish Parliament.

The Secretary of State for Scotland is a member of the UK Cabinet. He acts as the conduit between the UK and Scottish parliaments. The administration of reserved matters in Scotland is the responsibility of the Department of Constitutional Affairs. The Secretary of State for Constitutional Affairs is also a member of the Cabinet. Scotland will continue to elect M.P.s to the Westminster Parliament, but section 86 of the Scotland Act 1998 removes the requirement that there must be at least 71 constituencies in Scotland returning M.P.s to the UK Parliament. Moreover, the electoral quota to be used in calculating the number of seats for Scotland is now the same as for England. This will lead to a reduction in the number of Scottish constituencies returning M.P.s to the UK Parliament.

Key Concepts

The UK after devolution is a **unitary system**.

The **UK Parliament** retains power to legislate on all matters.
Certain matters are **reserved** exclusively to the UK Parliament.

SCOTTISH PARLIAMENT

4–04 The Scottish Parliament is a creature of statute and is not a sovereign body in its own right. Its powers, functions and duties derive from statute. As a subordinate body it is subject to the control of the Scotland Act and thus to the UK Parliament. A report, *Shaping Scotland's Parliament*, published in January 1999, included comprehensive proposals for the working of the new Parliament. Four key principles were identified:

Key Concepts

Key principles for the Scottish Parliament

(1) **Sharing the power**: The Scottish Parliament should embody and reflect the sharing of power between the people of Scot-land, the legislators and the Scottish Executive;

(2) **Accountability**:	The Scottish Executive should be accountable to the Scottish Parliament and the Parliament and Executive should be accountable to the people of Scotland;
(3) **Access and participation**:	The Scottish Parliament should be accessible, open, responsive and develop procedures which make possible a participative approach to the develop-ment, consideration and scrutiny of policy and legis-lation; and
(4) **Equal opportunities**:	The Scottish Parliament in its operation and its appointments should recognise the need to promote equal opportunities.

Powers of the Scottish Parliament

Parliament is given power to call for witnesses and documents. Anyone who is summoned to attend or to produce documents and fails to do so is guilty of an offence punishable by a fine or up to three months' imprisonment.[3] This punishment is not imposed by the Parliament itself but by the courts. **4–05**

Privileges

MSPs are protected against action in defamation arising from statements which they make in Parliament.[4] Such remarks are held to be absolutely privileged. The publications authorised by Parliament are also protected by the Scotland Act and other reports of proceedings which are fair and accurate and made without malice are protected by the Defamation Act 1996, s.15. MSPs are not entirely exempt from the general law on contempt of court and must therefore refrain from discussing matters which are *sub judice.* However a limited form of immunity is granted by s.42 whereby proceedings in relation to a Bill or subordinate legislation will not be covered by the strict liability rule of the Contempt of Court Act 1981. The Inner House considered the extent of the privilege afforded to the Scottish Parliament and MSPs by the Scotland in the case of *Whaley v Lord Watson of Invergowrie.* **4–06**

Whaley v Lord Watson of Invergowrie

2000 S.C. 340

The case was an appeal against a decision of the Lord Ordinary to refuse to grant an interim interdict against a member of the Scottish Parliament, restraining him from promoting, and introducing a Bill to outlaw hunting with dogs. Whalley claimed that the MSP had assistance from a pressure group, the Scottish Campaign Against Hunting with Dogs, which breached the rules relating to members' interests.[5]

The Inner House held that although the Scottish Parliament was a body created by statute and was subject to the jurisdiction of the courts in the same way as any other statutory body, Parliament was afforded some immunity from court orders by the Scotland Act.[6] This does not mean, however, that the protection against court orders

3 Scotland Act 1998, s.23.
4 Scotland Act 1998, s.41.
5 Scotland Act 1998 (Transitory and Transitional Provisions) (Members' Interests) Order 1999, art.6.
6 Scotland Act 1998, s.40(4).

will always apply to individual MSPs. A standards committee decision on an act of an MSP did not bar the courts from considering the matter or the Crown from investigating and prosecuting a suspected offence. The balance of convenience in the particular case, however, did not favour the grant of interim interdict as an interdict in these circumstances would have had the effect of preventing the Parliament from considering a Bill which was within its competency.

Composition of the Scottish Parliament

4–07 The Scottish Parliament is unicameral, that is to say it has only one chamber, unlike the bicameral UK Parliament, which includes the House of Commons and the House of Lords. There is no equivalent to the House of Lords in the Scottish Parliament. The Scottish Parliament is made up of 129 elected Members of the Scottish Parliament, known as MSPs. One of the MSPs is elected by the Parliament to serve as the Presiding Officer. There are also two deputy Presiding Officers.

Members of the Scottish Parliament

4–08 The elected representatives in the Scottish Parliament are known as Members of the Scottish Parliament or, more commonly, as MSPs.

MSPs can be elected in two ways:

(1) Seventy three constituency members are elected, based on the UK Parliament constituencies, using the "first past the post" system.
(2) A further 56 regional members are elected, seven for each of eight regions (based on the regions used in the European Parliament elections). These members are elected using the "Additional Member" System. This is a form of proportional representation using party lists, which ensures that each party's representation in the Parliament reflects its overall share of the vote.

Despite the fact that some MSPs are elected to represent a constituency and others are regionally elected members, they all have equal status once they are elected. Elections are normally held every four years. An extraordinary General Election may be held if either Parliament resolves to dissolve itself with a two-thirds majority, or there is no nomination for the office of First Minister within the first 28 days after a vacancy occurring. The holding of an extraordinary General Election will not normally disturb the four year cycle of elections unless the extraordinary General Election has been held within six months of an ordinary General Election. In such circumstances the extraordinary General Election replaces the ordinary one.

The Scottish Parliament is required to meet within seven days of the result of the poll being announced. MSPs may work from the Parliament Headquarters in Edinburgh but many also have a local office within their constituency or region, where they may hold surgeries. A Member may resign his or her seat by giving notice in writing to the Presiding Officer. Seats will also become vacant if an MSP dies or becomes disqualified. If this causes a constituency seat to become vacant, the vacant seat will be filled by holding a by-election, unless there is less than six months to the next General Election.[7] If a regional seat becomes vacant there is no by-election. If the Member who resigns was elected as an individual the seat will remain vacant until the next election. If he was returned from a political party's regional list, the next unelected person on the list will take the seat. If there is nobody left on the list to take the seat, the seat remains vacant.

In general, persons who are disqualified from membership of the UK Parliament by the House of Commons Disqualification Act 1975 are also disqualified from membership of the Scottish Parliament.[8] However, there are some differences: citizens of the EU who are resident in the UK

---

[7] Scotland Act 1998, s.10.
[8] Scotland Act 1998, s.15.

are not disqualified, neither are peers and peeresses nor priests and ministers of any religious denomination. The Scotland Act makes provision for further disqualifications for the holders of certain public appointments. Members of the UK Parliament are not disqualified from membership of the Scottish Parliament. All MSPs must take the oath of allegiance, usually at the first meeting after a General Election. A member may not participate in the proceedings of Parliament or accept a salary until he has taken the oath.

Presiding Officer

The Parliament is required to elect a Presiding Officer and two deputies at its first meeting after a General Election. They hold office until the next election, which would normally occur at the first meeting of the next Parliament. The Presiding Officer has several roles. **4–09**

Key Concepts

The **Presiding Officer**:

- chairs the meetings of the Parliament;
- convenes and chairs weekly meetings of the Parliamentary Bureau, where the future business of the Parliament is agreed;
- declares the date of the next General Election;
- chairs the Corporate Body;
- decides on questions raised regarding the meaning of the rules for Parliamentary proceedings;
- represents the Parliament at home and abroad and with such bodies, for example, as the UK Parliament, the Devolved Assemblies, European institutions and Parliaments from across the world; and
- submits Bills for Royal Assent.

Scottish Executive

The term "Scottish Executive" is the statutory term for the senior Ministers of the devolved Scottish government. The Scottish Executive is formed from the party or parties holding a majority of seats in the Parliament. The members of the Executive, collectively referred to as "the Scottish Ministers", are: **4–10**

Key Concepts

Scottish Executive

- The First Minister
- The Lord Advocate and the Solicitor-General (also known as the Law Officers)
- Other Ministers appointed by the First Minister

First Minister

4–11 The MSPs select a nominee who is then formally appointed by the Queen. He holds office at her Majesty's pleasure and, in theory, could be dismissed by the Sovereign. He will cease to hold office as soon as another First Minister is appointed. The First Minister may resign at any time and is required to do so if Parliament passes a vote of no confidence in the Scottish Executive. As head of the Scottish Executive, the First Minister has a direct relationship with the Sovereign in appointing Ministers and law officers. The First Minister is, in effect, Scotland's counterpart of the Prime Minister in the UK Parliament. He may appoint Ministers with the agreement of Parliament and may dismiss them without any requirement for such agreement.[9]

Scottish Law Officers

4–12 There are two Scottish Law Officers, the Lord Advocate and the Solicitor-General for Scotland who are part of the Scottish Executive. They advise the Scottish Executive on legal matters and represent its interest in court. The Lord Advocate is head of the systems of criminal prosecution and investigation of deaths in Scotland. Both are appointed by the Queen on the recommendation of the First Minister, made with the approval of the Scottish Parliament. Since their work is highly specialised, it may not be possible to appoint them from amongst the elected MSPs. If this is the case, they can still participate in the work of the Parliament but cannot vote.

Organisation of the Scottish Executive

First Minister

—

Deputy First Minister

—

Ministers

(Justice,[10] Education and Young People, Enterprise, Transport and Lifelong Learning, Finance and Public Services, Environment and Rural Development, Parliamentary Business, Social Justice, Tourism, Culture and Sport, Health and Community Care)

—

Law Officers

(Lord Advocate, Solicitor-General for Scotland)

Scottish Ministers

4–13 The members of the Scottish Executive are referred to by the statutory collective term "The Scottish Ministers".[11] This term is used for various legal purposes. Where an Act of Parliament conferred a power or a duty on a specific minister with regard to what is now a devolved function, such a power or duty is now exercisable by the "Scottish Ministers". This allows any one of them to exercise such powers interchangeably. There are some functions however, which are exclusively exercised by the First Minister and others which are exercisable only by the Law

---

[9] Scotland Act 1998, s.49.

[10] The office of Deputy First Minister and Minister for Justice are currently held by the same person. There is no legal requirement that this should be so.

[11] Scotland Act 1998, s.44(2).

Officers. Legal challenges, such as judicial review of the acts of members of the Scottish Executive, are brought against the "Scottish Ministers", rather than against the specific ministerial office with responsibility for the decision which is being challenged. The term "Scottish Ministers" is also used descriptively and informally to apply to all Ministers including Junior Ministers. The Scottish Ministers are appointed by the First Minister who determines the number of Ministers and their responsibilities, also known as portfolios. The First Minister can also appoint Junior Ministers to assist the Scottish Ministers with government business. A Minister's portfolio may be covered by one or more committees of the Parliament. The committees' members are chosen with regard to the political parties and groupings in the Parliament. A Minister can be called to appear before a committee to explain policies or to participate in inquiries.

Ministers who are not Members of the Scottish Executive are called "Junior Scottish Ministers". All Ministers are MSPs. There is no limit to the number of Ministers who may be appointed. Ministers are part of two separate organisations: the Scottish Executive (Ministers) and the Scottish Parliament (MSPs). In addition to a constituency or regional office dealing with local matters, a Minister may have a ministerial office within a Scottish Executive building. Local and ministerial offices remain completely separate and have different contact details. Local offices cannot deal with ministerial queries and, similarly, ministerial offices cannot deal with constituents' concerns. A Minister cannot sit on a parliamentary committee dealing with a subject for which he or she is Minister. At present it is general practice that no Ministers sit on committees.

Major government policy initiatives are announced to the Parliament by the Scottish Executive. These often take the form of ministerial statements made during meetings of the Parliament. Ministers may also use the practice, common at Westminster, of using the answers to written questions from MSPs as a way of announcing decisions and publicising documents. Political parties represented within the Parliament may also make statements regarding their own policies during meetings of the Parliament. The Executive often produces policy and consultation documents (similar to the "White" and "Green" Papers produced by the UK Government) which outline the Executive's proposals for legislation. The Scottish Parliament is not involved in this consultation stage. Consultation Papers are Executive documents and are available through the Scottish Executive rather than the Scottish Parliament. After the consultation has been considered by the Executive, the Executive may introduce a Bill into Parliament. This is known as an Executive Bill. Like all Bills, Executive Bills will be scrutinised by Committees and by the whole Parliament. It is for the Parliament to decide whether proposed legislation should be passed. Once this is achieved, responsibility is then passed back to the Executive who will draw up a time scale for the implementation of the Act.

Ministerial Responsibility

The Scottish Ministerial Code,[12] published in August 1999, defines the doctrine of collective **4–14**
responsibility which applies to members of the Scottish Executive, including Deputy Ministers.

> **Key Concepts**
>
> **Collective Responsibility**
>
> 2.1. The Executive operates on the basis of collective responsibility. The internal processes through which a decision has been made should not be disclosed. Decisions reached by the executive are binding on its members...

[12] wwww.scotland.gov.uk/library.

> 2.3. Collective responsibility requires that Ministers should be able to express their views frankly in the expectation that they can argue freely in private while maintaining a united front when decisions have been reached. This in turn requires that the privacy of opinions expressed and advice offered within the Executive should be maintained. It is therefore essential that, subject to the guidelines on the disclosure of information set out in the Code of Practice on Access to Scottish Executive Information, Ministers take the necessary steps to ensure that they and their staff preserve the privacy of Executive business and protect the security of Executive documents.
>
> 2.4. Collective Responsibility as defined above also applies to any junior Scottish Ministers who are appointed by the First Minister under the terms of Section 49 of the Scotland Act even though they are not members of the Executive. (This refers to Deputy Ministers).

Parliamentary Bureau

4–15 The Parliamentary Bureau comprises the presiding officer and:

- one representative of each political party represented by more than five members;
- one representative of any group formed by members who represent a political party with fewer than five representatives.

The main function of the Parliamentary Bureau is to propose the business programme. It allocates time during the meetings of the Parliament for matters such as debates and decision on the general principles of Bills. The membership of each committee is approved by the Parliament on a motion of the Parliamentary Bureau. It refers draft proposals for Bills from MSPs to committees. The Parliamentary Bureau also resolves any questions about committee remits.

Scottish Parliament Committees

4–16 The important role played by committees is a distinctive feature of the Scottish Parliament. The use of committees is one of the methods of furthering the principle that Scottish Parliament should be accessible, open and responsive. The committee procedures ensure that there are opportunities for the general public to participate in the development, consideration and scrutiny of policy and legislation.

Mandatory committees

4–17 Certain committees must be set up by the Scottish Parliament. Procedures, Standards and Finance committees must be established within 21 sitting days of a General Election. Other mandatory committees must be established within 42 sitting days. Mandatory committees will be established for the entire Parliamentary session.

> **Key Concepts**
>
> **Mandatory Committees and their remits**
>
> **Procedures:** Practice and procedures of Parliament.
>
> **Standards:** Members' conduct.
> Member's rights and privileges.

Finance:	Proposals for public expenditure or taxation. Responsibilities with regard to Budget Bills. Handling of financial business.
Audit:	Accounts laid before Parliament.
European:	Proposals for European Communities legislation. Implementation of EC legislation. European Communities or European Union issues.
Equal Opportunities:	Matters relating to equal opportunities, including their observance within the Parliament.
Public Petitions:	Admissibility of public petitions and proposals for action is to be taken.
Subordinate legislation:	Any delegated legislation laid before Parliament. Proposed powers to make subordinate legislation in Bills. General issues about subordinate legislation-making powers.

Subject committees

All committees that are not mandatory committees will be known as subject committees. Subject committees may be established to deal with a particular subject by Parliament on a motion of the Parliamentary Bureau. The Bureau must also propose membership, remit and duration of subject committees. Any MSP may propose by motion the establishment of a subject committee. The remits for each subject committee will be fixed by the Parliament. Any question about committee remits will be resolved by the Parliamentary Bureau. Where a matter falls within the remit of more than one committee, Parliament may identify one as the lead committee for that matter. The lead committee will then take into account the views of the other committees. Although committees are responsible for distinct subject areas the matters which they considers in relation to their subject area are the same. **4–18**

Key Concepts

Matters considered by subject committees

- the need for law reform;
- the policy and administration of the Scottish Administration;
- proposals for legislation before the Scottish or UK Parliaments;
- EC legislation and international conventions; and
- financial proposals of the Scottish Administration.

A committee may introduce Bills relating to its subject area.

Committee meetings

Each committee will have between 5 and 15 members, including a convener and deputy convener. The quorum for a meeting of a committee is three members. Committees may invite any person to attend its meetings to give evidence or produce documents. Committee meetings will be public unless the committee decides to hold all or part of a meeting in private. **4–19**

Meetings will be held in public if the committee is considering:

- proposals for legislation by the Scottish or UK Parliaments;
- EC legislation or international conventions or agreements; or
- the need for law reform.

Scottish Parliament Corporate Body

4–20 The members of the Scottish Parliament Corporate Body are the Presiding Officer and four other MSPs. The Corporate Body is required because the Scottish Parliament is not a body corporate and cannot hold property, enter into contracts or bring or defend legal actions. The Corporate Body may enter into contracts, charge for goods and services, make investments and accept gifts.[13] The Corporate Body is responsible for the financing of the Parliament and allocation of the budget, the staffing of the Parliament, accommodation and the use and security of Parliamentary facilities. It also acts as the client in the project for the building of a permanent Parliament at Holyrood. It meets at regular intervals and acts in a politically neutral way.

The administration of the Parliament is supported by its own staff, headed by the Clerk/Chief Executive of the Parliament. The Clerk, as the Parliament's most senior official, has the ultimate responsibility for ensuring it operates smoothly and efficiently. These officials are employed by the Parliament itself. Although, in some respects they can be regarded as being equivalent to the government's civil servants, they are independent of the Government and act impartially solely on behalf of the Parliament. Like the Presiding Officer, they must remain politically neutral There are many groups of staff performing a wide range of tasks, from clerks (who advise MSPs on detailed matters of parliamentary procedure) to security and IT staff. The Presiding Officer and the Clerk are each supported by their own offices. All other staff members of the Parliament are organised into five directorates:

(1) Legal Office.

- Provides legal advice to the Presiding Officer, the Parliament and its Committees, and the Parliamentary Corporation and its staff.
- Provides legal support to the Subordinate Legislation, Procedures, Standards and European Committees.
- Advises the Scottish Parliamentary Corporate Body on a wide range of matters.
- Advises the Presiding Officer on the legislative competence of Bills.
- Advises the Subordinate Legislation Committee on provisions in Bills giving power to make delegated legislation, and on the competence of every Statutory Instrument put to the Parliament.

(2) Clerking Directorate. Consists of two offices:

(a) Committee Office:

- Provides clerking and administrative support to 13 of the Parliament's 16 committees.
- Advises the committees on the application of procedures and Standing Orders.
- Provides support to members in connection with proposals for Members Bills.
- Liaises with the Scottish Executive and members to ensure that Bills comply with the requirement of Standing Orders.

(b) Chamber Office:

- Provides support to the Presiding Officer and Deputy Presiding Officers for all meetings of the Parliament.

[13] Scotland Act 1998, Sch.3, para.4.

- Processes all written and oral questions for Question Time and First Minister's Question Time, and the Written Answers Report.
- Advises members on the admissibility of motions and amendments for debate.
- Provides administrative support to the Parliamentary Bureau, the Procedures Committee, the Standards Committee and the Petitions Committee.

(3) Communications Directorate.

- Responsible for both communications with the public and for communications within Parliament.
- Provides a parliamentary information system to the public.
- Responsible for the visitor centre, enquiry unit and education service.
- Responsible for the Official Report of parliamentary proceedings.

(4) Corporate Services.

- Manages general financial affairs, the Allowances Office, which is responsible for making payments to Members in respect of their allowances, and the Procurement Office which purchases of all goods and services for the Scottish Parliament.
- Manages the buildings.

(5) Holyrood Project Team.

- Acts as the representative of the SPCB in negotiating the building of the new Scottish Parliament complex at Holyrood.

SCOTTISH PARLIAMENT LEGISLATION

Section 28(1) of the Scotland Act 1998, provides that the Parliament may make laws, to be known as Acts of the Scottish Parliament. Section 29 sets a limit on that power to legislate. The power to legislatc is referred to as "legislative competence". Legislative competence is defined according to five criteria. **4–21**

Key Concepts

Criteria for legislative competence

- the Parliament can only legislate for or in relation to Scotland;
- it cannot legislate in relation to the "reserved matters" set out in Sch.5 to the Act;
- it cannot modify certain enactments set out in Sch.4 to the Act (which include the Human Rights Act 1998 and certain provisions of the Acts of Union and the European Communities Act 1972);
- its legislation must be compatible with the European Convention on Human Rights and with European Community law; and
- it cannot remove the Lord Advocate from his position as head of the system of criminal prosecutions and the investigation of deaths.

The precise boundaries of the Parliament's powers to legislate can ultimately be decided only by the courts.

Proposed Acts of the Scottish Parliament are called Bills. Most Bills are "public Bills". If they are passed the resulting Act will alter the general laws of Scotland. Private Bills are Bills introduced by private individuals or bodies, seeking powers or benefits in excess of or in conflict with the general law. Private Bills are subject to distinct Rules.

Bills may be proposed by:

- the Scottish Executive: these Bills are known as Executive Bills;
- a committee of the Parliament: such Bills are called Committee Bills; or
- an individual member: these Bills are called Members' Bills.

Public Bills

4–22 A Bill sets out proposals for legislation. Many Bills are introduced into the Parliament by Ministers but they may also be introduced by parliamentary committees or by MSPs. An important aspect of the arrangements for introducing new legislation is the provision for pre-legislative examination. Prior to introducing a Bill, a Minister can advise the relevant committee on proposals for legislation and outline the proposed consultation exercise. The committee may wish to speak to the Minister at this stage. The committee monitors the consultation and may take its own evidence. In many cases, there will be a public consultation process. This may involve the publication of an Executive consultation document (referred to as a "Green Paper") and/or detailed proposals (referred to as a "White Paper"). This allows the Parliament and interested individuals and groups in society to have a significant impact on the formation of policy. It also allows interested parties to influence the translation of this policy into proposals for new laws.

Once the Executive has finalised the text of the draft Bill, there is a three week period during which officials of the Parliament take certain steps preparatory to formal introduction. The Scotland Act requires the legislative competence of any Bill to be assessed before it is introduced in the Parliament. The Member of the Scottish Executive in charge of a Bill has therefore, on or before the introduction of the Bill, to state in writing that, in his view, the provisions of the Bill would be within legislative competence. During the three week preintroduction period, the Parliament's Legal Adviser prepares advice to the Presiding Officer on legislative competence. The Presiding Officer then decides whether or not he agrees with this view and states his decision.[14]

Key Concepts

All **Bills** must be accompanied by the following documents:

(1) A written statement from the Presiding Officer stating whether the provisions are within the legislative competence of the Parliament. This must identify which provisions, if any, are outside the legislative competence.

(2) A Financial Memorandum estimating the cost of any proposed changes. This contains estimates of the administrative, compliance and other costs which the Scottish Executive, local authorities and other bodies, businesses and individuals would have to meet, if the Bill's provisions became law.

(3) An Auditor-General's report as to whether any proposed charge on the Scottish Consolidated Fund is appropriate.

The Parliament may decide to allow a Bill to be introduced without one or more of the accompanying documents required by Standing Orders but it may not waive the requirement for a Presiding Officer statement on legislative competence. This is because the statement on legislative competence is required by the Scotland Act. The Presiding Officer's statement may indicate a view that the Bill is (or specified provisions of it are) outwith legislative competence, giving reasons. A statement that a Bill is outside the legislative competence does not prevent the Bill

[14] Scotland Act 1998, s.31.

from being introduced. The Presiding Officer's statement is only an opinion and does not preclude the Parliament, or any committee, from critically examining a Bill on grounds of legislative competence during its passage.

Bills which are introduced by the Scottish Executive are also accompanied by:

(1) explanatory notes summarising objectively each provision of the Bill; and
(2) A policy memorandum setting out:

- the Bill's policy objectives;
- consideration of any alternative approaches;
- details of consultation exercises and their outcome; and
- assessment of the effects, if any, of the Bill on equal opportunities, human rights, islands communities, local government, sustainable development, and any other matters which the Executive considers relevant.

The Parliament may decide to allow a Bill to be introduced without a Policy Memorandum. Scottish Executive Bills are drafted by the Lord Advocate's Department. Private Members must draft their own Bills. Bills in the Scottish Parliament are very similar, in terms of layout, structure and the conventions of legislative drafting, to Bills in Westminster. Once the Presiding Officer has made a statement on legislative competence, and the other pre-introduction steps have been taken, the Bill may be formally introduced. A Bill may be introduced on any sitting day by being lodged with the clerks. It must be signed by the Member introducing it and by any supporters whose names are to appear on the published version. The Member who introduces the Bill is also the "member in charge" of it. This gives the Member who introduced the Bill an assurance that any necessary procedural steps can still be taken should he or she be unavailable for a period or on a particular occasion.

Section 36(1) of the Scotland Act 1998 requires there to be at least three distinct stages to which Bills are subject:

Key Concepts

Three stage process

(1) general debate on a Bill with opportunity for members to vote on its general principles;

(2) consideration of, and an opportunity for members to vote, on the details of a Bill;

(3) a final stage at which a Bill can be passed or rejected.

This three-stage model may be departed from in relation to specific types of Bill, and an additional stage must be provided for where a Bill is subject to challenge after being passed.

Stage 1

Once a Bill has been introduced, the Parliamentary Bureau refers it to whichever subject **4–23**
committee has the Bill within its remit. This committee is referred to as the lead committee. A Bill which includes provision to make subordinate legislation is also referred to the Subordinate Legislation Committee, for consideration. The Subordinate Legislation Committee considers whether any of the powers delegated by the Bill concern matters which should be the subject only of primary legislation and whether the parliamentary control proposed in each case is appropriate. Other committees may be involved such as the Equal Opportunities Committee, the Finance Committee and any other subject committee with an interest in some aspects of the proposed Bill. The other committees report back to the lead committee and their views are included in the Report.

The lead committee may also take evidence from other bodies or individuals when it is considering whether to introduce a Bill. The lead committee's role is to report to the Parliament on the general principles of the Bill rather than the detailed provisions. The report from the lead committee will usually include a recommendation to the Parliament as to whether the general principles of the Bill should be agreed to.

Once the lead committee has reported on the Bill, the Parliamentary Bureau allocates time for a debate and decision on the general principles of the Bill at a meeting of the Parliament. The Bill may be referred back to the lead committee before the Parliament makes its decision if a Member lodges a motion that the Bill be referred back to the Committee for a further report. Such a motion may relate to the general principles of a Bill or only to specific sections. On the day scheduled for debate the Parliament decides whether to agree the general principles of the Bill. This decision is taken in light of the lead committee's report. More evidence may be taken at this stage. If the Parliament does agree to the general principles then the Bill proceeds to Stage 2. If Parliament does not agree, the Bill falls and ceases any progress at this stage. Withdrawal of Bills is only possible during Stage 1. The Member in charge of the Bill may withdraw it at any time during Stage 1 by writing to the Clerk. After Parliament has agreed the general principles of a Bill, it is treated as the property of the Parliament as a whole, and can only be withdrawn if the Parliament agrees.

Stage 2

4–24 In this stage the Bill receives more detailed "line-by-line" consideration. The procedure adopted at this stage may vary according to the nature of the proposal.

Detailed consideration may be:

(a) entirely by the lead committee;
(b) entirely by a Committee of the Whole Parliament;
(c) entirely by a Parliamentary committee or committees other than the lead committee;
(d) partly by the lead committee and partly by a Committee of the Whole Parliament or a Parliamentary committee or committees other than the lead committee.

Each schedule, long title to and section of the Bill is considered separately in Stage 2, when amendments may be proposed and made. Amendments may be made which would insert or substantially alter any provisions to confer powers to make delegated legislation. If that is the case then the amended Bill is referred to the Subordinate Legislation Committee for its consideration and report.

Stage 3

4–25 The amended Bill is then considered by the Parliament, which can further consider and make amendments to its provisions. At this point, up to half the sections of the Bill may be referred back for further Stage 2 consideration by the relevant committee or committees. On the Bill's return to the Parliament after this, further amendments may be made only to its referred-back provisions. The Member in charge may move, immediately after the last amendment is disposed of, "That further Stage 3 consideration of the Bill be adjourned to a later day". If the motion is agreed to, no further proceedings take place on the Bill until the day named in the motion. In the interim, the member in charge may lodge further amendments, but only for the purpose of clarifying uncertainties or giving effect to commitments given at the earlier proceedings at Stage 3. The Parliament then debates and decides whether the Bill, in this final form, should be passed. At least a quarter of all MSPs must vote, whether for, against or in abstention. Once a Bill has been passed or approved, it is then submitted by the Presiding Officer to the Sovereign for Royal Assent. On receiving Royal Assent a Bill becomes an Act of the Scottish Parliament.

Members Bills

An individual MSP who is not a member of the Executive may seek to introduce a Bill either by encouraging a committee to make a proposal for a Committee Bill or by lodging a proposal for a Member's Bill. Such a proposal is printed in the Business Bulletin for one month. If it attracts at least 11 supporters in that time, the Member who lodged it has the right to introduce the Bill at any time during the four year session. If the proposal does not attract 11 supporters within a month, it falls and no similar proposal may be introduced for a period of six months. An example of an Act which was introduced as a Member's Bill is the Marriage (Scotland) Act 2002, which allows civil marriages to take place elsewhere than Registry offices. **4–26**

A Member's Bill proposal sets out:

(a) the Member's name;
(b) the proposed short title of the Bill; and
(c) a brief summary of the purpose of the Bill.

Each Member may only introduce two Members' Bills in any four-year session; however there is no limit to the number of proposals that each member may lodge. Members may be assisted in drawing up their proposals and draft Bills by the Non-Executive Bills Unit. The Bill must be accompanied by a Financial Memorandum, a statement by the Presiding Officer on legislative competence and an Auditor General's report (if relevant). The Member may choose to give Explanatory Notes or a Policy Memorandum but he is not obliged to do so. A Member's Bill follows the same three stages for debate as an Executive Bill.

Committee Bills

A proposal for a Bill may come from any committee. An example of an Act initiated as a committee Bill is the Scottish Parliamentary Standards Commissioner Act 2002, which was introduced by the Standards Committee. A member of the committee who wishes the committee to make a proposal should raise the matter with the convener, who can then invite the committee to decide whether to conduct an inquiry on the subject. Any MSP, whether he is a member of the committee or not, may submit a draft proposal for a Committee Bill to the Parliamentary Bureau. The draft proposal is then referred by the Bureau to an appropriate committee. The committee is then required to consider a draft proposal in order to decide whether or not to make a proposal. A proposal from a committee is made in the form of a report to the Parliament. The report must give a detailed account of the proposed Bill. It may include the whole draft Bill but if it does not it must be sufficiently detailed to allow the Parliament to make a properly-informed decision as to whether to support it. The Bureau must allocate time in a Business Motion for consideration of the proposal on the basis of the committee's report. If the Parliament agrees to the proposal, the committee convener may introduce the Bill after five sitting days have elapsed since the debate. The Bill may not be introduced if the Executive has indicated an intention to introduce an Executive Bill to give effect to the same proposal. **4–27**

The Committee Bill which is introduced must be broadly consistent with the terms of the proposal that was agreed to by the Parliament. If the Committee decides to make substantial changes, it would need to obtain the Parliament's agreement to a new report containing a revised proposal. A Committee Bill is introduced by the convener of the committee. It must be accompanied by a Financial Memorandum and Presiding Officer's statement on legislative competence. Explanatory Notes are normally provided. A Committee Bill is not referred at Stage 1 to a lead committee for a report on its general principles, but is referred to the Finance Committee for a report on the Financial Memorandum. It may also be referred to the Subordinate Legislation Committee if it contains provisions that will give rise to delegated powers. Once any committees have reported to the Parliament, the Stage 1 debate takes place in the normal way and thereafter a Committee Bill follows the same procedures as an Executive Bill.

Different procedures may be used for:

- Budget Bills;
- Bills which restate the law;
- Bills which repeal spent enactments;
- Emergency Bills;
- Private Bills.

Budget Bills are considered at Stage 2 by the Finance Committee and are subject to an accelerated time scale. Consolidation Bills, which bring together existing statutory provisions into one enactment, are considered by a specially convened Consolidation Committee. Only very limited amendments are permitted. Statute Law Repeal Bills and Statute Law Revision Bills also follow a simplified procedure. It is also possible to enact Emergency Bills by a process under which all stages are taken in as short a period as necessary, even in one day.

Private Bills

4–28 A Private Bill is a Bill introduced by an individual person, a body corporate or an unincorporated association of persons for the purpose of obtaining for the promoter particular powers or benefits in excess of or in conflict with the general law. It may relate to the estate, property, status or style, or other personal affairs, of the promoter.[15] An example of a Private Bill is the Robin Rigg Offshore Wind Farm (Navigation and Fishing) Scotland Bill. Unlike Public Bills which seek only to alter the general law of the land, Private Bills involve measures to benefit the private interests of the promoter. Other organisations or individuals may object and a procedure needs to be followed which allows their objections to be considered.

Before devolution, most Private Bills affecting Scotland were subject to the procedures established by and under the Private Legislation Procedure (Scotland) Act 1936. Other UK private legislation is subject to the Private Bill Standing Orders of the Westminster Parliament. Following the implementation of the Scotland Act, Private Bills dealing with devolved matters must be introduced into the Scottish Parliament. However Scottish Private Bills which deal in part with reserved matters must continue to use the 1936 Act system. They take the form of a draft Provisional Order which is subject to confirmation by a Bill introduced in the Westminster Parliament.

Key Concepts

Every **Private Bill** must be accompanied on introduction by:

(1) a statement by the Presiding Officer on legislative competence;

(2) Explanatory Notes;

(3) a Promoter's Memorandum;

(4) a Promoter's Statement; and

(5) an assignation of copyright/licensing agreement or agreements with the Scottish Parliamentary Corporate Body.

The purpose of the Promoter's Memorandum is to explain:

(a) the policy objectives of the Bill;
(b) whether alternative ways of achieving these policy objectives were considered, what these alternatives were and why the approach chosen was adopted; and

---

[15] Standing Orders of the Scottish Parliament, rule 9A.1.

(c) what consultation, if any, was undertaken on these objectives and the ways of meeting them and on the detail contained in the Bill together with a summary of the outcome of that consultation.

The purpose of the Promoter's Statement is to detail all the arrangements made by the promoter with regard to notification, discussion or consultation, advertising and distribution of the Bill and accompanying documents. The requirements for the statement vary according to the nature of the Bill for example if the Bill will affect heritable property, the statement should indicate that notice has been given to those with an interest in the property. The promoter must undertake to cover all of the costs of promoting the Bill.

Bills which seek to authorise the construction or alteration of certain classes of works or the compulsory acquisition or use of any lands or buildings must be accompanied on introduction by:

- an estimate of expense and funding statement;
- certain maps, plans, sections and book of reference (or a statement as to why they are not provided); and
- an environmental statement.

Introduction of the Bill

A Private Bill can be introduced on any sitting day. The fee fixed by the SPCB to cover the costs must also be paid at this time. Any person, body corporate or unincorporated association may lodge an objection to a Private Bill which would adversely affect their interests. Objections must be lodged with the Clerk within 60 days of the Bill being introduced, although the Private Bill Committee has a discretion to allow objections received after the objection period and before the completion of the Preliminary Stage. The Committee will exercise its discretion only if it is satisfied that the objector had good reason for not lodging the objection within the objection period. An objection may be lodged only if it is in proper form. **4–29**

Key Concepts

All **objections** must:

- be signed and dated;
- be in English;
- be printed, typed or clearly hand-written; and
- set out clearly the name, address and (where relevant) other contact details of the objector (telephone, email and fax).

There are criteria for the admissibility of objections.

Key Concepts

The **objection** must:

- be in proper form;
- set out clearly the nature of the objection;
- explain whether the objection is to the whole Bill or only to certain provisions;
- specify how the objector's interests would be adversely affected by the Bill; and
- be accompanied by the lodging fee determined by the Scottish Parliamentary Corporate Body.

Private Bill Committee

4–30 A Private Bill Committee is established once a Private Bill has been introduced. If there are two or more Private Bills in progress at the same time, separate Committees will be established for each. The remit of a Private Bill Committee will be to consider and report to the Parliament on the Bill in question. A Committee will normally be established only for the duration of the Bill. A Private Bill Committee will have five members, chosen to ensure impartiality. An MSP may not be appointed to a Committee if: he or she resides in an area which would be affected by the Bill; or the constituency or region which he or she represents, or any part of it, falls within the area affected by the Bill. An MSP will also not be appointed to a Private Bill Committee if the Register of Members' Interests indicates that he or she has a financial interest in the matter under consideration. Private Bill Committees normally meet in public. Any committee may meet in private if it so decides, for example when considering evidence which is commercially sensitive. All meetings at which legislation is considered must be in public.

All Private Bills will be subject to a three-Stage process. These are:

Preliminary Stage:	A Private Bill Committee considers the general principles of the Bill, decides whether the Bill should proceed as a Private Bill and considers of preliminary objections.
Consideration Stage:	The Committee takes evidence (including cross-examination) on the details of the Bill and considers amendments.
Final Stage:	The Parliament considers further amendments and decides whether or not to pass the Bill.

A separate Reconsideration Stage is also possible in certain circumstances.

Pre-enactment scrutiny of Scottish legislation

4–31 The Scotland Act 1998 gives powers to various bodies to correct defects in legislation, where the legislation is outwith the legislative competence. The powers are intended to allow amendments to be carried out as quickly as possible using a "fast track" procedure. The Secretary of State may intervene to pass an order preventing the Presiding Officer of the Scottish Parliament from submitting a Bill for Royal Assent where it is beyond the legislative competence.[16] Such an order, which must specify the provisions of the Bill objected to and the reasons, prohibits the Presiding Officer from submitting the Bill for Royal Assent.

The Lord Advocate and the Advocate General for Scotland have the power to refer any Bill which has been passed by the Scottish Parliament to the Judicial Committee of the Privy Council to determine whether the legislation is within the legislative competence of the Parliament. This must be done in the period before the Bill receives the Royal Assent and within four weeks of the passing of the Bill.[17] Once such a reference has been made, the Bill cannot make further progress towards Royal Assent until the Judicial Committee of the Privy Council has either decided the reference, or has referred a question arising from it on the compatibility of a Bill with European Law to the European Court of Justice.

The Presiding Officer may, however, submit the Bill for Royal Assent after less than four weeks if he has been notified by all three Law Officers and the Secretary of State that they do not intend to exercise those powers.

---

[16] Scotland Act 1998, s.35.
[17] Scotland Act 1998, s.33.

Reconsideration Stage

Where a Bill or a part of a Bill has been held to be outside the legislative competence it may be reconsidered by the Parliament so that it may be amended to the extent necessary to bring it within the legislative competence. This may arise after the Judicial Committee of the Privy Council has decided that a Bill is outside the legislative competence or after it has referred it to the European Court of Justice. Since the ECJ can often take two years or more to decide a question referred to it, s.34 of the Scotland Act allows the Parliament to reconsider the Bill or the part of the Bill in question without waiting for the decision from the ECJ. The Member in charge of the Bill may move that the Bill be reconsidered in advance of a decision from the ECJ. If the motion is agreed to, the Presiding Officer informs the Law Officers. The Law Officer who made the original challenge must then request withdrawal of the reference to the Judicial Committee of the Privy Council.[18] The reconsideration stage may not take place until the withdrawal of the Judicial Committee of the Privy Council reference has been formally confirmed. Proceedings at Reconsideration Stage are similar to those at Stage 3. Once the amendments have been disposed of, the Bill may be further debated before the Parliament decides whether to approve the Bill. However only a simple majority of those voting is required to pass a Bill at this stage. A Bill approved after reconsideration is again subject to legal challenge by the Law Officers or to the making of an order by the Secretary of State in exactly the same way as it was after it was first passed. There is no limit to the number of times the Parliament may approve a Bill, or to the number of times it may be challenged. **4–32**

Royal Assent

The Presiding Officer submits Bills for the Royal Assent when the statutory four-week period for pre-enactment scrutiny has passed without challenge or if the Secretary of State and all three Law Officers have confirmed that they will not challenge the Bill. The Bill, together with draft Letters Patent, is sent to the Palace for Royal Assent. A Bill receives Royal Assent at the beginning of the day on which Letters Patent under the Scottish Seal, signed by Her Majesty's own hand are recorded in the Register of the Great Seal. The date of Royal Assent is written on the Act of the Scottish Parliament by the Clerk and forms part of the Act. **4–33**

Procedural defects

The validity of an Act of the Scottish Parliament is not affected by any invalidity in the proceedings of the Parliament leading to its enactment. Every Act of the Scottish Parliament shall be judicially noticed. **4–34**

> **Key Concepts**
>
> The **Scotland Act 1998** enables the Scottish Parliament to legislate for Scotland on a wide range of matters.
>
> It may, however, only act within its **legislative competence** as defined in the Scotland Act.
>
> Acts of the Scottish Parliament are either **Public Acts**, which deal with matters of public policy and change the general law, or **Private Acts**, which confer powers or benefits on an individual or an organisation.

---

[18] Scotland Act 1998, s.34(2).

PETITIONS

4–35 An interesting aspect of the Scottish Parliament's ethos of openness and accessibility to the public is that a member of public may petition the Scottish Parliament on a matter which falls within its legislative competence. A Public Petitions Committee has been established to consider petitions.

Subject-matter of petitions

4–36 A petition can make a request for the Parliament to:

(1) take a view on a matter of public interest or concern; or
(2) amend existing legislation or introduce new legislation.

There are some restrictions on the subject-matter of petitions:

(1) The Parliament can only amend or introduce legislation within its legislative competence.
(2) The Parliament may not interfere with the executive decisions of other public bodies in Scotland.
(3) Petitions which relate to cases which have been subject to legal or court proceedings, industrial tribunals, appeals procedures and the like may not be considered. However, general issues arising out of such cases, such as a petition to change a legal procedure may be considered.
(4) Petitions should be in the public interest.
(5) Petitions should not ask the Parliament to do something unlawful.
(6) The wording of a petition should not amount to a breach of interdict or of commercial confidentiality.
(7) Petitions should not relate to matters that are *sub judice* (*i.e.* matters which are the subject of any court proceedings).
(8) Petitions should not include false statements or information. They must be submitted in good faith.

Action prior to submission of petitions

4–37 Before presenting a petition the petitioner should have taken all reasonable steps to resolve the issues by other means. In many cases, representations to the Scottish Ministers should be made in the first instance. At the very least, a petitioner should have sought the assistance of his MSP Evidence of the attempts to resolve the problem, including the details of persons who have been approached should be submitted as supporting information with the petition. If this information is not submitted, the petition may be returned to the petitioner. The petition should include a brief title and a short, clear and concise statement covering the subject-matter of the petition. The petition should make it clear what action the petitioner wishes the Parliament to take.

Key Concepts

Criteria for petitions

- Petitions must include (a) the name of the petitioner, (b) the address of the petitioner to which all communications concerning the petition should be sent, and (c) the name and address of any person supporting the petition.
- Petitions must be in English. Petitions may also be submitted in Scots Gaelic—or any other language—but only in addition to the English version.
- Petitions must not contain offensive language.
- Petitions which are unclear as to their purpose will be returned to the petitioner for clarification.

The Public Petitions Committee will consider each admissible petition and make a decision on the action to be taken in each case. The Committee may:

(1) agree to take no further action;
(2) forward to another committee of the Parliament or to another body or person within the Parliament such as the Presiding Officer, the Parliamentary Bureau or the Scottish Parliamentary Corporate Body for its consideration;
(3) forward to another body or organisation (outwith Parliament) *e.g.* the Scottish Executive, for consideration and response;
(4) recommend to the Parliamentary Bureau that the petition be debated at a meeting of the Parliament;
(5) invite the petitioner(s) to appear before it;
(6) invite the petitioner(s) to provide additional information; or
(7) take any other action it considers appropriate.

When it has considered the petition and decided what action to take the Public Petitions Committee responds formally to the petitioner stating clearly the action which is to be taken or to give notice in cases where no action is to be taken. The Public Petitions Committee monitors the action taken in respect of all petitions submitted to the Parliament. It publishes an annual report, which will provide a summary of its activities.

SCRUTINISING THE WORK OF THE SCOTTISH EXECUTIVE

As well as scrutinising Executive Bills, there are a number of other ways that all MSPs can **4–38** examine and question the work of the Executive. The main method of ensuring that the Executive is accountable to the Scottish Parliament is by questioning ministers during sittings of the Parliament. At Question Time, MSPs can ask oral questions of the Ministers and First Minister. These questions can be about any matter within the general responsibility of the Scottish Executive. Additionally, MSPs can submit written questions to the Executive. Both oral and written questions and their answers are published and are available to the public.

SCOTTISH ADMINISTRATION

The "Scottish Administration" is the statutory term which denotes both the political and **4–39** administrative side of the Scottish Government. The Scottish Administration is made up of four elements: the Scottish Executive, Junior Ministers, non-ministerial office-holders and civil servants. Rather confusingly, the term "Scottish Executive" is used by the present Scottish Government for the overall devolved administrative system of government in Scotland (including the ministerial Scottish Executive) instead of the statutory term "Scottish Administration".[19]

Key Concepts

The Scottish Administration

- Members of the Scottish Executive.
- Junior Scottish Ministers.
- Holders of non-ministerial offices such as: Registrar General of Births, Deaths and Marriages for Scotland, Keeper of the Registers of Scotland, Keeper of the Records of Scotland and others specified by Order in Council.
- Civil Servants.

[19] Scotland Act 1998, s.126(6)–(8).

The Scottish Executive, *i.e.* the statutory Scottish Administration, is the Government in Scotland for all devolved matters. When the Scottish Executive was established in 1999 the responsibilities previously held by the Scottish Office were divided between the newly-formed Scottish Executive and the Scotland Office. The powers and duties exercised by Ministers in the Scottish Office, relating to devolved matters, were transferred to the Scottish Ministers.

Key Concepts

Scottish Executive Departments

- Scottish Executive Justice Department (SEJD).
- Scottish Executive Health Department (SEHD).
- Scottish Executive Environment and Rural Affairs Department (SEERAD).
- Scottish Executive Development Department (SEDD).
- Scottish Executive Education Department (SEED).
- Scottish Executive Enterprise and Lifelong Learning Department (SEELLD).
- Corporate Services (SECS).
- Finance and Central Services Department (FCSD).

CHALLENGES TO ACTIONS OF THE PARLIAMENT OR THE SCOTTISH EXECUTIVE

4–40 Although the courts have no power to declare a provision in an Act of the Westminster Parliament invalid, the same principle does not apply to Acts of the Scottish Parliament. Acts of the Scottish Parliament are only valid if they are within the legislative competence, which has been devolved by the Scotland Act.[20] Acts of the Scottish Parliament and Scottish subordinate legislation are to be read as narrowly as is required for them to be within competence. An action taken under the Scotland Act raising an issue of the competence of the Parliament or the executive is referred to as a "devolution issue". Devolution issues are defined as the following questions:

Key Concepts

Devolution Issues:

- whether an Act of the Scottish Parliament, or a provision within it, is within the legislative competence of the Parliament;
- whether a function is a function of a Scottish Minister or the First Minister or the Lord Advocate;
- whether the exercise of a function by a member of the Scottish Executive would be within devolved competence;
- whether the exercise of a function by a member of the Scottish Executive is or would be incompatible with EC law or Convention rights;
- whether a failure to act by a member of the Scottish Executive is incompatible with EC law or Convention rights; and
- any other question as to whether a function is within devolved competence and any other question arising by virtue of the Act about reserved matters.

[20] Scotland Act 1998, s.54

A devolution issue may arise in any case, civil or criminal, anywhere in the UK. The issue may be raised by any party to the case but in criminal proceedings there are time limits for raising the issue. In cases on indictment the issue must be raised within seven days of the indictment being served and in summary cases the notice of devolution issue must be given before the accused is asked to plead.[21] Schedule 6 sets out the rules as to which court or tribunal may hear the devolution issue and the appropriate rules of the courts in Scotland were amended accordingly.[22] Courts and tribunals elsewhere in the UK are also detailed in the Schedule.[23]

As the Lord Advocate and the Advocate General for Scotland have a special interest in ensuring that devolution issues are resolved, the Scotland Act provides that either officer may institute proceedings to determine a devolution issue.[24] Devolution issues can also be raised by parties in any legal proceedings, whether they are proceedings instigated for the specific purpose of determining a devolution issue, or proceedings where the original purpose was the resolution of another matter but a devolution issue has arisen during the course of the proceedings. Devolution issues may be raised in both civil and criminal courts. They may be raised in courts at any level of the hierarchy. This means that in civil cases devolution issues may be raised in the Sheriff Court, the Court of Session and the House of Lords and in criminal cases devolution issues may be raised in the District Court, Sheriff Court and High Court of Justiciary. If neither the Lord Advocate nor the Advocate General is a party to the legal proceedings, notice must be given to both the Lord Advocate and the Advocate General that a devolution issue is to be raised so that they may participate in the proceedings.

Legal challenges to Acts of the Scottish Parliament

A challenge to the validity of a provision in an Act of the Scottish Parliament came before the Privy Council in October 2001. **4–41**

A v Scottish Ministers

2002 S.C. (P.C.) 63

A had previously challenged the lawfulness of a restriction order, under which he was detained in a hospital after being convicted of homicide. This challenge was unsuccessful and A appealed. He argued that the Mental Health (Public Safety and Appeals) (Scotland) Act 1999, s.1, which had amended the Mental Health (Scotland) Act 1984, was incompatible with the Human Rights Act 1998, Sch.1, Pt I, Art.5. Article 5 is concerned with the right to liberty. The Article includes a list of exceptions to the right of liberty and provides that persons who are of unsound mind may be detained. However in the case *Winterwerp v Netherlands*[25] the European Court of Human Rights held that compulsory detention in a hospital is only lawful where there is medical evidence that it is justified.

The Privy Council dismissed the appeal. They held that the Mental Health (Public Safety and Appeals) (Scotland) Act 1999, s.1 was not outside the legislative competence of the Scottish Parliament. It was not incompatible with Art.5 of the European Convention on Human Rights as there is nothing in that Article to the effect that persons of unsound mind may only be detained for the purpose of receiving medical treatment.

---

21 Rules of Court, 1999, Chap.40.

22 Act of Sederunt (Devolution Issue Rules) 1999 (SI 1999/1345) for civil proceedings and Act of Adjournal (Devolution Issue Rules) 1999 (SI 1999/1346) for criminal proceedings.

23 Scotland Act 1998, Sch.6, para.1.

24 Scotland Act 1998, Sch.6, para.4(1).

25 *Winterwerp v Netherlands* (1979–80) 2 E.H.R.R. 387.

The validity of the legal aid regulations came under consideration by the Privy Council in the case of *McLean v Buchanan*. Aspects of the Children's Hearing System in Scotland have also been challenged as devolution issues.[26]

McLean v Buchanan

2002 S.C. (P.C.) 1

In the course of a criminal appeal Maclean contended that the inadequate legal aid funding that he and his co-accused had been awarded under the Criminal Legal Aid (Fixed Payments) (Scotland) Regulations 1999, unfairly prejudiced them. He claimed that the inadequacy of legal aid provision was a devolution issue. The regulations were outside the legislative competence as they were incompatible with the right to a fair trial under Art.6(3) of the European Convention on Human Rights.

The Privy Council held that the inadequacy of the legal aid funding was not incompatible with Maclean's right to a fair trial. In his case the solicitors and counsel had continued to act even though funding had run out. However, it was noted that in a case where no legal representation was available as a result of the 1999 Regulations but under his Convention rights a defendant should be afforded representation then a breach might arise.

Normally when a legal provision or action is found to be *ultra vires* the provision or action is treated as null and void. However actions in court to challenge the validity of a provision or action made under the Scotland Act will take time to be heard and decided and before the case is raised the provision or action may have been acted upon. This would lead to uncertainty, as people could not rely on the provision in case a retrospective decision of invalidity was made. The Scotland Act therefore allows that a court or tribunal may remove or limit any retrospective effect of the decision, or suspend its effect for a period to allow correction of the defect if it decides that provisions are *ultra vires*.[27] The court is also required to have regard to the effect of an order on persons who are not parties to the proceedings.

Challenges to the validity of Acts of the Scottish Parliament may only be brought by a person who has title and interest to sue. He or she must be able to show that they are directly affected by the Act. Furthermore, the Scotland Act states that a person may not bring any proceedings in a court or tribunal on the ground that the Act is incompatible with Convention rights unless he would be a victim, in for the purposes of Art.34 of the Convention, if proceedings in respect of the Act were brought before the European Court of Human Rights.[28]

Adams v Scottish Ministers

July 31, 2002, 2002 G.W.D. 26–879

Adams brought a petition for judicial review of the Protection of Wild Mammals (Scotland) Act 2002, which rendered mounted foxhunting unlawful. He contended that the Act was partly incompatible with the Human Rights Act 1998, Sch.1, Pt I, Art.8 and Art.14 as it amounted to an infringement of the right to respect for private and family life and was discriminatory. He claimed therefore that the Act was beyond the legislative competence of the Scottish Parliament, and was *ultra vires*. (Adams was a manager of foxhounds, who lived in a house provided in the course of his employment.)

[26] *S v Principal Reporter (No.1)*, 2001 S.C. 977; 2001 S.L.T. 531.

[27] Scotland Act 1998, s.102.

[28] Scotland Act 1998, s.100(1).

The petition was dismissed because Adams was held not to qualify as a victim with a right to bring proceedings on the grounds of incompatibility of an Act with Convention rights.[29] In the opinion of the Lord Ordinary, foxhunting did not amount to an activity of private life for the purposes of Art.8 of the Human Rights Act. The Act could affect Adams' right to property but it was within the legislative competence to infringe such a right in order to further the general interest in preventing cruelty to animals. No breach of Art.14 of the Human Rights Act had been made as Adams had been unable to establish that he had been discriminated against.

Investigation of maladministration within the Scottish Parliament

The Scottish Parliamentary Standards Commissioner Act 2002, which received Royal Assent on July 30, 2002, creates the post of Scottish Parliamentary Standards Commissioner. The Scottish Parliamentary Corporate Body appoints the Commissioner with the agreement of the Parliament. His function is to investigate the conduct of MSPs. **4–42**

The Scottish Parliamentary Standards Commissioner investigates whether a Member of the Parliament has breached:

- a provision of the Code of Conduct;
- the Members' Interests Order;
- any provision in an Act of the Scottish Parliament (asp) that replaces that Order; or
- any provision of the standing orders of the Parliament.

A Code of Conduct for members of the Scottish Parliament was adopted and approved by the Parliament on February 24, 2000. Contravention of the Code of Conduct is an offence. As a temporary measure, a Scottish Parliamentary Commissioner for Administration was appointed to deal with complaints about maladministration in the Scottish Parliament. The post was filled by the same person as the Parliamentary Commissioner for Administration, The Health Services Ombudsman and the Welsh Administration Ombudsman. There were however separate investigating officers dealing with each aspect of his role. The creation of the office of a Scottish Parliamentary Standards Commissioner and the arrangements for investigating complaints supersede the temporary investigation provisions set out in the Code of Conduct.

Key Concepts

Appointment of the Commissioner

The following people are not eligible for the appointment of Commissioner:

- Members of the Parliament;
- staff of the Parliament; and
- any person who has been a Member of the Parliament or a member of staff of the Parliament during the preceding two years.

The maximum period of initial appointment is five years and there can only be one reappointment which, cannot be for more than another five years. Therefore the maximum period of time which one person can serve as Commissioner is 10 years. The Commissioner may resign from office or be removed from office by the SPCB after a resolution by the Parliament. An acting Commissioner may be appointed if required, for example if there are a large number of investigations. The Commissioner is required on receipt of a complaint to investigate whether a Member of the Parliament has committed the conduct complained of and whether the relevant

[29] Scotland Act 1998, s.100; Human Rights Act 1998, Sch.1, Pt I, Art.34.

provisions cover that conduct. The Commissioner may not investigate any other conduct without a specific complaint. The Commissioner can investigate complaints about former Members of Parliament in relation to conduct that took place when they were Members. He can also investigate the conduct of Scottish Law Officers and former Scottish Law Officers if they are not members of the Parliament.

The standing orders or the Code of Conduct may specify classes of complaints that are to be excluded from the investigation powers of the Commissioner. Nevertheless excluded complaints may still be investigated by the Commissioner if the Standards Committee considers this to be appropriate and makes a direction to this effect (s.12).

The Act has retrospective effect in relation to the time when the conduct complained about takes place. This is necessary to ensure the smooth transition of investigations from the previous arrangements to those under the Act as otherwise the Commissioner would be handling some complaints and the PCA, in his role as SPCA, would be handling others. The Commissioner may give advice on the procedure for making a complaint but may not give advice to a Member of the Parliament or to a member of the public in relation to whether any proposed or previous conduct would constitute a breach of the relevant provisions. The Commissioner must comply with the directions of the Standards Committee. These could include such matters as requiring the Commissioner to ensure that all persons interviewed by him or her are given a right to have a third party present and are advised of this right. Directions may not be given in relation to a particular investigation as that would compromise the independence of the Commissioner.

Key Concepts

Investigation process

Stage 1: Initial consideration by the Commissioner.

Stage 2: Investigation by the Commissioner and report to Parliament.

Stage 3: Parliamentary procedures (probably involving Standards Committee).

Stage 4: The Parliament decides whether to impose sanctions.

Stage 1

4–43 A complaint may be dismissed at this stage if the Commissioner considers that it is inadmissible. In certain circumstances he may also proceed at this stage to report a procedural defect to the Standards Committee who would be able to instruct that the investigation proceed or that the complaint be dismissed. Otherwise the Commissioner would be required to consider the complaint and carry out an investigation.

Stage 2

4–44 The investigation by the Commissioner is conducted in private. He may make an interim report to the Standards Committee at any time on the progress of an investigation. The Standards Committee can also request a report on the progress of an investigation from the Commissioner. The Commissioner decides when and how to carry out an investigation. After investigating, the Commissioner reports his findings to the Parliament. He reports on the conclusions which he has reached but does not express a view upon what sanctions would be appropriate for any breach of the Members' Interests Order or the Code of Conduct.

Stage 3

The procedures, which are followed after the Commissioner has made his report are a matter for Parliament to decide for itself as it is master of its own procedures. The Scottish Parliamentary Standards Commissioner Act does not deal with the conduct of Stages 3 and 4 of the process. The Standards Committee considers the report of the Commissioner and may conduct their own investigations or require the Commissioner to carry out further investigations. The Standards Committee then reports to the Parliament on the complaint with any recommendations for actions to be taken where they consider tat the complaint should be upheld. The Standards Committee can also investigate the conduct of MSPs where the conduct has been brought to their attention by other means **4–45**

Stage 4

The Parliament decides whether to accept the Committee's report and if appropriate impose sanctions. **4–46**

Admissibility

The Scottish Parliamentary Standards Commissioner applies three tests in order to decide whether or not a complaint is admissible: **4–47**

(1) the complaint must be relevant;
(2) the complaint must comply with certain specified procedural requirements; and
(3) the complaint must warrant further investigation.

Three matters need to be established for a complaint to be relevant:

(1) the complaint must relate to conduct of a Member of the Parliament;
(2) the complaint must be within the jurisdiction of the Commissioner; and
(3) some part of the conduct complained about must relate to a matter that the Commissioner considers may be covered by the relevant provisions.

There are also certain procedural requirements which must be met:

(1) the complaint must be made in writing to the Commissioner;
(2) the complaint must be from an individual and must include the complainer's name and address as well as being signed;
(3) the Member must be named;
(4) details of the facts relating to the alleged conduct must be given, and any evidence which supports the allegation must be provided; and
(5) the conduct complained about must have occurred within one year of the date when the complainer could reasonably have become aware of it.

The third test, that further investigation of a complaint is required, is satisfied when the Commissioner having carried out an initial investigation, decides that there is enough evidence to suggest that the conduct complained about may have taken place

Legal challenges to Acts of the Scottish Executive

Section 57(2) of the Scotland Act states that a member of the Scottish Executive has no power to make any subordinate legislation, or to do any other Act, so far as the legislation or Act is incompatible with any of the Convention rights. Excesses and abuses of power may be prevented in two ways: **4–48**

(1) the Scotland Act provides that a Secretary of State may make an order to prevent an action of a member of the Scottish Executive which the Secretary of State believes is incompatible with an international obligation, other than the ECHR; and
(2) a Secretary of State may also make an order requiring a member of the Scottish Executive to implement an international obligation.

The legality of actions or decisions of the Scottish Executive may also be challenged in the courts, after they have taken place, through judicial review procedure. The validity of an action may also be raised in the course of legal proceedings in certain circumstances, for example as a defence to a criminal prosecution. If a court or tribunal finds that an action of the Scottish Executive infringes a Convention right or a principle of European Law or is otherwise *ultra vires* the court or tribunal has power to strike down the offending action. The remedies which may be granted are the same as those which may be awarded by the court in any other action. Therefore if the Court of Session finds in favour of the petitioner in relation to a devolution issue, the court may order, reduction, declarator, specific implement or damages.

The Lord Advocate is a member of the Scottish Executive and many of the notable challenges to actions of the Scottish Executive relate to his functions with regard to the Scottish judicial system. Challenges have been brought in relation to such matters as the procedures for judicial and shrieval appointments, the provision of legal aid, the Childrens' Hearing System and delays in the prosecution of crimes. Where successful challenges have been made, the Scottish Parliament has acted promptly to introduce reforms by measures such as the Convention Rights (Compliance) (Scotland) Act 2001 which dealt with a wide range of procedures or by specific reforms, such as the Bail, Judicial Appointments etc. (Scotland) Act 2000. Two examples of challenges are given below:

Starrs v Ruxton

2000 J.C. 208; 2000 S.L.T. 42

A prosecution before Temporary Sheriff David Crowe in Linlithgow Sheriff Court was challenged on the basis that a temporary sheriff could not be regarded as impartial when his future employment prospects were subject to influence by the Lord Advocate. The Lord Advocate had a key role in the appointment, dismissal and non-reappointment of temporary sheriffs. He is also head of the public prosecution system in Scotland. Temporary sheriffs may be reluctant to reach decisions that may cause the Lord Advocate to look upon them with disfavour. Consequently, temporary sheriffs could not be regarded as sufficiently independent of the Executive to meet the requirements of Art.6 that an accused have a fair hearing before an "independent and impartial tribunal". It was held that the independence of a member of a court was to be established by reference to the manner of appointment, the term of office, the guarantees against outside pressure and the appearance of independence. Temporary sheriffs were appointed by the Secretary of State for Scotland,[30] however, the Lord Advocate played an important role in that he decided what appointments were required and advised the Scottish Courts Administration on selection. Appointments were generally for one year only. Appointment as a temporary sheriff was widely regarded as a step towards appointment as a permanent sheriff. Possible hopes of such advancement, as well as the short-term nature of the office, compromised the independence of the temporary sheriff. The absence of security of tenure was the most important factor in casting doubt on the independence of temporary sheriffs. While there was no suggestion that the Scottish Executive had ever acted contrary to the principles of judicial independence, it was necessary that legal guarantees of the independence of the judiciary be in place.

---

[30] Sheriff Courts (Scotland) Act 1971, s.11.

Clancy v Caird (No.1)

2000 S.L.T. 546; 2000 S.C.L.R. 526

An action of damages went to proof before a temporary judge. During avizandum the decision in *Starrs v Ruxton* was issued. On the basis of that decision, one of the parties in the damages action sought to raise as a devolution issue that a temporary judge was not an independent and impartial tribunal. It was held that the appointment and use of temporary judges to hear cases, where the Crown itself was not involved in the claim, did not breach a party's Convention rights. Temporary judges have security of tenure and enjoy the same status and immunities as a permanent judge. The absence of a guarantee of reappointment did not affect a temporary judge's independence. The Lord President decided whether or not to use a temporary judge and had laid down restrictions on the use of temporary judges in potentially sensitive cases, such as judicial review. Though the temporary judge remained in legal practice, there were institutional safeguards such as the judicial oath, and so this factor did not breach Art.6.

These two cases brought the issue of judicial appointments into the limelight and caused the Scottish Ministers to recognise the need for a review of the process of judicial appointments. Following a process of consultation, the Justice Minister announced judicial appointment reforms, which include the advertising of all appointments of the Court of Session Judges, Sheriff Principals and Sheriffs and an independent Judicial Appointments Board. The Judicial Appointments Board scrutinises candidates' applications and recommends the best person for nomination to the First Minister.[31]

Scottish Public Services Ombudsman

Under s.91(1) of the Scotland Act 1998 the Parliament is under a duty to make provision for the **4–49** investigation of maladministration complaints against members of the Scottish Executive in the exercise of functions conferred on the Scottish Ministers and against other office-holders in the Scottish Administration. The Scotland Act 1998 (Transitory and Transitional Provisions) (Complaints of Maladministration) Order 1999 (SI 1999/1351) put in place temporary arrangements for investigation of complaints of maladministration. A more permanent framework for the investigation of complaints against a wide range of public bodies has now been provided.

The Scottish Public Services Ombudsman Act 2002 established a Scottish Public Services Ombudsman to deal with complaints against public bodies which were previously dealt with by:

(1) the Scottish Parliamentary Commissioner for Administration;
(2) the Health Service Commissioner for Scotland;
(3) the Commissioner for Local Administration in Scotland; and
(4) the Housing Association Ombudsman for Scotland.

The Public Services Ombudsman also has responsibility for:

(1) the Mental Welfare Commission's function of investigating complaints relating to mental health; and
(2) complaints against Scottish Enterprise and Highlands and Islands Enterprise.

The Ombudsman is supported by up to three deputy Ombudsmen. The Act establishes a standardised set of procedures for dealing with all relevant complaints against a wide range of public authorities. The authorities which may be subject to investigation by the Public Services Ombudsman are listed in Sch.2. The list includes 89 different organisations. They fall into six categories:

[31] Bail, Judicial Appointments etc. (Scotland) Act 2000.

Key Concepts

Authorities which may be investigated:

- Scottish Parliament and Scottish Administration;
- health service;
- local government;
- housing;
- Scottish public authorities; and
- Cross-border public authorities.

The category "Scottish Parliament and Scottish Administration" comprises, the Parliamentary Corporation, members of the Scottish Executive and other office-holders in the Scottish Administration. The health service includes health service bodies, such as National Health Service trusts and family health service providers. As well as the local authorities themselves, the local government category includes any committee, joint committee or joint board whose members are appointed by one or more local authorities and any person who discharges any of the functions of a local authority. The Ombudsman may also investigate joint police and fire service boards and licensing boards. All registered social landlords may be investigated. The Scottish public authorities which may be investigated include: Highlands and Islands Enterprise, the Local Government Boundary Commission for Scotland, Scottish Enterprise, the Scottish Environment Protection Agency, the Scottish Higher Education Funding Council and the Scottish Qualifications Authority. The cross-border public authorities include: the Criminal Injuries Compensation Authority, the Forestry Commissioners, the National Consumer Council, and the UK Sports Council.

Investigations by the Ombudsman

4–50 The Ombudsman may investigate any matter, whenever arising, if:

(a) the matter consists of action taken by or on behalf of a person liable to investigation under the Act;
(b) the matter is one which the Ombudsman is entitled to investigate; and
(c) a complaint in respect of the matter has been duly made to the Ombudsman.

The Ombudsman decides whether to initiate, continue or discontinue an investigation. He may take such action in connection with the complaint or request as he thinks may be of assistance in reaching any such decision or resolving the complaint or request.

Matters which may be investigated

4–51 The following matters may be investigated:

(a) actions taken by or behalf of a listed in the exercise of administrative functions of the authority;
(b) actions taken by or on behalf of a health service body or an independent provider;
(c) service failure by a listed authority (except a family health service provider or a social landlord);
(d) actions taken by or on behalf of a family health service provider, in connection with any family health services provided by that provider; and
(e) actions taken by or on behalf of a registered social landlord.

The Ombudsman may only investigate a matter if a member of the public claims to have sustained injustice or hardship in consequence of the acts which amount to maladministration or failure to act. The person making the claim is referred to in this Act as the "person aggrieved". The Ombudsman may only investigate if he is satisfied that:

(a) it has been alleged publicly that one or more members of the public have sustained injustice or hardship; and
(b) the listed authority in question has taken all reasonable steps to deal with the matter to which the allegation relates.

Restrictions on the matters which may be investigated

The Ombudsman is not entitled to question the merits of a decision unless there has been **4–52** maladministration. The Ombudsman must not investigate action taken by or on behalf of a member of the Scottish Executive unless the action was taken in the exercise of functions conferred on the Scottish Ministers or of functions conferred on the First Minister alone. He must not investigate action taken by or on behalf of a listed authority which is a cross-border public authority unless the action taken concerned Scotland and did not relate to reserved matters. He may only investigate action taken in the exercise of the functions of a public nature. He may not investigate when there are other remedies available, such as a right of appeal to a Minister or a remedy by way of proceedings in any court of law. However, he has a discretion to investigate if he is satisfied that, in the particular circumstances, it is not reasonable to expect the person aggrieved to resort or have resorted to the right or remedy.

Persons who may complain

A complaint may be made to the Ombudsman: **4–53**

(a) by the person aggrieved; or
(b) by a person authorised in writing for the purpose by the person aggrieved.

The persons who may be authorised by the person aggrieved include:

(a) a member of the Scottish Parliament;
(b) a listed authority;
(c) a member, officer or member of staff of a listed authority.

After conducting an investigation, the Ombudsman must send a report of the investigation to the Scottish Ministers and must lay a copy of the report before the Parliament.

Key Concepts

The first Schedule to the Act gives statutory authority to the independence of the Ombudsman, his deputies and his staff. It states that are not to be regarded as servants or agents of the Crown. The Ombudsman, in the exercise of that officer's functions, is not subject to the direction or control of:

(a) any Member of the Parliament;

(b) any Member of the Scottish Executive; or

(c) the Parliamentary corporation.

LOCAL GOVERNMENT IN SCOTLAND

4–54 The structure, function and financing of local government are devolved matters and, as such are the responsibility of the Scottish Parliament. The current framework for local government in Scotland dates from 1996, when the Local Government etc. (Scotland) Act 1994 was implemented. The Local Government etc. (Scotland) Act 1994 set out provisions for comprehensive reform of the system of local government. Between 1975 and 1996, local government was operated as a two-tier structure consisting of 9 regional councils and 53 district councils on mainland Scotland. There were also three islands councils. This framework was abolished and replaced with a unitary system of local government. The structure of the three island authorities remained unchanged. The 1994 Act also provided for the creation of joint boards, consisting of elected members from constituent councils, with responsibility for overseeing the delivery of police, fire and valuation services.

Structure of local government

4–55

Key Concepts

Structure:

- 32 multi-purpose councils (29 councils on mainland Scotland and 3 island authorities);
- 6 joint police boards;
- 6 joint fire boards;
- 10 valuation joint boards.

The 1996 reorganisation restructured the boundaries and brought most of the services provided by the former regions and districts together into one authority. The unitary councils range in population size from over 62,000 in the City of Glasgow to only 48,000 in Clackmannan. Overall, 10 councils serve populations of under 100,000 and eight serve populations of more than 200,000. They also vary considerably in size. Clackmannan is about 300 square miles whereas Highland is about 160,000 square miles. The powers and functions of local authorities as a whole were not altered by the 1994 Act. Some of the powers and duties of local authorities to provide particular services such as education or social work are contained in separate legislation.

The Local Government etc. (Scotland) Act 1994 removed responsibility for water and sewerage services from the councils and transferred them to three newly created quangos whose boards were selected by the Secretary of State. These have subsequently combined to form one water authority for Scotland. The Act gave power to the Secretary of State (now the Scottish Ministers) to create joint boards for the provision of a service where it is considered that the function should be carried out jointly so as to maximise efficiency and economy. The Act also allows councils to set up joint committees for services. Each council retains the responsibility for the service but it is carried out jointly. Councils may also contract with one another to provide a service, for example it may be cheaper for a small council to contract out the rubbish collection and disposal service to a council which is better placed geographically to provide the service. Alternatively, two or more councils may set up a consortium to provide a service. Councils have resisted setting up joint arrangements, although they have contracted with other organisations for the provision of some services. Joint action for anything other than a very limited range of services is regarded as equivalent to introducing another tier of government which would undermine the position of the unitary authorities.

The 1994 Act did not change the way in which councils in Scotland operate. They are made up of councillors who are elected for a three year term of office. Full meetings of the council establish the policies to be followed. Specific matters are delegated to a range of committees. The functions are carried out by officers, headed by a chief executive and a number of chief officers in charge of departments which provide either a service such as housing or education or provide administrative support to the council itself.

Functions of local government

4–56

Key Concepts

Functions:

Provision of services: Planning, resourcing and direct provision of services including education, housing, local roads, social work, economic development, public protection, planning, leisure and recreation.

Strategic planning: Strategic planning framework setting objectives based on the needs and priorities of their constituents.

Regulation: Regulatory functions include: (a) granting licences for such things as the sale of alcohol or the operation of taxis, and (b) registration and inspection functions (*e.g.* private residential homes); trading standards.

Community leadership

The Local Government Committee has the main responsibility for local government affairs within the Scottish Parliament. There are, however, aspects of the work of local authorities which fall within the remit of a number of other committees, for example education, culture and sport, health and community care, rural affairs and social inclusion, housing and voluntary sector. The 1994 Act gave the Secretary of State for Scotland, and so now the Scottish Ministers, over 100 new powers to make orders and directions in relation to local government.

Throughout the UK, local councils may only do those things which are provided in the legislation setting them up. In Scotland, The Local Government (Scotland) Act 1973 is still the source of authority for the powers and duties of councils. Local authorities may only incur expenditure and provide services within the statutory framework. The 1973 Act gave limited power to a local authority to spend money where the authority considered it to be in the best interests of the inhabitants of their area. This limited power was, however curtailed by s.164 of the 1994 Act which states that councils may only incur expenditure which is in the interest of their area and will bring "direct benefit" to it.[32] There are further restrictions on the power under s.164, including an obligation to ensure that the direct benefit is commensurate with the expenditure. The Scottish Ministers may set a limit on the expenditure that may be incurred under this section. Should a local authority provide services outside the current statutes it would be acting *ultra vires*, literally *beyond its powers*, and may be subject to legal challenge in the courts.

---

[32] See s.83(1) of the Local Government (Scotland) Act 1973 (as amended by s.164 of the Local Government etc. (Scotland) Act 1994).

Key Concepts

Powers and duties of local authorities

Mandatory: Services which must be provided (*e.g.* education for school age children).

Permissive: Services which may be provided (*e.g.* economic development).

Discretionary: A general power to spend a limited amount of money which will bring direct benefit to the council area.

The Scottish Ministers have powers to control local government finance and expenditure. The Scottish Ministers are responsible for most of the costs of funding local councils. Permission must be sought before certain expenditure is incurred by a local authority.

The Police

4–57 The duties of a police officer in Scotland are given in the Police (Scotland) Act 1967, s.17(1). They include:

- duty to guard, patrol and watch to prevent commission of offences;
- duty to guard, patrol and watch to preserve order; and
- duty of protect life and property.

The performance of a police officer is subject to the direction of the Chief Constable, who has operational control of his force and enjoys considerable autonomy. He cannot be instructed to do something unless that instruction comes from the Sheriff Principal or appropriate prosecutor. The Lord Advocate may issue instructions as to the reporting of offences for prosecution. There are eight police forces in Scotland. Since the reorganisation of local authorities in 1996 only two correspond to the boundaries of new authorities: Fife and Dumfries and Galloway. The other six (Strathclyde, Central, Lothian and Borders, Tayside, Grampian and Northern) have a number of local authorities within their areas and thus the police authority for these forces is a joint board. This means that each local authority sends representatives to the meetings of the joint police authority, which is not under the control of a single authority.

Quick Quiz

- What is a unicameral Parliament?
- What functions are carried out by the Presiding Officer of the Scottish Parliament?
- List three examples of matters which are reserved for the UK Parliament.
- What are the four principles which underpin the operation of the Scottish Parliament?
- Give four examples of matters which are devolved to the Scottish Parliament.
- What function is carried out by the Parliamentary Bureau?
- Give two examples of the mandatory committees which must be set up by the Scottish Parliament.
- What is a devolution issue?
- Who would consider a complaint from a member of the public against a Scottish local authority?
- Are the following statements true or false?
  - (a) The Secretary of State for Scotland is a Member of the Scottish Executive.
  - (b) The UK Parliament may legislate on matters which have been devolved to the Scottish Parliament/
  - (c) A Bill may be introduced by an individual MSP
  - (d) There is no guaranteed minimum number of Scottish M.P.s in the UK Parliament.
  - (e) Each MSP represents a constituency.
  - (f) The Scottish law Officers need not be MSPs.
  - (g) An Act of the Scottish Parliament must be compatible with the European Convention on Human Rights.
  - (h) A member of the public, by submitting a petition, can ask the Scottish Parliament to reform the Law.
  - (i) All Scottish Parliament Committee meetings are held in private.
  - (j) The validity of an Act of the Scottish Parliament cannot be challenged.
  - (k) The Scottish Parliamentary Commissioner can provide a remedy for a person who has suffered a loss because of maladministration by an MSP
  - (l) The Scottish Parliament cannot enter into contracts.

Further Reading

Books

C. Ashton and V. Finch, *Constitutional Law in Scotland* (W. Green, 2000). This book provides an introduction to constitutional law in Scotland with chapters on the Scottish Parliament and Scottish Local Government. It provides more detail on the historical development of constitutional law in Scotland, legal redress for individuals against the State, elections and individual rights.

C.M.G. Himsworth and C.R. Munro, *Scotland Act 1998* (W. Green, 1999). This book provides explanations of the provisions of the Scotland Act 1998 and includes the provisions of the Act.

J. McFadden and M. Lazarowicz, *The Scottish Parliament: An Introduction* (Butterworths, 1999). This book gives an account of the operation of the Scottish Parliament.

Internet sources

Internet sources are particularly useful in the context of constitutional law. The following sites are particularly useful:

- Acts of the Scottish Parliament:

  www.scotland-legislation.hmso.gov.uk/legislation/scotland/s-acts.htm

  This site has all Acts of the Scottish Parliament. It also includes the explanatory notes to the Acts.

- Scottish Executive homepage: *www.scotland.gov.uk*
- Scottish Parliament homepage: *www.scottish.parliament.uk*

  The Scottish Parliament website is a very useful source of information on the day-to-day operation of the Scottish Parliament. Includes official report of the meetings of Parliament.

- Scotland Office homepage: *www.scottishsecretary.gov.uk*

Chapter 5

CONTRACT

Alasdair Gordon[1]

INTRODUCTION

At the risk of over-simplification, the basics of all contracts are the same, whatever the value of **5–01**
the subject-matter. A contract is a binding obligation which can be enforced by the parties to it.

[1] Formerly Lecturer in Law, Aberdeen College.

Most contracts are not expressed in writing, although there are cases where writing is essential or desirable.

In Scotland, contract law is largely based on common law. Whilst there have been major statutory inroads in certain areas,[2] the basic law of contract has been developed by the courts rather than Parliament. In today's complex society, the trend is towards a higher degree of statutory or regulatory control. In the 1990s, the Scottish Law Commission presented five significant reports on various aspects of contract law which it saw as in need of reform. In that decade, the recommendations from only one of these reports passed into legislation.[3] This raises the likelihood of further reforming legislation in the present century.

WHAT IS A CONTRACT?

5–02 A much quoted definition of a contract is "an agreement which creates, or is intended to create, a legal obligation between the parties to it."[4]

Key Concepts

A contract has three **essential elements**:

(1) agreement about the same thing;

(2) at least two contracting parties; and

(3) "legal" obligations.

Unless all three elements are present, the agreement is not a legally enforceable contract.

(1) Agreement about the same thing

5–03 In the traditional textbooks, this concept appeared under the maxim *consensus in idem*[5] and lies at the heart of contract law. If there is no real agreement—or the apparent agreement is really about different things—there is no contract. Party A may have two cars, car 1 and car 2. One of them, car 1, is for sale. If Party B makes A an offer for car 2, thinking that is the car for sale—and A accepts the offer, believing that B is actually offering for car 1—both parties think they have a contract. In fact, there is no contract, since there is no real agreement. In other words the essential *consensus in idem* ("consensus") is lacking. In *Raffles v Wichelhaus*,[6] a cargo was to be transported on a ship "Peerless" from Bombay to England. Unknown to both parties when the contract was formed, there were two ships of the same name in Bombay harbour, one sailing in October, the other in December. One party had meant the October ship, the other had intended December. There was no consensus, thus no contract.[7]

---

2 *e.g.* Sale of Goods Act 1979.

3 Contract (Scotland) Act 1997.

4 Jenks, *Digest of English Civil Law*, 2.1.

5 Agreement about the same thing.

6 (1864) 2 H. & C. 906.

7 See also *Mathieson Gee (Ayrshire) Ltd v Quigley*, 1952 S.C. (H.L.) 38.

(2) At least two contracting parties

Common sense dictates that it is impossible to have a contract between less than two parties. There is no legal upper limit, unless created by statute.[8] All parties to the contract must also have the necessary capacity,[9] *i.e.* legal capability to enter a contract. **5–04**

(3) "Legal" obligations

The agreement must create obligations which the law recognises as appropriate to enforce. The courts will not enforce agreements which are clearly illegal, criminal or immoral. However, there are agreements which are perfectly legal, but which the courts will not uphold. A so-called "social contract", such as a dinner date, is perfectly legal, but if one party fails to turn up, the disappointed host will not be able to compel performance or seek damages. Social workers, counsellors and others whose provide personal or emotional support increasingly make "contracts" with their clients. Such agreements are intended to be moral, not legal, obligations so that the parties are clear as to boundaries and expectations on both sides. **5–05**

Traditionally, courts will not enforce betting and gaming wagers, called *sponsiones ludicrae*[10] or sportive promises.[11] In *Kelly v Murphy*,[12] K was unsuccessful in an action against M, a pools promoter, for the prize money which K was due as winner of the pool. In *Ferguson v Littlewoods Football Pools Ltd*,[13] a syndicate completed pools coupons and gave them to a party who failed to pass them to Littlewoods. If the coupons had been received, a dividend of some £2.5 million would have been payable. The syndicate unsuccessfully sought payment. However, in *Robertson v Anderson*,[14] two friends played bingo together. One of them won the national jackpot. There was a long standing agreement between the two parties that winnings would be split. This agreement was *not* a gambling debt as it was collateral[15] to the wager itself.

There is the occasional problem of the so-called "gentleman's agreement" or honourable understanding. In *Ritchie v Cowan & Kinghorn*,[16] R was unable to pay his creditors, C&K, in full but arranged to pay 10s. (50p) in the £1. C&K gave him a receipt stating that they were acccpting his payment "*in full*" but added that it was understood that R would pay the balance "*whenever he is able to do so*." These additional words were an honourable understanding and not legally enforceable.

FORMATION OF CONTRACT

A contract is formed (made) when the parties reach agreement on the essential features of the bargain, *i.e.* when they achieve consensus. Either expressly or by implication, there will be an offer and an acceptance. **5–06**

---

[8] *e.g.* Companies Act 1985, s.716. It is not possible for more than 20 people to enter into a partnership agreement (subject to certain important exceptions).

[9] Considered further below.

[10] Obligations in jest.

[11] There is considerable statutory control of the gambling industry.

[12] 1940 S.C. 96. See also *Robertson v Balfour*, 1938 S.C. 207; *County Properties & Developments Ltd v Harper*, 1989 S.C.L.R. (Sh. Ct) 597.

[13] 1997 S.L.T. 309.

[14] 2001 G.W.D. 17–669.

[15] Connected to, but separate from.

[16] (1901) 3 F. 1071.

Offer

5–07 The offer must come before the acceptance. Equally, there can be no acceptance unless there is an offer which is capable of being accepted. The offer may be made verbally, in writing, or by any other suitable means of communication, such as fax, text message or email. Some contracts require to be formed in writing.[17] If the offer is communicated through any of the above means, this is called an *express* offer. The offer may also be inferred from the actings of the parties, *i.e.* the offer is not express, but is by *implication*. If a customer goes into a shop, lifts up an item and hands the money to the sales assistant, a valid contract is formed: both offer and acceptance are implied. Equally, a vending machine permanently offers to supply a particular commodity. By placing the appropriate coin in the slot, the consumer implies acceptance. A self-service petrol pump similarly makes an open-ended offer which is accepted by implication when a customer "helps himself".[18]

Contrast an offer with a willingness to negotiate

5–08 A proposal to do business is not the same as an offer. Party A might say to Party B that he was thinking of selling a particular item of property for £50. If B says "I will take it", there is no contract. Party A was not making an offer, he was only indicating a willingness to negotiate or extending an "invitation to treat". What B thought was an acceptance was really an offer. Until A accepts the offer, there is no contract.

Key Concepts

There is one hard and fast rule to which there are no exceptions: **an offer must always come before an acceptance**. To put this another way, no one can accept what is not on offer.

Shops, in law, do not offer goods for sale: they merely indicate a willingness to negotiate, quite different from the open-ended offer made by a vending machine. It is confusing, of course, when shops display signs such as "special offer", when, in fact, they are not offering anything. However, a shop owner does not have to sell any goods against his will and has an absolute right to refuse an offer to buy.

Pharmaceutical Society of Great Britain v Boots Cash Chemists Southern Ltd[19]

[1952] 2 Q.B. 795

Legislation required that listed poisons could only be sold under the supervision of a registered pharmacist. Such a poison had been sold in a self-service store. There was no pharmacist near the shelves where the goods were displayed but there was a pharmacist at work beside the checkout. The question was—when did the actual sale take place? Was it (a) when the customer took the goods off the shelf or (b) when the goods were presented at the checkout? The display of goods on the shelf did not comprise an offer. It was the customer who made the offer by taking the goods to the checkout. The sales assistant, as agent for the company, accepted the offer and the contract was thus formed, under the supervision of the pharmacist. B was not in breach of the Act.

---

17 Explained below.

18 See *Chapleton v Barry Urban DC* [1940] 1 K.B. 532 where, in context, a contract was formed when a consumer helped himself from a pile of deck chairs.

19 See also *Fisher v Bell* [1961] 1 Q.B. 394.

Other good examples of willingness to negotiate are advertisements or illustrations of goods in catalogues.

So, how is it possible to tell whether a particular statement is an offer (in which case it can be accepted) or a mere willingness to negotiate (which cannot be accepted)? There are no hard and fast rules. As a rule of thumb, if the first party publicly communicates a statement which is *non-discriminatory*, that statement is likely to be an offer. Thus the self-service petrol pump offers to supply petrol at the given price to whoever chooses to help himself. A shop keeper, on the other hand, does not have to sell any item of his stock to a customer if he does not wish to.

Quotation of price

If a potential supplier of goods or services indicates the price of his commodity in advance, this will normally be taken to be an estimate or quotation, *i.e.* an indication of willingness to negotiate. In context, however, it could be taken to be a tender or a firm offer. **5–09**

Harvey v Facey

[1893] A.C. 552

H sent a telegram to F "Will you sell us Bumper Hall Pen?[20] Telegraph lowest cash price". F telegraphed in reply "Lowest price for Bumper Hall Pen £900". H then telegraphed to F "We agree to buy Bumper Hall Pen for £900 asked by you". H received no reply to his telegram but argued that there was a valid contract. F's telegram was merely a statement of the lowest price at which he might be prepared to sell. It was not an offer to H nor was it an affirmative reply to the question in H's first telegram.

By contrast, in *Philp & Co. v Knoblauch*,[21] K wrote to P, oil-millers, "I am offering today plate linseed for January/February and have pleasure in quoting you 100 tons at 41/3d usual plate terms. I shall be glad to hear if you are buyers and await your esteemed reply". The following day, P telegraphed "Accept hundred January/February plate 41/3d". The telegram was confirmed by letter. K then attempted to recall his original quotation by sending a telegram to that effect. K's original letter/quotation *was* an offer to sell and not merely a statement of the current price. A contract had been formed by P's acceptance telegram. K's subsequent telegram was too late to have any effect.

There are always potential problems since the words, "offer", "estimate", "quotation" and "tender" are frequently used loosely in colloquial speech. It is a question of interpretation as to what words actually mean in context.

Expression of intention

An announcement by one party that he has something for sale for which offers may be made is normally only an indication of willingness to negotiate. In *Paterson v Highland Ry*,[22] the fact that a railway company had announced reduced rate tickets for a particular period of time did not prevent it from withdrawing the concession before the period expired. In *Dawson International plc v Coats Paton plc*,[23] directors of CP agreed to recommend to company members that an offer from DI to buy their shares should be accepted. The recommendation was duly made but was later withdrawn when a higher bid was received from a third party. DI were unsuccessful in their claim for **5–10**

[20] "Bumper Hall Pen" was the name of a farm in Jamaica. The case came to the Privy Council by way of appeal.

[21] 1907 S.C. 994.

[22] 1927 S.C. (H.L.) 32. *Mason v Benhar Coal Co.* (1882) 9 R. 883, the fact that a company had proposed to issue new shares, did not commit it to do so.

[23] 1993 S.L.T. 80.

damages for breach of contract since there was no contract. It is not easy to glean precise principles out of the case law.

If a party invites offers, such as is common in the sale of heritable property, he is not bound to accept any offer, even the highest. When property is advertised at a "fixed price", this is no more than a willingness to negotiate. A prospective buyer can offer a lower or even a higher price. A sale by auction is completed by the fall of the hammer, or equivalent. At this point, the auctioneer, as agent for the seller (exposer), "prefers" (accepts) the highest bid (offer). Until that moment, the bidder may withdraw his offer. In *Fenwick v Macdonald Fraser & Co.,*[24] it was held that the exposer was similarly free to withdraw his goods before the hammer fell. Occasionally, the so-called "referential" bid may be encountered in sealed competitive bids, such as an offer to "top" the highest bid by £X or by a given percentage. Bids of this kind were held to be invalid in *Harvela Instruments Ltd v Royal Trust Co. of Canada Ltd*[25] unless the prospective bidders are all given reasonable notice that this method may be employed.

Withdrawal of offer

5–11 An offer can be withdrawn, in most cases, at any time before it is accepted. This is an important feature of offers and the period, before acceptance, when the offerer is still free to withdraw is traditionally referred to as *locus poenitentiae*.[26]

> **Key Concepts**
>
> If a **time limit** is placed on the offer and that limit passes without an acceptance, the offer automatically lapses. If an offerer undertakes to keep his offer open for a certain time, this undertaking will be binding. This is because, in Scots law, a promise can be a binding obligation and breach of that promise could give rise to a claim for damages.

In *Littlejohn v Hawden,*[27] the solicitor for the seller of an estate indicated by letter that the potential buyer had an option to purchase which would remain open for ten days. This undertaking was legally binding. If, as in *Effold Properties v Sprot,*[28] the offer simply states that it must be accepted within a certain time, this does not count as an undertaking and the offerer can still withdraw his offer.[29]

How long does an offer last?

5–12 When a time limit is stated, the matter is clear. If the offer is not accepted within the time limit, it automatically falls. If no time limit is stated, the offer remains open for a "reasonable" time. There are times when it is only fair to give the second party some days to consider the offer. Equally, there are occasions when it is obvious that an offer must be accepted promptly.[30]

In the following two cases, the original offer *had* lapsed due to the length of time. *Wylie & Lochhead v McElroy & Sons*[31]: an offer to carry out certain iron work on a new building had not been "accepted" until five weeks had passed, during which time there had been a considerable rise

[24] (1904) 6 F. 850.
[25] [1986] 1 A.C. 207, HL.
[26] Literally meaning "room for repentance".
[27] (1882) 20 S.L.R. 5.
[28] 1979 S.L.T. (Notes) 84.
[29] In *McMillan v Caldwell*, 1991 S.L.T. 325, it was held that a formal written offer to buy heritable property can be withdrawn verbally, provided the withdrawal reaches the offeree before he accepts.
[30] *e.g.* if the subject-matter is raw materials which have a volatile price movement or where perishable goods are involved.
[31] (1873) 1 R. 41.

in the price of iron. *Glasgow Steam Shipping Co. v Watson*[32]: an offer made on August 5 to supply coal had not been "accepted" until October 13, by which time coal had risen substantially in price. By contrast, the court decided in *Murray v Rennie and Angus*,[33] that an offer dated June 10 to carry out certain mason work was still open for acceptance on June 21.

Death, insanity and bankruptcy

Provided the offer has not been accepted, it will automatically lapse on the death, insanity or bankruptcy of the offerer, unless the latter was acting purely as an agent for another party. **5–13**

Acceptance of an offer

Key Concepts **5–14**

If there is no **acceptance** of an offer, there is no contract. An acceptance must "meet" the offer, *i.e.* there must be consensus. If (and this is quite common) there are new terms or conditions in the so-called acceptance, no contract has yet been formed. What the original offerer has received is confusingly called a "qualified acceptance". Without exception, a qualified acceptance never concludes the process of formation of a contract.

The so-called qualified acceptance is really a new or counter offer. This new offer must be met by an unqualified acceptance before the parties can achieve consensus.[34]

In *Wolf & Wolf v Forfar Potato Co. Ltd* [35] F offered, by telex, to sell a quantity of potatoes to W. The offer was open for acceptance by 5pm on the following day. W sent an "acceptance" by telex on the following morning, but it contained new conditions. F telephoned W and informed them that the new conditions were unacceptable. W sent a second telex, still within the time-limit, purporting to accept the terms of the original offer. There was no contract. The first "acceptance" was a counter-offer, which killed off the original offer. The original offer could no longer be accepted. The counter offer or qualified acceptance from W had never been accepted by F.

The acceptance does not require to repeat the offer word for word. It is sufficient that it shows acceptance of the offer as a whole. Like an offer, an acceptance may be either express or implied. In most cases, express acceptance is required in order to achieve consensus but sometimes it may be implied, *e.g.* an order for goods may not require an express acceptance, since acceptance is implied by the act of supplying the goods. Acceptance can also *sometimes* be implied from a failure to reject an offer, but this can only arise if there have been similar dealings between the parties in the past. The law, in general, does not take kindly to contracts being imposed on people against their will.[36]

Method of acceptance

A person making an offer is entitled to state the method by which the acceptance should be communicated, *e.g.* letter, telephone or fax. If the precise method and/or time for acceptance is **5–15**

---

[32] (1873) 1 R. 189.

[33] (1897) 24 R. 965.

[34] *Nelson v The Assets Co. Ltd* (1889) 16 R. 898. See also *Stobo v Morrisons (Gowns) Ltd*, 1949 S.C. 184.

[35] 1984 S.L.T. 100. Followed in *Rutterford Ltd v Allied Breweries Ltd*, 1990 S.C. 249; distinguished in *Findlater v Maan*, 1990 S.C. 150.

[36] The practice whereby certain unscrupulous traders would send unsolicited goods to persons, and demand payment if the goods were not returned within a specified time, was largely curbed by the Unsolicited Goods and Services Act 1971. Persons who receive unsolicited goods can keep these goods if the sender does not take steps to recover them within a certain period.

stated, it must be adhered to. If no special conditions are laid down, acceptance can be given in any competent manner.

Offers to the general public

5–16 As demonstrated earlier, an advertisement is not an offer, merely an indication of a willingness to negotiate. However, there have been rare occasions where the courts have decided that particular advertisements go beyond being mere willingness to negotiate and are really offers to the general public. The most celebrated occasion must be:

> **Carlill v Carbolic Smoke Ball Co. Ltd**
>
> [1893] 1 Q.B. 256
>
> CSB, through newspaper advertisements, offered to pay £100 to any member of the public who bought a patent preventative "smoke ball" and, having used it according to instructions, contracted influenza. C bought a smoke ball, used it according to instructions and still contracted influenza. She sought payment of £100. CSB refused payment, claiming that there was no contract. They submitted that the advert was no more than a willingness to negotiate and thus could not be accepted. This particular advertisement was held to be an offer to the general public. C had accepted the offer when she bought the smoke ball and used it according to the instructions. There was a contract between CSB and C and she was entitled to her payment of £100.[37]

Withdrawal of acceptance

5–17

> **Key Concepts**
>
> The general rule is simple. Once an acceptance is given, provided it is final and not qualified, it cannot be **withdrawn**.

The parties are now in a mutually binding contract. Under the so-called postal rules (below), there is one interesting and illogical quirk in this rule.

THE POSTAL RULES

Offering and accepting

5–18 Where parties are negotiating *entirely* by post they rely on an agent, *i.e.* the postal service, to convey offers, counter offers, qualified acceptances and final acceptances. Over the years, certain common law "rules" have grown up but, it is always possible for parties to agree their own provisions or even for certain rules to be inferred.

Starting with the obvious—if an offer is posted, it must actually reach the second party (offeree).

---

[37] This case, though very famous, is somewhat of a "maverick". See also *Hunter v General Accident, Fire and Life Assurance Corporation*, 1909 S.C. (H.L.) 30.

Key Concepts

A potential problem arises as to when a posted acceptance actually achieves **consensus**. Under the postal rules, consensus is achieved when the second party posts his acceptance.

The acceptance rule is unsatisfactory in that the offerer can be in a binding contract, without being aware of it, since the acceptance could have been posted but not yet delivered. It has a further knock-on effect: if an offer is open for acceptance within a specified period, acceptance is effective if it is *posted* within that time limit. In *Jacobson Sons & Co. v Underwood & Son Ltd*,[38] the offer stated "for reply by Monday 6th". The acceptance was posted on the 6th but it did not arrive until 7th. The offer *had* been accepted on time because the reply had been in the hands of the Post Office on the 6th.

Withdrawal of offer

An offerer might post his offer and then have second thoughts and wish to withdraw it. His withdrawal is only effective if it reaches the offeree before the acceptance is placed in the post. In *Thomson v James*,[39] J made a written offer to buy an estate from T. Some days later, T posted an acceptance. On the same day on which T posted his acceptance, J posted a letter withdrawing his offer. There was a binding contract since consensus had been achieved when T posted his acceptance. J was too late to withdraw his offer. **5–19**

Withdrawal of acceptance

From the point of logic, the above rules ought to mean that once an acceptance is posted, it is irrevocable since consensus has been achieved. However, there appears to be a quirk in the law, based on an old case of *Countess of Dunmore v Alexander*.[40] A wrote to D, offering her services as a maid-servant. On November 5th, D wrote to A accepting her offer. On the 6th, D changed her mind and wrote to A withdrawing her acceptance. A received both letters at the same time. The court decided that D's withdrawal of acceptance was effective: there was no contract.[41] **5–20**

Contracts not covered by the postal rules

In contracts made with overseas parties, if they are made under the Uniform Laws on International Sales Act 1967, the postal rules do not apply. A contract will only be deemed to be completed when an acceptance arrives in the office of the offering party. **5–21**

The postal rules do not apply to communications made by telex which are treated in the same way as oral communications.[42] An acceptance by telex is effective when it is printed out at the offerer's end. It is assumed that similar rules apply to fax. Modern technology throws up other problems in the use of email and text messages. An email does not come under the postal rules. Opinion is that an email or text message has to be received, not merely sent. Presumably, the recipient would be expected to access the email or text at reasonable intervals.[43]

[38] (1894) 21 R. 654.
[39] (1855) 18 D. 1.
[40] (1830) 9 S. 190.
[41] If the acceptance had reached A before the recall, there would have been a contract. The Scottish Law Commission has recommended the abolition of the postal rules (Report 1993 No.144).
[42] *Brinkibon Ltd v Stahag Stahl* [1983] 2 A.C. 34.
[43] Consumers who buy goods and services "at a distance" have important protection under the Consumer Protection (Distance Selling) Regulations 2000 (SI 2000/2334).

PROMISES

5–22 A particular feature of the Scottish law of obligations is the possibility of a binding agreement even when nothing is asked in return. Most contracts contain an element of reciprocity, *i.e.* both parties will give and take something of value. This is usually referred to as "consideration". The tradition, in English law, is that if there is no element of consideration, the contract is not legally enforceable.[44]

> **Key Concepts**
>
> In Scotland, consideration is not an absolute requirement for an undertaking to be **legally binding**. An obligation to do or give something gratuitously can be as enforceable as any mutual contract. In *Morton's Trustees v Aged Christian Friend Society of Scotland*,[45] M wrote to a new charitable society, offering to provide pensions for elderly people, funded by annual capital payments. The obligation to meet these payments was a binding contract.

In law, however, there is a general presumption against donation. Also, mere verbal promises are not legally enforceable in every case. Under the Requirements of Writing (Scotland) Act 1995[46] "writing" is required to constitute a gratuitous unilateral obligation, except where undertaken in the course of a business.

It appears that a true gratuitous *contract*, as distinct from a gratuitous unilateral obligation, does not require to be in writing.[47]

THE REQUIREMENTS OF WRITING

5–23 The general rule is that no special formalities are required for parties to enter into a contractual obligation. There are, however, exceptions to this general rule and some contracts do require writing for their constitution. Until August 1, 1995, when the Requirements of Writing (Scotland) Act 1995 came into force, there were certain contracts, known as the *obligationes literis*, which required to be expressed in writing.

Under the 1995 Act, this entire area of law was modernised.[48] A written document is required[49] for: (i) creation, variation or extinction of an interest in land[50]; (ii) gratuitous unilateral obligations, unless undertaken in the course of business; (iii) creation of a trust where a person declares himself to be sole trustee of his own property.[51]

> **Key Concepts**
>
> Under the 1995 Act a document is **formally valid if it is subscribed by the granter**. In other words, a simple signature is sufficient formality to make the document binding. Thus most contracts only require the signatures of the parties.

44 *Stilk v Mayrick* (1809) 2 Camp. 317.
45 (1899) 2 F. 82.
46 s.1(2)(a)(ii).
47 This distinction between the two can be obscure. See *Bathgate v Rosie*, 1976 S.L.T. (Sh. Ct) 16.
48 The old law continues to apply to documents executed before the 1995 Act came into force.
49 s.1(2).
50 With the exception of leases of not more than one year's duration.
51 There are also statutory instances where certain documents (not all of them contracts) require writing, *e.g.* testamentary documents, life assurance, bills of exchange, hire purchase and regulated credit agreements.

If a document is to be regarded as self proving[52] it requires to be attested. This means it is signed, or the signature is acknowledged, by the granter before one witness aged at least 16, who signs as a witness. If a document is not self proving, *i.e.* if the signature was not witnessed, an application can be made to the Sheriff Court to give it self proving status should that be required.

In the case of a basic contract, a signature is required on the last page. Annexations only require to be signed if the contract relates to land. However, an annexation is only incorporated into any contract if it is referred to in the main document and identified on its face as being the annexation referred to. This rule applies whether the annexation requires to be signed or not.[53]

Personal bar

If a contract requires to be in writing, but is not (or is only partly in writing) and the party "loyal" to the defective contract (*i.e.* who wants it to continue—called the "first party" in the Act) acts, or refrains from acting, with the knowledge and acquiescence of the other party (the "second party"), the latter is said to be *personally barred* from withdrawing from the contract on the grounds of lack of writing. Personal bar will only operate if the position of the first party has been materially affected by his own actings and would be similarly affected if the second party were allowed to withdraw from the contract.[54] **5–24**

Electronic communication

The Electronic Communications Act 2000 made future provision for electronic communication to be recognised as the equivalent of a written document, including the possibility of electronic signatures. **5–25**

VALIDITY OF CONTRACTS

Key Concepts **5–26**

Parties may have a contract which is ***ex facie*** [55] **valid** but which, in some way, is **defective**. Depending on the form of the defect, the contract may turn out to be:

- void;
- voidable;
- unenforceable.

Void contracts

A contract is void if, for any reason, true consent[56] is lacking. Strictly speaking, it is illogical to refer to any contract as void. If a contract is void, there is no contract.[57] **5–27**

Lack of true consent may arise in a number of situations. It might be that one or both of the parties is not recognised in law as having the required capacity to give consent, *e.g.* young children

---

[52] When a document is self proving, its subscription is presumed valid without need for further evidence.
[53] It is easy to overlook this requirement.
[54] A concise account of the various categories of personal bar can be found in Gordon, *Contract Law Basics* (2nd ed., 2003), Chap.2.
[55] On the face of it.
[56] *i.e.* the element of consensus.
[57] Law is not an exact science nor is it always logical.

or insane persons. Lack of consent could also arise where there is essential error, *e.g.* as to the subject-matter of the contract.[58]

If an apparently valid contract is void, for whatever reason, it has no legal effect and must be treated as though it has never existed. Thus, if Smith purports to sell goods to Jones and the contract of sale is void, the goods still belong to Smith, even if Jones has paid full value.

Third parties may also be affected if a contract is void. Even though third parties act in good faith, they cannot acquire rights. If Jones meantime had sold goods to Brown (the third party) who paid for them and acted in good faith, the goods still belong to Smith.[59]

A simple example of a void contract is where the subject-matter is stolen goods, which will always belong to their original owner no matter how much time has elapsed nor on how many occasions they have changed hands, even if in good faith.

O'Neil v Chief Constable of Strathclyde

1994 S.C.L.R. 253

One car was exchanged (bartered) for another car which turned out to have been stolen. The car which had *not* been stolen was sold to a third party who took in good faith and for value. Because one stolen car had been involved, the original contract of barter was void. The third party could not acquire rights to the non-stolen car.

Voidable contracts

5–28 If a defect in a contract does not strike at the root of the agreement and does not, therefore, remove the basic consensus, the contract is not void, merely voidable. A contract could also be voidable because of some defect in its formation, *e.g.* if a contract for the sale of a house is not in writing. The contract, as it stands, is not invalid and it could still be honoured by the parties to it, or personal bar might operate.

In other words, if a contract is voidable, it is valid until steps are taken to have it set aside or "avoided".[60] The parties have two options: either they can ignore the defect and treat the contract as fully binding or one of them can use the defect as a means of getting out of the contract.

Key Concepts

A particularly important point to is the position of **third parties** under a voidable contract. If goods, property or rights which have changed hands under such a contract are subsequently transferred to a third party, that party *does* acquire ownership of them, so long as he has acted in good faith and for value and, at the time of transfer, the original contract has not been avoided.

The right to cancel a voidable contract may be lost in certain cases, such as where the parties cannot restore each other to their former positions, known as *restitutio in integrum*.[61] As indicated above, a third party cannot be required to give up goods acquired in good faith and for value. This has a further knock-on effect. If the third party has acquired goods in such a manner, the original voidable contract can no longer be set aside.

---

[58] As in *Raffles v Wickelhaus*, above.
[59] Brown can sue Jones for return of the money paid. Equally Jones can sue Smith.
[60] Which basically means "cancelled".
[61] Entire restoration.

Unenforceable contracts

These are contracts which are not necessarily void nor voidable but, because of their nature, cannot be enforced in the courts. The obvious examples are social agreements and *sponsiones ludicrae*, dealt with earlier. **5–29**

The main reasons for a contract being either void or voidable[62] are: lack of contractual capacity, error, misrepresentation and illegality.

CONTRACTUAL CAPACITY

The capacity, *i.e.* the legal capability, of certain persons to make a contract may be limited either at common law or by statute, because it is considered, for one reason or another, that they cannot give valid consent. **5–30**

Children and young people

The Age of Legal Capacity (Scotland) Act 1991 came into force on September 25, 1991. The centuries old division of young people under the age of majority into pupils and minors disappeared and a new single tier system took its place. **5–31**

> **Key Concepts**
>
> Young people **under the age of 16** ("children") have *no* contractual capacity subject to certain exceptions.

So, "reasonable transactions" commonly entered into by persons of their age and circumstances are valid.[63] These would include children buying items such as sweets or travelling on a bus. A positive aspect of the 1991 Act is the element of flexibility through age and circumstances, recognising that growing up is a gradual process. A nine-year-old is unlikely to be spending large sums of money, whereas a 15-year-old could have substantial spending power.

> **Key Concepts**
>
> Young people **aged 16 and 17** have full contractual capacity, although transactions which cause them "substantial prejudice" may be set aside on application to the court.

The young person has until age 21 in which to apply. The court would only set aside a transaction if[64] an adult exercising reasonable prudence would not have entered into it and it has caused, or is likely to cause, substantial prejudice to the applicant. This does not imply that any contract which does not work out as well as expected can be easily set aside.

Parties might well be ultra-cautious about entering into a transaction with any young person aged between 16 and 17, particularly if buying heritable property. The Act[65] introduces a procedure for making a proposed transaction unchallengeable by judicial ratification. This is achieved by joint action under summary cause and the sheriff's decision is final.

---

[62] Apart from the requirements of writing, considered above.
[63] s.2(1).
[64] s.3(2).
[65] s.4.

Insane persons

5–32 At common law, an insane[66] person has no capacity to contract, although he must pay a reasonable price for "necessaries". Traditionally, someone certified insane might have had a *curator bonis*[67] appointed by the court and all contracts would made through him.

The Adults with Incapacity (Scotland) Act 2000 provides a whole new mechanism. Depending on circumstances a guardian, intromitter or intervener can be appointed and applications for appointment of a *curator bonis* are now incompetent. A fundamental principle of the Act is that there must be no intervention unless it is for the benefit of the adult and the outcome cannot be achieved in any other way. So far as is possible, the views of the adult must be taken into account. Any intervention must take the least restrictive option.

Under the Law Reform (Miscellaneous Provisions)(Scotland) Act 1990,[68] a power of attorney signed after January 1, 1991 will continue in force, even if the granter subsequently becomes mentally incapable. The provision is not retroactive.

Intoxicated persons

5–33 Intoxication, like insanity, is a question of fact and degree. As a general rule, drunkenness is not a ground on which a contract is either void or voidable unless the drunkenness has reached the stage where the person has lost his reason and could give no true consent. There is no modern Scottish case in which a contract has been set aside on the grounds of intoxication.[69]

EFFECT OF ERROR ON CONTRACTS

5–34 Either or both parties to a contract may have entered into it under some form of error and this may well affect the validity of the contract. In the first instance, errors can be divided into two distinct categories:

- **Errors as to law**: These could arise where one or other of the parties was in error in relation to his rights or to the legal effect of the contract. The general rule is that an error as to law does not affect the validity of a contract. There is a well-known legal maxim *ignorantia juris neminem excusat.*[70]
- **Errors as to fact**: One or both of the parties may be mistaken as to some fact connected with the contract, *e.g.* the price of the goods. Errors as to fact can affect the validity of a contract in different ways. What follows hereafter is an examination of the legal effect of errors of fact, in different situations.

Error of expression

5–35 Errors of expression can arise where there is no doubt what both parties meant but, owing to a clerical error of a third party, the written contract is not expressed in the terms originally agreed by the parties. In *Anderson v Lambie*,[71] the owner of an estate, of which a farm formed part, agreed to sell only the farm. Due to a mistake by his solicitor, the entire estate was conveyed to the buyer.

---

66 Insanity is not a very precise concept at common law. In law, there is a presumption of sanity. The contrary must be proved or admitted.

67 One who has a care of goods.

68 s.71.

69 *Pollok v Burns* (1875) 2 R. 497; *Taylor v Provan* (1864) 2 M. 1226.

70 Ignorance of the law is no excuse.

71 1954 S.C. (H.L.) 43. See also *Krupp v John Menzies Ltd*, 1907 S.C. 903; *Aberdeen Rubber Ltd v Knowles & Sons (Fruiterers) Ltd*, 1995 S.L.T. 870.

As the disposition[72] did not give effect to the original agreement, the court reduced the disposition so that a correct version could be recorded in its place.

In some ways, this is not so much an error of fact as a defect in the way in which the contract is expressed. At common law, there is equitable power to deal with such situations by reducing the written document. This requires an action of reduction in the Court of Session.

There is a simpler statutory procedure under the Law Reform (Miscellaneous Provisions) (Scotland) Act 1985[73] to rectify documents which fail to express what the parties had intended. An advantage of the statutory procedure is the power given to the court to change the wording of a document. At common law, the court can uphold or reduce a document (or parts of it) but cannot change it. A statutorily rectified document is counted as though it had always been in its rectified state. There is protection of third parties who have acted in good faith in reliance on the document in its original state.

Error of expression can also occur when a person expresses an offer in terms which he did not intend and the incorrect offer is accepted. An example would be quoting a lower price than intended. If the person accepting the offer knows that there is a mistake, the contract is probably void. If he does not know of the mistake, the position is less clear and all one can say is that the contract could be voidable in some circumstances.[74]

If there is a faulty transmission of an offer, there will be no contract if the message delivered is substantially different from the original. In these days of fax and email, such problems are less common than they were when telegrams were sent down land-lines in Morse code.[75]

Error of intention

For there to be an error of intention, one or both of the parties must be mistaken as to the nature or subject-matter of the contract which they are entering. This area can be divided into three aspects: **5–36**

(1) unilateral error;
(2) common error; and
(3) mutual error (incidental and essential).

(1) Unilateral error

The general rule is that if the error is of one party only, this does not affect the validity of the contract. So, if a person with full contractual capacity freely and willingly pays more for something than it is worth or sells something for less than its true value, the contract cannot be set aside on these grounds alone provided the party was not induced to enter the contract by fraud or misrepresentation.[76] **5–37**

Both common error and mutual error, which are dealt with below, are sometimes said to be forms of bilateral error. The latter is a somewhat misleading term as it could be taken to imply that both parties must be in error, which is not always the case. If parties are genuinely at cross-purposes, they need not both be in error. Where both parties are in error or have so confused the situation that they cannot have achieved consensus, these situations are more accurately classified as errors of intention.

---

72 The deed which conveys heritable property.
73 ss.8 and 9.
74 *Seaton Brick and Tile Co. Ltd v Mitchell* (1900) 2 F. 550; *Wilkie v Hamilton Lodging-House Co. Ltd* (1902) 4 F. 951.
75 *Verdin Bros v Robertson* (1871) 10 M. 35.
76 *Stewart v Kennedy* (1890) 17 R. (H.L.) 25; *Spook Erection (Northern) Ltd v Kaye*, 1990 S.L.T. 676.

(2) Common error

5–38 Common or shared error can arise when both parties have made the *same* mistake about a matter of fact. To put it another way, they both share the same mistaken belief. If the error is material and goes to the root of the contract, that contract will be void. A statutory example is where there is a contract of sale of specific goods, *e.g.* a particular painting, which, unknown to the seller, have perished at the time the contract is made.[77]

Where the common error was really just a matter of opinion, as distinct from an error of fact, the contract will be valid. In *Dawson v Muir*,[78] M sold certain vats to D for £2. Both parties were of the opinion that they were only of scrap value. Subsequently, it was found that they were worth £300. The contract stood.[79]

(3) Mutual error

5–39 This refers to a situation where, for reasons good or bad, the parties have misunderstood one another. Each party thinks consensus has been achieved, but each has a different perception of what has been agreed. In such a situation, the courts will have to look at the terms of any written contract or the prior negotiations.

Key Concepts

If the **misunderstanding** does not go to the heart or root of the contract, *i.e.* is "incidental", the contract will stand unless the error was induced by misrepresentation, in which case, the contract may be voidable. If, however, the error goes to the root of the contract, *i.e.* is "essential" (of the essence), the contract is void.

Incidental error

5–40 This form of error, also known as *error concomitans*,[80] refers to matters which do not go to the root of the contract or are only incidental. Incidental errors do not prevent basic consensus and therefore the contract will stand, unless the error was induced by misrepresentation, in which case the contract may be voidable. In *Cloup v Alexander*,[81] the manager of a company of French comedians hired an Edinburgh theatre "for their performances". The comedians subsequently discovered that it was illegal for them to perform in that particular theatre. They were still obliged to pay the rent. The error in this case was an incidental or collateral issue, namely what kind of act could be put on in the theatre.

Essential error

5–41 Where error is of the essence[82] of the contract there is no consensus, which makes the contract void, not merely voidable. Error is said to be essential "*whenever it is shown that but for it one of*

[77] Sale of Goods Act 1979, s.6.

[78] (1851) 13 D. 843.

[79] There was a similar result in *Leaf v International Galleries* [1950] 2 K.B. 86, when both buyer and seller mistakenly, but genuinely, believed that a particular painting was a genuine work of John Constable.

[80] Collateral error.

[81] (1831) 9 S. 448.

[82] Also known as error *in substantialibus* (in the substantials).

the parties would have declined to contract".[83] Traditionally, essential error occurs in five possible situations, although these should not be regarded as final or watertight.

Subject-matter

This arises when the parties believe they are in agreement as to which item or service forms the subject-matter whereas, in fact, they have different things in mind. One of the classic cases is *Raffles v Wichelhaus*,[84] considered earlier. **5–42**

Price

The fact that a price has not been fixed does not make a contract void as a matter of course. If it has not been fixed (or some clear reference system put in place to ascertain the price), this usually means that the parties are still at the pre-contract stage of negotiation. However, it is possible for both parties to think that a price has been fixed whereas, in fact, they have different prices in mind. In such circumstances, the contract will be void. **5–43**

If the goods cannot be returned to their original owner, the courts have power both at common law and by statute[85] to fix a reasonable price.

Identity

In many cases, it matters little with whom a party actually contracts. However, there arc times when identity can be of the essence of a contract. There are certainly cases where *delectus personae*[86] applies. Common sense indicates that if A wants his portrait painted by X, he need not accept a portrait painted by Y. But, in the case of less personal contracts, what would be the effect of B thinking that he is contracting with C but, in fact, is contracting with D? **5–44**

Morrisson v Robertson

1908 S.C. 332

In this case, a confidence trickster named Telford ("T") introduced himself to M, a cattle dealer, fraudulently claiming to be the son of Wilson, a dairy farmer of good credit, who was known to M. T claimed authority from his father to buy cows from M on "the usual credit terms". M was totally deceived and gave the cows to T without hesitation on the basis of Wilson's good standing. T had no intention of paying for the cows. He sold them on to a third party, R, who bought in good faith, without knowing that they had been improperly obtained. When M realised that he had been tricked, he made enquiries and found that the cows were in R's possession. The original contract between M and T was void because of the error in M's mind as to the true identity of T. The latter had never owned the cows and could not pass ownership to R, the third party, even though R acted in good faith.

---

[83] Lord Watson in *Menzies v Menzies* (1893) 20 R. (H.L.) 108.

[84] (1864) 2 H. & C. 906. See also *Scriven v Hindley* [1913] 3 K.B. 564.

[85] Sale of Goods Act 1979, s.8; *Stuart & C v Kennedy* (1885) 13 R. 221; *Wilson v Marquis of Breadalbane* (1859) 21 D. 957.

[86] Choice of person.

This case should be contrasted with:

MacLeod v Kerr

1965 S.C. 253

K advertised his car for sale. A con-man named Galloway, who told K his name was Craig, responded to the advertisement and agreed to buy the car. He wrote out a cheque and signed it "L Craig" and K gave him the registration document. The chequebook was stolen and the signature was a forgery. A few days later, Galloway, now giving his name as Kerr, sold the car to Gibson, a garage proprietor, who bought in good faith. In an action of multiple poinding,[87] K argued that there had been essential error of identity and that the car still have belonged to him. The court held that the car belonged to Gibson, the third party. The original contract between K and Galloway had not been void, merely voidable. When the contract was formed, there was no error in K's mind as to the identity of the person with whom he was contracting: it was the man in front of him, whether he called himself Galloway or Craig. This was *not* a case of essential error as to identity, so *Morrisson v Robertson* was not applied. Even although the original contract had been voidable, it could no longer be set aside, because the third party (Gibson) had acquired rights.

It is probably fair comment to suggest that the courts today are more likely to follow *MacLeod v Kerr* than *Morrisson v Robertson*.[88]

Quantity, quality or extent

5–45 Some authorities suggest that this is an example of error as to the subject-matter (above) rather than a distinct category of its own. In *Patterson v Landsberg & Son,*[89] P, a dealer, bought from a London dealer items of jewellery, which appeared to be antique. In fact, they were reproductions. The contract was void. There had been a crucial misunderstanding as to the quality of the goods.

Nature of the contract

5–46 This category of error can only arise in a written contract. It could arise when a party signs a document which he did not intend,[90] or in a capacity in which he did not intend.

However, the law is not generally sympathetic to individuals who, without being induced by misrepresentation, sign solemn undertakings and subsequently claim not to have understood them.

Royal Bank of Scotland plc v Purvis

1990 S.L.T. 262

A wife signed an undertaking as cautioner[91] for money lent by R to her husband. When he defaulted, R raised an action against the wife for payment of all sums due. The wife claimed she had signed at the request of her husband and that she was unfamiliar with business. Since the wife must have known she was signing a document which gave rise to obligations, the court could not look into what was in her mind when she signed and she was thus bound by it.

---

[87] A form of action used where the ownership of property is in dispute.

[88] In two English cases involving identity, the contracts were voidable: *Phillips v Brooks*, 1919 2 K.B. 243; *Lewis v Averay* [1971] 3 All E.R. 907.

[89] (1905) 7 F. 675.

[90] *McLaurin v Stafford* (1875) 3 R. 265.

[91] Guarantor.

Although the courts are unwilling to overturn clear written agreements, it was held in *Smith v Bank of Scotland*[92] that a bank is under a duty to advise a cautioner spouse to take independent advice.

MISREPRESENTATION

Misrepresentation is an aspect of error. In some cases considered so far, the "misunderstanding" between the parties arose from conduct or statements of a fraudulent or careless nature. **5–47**

Key Concepts

Misrepresentation arises in three distinct situations, which are partly self-explanatory:

- innocent;
- fraudulent;
- negligent.

One preliminary, but very important, comment requires to be made: innocent misrepresentation does not give rise to a claim for damages.[93] The other two forms of misrepresentation do, at least potentially.

Innocent misrepresentation

If a person makes a statement, honestly believing it to be true and unaware that it is false, the misrepresentation counts as innocent, provided it is not actually negligent. If the error induced by the innocent misrepresentation is essential, the contract will be void, otherwise it will be voidable. However, before a contract can be reduced on the grounds of innocent misrepresentation, the misrepresentation must have been more than merely trivial and must have been relied on by the party misled, inducing him to enter the said contract. In addition, the party wishing to reduce must be in a position to give *restitutio in integrum*.[94] If this is not possible, the contract will generally have to stand. **5–48**

Boyd & Forest v Glasgow & South Western Railway Co. (No.1)
1912 S.C. (H.L.) 93

B, contracting engineers, agreed to build a new stretch of railway track for G. The price was fixed by B at £243,000 based on data provided by G. B subsequently found that the information was materially inaccurate, making the work more difficult and expensive. The original data had been the work of independent surveyors and were accurate. However, G's own engineer disagreed with some of the figures and had altered them in good faith. Despite many problems, B completed the track at a cost of £379,000. B sued G for damages claiming they been supplied with misleading information, inducing them to enter the contract by fraudulent misrepresentation. The House of Lords held there was no fraud. G's engineer had altered the figures only

---

[92] 1997 S.C. (H.L.) 111; this appeared to bring Scots law into line with the English case of *Barclays Bank plc v O'Brien* [1994] 1 A.C. 180. In fact, Scots law is still developing in this area: *Forsyth v Royal Bank of Scotland plc,* 2000 S.L.T. 1295; *Clydesdale Bank plc v Black,* 2002 S.L.T. 764.

[93] *Ferguson v Wilson* (1904) 6 F. 779.

[94] Entire restoration to the original position.

because he honestly believed them to be inaccurate. Any misrepresentation was innocent and no damages could be awarded.

Fraudulent misrepresentation

5–49 Like innocent misrepresentation, fraudulent misrepresentation may induce error, making the contract void or voidable. If the error is essential, the contract is void, otherwise it is voidable. "Trade puffs" or *verba jacantia*[95] are allowed some degree of latitude in practice, since few people take claims such as "good value" or "superior quality" too seriously.[96] It is not fraud to express a genuinely held opinion, even if it is wrong, although, nowadays, this might give rise to an action on the grounds of negligent misrepresentation. In *Hamilton v Duke of Montrose*,[97] a statement which had been made about the capability of certain land to sustain a particular number of livestock turned out to be incorrect. There had not been any misrepresentation of fact, merely a statement of opinion. The contract was valid.

Where a statement of opinion—which turns out to be wrong—is made in the course of business and, in context, is reasonably relied on, it may count as a misrepresentation. It is more likely to be counted as negligent than fraudulent. A statement of pure future intention such as "I am hoping to expand my business over the next five years" is not a misrepresentation since, as a pure future statement, it is neither true nor false. If, however, a future statement relies on some present fact and is unreliable, it is not "pure" and may count as misrepresentation.[98]

Misrepresentation is not fraudulent unless it was known to be untrue and conscious dishonesty must be proved. Mere carelessness is not fraud but it may amount to negligence. *Bile Bean Manufacturing Co. v Davidson*[99] gives a classic example of fraud. B advertised "Bile Beans" as being manufactured from secret ingredients, previously known only to Australian Aborigines. These claims were totally fictitious.

In *Derry v Peek*,[1] directors of a tramways company issued a share prospectus stating that the company had the right to use steam power in its trams. D bought shares on the strength of that statement. In fact, the company was only entitled to use steam power if it was issued with a Board of Trade certificate. The Board declined to issue such a certificate. D failed in his action for damages against the directors of the company since the statement had been made in the honest belief that it was true, even although the directors had not taken all reasonable care to check their statements.[2]

Reference is made above to the 1912 case of *Boyd & Forest*. Having lost their first action, B raised a second action,[3] this time for reduction of the original contract claiming that G's innocent misrepresentation made it voidable. If B had succeeded in they could have claimed the *actual* cost of the railway. The House of Lords was not convinced that there had been any misrepresentation. Even if there had been, B's claim failed. B had not proved that the alleged misrepresentation had actually induced them to enter the contract.

Today, no contractor would give a fixed price on such a large undertaking. If a similar situation did arise, an action would probably be on the grounds of negligent misrepresentation.

Negligent misrepresentation

5–50 This area of law has developed in more recent times.

---

[95] Words thrown about.
[96] The Trade Descriptions Act 1968 provides criminal sanctions where there is material misdescription of goods or services.
[97] (1906) 8 F. 1026; *Flynn v Scott*, 1949 S.C. 442.
[98] *British Airways Board v Taylor* [1976] 1 All E.R. 65.
[99] (1906) 8 F. 1181.
[1] (1889) App. Cas. 337.
[2] The law on company prospectuses was changed by statute shortly afterwards.
[3] *Boyd & Forest v Glasgow & South Western Railway (No.2)*, 1915 S.C. (H.L.) 20.

Key Concepts

A representation is **negligent** if the person making it failed to take reasonable care in making the representation *and* he was under a legal duty to do so.

A foundation case is:

Hedley Byrne & Co. Ltd v Heller & Partners Ltd

[1964] A.C. 465

HB were advertising agents. They were asked by Easipower Ltd to arrange advertising. HB enquired into the financial soundness of E by requesting their own bank to write to H&P, bankers to E. H&P stated that E were financially stable enough to honour the contract. The letter from H&P was headed "*Confidential. For your private use and without responsibility on the part of this Bank*". In reliance on the information, HB placed advertisements. Shortly afterwards, E went into liquidation, leaving HB with a substantial loss. It was clear, from subsequent enquiries, that E had been in financial difficulties when H&P had made their reassuring statement. HB sued H&P claiming negligent misrepresentation. The case established that bankers owe a duty of care in answering such enquiries where it is clear that recipients rely on them.

Although the case only dealt with a matter of delict, the basic principle was basic extended to contractual matters.[4] To put the matter beyond doubt, the Law Reform (Miscellaneous Provisions) (Scotland) 1985[5] provided that damages for negligent misrepresentation are recoverable in Scotland.

Silence or concealment as misrepresentation

When parties enter a contract, they normally do so after negotiating *at arm's length*. Neither party **5–51** is going to volunteer information, unless he has to. X may be negotiating to buy an article from Y for £20. X does not have to disclose to Y that he already has a third party buyer lined up who will pay £50 for it. As a general rule, contracting parties are expected to see to their own interests and satisfy themselves.[6] Although beyond the scope of this chapter, a buyer frequently has important statutory protection, particularly under the Sale of Goods Act 1979. What follows is basically the common law position.

If a direct question is put, it must be answered truthfully, otherwise the reply could count as fraudulent. Problems can arise, however, when nothing is said. Can silence count as misrepresentation? In *Gillespie v Russell*,[7] G, a land owner, sought to cancel a lease of mineral rights he had given to R. R had known that the land in question contained a particularly valuable seam of coal, but G had been unaware of this fact. The lease was valid as the concealment of such information by R was not fraud.

However, there can be cases in which silence is, in fact, a subtle form of misrepresentation, as in *Gibson v National Cash Register Co.*,[8] where G ordered two new cash registers. He was actually supplied with two second-hand machines, reconditioned to look like new. This was clearly fraudulent.

---

[4] *Esso Petroleum Co. v Mardon* [1976] Q.B. 801; *Kenway v Orcantic Ltd*, 1980 S.L.T. 46; *Foster v Craigmiller Laundry Ltd*, 1980 S.L.T. (Sh. Ct) 100.

[5] s.10.

[6] This is sometimes expressed in the maxim *caveat emptor* (let the buyer beware).

[7] (1856) 18 D. 677; *Royal Bank of Scotland v Greenshields*, 1914 S.C. 259.

[8] 1925 S.C. 477.

A potentially problematic area is where parties are "economical with the truth". In fact, half-truths can be every bit as misleading as complete untruths.[9] A second-hand car dealer might truthfully tell a prospective customer that a particular car has been "thoroughly checked". But if nothing had been done to cure the many faults discovered by the check, the assurance would be worthless.

Contracts not subject to "arm's length" rule

5–52 Having established the general "arm's length" rule, there may be occasions where parties to a contract *do* require to make full disclosure to one another. Contracts which are not subject to the arm's length rule fall into two main categories:

Contracts *uberrimae fidei*[10]

5–53 Insurance or partnership are the two generally accepted categories. In all insurance contracts, the policy will be voidable if the party insured fails to disclose some material fact which might affect the risk being undertaken by the insurer, even if the insurer did not ask a specific question relating to it. This is powerfully illustrated by the following case:

The Spathari
(1925) S.C. (H.L.) 6

D, a Greek ship broker, resident in Glasgow, bought the *SS Spathari*, a Finnish ship at Hull, with the intention of selling her to a syndicate of Greeks at Samos. At the time, Greek vessels had great difficulty in getting insurance. D arranged with B, a Glasgow ship broker, that she would be transferred into B's name, that the latter would register and insure her, ostensibly as owner, until the voyage to Samos was complete. On the voyage, the *Spathari* sank. The insurance company was entitled to refuse payment on account of B's failure to disclose a material fact, namely the "Greek" element of the boat.

Contracts involving a fiduciary relationship

5–54 These are contracts where the parties stand in a relationship of trust to one another, *e.g.* parent and child, agent and principal, solicitor and client. Common sense indicates that such parties do not contract with each other as strangers. Solicitors have strict professional rules about making contracts with clients outwith the provision of normal professional services.[11]

OTHER FACTORS AFFECTING VALIDITY

5–55 In the following cases, the validity of the contract is affected, as the consent of one of the parties has been improperly obtained.

[9] *Shankland v Robinson*, 1920 S.C. (H.L.) 6.
[10] Of utmost good faith.
[11] *McPherson's Trustees v Watt* (1877) 5 R. (H.L.) 9.

Facility and circumvention

A contract can be reduced where the party misled is not insane but is suffering from weakness of mind due to old age or ill health, *i.e.* there is a "facility". Circumvention is the motive to mislead, falling short of actual fraud. If both factors are present and the party misled suffers some kind of harm or loss as a result of the contract, it is voidable.[12] 5–56

Undue influence

A contract is voidable if one person is in a position to influence another and abuses this position to induce this other party to make the contract to his disadvantage. It is most likely to occur in fiduciary relationships, such as parent and child,[13] doctor and patient, solicitor and client, but it could take place in any relationship where there an element of confidence. There is no need, however, to prove that the weaker party was subject to any facility. 5–57

Force and fear

Generally, if a contract is entered into because of force or fear, it is void through lack of true consent. The threats may be physical or mental, *e.g.* "blackmail", and could be made in respect of a near relative as well as to the victim himself. In *Gow v Henry*[14] a threat to dismiss a workman from his post, without just cause, counted as force and fear. However, a threat to do something legal, such as pursuing a legitimate debt, or asking a dishonest employee to resign rather than call in the police, is not force and fear. In the very old case of *Earl of Orkney v Vinfra*,[15] the Earl commanded V to sign a contract. V refused, then did so when the Earl threatened to kill him. The contract was void. 5–58

Extortion

The general rule is that a contract is neither void nor voidable merely on the grounds of being a poor bargain. Parties normally contract at arms length and should look to their own interests. In *McLachlan v Watson*,[16] M took a 10-year lease of a Glasgow hotel under an arrangement which were clearly a poor bargain. M died four years into the lease but his widow was unsuccessful in her attempts to have it reduced. 5–59

ILLEGAL AGREEMENTS

A contract must be lawful both in its objects and in the way in which it is performed. If either of these elements is not satisfied, the courts will not enforce the agreement. Such agreements are known as *pacta illicita*.[17] It is not necessarily criminal, to set up such agreements, but the court will not enforce them nor award damages in the event of breach. Some of these agreements would more properly be called unenforceable. The general principle is *ex turpi causa non oritur actio*.[18] 5–60

[12] *Cairns v Marianski* (1850) 12 D. 919; *MacGilvray v Gilmartin*, 1986 S.L.T. 89; *Anderson v The Beacon Fellowship*, 1992 S.L.T. 111.

[13] *Gray v Binny* (1879) 7 R. 332.

[14] (1899) 2 F. 48. See also *Priestnell v Hutcheson* 19 D. 495; *Hunter v Bradford Trust Ltd*, 1977 S.L.T. (Notes) 33; *Hislop v Dickson Motors (Forres) Ltd*, 1978 S.L.T. (Notes) 73.

[15] (1606) Mor. 16481.

[16] (1874) 11 S.L.R. 549.

[17] Illegal agreements.

[18] No action arises out of an immoral situation; *Hamilton v Main* (1823) 2 S. 356.

Another maxim in this area of law is *in turpi causa melior est conditio possidentis.*[19] Thus, the loss is allowed to lie where it falls, *e.g.* a person pays money for an illegal drug, which is not supplied. He will not be able to take legal steps to recover the money from the drug dealer.

However, when the parties are not *in pari delicto*,[20] the court may assist the party who is less blameworthy.

Statutory illegality

5–61 An Act of Parliament can place a limit on the freedom of a person to make a contract. Sometimes it may even declare a certain type of contract to be illegal making it null and void. However, the courts may give effect to rights which are incidental to the contract, to prevent one party from gaining an unfair advantage over another. In *Cuthbertson v Lowes*,[21] C sold L two fields of potatoes at £24 per Scots acre. This contract was void, as imperial measure was obligatory. Even though the contract could not be enforced by the court, C was entitled to the market value of the potatoes at the time of harvesting.[22]

Illegality at common law

5–62 A contract is illegal at common law, if its purpose is criminal, fraudulent, immoral[23] or contrary to public policy.

Agreements contrary to public policy

5–63 Public policy is notoriously difficult to define. Some agreements are clearly against public policy, *e.g.* contracting with an enemy alien or interfering with the administration of justice. Less easy, are contracts which seek to restrict a person's freedom to work or to trade, *i.e.* contracts in restraint of trade, although these are mainly governed now by the Competition Act 1998.

Closely related are restrictive covenants, which are governed by common law. A restrictive covenant seeks to restrict a person's freedom to work where he pleases, for whom he pleases and in what line of business he pleases.

Key Concepts

The very general common law rule is that contracts in **restraint of trade** or **restrictive covenants** are void unless it can be shown that the restrictions are reasonable both for the parties to the contract and for the public. The courts will also want to be convinced that the parties are contracting on equal terms.[24]

Agreements between employers and employees

5–64 A restrictive covenant seeks to prevent an employee from working in competition with his former employer in the future. This may be part of the employee's contract of employment and normally will only take effect when the employment comes to an end. Even if the employee is wrongfully

[19] In an immoral situation, the position of the possessor is the better one; *Barr v Crawford*, 1983 S.L.T. 481.
[20] Equally at fault; *Strongman v Sincock* [1955] 2 Q.B. 525.
[21] (1870) 8 M. 1073.
[22] Contrast *Jamieson v Watt's Trustee*, 1950 S.C. 265.
[23] *Pearce v Brooks* (1886) L.R. 1 Ex. 213.
[24] *Schroeder Music Publishing v Macaulay* [1974] W.L.R. 1308.

dismissed, the restrictive covenant may still apply. Such covenants are most common in service industries or where there are trade secrets or sensitive information.

> **Key Concepts**
>
> The courts do not generally take kindly to an individual being **unreasonably restrained** and such an agreement will not be enforced unless the employer can show that he is protecting his legitimate interests.
>
> - It *is* legitimate for an employer to protect his trade secrets or his customer base.
> - It *is not* legitimate to prevent fair competition.

If the courts are asked to uphold a restrictive covenant, it will have to pass the reasonableness test. Thus, the courts will look at all the factors involved, *e.g.* the type of business, radius or customer area, location and the status of the employee. The courts tend to interpret "reasonable" more strictly in the relationship of employer and employee than between buyer and seller of a business. There is a large body of case law, of which only a sample can be given.

In *Mason v Provident Clothing & Supply Co. Ltd*,[25] M was employed as a salesman with P. The company had branches all over England, but M was employed only in a limited area of London. He had agreed that he would not become employed in a similar business within a radius of 25 miles of London and within a period of three years. As M was employed in a relatively minor capacity and, considering the dense population of London, the restraint was far wider than reasonably necessary and was unenforceable.

In *Fitch v Dewes*,[26] F was employed as managing clerk to D, a solicitor. F was well known to D's clients. F had agreed that he would not become engaged in the business of a solicitor within a radius of seven miles of D's office. This restriction was reasonable and enforceable. D had done no more than attempt to prevent his clients being enticed away from him. On the other hand, in *Dallas McMillan & Sinclair v Simpson*[27] the court refused to prevent an outgoing partner of a firm of solicitors from practising within 20 miles of Glasgow Cross.

An important factor is the right, referred to above, of an employer to protect his trade secrets. A classic modern example is *Bluebell Apparel v Dickinson*.[28] D was a management trainee with B, manufacturers of "Wrangler" jeans. Within a few months, D was in sole charge of one of B's Scottish factories. Shortly afterwards, he intimated that he was taking up a position with a rival manufacturer. Both companies operate on a world wide basis. B was in possession of trade secrets[29] which would be of value to a business competitor. The two year and world wide restriction in his original contract was reasonable.

The courts have no power to change an agreement into which parties have voluntarily entered. Either the agreement stands or falls as illustrated in *Empire Meat Co. v Patrick*.[30] P was manager of a butcher's shop whose customers came mainly from within a one-mile radius. P had agreed that he would not set up business nor work for another butcher within a five-mile radius of his employer's premises. This restriction was too great and thus entirely unenforceable. A one-mile radius would have been acceptable but the court had no power to change the agreement.

---

[25] [1913] A.C. 724; contrast *The Scottish Farmers' Dairy Co. (Glasgow) Ltd v McGhee*, 1933 S.C. 148 and *Rentokil Ltd v Kramer*, 1986 S.L.T. 114.

[26] [1921] 2 A.C. 158.

[27] 1989 S.L.T. 454; contrast *Stewart v Stewart*, 1899 1 F. 1158.

[28] 1980 S.L.T. 157.

[29] A trade secret need not necessarily refer to a technical process. It could refer to any confidential information, such as the business of a bank: *TSB Bank plc v Connell*, 1997 S.L.T. 1254.

[30] [1939] 2 All E.R. 85.

If there are two parts to the agreement, one of which seems reasonable and the other does not, the court may be prepared to allow one part to stand but to delete ("blue pencil") the other part, provided the two parts are severable, *i.e.* capable of being separated and standing on their own.[31]

Agreements between buyer and seller of a business

5–65 When a purchaser buys the goodwill of a business, he will usually insist that the seller binds himself not to set up in competition within a certain area and/or time. The courts are more willing in these cases to enforce the agreement, but the test of reasonableness will still apply. The agreements must not cover a longer period of time, nor a wider area of operations, than is necessary. A famous case is *Nordenfelt v Maxim Nordenfelt Guns and Ammunition Co. Ltd.*[32] N, the owner of a cannon manufacturing business, sold it to M and agreed not to engage in the making of cannon anywhere in the world for 25 years. As the business was unique and customers few, the restriction was not too wide nor contrary to the public interest.

Joint agreements between manufacturers or traders

5–66 These agreements, although not unknown in common law, are mainly regulated by statute and delegated legislation to protect the interests of the public.

The current law is found in the Competition Act 1998 and Arts 81 and 82 of the EC Treaty. Competition law is a subject in its own right and only a few basic comments can be included in this chapter. The 1998 Act introduced a requirement to interpret its provisions in the light of the competition law of the European Community. The Act covers, for example, agreements which fix buying or selling prices, limit production, markets or investment or which share markets or sources of supply. There is provision for exemption. The Act also set up the Competition Commission, taking the place of the former Monopolies and Mergers Commission.

Solus agreements

5–67 These are agreements between the supplier of goods and the distributor or retailer under which the retailer sells only one brand of goods, in return for which he receives special discounts or privileges. Such *solus*[33] agreements are quite common but, if challenged, must again meet the reasonableness test. The relative bargaining position of the parties might also be taken into account.[34]

EXCLUSION CLAUSES IN CONTRACTS

5–68 At an early stage in the Chapter, it was emphasised that, before anyone can claim that a contract exists, there must be consensus. Sometimes, one of the two parties may have greater bargaining power than the other and will try to bring conditions into the contract of which the other party has no knowledge or does not quite understand or realise their significance. The party with the greater bargaining power might attempt to incorporate an exclusion (of liability) or an exemption in his own favour by printing appropriate wording[35] on a "ticket", notice or display.

---

[31] *Mulvein v Murray*, 1908 S.C. 528.
[32] [1894] A.C. 535; contrast *Dumbarton Steamboat Co. Ltd v MacFarlane* (1899) 1 F. 993.
[33] Alone, only.
[34] *Petrofina (GB) v Martin* [1966] Ch. 146; *Esso Petroleum Co. Ltd v Harpers Garages (Stourport) Ltd* [1968] A.C. 269.
[35] *e.g.* "PERSONS ENTER THESE PREMISES AT THEIR OWN RISK".

When a ticket is issued, it can be either a receipt for money paid or a voucher to claim property or services. The ticket will have conditions printed on it, or it may refer to conditions published elsewhere. Sometimes there will be no ticket, but a notice may be displayed on business premises, intended as a written clause in an otherwise unwritten contract. Sometimes, the clause will appear both on a ticket and on a notice.

Key Concepts

The purpose of the clause is to **exclude or limit liability**, particularly for negligence. Whether or not such a clause is effective depends partly on the nature of the ticket or notice and partly as to whether the other party's attention has been properly drawn to it.

Attempts to impose post-formation conditions

New conditions cannot be added after a contract has been formed, unless with the consent of both parties. In *Olley v Marlborough Court Ltd*,[36] Mr and Mrs O made a hotel booking. On the wall of their room was a notice "*THE PROPRIETORS WILL NOT HOLD THEMSELVES RESPONSIBLE FOR ARTICLES LOST AND STOLEN*". They locked the room and gave the key to the receptionist. A thief obtained the key and stole goods. The hotel company attempted unsuccessfully to rely on the notice on the wall. The condition was not known to Mr and Mrs O until after the contract had been formed and was not part of it. **5–69**

The nature of the ticket

For a condition printed on a ticket to be an integral part of, the contract, the ticket itself must be *more* than just a voucher or receipt. Usually a ticket is an integral part of contracts of carriage (*e.g.* a train journey) or deposit (*e.g.* left luggage) and the courts would expect a reasonable person to be aware that such contracts are normally subject to published conditions. **5–70**

If the ticket is not an integral part of the contract and is merely a receipt or voucher, conditions printed on it will not generally be binding.[37]

Sometimes, even though no notice is given of a specific exclusion, a person may still be bound by it because he is aware of it due to previous dealings between the parties. However, before allowing this, the courts would have to be convinced that the previous dealings had been consistent.[38]

Was attention adequately drawn to the condition?

Even if the ticket is integral to the contract, the existence of conditions must still be adequately brought to the attention of the customer. If the conditions are not adequately drawn to his attention, the contract itself is still valid but the conditions on the ticket are not binding.[39] **5–71**

[36] [1949] 1 K.B. 532; *Thornton v Shoe Lane Parking Ltd* [1971] 2 Q.B. 163.

[37] *Chapelton v Barry UDC* [1940] 1 K.B. 532; *Taylor v Glasgow Corporation*, 1952 S.C. 440.

[38] *McCutcheon v David MacBrayne Ltd*, 1964 S.C. (H.L.) 28.

[39] *Henderson v Stevenson* (1875) 2 R. (H.L.) 71. There was a similar result in *Williamson v North of Scotland Navigation Co.*, 1916 S.C. 554 where conditions had been printed on the front of a steamer ticket but in the smallest typeface known. Contrast *Hood v Anchor Line*, 1918 S.C. (H.L.) 143.

Exclusions at arm's length

5–72 If parties who are in business elect to sign contracts at arm's length, they will be bound by them, subject to "standard form" contracts requiring to be fair and reasonable under the Unfair Contract Terms Act 1977, considered further below. In *Photo Production Ltd v Securicor Transport Ltd*,[40] S agreed to provide security inspection at a factory. One of their employees criminally started a fire in the factory, resulting in a loss of £615,000. The factory owners sued for damages. S successfully relied on a clause in its standard conditions which excluded liability in most situations including acts such as that of its employee.

Signing a ticket

5–73 It would seem that if a person actually signs a ticket, he is presumed to have read and accepted the conditions, unless misrepresentation took place.[41]

Key Concepts

Summary of exclusions through tickets

(1) An exclusion clause cannot usually be brought in through the use of a ticket if it is only a voucher or receipt. In contracts of carriage or deposit, parties normally understand that the contract will be subject to certain published conditions.

(2) If it is more than a mere voucher or receipt and the person knew that there were conditions but did not read them, he will still be bound by them if they are of the type expected in that kind of contract, subject to the Unfair Contract Terms Act 1977 ("UCTA").

(3) If the person has actually read the conditions, he will be bound by them (subject to UCTA).

(4) If he did not know of the conditions, he will only be bound by them (subject to UCTA) if they have been properly brought to his attention. In the light of decided cases, that seems to mean that either the conditions must be clearly printed on the front of the ticket or, if the actual conditions are to be found somewhere else, there must be a clear reference on the front of the ticket that this is the case.

UNFAIR CONTRACT TERMS ACT 1977

5–74 The title of this Act is misleading as it does not cover all unfair contract terms—only exclusion clauses. Under UCTA, certain exclusion clauses are declared void whereas others are subject to a test of being "fair and reasonable". UCTA only applies to attempts to exclude liability by businesses. In this situation, "business" includes companies, partnerships, sole traders, professionals, local authorities and government departments. It does *not* include individuals who act in a personal or private capacity.

Part I of UCTA applies to England and Wales, Part II to Scotland and Part III to all of the UK. The Act applies to the following types of contracts:

---

[40] [1980] A.C. 827; *Ailsa Craig Fishing Co. v Malvern Fishing Co.,* 1982 S.C. (H.L.) 14.

[41] *Curtis v Chemical Cleaning & Dyeing Co. Ltd* [1951] 1 All E.R. 631.

- **Contracts in the course of a business**:
  - *Consumer contracts*: where one of the parties deals in the course of a business and the other does not and the goods are of a type normally bought by a consumer.
  - *Standard form contracts*: the contract is only offered, or accepted, on the basis of the party's "standard" conditions. These, in fact, are often consumer contracts but a contract between two businesses can be brought into the provisions of the Act where it is "standard form" (see further below).
- **Contracts for the sale of goods**: This includes goods bought under credit or hire purchase agreements.
- **Contracts for the hire of goods**: This would include moveable items such as a car or television set, but not a lease of heritable property.
- **Contracts of employment**: This also includes contracts of apprenticeship.
- **Contracts for services**: This covers a wide area including services provided by a law agent, accountant, builder, dry-cleaner, car-park owner, bus company, left luggage.
- **Contracts allowing entry to someone's property**: Included are items such as a ticket for admission to a sports ground, cinema, safari park, museum, swimming pool. Also included, are parties who are given permission to enter property, *e.g.* to carry out repairs.

Certain contracts are, however, excluded from the Act. These include insurance and contracts for the transfer of an interest in land. A condition in a contract to which UCTA applies is void if it relates to exclusion of liability for death or personal injury. The condition is of no effect in other cases unless it was fair and reasonable when the contract was made. The contract itself is not voided; only the purported exclusion.

The burden of proving that a term is fair and reasonable lies with the party who is seeking to rely on it, *i.e.* that party will always be a business.

Unfair Terms in Consumer Contracts Regulations 1999

The above Regulations[42] came into effect on October 1, 1999 and were subsequently amended.[43] A **5–75**
consumer (a natural person acting outside his trade, business or profession) can avoid a term in a contract for goods or services by showing that it is unfair, contrary to good faith or causes imbalance to his detriment. This goes further than UCTA which only deals with exclusions of liability.

The basic premise that parties are free to contract at arm's length is not affected. Thus if parties individually negotiate the selling price of a particular item at arm's length, the Regulations do not apply. However, they *do* apply to standard term contracts and to contracts of insurance.

The "battle of forms"

It is common for businesses when sending an order, *i.e.* an offer, to do so subject to their own **5–76**
standard pre-printed conditions. A problem could arise when the second party accepts the offer on its own standard form acceptance—but the terms of offer and acceptance do not meet and may even contradict. Sometimes each set of conditions may say that, in the event of a dispute, its terms will rule.

If a dispute arises, there can be major problems, not least whether or not a contract even exists. Usually the courts decide there *is* basic consensus, although that may not always be entirely logical. Frequently, the terms of the contract will be those of the party who "fired the last shot".[44]

---

[42] SI 1999/2083.

[43] SI 2001/1186.

[44] *Butler Machine Tool Co. v Ex-Cell-O Corporation* [1979] 1 All E.R. 965; followed in *Uniroyal Ltd v Miller & Co. Ltd*, 1985 S.L.T. 101.

REMEDIES FOR BREACH OF CONTRACT

5–77 At this stage, it is assumed that a contract has been validly formed and is free from vitiating factors. Fortunately, the majority of contracts are performed uneventfully but there will always be some defaulters. When one of the parties to a contract fails to carry out his side of the obligation, he will be considered in breach of contract, unless the reasons for his non-performance are recognised as valid in law, *e.g.* supervening impossibility, further considered later in the Chapter.

Breach can arise, in practice, in three different ways: total non-performance, partial performance and defective performance.

Specific implement and interdict

5–78 An innocent party can ask the court for a decree to make the party in breach fulfil the terms of his obligation under the contract. If the action is in the positive, *i.e.* to make the party in breach do something, the court may award a decree *ad factum praestandum*.[45]

If the action is in the negative, *i.e.* to stop the party in breach from doing something he agreed not to do, the court may award a decree of interdict. If an employer wanted to prevent a former employee from working for a competitor, in breach of a restrictive covenant, he could use such a remedy as in *Bluebell Apparel v Dickinson*[46] cited earlier in the Chapter.

Interdict can never be used to enforce a positive obligation. In *Church Commissioners for England v Abbey National plc*,[47] AN intended closing a branch office. C, the landlords, considered this to be in breach of the lease. However, they were unable to make AN keep the branch open by means of the remedy of interdict. It is, however, possible to specifically implement a positive obligation in a lease to "keep open" certain premises, provided it is not impossible nor unreasonable.[48]

If the party in breach wilfully fails to obey the decree, whether it be positive or negative, he puts himself in contempt of court, the result of which could be a fine or even imprisonment. In practice, the court will not lightly taking these draconian steps.

Under Scots law, specific implement is, in theory, the primary remedy to which an innocent party is entitled in the case of breach of contract. In practice, it is not particularly common. In addition, there are a number of situations where the courts do not consider specific implement as an equitable or suitable remedy and will not grant a decree. The following are the main areas where a court will *not* grant a decree *ad factum praestandum*.

(1) Where the obligation is to *pay a sum of money*. A debtor in default could find himself in contempt of court and thus liable to imprisonment for non-payment. As a matter of public policy, debtors are not normally sent to prison. In Scotland, a creditor can enforce payment by simpler processes, such as action for payment and diligence.

(2) Where a contract involves *personal relationships*, *e.g.* employment or partnership. If A and B are business partners and B does not wish the partnership to continue, common sense indicates that there is nothing to be gained by A taking B to court and trying to force the issue.[49]

(3) Where the subject-matter of the contract has *no special significance in itself*, such as 100 bags of flour. The remedy for the innocent party would be to rescind[50] the contract, obtain the goods elsewhere and claim damages. An action *ad factum praestandum* could be

---

45 For the performance of an act.

46 1980 S.L.T. 157.

47 1994 S.L.T. 959.

48 *Retail Parks Investments Ltd v The Royal Bank of Scotland plc (No.2)*, 1996 S.L.T. 669; followed in *Highland and Universal Properties Ltd v Safeway Properties Ltd*, 2000 S.L.T. 414.

49 *Skerret v Oliver* (1896) 23 R. 468 (a minister of a Presbyterian church) and *Page One Records Ltd v Britton (t/a The Troggs)* [1967] 3 All E.R. 822 (the manager of a pop group). Under employment legislation, an employee who has been unfairly dismissed may be awarded reinstatement by an industrial tribunal.

50 See further below.

appropriate if the contract concerned a specific item such as a unique painting, as that is said to have a *pretium affectionis*.[51]

(4) Where the contract is *illegal or impossible* to perform or where the court could not enforce the decree, *e.g.* if the party in breach is furth of Scotland.

(5) Where, in the opinion of the court, it would be *unjust* to grant such a remedy.

At common law, an interdict can be obtained quite speedily on an interim basis. Although there is no such common law equivalent in the case of specific implement, there are appropriate statutory provisions under the Court of Session Act 1988.[52] In either case, the interim award is at the discretion of the court and without prejudice to its decision at a subsequent hearing.

Rescission

The innocent party may, in certain circumstances, bring the contract to an end without going near a court of law. Clearly, if such a remedy was too widely available, it would favour "hotheads" who might call off a contract for the most trivial of reasons. **5–79**

Key Concepts

For **rescission** to be appropriate, the breach must be material and go to the root of the contract. An inappropriate rescission counts as a repudiation and can give rise to a claim in damages.

Wade v Waldon

1909 S.C. 571

Wade, a comedian, better known by his stage name "George Robey", contracted with Waldon to appear in one year's time at a Glasgow theatre. A clause in the contract provided that Wade was to give 14 days' notice before the performance and also to supply publicity material. He failed to do either. Waldon called off the entire contract, although Wade was more than willing to appear at the theatre as agreed. Wade *was* in breach of contract, but it was *not* a material breach and could not justify rescission on Waldon's part. The essence of the contract was Wade's appearing on stage, which he had always been willing to do. Waldon was thus liable in damages, as he had repudiated the contract.

Rescission means the justifiable cancellation of a contract. By contrast, repudiation is the unilateral act of a party to a contract whereby he indicates, expressly or by implication, that he does not intend to perform his part of the obligation. It would then be open to the innocent party to rescind the contract in view of the material breach, and claim damages. Total non-performance would always be material. If the innocent party still wishes the party in breach to perform, obviously he will not rescind[53] as long as he believes that there is life in the contract.

In any contract, both parties are bound to perform their respective obligations. The implication is that one party cannot insist on performance by the other if he himself is not willing to carry out his part of the agreement. An employee is entitled to pay for duties performed but if he chooses to take time off, without permission, he cannot expect to be paid for it.[54] Material breach also

[51] Literally, "price of affection" meaning that it has value in itself.

[52] ss.46 and 47.

[53] The verb of rescission is "rescind". Sometimes, particularly in the area of contracts to buy and sell heritable property, the verb used is "resile"; the two verbs appear to mean the same thing.

[54] *Graham v United Turkey Red Co.*, 1922 S.C. 533 (an agent in material breach of his contract was not entitled to commission).

occurred when a club manager refused to carry out certain tasks in the honest, but mistaken, belief that they were not part of his duties.[55]

If the innocent party rescinds, he cannot then enforce performance of any part of the contract. He can only claim damages. In *Lloyds Bank plc v Bamberger,*[56] the innocent party rescinded and then sought certain interest payments, as specified in the contract. This was not possible since the innocent party had rescinded the entire contract and could not now seek to invoke parts of it. This decision is in line with the established principle of "approbate and reprobate", which means that a party cannot take advantage of one part of a written document and reject the remainder. However, provisions can be built in to a contract which keep certain parts of it alive, even if the material parts are rescinded.

One of the problems is knowing when a breach of contract is material. Parties may agree between themselves at the outset which breaches would count as material. In some cases it will be clearly implied. Common sense dictates that a wedding dress would be required in time for a wedding. In such a case, it is said that *time is of the essence* of the contract.

Usually time is not of the essence unless expressly stated or circumstances, such as the involvement of perishable goods, make it clearly implied. In contracts for the sale of heritable property, payment of the purchase price on the date of entry is not of the essence.[57]

Parties are not expected to wait for ever for contracts to be performed. The normal practice is to issue a "warning" to the other side and, frequently, impose a reasonable time limit for performance.

Particular problems can arise where the breach is one of several stipulations as in *Wade v Waldon* (above) or involves defective performance. Just how defective does performance have to be to count as material breach? At common law, that is not always easy to answer.[58]

Retention

5–80 Retention is the withholding of payment of a money debt until such time as the other party performs his obligation in full, *e.g.* a tenant may wish to withhold his payment of rent until the landlord carries out his legal duty to make the house habitable. There are restrictions as to when this measure can be used since, as a general rule, a debtor cannot refuse to pay a debt simply because he has another claim against the creditor. Retention, like lien (below), is not so much a remedy as a defensive measure. Retention can only be used in the following situations:

(1) Where both claims arise under the *same* contract (as in the example of landlord and tenant given above).
(2) Where "compensation" can be pleaded, *i.e.* both debts must be liquid[59] and the parties are debtor and creditor in the same capacity at the same time. To put this another way, there has to be *concursus debiti et crediti.*[60]
(3) Where the creditor in a money obligation is bankrupt.

---

55 *Blyth v Scottish Liberal Club*, 1983 S.L.T. 260.
56 1994 S.L.T. 424.
57 *Rodger (Builders) Ltd v Fawdry*, 1950 S.C. 483. It is common for the seller to qualify his acceptance by stating that time is of the essence as regards payment in full at the date of entry.
58 Sometimes a statute itself may give guidance, such as the Sale of Goods Act 1979, s.15B.
59 Actually due and of an ascertained amount.
60 Concurrence of debt and credit; *Stuart v Stuart* (1869) 7 M. 366.

Lien

Key Concepts 5–81

Lien (pronounced "lean") is the withholding of property which would normally be delivered to the other party. There are two kinds of lien, general and special. The special lien is by far the more common.

A special lien allows a person who has done work on the moveable property of another, or has not been paid the purchase price of goods, to retain possession of that property until he has received the payment due. So, if X takes his car to be repaired and is unable to pay the bill, the garage may retain his car until payment is made. This is exercising a right of lien against these "special" or specific goods. Two other points should be noted:

(1) Lien is a possessory right. The car in the above example, does not become the property of the garage, it is merely in the garage's possession. Furthermore, if the garage proprietor does let X take his car away without paying the bill, he cannot later re-exercise the lien.[61]
(2) A special lien can only be exercised against the goods which are specific or special to the contract.

Much less common is the general lien which allows the holder of the article to retain it until a general balance due by the owner of the goods is satisfied. Certain trades and professions have the right in law to do this. The courts do not favour extending these categories.

A law agent may retain title deeds and share certificates in his possession until a client had paid his professional account. In *Paul v Meikle*,[62] Mrs D bequeathed property to her son. The will had been drawn up by M, her solicitor, who was also her creditor in respect of unpaid professional fees extending over many years. M was entitled to retain the will until his fees were paid.[63] When a document or title deed subject to a lien is the property of sequestrated debtor, the permanent trustee in the sequestration can require delivery of the document in question.[64]

In practice, it is relatively simple to defeat a lien over a document where a duplicate or certified copy can be obtained. An accountant does not enjoy a right of general lien, although it is well established that he has right of special lien.[65] A banker has a general lien on bills of exchange, cheques and promissory notes belonging to a customer provided these have come into his possession in the course of banking transactions. This general lien does not extend to articles left with the bank for safe keeping. An innkeeper has a general lien over a guest's luggage, pending payment of the hotel bill.

Although it is only a defensive measure, lien is common in practice and highly persuasive in making payment forthcoming. It is useful where the innocent party does not wish to rescind or where it would be pointless to do so because he has, in fact, performed his part of the contract.

Action for payment

The commonest breach of contract is non-payment of money. A short delay in payment is not necessarily material breach. There is sometimes a fine line between delay in payment and actual non-payment. Thus rescission must not be exercised too hastily. In any event, it would normally be inept to rescind a contract unless *restitutio in integrum* is possible. Where the contract price is 5–82

[61] *Hostess Mobile Catering v Archibald Scott Ltd*, 1981 S.L.T. (Notes) 125.
[62] (1868) 7 M. 235.
[63] A solicitor's right of lien is well established, being traced back to the old case of *Ranking of Hamilton of Provenhall's Creditors* (1781) Mor. 6253.
[64] Bankruptcy (Scotland) Act 1985, s.38(4).
[65] *Meikle & Wilson v Pollard* (1880) 8 R. 69.

unpaid but goods have been delivered or services performed, the creditor can recover payment by means of a court action.

The Late Payment of Commercial Debts (Interest) Act 1998 has given rights to businesses to charge interest on late payment of money debts due by other businesses or by bodies in the public sector. Whilst parties can contract out of these provisions, they can only do so *after* the creation of the debt.

DAMAGES

5–83 "It is impossible to say that a contract can be broken, even in respect of time, without the party being entitled to claim damages—at the lowest, nominal damages."[66]

Under Scots law, wherever there is an established breach of contract, however small and no matter what other remedies or measures have been used by the pursuer, a claim for damages is always open.

Key Concepts

The purpose of damages is simple: it is to compensate the innocent party for his loss and to place him in the position he would have been in had the contract been fully performed, in so far as money alone is capable of doing this. This means that the actual breach of contract must have caused some loss.

Irving v Burns

1915 S.C. 260

B, secretary of a company, engaged Irving to carry out plumber work, although B had no authority to do so. Irving performed his part of the contract but received no payment since the company was now insolvent. Irving was unsuccessful in an action for damages against B. Even if the latter had been given authority to form the contract, Irving would have received nothing, due to the insolvency. He was thus no worse off as a result of B's conduct.

Even if no actual loss is sustained, the court may award nominal damages to compensate for trouble and inconvenience. In *Webster* (above), C agreed to supply pipes for a mill. There was a delay of three months in supply. W, the mill owners, claimed £300 damages for the loss sustained by the delay but were unable to prove that they had suffered any financial loss. They were able to prove that they had been put to considerable trouble and inconvenience. They were awarded nominal damages of £10.

In more recent times, the courts have shown an increasing willingness to award more realistic damages in respect of the irritation and disappointment which can be caused by breach of contract. Realistic amounts were awarded in *Jarvis v Swan Tours*,[67] where there was a disastrous failure by a tour company to match the expectations arising from its brochure.

There are three important points to note about damages:

---

[66] These are the often quoted words of Lord President Inglis in *Webster & Co. v Cramond Iron Co.* (1875) 2 R. 752.

[67] [1973] 1 All E.R. 71. See also *Diesen v Samson*, 1971 S.L.T. (Sh. Ct) 49.

Key Concepts

1. Damages are never to be considered as a penalty or civil punishment of the party in breach. There is no place for so-called "punitive" damages in Scots law. The purpose of damages, as stated above, is to compensate the innocent party for loss incurred.

2. The innocent party is expected to take reasonable steps to minimise his loss, *i.e.* to keep it as low as possible, otherwise his claim for damages could be restricted to the amount he could have claimed if he had taken such steps.

Thus, if a party is not supplied with goods, but then delays in buying in suitable goods elsewhere until the price has risen, his claim for damages will be restricted.[68]

However, the innocent party is only expected to take *reasonable* steps to minimise his loss.[69]

Key Concepts

3. The *quantum*[70] of damages is worked out on the principle that only loss which is a direct and foreseeable result of the breach of contract can be claimed.

Damages in the latter case are referred to as "general" or "ordinary" damages. If there are special or "knock-on" circumstances which lead to an unusual or special loss, the party in breach is not held liable, *i.e.* to pay special damages, unless he knew of the special circumstances *at the time the contract was formed*. The basic effect is that a party will not normally bc liablc for *all* the consequences of his breach. This basic principle is often referred to as the "rule in *Hadley v Baxendale*".

Hadley v Baxendale

(1854) 9 Ex. 341

H's flour mill was at a standstill because the cast-iron crankshaft from a steam engine had fractured. The broken crankshaft had to be sent from Gloucester to a foundry at Greenwich, as a pattern for a replacement. B, a carrier, was given the task of transporting it. He was told it was a crankshaft for a mill but he was not made aware that, on account of the broken crankshaft, the mill was at a standstill. B was negligent and caused a delay in delivering the new crankshaft. He was in breach of contract, because he had undertaken to complete his work within two days. However, H was not entitled to claim special damages for the loss of profits when the mill was at a standstill because these special circumstances had not been properly explained to B when the contract was formed. Thus, this special loss of profit was beyond what the carrier could have been expected to foresee.

In *Victoria Laundry v Newman Industries*,[71] N agreed to supply a boiler to V, who required it (a) to expand their business and (b) to permit them to take up a large government contract. The boiler was delivered late, by which time the government contract had been lost. As N had no way of knowing about the government contract when they agreed to supply the boiler, they were only liable for ordinary or general damages for the foreseeable loss of business and not for any special damages in respect of the lost contract.[72]

---

68 *Ireland v Merryton Coal Co.* (1894) 21 R. 989.
69 *Gunther v Lauritzen* (1894) 1 S.L.T. 435.
70 How much.
71 [1949] 2 K.B. 528.
72 There was a similar result in *"Den of Ogil" Co. Ltd v Caledonian Railway Co.* (1902) 5 F. 99.

By contrast, in *Macdonald v Highland Railway Co.*,[73] confectionery for a celebration on the Isle of Skye was sent by rail from Inverness via Dingwall. The cartons were clearly marked "PERISHABLE". Due to the company's negligence, the cartons were held up at Dingwall. When they reached Skye, the celebration was past and the confectionery had perished. The railway company were liable for all the loss, because the special circumstances, *i.e.* that the goods were perishable, had been clearly brought to their notice at the time the contract was formed.

More recently, in *Balfour Beatty Construction (Scotland) Ltd v Scottish Power plc*,[74] B were constructing an aqueduct. This required a long "continuous pour" of concrete. Work on the first stage was almost complete when the electricity supply failed. As a result, the first stage had to be entirely demolished. B were unsuccessful in a claim for special damages of some quarter of a million pounds. It would have required a high degree of technical knowledge of the construction industry on the part of S for them to have foreseen the results of an interruption of the electricity supply.

LIQUIDATE DAMAGES

5–84 In the cases considered so far, the courts have been required to assess the *quantum* of damages to be paid. Parties can, however, agree at the outset how much will be paid as damages in the event of a breach taking place. This form of damages is called liquidate damages and is perfectly legitimate and enforceable *provided* it is a genuine pre-estimate of loss. Confusingly, such a provision in a contract is often called a "penalty clause". This is an unsatisfactory title since, as demonstrated, damages for breach of contract are intended to be compensatory, not penal.

Key Concepts

The name given to the clause is unimportant. What matters is its **actual effect**. Where it is clear that the clause is intended to punish rather than to compensate, it is invalid and unenforceable and the court would assess damages using the usual criteria.

Where there is a genuine liquidate damages clause, whatever it may actually be called, the amount recoverable by the innocent party is restricted to that amount even if the actual loss is larger or smaller than the sum specified.

In distinguishing between penalty clauses and liquidate damages clauses, the courts have frequently had regard to the principles set out by Lord Dunedin,[75] summarised as follows:

(a) the use of the words "penalty" or "liquidate damages" is not conclusive in itself;
(b) a penalty punishes; liquidate damages is a genuine pre-estimate of loss;
(c) whether a sum is a penalty or liquidate damages is a question judged at the time of the formation of the contract, not at the time of the alleged breach;
(d) if a sum is clearly extravagant, it will be counted as penal and thus unenforceable;
(e) if the same single lump sum is payable on the occurrence of several different situations, it will be presumed to be penal.

In *Lord Elphinstone v Monkland Iron & Coal Co.*,[76] tenants in a mineral lease had undertaken to level and soil-over ground by a certain date under a "*penalty of £100 per imperial acre for all ground not so restored.*" The sum was liquidate damages, not a penalty as it was a genuine

---

[73] (1873) 11 M. 614.
[74] 1994 S.L.T. 807.
[75] *Dunlop Pneumatic Tyre Co. v New Garage and Motor Co.* [1915] A.C. 79.
[76] (1886) 13 R. (H.L.) 98. See also *Cameron-Head v Cameron & Co.*, 1919 S.C. 627.

pre-estimate of loss. By contrast, in *Dingwall v Burnett*[77] a lease of a hotel provided for a "*penalty of £50*" to be paid in the event of any breach of the lease provisions. The tenant totally non-performed but maintained that he was only liable to pay the £50 "penalty". The court found that the £50 was a penalty and thus unenforceable. This left the way was open for the landlord to claim a higher amount according to the normal rules for assessing the *quantum* of damages.

Finally, and very rarely, there could be circumstances in which it is impossible to give a genuine pre-estimate of loss. If this is so, any sum agreed on by the parties will be accepted as liquidate damages, even if in normal circumstances it would appear penal.[78]

It has long been recognised that the law on penalty clauses is in need of modernising. The Scottish Law Commission (Report No.171) has recommended that agreed damages clauses should be enforceable unless manifestly excessive.

ANTICIPATORY BREACH

It might seem strange for a party to a contract to claim a remedy for breach until a breach has actually occurred. However, it is possible that one of the parties could indicate in advance of performance, by his words or actions, that he does not intend to fulfil his obligations. This is known as anticipatory breach. **5–85**

Suppose a performer makes a contract in January to appear at a concert in July. In April, he states that he will not perform; in other words, come July, he will be in breach of contract. The promoter would have a choice. He could (1) treat this as a repudiation of the contract by the singer, rescind on the grounds of material breach, and claim damages; or (2) he could wait until the time of performance and see what happens, leaving the contract alive.

Key Concepts

For an **anticipatory breach** to take place, the refusal to give performance must be definite. If one party merely expresses doubts about ability to perform, that is not anticipatory breach.

White & Carter (Councils) Ltd v McGregor

1962 S.C. (H.L.) 1

W supplied street litter bins to local authorities on condition that W could sell advertising space on the bins. One of W's representatives called at M's garage and agreed a new advertising contract for three years. Later in the day, M telephoned W to cancel the contract. W chose to ignore this purported cancellation. They duly prepared the advertisements and displayed them for the three year period. W were held to have been entitled to proceed with the contract and to sue for the contract price, even although M had already intimated that he would not perform his side of the obligation.

The above case is not without its critics and, although a House of Lords appeal on a Scottish case, the verdict was by a 3:2 majority. It has been pointed out[79] that there is a paradox in the decision since the pursuers were able to overcome the normal principle of minimisation of loss as they were suing for a money debt and not for damages.

---

[77] 1912 S.C. 1097.
[78] *Clydebank Engineering and Shipbuilding Co. v Castaneda* (1914) 7 F. (H.L.) 77.
[79] Woolman and Lake, *Contract* (3rd ed.), p.147.

The English courts have shown a marked reluctance to follow this decision. In *Clea Shipping Co. v Bulk Oil International (The Alaskan Trader)*,[80] it was held that the innocent party's keeping a ship at anchor off the Piraeus for seven months after an anticipatory breach, was wholly unreasonable.[81]

TERMINATION OF CONTRACT

5–86 **Key Concepts**

The parties to a contract have reciprocal rights and duties, *i.e.* they are both debtor and creditor to one another. A "debt" is not only an obligation to pay money; it can equally be a duty to perform.

If X agrees to sell goods to Y, we get the following picture. X is Y's debtor, in so far as X is due to deliver goods to Y. X is also Y's creditor, in so far as X is entitled to be paid by Y. Equally, Y is X's debtor, as he is due to pay for the goods, but Y is also X's creditor because he is entitled to have the goods delivered.

When these reciprocal arrangements are satisfied in full, the contract is terminated by performance. Strictly speaking, a void contract cannot be ended, because it never existed. Nevertheless, a court may have to declare that the contract is void and make judgement as to the respective rights of parties. A voidable contract continues to run unless it is set aside. Termination by rescission has been considered above.

However, there are other ways in which a contract can be ended and these have a particular significance, in so far as none of them gives rise to damages. These ways are now considered.

Performance

5–87 This is the most common way of ending a contract. Partial performance does not count as performance but there is a legal maxim *de minimis not curat lex*[82] which means that very minor discrepancies are not suitable matters for litigation nor valid grounds for rescission. Frequently the missing element of performance is payment. Work is done, or goods are delivered, but payment is not forthcoming.

Payment should be made in the proper manner, usually at the creditor's place of business or his residence. A creditor can insist (unless agreed to the contrary) on being paid in legal tender, which under the Coinage Act 1971 (as amended) is:

- £1 or £2 coins up to any amount;
- 20p and/or 50p coins up to a maximum of £10;
- 10p and/or 5p coins up to a maximum of £5; and
- bronze up to a maximum of 20p.

In Scotland, no Bank of England notes are legal tender. Scottish clearing banks have the historic right to issue their own bank notes but they are not legal tender, even in Scotland. Certain "special issue" coins, such as £5 crowns, are given the status of legal tender.

Payment by credit, charge or "switch" debit card is not legal tender, though widely accepted, subject to conditions or limits. Payment by cheque is only conditional payment of a debt. If the cheque is accepted, the money debt is extinguished, but it is revived if the cheque is dishonoured.[83]

---

[80] [1984] 1 All E.R. 129.

[81] In the subsequent Scottish case of *Salaried Staff London Loan Co. Ltd v Swears & Wells*, 1985 S.C. 189, the *White & Carter* interpretation was followed.

[82] The law does not concern itself with trifles.

[83] This is known as a resolutive condition.

In *Charge Card Services*,[84] it was held that payment by a credit or charge card counts as absolute and not conditional payment.

Acceptilation

A debtor may have non-performed or part performed, or even defectively performed his part of the obligation, yet the creditor is prepared to accept this as though it was full performance. Giving discount is a common form of acceptilation. **5–88**

Novation

A creditor and debtor may expressly agree that the debtor will substitute a new obligation for the one originally undertaken, *e.g.* that apples will be supplied instead of pears. It is important that the original obligation is expressly discharged, as there is a general presumption against novation. **5–89**

Delegation

Delegation is a form of novation. It involves the substitution of a new debtor, as distinct from a new obligation. It requires the express consent of the creditor and would be inappropriate in a contract involving *delectus personae.*[85] If someone has arranged for his portrait to be painted by a famous artist, he is unlikely to accept that "debt" being contracted out to a third party. There is a general rule that an agent has no implied authority to delegate the performance of his duties. This is summed up in the maxim *delegatus non potest delegare.*[86] There are some notable exceptions. It is well recognised that a solicitor may delegate the searching of public registers to a professional searcher. Similarly, an architect may delegate measurement of final plans to a surveyor.[87] **5–90**

Confusion

Confusion, occasionally known as "combination", operates where the same person in the same capacity becomes both creditor and debtor in an obligation. A person cannot be his own debtor. If he finds himself in such a position, the debt is normally extinguished. Examples are not common in practice. Suppose a tenant buys his landlord's right in the property which he occupies as tenant. The contract of lease ends. If, however, the tenant had bought the landlord's right as director of a property company, confusion would not operate. As a tenant, he would be a private individual but as a director he would be acting for the company, *i.e.* in a different capacity. **5–91**

Compensation

This can be traced back to the Compensation Act 1592. If one party is both debtor and creditor to the other party, he can offset one claim against the other, reducing or extinguishing the amount due. **5–92**

If John owes Jean £500 and Jean owes John £200, John need only pay Jean the net sum of £300. However, compensation can only operate if certain conditions are fulfilled:

---

84 [1988] 3 All E.R. 702.
85 Choice of person.
86 The one to whom delegation has been made cannot delegate.
87 *Black v Cornelius* (1879) 6 R. 581.

- Compensation must be pleaded in an action for recovery of the debt. It does not automatically reduce or extinguish the debt. Thus, in the above example, Jean would be entitled to sue John for £500. John would plead compensation of £200, so the court would grant decree for £300.
- Unless both debts arise out of the same contract, or one of the parties is bankrupt, the debts must both be liquid.
- There must be *concursus debiti et crediti.*[88] This concept has been explored in relation to retention.

Prescription

5–93 Not all rights last for ever, although some do, such as the right to recover stolen property. Many rights do come to an end after a certain period of time, *i.e.* they "prescribe". Most obligations under contract prescribe after five years (short negative prescription) and this includes the right to payment.[89]

It is essential that the period of time is unbroken. If there is interruption, the running of the period goes back to "zero" and starts again. An interruption can take place by a "relevant claim"[90] or a "relevant acknowledgement".[91]

Prescription is of ancient origin. The modern law is found in the Prescription and Limitation (Scotland) Act 1973 as amended.

Impossibility

5–94 A valid contract may be formed, but subsequent or supervening events, outwith the power of both parties, make it impossible to perform.

> **Key Concepts**
>
> The obligation must be **literally impossible to perform**, not merely inconvenient or more expensive. In addition, the impossibility must not be due to the fault of the non-performing party.

In *The Eugenia*,[92] it was known that part of a ship's voyage, namely the Suez Canal, was a war zone, but the charterer ordered her to proceed by that route. The ship was detained in the canal, but the charterer could not escape damages. It was he who had been instrumental in causing the supervening event. The court conceded that performance was now impossible, but damages were still awarded.

A common example of impossibility is *rei interitus*[93] where the subject-matter of the contract is destroyed. In *Taylor v Caldwell*,[94] a music hall had been hired for a concert. After the hire had been agreed, the hall was badly damaged by fire. This was not due to the fault of the owner. The contract was terminated, without damages.

---

[88] Concurrence of debt and credit.
[89] Certain other rights, *e.g.* relating to land, are subject to the long negative prescription of 20 years. Also, certain rights may be acquired by positive prescription but this is not relevant to termination of contract.
[90] Creditor raises a court action or refers the matter to arbitration.
[91] Debtor has shown signs of performing or has admitted in writing that the obligation still exists.
[92] [1964] 2 Q.B. 226.
[93] Destruction of a thing.
[94] (1863) 3 B. & S. 826.

In a contract for the sale of heritable property, the risk, as distinct from the ownership, passes to the buyer as soon as there is an agreement to buy. This rule applies even although the buyer has not taken entry, paid the price nor been given a legal title.[95]

Sometimes subjects are not literally destroyed but, to all intents and purposes, the effect is the same. This is known as "constructive" destruction, as in *London and Edinburgh Shipping Company v The Admiralty*,[96] where a ship had been very badly damaged but had not actually sunk.

It might be impossible for a contract to be performed due to the condition of one of the parties. An example would be breakdown of health, as in *Robinson v Davidson*.[97]

The fact that a contract has become more expensive or more difficult does not make it impossible to perform. In *Davis Contractors v Fareham Urban District Council*,[98] a builder had agreed to construct 78 houses within eight months for a fixed sum. Due to shortages of labour and material, bad weather and inflation, the builder found himself substantially out of pocket. However, as performance was not impossible, the contract was not terminated.[99]

If the impossibility is due to the substantial neglect or default of one of the parties, the possibility of damages would be open. However, the courts will not grant a decree *ad factum praestandum* where an obligation is impossible.

Illegality

The rule is simple. If a valid contract is formed but a subsequent change in the law, or political **5–95**
circumstances such as outbreak of war, make performance illegal, the contract is at an end.[1] Indeed, it may be a criminal offence to continue with performance. If a contract is illegal when formed, it is void *ab initio*[2] and does not require to be terminated, although the court may have to adjudicate on the relative positions of the parties.

Frustration

Frustration[3] can terminate a contract which is valid and could be performed, but subsequent events, **5–96**
outwith the control of either party, have made the result of performance materially different from what the parties originally had in mind.

The concept of frustration can be well illustrated by the two "coronation cases", which arose from the postponement of the coronation of Edward VII due to his illness. In *Krell v Henry*,[4] a contract was formed for the hire of rooms to overlook the procession. It was possible for the contract to be performed, *i.e.* the hiring of the room, but the outcome—looking at the London traffic instead of the procession—would have been so radically different as to frustrate the contract. By contrast, in *Herne Bay Steamboat v Hutton*,[5] there was a contract for the hire of a pleasure boat to watch the review of the fleet off Spithead by the King. Although the King was unable to attend, the fleet was present and it was possible to enjoy the outing; the contract was not frustrated.

In *Jackson v Union Marine Insurance*,[6] a contract of charterparty[7] provided for a ship to proceed from Liverpool to Newport and pick up a cargo of iron for San Francisco. On her way to

---

[95] *Sloans Dairies Ltd v Glasgow Corporation*, 1977 S.C. 223. The Scottish Law Commission has recommended the statutory reversal of the common law rule (Report No.127).

[96] 1920 S.C. 309; *Tay Salmon Fisheries v Speedie*, 1929 S.C. 593; *Mackeson v Boyd*, 1942 S.C. 56.

[97] (1871) L.R. 6 Exch. 269; *Condor v Barron Knights* [1966] 1 W.L.R. 87.

[98] [1956] A.C. 696.

[99] Most building contracts routinely allow for rises in costs due to materials, wages, or inflation.

[1] *Fraser & Co. Ltd v Denny, Mott & Dickson Ltd*, 1944 S.C. (H.L.) 35.

[2] From the beginning.

[3] From the Latin *frustra* (in vain).

[4] [1903] 2 K.B. 740.

[5] [1903] 2 K.B. 683.

[6] (1874) L.R. 10 C.P. 125.

Newport, the ship grounded on a sandbank. It took several months to recommission her. Meanwhile, the charterer had put his goods on another ship. The original charterparty was frustrated. It would have been possible for the original ship to proceed to San Francisco, but the outcome would have been very different, due to the long delay.

By contrast, it should be noted that frustration, like impossibility, does not terminate a contract merely because performance has become more expensive. Where a ship bound for Britain had to take the longer route round the Cape of Good Hope due to the sudden closure of the Suez Canal in 1956, the charterparty was not frustrated.[8]

Money back?

5–97 In the case of frustration, impossibility or illegality, it is possible that money may have been paid in advance. This falls to be paid back, not under the law of contract but under an action for repetition (repayment) known as the *condictio causa data causa non secuta*.[9] In *Cantiere San Rocco SA v Clyde Shipbuilding and Engineering Co.,*[10] a Scottish company had agreed to supply engines to an Austrian company, payment to be by instalments. One instalment had been paid, but no engines were supplied as the outbreak of the First World War made performance illegal. After the war, the Austrian company was able to recover the deposit.

---

[7] Hire of a ship.
[8] *Tsakiroglou & Co. Ltd v Noblee Thorl GmbH* [1962] A.C. 93.
[9] Action applicable when consideration has been given and consideration has not followed.
[10] 1923 S.C. (H.L.) 105.

Quick Quiz

Contract law

- What is the distinction between an offer and a willingness to negotiate?
- Explain "error of expression".
- Distinguish contracts void and voidable.
- Outline the circumstances in which essential error might void a contract.
- Distinguish innocent and fraudulent misrepresentation.
- Outline the provision of the Unfair Contract Terms Act 1977.
- Explain specific implement, rescission, retention and lien.
- Outline the "Rule in *Hadley v Baxendale*".
- Explain liquidate damages.
- Explain acceptilation, novation and delegation.
- Outline how a contract can be "frustrated".

Further Reading

The leading textbook is **William W. McBryde, *The Law of Contract in Scotland*** (2nd ed., 2001) which is scholarly, detailed and authoritative. It is not a book for beginners. At the opposite end of the scale is **Alasdair Gordon, *Contract Law*Basics** (2nd ed., 2003) which gives a foundation treatment and is useful for revision.

The two textbooks written for student consumption are **MacQueen and Thomson, *Contract Law in Scotland*** (2000) and **Woolman and Lake, *Contract*** (3rd ed., 2001).

Reference can also be made to the ***Stair Memorial Encyclopaedia***, particularly under the heading "Obligations" and to ***Gloag and Henderson's Law of Scotland*** (MacQueen and others ed., 11th ed., 2001).

A useful resource book is **John A.K. Huntley, *Contract Cases and Materials*** (2nd ed., 2003).

Occasionally, courts might still refer to ***Gloag on Contract*** (2nd ed., 1929) which is a monumental work of scholarship, although now dated.

Chapter 6

EMPLOYMENT

Professor Vic Craig[1]

THE CONTRACT OF EMPLOYMENT

Introduction

An understanding of employment law requires a general awareness of: **6–01**

(a) the basic legal principles of contract law and delict[2];
(b) statute law; and
(c) the common law;

and how (b) and (c) relate to each other. Although the relationship of employment is regulated by both statute and common law, the bulk of modern employment is statutory and is dealt with by Employment Tribunals.

[1] Lecturer in Law, Heriot Watt University.

[2] See Chapters 5 and 9.

Generally, the common law develops incrementally, while more radical policy changes in the law regulating the employment relationship are the result of Parliamentary intervention in the form of statutes or regulations made by government departments and approved by Parliament.

The effect of this hybrid or dual approach to employment law in the UK is to require at least an understanding of the principles of contract law and the legislative rules created by Parliament which have, over recent years, attempted to counter employer power by creating basic or minimum rights for employees. These rights are often referred to as "a floor of rights" in the expectation that enlightened employers will seek to offer more advantageous provisions or do so as a result of collective bargaining. Unlike in continental legal systems the collective agreement in the UK does not create rights and duties for employers and employees throughout an industry or sector of an industry. Collective agreements therefore do not have any binding or normative or standard-setting effect; in the UK such a role is played by statute.

However, like in many areas of industry and society, the law of the European Community plays an important part in shaping employment law rights. Some articles of the European Economic Treaty create directly enforceable rights—without the need for domestic legislation—for all citizens of the European Union. In the field of employment law, the most notable example is Art.141 which provides for equal pay for men and women.

Courts and Employment Tribunals

6–02 Another result of the hybrid system is that some employment law disputes are dealt with by the ordinary courts. For example, if an employee acts in breach of his contract by disclosing confidential information, his employer may raise an action in the ordinary court; or an employee may sue for his wrongful dismissal in the ordinary court. Generally, actions for breach of contract whether brought by the employer or the employee must be brought in the ordinary courts and not the specialist Employment Tribunals.[3]

On the other hand, statutory employment rights are capable of being enforced only through the Employment Tribunals which are given an exclusive jurisdiction.

In Scotland, where a case is complicated a party may receive legal aid to assist in presenting his case.[4] Complaints usually have to be presented to the Employment Tribunals Office within three months of the right being infringed, although this can be extended. The three-months' time limit is generally strictly enforced by the tribunal so that complaints can be dealt with while recollections are fresh, without the need for detailed documentation and to allow the system to operate as speedily as possible.

The following disputes may be heard only by Employment Tribunals:

- National Minimum Wage and access to records;
- maternity leave and the right to return to work;
- redundancy payments, sex, race and disability discrimination;
- time off and holiday pay;
- unfair dismissal;
- unlawful deductions from wages;
- equal pay (strictly such claims may also be raised in the ordinary courts but seldom are);
- appeals against health and safety improvement, prohibition and non-discrimination notices;
- failure to consult employee representatives on business transfers;
- action short of dismissal on grounds of union membership or non membership;
- exclusion from trade unions;
- refusal of employment on grounds of union membership;
- written particulars of terms of employment;
- written statement of reasons for dismissal; and
- payment by Secretary of State where employer is insolvent.

---

[3] *cf.* Employment Tribunals (Extension of Jurisdiction) (Scotland) Order 1994.

[4] Advice and Assistance (Advice by Way of Representation) (Scotland) Regulations 2001.

Identifying the contract of employment

For many years the most important distinction in employment law was the contract of employment (or service) at one end of the spectrum and the contract for services at the other. Essentially, the distinction is between the paid servant or employee on the one hand and the independent businessman/woman on the other hand. The distinction was important for a variety of reasons. Many of the important legal rights contained in the Employment Rights Act 1996—the main source of individual employment rights—are given only to those who have a contract of employment or a contract of apprenticeship. **6–03**

Only relatively recently have other types of contracts under which work is done become significant for employment law. Statutes, such as the Sex Discrimination Act 1975, the Race Relations Act 1976 and the Disability Discrimination Act 1995 confer protection on the ever increasing group of economically active persons known as "workers". This concept is wider than the concept of "employee". A worker means an individual who has entered into a contract of employment as well as "any other contract ... whereby the individual undertakes to perform personally any work or services for another party to the contract" who is not a client or customer of any profession or business carried on by the individual.[5]

However, there has recently been created the "agency worker" who provides his/her services through the medium of an agency to a third party. For example, a typist (A) may enter a contract with an employment agency (B), which when work becomes available will assign her to work for different businesses (C, D, E). Some statutes now expressly apply to employees, workers and agency workers.[6]

Control and other tests

Important rights like unfair dismissal, redundancy pay, maternity pay and leave, and notice of termination are restricted to those who have contracts of employment and it is still necessary to be able to identify that contract and to distinguish it from others. At one time, if the employer could tell the individual what to do and how to do it there would be a contract of employment. This was sometimes referred to as the "control test". **6–04**

Performing Rights Society v Mitchell and Booker
[1924] 1 K.B. 762

The Performing Rights Society, which protects copyright in music on behalf of its composers, sued Mitchell and Booker who owned a dance hall. The Society argued that the band which played in the dance hall had played music without receiving the composer's or the Society's permission. If the band were employed under contracts of employment then Mitchell and Booker would be vicariously liable for their breach of the composer's right. On the other hand, if they were independent musicians they themselves could be liable for breaching the composer's right in his music. In the event, having examined the degree to which the members of the band were under the control of the dance hall owners, the court came to the conclusion that they were indeed employed under contracts of employment by the owners of the dance hall. The dance hall owners could specify the type of music to be played at particular times so that it was fair to conclude they directed not just the ends but also the means of performing the contract.

However, the simple control test was not suitable for more developed and sophisticated types of employment. As a result the courts began to relax the control test so that it was sufficient if an

---
[5] Employment Rights Act 1996, s.230.
[6] *e.g.* the Working Time Regulations 1998.

employer could merely direct a person's individual skill.[7] Similar difficulties were experienced with the advent of professionally qualified staff.[8]

In other circumstances, the courts have adopted what has become known as the "organisation test" or "integration test" which allows the courts to look at whether the services or work done under the contract is done as an integral part of the employer's activities or organisation.[9]

Multiple and variable test

6–05 Recently, courts and tribunals have developed a more flexible test that can be used to deal with many sorts of employment—the "multiple and variable" test. It permits the court to take into account a multiplicity of different factors or criteria and give a particular factor or criterion emphasis or weight according to the circumstances before the court. The test may have the advantage of being universal and flexible but it does have the disadvantage of making it difficult to predict in advance of a court decision what is the type of relationship in marginal cases.

Key Concepts

The following may be regarded as **factors** which are **relevant** in determining whether or not there is a contract of employment:

- **Control** — The criterion of control is clearly still an important one although it is no longer the decisive criterion.
- **Provision of equipment** — The extent to which the person doing the work has to provide equipment at his or her own expense is significant. Generally, incurring a large capital outlay to acquire equipment to perform a task is more readily associated with a contract for services rather than a contract of employment.
- **Hire of helpers** — If the task cannot be done by the individual but requires the individual worker to hire additional helpers, that would also suggest it is not a contract of employment; a contract of employment is a contract under which there is personal performance by the workman/woman.
- **Financial risk** — If the contract involves a degree of financial risk and requires exercising responsibility for the management of the work of the contract it suggests it is not a contract of employment but more likely to be a contract for services.
- **Opportunity to profit** — An opportunity to profit from the sound management of the contract will more readily be associated with a contract for services.
- **Label or name of contract** — Frequently, the parties to a contract, in an attempt to remove doubt as to the type of contract, will give the contract a particular name However, the name the parties give a contract will not be conclusive because the existence of a contract of employment is a matter for a court or tribunal to decide and cannot be determined by the name or "label" the parties give to the contract.
- **Change of status** — On the other hand where the parties have genuinely intended to change the status of the contract, the courts will bear this in mind in determining the relationship between the two parties.

---

7 *Stagecraft v Minister of Pensions*, 1952 S.C. 288.
8 *Cassidy v Minister of National Insurance* [1951] 2 K.B. 343.
9 *Whittaker v Minister of Pensions* [1967] 1 Q.B. 156.

- **Income tax and national insurance** — Seldom will the fact that the employer does or does not deduct income tax or pay national insurance Contributions as if the person was an employee be of much significance. In many cases whether such income tax or national insurance contributions should be deducted at source is the issue which has raised the issue of the status of the individual. How income tax is paid is of little significance.
- **Mutuality of obligation** — Is the employer required to provide work when it is available and is the individual required to do it when it is provided.

The status of workers is frequently resolved by having regard to the issue of "mutuality of obligation".

O'Kelly v Trusthouse Forte plc

[1983] I.C.R. 728

O'Kelly and others worked as casual waiters on a regular basis for banquets contracted to Trusthouse Forte. In many cases the banquets would take place in the same venues and when banquets were to be held preference would be given to staff like O'Kelly and work allocated to them. However, there was no obligation on Trusthouse Forte to give work to staff like O'Kelly when the work was available nor was there any obligation on staff like O'Kelly to do the work when it was offered to them. For that reason the court concluded there was insufficient mutuality of obligation for there to be a contract of employment.

Nethermere (St Neots) Ltd v Taverna

[1984] I.C.R. 612

Nethermere St Neots manufactured trousers in a factory where they employed about 70 operatives who were undoubtedly employees and from whose wages they deducted income tax and national insurance Contributions. The tribunal also found that the appellants also made use of the services of a number of home-workers from whose remuneration such deductions were not made. Mrs Taverna started as a home-worker in January 1978; her work consisted of mainly putting pockets into trousers for which she used a machine provided by the appellants. She worked about five hours each day and in that time she put in about 100 pockets. Later her work changed and she put in artificial flaps into trousers. She then worked for about six-seven hours per day. She had no fixed hours of work. The garments were delivered to her daily and sometimes twice a day. In the year 1979-1980 she did not work for 12 weeks; in the year 1980-1981 she did not work for 9 weeks. The arrangement came to an end in July 1981. During the period she worked in 1981 she worked in every week of the year. She was paid weekly, according to the garments that she completed.

The court accepted that there was a regular course of dealing between parties for years under which the garments were supplied daily to the home-workers, worked on, collected and paid for. The mere fact that the home-workers could fix their own hours of work, take holidays and time off when they wished and vary how many garments they were willing to take on or sometimes to take none on a particular day, were factors for consideration in deciding whether or not there was a contract of service. The fact that the home-workers could decide how much work to do subject to making it worthwhile for the van driver's time in collecting it, could be read as an obligation on operatives like Mrs Taverna to take a reasonable amount of work. Conversely, there was an obligation on the company to provide a reasonable share of work for each home worker.

The importance of mutuality of obligation and personal performance has been emphasised by the House of Lords in the following decision.

Carmichael v National Power plc
[2000] I.R.L.R. 43

Mrs Carmichael and Mrs Leese were employed as station guides at the Blyth Power Stations. Their jobs involved conducting visitors on tours of the power stations and the advertisement to which they responded prior to appointment explained that visits were normally two hours long and could be at any time during the day. Employment was to be on a "casual as required basis" at a certain hourly rate. Mrs Carmichael and Mrs Leese were appointed after interview and were told that National Power had noted that they were "agreeable to be employed" on a "casual as required" basis. They signed a pre-typed letter that stated "confirming acceptance of this offer" and after training they were paid for the hours they worked. When they did work they had to follow instructions of National Power in relation to first aid responses, uniform and the quality of the tours. National Power claimed that they did not have contracts of employment.

The House of Lords held that there was no evidence to support the inference that there was an intention to create an employment contract which subsisted when Mrs Carmichael and Mrs Leese were not actually working.

The Lord Chancellor (Lord Irvine of Lairg) stated: "[There were] no provisions governing when, how or with what frequency guide work would be offered; there were no provisions for notice of termination on either side; the sickness, holiday and pension arrangements for regular staff did not apply; nor did the grievance and disciplinary procedures. Significantly … in 1994 … Mrs Carmichael was not available for work on seventeen occasions and Mrs Leese on eight. No suggestion of disciplining them arose. The objective inference is that when work was available they were free to undertake it or not as they chose. This flexibility of approach was well suited to their family needs. Just as the need for tours was unpredictable so also were their domestic commitments. Flexibility suited both sides … The arrangement turned on mutual convenience and goodwill … Mrs Carmichael and Mrs Leese had a sense of moral responsibility to [National Power] but … no legal obligation."

Apprenticeship contracts

6–06 The contract of apprenticeship attracts the benefits of modern employment legislation. Thus, the Employment Rights Act 1996, s.230(2) states that a contract of employment also means a contract of apprenticeship. Similarly, the Disability Discrimination Act 1995, s.68 provides that "employment means … employment under a contract of service or of apprenticeship". In short, any statute that confers rights on a person with a contract of employment also protects a person with an apprenticeship contract.

The primary duty of the employer under an apprenticeship contract is to instruct the apprentice in the trade or profession concerned. In *Edmonds v Lawson* [2000] I.R.L.R. 391 Lord Bingham of Cornhill stated:

> "A contract of apprenticeship is in law a contract with certain features peculiar to itself. It is for instance less readily terminable by the employer than the ordinary contract of employment … [I]t is a synallagmatic contract in which the master undertakes to educate and train the apprentice in the practical and other skills needed to practise a skilled trade or profession and

the apprentice binds himself to serve and work for the master and to comply with all reasonable directions. These mutual covenants are in our view cardinal features of such a relationship."

Company directors

Generally, executive directors of limited companies will have contracts of employment, sometimes referred to as "service agreements" with the company. If the director is truly an employee with a contract of employment with the company, he or she will be protected against unfair dismissal and redundancy. The director will be entitled to have his or her salary and certain other debts due to him by the company protected and, in the event of the liquidator being unable to pay even these preferred debts, an employee will be entitled to receive payments such as arrears of wages, holiday pay, notice pay and redundancy pay, direct from the National Insurance Fund.[10] **6–07**

It is therefore important to determine whether or not a director is an employee of the company, having regard to all the relevant facts. If an individual had a controlling shareholding, that is certainly a fact which is likely to be significant in all situations and in some cases it might prove to be decisive. However, it is only one of the relevant factors and certainly is not to be taken as determinative without considering all the relevant circumstances. Other relevant matters include:

- how and for what reasons the contract had come into existence;
- the degree of control exercised by the company over the shareholder/employee;
- whether there were directors other than or in addition to the shareholder/employee;
- whether the shareholder/employee was, in reality, answerable only to himself and incapable of being dismissed.

A controlling shareholder may be an employee of the company, and whether a director is an employee of the company depends on all the circumstances and the size of the shareholding is merely one of those circumstances, and this is not in any way conclusive.[11]

Public employment

Many people work in the public sector, but that fact alone does not affect their status as employee. What it may mean, however, is that their terms of employment are not merely those set out in their contracts of employment, but have to be read as being supplemented by certain principles of the general law. **6–08**

Vine v National Dock Labour Board

[1957] A.C. 488

At the relevant time, in order to obtain employment in the nationalised dock industry, dockers had to be on the National Dock Register. Mr Vine had his name removed from the National Dock Register with the result that he was unable to obtain employment as a docker. However, the legislation set down the procedure which might lead to a docker's name being removed from the Register. However, according to the legislation removal of a docker's name from the register could only be done by the National Dock Labour Committee. The court held his name had been removed unlawfully and without proper authority from the Register of Dockers. In law that was a nullity and resulted in his "dismissal" as a docker being invalid.

---

[10] Insolvency Act 1986, s.386; Employment Act 1996, s.182.

[11] *Secretary of State for Trade & Industry v Bottrill* [1998] I.R.L.R. 120; *Fleming v Secretary of State for Trade & Industry* [1997] I.R.L.R. 682.

Another important aspect of employment in the public sector is that where the employment is regulated by public law, an employee may be entitled to argue that a dismissal is not merely a breach of his contract or terms of employment, but that it is illegal and therefore a legal nullity.[12]

European directives and employees of the state

6–09 Employees of the state or organisations which are "emanations of the state", for example, local government employees are entitled to enforce against their employer the provisions of EU directives.[13] However, a directive may only be relied on in this way if it is unconditional and sufficiently precise in its language to allow a domestic court to apply it.

Civil servants technically do not have contracts of employment, but are generally brought within the framework of modern employment law by provisions which deem them to have contracts of employment.[14]

The correct approach is to regard the civil servant as having a contractual relationship with the Crown but one which can be determined at pleasure by the Crown without penalty.[15]

> **Key Concepts**
>
> Historically, the most important distinction in employment law was the **contract of employment** (or service) at one end of the spectrum and the **contract for services** at the other.
>
> Statutes confer protection on the ever increasing group of economically active persons known as "**workers**"—a concept wider than the concept of "employee".

Formation of the contract of employment

6–10 Generally, the legal rules relating to the formation of the contract of employment are found in the law of contract.[16]

The general rule[17] is that the parties may enter into a contract of employment any way they choose. It is possible to create a contract of employment any of the following ways or by a mixture of them: entirely by a written agreement: entirely oral; by implication through the actings and conduct of the parties. However, it is clearly advisable that a contract of employment be entered into in writing.

In Scots law, contracts of employment for a fixed period of more than one year entered into before August 1, 1995 required to be in probative writing or improbative followed by *rei interventus*.

Written statement of particulars

6–11 An employer must give to each employee a written statement of the particulars of employment.[18] However this does not require the contract of employment—or even particular parts of it—to be in

---

[12] See *Malloch v Aberdeen Corporation*, 1973 S.L.T. 253.

[13] See *Marshall v Southampton & South West Hampshire Area Health Authority (No.1)* (C152/84) 42696 [1986] I.C.R. 335.

[14] See Employment Rights Act 1996, s.191 and the Trade Union and Labour Relations Consolidation Act 1992, s.273(1).

[15] See *Kodees Waaran v Attorney General of Ceylon* [1972] W.L.R. 456.

[16] See Chapter 5.

[17] Exceptions relate to merchant seamen (Merchant Shipping Act 1995); company directors (Companies Act 1985); no strike clause in collective agreements (Trade Union and Labour Relations (Consolidation) Act 1992).

[18] Employment Rights Act 1996, Pt I, giving effect to Directive 91/533.

writing but merely that certain information is given by the employer, in writing, to his employees. Therefore, a failure to issue a written statement of particulars of employment will have no effect on the validity of any contract, which might exist between the employer and the employee.[19] On the other hand, many employers and employees will accept that the written statement of particulars is at least prima facie evidence of the contract. However, since the statement is not a contract but merely a unilateral document issued by the employer to his employee, either party is free—in the context of a dispute about the contract—to argue that the written statement differs from the contract.

A written statement of particulars of employment must include the following:

- name of employer;
- name of employee;
- date employment with employer began and date continuous employment began if different taking into account employment with associated employers and previous business owners;
- scale, rate or method of calculating, and intervals of, remuneration and how it is paid;
- terms about hours of work including normal working hours;
- terms about holidays/pay and entitlement to accrued holiday pay on termination;
- terms about incapacity for work including sick pay provision;
- terms about pensions;
- notice requirements;
- job title or brief description;
- where job is not permanent, the likely period or the period of a fixed term contract;
- the place of work or if the employee is required to work in different places, that shall be stated as well as the address of the employer;
- any collective agreements which affect the terms of employment and the partied to such collective agreements; and
- where the employee is required to work outside the UK for more than a month, the period of time, the currency of remuneration, any additional remuneration and benefits payable, and terms about return to the UK.

A written statement must also: (a) specify any disciplinary rules and procedures applicable to the employee, or refer to a document which does so and which is reasonably accessible to the employee; (b) indicate the person to whom an employee can apply if he is dissatisfied with a disciplinary decision or if he has a grievance related to his employment; and (c) if there are appeals to higher levels of management.

The written statement must generally be given not later than two months after the employee begins employment. It may be given in installments, provided all are given within two months of the employee starting work and some must be included in a document given to each employee. The particulars of any other matters may be contained in a document to which the employee is referred, the document must be reasonably accessible to the employee.

Changes to terms of employment must be given not later than one month after the changes have occurred or before the employee is to leave the UK (if that is earlier).

The employee's remedy is to apply to an Employment Tribunal which may correct or complete a statement or, if no written statement has been issued, issue a statement which ought to have been issued. However, there is no provision for the Tribunal to enforce any of the particulars against an employer or for declaring what meaning is to be given to a written statement.

The written statement is not a contract; the written statement is a unilateral document issued by the employer to the employee and it merely represents the terms of employment which the employer believes to be in existence at the time it is issued and it is not possible to alter the terms of the contract merely by issuing a new written statement.[20]

---

[19] See *British Steel Corporation v Dingwall,* 1976 S.L.T. 230.

[20] *System Floors (UK) Ltd v Daniel* [1982] I.C.R. 54.

Written contracts of employment

6–12 Where the contract of employment is entirely in writing, it may be difficult to introduce evidence that it does not accurately represent the contract or to show the contract contains additional terms which are not set out in writing. This particularly applies where the contract has been set out in a formal document. As a result of the provisions of the Contract (Scotland) Act 1997, where a document appears to comprise all the express terms of a contract, it shall be presumed unless the contrary is proved, that the document does comprise all the express terms stated. However, extrinsic oral or documentary evidence is admissible to prove that the contract does include additional express terms.

Collective agreements

6–13 As a result of the practice of settling terms and conditions of employment through collective agreements, it is important to understand the precise legal relationship between a collective agreement and the individual employee's relationship with his employer.

Definition

6–14 A collective agreement is:

> "any agreement or arrangement made by or on behalf of one or more trade unions and one or more employer or employers' associations and relating to one or more of the following matters specified below:
>
> (a) terms and conditions of employment or the physical conditions in which any workers are required to work;
> (b) engagement or non-engagement or termination or suspension of employment or the duties of employment of one or more workers;
> (c) allocation of work or the duties of employment between workers or groups of workers;
> (d) matters of discipline;
> (e) a worker's membership or non-membership of a trade union;
> (f) facilities for officials of trade unions; and
> (g) machinery for negotiation or consultation, and other procedures, relating to any of the above matters, including the recognition by employers or employers' associations of the right of a trade union to represent workers in such negotiation or consultation or in the carrying out of any such procedures."[21]

Legal effect of collective agreements

6–15 The legal status of a collective agreement reflects the historical development of industrial relations in the UK, whereby neither side of industry has wanted their agreements to be subject to adjudication by the courts—the voluntarist approach to industrial relations.

Collective agreements are entered into on the grounds that they do not create legally enforceable contracts. Indeed that common law position is now endorsed by statute which provides that a collective agreement shall be not be a legally enforceable contract unless: (1) it is in writing; and (2) it contains an express provision that it is intended to be a legally enforceable contract. See s.179 of the Trade Union and Labour Relations (Consolidation) Act 1992.

---

[21] Trade Union and Labour Relations (Consolidation) Act 1992.

Incorporation of collective agreements

However, terms of the collective agreement (like those dealing with wages, hours of work and other conditions of employment) may be incorporated into the contract of employment between the employer and employees, and this results in certain terms of collective agreements giving rise to legal rights and duties between the employer and those employees into whose contracts of employment the collective agreement has been introduced or incorporated. **6–16**

Incorporation comes about by an express or implied reference or statement in the contract of employment to the collective agreement. The principle of incorporation is set out in the following case.

Galley v NCB

[1958] 1 W.L.R. 16

Mr Galley's contract of employment indicated that he accepted employment on "terms negotiated from time to time with the trade unions". Although his own contract of employment made no mention of overtime or weekend working, his employer, the National Coal Board, negotiated collectively with the relevant trade unions from time to time and, in one such negotiation, it was agreed that employees like Mr Galley could be required to do a reasonable amount of overtime when requested by the mine manager. When Galley was rostered for overtime, he refused to do it on the grounds that it was not in his contract of employment. The court held that his contract of employment was that he would work on such terms as were negotiated from time to time with the trade unions, and as the trade unions and the employer had negotiated a collective agreement whereby employees could be required to work overtime, his contract had incorporated these collectively agreed terms. Galley therefore was in breach of his contract by refusing to work the rostered overtime.

Once a collective agreement has been incorporated into the contract of employment, it remains in force and effective between the employer and the employee until a new collective agreement is arrived at, or until the individual employee and employer agree to other terms.

Gibbons v Associated British Ports

[1985] I.R.L.R. 376

Gibbons' contract of employment provided that his "wages and conditions of service shall be in accordance with national or local agreements for the time being in force". In 1970 a collective agreement regarding wages was arrived at and in 1982 a collective agreement provided that Gibbons would have a six-day guaranteed week payment but would lose his nightshift working allowance. In 1984 Gibbons' employers gave notice to the trade union that the six day guarantee payment was to be withdrawn. The trade unions responded by saying that they would then terminate the 1970 collective agreement regarding wages and the employers argued that if they did so Gibbons' wages would then become regulated by a national agreement which made no provision for rates of pay or any six day guarantee payment. The court held that the six day guarantee payment had been incorporated into Gibbons' contract and it was not affected by the trade union terminating the 1970 collective agreement itself. It could be removed or altered only by a new collective agreement or by Gibbons agreeing to its removal or alteration.

That a collective agreement expressly provides that it shall not be legally binding between the employer and the trade union, is of no relevance to the issue of whether a term originating in a collective agreement can become legally binding once incorporated into a contract of employment.[22]

Only in special circumstances will trade union representatives who negotiate a collective agreement be regarded as agents acting on behalf of the members (principals). The facts of *Edwards v Skyways Ltd* [1964] 1 All E.R. 494 were special in that the trade union representatives had been expressly authorised by employees like Edwards to conclude bargains on behalf of the group of employees with the employer.

Key Concepts

Collective agreements are entered into on the grounds that they do not create legally enforceable contracts between the trade union and the employer(s).

Incorporation comes about by an express or implied reference or statement in the contract of employment to the collective agreement and results in the incorporated term taking on the legally binding quality of a contractual term.

TERMS AND CONDITIONS OF EMPLOYMENT

6–17 This section deals with the main terms and conditions of employment; some of these are entirely contractual or statutory, while others are in part contractual and in part statutory. Thus the relationship between an employee and his employer today is a complex one involving a mixture of express and implied[23] contractual and statutory obligations and rights.

Wages

6–18 Entitlement to wages will normally be dealt with by an express term of the contract, and the written statement must give particulars of the scale or rate of remuneration or the method of calculating remuneration.[24]

Where an employee is hourly paid and the number of hours for the week or month is specified in the contract, the employee is entitled to wages for that number of hours at the agreed rate whether or not he actually works the specified amount. Where the contract is for piecework (where wages are in accordance with output) the employer is required to provide a steady supply of work, unless there is an established custom of a particular trade that the obligation to pay wages while the worker is idle may be suspended.[25]

A unilateral reduction of wages by an employer allows the employee to continue the contract and sue for damages.

Rigby v Ferodo Ltd

[1987] I.R.L.R. 516

Ferodo Ltd told its employees that it was going to reduce their wages, but Rigby and other employees refused to agree with their decision. However, the House of Lords confirmed that there is no principle of law, that any breach which the innocent party is

[22] *Marley v Forward Trust Group Ltd* [1986] I.R.L.R. 369.

[23] See Chapter 5.

[24] *cf. Thomson v Thomson's Tr.* (1889) 16 R. 333.

[25] See Bell's Principles, s.192 and *Devonald v Rosser & Sons* [1906] 2 K.B. 728; National Minimum Wage Regulations 1999.

entitled to treat as a repudiation of the contract, brings the contract to an automatic end. It was clear in this case that Rigby and his fellow employees had not accepted the employer's repudiation of the contract as bringing it to an end with the result that it had no effect on the terms of their contract with the employer. They were able to claim successfully that they were still entitled to be paid the (unreduced) wages as stated in their contracts of employment.

Late payment of wages may be a repudiation of the contract.

Hanlon v Allied Breweries

[1975] I.R.L.R. 321

Mrs Hanlon worked as a barmaid and received her wages late on two consecutive occasions. Her reaction was to rescind her contract. The tribunal held that she was entitled to do so because the employers, by their conduct, had indicated that they were not seriously intending to perform their obligations to Mrs Hanlon. This case must, however, be regarded as unusual and turning on its own facts.

Unless there is an express term to the effect, generally, the contract of employment does not require payment of wages or salary of an employee who is unable to work through sickness or injury. In 1982, however, Statutory Sick Pay (SSP) was introduced. The provisions are now contained in the Social Security Contributions and Benefits Act 1992. The SSP system requires employers to act as a paying agent on behalf of the state and disputes about entitlement to SSP are dealt with not by Employment Tribunals but by Social Security Tribunals. Employers pay an amount equivalent to what would have been paid by way of state Incapacity Benefit, for a maximum of 28 weeks to incapacitated employees. SSP is in addition to any contractual rights and cannot be limited or excluded by any agreement.

Until the Wages Act 1986, a manual worker could insist upon being paid in cash and any non-cash payment, for example by cheque or by credit transfer, was regarded as void. However the 1986 Act repealed that rule and the practice today is to include in the contract of employment, an express term dealing with how wages will be paid.

The Wages Act 1986 also revised the law regarding deductions from wages (and any payments the workers is required to make to the employer) and the current rules are now contained in Part II of the Employment Rights Act 1996.

Section 13 of the 1996 Act provides that "an employer shall not make a deduction from wages of a worker unless (a) the deduction is required or authorised to be made by virtue of a statutory provision[26] or a relevant provision of the worker's contract or (b) the worker has previously signified, in writing, his agreement or consent to the making of the deduction". Thus, a deduction is lawful only if it is required by statute or the worker has (a) agreed to it in writing or (b) has had written notice of the existence of the unwritten contractual term, giving the employer a right to make the deduction, before any deduction is made. However, where an employer has the right to transfer an employee to work which is less well paid, a fall in the wages to which the employee is entitled is not a deduction from wages.

Hussman Manufacturing Ltd v Weir

[1998] I.R.L.R. 288

Weir had been employed for 12 years by Hussman Manufacturing Ltd on night-shift duty, when his employers decided to alter their shift system and he was moved to a day-shift rota and paid at the day-shift rate. He carried on working under protest and complained to an Employment Tribunal that his employers had made an unlawful deduction from his wages.

---

[26] *e.g.* income tax or national insurance contributions.

The EAT held that an employer who moved an employee from a night-shift to a day-shift and reduced his salary to the day-shift rate had not made an unlawful deduction from the employee's wages.

There are special rules for retail workers. Section 18 of the Employment Rights Act 1996 provides that where an employer of a worker in retail employment makes a deduction on account of cash shortages or stock deficiencies, the deduction shall not exceed 10 per cent of the gross amount payable on that day.

However none of the above rules applies to the following:

- deductions to recover an overpayment of wages or expenses;
- deductions as a result of statutory disciplinary proceedings;
- a deduction the employer is required to make by law and to pay the amount over to a public authority;
- deductions agreed to in writing by the worker which the employer is required to pay over to a third person, an amount notified by that person (*e.g.* trade union subscriptions and payments to provident and benefit funds);
- deductions on account of the worker having taken part in a strike or other industrial action; or
- deductions agreed to in writing by the worker to satisfy a court or tribunal order requiring the payment to be made by the worker to the employer.[27]

Definition of wages

6–19 Wages are "any sums payable to the worker in connection with his employment including fee, bonus, commission, holiday pay or other emolument referable to his employment whether payable under his contract or otherwise".[28] The definition also includes various statutory payments, like Statutory Sick Pay and Statutory Maternity Pay. However, the following payments are excluded:

- advances of wages or loans;
- expenses incurred by the worker in carrying out his employment;
- pensions, allowances, gratuities, in connection with retirement or as compensation for loss of office;
- payments referable to redundancy; and
- payments to the worker otherwise than in his capacity as a worker.

In *Delaney v Staples*[29] the House of Lords held that pay in lieu of notice is made in respect of a period after the contract had been brought to an end and it could not be regarded as wages for the purpose of Part II of the Employment Rights Act 1996. Accordingly, non-payment of pay in lieu of notice is not an unlawful deduction under the Employment Rights Act. An alternative to paying an employee in lieu of notice is to place the employee on "garden leave" during the period of notice. This means that the contract of employment continues during the notice period, and should the employer fail to pay wages there will be an unlawful deduction from wages because the contract of employment does not come to an end until the garden leave has expired.

A worker can present a complaint in the Employment Tribunal that his employer has made an unlawful deduction from wages, and if the Tribunal upholds the complaint it shall order the employer to pay to the worker the amount of any deductions.

Employees are entitled to receive a written itemised pay statement containing particulars of:

[27] ERA 1996, s.14.
[28] ERA 1996, s.27.
[29] [1992] I.C.R. 483.

- the gross amount of wages or salary;
- the amounts of any variable and fixed deductions and the purposes for which they are made;
- the net amount of wages payable; and
- where different parts of the net amount are paid in different ways, the amount and method of payment of each part-payment.[30]

If an employer fails to give an employee an itemised pay statement, the employee may refer the matter to an Employment Tribunal which can order the employer to pay to the employee the aggregate of any unnotified deductions.

> **Key Concepts**
>
> **Deductions from wages** may generally only be made with the worker's written consent or by statutory authority.
>
> **Retail workers** have additional protection for deductions for cash or stock shortages.

National Minimum Wage

Until the National Minimum Wage Act 1998 there was no general protection against low pay. The 1998 Act with the National Minimum Wage Regulations 1999 introduces a scheme to ensure a minimum level of pay across all industry. The scheme applies to employees, workers and agency workers. Those who are under 18 are not protected and there are different rates for those between 18 and 21 and those 22 and over. (The Secretary of State may refer matters including the level at which the Minimum Wage is set to the Low Pay Commission (National Minimum Wage Act, s.6).) The rate is expressed as an hourly rate and the current rates are: £4.20 for those 22 and over and £3.60 for 18–21 year olds. **6–20**

In order to decide whether the appropriate rate is paid, it is necessary to determine the pay reference period, the total pay received and the total hours worked during that period. The pay reference period is one month or other shorter period; accordingly the reference period for workers paid weekly is a week, for those paid daily one day and for those paid at longer intervals *e.g.* two months, is one month.[31] The total pay is the gross pay which includes all commission, bonuses and gratuities paid through the payroll but does not include benefits in kind like luncheon vouchers and use of company car.[32] Accommodation provided by the employer is taken into account but up to the maximum of £22.75 per week.[33] Special shift rates are excluded.

The hours to be used in arriving at the hourly rate vary depending on whether it is time work (where the worker is paid according to the hours worked), salaried work (where the worker is paid for a basic number of hours per year for which he gets an annual salary paid in 12 equal monthly instalments or 52 equal weekly instalments), output work (where the worker is paid for the number of units of work completed) or unmeasured work (where there are no specified hours but the worker is required to work when needed or work is available).[34]

---

[30] ERA 1996, ss.8, 9.
[31] National Minimum Wage Regulations 1999, reg.10.
[32] reg.9.
[33] reg.36.
[34] regs 3–6.

Key Concepts

Time work: hours done in reference period.

Salaried work: basic hours plus any hours for which the worker received extra payments.

Output work: hours in a "fair estimate" agreement of the hours to be worked or the actual hours in the reference period.

Unmeasured work: hours in a "daily average" agreement or the actual hours in the pay reference period.

Enforcement

6–21 Employers are required to keep records to show that the worker is paid the National Minimum Wage and a worker has the right to see such records.[35]

Enforcement of payment of the National Minimum Wage is by the Inland Revenue issuing of an Enforcement Notice on an employer and by a worker making a complaint to an Employment Tribunal that there has been an unlawful deduction from wages under Part II of the Employment Rights Act 1996.[36] Where such a complaint is made, it is presumed the worker qualified for the Minimum Wage and that she was paid less than that wage.[37]

Hours of work and holidays

6–22 Until the Working Time Regulations 1998, generally employers and employees were free to make such contractual arrangements as they wished regarding hours of work and holidays.

The Regulations apply to employees, workers and agency workers but in some cases certain groups are partly excluded, for example domestic servants, while others are totally excluded, for example particular sectors of activity; namely: air, road, rail and sea transport, activities of doctors in training, activities of the armed forces and the civil protection services which inevitably conflict with the Regulations. However, Council Directive 2000/34 which becomes effective in 2003 will remove many of the existing exclusions.

Protection to other workers may be reduced if certain conditions are met. Regulation 21 contains many special circumstances in which the Regulations do not apply:

(a) place of work and residence or places of work distant from each other;
(b) security and surveillance requiring permanent presence;
(c) need for continuity of service and production;
(d) foreseeable surge of activity; and
(e) exceptional events and accidents.

"Working time" means any period during which the worker is working, at the employer's disposal and carrying out his activity or duty, any period during which the worker is receiving relevant training and "any additional period which is to be treated as working time … under a relevant agreement" so that if an employer and employee are in doubt about whether a period is to be treated as working time they are able to enter an agreement by which that uncertainty is removed. In *Sindicato de Medicos de Assistencia Publica (SIMAP) v Conselleria de Sanidad y Consumo de*

[35] reg.3.
[36] National Minimum Wage Act, ss.19–22.
[37] National Minimum Wage Act, ss.17, 18.

la Generalidad Valenciana[38] the European Court of Justice held that time spent on call by doctors must be regarded as working time where their presence at the health centre is required.

Maximum working week

A worker's average working time—including overtime—shall not exceed 48 hours for each seven day period.[39] The only exceptions permitted from the 48 hour limit are in respect of: **6–23**

- domestic servants;
- workers whose working time "is not measured or predetermined or can be determined by the worker himself"; and
- where the worker has agreed in writing to exceed 48 hours.[40]

Night work

Generally a night worker's hours shall not exceed an average of eight hours in a 24-hour period.[41] The limits on night work are excluded in many cases when certain conditions apply and may be excluded or modified by collective or workforce agreement.[42] **6–24**

Rest periods

There are exceptions for shift workers (reg. 22) but generally a worker is entitled to a daily rest break of 11 consecutive hours and a weekly rest period of not less than 24 hours. Where a worker's working day is more than six hours he is entitled to a rest break of not less than 20 minutes.[43] **6–25**

Annual leave

A worker is entitled to four weeks' paid annual leave,[44] and this cannot be modified or excluded by collective or workforce agreement and except where the employment is terminated, there can be no payments in lieu. **6–26**

Enforcement and remedies

There are three ways in which the Regulations can be enforced: **6–27**

(1) criminal offences under Health and Safety at Work Act 1974;
(2) breach of statutory duty by action in ordinary court; and
(3) worker's entitlements by complaint to the Employment Tribunal.

---

[38] [2000] I.R.L.R. 845.
[39] reg.4.
[40] regs 4, 19, 20.
[41] reg.6.
[42] regs 21, 23.
[43] reg.12.
[44] reg.13.

Time-off rights

6–28 Statute now provides that employees are entitled to time off for certain purposes. On some occasions time off is with pay, while on other occasions it is unpaid time off.

Trade union duties and activities

6–29 An official of an independent trade union recognised by an employer is entitled to paid time off to carry out his *duties* as an official connected with negotiations with his employer and concerned with the receipt of information and consultation (and for training associated therewith), relating to redundancies and business transfers. An employee is also entitled to unpaid time off to take part in the *activities* of a recognised trade union. In each case, the amount of time off to which an employee is entitled is such time off as is reasonable, in respect of the guidance given by the Code of Practice issued by ACAS and complaints that an employer has not permitted time-off, lie to an Employment Tribunal.[45] Time off for union learning representatives was introduced in 2003.[46]

Public duties

6–30 Employees who hold certain public offices, *e.g.* Justices of the Peace, or are members of certain public bodies, *e.g.* local authorities and statutory tribunals, are entitled to reasonable time off without pay to perform their public duties.[47] Jury service is treated by s.85 of the Criminal Procedure (Scotland) Act 1995 and jurors are entitled to expenses for loss of wages and benefits.

Finding work

6–31 An employee with two years' service and who is under notice of redundancy is entitled to reasonable time off with pay, (a maximum of half a week's pay) to look for other work or to arrange training for new employment.[48]

Maternity, paternity, adoption and parental leave, and flexible working

6–32 Periods of time off supported with rights to statutory payments for varying periods and at different rates in some cases are now available, and in certain conditions employees have the right to request contractual changes for childcare.[49] Briefly, the position is as follows:

(1) *Maternity*: Regardless of length of service all employee are entitled to 26 weeks Ordinary Maternity Leave (OML) followed by 26 weeks' Additional Maternity Leave (AML) for women who have accumulated 26 weeks continuous employment by the 15th week before their expected week of childbirth (EWC). A woman who has 24 weeks employment (with the employer) is entitled to Statutory Maternity Pay (SMP) which is at 90% of earnings for the first six weeks and at a flat rate of £100 (if less than the 90% of earnings).[50] The right to return to work is also secured.

---

[45] Trade Union and Labour Relations (Consolidation) Act 1992, ss.168, 170.

[46] Employment Act 2002, s.43.

[47] ERA 1996, s.50.

[48] ERA 1996, s.52.

[49] Detailed discussion is not possible here but see the Employment Rights Act 1996, Part VIII, Chapter I (Maternity Leave), Chapter II (Parental Leave) and Maternity and Parental Leave Regulations 1999 as amended by the Employment Act 2002 and Regulations made thereunder and the Employment Act 2002, ss.1–4 (Paternity and Adoption Leave and Pay) and s.47 (Flexible Working) and Regulations made thereunder.

[50] The Regulations require notices and responses to be given at particular times.

(2) *Paternity*: After 26 weeks' employment by the 15th week before EWC the biological father or the husband (or partner[51]) of the child's mother is entitled to two weeks' paternity leave either on the birth or adoption of a child provided the leave is taken for the purpose of caring for the child or supporting the mother and the employee has responsibility for the upbringing of the child. The leave must be taken within 56 days of the birth and is with pay at the rate of 90% of earnings. The right to return to work is secured as for a woman returning from OML.

(3) *Adoption*: After 26 weeks' employment by the date of being notified[52] of a match for adoption, an individual (or where the adoption is by a couple one of the couple[53]) is entitled to 26 weeks' Ordinary Adoption Leave (OAL) followed by 26 weeks' Additional Adoption Leave (AAL) with the same rights to return to work as a woman on OML or AML.[54] During OAL employees are entitled to Statutory Adoption Pay (SAP) at the same rates as those which operate for maternity pay.

(4) *Flexible working*: The right to a flexible working pattern was introduced by the Employment Act 2002, section 47 as part of the family friendly approach to employment. The right is available to an employee/parent (which includes mother, father, adopter, guardian or foster parent or a person married to, or the partner of, such a person and has the responsibility for the child's upbringing) of a child under six (or 18 if Disability Living Allowance is in payment) and has at least 26 weeks' continuous employment. It entitles the employee to apply to an employer for changes regarding his/her: (a) time/hours of work; (b) place of work as between home and place of business; and (c) other terms as regulations may specify. Only one application which must be per year is permitted but the employer's right to refuse is limited to the following: (a) additional costs; (b) detriment to customer demand; (c) quality performance; (d) inability to reorganise work among other staff or recruit other staff; (e) insufficiency of work; or (f) planned structural changes. The right is enforced by complaint to the Employment Tribunal which can order reconsideration of the request and make an award of compensation.

In addition a woman who is pregnant is entitled to paid time off for ante-natal care where the appointment has been made on the advice of a registered medical practitioner, midwife or health visitor.[55]

Domestic incidents

Employees are entitled to a reasonable amount of time off during working hours to deal with a domestic incident,[56] *e.g.*: **6–33**

- when a dependant falls ill, is injured or dies, or to arrange care for such a dependant;
- where the care arrangements for such dependant unexpectedly ends; or
- where the employee's child is involved in an unexpected incident at school.

Employee representatives

An employee who is a representative for purposes of redundancy or business transfer consultation is entitled to reasonable paid time-off to perform his duties or to act as a candidate in election of representatives.[57] **6–34**

[51] Same sex partners are included.
[52] Notification must be by an approved adoption agency.
[53] The other member of the couple may be entitled to Paternity Leave and Pay.
[54] The Regulations require notices and responses to be given at particular times.
[55] ERA 1996, s.56.
[56] ERA 1996, s.57A.
[57] ERA 1996, s.61.

Safety representatives

6–35 Safety representatives appointed by a recognised trade union and elected representatives of employee health and safety are entitled to such time off with pay as is reasonable in accordance with the HSC Code of Practice to perform their functions and to receive training.[58]

Study and training

6–36 Employees who are between 16 and 18 years of age and not in full-time education are entitled to reasonable time off with pay to undertake study or training which leads to a relevant qualification.[59]

Other contractual terms and duties

6–37 As indicated earlier, the contract of employment contains many implied terms. It is tempting to think of the implied duties of the contract of employment as specific or discrete. However, the underlying obligation in the relationship today may be expressed simply as an obligation on both parties not to act in such a way that is likely to, or calculated to, destroy or seriously damage the trust and confidence on which the employment relationship is ultimately based. The generality of the duty of trust and confidence is illustrated by the following two cases.

Malik v B C C I SA
[1997] I.R.L.R. 462

The House of Lords held that an employer could be in breach of the implied duty of trust and confidence by operating his business in a dishonest and corrupt way and an employee who was unable to secure employment in the future as a result of having worked for such an employer is entitled to damages for that loss.

Lord Nicholls of Birkenhead stated: "Employers may be under no ... implied contractual term of general application, to take steps to improve their employees' future job prospects. But failure to improve is one thing, positively to damage is another. Employment, and job prospects, are matters of vital concern to most people. Jobs of all descriptions are less secure than formerly, people change jobs more frequently, and the job market is not always buoyant. Everyone knows this. An employment contract creates a close personal relationship, where there is often a disparity of power between the parties. Frequently, the employee is vulnerable. Although the underlying purpose of the trust and confidence term is to protect the employment relationship, there can be nothing unfairly onerous or unreasonable in requiring an employer who breaches the trust and confidence term to be liable if he thereby causes continuing financial loss of a nature that was reasonably foreseeable."

---

[58] Safety Representatives and Safety Committee Regulations 1977; Health and Safety (Consultation with Employees) Regulations 1996.
[59] ERA 1996, s.63A(1).

TSB Bank plc v Harris

[2000] I.R.L.R. 157

Harris was unaware that customer complaints had been made against her. When Miss Harris sought another employment, the TSB were approached for a reference. The reference stated that seventeen complaints had been made against her, of which four were upheld and eight were outstanding, and as a result of that reference the new employers refused to engage Miss Harris. When Miss Harris discovered that there had been so many complaints against her, in respect of which she was given no opportunity to comment or explain she resigned and claimed a constructive dismissal. The Employment Tribunal held that the employers were in breach of the implied term of trust and confidence in providing a reference which made mention of previously unregistered complaints and was misleading and potentially destructive of the employee's career in financial services. That decision was upheld by the Employment Appeal Tribunal on the grounds that where an employer undertakes to give a reference in respect of an employee, there is an implied contractual obligation to ensure that it is a fair and reasonable reference, and a failure to do so may be a breach of the implied term of trust and confidence. While referring to previously lodged complaints was nothing more than true and accurate, that was not necessarily a reasonable and fair reference.

Nonetheless, having underlined the generality of the obligations on both the employer and employee it is convenient to categorise the implied duties of the employee under the following headings:

Obedience

An employee must carry out the instructions given to him by his employers for the purpose of performing his contract, provided it does not involve the employee doing an act that is illegal or immoral. Thus, an employee who was employed as a petrol pump attendant was entitled to refuse to falsify the sales records at a time when the business was to be put up for sale because it would have resulted in him performing an illegal and immoral act.[60] **6–38**

An employee is not required to perform an act which is outside the scope of his contract. Thus, it has been held that a shepherd was entitled to refuse instructions to tend cows.[61] However, an employee is expected to be flexible and co-operative in emergency situations.[62]

The scope of the contract may also be limited by terms of place and time.

Johnstone v Bloomsbury Health Authority

[1991] I.R.L.R. 118

Dr Johnstone, employed as a junior doctor by the health authority, was required by his contract to work a standard working week of 40 hours and additional availability on-call up to an average of 48 hours a week. Dr Johnstone contended his long working hours affected his health. The following statement of Sir Nicolas Browne-Wilkinson is probably an accurate reflection of law:

---

60 *Morrish v Henlys (Folkestone)* [1973] 2 All E.R. 137; and *Pagano v HGS Ltd* [1976] I.R.L.R. 9.

61 *Moffat v Boothby* (1884) 11 R. 501.

62 *Smith v St Andrew Ambulance* [1973] N.I.R.C. unreported, July 12, 1973 (ambulance driver); *Sim v Rotherham B.C.* [1986] I.C.R. 897 (school teacher).

> "There was in the contract of employment no incompatibility between Dr Johnstone's duty on the one hand and the authority's right, subject to the implied duty as to health on the other hand. The implied duty did not contradict the implied term of the contract. There must be some restriction on the authority's rights. In any sphere of employment other than that of a junior hospital doctor an obligation to work up to 88 hours per week would be rightly regarded as oppressive and intolerable. The authority's right to call for overtime under (the contract) was not an absolute right but must be limited in some way. Therefore not withstanding (the express term in the contract) the authority could not lawfully require the plaintiff to work so much overtime in any week as it was reasonably foreseeable would damage his health."

In some cases, the contract does not make clear where the place of employment is and this has to be determined by looking at all the facts and circumstances.[63] In some cases, the contract will include a term allowing the employer to move the employee from one place of work to another. However, a right to transfer an employee from one place of work to another is itself subject to the implied qualification that the employer will not use the right in such a way as to make it impossible for the employee to perform his contract.

United Bank Ltd v Akhtar

[1989] I.R.L.R. 507

There was a term in Mr Akhtar's contract of employment which allowed the bank to transfer him to any place of business which the bank had in the UK, either permanently or temporarily; the contract also provided that the bank may make a contribution to the employee's removal costs. The bank, in reliance on this term, required Mr Akhtar to move from one town in the Midlands to another, without indicating whether the move would be temporary or permanent and without indicating whether they would make a contribution to Mr Akhtar's removal costs. Initially, Mr Akhtar was given only a weekend's notice, which the bank later extended to almost a week. The court came to the conclusion that although the employer appeared to have an unfettered discretion to transfer Mr Akhtar from one place to another it could not use that contractual term in such a way as to make it virtually impossible for Mr Akhtar to perform his contract. It is clear therefore that even an express mobility clause in a contract of employment has to be operated in such a way that it is not virtually impossible for the employee to comply with it.

The scope of the contract is also limited by the implied understanding that employees will not be required to undertake unforeseen and unreasonable risks in carrying out the contract.[64] In *Ferrie v Western District Council*[65] an employee was entitled to refuse to clean ponds in remote locations where the ponds were deep and steep-sided and presented a serious risk to non-swimmers like Mr Ferrie, who might drown in the event of him slipping or falling into the pond while carrying out the cleaning operation. Instructions must be given in a way that does not undermine trust and confidence. In *Wilson v Racher*,[66] the employee had demonstrated a degree of disobedience to his employer but the court came to the conclusion that this was provoked by the employer's lack of respect for the employee, by humiliating him in front of others.

---

[63] *O'Brien v Associated Fire Alarms Ltd* [1968] 1 W.L.R. 1916: O'Brien's place of work was "the Liverpool area" and he could not therefore be required to work in Barrow-in-Furness.

[64] *Burton v Pinkerton* (1867) L.R. 2 Ex. 340.

[65] [1973] I.R.L.R. 162.

[66] [1974] I.R.L.R. 114.

Employee's duty of careful performance

An employee must perform his contract with reasonable care. The principle is exemplified in: **6–39**

Lister v Romford Ice and Cold Storage Ltd
[1957] A.C. 555

Romford Ice Cold Storage Ltd employed Mr Lister senior and Mr Lister junior (father and son). The son drove a lorry and the father acted as the driver's assistant. When Lister senior was giving manoeuvring instructions to his son, he was injured as a result of his son's careless driving. In accordance with the normal rules of vicarious liability Lister junior's employers, Romford Ice and Cold Storage Company Ltd, were liable to Mr Lister senior for his injuries. Romford Ice and Cold Storage Ltd called upon their insurance policy and their insurers duly made payment to Lister senior. However, relying on their subrogation clause in the contract of insurance, the insurers then insisted that Romford Ice and Cold Storage Company Ltd used their right to require Lister junior to perform his contract with reasonable care to recover from Lister junior the payments the insurance company had to make to Lister senior. The House of Lords reaffirmed the principle that an employee who breaches his contract by performing his obligations without reasonable care is required to indemnify the employer for any loss which follows.

Employee's duty of fidelity

This implied duty binds an employee to protect his employer's business in the form of commercial assets and trade secrets and other confidential information and is relevant to the freedom of an employee to take on secondary or part-time employment.[67] At its simplest, it requires the employee to use all reasonable means to advance his employer's business and, secondly, to refrain from doing anything which would injure his employer's business. **6–40**

Competition

There is no general rule that an employee may not deal in commodities in which his employer deals or is prohibited from working for a competitor of his employer in his own time (*Graham v Paton*). It depends on the work the employee does.[68] **6–41**

Trade secrets and confidential information

The duty of fidelity and loyal service requires that an employee protects and does not abuse or disclose his employer's trade secrets or confidential information. Even after the contract of employment has come to an end, a diluted form of this duty continues. **6–42**

---

[67] *Graham v Paton,* 1917 S.C. 203; *Faccenda Chicken v Fowler* [1986] I.C.R. 297; and see *Sanders v Parry* [1967] 1 W.L.R. 753.

[68] *Hivac v Park Royal Scientific Instruments Ltd* [1946] Ch. 169.

Faccenda Chicken v Fowler
[1986] I.C.R. 297

Fowler left his employment with Faccenda Chicken to set up in competition. There was no restrictive covenant in Fowler's contract of employment and Faccenda Chicken therefore could rely only on Fowler's implied duty not to disclose or use confidential information after the contract came to an end. The information which the employer claimed to be confidential in this case included the names and addresses of customers and their requirements, the most convenient routes for delivery vehicles and customers' preferences for delivery days and times and the price structure used for particular customers. The Court of Appeal held that while an ex-employee must not disclose secret processes of manufacture or other truly confidential information, the obligation of the ex-employee did not extend to information which was confidential only in that, had it been disclosed during the contract, it would have breached the implied duty of fidelity.

Key Concepts

The factors which are relevant to determining whether or not information is truly confidential include:

- the nature of the job;
- the nature of the information;
- can it be equated with a trade secret;
- has the employer stressed the confidentiality of the information during the period of employment; and
- can the confidential information be isolated from other general information to which an employee is exposed in the course of employment?

Of course an employee will develop his own skills and knowledge while in employment and they become part of the employee's own "stock in trade" which he is allowed to use in developing his career and earning potential.[69]

Restrictive covenants

6–43 Often employers seek to protect their legitimate interests like business connections, knowledge of customers and confidential information by inserting into contracts of employment restrictive covenants. A covenant which prevents an employee from competing with his employer is regarded as a *pactum illicitum* and will be unenforceable unless it is necessary to protect a legitimate interest of the employer. The mere exclusion of competition by an ex-employee is not itself a legitimate interest and in order to be enforceable a restrictive covenant must protect confidential information or trade connections.[70] However, even then for the covenant to be enforceable it must be reasonable and in the public interest.

Reasonableness can be determined by having regard to the time of the restriction, the area to which it applies and the job function to which it relates.

[69] *United Sterling v Mannion* [1974] I.R.L.R. 314.
[70] *A & D Bedrooms v Michael*, 1984 S.L.T. 297.

Bluebell Apparel v Dickinson
1980 S.L.T. 157

Dickinson's contract of employment provided that he would not, for two years after the termination of his employment, perform any services for any competitors anywhere in the world. Having regard to the nature of the jeans industry and the confidential information to which Mr Dickinson had access, the court upheld the validity of the covenant. The court noted the covenant was necessary to protect trade secrets in a world-wide industry. It remarked that "prohibition against disclosing trade secrets is worthless unless accompanied by a restriction upon the employee possessed of secrets against entering the employment of rivals".

The covenant must not be against the public interest which generally requires access to services in a free market.[71]

TERMINATION OF THE CONTRACT AND WRONGFUL DISMISSAL

Notice

Unless the contract is for a fixed period, the contract of employment can be ended by either party giving notice of termination. If the contract makes no provision (express or implied) for termination by notice the common law provides that either party may terminate the contract by giving reasonable notice of termination.[72] What is reasonable depends on the circumstances of the case, including the seniority of the employee and how long it is likely to take him to find other work or the employer to find a replacement. **6–44**

The Employment Rights Act 1996 provides for minimum periods of notice. Provided an employee has been continuously employed for a month or more he is entitled to the period of notice specified in the Act and any contractual term which deprives the employee of that right is void.[73] The length of minimum notice to which an employee is entitled depends on the length of his continuous employment and for every year of continuous employment an employee is entitled to one week's notice, until the maximum of 12 weeks is reached. Such a sliding scale does not apply to the notice the employee is required to give; under the Act an employee is not required to give more than one weeks' notice but his contract of employment will often require that he gives more.

Partnership dissolution

Many employees are employed by partnerships. In Scots law there are two kinds of partnerships. The first and most common type is that regulated by the Partnership Act 1890 which recognises that a partnership possesses a quasi-legal personality distinct from the personalities of the partners themselves but lacks the distinct legal personality of a limited company.[74] The dissolution of such a partnership will operate to terminate contracts of employment between the firm and employee. However, where the partnership continues, contracts of employment with the firm are deemed to include an implied term that the death, resignation or assumption of a partner or partners will be accepted by the firm's employees.[75] Since 2001, it has been possible to form a limited liability partnership under the Limited Liability Partnership Act 2000. Where such a partnership is the **6–45**

[71] *Bull v Pitney Bowes* [1967] 1 W.L.R. 273.
[72] *Forsyth v Heathery Knowe Coal Company* (1880) 7 R. 887.
[73] Employment Rights Act 1996, s.86(3).
[74] Partnership Act 1890, s.4(2).
[75] *Berlitz School of Languages v Duchene* (1903) 6 F. 181.

employer, the contract of employment is with the body corporate whose legal personality is not affected by any change in the partners who make it up.

Winding up, receiverships and administration orders

6–46 Where companies are wound up the effect on the contracts of employment depends on the nature of the winding up and the circumstances surrounding it but generally a court order which winds up a company (a compulsory winding up order) operates as notice of termination of the contracts of employment between the company and its staff.[76] On the other hand, a resolution to voluntarily wind up a company may operate to terminate contracts of employment depending upon the facts and circumstances of each case.[77] It may be necessary therefore to distinguish a compulsory winding up to cease business and insolvency[78] from a voluntary winding up, merely to facilitate a take-over or business reconstruction.[79]

Frustration

6–47 The contract of employment may become impossible to perform or "frustrated".[80] The death of either party frustrates the contract of employment,[81] as does the serious or protracted illness of either party. Where the illness of the employees is concerned a great deal depends on the circumstances of the employment and the nature of the illness as well as the prospect of recovery. In *Marshall v Harland & Wolff Ltd*,[82] the following were stated to be relevant:

- terms of the contract;
- the nature of the employment and its expected duration if no illness;
- nature of illness and prospects of recovery;
- period of past employment;
- possibility of acquisition of statutory rights by the replacement employee; and
- continued payment of wages during absence.

Being sent to prison or interned may result in the contract being frustrated although again it will depend on the length of the sentence and the nature of the employment.

F.C. Shepherd & Co. Ltd v Jerrom

[1986] I.R.L.R. 358.

The contract of an apprentice who, during his apprenticeship had been convicted of conspiracy to assault and affray, which resulted in him being given a borstal sentence, was frustrated after he had served 39 weeks in borstal.

Lawton L.J. stated: "The apprentice's criminal conduct was deliberate but it did not have by itself any consequences on the performance of the contract. What affected the contract was the sentence of borstal training which was the act of the judge and which he (the apprentice) would have avoided if he could have done ... In this case the facts did frustrate the contract."

[76] *Day v Tait* (1900) 8 S.L.T. 40.
[77] *Ferguson v Telford, Grier and McKay & Co.* [1967] I.T.R. 387.
[78] *Reigate v Union Manufacturing Company (Ramsbottom) Ltd* [1918] 1 K.B. 592.
[79] *Midland Counties Bank Ltd v Attwood* [1905] 1 Ch. 357.
[80] See Chapter 5.
[81] *Hoey v McEwan and Auld* (1867) 5 M. 814.
[82] [1972] 2 All E.R. 715.

A contract can also be frustrated by becoming illegal and this has meant that where an employee becomes legally disqualified from performing certain work, his contract may be brought to an end by frustration. Therefore where a contract of employment requires the employee to hold a valid qualification, a relatively short period of legal disqualification can result in the contract being frustrated.[83]

Rescission

The general rule is that one party cannot bring to an end his contractual obligations merely by repudiating the contract or breaking it in a material or fundamental way. Repudiation merely allows the innocent party to rescind the contract but in employment law there are exceptions while repudiation of the contract by a unilateral wage reduction did not itself terminate the contract. **6–48**

Rigby v Ferodo Ltd

[1988] I.C.R. 29

Ferodo Ltd gave its employees notice that it was going to reduce wage rates but Rigby and other employees refused to agree. When his wage was reduced Rigby sued for the difference between but Ferodo argued that the notice to reduce the wages should be construed as a 12–week notice to terminate the contract of employment with the offer of a new contract containing the reduced wage rate.

Lord Oliver stated: "There was no reason in law or in logic why, leaving aside the extreme cases of outright dismissal or walk out, a contract of employment should be on any different footing from any other contract, regarding the principle that an unaccepted repudiation was a thing writ in water and of no value to anybody."

Wrongful dismissal

Wrongful dismissal is the term which denotes dismissal in breach of contract and is to be contrasted with unfair dismissal which is primarily concerned with the reasonableness of the employer's actions. Although in unfair dismissal the question as to whether an employer has broken the contract in dismissing the employee will be relevant, it is only one of all the circumstances the Employment Tribunal is required to take into account. Dismissal by a public body can sometimes be challenged by judicial review by which an employer's action in dismissing an employee may be declared unlawful. **6–49**

Remedies

Scots law regards the contract of employment as a contract involving the provision of personal services—a personal relationship based on mutual trust and confidence. One result of this is that the common law provides that the remedy of specific implement is not available,[84] and this rule is now enshrined in s.236 of the Trade Union and Labour Relations (Consolidation) Act 1992 which provides: **6–50**

---

[83] *Tarnesby v Kensington & Chelsea & Westminster Area Health Authority* [1981] I.R.L.R. 369—doctor's registration being temporarily suspended; *Dunbar v Baillie Brothers*, 1990 G.W.D. 26-1487—HGV driver, losing licence following a heart attack.

[84] *Murray v Dumbarton County Council*, 1935 S.L.T. 239.

"No court shall be way of—

(a) and order for specific performance or specific implement of a contract of employment, or

(b) an injunction or interdict restraining breach of threatened breach of such a contract,

compel an employee to do any work or attend at any place for the doing of any work."

The result is that where a breach involves a resignation without giving the notice required by the contract or a dismissal without notice the courts will generally not grant any order whose effect would be to compel the continuation of the employment relationship. In England, the courts have restrained a wrongful dismissal by the granting of an injunction and the Scottish courts have followed this trend. Examples of the Scottish courts being prepared to grant interdicts to restrain a dismissal are found in *John Anderson v Pringle of Scotland*[85] and *Peace v City of Edinburgh Council.*[86]

Damages

6–51 The most common remedy for wrongful dismissal is an action of damages. If the contract is for a fixed term, damages will include the salary and other benefits which the employee would have received if the contract had run its full course. If the contract could have been lawfully ended by the employer giving notice, the damages will compensate the employee for what he would have received in salary and other benefits during the period of notice. By restricting the loss to the period of the contract or the notice it required, the court is giving effect to the right of the party in breach to perform the contract in the least burdensome way.

Morran v Glasgow Council of Tenants

[1998] I.R.L.R. 67

Morran was dismissed in breach of his contract. If his contract had been performed by the employers he would have received either four weeks' notice of termination or pay in lieu of notice. In fact he received neither and argued that if he had been given four weeks' notice he would have had enough continuous employment to claim unfair dismissal. He therefore claimed damages for loss of the right to claim unfair dismissal.

Held, that in an action for damages for breach of the contract, an employee is entitled to recover damages, which will put him in a position he would have been in had the employers fulfilled their contractual obligation. Where, as here, the contract gives the employer the option of terminating by giving due notice or making a payment in lieu thereof the less burdensome way for them is to dismiss the employee and make a payment in lieu of notice. If the employers had dismissed the employee with pay in lieu of notice, his employment would still have terminated before he had the necessary service to claim unfair dismissal.

Addis v Gramophone Company Ltd [87] has been regarded as precluding an award of damages in respect of injury to the employee's feelings. However, in *Malik v BCCI* [88] the House of Lords has distinguished *Addis* and has held that an employee is entitled to damages for the financial loss he suffered (through, for example, not being able to find other employment) as a result of the employer being in breach of the implied duty of trust and confidence by, for example, running his

[85] [1998] I.R.L.R. 64.

[86] [1999] I.R.L.R. 417.

[87] [1909] A.C. 488.

[88] [1997] I.R.L.R. 462.

business in a dishonest and corrupt way. Thus "stigma" damages may now be awarded for loss of reputation caused by such a breach of contract.

However, there is still no entitlement to damages for injury to feelings or anxiety for wrongful dismissal.[89]

Pay in lieu of notice

In Scots law, the employer has an implied right to terminate the contract by paying wages and giving other contractual benefits due to the employee in lieu of notice. It follows that where an employer does this in the ordinary case, no action for damages will lie, because no breach of contract will have occurred. Unless the conduct of the employee justifies summary dismissal, an employer who dismisses without notice or without paying in lieu of notice will be liable in damages to the employee for a sum equivalent to wages in lieu of notice and the employee may sue for such in either the ordinary courts or an Employment Tribunal. **6–52**

Key Concepts

The contract can be **terminated** by:

- notice of termination;
- dissolution or winding up of a partnership or company;
- impossibility or illegality of performance (frustration); or
- rescission following repudiation.

The remedy for **wrongful dismissal** is almost always damages.

UNFAIR DISMISSAL

Unfair dismissal describes a dismissal which is contrary to certain standards of reasonableness or other rules of law. These are currently contained in the Employment Rights Act 1996, the Transfer of Undertakings (Protection of Employment) Regulations 1981 and the Trade Union and Labour Relations (Consolidation) Act 1992 (TULRCA) as supplemented by the provisions of any relevant ACAS Code of Practice. Unfair dismissal is concerned with the employer's reason and motives for dismissal and how it is carried out; it is dealt with exclusively by Employment Tribunals and may lead to orders of reinstatement, re-engagement or compensation. **6–53**

To be protected against unfair dismissal, an employee must have been continuously employed for a period of one year at the effective date of termination.[90] The main exceptions to this are: dismissal for union membership/non-membership and dismissal for participating in union activities at an appropriate time[91]; dismissal for pregnancy[92]; dismissal for asserting a statutory right[93]; dismissal for certain health and safety reasons[94]; dismissal for making a qualifying disclosure[95]; dismissal in breach of the Working Time Regulations 1998[96]; dismissal in breach of the National Minimum Wage Act 1998[97]; and dismissal of employee representatives elected to consult on redundancies and the transfer of an undertaking.[98] In such special cases, no continuous employment is required before a complaint may be lodged.

---

89 *Johnson v Unisys Ltd* [2001] I.R.L.R. 279, HL.
90 Employment Rights Act 1996, s.108.
91 TULRCA, s.152.
92 Employment Rights Act 1996, s.99.
93 s.104.
94 s.100.
95 s.103A.
96 s.101A.
97 s.104A.
98 s.103(1).

Employees lose the right to complain of unfair dismissal when they reach the non-discriminatory normal retiring age for the position they hold or, in any other case, the age of 65.[99] Normal retiring age is determined by considering the age at which employees can be compulsorily retired (the contractual retirement age) and then considering whether that age has been departed from or abandoned in practice by the employer.[1]

Generally, an employee cannot contract out of his/her statutory right not to be unfairly dismissed or to complain to an Employment Tribunal.[2] However there are two important exceptions to this:

(1) where there has been agreement following action by an ACAS conciliation officer; and
(2) where the employee has entered into a settlement or compromise agreement having received independent legal advice (ERA, s.203).

Other employees who are excluded from unfair dismissal law are:

(1) those employed in the police service (ERA, s.200);
(2) members of the armed forces (ERA, ss.191, 192);
(3) certain civil servants (ERA, s.193, as replaced by the Employment Relations Act 1999, Sch.8)).

Continuous employment

6–54 Continuous employment is a statutory concept whose existence depends on the provisions contained in Employment Rights Act 1996, ss.210–219.

The rules relating to continuous employment may be summarised as follows:

(1) Periods of continuous employment are made of weeks that count.

(2) Except where there is a strike or lock out a week which does not count breaks continuity and the employee has to start accumulating continuity all over again.

(3) Once employment with an employer has begun it is presumed to be continuous unless the employer proves otherwise.

(4) The following weeks count as continuous employment:

(a) a week during the whole or part of which the employee's relations are governed by a contract of employment;
(b) a week in which the employee is incapable because of illness, pregnancy or childbirth;
(c) a week during which the employee is absent on account of a temporary cessation of work (for example a break between two fixed term contracts) or an arrangement whereby continuity is maintained;
(d) a week of absence because of pregnancy where a woman has exercised her statutory right to return to work;
(e) a week which occurs between dismissal and re-engagement or which occurs in the period of statutory notice the employee should have received.

Where a business or undertaking has been transferred, employment with the transferor counts along with employment with the transferee. Where an employee transfers to an employer who is

[99] s.109.
[1] *Waite v GCHQ* [1983] I.C.R. 653; *Hughes v DHSS* [1985] I.C.R. 419.
[2] Employment Rights Act 1996, s.109.

an "associated employer" of the other employer, the employment with both employers counts towards continuous employment.[3]

Dismissal

"Dismissal" is defined by ss.95 and 96 of the Employment Rights Act 1996, and if an employee cannot prove that he or she has been "dismissed" in accordance with the definition, the case is bound to fail. **6–55**

Where the employer, with or without notice, terminates the contract of employment, the employee is dismissed. Where a letter communicates dismissal, the dismissal does not take effect until the employee has read the letter or has had a reasonable opportunity of doing so, although an employee cannot avoid being dismissed by deliberately not reading the letter. Even unambiguous words of dismissal can be withdrawn if uttered in the heat of the moment; but the withdrawal must be almost immediate.[4]

Being told by an employer to "resign or be dismissed" is a dismissal even where the employee resigns.[5]

Where an employee is employed on a contract for a fixed term or a fixed task or until the occurrence of a particular event (except retirement) the expiry of that contract without its renewal is a dismissal of the employee.[6] Thus, if an employee is employed on a contract which is from January 1, 1998 until December 31, 1998, he is dismissed if the contract is not renewed on its expiry. Of course the dismissal may be fair but it is nevertheless a dismissal.

Where a contract is terminated by the employee, with or without notice, but in circumstances such that he/she is entitled to terminate without notice by reason of the employer's conduct, there is also a dismissal—referred to as a "constructive dismissal".

The test for whether an employee is entitled to terminate the contract without notice is contractual, and it is not enough for the employee merely to show that the employer's conduct had been unreasonable in some way.[7] The employer's actions must go to the root of the agreement or show that the employer no longer wishes to be bound by one or more of its essential terms.

In order to establish that he/she has been constructively dismissed, the employee must also show that the breach was what caused him/her to leave.

Reason for dismissal

In the normal case once the employee has satisfied the tribunal that he/she has been "dismissed" the onus transfers to the employer to show that the dismissal was for a potentially fair reason. These are set out in s.98(2) of the Employment Rights Act 1996. Assuming the employer can do this the tribunal then considers whether the employer has acted reasonably. Where the employee has less than one year's employment (the qualifying period for ordinary unfair dismissal claims) and is claiming that he/she has been unfairly dismissed for one of the special reasons mentioned later, the onus is on the employee to prove that he/she was dismissed for that specific reason. **6–56**

---

3 Employers are associated where one is a company that the other controls or where two or more are companies controlled by a third person: *Merton LBC v Gardiner* [1980] I.R.L.R. 472.

4 *Martin v Yeoman Aggregates Ltd* [1983] I.C.R. 314.

5 *Sheffield v Oxford Controls Ltd* [1979] I.R.L.R. 199.

6 Employment Rights Act 1996, s.95, as amended by the Fixed Term Employees (Prevention of Less Favourable Treatment) Regulations 2002.

7 *Western Excavating ECC Ltd v Sharp* [1978] I.C.R. 221; *GGHB v Pate* 1983 S.L.T. 90.

Fair reasons

6–57 (1) Related to the capability or qualifications of the employee for the work he is employed to do. Capability and qualifications are widely defined; the former includes skill, aptitude, health and mental capacity while the latter includes technical, academic and professional qualifications. The issue of capability must be resolved by reference to the work the employee was doing at the time of dismissal.

Shook v London Borough of Ealing
[1986] I.R.L.R. 46, EAT

Shook had a contractual term which allowed her employer to transfer her to any work for which her qualifications were appropriate. On her dismissal she argued that she was not incapable of doing all the kinds of work that her contract required. Her employers had therefore shown their reason for her dismissal was not related to her capability for the work she was employed to do.

The EAT held it was not necessary for the employer to show Shook was incapable of doing all the tasks which the employer was entitled by law to call upon her to discharge. In this case, however widely her contract was construed, her incapability related to her performance of her duties under her contract, even although her performance of all of them may not have been affected. There is a distinction between the reasons set out in Employment Rights Act 1996, s.98(2)(a) (capability) and (2)(b) (conduct) and the reasons in s.98(2)(c) (redundancy) and (d) (breach of statute).

According to the EAT the former two are couched in terms of "relation" whereas the latter two are couched in terms of actuality.

(2) Related to the conduct of the employee. Although statute does not state expressly, it is implied that there must be a connection between the conduct and the employee's responsibilities to his/her employers. This is sometimes referred to as the "conduct in context test". *Thomson v Alloa Motor Co. Ltd*[8] indicates that the conduct must in some way reflect on the employer/employee relationship. Thus, damage caused to employer's property when a learner driver was leaving the garage forecourt after her duties had ended (which did not involve driving), was not a reason related to her conduct. It follows therefore that acts of misconduct including criminal activities away from work can have a sufficient connection with the employment relationship to relate to the conduct of the employee; this would particularly be the case where dishonesty was involved and the employee had responsibility for money or property or where the employee held a senior (management) position.[9]

(3) The redundancy of the employee. "Redundancy" is legally defined in s.139(1) of the Employment Rights Act to mean a reduction in the needs of the business for employees to do work of a particular kind or a cessation (temporary or permanent, actual or expected) of the business, completely or in the place where the employee is employed. This is dealt with in more detail later.

(4) Contravention of a statutory enactment, either by the employer or employee, if the employee's employment were to be continued. This would apply to the continued employment of a doctor whose registration had been terminated or an employee who required to have a work permit but whose permit had expired.

[8] [1983] I.R.L.R. 403.
[9] *Norfolk County Council v Bernard* [1979] I.R.L.R. 220.

(5) Some other substantial reason (SOSR) justifying the dismissal of the employee from the position he/she held. This reason is frequently pleaded as an alternative to conduct particularly where the employer is unsure of overcoming the "conduct in context test". It usually involves establishing that the particular ground will have a negative impact upon the employer's business. It has been successfully pleaded in the following situations:

- criminal conviction unconnected with work (*Singh v London Country Bus Services Ltd*[10]);
- personality clashes resulting from disclosures of private life(*Treganowan v Robert Knee & Co. Ltd*[11]);
- reaction of best customer against conduct of employee (*Scott Packing & Warehousing Ltd v Patterson*[12]); and
- sexual proclivities of employee which made parents less likely to send their children to the camps (*Saunders v Scottish National Camps Association*[13]).

There will be SOSR for a dismissal where business conditions require the employer to introduce changes in conditions or terms of employment which employees refuse to accept, so long as it can be shown that there are pressing business needs constituting the to reason for the introduction of the changes. In such circumstances an employer would be justified in dismissing those employees who refused to accede to the new conditions.[14]

Statute also provides:

(1) that the dismissal of an employee to accommodate the return of a woman from maternity leave or from medical suspension is for SOSR (Employment Rights Act 1996, s.106); and
(2) where there has occurred a transfer of a business and there is an economic, organisational or technical reason entailing changes in the workforce of the transferee or transferor either before of after transfer, the dismissal of an employee shall be for SOSR (Transfer of Undertakings (Protection of Employment) Regulations 1981, reg.8).

Admissible evidence

Contrary to the position in cases involving alleged wrongful dismissal, in unfair dismissal employers are restricted to producing evidence of which they were aware at the time they took the decision to dismiss. Thus information or evidence of misconduct which comes to light after the decision to dismiss has been taken, cannot be relied on by the employer to show the reason for the dismissal or that its conduct in dismissing the employee was reasonable.[15] **6–58**

The next question is whether the employer has acted reasonably and shown a sufficient reason for dismissing the employee.[16] In considering the issue of reasonableness, it is recognised that there is a "band" of reasonable responses to the employee's conduct, of which one employer might reasonably take one view and another quite reasonably take another. Ultimately, it is for the tribunal as an industrial jury to decide whether the employer's decision fell within this band. It is not for the tribunal to substitute their views for those of the employer.[17] A tribunal which seeks to avoid the band of reasonable response approach and substitute their views for those of the employer commits an error of law.[18]

---

[10] [1976] I.R.L.R. 176.
[11] [1975] I.C.R. 405.
[12] [1978] I.R.L.R. 166.
[13] [1981] I.R.L.R. 277.
[14] *Hollister v NFU* [1979] I.R.L.R. 238.
[15] *Devis & Sons Ltd v Atkins* [1977] I.C.R. 662.
[16] Employment Rights Act 1996, s.98(4).
[17] *Iceland Frozen Foods Ltd v Jones* [1983] I.C.R. 17.
[18] *Post Office v Foley* [2000] I.R.L.R. 827.

The issue of reasonableness—procedural matters

6–59 To determine whether an employer acts reasonably it is necessary to have regard to the guidance given by the House of Lords in *Polkey v A E Dayton Services Ltd*,[19] overruling *British Labour Pump v Byrne*.[20]

The rule in *Polkey* may be summarised that where there is a serious flaw in the employer's pre-dismissal procedure, the dismissal will be unfair unless the employer, on the information available to it, would be acting reasonably by adopting no (or no further) procedure because such a (further) procedure would be "utterly futile". Thus, the issues for the tribunal are:

- What did the employer do or fail to do?
- Was that failure/defect serious?
- What would a reasonable employer do?
- Was further procedure utterly futile?

In relation to this last question if the answer is Yes, the dismissal will be procedurally fair; if No, the dismissal will be unfair.

Key Concepts

- Employee must prove he/she has been dismissed.
- Employer must prove reason for dismissal is one recognised by s.98.
- Whether a dismissal is fair depends on whether it falls within the bands of reasonable responses.
- The Employment Tribunal must not simply substitute its own view of whether the employer acted reasonably.

Employment Act 2002

6–60 The Employment Act 2002 will affect the position when it becomes effective in 2004. It seeks to encourage workplace resolution of disputes by requiring employers and employees to follow certain statutory disciplinary and grievance procedures.

Statutory procedures

6–61 The standard[21] statutory procedure for discipline or dismissal requires: (1) the employer to set out in writing the alleged conduct of the employee; (2) send it to the employee; (3) invite him to a meeting to discuss it; (4) hold the meeting before disciplinary action (except suspension[22]); (5) inform the employee of the decision and of the right to appeal; and (6) after any appeal inform the employee of the final decision. However the Act[23] also permits regulations to be made about a variety of matters including: (a) the application of the statutory procedures; (b) when a procedure is to be taken to be completed; and most importantly; (c) what constitutes compliance with a statutory procedure.

The 2002 Act will also insert into the Employment Rights Act 1996 a new section 98A on "procedural fairness". This provision will oblige Employment Tribunals, when assessing fairness,

[19] [1987] I.R.L.R. 503.
[20] [1979] I.C.R. 347.
[21] The standard procedure operates where the decision to discipline has not yet been taken but is modified where dismissal has already occurred: Sch.2.
[22] Presumably this means suspension to permit investigation to take place and not disciplinary suspension.
[23] s.31(6).

to disregard employers' failures to take procedures which are additional to the prescribed statutory procedures if following such (additional) procedures would have had no effect on the decision to dismiss and to that extent the rule in *Polkey* has been modified. On the other hand the Tribunal would be bound to hold unfair any dismissal which did not follow or "complete" the statutory procedures. Thus when these provisions of the 2002 Act are brought into effect only in a case of a failure to follow the statutory procedure will an employer be prevented from arguing that following the procedure would have made no difference. In such a case the Tribunal will be compelled to hold a dismissal unfair for want of following the statutory procedure. In all other cases a Tribunal will be able to hold that although a procedure was not followed the dismissal was still fair if the employer would have been dismissed even if he had followed the procedure.

Special situations

What has been stated above applies to dismissal for the ordinary reasons, namely: conduct, **6–62**
capability, redundancy, breach of statute and some other substantial reason. However, special rules exist for some special categories of dismissal and these are discussed now.

Industrial action and lock-outs

Where the industrial action is official (broadly this means that the action has been authorised by the employee's trade union) or where the dismissal is during a lock-out, the position is regulated by s.238 of TULRCA, and an Employment Tribunal may only entertain an application if one or more relevant employees has not been dismissed. Where the action is unofficial employees who are dismissed while taking part have no right to claim unfair dismissal even if other employees who also took part were not dismissed.[24]

Protected industrial action

Where an employee takes part in protected industrial action (action for which the trade union has immunity) his/her dismissal will be unfair if one of three conditions is satisfied. First, where the dismissal took place within eight weeks of the start of the action. Secondly, where the dismissal took place outwith the eight week period but the employee had stopped taking part in the action before the eight week period ended. Thirdly, where the dismissal is outwith the eight-week period and the employee is still taking part in it but the employer has failed to take reasonable procedural steps to resolve the dispute.[25]

Union membership and activities

Individual employees receive certain rights to allow them to join and to participate in the activities **6–63**
of an Independent Trade Union (ITU). Thus, ss.152 and 153 of the TULRCA provided it is unfair to dismiss (or select for redundancy) an employee who:

(a) is or proposes to become a member of an ITU;
(b) has taken part or proposes to take part in the activities of an ITU at an appropriate time;
(c) is not a member of any trade union or of a particular trade union; or
(d) has refused to become or remain a union member.

---

[24] TULRCA, s.237.
[25] TULRCA, s.238A.

It is also unfair to dismiss an employee who refuses to pay a sum or suffer deduction from wages in lieu of membership. In the case of the dismissal of a non-union member, a third party (for example, the trade union itself) may be "sisted" or joined as a respondent in the proceedings as well as the employer.

Union recognition dismissals

6–64 Until the Employment Relations Act 1999 an employer could not be compelled to recognise a trade union for collective bargaining purposes. The 1999 Act has introduced such a right (see TULRCA, Sch.A1) and special rules now make it unfair to dismiss employees in connection with union recognition. It is unfair to dismiss employees who seek to obtain, support or prevent union recognition or the ending of bargaining arrangements or who vote or seek to influence the way others vote in a ballot about union recognition.[26] It is also unfair to select employees for redundancy in a discriminatory way if the reason for their selection was one concerned with union recognition.[27] There is no qualifying period or upper age limit for such dismissals.

Health and safety dismissals

6–65 The present provisions are to be found in Employment Rights Act 1996, s.100 where it is declared that dismissal of an employee for any of the following reasons will be unfair:

(a) carrying out health and safety duties by an employee designated by the employer to carry out such duties (for example a safety officer);
(b) carrying out functions as health and safety representative or safety committee member;
(c) taking part in consultations with the employer as a representative of employee safety or seeking election to such a post;
(d) where there are no safety representatives or safety committee or it is not reasonably practicable to use them and the employee reasonably believes these circumstances were harmful to health or safety;
(e) leaving the place of work in circumstances of danger which the employee reasonably believed to be serious and imminent and which he/she could not reasonably be expected to avert;
(f) taking appropriate steps to protect himself/herself or others (including members of the public).

There is no qualifying period or upper-age limit for the above protections.

Asserting a statutory right

6–66 It is unfair to dismiss an employee if the reason was one of the following;

- he/she brought proceedings against the employer to enforce a statutory employment right;
- he/she alleged that the employer had infringed a statutory employment right.[28]

It is not necessary to show that the employee actually had the right in question so long as the claim to the right is made in good faith and the rules about qualifying period and upper age limit do not apply. While this provision only applies to certain statutory rights namely those described in s.104(4) of the Employment Rights Act 1996. They include:

---

[26] TULRCA, Sch.A1, para.161.
[27] TULRCA, Sched.A1, para.162.
[28] Employment Rights Act 1996, s.104.

- rights conferred by the Employment Rights Act 1996 which can be enforced by Employment Tribunals;
- the right conferred by s.86 of the Employment Rights Act 1996 (to minimum notice of termination);
- rights conferred by ss.68, 86, 146, 168, and 170 of the TULRCA (*i.e.* deductions from pay, union activities and time off); and
- rights conferred by the Working Time Regulations 1998.

Dismissals on the transfer of an undertaking

Until 1981 employees who worked in businesses that were sold or acquired by another employer could find that the person who acquired the business did not wish to employ the existing workforce at all. To remedy this situation the EC Acquired Rights Directive was adopted. The Directive has been implemented in the UK by the Transfer of Undertakings (Protection of Employment) Regulations (TUPE) 1981. The Regulations do essentially two things for employees who work in businesses which are sold or transferred to a new owner (the transferee). First, the contractual rights and duties that the employees enjoyed with the old owner (the transferor) are automatically transferred and become binding on the new owner (reg.5). Secondly, in order to complement this transfer of contracts the dismissal of an employee because of the transfer (or a reason connected with it) is unfair (reg.8(1)). An employee who is dismissed for a reason connected with the transfer of an undertaking or business has the right to complain that he/she was unfairly dismissed so long as the normal qualifying period for unfair dismissal is satisfied. However, it is a defence for the employer to show that the dismissal was for an economic, technical or organisational reason entailing changes in the workforce (reg.8(2)). In such a case the dismissal is deemed to have been for a substantial reason and whether it is fair or unfair will depend upon the general issue of reasonableness. **6–67**

Pregnancy and family leave

By s.99 of the Employment Rights Act (which is not dependent on a period of continuous employment) a dismissal is unfair if the reason or the principal reason for it is prescribed by the Maternity and Parental Leave Regulations 1999. **6–68**

Regulation 20 provides that an employee who is dismissed (or selected for redundancy) is unfairly dismissed if: (a) the principal reason for the dismissal (or selection for redundancy) is specified in the regulation; or (b) the principal reason for the dismissal is that the employee is redundant and alternative employment has not been offered in accordance with reg.10 of the 1999 Regulations.

The Regulation specifies the following as reasons which make the dismissal (or selection for redundancy) automatically unfair:

(a) the pregnancy of the employee;

(b) the employee has given birth to a child and dismissal ends her maternity leave;

(c) because of a legal requirement or a recommendation under a Health and Safety Code of Practice, the employee was suspended from work on the ground that she was pregnant, had recently given birth or was breast-feeding;

(d) she took, sought to take or availed herself of the benefits of, ordinary maternity leave;

(e) she took or sought to take—

(i) additional maternity leave;

(ii) parental leave;

(iii) time off for family emergencies;

(f) she declined to sign a workforce agreement relating to maternity, parental or family emergencies;

(g) performed (or proposed to perform) any functions or activities as a representative or candidate in relation to a workforce agreement.

Similar protection is now extended to employees who take Adoption or Paternity Leave.

Whistle-blowing

6–69 The effect of s.103A of the Employment Rights Act 1996 is to make it unfair to dismiss an employee who makes any disclosure of information which in the reasonable belief of the person making it tends to show one or more of the following:

(a) a criminal offence has been committed;
(b) someone is failing to comply with a legal obligation;
(c) a miscarriage of justice has occurred or may occur;
(d) the health and safety of any individual is likely to be endangered;
(e) the environment is likely to be damaged; or
(f) information regarding any of the above is likely to be deliberately concealed.

However this is not a "whistle-blowers' charter" in that dismissal is unfair only where the disclosure is made to certain people, *i.e.* an employer, a legal adviser, a Minister of the Crown who has appointed an employer, or a person designated by the Secretary of State (see the Public Interest (Prescribed Persons) Order 1999 (SI 1999/1549)) to whom the disclosure may be made.[29]

Other special cases

6–70 Employees and workers are also protected from dismissal in connection with their rights under the Working Time Regulations and the National Minimum Wage Act and in relation to tax credits. It is also unfair to dismiss employees who are trustees of an occupational pension scheme or employee representative for the purposes of consultation on redundancy or the transfer of an undertaking. There is no qualifying period or upper age limit in any of these cases.

Remedies for unfair dismissal

6–71 The Employment Rights Act (ss.111–132) creates a framework of remedies for unfair dismissal. The primary remedy is supposed to be re-employment (either re-instatement or re-engagement) but this has not been the case in practice. There is also a right to compensation where either the Tribunal refuses to order re-employment or the employee does not seek this remedy. Compensation is made up of two elements—the basic award and the compensatory award. There is also a right to an additional award where the tribunal has ordered re-employment and this has not been complied with by the employer.

[29] Employment Rights Act 1996, ss.43C–43F.

Reinstatement and re-engagement

An order of reinstatement is an order from the tribunal requiring the employer to treat the complainant in all respects as if he/she had not been dismissed.[30] A tribunal can make an order of re-engagement on such terms as it may decide that the complainant be engaged by the employer, or by a successor employer, or by an associated employer, in employment comparable to that from which he/she was dismissed or other suitable employment (see the Employment Rights Act 1996, s.115(1)). **6–72**

There is a clear order of priorities as regards re-employment. First, the tribunal must consider reinstatement and only if this is not ordered should it consider re-engagement and on what terms. In conducting this exercise the tribunal must consider the following:

(a) the wishes of the complainant;
(b) whether it is practicable for the employer to comply;
(c) where the complainant caused or contributed to the dismissal, whether it would be just to make the order (see the Employment Rights Act 1996, s.116(1)).

Where the employer fails to comply with the order, the tribunal can make an additional award (subject to the practicability issue again).

Compensation

A complainant's compensation is made up of two elements—a basic award and a compensatory award. **6–73**

The basic award

The basic award is calculated by reference to the period, ending with the effective date of termination (EDT), during which the employee has been continuously employed, by starting at the end of that period and reckoning backwards the number of years of employment and allowing: **6–74**

(a) one-and-a-half weeks' pay for each year in which the employee is over 41;
(b) one week's pay for each year in which the employee was between 22 and 41; and
(c) half a week's pay for each year of employment under 22.[31] The maximum number of years that can be taken into account is 20 and the maximum amount of a week's pay is currently £250.

In cases of dismissal for union membership or activities, or for carrying out duties of: (1) a health and safety representative; or (2) a representative in connection with the Working Time Regulations; or (3) a trustee of an occupational pension scheme there is a minimum basic award.[32]

Compensatory award

Section 123(1) of the Employment Rights Act declares that the amount of the compensatory award will be such amount as the tribunal considers just and equitable in all the circumstances having regard to the loss sustained by the complainant in consequence of the dismissal, in so far as that action is attributable to action taken by the employer. The award is subject to a statutory maximum that is currently £51,700. **6–75**

---

[30] Employment Rights Act 1996, s.114(1).
[31] Employment Rights Act 1996, s.119(2).
[32] Employment Rights Act 1996, s.120.

The principles for calculation of the compensatory award were first discussed in *Norton Tool Co. Ltd v Tewson*[33] where the most important heads of loss were stated to be as follows:

(a) *Immediate loss of wages*: This is compensation for actual loss of wages and other benefits from the date of dismissal to the date of the hearing.
(b) *Future loss*: Where the complainant is still out of work at the date of the hearing the tribunal can make an award to cover future loss of wages.
(c) *Loss of pension rights*: The sum here might be substantial, particularly where the complainant contributed to an occupational pension scheme and remains unemployed.
(d) *Loss arising from the manner of the dismissal*: An employee has no general right to compensation for the distress caused by dismissal or for injury to feelings. However, occasionally, employees may be entitled to compensation where there is cogent evidence that the manner of dismissal may have caused financial loss.
(e) *Loss of statutory protection*: There may be occasions where the loss of service-related rights, such as the right to long notice, can be compensated under this head.

Interim relief

6–76 In certain cases (union membership dismissals, health and safety and working time cases, employee representative dismissals and dismissals for making a protected disclosure) employees can apply to an Employment Tribunal for interim relief. This is an order that the employee's contract, if terminated, will continue in force as if it had not been terminated and, if not terminated, that it will continue in force, in either case until the complaint is settled or determined by the Tribunal. The continuation covers pay and other benefits such as pensions and seniority rights and for determining the period of continuous employment.

Key Concepts

Ordinarily an employee who is over 65 is not protected against **unfair dismissal**.

Ordinarily an employee is not protected against unfair dismissal until he/she has **one years' continuous employment**.

In specific situations whether a dismissal is unfair does **not** depend on the **reasonableness** of the employer's actions.

The **remedies** for unfair dismissal are reinstatement, re-engagement and compensation.

REDUNDANCY PAYMENTS

6–77 The system for compensating employees for loss of employment on account of redundancy was first introduced by the Redundancy Payments Act 1965.

General principles

6–78 The provisions relating to redundancy payments are now contained in the Employment Rights Act 1996, Pt XI. Provided an employee has two years' continuous employment and is under 65, he

[33] [1972] I.C.R. 501.

becomes entitled to a redundancy payment on being dismissed for redundancy or after a spell of lay-off or short time.[34]

Dismissal

6–79 Dismissal is defined variously and includes the failure to permit return of pregnant employee and implied termination.[35] For redundancy payments law, a lock-out will not support a constructive dismissal and where an employee is under notice of redundancy and wishes to leave before the expiry of the employer's notice, his notice must be in writing and given during the "obligatory period". Where in accordance with an enactment or rule of law (a) an act on the part of an employer or (b) an event affecting an employer (including an individual employer's death) operates to terminate the contract of employment, that act or event shall be taken to be a termination of the contract by the employer.[36] The result is that certain circumstances which would otherwise be regard as a frustration of the employment contract are deemed to be dismissals thereby preserving the employee's right to claim a redundancy payment.

Where an employee volunteers for redundancy there are two possible analyses: (1) he agrees to be dismissed in which case he is entitled to a redundancy payment; and (2) the contract is ended by mutual consent in which case there is no dismissal and he is not entitled to a payment. Thus where an employee "volunteers" for redundancy, there is a dismissal provided the causative act (to bring the employment to an end) is that of the employer alone, so that where employees applied for early retirement and the employer accepted their applications there was no dismissal but rather termination by mutual consent.[37]

An employee laid off or on short-time may serve notice on his employer that he intends to terminate the employment and claim a redundancy payment. Unless the employer can show that full time employment is to be resumed, the employee will become entitled to a redundancy payment.[38]

Redundancy

6–80 For purposes of redundancy payments, the definition of redundancy is set out in s.139 of the Employment Rights Act 1996. An employee is dismissed by reason of redundancy if the dismissal is attributable wholly or mainly attributable to the following:

(a) the fact that his employer has ceased or intends to cease, (i) to carry on the business for the purposes of which the employee was employed by him or, (ii) to carry on that business in the place the employee was employed; or
(b) the fact that the requirements of that business, (i) for employees to carry out work of a particular kind or, (ii) for employees to carry out work of a particular kind in the place the employee was employed have ceased or diminished either permanently or temporarily.

There are thus two "limbs" to the definition of redundancy. The first is where the employer ceases the business for the purpose of which the employee was employed, either completely or at the place the employee has been employed. The second deals with whether the requirements of the business for employees to do "work of a particular" have ceased or diminished. Whether a "business" ceases is a question of fact and the judicial approach is illustrated by

---

[34] Employment Rights Act 1996, ss.135, 155.
[35] Employment Rights Act 1996, ss.136, 137.
[36] Employment Rights Act 1996, s.136(5).
[37] *Birch & Humber v Liverpool University* [1989] I.R.L.R. 165.
[38] Employment Rights Act 1996, ss.135, 147.

Melon v Hector Powe Ltd
1981 S.L.T. 74, HL

A company (Hector Powe Ltd) owned a factory at which men's suits were made for sale in the company's retail outlets. They sold the factory and its equipment to another company (Executex Ltd) which made suits for sale in the retail market generally. The employees remained and did the same kind of work (making suits) working for Executex but the House of Lords held that this resulted in there being the transfer of assets of the business but not the transfer of a business. Making suits for dedicated retail outlets also owned by the factory, was a different type of business from making suits for sale to any wholesale for onward retail sales. Hector Powe Ltd had ceased to carry on the business of making suits for its own retail outlets when it sold the factory and its equipment to Executex Ltd.

In the definition of redundancy, the place the employee is employed is important. To establish the place of employment and the kind of work for which there is a reduced requirement, until recently the contract test was applied.[39]

The "contractual" approach to determining what is the employee's place of employment has now been expressly rejected by the EAT and the Court of Appeal.[40]

Requiring employees to work different hours will generally not mean that an employee who is dismissed because he is unwilling or unable to work the new hours will be dismissed for redundancy. The critical question is whether the change in working hours is such that it can be said that the requirements of the business to do work of a particular kind has ceased or diminished.[41]

Archibald v Rossleigh Commercials Ltd
[1975] I.R.L.R. 231

Archibald had been employed as a night shift mechanic whose hours of work were from 10pm to 8am six nights a week. When the employer decided that it would no longer keep the premises open 24 hours a day, Archibald was offered work as a day mechanic but refused and claimed a redundancy payment. The Employment Tribunal upheld his claim because the employers requirement for employees to do work of a particular kind which the applicant was employed to do—work of a night mechanic—had ceased. The Tribunal pointed out that his duties were different from those of the day shift, in that Archibald was required to attend to emergencies which arose during the night; it was not merely a change of the time at which the work was done.

To determine whether the requirements of the business, for employees to do work of a particular kind, it may be necessary to distinguish an employee's skills or abilities from other attributes and the critical issue in each case is: "Have the requirements for work of a particular kind ceased or diminished?" and that requires a careful examination of the work the employer requires to be performed.[42]

The dismissal of one employee to accommodate, and prevent the dismissal of another redundant employee, is also to be regarded as a dismissal on the grounds of redundancy. The concept known as "bumping" means that an employee whose job continues, may nevertheless be seen to have been dismissed by reason of redundancy. The reason for this definition of redundancy contained in s.131(1)(b) of the Employment Rights Act 1996 does not expressly require that the redundant

[39] *Haden Ltd v Cowen* [1982] I.R.L.R. 314.

[40] *Bass Leisure Ltd v Thomas* [1994] I.R.L.R. 104; *High Table Ltd v Horst* [1997] I.R.L.R. 513.

[41] *Johnson v Nottinghamshire Combined Police Authority* [1974] I.C.R. 170, CA.

[42] *Sartin v Co-operative Retail Services Ltd*, 1969 VII K.I.R. 382.

employee be an employee who is employed on the particular kind of work the requirements of which have ceased or diminished.[43]

Where an employee is dismissed by reason of redundancy his entitlement to a redundancy payment may be lost if he refuses an offer of suitable alternative employment made by his employer or an associated employer.[44] The offer need not be in writing; it may be a collective one (or advertised on a notice board) but it must be made before the end of the prior contract and must begin within four weeks of end of prior contract. If the employment offered is not suitable the employee is entitled to receive a redundancy payment.

Whether alternative employment offered is suitable, and whether the employee's refusal is reasonable, requires a consideration of all facts and circumstances.

Cahuc, Johnson & Crouch v Allen Amery Ltd

[1966] I.T.R. 313

The three employees were previously employed in Hackney, London E2 and were offered, but refused, alternative employment in EC1. The Employment Tribunal held that the offer was unsuitable because each employee lived very close to the old premises but the new premises involved a bus journey of at least 40 minutes. One employee had a widowed mother whom she had been able to look after while she worked at the old premises but would not be able to do so at the new ones. The tribunal observed "The third factor ... was the inconvenience and the time in travelling. It is manifest that it is a great advantage to have a job which does not involve travel in London. If she accepted the offer it would take about 40 minutes in each direction. There is no need to underline the inconveniences of waiting for and the difficulty of catching buses in rush hours, bad weather etc ... We find ... the offer was not of suitable employment in relation to the employees."

Bruce v NCB

[1967] I.T.R. 159

As the alternative employment offered to Bruce, who was a diabetic, would have involved him working three shifts instead of two, his routine would be sufficiently disturbed to allow him to reasonably reject the offer.

Where the employer has given notice of termination but the employer justifiably terminates for misconduct of the employee, entitlement to a redundancy payment depends on whether an Employment Tribunal thinks it is just and equitable to make a payment.[45]

Once the employee has proved he has been dismissed and that he is not excluded from entitlement, an employee can rely on presumption that the reason for dismissal is redundancy.[46]

To preserve his entitlement the claimant must, within six months: (1) agree and receive a payment; (2) serve written notice of claim on ex-employer; (3) refer entitlement to an Employment Tribunal; or (4) present unfair dismissal claim.[47]

Exclusions

The main exclusions operate in relation to: (i) domestic servants related to the employer and employed in a private household[48]; and (ii) employees on fixed term contract for more than two **6–81**

[43] *Murray v Foyle Meats Ltd* [1999] I.R.L.R. 562, HL.
[44] Employment Rights Act 1996, s.141.
[45] Employment Rights Act 1996, ss.140, 143.
[46] Employment Rights Act 1996, ss.163(1), 210(5).
[47] Employment Rights Act 1996, s.164(1).
[48] Employment Rights Act 1996, s.161(1).

years.[49] An employee who is employed under a fixed term contract for more than two years may agree to exclude or waive his right to receive a redundancy payment when his contract expires without being renewed. However, the opportunity to exclude the right to redundancy payment in this way has been removed by the Fixed Term Employees (Prevention of Unfavourable Treatment) Regulations 2002 for fixed term contracts entered into after July 10, 2002.

Payments

6–82 Payments are calculated in accordance with statutory rules which apply a formula consisting of: (i) the length of the employee's continuous employment prior to the relevant date (which usually the date the notice of termination expires); (ii) the employee's week's pay; and (iii) the age of the employee.[50] Service below 18 years does not count and employment after 64 years results in reduction of payment by 1/12 for every month worked over 64.[51] The week's pay is subject to variable statutory limit, currently £260.

Key Concepts

Redundancy is a legal concept.

To be entitled to a redundancy payment an employee must have **two years' continuous employment**.

Refusing an offer of suitable employment can result in loss of entitlement to a redundancy payment.

DISCRIMINATION

6–83 Until the 1970s the law of the UK did little to prevent employers treating less favourably job applicants and employees on account of their sex, sexual orientation, race, colour, nationality, religion, political opinions, age or disability. Legislation now makes it unlawful to treat applicants and employees less favourably on various grounds. Legislation now deals with discrimination on grounds of (1) sex, transsexualism, sexual orientation, pregnancy and marital status; (2) race, colour, ethnic and national origins and nationality; (3) disability; (4) religion; (5) being part-time workers; and (6) being fixed term contract employees.

Sex discrimination

6–84 The Sex Discrimination Act 1975 (SDA) and the Equal Pay Act 1970 (EPA), as supplemented by their respective Codes of Practice, make it unlawful to discriminate on grounds of sex, pregnancy, marital status and transexualism.

Although the UK courts were unsure of whether discrimination on the grounds of pregnancy fell within the ambit of sex discrimination that matter has been resolved by the European Court of Justice in the following case.

[49] Employment Rights Act 1996, s.197(3).
[50] Employment Rights Act 1996, s.162(1), (2).
[51] Employment Rights Act 1996, ss.162(4), 211(3).

Dekker v VJV Centrum

[1991] I.R.L.R. 27, ECJ

Mrs Dekker applied for a post with VJV Centrum but was refused employment because the employer would have suffered financially during a period of maternity leave to which Mrs Dekker would have been entitled.

The ECJ held that whether a refusal to employ results in direct sex discrimination on grounds of sex depends on whether the most important reason is one which applies without distinction to employees of both sexes, or whether it exclusively applies to one sex. As employment can only be refused because of pregnancy to women, such a refusal is direct discrimination on grounds of sex, and an employer acts contrary to the principle of equal treatment contained in the Equal Treatment Directive if he refuses to enter a contract with a female applicant who is suitable for the post in question because of the possible adverse financial consequences of employing a pregnant woman; it is not important that there are no male applicants.

Direct sex discrimination occurs where an employer treats (or would treat) a person less favourably than a person of the opposite sex on the grounds of his or her sex.[52] Direct marital status discrimination occurs where an employer treats (or would treat) a married person less favourably than an unmarried person of the same sex.[53] In each case the relevant circumstances must not be materially different[54] but the subjective motive of an employer is not relevant; the question is whether but for his/her sex the employee would not have been treated less favourably. In *James v Eastleigh Borough Council*,[55] in which female pensioners were not required to pay for entry into a local authority pool while male pensioners like Mr James were, the House of Lords held that the test which should be applied in assessing whether there was direct discrimination was the "but for" test, namely, would the applicant have received different treatment from the respondent but for his or her sex? But for Mr James's sex he would have been entitled to free entry to the swimming pool.

Generally, positive discrimination, which means the more favourable treatment of a person on grounds of sex in order to overcome the fact that his or her sex is under-represented in a work group, is not permitted. The only exceptions to this relate to offering training opportunities to existing employees,[56] but an employer is not permitted to recruit an applicant of one sex in preference to a better qualified applicant of the other sex.

The law recognises there are genuine occupational qualifications (GOQs) which permit discrimination:

(1) where the essential nature of the job calls for a man (or woman) for reasons of physiology or, in dramatic performances, authenticity;
(2) where the job needs to be held by a man (or woman) in order to preserve decency or privacy because it is likely to involve physical contact with women in circumstances in which they may reasonably object, or women might object to the job being done by a man because they are in a state of undress or using sanitary facilities, or the job involves working in a private home and objection may be taken to a woman having social contact or knowledge of intimate details of life of a person living there;
(3) where the nature of the establishment makes it impracticable for the job holder to live elsewhere than in premises provided by the employer (*e.g.* lighthouse keepers, oil rig workers) and (i) there are sleeping or sanitary facilities for one sex and (ii) it is not

52 Sex Discrimination Act 1975, s.1(2).
53 Sex Discrimination Act 1975, s.3.
54 Sex Discrimination Act 1975, s.5(3).
55 [1990] I.C.R. 554.
56 Sex Discrimination Act 1975, ss.47, 48. And see *Kalanke v Freie Hansestadt Bremen* [1995] I.R.L.R. 660 and *Marschall v Land Nordrhein-Westphalen* [1998] I.R.L.R. 39.

reasonable to expect employer to provide separate or alternative facilities for the opposite sex;

(4) where the work is to be done in an establishment (or part of one) like a hospital or prison for persons (who are all men (women)) requiring special care or supervision and that its reasonable that the job should not be held by a woman (man);

(5) where the job holder provides persons with personal services promoting their welfare or education or similar personal services which can most effectively be provided by a member of a particular sex, *e.g.* rape crisis centre workers or even relationship counsellors;

(6) where the job is likely to involve performance of duties in a country (*e.g.* certain Middle East countries) whose laws or customs would mean that a woman could not effectively perform the duties; and

(7) the job is one of two to be held by a married couple so that it need not be offered to an unmarried couple or two men or women.

A GOQ may not be pleaded where the employer has sufficient employees of the appropriate sex who are capable of doing the GOQ part of a job and it would be reasonable to employ them on these duties.[57]

Indirect sex discrimination occurs where an employer applies a practice, provision or criterion (*i.e.* what looks like a gender-neutral criterion) which is to the detriment of a considerably larger proportion of women than men. In practice, it would be to the detriment of more women and it is unlawful unless the employer can show it is justifiable criterion having regard to the duties of the job.[58]

Examples of criteria being to the detriment of more women than men are:

- full time hours only;
- age limits;
- length of service before rights are obtained; and
- benefits to permanent employees only.

Indirect discrimination requires consideration of proportions and not merely numbers, and that the definition of the pool or population in relation to which proportionality is to be measured is vitally important. There is no hard and fast rule as to the selection of the appropriate pool and much depends on the nature of the alleged discriminatory act.

London Underground v Edwards (No.2)

[1998] I.R.L.R. 364

In this case it was proposed to introduce new flexible work rostering of train operators. Ms Edwards argued that the rostering was to the detriment of a considerably larger proportion of women. She was only one of 21 women employed as train operators and only she could not comply. All the other operators (2,023) were men and all of them could comply. When dealing with the identification of the pool Potter L.J. stated:

"The identity of the appropriate pool will depend on identifying that sector of the relevant workforce which is affected or potentially affected by the application of the particular requirement or condition in question and the context or the circumstances in which it is sought to be applied. In this case the pool was all the members of the workforce of the Underground, namely train operators to whom the new rostering requirements were to be applied. [I]t did not include all employees of the London Underground. Nor did the pool extend to include the wider field of potential new applicants for the job of train operator ... because the discrimination complained of

[57] Sex Discrimination Act 1975, s.7(4).

[58] Sex Discrimination Act 1975, s.1(2).

> was the requirement for existing employees to enter a new contract embodying the new rostering arrangement; it was not a complaint brought by an applicant from outside complaining about the terms of the job applied for."

Whether being unable to comply with the requirement is to the complainant's detriment is a matter of fact but the standard is not high and it is enough if the complainant can show that he or she has been placed at some disadvantage.[59]

There is no indirect discrimination if the provision, practice or criteria is justified. The most useful analysis is in the race case of *Hampson v Department of Education and Science*[60] in which it was emphasised that whether a requirement or condition is "justifiable" requires an objective balance to be struck between the discriminatory effect of the provision and the reasonable needs of the employer's business. This reflects the views of the European Court of Justice in equal pay cases like *Bilka-Kaufhaus v Hartz*[61] where it was held that to justify a requirement or condition the employer must show that the means chosen correspond to a real need on the part of the business, are appropriate to achieve that objective and are necessary.

For the Sex Discrimination Act 1975, employment means "employment under a contract of service or of apprenticeship or a contract personally to execute any work or labour".[62] Clearly, this definition embraces, but is also wider than, a contract of employment and can include some self-employed workers.[63]

It is unlawful for an employer to discriminate against a person in relation to the following:

(a) the arrangements he makes for determining who should be offered employment for example the recruitment and selection process;
(b) the terms on which he offers employment, *e.g.* requiring that the job-holder works full time;
(c) by refusing to offer employment for example rejecting a job applicant;
(d) in the way he affords access to promotion, training, transfer, benefits, facilities or services; or
(e) by dismissing or subjecting a person to some other detriment.[64]

Transsexuals

In its original form, the Sex Discrimination Act 1975 did not confer protection against discrimination on the grounds of transsexuality. However, in *P v S & Cornwall County Council*,[65] the ECJ concluded that it is contrary to the Equal Treatment Directive to dismiss a person on the ground that he/she was intending to undergo or had undergone gender reassignment; that was to treat him/her unfavourably in comparison with persons of the sex to which he/she was deemed to belong before undergoing gender re-assignment. The Sex Discrimination (Gender Re-assignment Regulations) 1999 made it unlawful to discriminate against a person on the grounds of transsexuality subject to special GOQs that apply. **6–85**

Sexual orientation

The Sex Discrimination Act 1975 does not extend to discrimination on the grounds of sexuality. **6–86**

[59] See *Ministry of Defence v Jeremiah* [1980] I.C.R. 13 and *Barclays Bank v Kapur (No.2)* [1995] I.R.L.R. 87.
[60] [1989] I.C.R. 179.
[61] [1987] I.C.R. 110.
[62] Sex Discrimination Act 1975, s.82(2).
[63] *Hugh-Jones v St John's College, Cambridge* [1979] I.C.R. 848; *Gillick v Roevin Management Services Ltd and BP Chemicals Ltd* [1993] I.R.L.R. 437.
[64] Sex Discrimination Act 1975, s.6. Subjecting a person to a detriment covers harassment. See *Porcelli v Strathclyde Regional Council* [1986] I.C.R. 564.
[65] [1996] I.R.L.R. 347.

Ministry of Defence v MacDonald
[2001] I.R.L.R. 431

The Court of Session has held that in the Sex Discrimination Act 1975, the phrase "on the ground of sex" means discrimination on the basis of gender, and does not include discrimination on the ground of sexual orientation, and that such an interpretation was not incompatible with the European Convention on Human Rights because the decision of the European Court of Human Rights in *Salgueiro da Silva Mouta v Portugal* [2001] 1 F.C.R. 653 (relied on by the EAT in its decision) did not mean that "sex" as used in Art.14 of the Convention included sexual orientation.

The court further held (by a majority of 2:1) that s.5(3) of the Sex Discrimination Act required that the relevant circumstances of cases to be compared were the same or not materially different, and in the context of the present case where the Ministry of Defence had terminated Mr MacDonald's employment on the grounds of his being attracted to males, the correct comparator was a female who was attracted to females. As it was not disputed that a female homosexual (*i.e.* a female attracted to other females) would have been treated in the same way as Mr MacDonald, there had been no breach of his right not to be discriminated against on the grounds of his sex.

However, as a result of the European Community Directive 2000/78, UK law will have to render unlawful discrimination by employers on the ground of sexual orientation by December 2, 2003—to this effect the Employment Equality (Sexual Orientation) Regulations 2003 have been passed. The Regulations make it unlawful for employers to discriminate against a person, directly or indirectly, on grounds of sexual orientation. However certain exceptions apply where the nature of the employment or the context in which it is carried out requires it.

Race discrimination

6–87 The Race Relations Act 1976 (RRA) is modelled on the Sex Discrimination Act 1975 (SDA) and it is dealt with here only in so far as it contains significant differences.

A person commits an act of direct discrimination if "on racial grounds he treats a person less favourably than he treats or would treat other persons". This includes treating someone (A) less favourably because of another person's (B) race[66] as where Mr Owens, who was white, was dismissed from his job as manager of an amusement centre for failing to comply with an instruction to exclude young black people from the centre; the words "on racial grounds" in s.1(1)(a) are perfectly capable of covering any reason for an action based on race, whether it be the race of the person affected by the action or of others.

Racial grounds

6–88 "Racial grounds" covers colour, race, nationality, ethnic[67] or national origins and "racial group" means a group of persons defined by reference to these characteristics.[68] Nationality covers nationality or citizenship of a state, whether acquired at birth or subsequently.[69]

The Race Relations Act applies to racial groups within the UK as well as those outside the UK and "national origins" means more than nationality, in the legal sense, acquired by an individual at birth.[70]

---

[66] RRA, s.1(1)(a); and see *Showboat Entertainment Centre Ltd v Owens* [1984] I.C.R. 65.
[67] *Mandla v Lee* [1983] I.C.R. 385.
[68] RRA, s.3.
[69] RRA, s.78(1).

Indirect discrimination

In relation to indirect discrimination, the requirement or condition imposed by the employer must 6–89
be such that the proportion of persons of one racial group who can comply with it, is considerably smaller than the proportion of persons not of that racial group who can comply. With regard to indirect racial discrimination, the following requirements or conditions have been held to be justifiable in particular circumstances:

- forbidding a beard on the grounds of hygiene[71];
- requiring that a Muslim female nurse conform with the uniform prescribed by regulations by not wearing trousers,[72] but in *Malik v Bertram Personnel Group Ltd*[73] the ET held that requiring Muslim women sales assistants to wear a skirt was not justified; and
- requiring highly qualified and skilled employees to produce written reports in English promptly.

The following have been held not to be justifiable:

- a requirement that labourers complete application forms in English in their own handwriting;
- a requirement that pupils attending a Christian school do not wear a turban[74]; and
- a requirement that students who have not been ordinarily resident in the European Community for three years pay higher fees.[75]

The Race Relations Act contains only limited opportunities for positive discrimination. It permits an employer to discriminate positively only in relation to providing existing employees with training where employees of that race are not well represented in a work group. However while an employer may encourage the participation of under-represented racial groups he may not positively discriminate by employing a candidate of one racial group who is worse than a candidate of another racial group who has been rejected.[76]

GOQ provisions operate where:

- the job involves participation in a dramatic performance or entertainment which requires person of a particular racial group for authenticity, for example refusing to engage a black person to play the part of a Scot;
- the job involves work as a model in the production of a work of art which requires a person of a particular racial group for authenticity, for example an artists or photographer's model;
- the job involves working in place where food or drink is provided to the public in a particular setting which requires a person of particular racial group for authenticity, for example, refusing to employ a native Scot as waiter in a Chinese restaurant; and
- the job-holder provides members of a particular racial group with personal services which can most effectively be provided by one of the same racial group, *e.g.* not appointing an English person to work as a social worker for the Afro-Caribbean community.

Exceptions and special provisions

In addition to the GOQs mentioned earlier, the SDA and the RRA do not apply in certain 6–90
circumstances. The main exceptions are as follows:

---

[70] *BBC Scotland v Souster* [2001] I.R.L.R. 150; *Northern Joint Police Board v Power* [1997] I.R.L.R. 610.
[71] *Singh v Rowntree Mackintosh Ltd* [1979] I.C.R. 199.
[72] *Kingston and Richmond Area Health Authority v Kaur* [1981] I.C.R. 631.
[73] 1979, unreported.
[74] *Mandla v Lee* [1983] I.C.R. 385.
[75] *Orphanos v Queen Mary College* [1985] I.R.L.R. 349.
[76] RRA, ss.37, 38.

- *Charities*: SDA, s.43 and RRA, s.34 exempt acts by bodies set up for charitable purposes but only in relation to conferring benefits and not in relation to employment.[77]
- *Sport*: SDA, s.44 and RRA, s.39 exempts certain sports competitions so that single sex competitions are lawful as are rules relating to representative competitions.
- *Statutory authority and national security*: Limited exceptions are provided by SDA, ss.51 and 52 and RRA, s.42 which make lawful discrimination for health and safety purposes.
- *Training*: Limited positive discrimination is permitted to make certain employment available to a sex or racial group that is underrepresented in particular types of work (RRA, ss.35–38 and SDA, ss.47, 48).
- Special provisions relate to police (SDA, s.17, RRA, s.16), prison officers (SDA, s.18), and ministers of religion (SDA, s.19).

Disability

6–91 The Disability Discrimination Act 1995 (DDA) applies to all employers with 15 or more employees.[78] The Act is to be read along with a Code of Practice relating to employment, regulations dealing with the meaning of disability and discrimination in employment as well as statutory guidance on matters to be taken into account regarding the meaning of the definition of disability.

The Act renders unlawful discrimination against disabled persons and victimisation of those who have brought complaints or have helped other to do so[79] but makes no distinction between direct and indirect discrimination.

Definition of disability

6–92 A disability is a "a physical or mental impairment which has a substantial and long-term adverse effect on a person's ability to carry out normal day-to-day activities".[80] This definition is further refined by provisions to the effect that: (1) mental impairment includes an impairment resulting from a mental illness if clinically well recognised; (2) long term effect means an impairment has lasted or likely to last 12 months or life; (3) an impairment which has ceased to have substantial adverse effect is treated as continuing if its effect is likely to recur; (4) severe disfigurement has substantial adverse effect; (5) progressive conditions (including HIV) which are likely to impair day-to-day activities are to be regarded as impairments with substantial adverse effect even although they are not yet in an advanced stage; and (6) one must judge the adverse effect of an impairment by ignoring medical treatment or prosthesis (except spectacles).[81]

An impairment will be of long-term effect if it has lasted or is expected to last 12 months or for life and if an impairment has ceased to have a substantial effect on normal day to day activities it is to be treated as having that effect if it is likely to recur (*e.g.* epilepsy, rheumatoid arthritis).[82]

An impairment is measured in terms of normal day-to-day activities under one of the following prescribed headings:

- mobility;
- manual;
- manual dexterity;
- physical co-ordination;
- continence;
- memory, powers of concentration, learning and understanding;

---

[77] *Hugh-Jones v St John's College Cambridge* [1979] I.C.R. 848.
[78] DDA, s.7.
[79] DDA, ss.4, 55.
[80] DDA, s.1.
[81] DDA, Sch.1.
[82] DDA, Sch.1.

- perception of risk of physical danger;
- ability to lift/carry everyday things;
- speech, hearing, sight.

An employer may discriminate against a disabled person in two ways. First, where for a reason which relates to a disability, he treats (or would treat) a person less favourably than a person to whom that reason does not apply and he (the employer) cannot show that the treatment is justified.[83] Secondly, where a physical feature of an employer's premises, the arrangements for offering employment or the terms on which employment is offered, puts a disabled person at a disadvantage and the employer fails to make a reasonable adjustment to such physical features, arrangements for offering employment or terms of employment in order to prevent the premises, arrangements or terms of employment having that effect.[84] This second type of discrimination only arises if the employer knows, or ought to have known, of the person's disability (s.6(6)) so that an employer (by failing to make an adjustment) did not discriminate against a person who had epilepsy when that person gave the employer an assurance that his epilepsy was under control.[85]

In each type of case an employer may show that the treatment afforded or the failure to make an adjustment was justified.[86] Reasonable adjustment will require consideration of the practicability of an adjustment, the financial cost and disruption to the employer's business, the employer's resources and the availability of help from public or other funds but may require any of the following:

- altering premises;
- providing or modifying equipment;
- providing training;
- allocation of duties to another person;
- transferring to a vacancy;
- assigning to a different place of work;
- providing a reader or interpreter or supervision;
- altering working hours; and
- permitting absence for treatment.

When considering whether an employer has treated a disabled person less favourably the comparison is not between how an employer treats a disabled.

Clark v TDG Ltd (Trading as Novacold)

[1999] I.R.L.R. 318

The applicant had suffered an injury at work and did not work again until his dismissal. At the date of dismissal the employers did not believe he would be able to perform his duties for another year. The applicant presented a complaint to an Employment Tribunal alleging unlawful disability discrimination. The employers accepted that the applicant had a disability falling within the Act but contended that if one compared the applicant's position with that of a person not suffering from a disability, then they would have acted no differently, and that he had not been treated less favourably because of his disability.

The Court of Appeal held that the Employment Tribunal erred in holding that the applicant had not been treated less favourably when he was dismissed on the grounds of his absence due to disability, on the reasoning that the applicant was treated no differently than a person who was off work for the same amount of time but for a reason other than disability. For the Disability Discrimination Act it is simply a

[83] DDA, s.5(1).
[84] DDA, s.6.
[85] DDA, s.6(6); and see s.6(11) re occupational pension schemes.
[86] DDA, s.5(2).

> case of identifying others to whom the reason for the treatment does not, or would not, apply. The test of less favourable treatment is based on the reason for the treatment of the disabled person and not the fact of his disability. It does not turn on a like-for-like comparison of the treatment of the disabled person and of others in similar circumstances and it is therefore not appropriate to make a comparison of the cases in the same way as in the Sex Discrimination and Race Relations Acts.

Enforcement and remedies

6–93 The method by which discrimination by employers may be challenged is similar whether the discrimination falls under the Sex Discrimination Act, the Race Relations Act or the Disability Discrimination Act which was amended by the Disability Rights Commission Act 1999 (DRCA). The DRCA replaced the National Disability Council with the Disability Rights Commission (DRC) and gave it powers analogous to those held by the Commission for Racial Equality (CRE) and the Equal Opportunities Commission (EOC). In each case enforcement of the obligations of employers under the three Acts may be by the EOC, CRE or the DRC respectively or by complaints made by individuals.

The EOC, CRE or the DRC may enforce the obligations on employers (and others) by way of conducting formal investigations,[87] issuing of non-discrimination notice,[88] taking action where there is persistent discrimination[89] and in respect of discriminatory advertisements and instructions or pressure to discriminate.[90] The Commissions also have powers to draw up and issue Codes of Practice containing practical guidance to employers on how to avoid discrimination and any such Code is admissible in Employment Tribunal proceedings[91] and Codes have been issued in respect of sex, race and disability discrimination.

The remedy for an individual who believes he/she was the victim of unlawful discrimination is to apply to an Employment Tribunal within three months of the act complained of although this may be extended if the tribunal considers it just and equitable to do so[92] and in the event of the complaint being upheld the tribunal may grant any or all of the following remedies:

(1) a declaration of the rights of the parties;
(2) an award of compensation which may include a sum in respect of injury to feelings and interest;
(3) a recommendation that the employer takes action for the purpose of obviating the effect on the complainant of any act of discrimination.

An important tool for a person who believes that he/she has been the victim of unlawful discrimination is the questionnaire procedure. This allows such a person to serve on the employer a statutory questionnaire in which certain questions may be addressed to an employer (or prospective employer). While there is no obligation on the employer to respond to the questionnaire, any response is admissible in tribunal proceedings and if an employer's responses are absent, evasive or delayed, a tribunal may draw that an act of discrimination has been committed.[93]

---

87 SDA, s.57; RRA, s.48; DRCA, s.3.
88 SDA, s.67; RRA, s.58; DRCA, s.4.
89 SDA, s.71; RRA, s.62; DRCA, s.6.
90 SDA, s.72; RRA, s.63.
91 SDA, s.56A; RRA, s.47; DDA, s.53A.
92 SDA, s.76(1), (5); RRA, s.68; DDA, s.8.
93 SDA, s.74; RRA, s.65; DDA, s.56.

Vicarious liability

Liability for an act of discrimination committed by an employee in the course of his employment falls on the employer. Thus, all of the three Acts provide that anything done by a person in the course of his employment shall be treated for the purposes of this Act as done by his employers as well as by him, whether or not the act is done with the employer's approval or knowledge, although it is a defence if an employer can show that he took reasonably practicable steps to prevent the employee doing such an act, *e.g.* by drawing up and applying a policy to eliminate discriminatory acts and behaviour and by disciplining those who contravene it.[94] However, the approach of tribunals to what is or is not in the course of employment has been generous. 6–94

Chief Constable of the Lincolnshire Police v (1) Stubbs, (2) Taylor And (3) The Chief Constable Of The North Yorkshire Police

[1999] I.R.L.R. 81

Constable Deborah Stubbs and Sergeant Walker were police officers and while working together incidents occurred which resulted in Stubbs complaining that she was being sexually harassed by Walker. One of these incidents occurred when Stubbs went for a drink at a pub after work with several fellow officers including Walker and a subsequent incident with Walker which also took place in a pub after an office leaving party. She complained that acts of sexual discrimination (harassment) alleged to have been committed by Walker were in the course of his employment for which the Chief Constable would be vicariously liable. Held: what happened between Stubbs and Walker occurred in circumstances that were "an extension of their employment". In this particular case although the incidents did not occur at the employer's premises, they were nevertheless, social gatherings involving officers from work either immediately after work or for an organised leaving party. The incidents therefore came within the concept of course of employment as explained by the Court of Appeal in *Jones v Tower Boot Company*.[95] It would have been different if the acts had taken place during a chance meeting.

Religion

Apart from in Northern Ireland, religious discrimination in employment is strictly not unlawful in the UK. However, certain ethnic groups are also religions and certain employer policies and dress codes may indirectly discriminate against Muslims by virtue of their being Asians. However, the European Convention on Human Rights (Art. 9) to which effect is given by the Human Rights Act 1998, guarantees freedom of religion and belief and the right to manifest one's religious belief. Article 9 rights have been afforded considerable protection from attack. Religion and belief have been widely construed to include Druidism,[96] veganism,[97] pacifism and even non-belief. Political or idealistic movements are not covered. There have been a number of challenges in respect of expression and manifestation of belief and time off work for religious beliefs. In *Ahmad v United Kingdom*[98] where a Muslim teacher was refused permission to attend weekly prayers it was held there was no breach of Art.9, as the teacher had willingly accepted his contract of employment in the knowledge that it may interfere with prayers and a similar approach was adopted in *Stedman v United Kingdom*[99] which involved a refusal to work on Sunday. However the EC Council of 6–95

[94] SDA, s.41; RRA, s.32; DDA, s.58.
[95] [1997] I.C.R. 254.
[96] *Chappell v United Kingdom* 1987 53 D.R. 241.
[97] *X v United Kingdom*, Commission Decision, February 2, 1993.
[98] (1982) 4 E.H.R.R. 126.
[99] (1997) 23 E.H.R.R. 168.

Ministers has adopted Directive 2000/78 which will by December 2003 proscribe discrimination on grounds of religion or belief so that Muslims, Rastafarians and other religions will enjoy protection not available directly under the Race Relations Act. The Directive has been implemented by the Employment Equality (Religion or Belief) Regulations 2003 which make it unlawful to discriminate against a person, directly or indirectly, on grounds of religion or belief. However certain exceptions apply where being a particular religion is a genuine requirement for a job or where the employer has an ethos based on religion or belief.

Part-time workers

6–96 Prior to the passing of the Part-time Workers (Prevention of Less Favourable Treatment) Regulations 2000 it had been possible for women and married persons to argue that treating part-time employees less favourably than full-time employees constituted either indirect sex or marital status discrimination. Thus by excluding part-time employees from promotion or training opportunities an employer could commit an act of sex discrimination on the grounds that fewer women than men or fewer married persons than unmarried persons would work full-time so as to be able to apply for promotion or a training opportunity.

The Part-time Workers (Prevention of Less Favourable Treatment) Regulations 2000 have, since July 2000, enabled less favourable treatment of part-time workers to be challenged without the need for indirect sex discrimination to be established.

Fixed term contracts

6–97 Directive 1999/70, with effect from July 10, 2001, requires: (1) that fixed term contract workers shall not be treated less favourably than comparable permanent workers solely because they have a fixed term contract unless different treatment is justified on objective grounds; and (2) that successive fixed term contracts shall be justified on objective grounds or be regulated in terms of duration or the number of renewals. Regulations have been introduced to give effect to the Directive. With effect from July 10, 2002, it is unlawful to treat fixed term employees less favourably than those on contract.[1]

Equal pay

6–98 The Equal Pay Act 1970 (EPA) seeks to ensure equal pay for men and women doing work of equal value. The short title states that it is "An Act to prevent discrimination, as regards terms and conditions of employment between men and women" and is concerned with contractual terms of employment including, but not limited to, those concerning pay. Every contract of employment contains an equality clause.[2] The Act only gives equality of pay between men and women in the same employment.[3]

The three entitlements

6–99 A woman (or a man) is entitled to equal pay with a man (or a woman) in the following three situations:

[1] Fixed Term Employees (Prevention of Less Favourable Treatment) Regulations 2002.
[2] EPA, s.1(1).
[3] EPA, s.1(2)(b).

(1) where the man and the woman are engaged on "like work" (s.1(2)(a));
(2) where the man and the woman are engaged on "work rated equivalent", namely where a job evaluation study has been carried out in respect of the work (s.1(2)(b)); and
(3) where the man and the woman are engaged on in "work of equal value (s.1(2)(c)).

However, when comparison is being made between the pay of a woman and the pay of a man, in order to ensure transparency in the pay scheme each individual item of the contract has to be compared.

Like work

This occurs where a woman and a man do work which is of the same, or a broadly similar nature **6–100** and if there are any differences in the things that the man and the woman do they must not be of practical importance in relation to terms and conditions of employment.

Work rated equivalent

This occurs when a woman's job, and that of the man, have been given an equal value in terms of **6–101** the demands made on the worker under several headings like effort, skill, decision-making, etc., in a job evaluation study.

Equal value

This is a flexible route to equal pay and may be used where men and women are not engaged on **6–102** like work or where there has been no proper job evaluation study undertaken. This permits a woman who is employed, *e.g.*, as a cook or a kitchen assistant to compare her pay and other contractual conditions with those of male workers employed as, for example, joiners, plumbers, engineers or accountants.

Genuine material factor

An employer faced with an equal pay claim may defend it by showing that the difference in pay is **6–103** genuinely due to a material difference (or factor) between the woman's case and the man's.[4] Provided the difference is genuine and is due to factor other than sex the defence will be effective.

Wallace v Strathclyde Regional Council

[1998] I.R.L.R. 146

Wallace and others were female teachers who did the same work as male principal teachers but were paid at a lower rate and not given the opportunity of promotion. The Council could not create new promoted posts because of restraints imposed by government. As a result, the appellants were doing the work of principal teachers without having been promoted to that grade and without receiving the salary commensurate with it. Relying on the Equal Pay Act these unpromoted female teachers sought equal pay with male principal teachers. An Employment Tribunal held that the Council had not shown that the difference was genuinely due to a material difference which was not the difference of sex.

---

[4] EPA, s.1(3).

Held: Provided that there is no element of sexual discrimination, an employer establishes a s.1(3) defence by identifying the factors which he alleges have caused the disparity, proving that those factors are genuine and proving further that they were causally relevant to the disparity in pay complained of.

Remedies

6–104 The majority of equal pay claims are raised in the Employment Tribunal but such claims may also be raised in the form of breach of contract actions in the ordinary court.

Where a woman's claim to equal pay is upheld her contract is modified with regard to the future.[5] With regard to the period before the claim is upheld the tribunal may award arrears of remuneration or damages.[6]

European Community law

6–105 In the field of sex discrimination, Art.141 of the Treaty of Rome states, *inter alia*, that "each member state shall … ensure and subsequently maintain the application of the principle that men and women should receive equal pay for equal work". This obligation is amplified by the Equal Pay Directive (75/117) and the Equal Treatment Directive (76/207) prohibits discrimination in conditions of employment including dismissal. Article 141 creates rights which can be enforced by individuals against employers and overrides any contrary domestic law.

In order to enforce any right conferred by Art.141 an employee should still raise the case by way of a complaint to an Employment Tribunal which must then hear the complaint under the Equal Pay Act by ignoring or "disapplying" any provision of that Act which is contrary to Art.141.[7]

Key Concepts

UK law now makes it unlawful for an employer to **discriminate** on the following grounds:

- sex, pregnancy, marital status, transsexualism and sexual orientation;
- race, national and ethnic origins and nationality;
- disability;
- religion or belief;
- being a part-time worker or fixed-term employee.

Direct discrimination is less favourable treatment of an employee simply because of his/her sex, race, etc.

Indirect discrimination occurs where the same criterion is applied to all but impacts adversely and disproportionately on members of one race, sex, etc. who cannot meet the criterion.

---

5 EPA, s.1(2).
6 EPA, s.2(1).
7 *Biggs and Barber v Staffordshire County Council* [1996] I.R.L.R. 209.

Quick Quiz

Employment law

- What formalities are necessary to create the contract of employment?
- How do courts identify the contract of employment? List four criteria the courts often take into account. What is meant by "mutuality of obligation"?
- What is the legal status of a Written statement of Particulars issued under the Employment Rights Act 1996? List six things it must contain.
- What is a collective agreement and how can it become a contract between the union and the employer?
- What is meant by, and what is the result of, incorporation of a collective agreement?
- List two duties on the employee that are implied into the contract of employment.
- What are the main entitlements under the Working Time Regulations?
- List three situations in which employees are entitled to paid leave.
- Explain what is a wrongful dismissal and how it differs from an unfair dismissal.
- What is the main remedy for wrongful dismissal?
- What is meant by the least burdensome performance rule?
- List two situations in which an employee is deemed to be dismissed for unfair dismissal.
- List three reasons which an employer can prove to support an unfair dismissal.
- Which court or tribunal can deal with unfair dismissal complaints?
- What are the remedies for unfair dismissal?
- How does the law define indirect sex discrimination?
- List the areas in which the law makes it unlawful for an employer to discriminate against employees.

Further Reading

V.Craig and K.Miller, ***A Student Guide to Employment Law*** (W. Green, 2002) – a brief guide to employment law with sample Q&As; **V.Craig and K.Miller,** ***Employment Law in Scotland*** (3rd ed., Butterworths) – an up-to-date account of individual and collective employment law in Scotland; ***Selwyn's Law of Employment*** (12th ed., Butterworths, 2002) – a comprehensive statement of employment law; and **Honeyball and Bowers,** ***Textbook on Labour Law*** (7th ed., Oxford University Press, 2002).

Chapter 7

AGENCY

Stuart R. Cross[1]

THE MEANING AND CHARACTERISTICS OF AGENCY

Agency is the contract which exists when one party allows or engages another party to act for them in a legal arrangement with a third party. Of the three parties involved, the agent is the one engaged to act, the principal is the one who engages or allows the agent to act and the third party is bound into the legal arrangement by the agent. The tripartite arrangement has the distinctive effect of creating a binding contractual relationship between the principal and the third party to which the agent will not generally be a party. **7–01**

Agency performs an essential role in allowing a wide range of commercial transactions and other contractual arrangements to operate effectively. In the law of partnership partners are agents of the partnership[2] and in company law directors are considered to be agents of their company. While there is no precise legal definition of what agency is, the courts are more concerned with the consequences of an arrangement and the effect on the parties involved and will look to the effects of rather than the description given to the relationship. It has been argued that:

> "Commerce would literally come to a standstill if businessmen and merchants could not employ the services of factors, brokers, estate agents… and the like and were expected to do everything themselves."[3]

---

[1] Senior Lecturer in Law, University of Dundee.
[2] Partnership Act 1890, s.5.
[3] B. S. Markesinis and R. J. C. Munday, *An Outline of the Law of Agency* (1992), p.3.

DIFFERENT KINDS AND EXAMPLES OF AGENTS

Kinds of agents

7–02 There are many different types of agents and many different names and labels are used to describe agency relationships. Such names and labels are not necessarily conclusive and some commentators do not consider them to be of much use or assistance. Where they may continue to be of use is in offering guidance as to what the intentions of the parties may have been in creating the relationship in question and what the actual nature of the relationship may be. When differing kinds of agency are categorised, one of the main distinctions made is between "general" and "special" agents.

General and special agents

7–03 A general agent is one who has authority to act for the principal in respect of all matters or in respect of those matters which a person in the agent's trade, business or profession would expect to deal with. A solicitor or the managing director of a company would be examples of general agents. A special agent has a different relationship with the principal in respect of the agent's authority and can only act for the principal in respect of a particular transaction.

Morrison v Statter

(1855) 12 R. 1152

Lord Young: "Where you have a particular agent employed by a principal, to perform a particular piece of business for him, he must act within the instructions given for the particular occasion, and does not bind his principal if he acts otherwise. If you have a general agent, employed generally in his master's or principal's affairs, or in a particular department, he is assumed to have all the authority which is necessary to enable him to serve his master as such general agent ..."

Examples of agents

Solicitors

7–04 A solicitor can be both a general and a special agent and the true nature of the relationship will depend on the circumstances. Traditionally, the "law agent" was engaged for relatively narrow purposes but it is now much more common to see a solicitor engaged on a broad range of agency work, both specialist and general. The relationship is in all respects fiduciary in nature[4] and as such the solicitor must carry out the instructions given by the client (principal). The other elements of the fiduciary relationship between a solicitor and client dictate that a solicitor should not make a secret profit from his client as a result of a transaction in which the solicitor is a party.[5] A solicitor engaged in a court matter has authority in respect of a number of matters. There is an implied authority to instruct Counsel[6] to pursue the court process and take all necessary steps involved including the instruction of a local agent.[7]

---

4 *Brown v Inland Revenue Comrs*, 1964 S.C. (H.L.) 180.

5 See *Brown v Inland Revenue Comrs* at 197.

6 *Torbat v Torbat's Trs* (1906) 14 S.L.T. 830.

7 *Bannatyne, Kirkwood, France & Co.*, 1907 S.C. 705.

In Scotland, the Law Society of Scotland is the professional body for solicitors and regulates the activities of solicitors. Law Society rules reflect the fiduciary nature of the solicitor/client relationship and solicitors would not be expected to act for more than one principal where their interests conflict.

Advocates

Although also acting in respect of legal issues, advocates are more likely to be special agents. They will normally be instructed to carry out a specific task or item of business and their authority to act will be restricted by the nature of the instructions. Where, for example, an opinion is sought from an advocate, a memorial setting out the facts involved and the legal issues upon which an opinion is sought will normally be drafted by a client's solicitor and submitted to an advocate for an opinion. No authority to act beyond the preparation of the opinion will normally be given. Where an advocate is instructed in respect of a court matter, the extent of the authority given appears to be much wider. In *Brodt v King*[8] the court held that the advocate had the right to conduct the case without regard to the client's wishes provided that his mandate had not been recalled and his actions in good faith would bind the client. **7–05**

While the advent of the solicitor advocate might appear to confuse matters, the role in which the solicitor is acting and the instructions involved remain the crucial elements involved in establishing the nature of the agency relationship.

Partners

An important example of an agency relationship is that which exists between partners and their partnership. Section 5 of the Partnership Act 1890 says that: **7–06**

> "Every partner is an agent of the firm and his other partners for the purpose of the business of the partnership..."

This means that the partnership (the firm) will be bound as principal in respect of any transactions entered into by any of the partners on behalf of the partnership, if those transactions were carried out in the course of the business. As the agency relationship only exists when the activity is for the purpose of the business of the partnership, the nature of the partner's authority may vary. It may be actual or (as will be seen later) implied.

Company directors

While companies are treated by the law as having a separate legal personality[9] from those who are shareholders and directors of the company, that personality is artificial. Companies need human beings to act on their behalf. The responsibility for acting on behalf of companies is normally delegated to the directors of the company. The articles of association of a company deal with the delegation of authority to directors and that delegation of authority places them in the role of agents for the company. The authority granted to directors is normally extensive, *e.g.* reg.70 of the Companies (Tables A to F) Regulations 1985 specifies that: **7–07**

> "[T]he business of he company shall be managed by the directors who may exercise all the powers of the company."

---

[8] 1991 S.L.T. 272.

[9] *Salomon v Salomon & Co.* [1897] A.C. 22.

Mercantile agents

7–08 A mercantile agent is a statutory creation and s.1(1) of the Factors (Scotland) Act 1890 provides that:

> "The expression 'mercantile agent' shall mean a mercantile agent having in the customary course of his business as such agent, authority either to sell goods or consign goods for the purpose of sale, or to buy goods, or to raise money on the security of goods."

Within the category of mercantile agent there is a further sub-division and in Scotland they may be known as either a factor or a broker.[10] What they have in common is that they are both employed to buy and sell goods on behalf of the principal and they have authority to act on the basis of custom and practice in the markets in which they deal. Where they differ is that a factor has possession of the principal's goods and is entitled to sell those goods in his own name. The broker, on the other hand, does not have possession of the goods and is simply arranging something in respect of the principal's goods. A good example of a factor would be an auctioneer who physically has possession of the goods for the purpose of selling them, while a stockbroker is a broker who arranges something for the principal in respect of shares but does not have possession of the goods. An important consequence of the absence of possession is that the broker will have no right of lien over the goods being dealt with.[11]

Del credere agents

7–09 This is a somewhat specialised form of agency where the agent promises to indemnify or pay the principal if the third party involved fails to meet an obligation to pay the principal. In effect, the agent is acting as a guarantor for the third party. The *del credere* agent is usually a mercantile agent and this type of relationship was often used where goods were being sold abroad and the principal wished to minimise any risk of not being paid for the goods. Where the agency is disclosed, the agent will not normally be liable to the third party and is not a party to the contract between the principal and the third party. The principal has to look to the third party in the first instance to make payment and the agent will normally seek a higher than normal rate of commission given the nature of the obligation being undertaken.

This type of agency arrangement is far less common now as more sophisticated mechanisms such as credit guarantee schemes are available. These may often be state supported.

Commercial agents

7–10 Historically, the law of agency in Scotland has been found largely in the common law. The category of agents known as commercial agents has a different origin and was created in the UK by the Commercial Agents (Council Directive) Regulations 1993.[12] The regulations apply to agents known as commercial agents and these are defined as:

> "a self-employed intermediary who has continuing authority to negotiate the sale or purchase of goods on behalf another person (the 'principal'), or to negotiate and conclude the sale or purchase of goods on behalf of and in the name of that principal".[13]

The importance of this definition is that it does not automatically include some people who would normally be considered by Scots law to be commercial agents but also extends to cover people and organisations who might normally not have been considered to be agents. Anyone who is

[10] Lord President Inglis discusses the distinction in *Cunningham v Lee* (1874) 2 R. 83.
[11] *Glendinning v Hope & Co.*, 1911 S.C (H.L.) 73.
[12] SI 1993/3053. This has since been amended by the Commercial Agents (Council Directive) (Amendment) Regulations 1993 (SI 1993/3173). The Regulations came into force with effect from January 1, 1994.
[13] reg.2(1). The definition was also considered in *King v T. Tunnock Ltd*, 1996 S.C.L.R. 742.

employed, such as a manager or a sales assistant, falls outside the definition. On the other hand, a company can be a commercial agent but anyone who is a partner in a firm or an officer of a company is not a commercial agent if they are acting on behalf of their organisation.[14] In addition, the regulations do not apply to commercial agents who are unpaid and do not apply where a single transaction is involved which is not repeated.

In acting as a commercial agent, the agent must look after the interests of the principal and act dutifully and in good faith.[15] The regulations elaborate on this and, in particular, the agent must:

- make proper efforts to negotiate and, if appropriate, conclude transactions which the agent has been instructed to take care of;
- communicate to the principal all the necessary information available to the agent; and
- comply with all reasonable instructions given by the principal.[16]

There are also obligations on the principal. Generally, the principal must act dutifully and in good faith towards the agent and, in particular, the principal must:

- provide the agent with the necessary documentation relating to the goods involved;
- obtain for the agent the information which is needed for the performance of the contract; and
- inform the agent within a reasonable period of the principal's acceptance or refusal or non-performance of a transaction which the agent has arranged.[17]

An important issue which is dealt with at some length in the regulations is the remuneration of the agent.[18] How and to what extent the agent is to be paid may be dealt with by means of agreement between the agent and the principal. Where there is no agreement, the agent is entitled to be paid what is customarily paid to agents appointed in relation to the type of goods involved. If there is no such customary practice, the agent is entitled to reasonable remuneration taking into account all the elements of the transaction.[19] Normally, the method of payment involved will be commission and commission becomes due and payable when one of these events takes place:

- the principal has executed the transaction; or
- on the basis of the agreement with the third party, the principal should have executed the transaction; or
- the third party has executed the transaction.[20]

To provide further protection to the agent it is specified that the commission must be paid when the third party has completed his part of the transaction or would have completed had the principal also completed his part of the transaction at the very latest.[21] The right to receive commission will come to an end if it can be shown that the contract between the principal and the third party will not be completed and that this is because of something for which the principal is not to blame.[22]

The regulations also contain detailed provisions relating to termination of the agency relationship. As a starting point, both the agent and the principal are entitled to receive from the other a copy of the terms of the contract.[23] When an agency contract is entered into for a period which is indefinite then either party may terminate it by giving notice to the other. The period of notice is:

[14] regs 2(1)(i) and 2(1)(ii).
[15] reg.3(1).
[16] reg.3(2).
[17] reg.4(3).
[18] Dealt with in regs 6–12.
[19] reg.6(1).
[20] reg.10(3).
[21] reg.10(2).
[22] reg.11(1).
[23] reg.13(1).

- one month for the first year of the contract;
- two months for the second year; and
- three months for the third year and any subsequent years.

The parties cannot agree on shorter periods of notice but they can specify longer periods. If they do opt for longer notice periods then the period of notice to be observed by the principal must be at least the same as that observed by the agent.[24] The agency arrangement can be brought to an end immediately when either party fails to carry out all or part of their obligations under the contract or because exceptional circumstances arise.

However, where the agency comes to an end the regulations provide for circumstances where the agent is entitled to compensation.[25] Regulation 17 provides that the agent is entitled to an indemnity where the agent has:

- brought the principal new customers or significantly increased the level of business with existing customers and the principal is continuing to benefit from these actions; and
- payment is equitable taking into account all the circumstances, especially the commission lost by the agent on the business with these customers.[26]

There will also be an entitlement to an indemnity or compensation where the agent dies or suffers damage as a result of the termination of the agency relationship.[27]

> **Key Concepts**
>
> **Agency** is a tri-partite relationship involving the agent, the principal and a third party. If properly constituted the agent enters into a contract with the third party which will be binding on the principal and the third party but which will not be binding in any way on the agent.

CREATING AGENCY

7–11 As with many other contractual relationships there are a variety ways in which agency may be created. These are:

- express creation;
- implied creation;
- creation by necessity;
- holding out;
- necessity;
- ratification; and
- by statute.

Express creation/appointment

7–12 There is no special form or process required for the creation and it can be created expressly either orally or in writing.[28] Differing types of documents may be used to create agency and the extent of the formality involved can vary. In a commercial agency relationship both the agent and principal are entitled to request a signed written document setting out the terms of the agency arrangement.[29] Sometimes, where the agency relationship is of particular importance, the document creating the

---

24 reg.15(3).

25 For a general discussion of compensation on termination, see Smith, "Death of the Salesman" 2000 S.L.T. 289–295 and *King v T. Tunnock Ltd*, 1996 S.C.L.R 742.

26 reg.17(3).

27 reg.17(8) and (6).

28 *Robert Barry & Co. v Doyle*, 1998 S.L.T. 1238.

29 Commercial Agents (Council Directive) Regulations 1993 (SI 1993/3053), reg.13.

agency will itself be formal and the nature and extent of the agency clearly stated. A good example of such an arrangement is where one party (the principal) grants a power of attorney in favour of another (the agent) which permits the principal's affairs to be looked after by the agent.

In the majority of instances, agency will be created by less formal means. This may be orally, or by other informal means. Provided issues of proof can be dealt with satisfactorily there is no reason why agency cannot be created by more modern means of communication such as email or text message.

Implied creation/appointment

The agency relationship may also be created by implication. In many instances the creation of agency will be obvious from the circumstances involved. This may be because of the actings of the parties or because of a statement of law which implies the creation of agency. For example, in the case of a partnership every partner is deemed or implied to be an agent of the firm and the other partners because of s.5 of the Partnership Act 1890. In the case of a senior employee or manager, the circumstances of the employment may imply an agency relationship.[30] **7–13**

Creation by necessity

Strictly speaking, the creation of agency by necessity is a concept of English law. The cases involve one person being seen as justified in taking action on behalf of another in an emergency where there may have been no pre-existing relationship between the parties in question.[31] In Scots law, situations in which agency has been created by circumstances amounting to necessity have been treated as arising under the rather broader doctrine of *negotiorum gestio* which is one of the forms of agency by necessity. The clearest example of where this type of agency exists is in an emergency situation where one person who has no authority takes action on behalf of someone else. All of this takes place in circumstances where it is impossible to communicate with the person on whose behalf action is being taken. As modern communications are now so much improved and more reliable the likelihood of this type of agency having to be relied upon has lessened. Where it is relied upon, the actions taken in necessity should be taken in good faith, should be reasonable and should be in the best interests of the person on whose behalf they are taken. **7–14**

Creation by holding out

Agency may be created when one person is "held out" by another as being an agent. In this situation, a third party comes to believe that agency exists as a result of the holding out. This type of agency often results from a situation where agency proper did in fact exist at one time and the agent did in fact have authority to act on behalf of the principal, but that authority has now in fact been withdrawn and third parties have not been notified. Where someone allows the representation to continue that agency exists, then that person is debarred from arguing that agency does not in fact exist. The principle which is operating is that the person allowing the representation of agency to be made is personally barred from arguing at a later stage that agency does not exist. In English law, this type of agency is known as agency by estoppel. **7–15**

In this type of agency it is important that it can be shown that the third party involved relied on the holding out or representation and that the agent acted in a fashion which was consistent with the existence of agency.

---

[30] See *Neville v C and A Modes*, 1945 S.C. 175 and *Mackenzie v Cluny Hill Hydropathic Co. Ltd*, 1908 S.C. 200.

[31] See Reynolds, *Bowstead & Reynolds on Agency* (2001), p.125.

Creation by ratification

7–16 Usually, an agency relationship is created by the agent and principal before the agent takes any action on behalf of the principal. In some situations this is not always the case and one person acts on behalf of another without actually having prior authority to do so. This does not mean that agency cannot exist in such a situation and it is possible for the person for whom the act was done to ratify the act at a later stage. The effect of ratification at a later stage is to retrospectively approve what has already taken place[32] and make what has happened as valid as if it had been approved by the principal from the beginning. The ratification can be express or implied from the way the principal behaves. In deciding whether ratification has taken place any act, behaviour or statement by the principal which clearly shows an intention to ratify will be sufficient. If the principal does not take any action to ratify the action which has been taken by the agent then the agent will be personally liable for the action which has been taken. The overall effect of ratification is therefore to place the agent and principal in the same position they would have been had agency been agreed before any action was taken by the agent.

Before ratification can take place and become effective a number of conditions have to be fulfilled:

- the principal must exist;
- the principal must have had legal capacity;
- the ratification must take place in time; and
- other relevant conditions must have been fulfilled.

Principal must exist

7–17 At the time the agent purported to act the principal must have been in existence. The principal must, of course, also exist at the time of purported ratification. This condition has been of significance in relation to company law where problems have arisen when a company attempts to ratify an earlier action when the company did not exist.[33]

Tinnevelly Sugar Refining Co. Ltd v Mirrlees, Watson and Yaryan Co. Ltd
(1894) 21 R. 1009

Two men purchased items of machinery from Mirrlees Watson, stating that they were acting on behalf of Tinnevelly. In fact the company was not formed for another two weeks. The machinery supplied was defective and Tinnevelly (which by this stage had been registered) tried to sue. It was held that Tinnevelly had no rights under the contract because it was not a party to it. It had not existed at the time the contract was entered into.

Principal must have had legal capacity

7–18 The next condition to be satisfied if ratification is to be effective is that the principal must have been legally capable of authorising the agent's activities when they took place.[34]

[32] *Alexander Ward & Co. Ltd v Samyang Navigation Co. Ltd*, 1975 S.C. (H.L.) 26.
[33] *Kelner v Baxter* (1866) L.R. 2 C.P. 174.
[34] *Boston Deep Sea Fishing and Ice Co. Ltd v Farnham* [1957] 3 All E.R. 204.

Ratification in time

If the ratification of an action has to be done within a set or certain period of time then ratification must take place within that period of time if it is to be effective. **7–19**

Goodall v Bilsland

1909 S.C. 1152

In this case, a wine merchant applied to a Licensing Board to have a wine and spirits licence renewed. There were opponents to the application who employed a solicitor to act for them in opposing the application. The licence was issued. A period of 10 days was allowed for the lodging of an appeal and the solicitor for the opponents, without consulting his principals, submitted an appeal. This was successful. The Inner House of the Court of Session held that the ratification was ineffective as it had taken place after the period for the appeals procedure.

Other conditions

As well as the conditions listed, it is also accepted that it is a condition of valid ratification that the principal must have been aware of all the relevant facts at the time the ratification took place, unless it can be shown that the principal has shown a willingness to ratify whatever the circumstances. **7–20**

It is also generally believed to be a condition of ratification that the agent must have claimed to have been acting on behalf of a known or identified principal. In so doing, the agent will have made it clear that the action taken was as an agent and not in an individual capacity. This condition has been described as demonstrating that an undisclosed principal cannot ratify. In the case of:

Keighey, Maxsted & Co. v Durant

[1901] A.C. 240

A corn merchant named Roberts was authorised by Keighly, Maxsted to buy wheat with a limit as to the price he could pay. He failed to buy at the specified price and agreed to buy wheat from another merchant at a higher price. He did not tell the other merchant that he was also acting as an agent for Keighly, Maxsted. While they agreed the next day to take the wheat, Keighly, Maxsted subsequently did not take delivery. It was held that they could not be liable on the basis of having ratified the contract because at the time the contract was made the merchant did not know that Roberts was acting on behalf of Keighly, Maxsted.

Creation by operation of law

In certain situations agency comes into existence as a result of the operation of law. This usually takes place when a statute specifies that this is the case. An important example of this is in respect of partners and their authority to bind their fellow partners as agents. Section 5 of the Partnership Act 1890 provides that "Every partner is an agent of the firm and his other partners for the purpose of the business of the partnership …'. Receivers, liquidators and administrators who have been appointed in connection with a company are also recognised as being agents for certain purposes.[35] **7–21**

[35] See the Insolvency Act 1986, ss.14(5), 57(1),(1A); and see also *Knowles v Scott* [1891] 1 Ch. 717, Ch.D, *per* Romer J.

Key Concepts

Creation of agency can take place in a variety of ways. What is important to note is that whatever the manner of creation, provided it is valid the contractual relationship created will be binding on the principal and agent.

THE AGENCY RELATIONSHIP

Authority of an agent

7–22 The authority which an agent has to act on behalf of a principal is particularly important as it is crucial to the question of whether and to what extent the principal will be bound to a third party. Normally a principal will not be bound to a third party if the agent acts without the principal's authority. If authority has been given it is important to identify what type of authority has been given. There are four recognised categories used to identify types of authority given to an agent. These are:

- express;
- implied;
- ostensible (sometimes refereed to as apparent); and
- presumed.

The phrase "actual authority" is often used in connection with express and implied and refers to the fact that the authority arises out of the contract between the principal and the agent.

Express authority

7–23 This is perhaps the clearest and most straightforward type of authority. In this situation the principal will have stipulated the agent's authority in the agreement they reached, irrespective of whether the agreement is or is not in writing. At the time of dealing with the agent the third party may not know the exact extent of the authority which has been expressly given by the principal. Even if this is the case, the third party is entitled to rely on the scope of the express authority when it becomes known and in any dispute with the principal. Where the agent exceeds the extent of the express authority which has been given and there is no other type of authority (or ratification) which the third party can rely on, then the principal will not be liable to the third party.

Implied

7–24 In many instances, an agent's authority will not in fact be stated expressly. The absence of express authority does not necessarily mean that the agent has no authority. The agent may have implied authority to act which arises from the particular appointment, from the specific type of agency which exists or simply from all the circumstances surrounding the particular agency and appointment. Where implied authority exists then the extent of that authority is to do whatever is necessary to carry out the agent's particular task. This may vary widely. For example, a general agent will have no authority to borrow money. In the case of *Sinclair, Moorhead & Co. v Wallace*,[36] the general manager of a branch of a large firm borrowed money on behalf of the firm and then disappeared with the money. It was held that his employers were not bound to repay the loan as the manager's implied authority did not extend to borrowing money. Conversely, sales staff do have implied authority to take purchase orders. In *Barry, Ostlere & Shepherd Ltd v*

[36] (1880) 7 R. 874.

Edinburgh Cork Importing Co.,[37] a contract was made by Barry, Ostlere and Shepherd through a salesman of Edinburgh Cork for the sale of cork shavings. The Cork Co. didn't deliver. B, O and S brought an action for breach contract against The Cork Co. They denied that the salesman had authority to conclude a contract. It was held that the pursuers were entitled to assume that the salesman did have authority to complete a contract.

Where a principal wishes to restrict the extent of the agent's powers and authority this will only be effective when it has been intimated to third parties.[38]

Apparent or ostensible

In addition to the "actual authority" given to agents when they have express or implied authority, **7–25**
agents may also bind principals with authority which is referred to as being apparent or ostensible in nature. This type of authority has not been given to the agent by the principal expressly but it is authority which the agent appears to have. The appearance arises because of the way the principal and the agent have acted. In particular, some form of representation by the principal which makes it appear as if thé agent had in fact been given authority. There is a binding relationship between the principal and the third party because the principal has held out the agent as having the necessary authority. On the basis of the principle of personal bar the principal cannot deny that the agent has this type of authority.[39] There are two common situations in which this type of authority arises. The first is where a principal has conferred authority on an agent at some earlier stage but that authority has been withdrawn without notice having been given to third parties. For withdrawal of authority to be effective it is vital that the principal properly intimates the change in authority to third parties. The second situation where this type of authority commonly arises is where the principal has made an arrangement with the agent which limits the agent's authority but the agent exceeds that actual authority in dealings with third parties. Where the third party believes, *e.g.*, on the basis of previous dealings that the agent continues to have the original degree of authority, that "apparent" authority will continue to exist until the principal takes action to properly notify third parties. A case which is often cited as a good example of this type of authority is:

International Sponge Importers v Andrew Watt and Sons

1911 S.C. (H.L.) 57

A travelling salesman for a company was in the normal practice of selling sponges which he carried with him. He had no authority to take any form of payment other than crossed cheques in favour of his employer. On a number of occasions he took payment for goods by means of cheques made payable to him personally. His employers knew that this had taken place. The travelling salesman eventually absconded with money which had been made payable to him personally. His employers sought to recover the money from the third party who had paid it to the salesman. It was held that the salesman's employer could not recover from the third party as it was reasonable for them on the basis of the earlier course of dealings to conclude that the salesman did have authority to accept payment personally.

Where a third party knows that an agent is acting in his own interest and not on behalf of the principal then, relying on the same principle of personal bar which lies at the heart of the ostensible authority, the third party cannot argue that the agent was acting on the basis of ostensible authority.

---

[37] 1909 S.C. 1113.

[38] *Watteau v Fenwick* [1893] 1 Q.B. 346. For another example see Partnership Act 1890, ss.5 and 8.

[39] *Thomas Hayman & Sons v American Cotton Oil Co.* (1907) 45 S.L.R. 207; *British Bata Shoe Co. Ltd v Double M Shah Ltd*, 1980 S.C. 311; *Armagas Ltd v Mundogas SA* [1986] 1 A.C. 717

Presumed authority

7–26 In certain situations, the law will presume that authority has been given. The presumption is that, had there been some form of consultation with the principal in advance, this is the type of authority which would have been granted. The case of agency by necessity (*negotiorum gestio*) is the most obvious example.

> **Key Concepts**
>
> **Authority of an agent** is crucial as it is this which will determine whether and to what extent a principal is bound to a third party by the actings of an agent. If an agent acts within the limits of the authority which has been granted by a principal, then the principal will be bound. If an agent acts outwith the limits of the authority which has been granted, then the principal may not be bound.

Duties of an agent

7–27 The agency relationship is like most contractual relationships in involving the parties in mutual rights and obligations. In an ideal situation, the duties an agent must observe will be clearly stated in the agreement between the agent and the principal. There will be times when no such agreement exists or if it does it is silent as to rights and duties. When this is the case, the law will imply a number of duties provided the express terms of the contract do not conflict.

To perform instructions

7–28 An agent must perform what he or she has been instructed to do by the principal. Often it will be the case that the agent has only been given general instructions by the principal or may not in fact have received instructions at all. In such situations the agent should act in a manner which reflects his or her best judgement and the generally established customs of his/her profession.[40]

Where the agent does not comply with express instructions from the principal then the agent will be liable personally to the principal.

> **Gilmour v Clark**
>
> (1853) 15 D. 478
>
> An Edinburgh merchant called Gilmour gave instructions to Clark, a carrier, to take a consignment of goods to Leith docks to be put on board a ship called the Earl of Zetland. Someone working for Clark put them on a ship called The Magnet instead. This ship sank and the goods were lost. It was held that Clark was liable to Gilmour for the value of the goods.

As well as being personally liable to the principal for not following express instructions, an agent also loses the right to claim the agreed payment or commission for the period of the breach.[41]

---

[40] *Fearn v Gordon and Craig* (1893) 20 R. 352.

[41] *Alexander Graham & Co. v United Turkey Red Co. Ltd*, 1922 S.C. 533.

To exercise skill and care

An agent must act in a way which shows due care and skill. If an agent does not exercise skill and care then the agent will be liable for any damages which results.[42] If the agent is not a member of a particular profession then the standard of skill and care expected is that which would be expected of an ordinary prudent man managing his own affairs.[43] Where the agent is also a member of a particular profession or trade then the agent has to exercise the degree of skill and care and demonstrate the knowledge which could be expected of a reasonably competent and careful member of that trade or profession.[44] Even where the agent is acting gratuitously and receiving no payment in acting for the principal, the agent must still act with due care and skill.[45] An agent will not be liable where any action taken turns out not to be in the interests of the principal when the action taken is on the basis of instructions given by the principal. Similarly, an agent who is a member of a particular trade or profession will not be held to have breached this duty if they make an error of judgement but can still be shown to have acted in a manner which demonstrates reasonable knowledge, skill and care.[46] **7–29**

To act personally

The basic assumption in an agency relationship is that the agent has a duty to act personally for the principal and must not delegate the work to anyone else.[47] While this is the generally accepted rule it is also recognised that there are and can be many exceptions to this rule. The agency agreement itself may expressly permit delegation. Delegation might also be implied from the circumstances of the case in question and may be common in particular trades or professions.[48] Where delegation is permissible then rights and duties will also exist between the principal and the sub-agent appointed by delegation.[49] Nonetheless, even when delegation is permitted the agent may remain liable for acts and omissions of the sub-agent and in instances where delegation is not permissible the agent remains liable to the principal for breach of the agreement. **7–30**

To account

An agent must keep accounts and has a duty to account to the principal for actions taken on the principal's behalf. If there is any deficiency which the agent cannot explain then this has to be made good by the agent even although there may be no suggestion of dishonesty.[50] **7–31**

To act in good faith

A fundamental element of an agency relationship is that it is described as being of a fiduciary nature in character. The agent is generally bound by a fundamental duty to act in good faith and solely for the benefit of the principal. This does not mean that an agent is automatically barred from acting for other principals and if questions arise as to whether or not a conflict of interest **7–32**

---

[42] *Stiven v Watson* (1874) 1 R. 412.
[43] Bell, *Commentaries* I, 516.
[44] *Cooke v Falconer's Representatives* (1850) 13 D. 157.
[45] *Copland v Brogan*, 1916 S.C. 277.
[46] *Simpson v Kidstons, Watson, Turnbull & Co.*, 1913 S.L.T. 74.
[47] The latin phrase which is often cited in this connection is *delegatus non potest delegare.* This simply translates as meaning that an agent cannot delegate.
[48] In *Cornelius v Black* (1879) 6 R. 581 it was recognised that an architect has the right to delegate certain work to a surveyor.
[49] *De Bussche v Alt* (1878) 8 Ch. D. 286. In this case the principal, De Bussche, had appointed an agent to sell a ship at a specified price. The agent had been given permission to appoint a sub-agent and Alt was appointed as sub-agent to sell the ship in Japan. It was held that this action was not a breach of duty and as Alt had in fact been appointed as a substitute agent there was a contract between the principal and Alt.
[50] In *Tyler v Logan* (1904) 7 F. 123 there was a discrepancy of £62 when a stocktaking was taken in a Dundee shoeshop. The shop manager (Logan) was held liable to pay this amount even although there was no evidence of dishonesty.

exists then reference must be made to the agency contract to ascertain whether an express or implied term exists which restricts the agent's capacity to contract with other principals.[51]

Although not separate duties, there are a number of situations which tend to show clearly the nature of the fiduciary duties owed by an agent to a principal. In acting as an agent it is common for confidential or sensitive information to be passed to an agent. If this is the case then the agent is bound not to disclose that information.

Liverpool Victoria Friendly Society v Houston

(1900) 3 F. 42

Houston worked as an insurance agent for Liverpool Victoria and over a period of four years saw a detailed list of people insured by them. After being dismissed Houston offered the lists to a competing society which approached the people on the list. It was held that Houston had a duty to treat the information as confidential and was liable in damages for the loss of business suffered by Liverpool Victoria.

If, while acting in the course of the agency, the agent's personal interests conflict with the duties owed to the principal then the agent should disclose this to the principal who may then decide whether or not to consent to what the agent has done or intends to do. If the agent does not do this then the risk arises that anything the agent does which generates a benefit to the agent may be seen as the agent generating what is known as a secret profit and being liable to account to the principle for that profit.[52] If, on the other hand, the agent tells the principal about any additional benefit which is being obtained and the principal agrees to this, the benefit may be retained by the agent. Secret profits may take a number of differing forms. While generally it is regarded as being any sort of benefit which the agent obtains over and above what is being provided by the principal,[53] it may be a direct bribe, a special discount a gift or a simple direct payment.[54] If the principal discovers a secret profit which has not been disclosed then the principal may terminate the contract[55] and the agent is liable to lose any right to payment for the period of the contract during which the breach continues. In addition to rights against the agent, the principal may also chose not to proceed with the transaction with the third party who has been involved in the transaction and who is aware of the agent's secret profit.[56] Finally, in property transactions between the agent and the principal, the agent should not sell his or her own property to the principal without telling the principal and obtaining consent[57] and the agent should not buy property from the principal without indicating that this is the case.[58]

Key Concepts

The **duties of an agent** are important as they specify the manner in which the agent should carry out the tasks allocated by the principal. Duties may be specified in the contract between the agent and principal if this exists. If there is no express agency agreement between the agent and the principal then a number of duties will be implied by common law.

---

[51] In *Lothian v Jenolite Ltd*, 1969 S.C. 111, Lothian agreed to sell some of Jenolite's products in Scotland on a commission basis. The initial agreement was for a four year period but it was terminated by Jenolite after just over a year. Lothian raised a damages action for breach of contract. Lothian counterclaimed and stated that as Lothian had bought and sold products from competitors this was itself a breach of contract. It was held that as the contract had not stated that Lothian was restricted to selling only Jenolite's products then Lothian was permitted to sell other products.

[52] *Boardman v Phipps* [1967] 2 A.C. 46, HL.

[53] *Industries and General Mortgage Co. v Lewis* [1949] 2 All E.R. 573.

[54] *Trans Barwil Agencies (UK) Ltd v John S Braid & Co. Ltd*, 1988 S.C. 222.

[55] *Boston Deep Sea Fishing and Ice Co. v Ansell* (1888) 39 Ch. D. 339.

[56] *Logicrose Ltd v Southend United Football Club* [1988] 1 W.L.R. 1256.

[57] *Armstrong v Jackson* [1917] 2 K.B. 822.

[58] *McPherson's Trs v Watt* (1877) 5 R. (H.L.) 9.

Rights of an agent

The principal rights attributed to an agent are the right: **7–33**

- to be remunerated;
- to relief; and
- of lien/retention.

To be remunerated

Often the most practically important right for an agent will be the right to be remunerated. The **7–34**
amount of the agent's commission or payment will depend on the express or implied terms and conditions of the contract between the agent and principal. If there is an express statement as to payment then the prospects for confusion are limited. If no such express statement exists then the normal practice is to consider what is custom and practice in the particular field or trade and profession and attempt to assess a level of payment on this basis. If even this is not achievable then the amount to be paid will be fixed by reference to the amount the agent has actually earned.[59] If there is any question as to whether it was ever intended that the agent should be paid anything at all then the courts will look at all the circumstances surrounding the agency relationship in deciding whether payment should be made.

The right of the agent to be paid and the duty of the principal to make payment only arises when the agent has earned payment. Understandably, this is an area where dispute is common and an agent may feel that everything possible has been done and commission earned and the principal may take an entirely opposing position. The question is a matter of fact and the courts will review the agent's contribution to the transaction in question.[60]

Right of relief

An agent is entitled to be relieved by the principal of all liabilities and to be reimbursed for all **7–35**
losses and expenses properly incurred by the agent in carrying out the duties assigned by the principal.[61] The principal's obligation may be stated expressly in the agreement with the agent but more commonly it will be implied and the extent of the principal's obligation will depend on exactly what the agent has been instructed to do. The agent does not have a right to be indemnified where the agent has acted in a fashion which is illegal or negligent.[62] Similarly, the principal will be under no duty to relieve the agent when liabilities have been incurred which are outwith the extent of the agent's authority.

Right of lien/retention

An agent has the right to retain any of the principal's property which is held by the agent as **7–36**
security for the payment of the agent's remuneration or any other sums properly due and payable to the agent. This right of lien is known as a general lien where it is recognised by custom and practice that particular trades may exercise this right.[63] Mercantile agents are also recognised as having a general lien which they may exercise over any of the principal's property which comes

---

[59] This method of calculation is referred to as being *quantum meruit*, *i.e.* the amount which has been earned: *Kennedy v Glass* (1890) 17 R. 1085.

[60] *Walker, Fraser and Steele v Fraser's Trs*, 1910 S.C. 222.

[61] *Stevenson & Sons v Duncan* (1842) 5 D. 167; *Robinson and Fleming v Middleton* (1859) 21 D. 1089.

[62] *Thacker v Hardy* (1878) Q.B.D. 685.

[63] Bankers and solicitors are just two professions where a general lien is recognised as existing. See, *e.g.*, *Drummond v Muirhead and Guthrie Smith* (1900) 2 F. 585.

into their possession during the course of their agency.[64] While the right to exercise a lien is well known and recognised in a variety of trades and professions,[65] the general lien is not an automatic right which exists in all cases of agency. In those instances where a general lien does not exist then the right which is granted is known as a special lien. The special lien is more specific and only entitles the agent to retain a particular piece of property until such time as the amount due to the agent in relation to that property have been paid. Accountants, for example, do not have a general lien but do have the right to a special lien over papers they may be holding in relation to a piece of work until that work has been paid for.

It is important to note that that the right of lien only entitles the agent to retain the items belonging to the principal. The agent does not have a right to sell or dispose of the items in question unless that has been expressly agreed with the principal.

Key Concepts

The **rights of an agent** may also be set out in the contractual arrangements entered into by the agent and principal. Once again, if no such express arrangement exists then the agent is afforded a number of rights by operation of law.

THIRD PARTIES

7–37 The simple purpose of agency is to provide a mechanism which permits the agent to enter into transactions which are binding on the principal and the third party involved. Whether this is achieved or not can be influenced by the manner in which the agent acts. The crucial issue which concerns all the parties to the relationship is where responsibility lies for the agent's actions. Generally speaking, the agent may act in two different ways. The agent may act on behalf of the principal and disclose this to the third party. In this situation the agent may, or may not, tell the third party the principal's name. Alternatively, the agent may not disclose to the third party that agency exists leaving the third party to possibly believe that the transaction is being entered into with a principal and not an agent. A brief statement of the main rules in this area is to be found in:

A. F. Craig & Co. Ltd v Blackater

1923 S.C. 472

Lord Anderson (at 486): "If A contracts as agent of a disclosed principal, A cannot competently sue or be sued with reference to the contract. Again, if A contracts for an undisclosed principal, A may sue and is liable to be sued as principal, the third party having no knowledge that he is anything but a principal. If, however, A contracts for an undisclosed principal who is subsequently disclosed to the third party, the later may sue either agent or principal. He cannot, however, sue both. If an action is raised against the third party he may insist that it be at the instance of the disclosed principal."

[64] *Powdrill v Murrayhead Ltd*, 1996 G.W.D. 34–2011; *Sibbald v Gibson and Clark* (1852) 15 D. 217.

[65] In addition to bankers and solicitors who have already been mentioned auctioneers and stockbrokers also have the right to exercise a general lien. See *Glendinning v John D. Hope & Co.*, 1911 S.C. (H.L.) 73.

Agent acts as agent

Where principal is identified

The basic rule is that where an agent has acted on behalf of a named principal and had authority to do so, the agent is not regarded as having any part in the contract which is simply between the agent and the right. The agent has no right to sue on the contract and cannot be sued.[66] The important point is that the agent has acted within the authority which has been given. The same rule will also apply where the principal's name is not actually given but can be identified by the third party.[67] Again, the same rule applies where the agent is acting on behalf of a foreign principal.[68] There can be exceptions to the general rule in this area. It may be the case that the agent will be personally liable if that is the intention of the parties or if the contract makes it clear that this is the case. It is also the case that in certain trades and professions as a result of custom and practice the agent will be personally liable even although clearly acting as an agent for a named and disclosed principal. Examples of this being the case can be seen in the legal profession where a solicitor may be held liable for undertakings given during the course of a transaction.[69] Solicitors may also be held liable for fees and outlays when they have instructed another solicitor on behalf of a client.[70] Where an agent can show that he/she has an interest in the transaction which has been entered into on behalf of the principal then the agent will be entitled to sue.[71] Finally, an agent will be personally liable if the principal is not actually a legal person and cannot be sued. A good example of such a situation is where an agent purports to act on behalf of a company which does not yet exist. Section 36(C) of the Companies Act 1985 states that where a company has not yet been registered then the agent is personally liable.[72] The position is the same when the principal is an unincorporated body which cannot be sued in its own name,[73] although it may be possible to establish who has actually been responsible for decision making in such an organisation and hold them liable for the actions taken.[74] **7–38**

Where principal is not identified

There can be situations where an agent acts in the capacity of agent but does not name the principal. The general rule in this situation is very similar to instances where the principal has been named. The third party knows that the agent is acting as an agent and accordingly cannot sue the agent.[75] The position can differ when the agent refuses to disclose the identity of the principal. The effect of this is to deny the third party any remedy against the principal and the agent can be held personally liable in such situations.[76] **7–39**

---

[66] *Stone & Rolfe Ltd v Kimber Coal Co. Ltd*, 1926 S.C. (H.L.) 45.

[67] In *Armour v TL Duff & Co.*, 1912 S.C. 120 it was argued that the agent was acting on behalf of an undisclosed principal. This argument failed because the principals were known to be the owners of a particular ship and their identity could readily be discovered by looking at the Register of Shipping.

[68] *Millar v Mitchell* (1860) 22 D. 833.

[69] *Digby Brown & Co. v Lyall*, 1995 S.L.T. 932

[70] *Livesey v Purdom & Sons* (1894) 21 R. 911. See also Solicitors (Scotland) Act 1980, s.30.

[71] In *Mackenzie v Cormack*, 1950 S.C. 183. An auctioneer was acting on behalf of a named and disclosed principal. The bidder for a particular item failed to pay the price and it was held that the auctioneer could sue because as a mercantile agent the auctioneer was entitled to exercise a lie over the goods for commission and charges.

[72] The wording of the section does permit novation when the new company is registered.

[73] *Cromarty Leasing Ltd v Turnbull*, 1988 S.L.T. (Sh. Ct) 62.

[74] In *Thomson and Gillespie v Victoria Eighty Club* (1905) 43 S.L.R. 628, the members of the committee and not the ordinary members or the club were held liable.

[75] *Matthews v Auld & Guild* (1873) 1 R. 1224.

[76] In *Gibb v Cunningham and Robertson*, 1925 S.L.T. 608, a firm of solicitors, Cunningham and Robertson, acted for a client in buying shares in a company and buying a house belonging to Gibb. The paperwork showed that they were acting for a client but did not disclose the identity of the client. The price was not paid and Gibb asked for the name of the client. The solicitors did not reply and it was held that Gibb was entitled to sue the solicitors for the purchase price.

Agent acts as apparent principal

7–40 If an agent acts but does not disclose the existence of a principal, it may well appear to the third party that the agent is in fact acting as a principal. In such a situation the agent risks the possibility that the third party will hold the agent liable on the contract. The general position is that in cases where the principal remains undisclosed the agent can be sued under the contract with the third party. In instances where the agent is acting within the boundaries of his/her authority then the principal may disclose his/her identity at any time and at that stage may sue or be sued under the contract.

Bennett v Inveresk Paper Co.

(1891) 18 R. 975

Bennett owned a newspaper in Sydney, Australia and asked his London agent to arrange for the supply of paper for the newspaper. They contracted with Inveresk to supply the paper and ship it to Australia. Inveresk had no knowledge of Bennet's existence at this stage. When the paper arrived in Australia it was damaged. Bennett brought an action against Inveresk for breach of contract. It was held that had title to sue.

When the principal does reveal his/her identity then the third party must elect whether to sue the agent or the principal. Once this election has been made then it is final.[77] Issues do arise as to whether or not an election has been made. This can be established in a variety of ways, including conduct, but the common feature is that the choice must be clear. Simply raising a court action is not in itself sufficiently clear or conclusive to establish that an election has taken place.[78] However, when an action was raised against an agent, the identity of the principal came out during the course of the action and the third party pursued the action through to the grant of a decree this amounted to an election by the third party to treat the agent as the debtor.[79]

Agent acting outwith authority

7–41 When an agent acts without the principal's authority then there is no relationship created which is binding upon the principal unless the principal chooses to ratify the action taken by the agent. The agent will almost certainly be personally liable to the third party. The third party has no right to sue the agent on the basis of the contract which was apparently entered into but does have the right to sue on the basis that there exists an implied undertaking from the agent that he/she had the necessary authority to create a binding contract between the third party and the principal. If the principal has in fact withdrawn or limited the agent's authority then it is the principal's responsibility to ensure that third parties dealing with the agent know about the alteration in the agent's authority.

When the actions of the agent are fraudulent then the agent may also be liable in damages to the third party. If the actions of the agent are innocent then again the agent may be liable in damages to the third party. This liability arises because the agent is regarded by the law as having impliedly warranted to the third party that the necessary authority existed when in fact it did not. The agent is liable for having breached that authority.[80]

---

[77] *Ferrier v Dods* (1865) 3 M. 561.

[78] *Meier & Co. v Kuchenmeister* (1881) 8 R. 642.

[79] *A.F. Craig & Co. Ltd v Blackater*, 1923 S.C. 472; *James Laidlaw and Sons Ltd v Griffin*, 1968 S.L.T. 278.

[80] In *Anderson v Croall and Sons Ltd* (1903) 6 F. 153, a horse was accidentally auctioned by Croall. The price was paid but the owner of the horse refused to deliver it to the buyer as the sale had not been authorised by him. It was held that Anderson was entitled to the return of the price paid for the bhorse plus damages from Croall and Sons.

ENDING AGENCY

Agency can be terminated in a variety of ways. The parties to the agency may terminate it. The agency contract itself may specify how the relationship may be brought to an end and the relationship may also be brought to an end by virtue of the operation of the law. **7–42**

Ended by agent or principal

The agent and the principal can mutually agree that the agency relationship between them is to be terminated. In certain situations such termination will not be effective unless notification of the termination is given to third parties, particularly those with whom the agent has had dealings.[81] The principal may also seek to terminate the agency without the agent's consent. Where such termination is possible the principal must again give notice to third parties to ensure that the principal is not held liable on the basis of the agent's ongoing ostensible authority. Certain agency relationships cannot be brought to an end by the principal without the agent's consent. In these situations the agent has been given authority by the principal which allows the agent to do something in the agent's own interests, the agent is recognised as having a "procuratory *in rem suam*".[82] Where the agent has this authority to also do something which takes the agent's interests into account then the principal cannot terminate the agency until the agent the interest in question or agreed that the agency may be terminated. Where the principal has terminated the agency it is possible that the principal may still be liable to the agent in damages if there has been a breach of an express or implied term of the agency contract.[83] **7–43**

By contract

The agency contract itself may specify when the agency is to come to an end. The simplest manner in which an agency relationship may be terminated is the completion of the transaction for which the agency was formed or the expiry of a fixed period of time for which it was agreed the agency would endure.[84] **7–44**

By operation of law

There are a variety of ways in which agency may be brought to an end by virtue of the operation of law. These are: **7–45**

- frustration;
- death;
- bankruptcy;
- insanity; and
- discontinuance of business.

---

[81] See, *e.g.*, s.36(1), (2) of the Partnership Act 1890. This specifies that a retiring partner's authority is not terminated unless notice is given to third parties and also intimated in the *Edinburgh Gazette*.

[82] See *Premier Briquette Co. Ltd v Gray*, 1922 S.C. 329.

[83] *Galbraith and Moorhead v Arethusa Shipping Co. Ltd* (1896) 23 R. 1011; *North American and Continental Sales Inc v Bepi (Electronics) Ltd*, 1982 S.L.T. 47.

[84] *Brenan v Campbell's Trs* (1898) 25 R. 423.

Frustration

7–46 The agency relationship may be terminated through frustration which operates just as it does in the general law of contract. The relationship is terminated by events outwith the control of the agent or the principal. The situations in which frustration most commonly operates are often grouped into four categories: death, bankruptcy, insanity and the discontinuance of the principal's business.

While these situations are recognised as being those in which it most likely to encounter frustration they are not exhaustive. Drawing again on the general law of contract where it becomes illegal to perform the contract or where it becomes impossible to do so (one of the parties may, for example, be unavailable due to long term illness) then the contracted is terminated by operation of law.[85]

Death

7–47 The death of the principal will normally bring the agency to an end. In fact, where there is more than one principal then the death of one may end the agency relationship.[86] Where the agent knows of the death of the principal the agent may continue to complete the transaction which is ongoing at the time of death.

The death of the agent will likewise normally bring the agency to an end. The contract of agency is one which involves *delectus personae* and because it is a personal relationship it cannot be performed by someone else who has been delegated to act instead of the agent. In similar fashion to cases of more than one principal where there is more than one agent then in certain situations where there is more than one agent the death of one may end the authority of all of the agents.[87]

Bankruptcy

7–48 Agency will also be terminated by the bankruptcy of the principal. The bankruptcy is seen as ending the principal's capacity to act.[88] The bankruptcy of the agent will also normally terminate the agency. Again, because the agent is appointed on the basis of *delectus personae* the trustee in bankruptcy cannot adopt the agency and continue to act. There can be limited circumstances in which the agency is not terminated as a result of the agent's bankruptcy but this will largely be dictated by the terms of the agreement between the agent and principal and whether it is an express or implied term of the contract that the agent would continue to be solvent.[89]

Insanity

7–49 In the case of the principal, insanity will bring the agency to an end if it is permanent.[90] In situations where the principal's insanity is temporary then the agency will not be terminated and the agent will still be entitled to remuneration for anything which had been done during the period of incapacity.[91] Where an agency relationship has been formally created then it is now the case that the insanity of the principal after the creation of the agency will not terminate the agency.[92]

---

85 *Boston Deep Sea Fishing and Ice Co. Ltd v Farnham* [1957] 3 All E.R. 204.
86 *Life Association of Scotland v Douglas* (1886) 13 R. 910.
87 *Friend v Young* [1897] 2 Ch. 421.
88 *McKenzie v Campbell* (1894) 21 R. 904; *Dickson v Nicholson* (1855) 17 D. 1011.
89 *Hudson v Grainger* (1821) 5 B. & Ald. 27.
90 *Daily Telegraph Co. v McLaughlin* [1904] A.C. 776.
91 *Wink v Mortimer* (1849) 11 D. 995.
92 See Law Reform (Miscellaneous Provisions) (Scotland) Act 1990, s.71. This section has effect in respect of agency agreements entered into after January 1, 1991 but does not have effect to agency entered into before that date.

Where the principal becomes insane after entering into an agency relationship and a third party enters into a relationship unaware of the principal's insanity then there is authority for the view that where the third party is acting in good faith the agent can be viewed as still having authority until notification of the insanity had been given.[93]

Where the agent becomes insane after entering into the agency relationship then the agency is terminated.

Discontinuance of business

If the principal decides to discontinue the business with which the agent is associated then the agency relationship will be terminated. The agent will not be entitled to claim damages for breach of the contract unless it can be shown that it was an express or implied term of the agency contract that the principal should continue the business for a specified period of time.[94] **7–50**

A good example can be seen in the case of:

S.S. "State of California" Co. Ltd v Moore

(1895) 22 R. 562

For many years regular sailings had been provided between Glasgow and New York by the State Steamship Co. Ltd. In 1889 a number of the company's shareholders decided to form a new company which was to purchase a new and modern steamer. The two companies entered into an agreement which specified that the State Steamship Company would give it regular slots on the transatlantic run for a period of 10 years after the launch of the new steamer. Around one month after the new steamer was launched the State Steamship Co. Ltd passed a winding-up resolution. It was held that the agreement between the two companies had to be read as being subject to a condition that the arrangement would only last as long as the State Steamship Co. Ltd carried on business. No damages were awarded for breach of contract.

---

[93] *Pollock v Patterson*, December 10, 1811, F.C.

[94] *Patmore & Co. v B. Cannon & Co. Ltd* (1892) 19 R. 1004.

Quick Quiz

Agency

- Who are the parties in an agency relationship?
- What is the difference between a general and a special agent?
- What duties does a commercial agent owe to the principal in an agency relationship?
- Explain the differences between the creation of agency expressly, by implication and by necessity.
- Distinguish the express and implied authority of an agent.
- Outline the main duties owed by an agent to a principal.
- Explain how an agent may become bound to a third party.
- Outline how an agency relationship may be brought to an end.

Further Reading

There are a number of textbooks to which students may refer. One which is aimed directly at students is **A. ODonnell, *Agency*** (1998), which is part of the W.Green ***Law*Basics** series.

The chapters on agency in **Forte's *Scots Commercial Law*** (1997) and in ***Scots Law A Student Guide*** (2000) are also useful.

Reference can also be made to the ***Stair Memorial Encyclopaedia*** and to **Gloag and Henderson's *Law of Scotland*** (MacQueen and others, W.Green, 11th ed., 2001).

Although they are English textbooks, ***Fridman on the Law of Agency*** (1996) and ***Bowstead and Reynolds on Agency*** (2001) are both useful.

Chapter 8

UNJUSTIFIED ENRICHMENT

Professor Hector MacQueen[1]

INTRODUCTION

What is meant by unjustified enrichment?

The basic idea of the law of unjustified enrichment, which first began to emerge long ago in Roman law,[2] is that a person who has been unjustifiedly enriched at another's expense must restore the enrichment to that other. At first sight, this seems odd: one of the fundamental tenets of Western society is the lawfulness of making yourself richer, even if that involves loss to another, as for example when I compete successfully with you in business so that I make profits and you lose customers you used to have. More violent, dishonest or comparable methods of enriching yourself at another's expense, such as robbery, theft and fraud, are of course prohibited by the criminal law. But Scots civil (or private) law (like most modern legal systems) recognises that *some* enrichments arising in contexts going beyond the criminal ones just mentioned are also *unjustified*, so that the enriched person has to give it back to the person at whose expense it was obtained, or, if restoration is not possible, pay for the enrichment. **8–01**

[1] Professor of Private Law, University of Edinburgh.
[2] See Digest 12.6.14; 50.17.206 (for this by nature is equitable, that no-one be enriched at the expense of another).

Key Concepts

Three key concepts triggering the obligation to give enrichment back, are, therefore:

- **enrichment** of one party (the defender); see further below, paras 8–04 to 8–11;
- **at the expense** of another party (the pursuer); see further below, paras 8–12 to 8–16; and
- **unjustified** for the first party to retain the enrichment; see further below, paras 8–17 to 8–27.

It is the job of the law to define each of these concepts so that parties, lawyers and courts can have a reasonably clear idea when the obligation arises and, equally or even more important, when it does not. Essentially this comes down to working out what justice requires, but it is important to realise that this working out has been done, and continues to have to be done, in accordance with principles and rules contained in the definitions of the law's fundamental concepts, and not just as an instinctive or intuitive response to the various enrichment situations which life throws up from time to time.

For this reason, the better name of our subject is *unjustified rather than unjust enrichment* (a usage which is nonetheless found in both texts and cases).[3] As the point has been well expressed by one writer:

> "'Unjustified' is more accurate, though less specific. 'Unjust' normally refers to a moral criterion. So if it is used in the present context a lot of effort has to go into explaining that it does not mean unjust in the normal sense but has a very special and unusual meaning."[4]

The development of Scots law

8–02 Until the 1990s, the approach of Scots law was to start analysis of this subject under three headings, as follows:

Key Concepts

The remedies/obligations of repetition, restitution, and recompense (the "**three Rs**"):

- **repetition**—claims for the return of money
- **restitution**—claims for the return of other forms of property
- **recompense**—claims for other benefits resulting from the expenditure or actings of the pursuer

Under each of these headings were defined the categories of enrichments which the law recognised as unjustified. In the actions of repetition and restitution in particular, Scots law used Roman law to help it make these definitions. Roman law too divided enrichment law up into a series of actions, the most important of which were known as the *condictiones*.[5] For our purposes the most significant of these were:

---

3 The name "quasi-contract" will often be found in older materials, but has been abandoned in the modern law as misleading about the nature of the subject.

4 E. M. Clive, *Draft Rules on Unjustified Enrichment and Commentary*, Appendix to Scottish Law Commission Discussion Paper No.99 (1996), pp.19–20.

5 See Digest 12.4 (*causa data causa non secuta*), 12.5 (*ob turpem vel injustam causam*), 12.6 (*indebiti*) and 12.7 (*sine causa*). Note too the *actio de in rem verso* (Code 4, 26, 7, 3), also received in Scots law.

Key Concepts

The ***condictiones***:

- ***condictio indebiti*** (action for return of an undue payment);
- ***condictio causa data causa non secuta*** (action for return of a payment rendered for a purpose which failed to materialise);
- ***condictio ob injustam vel turpem causam*** (action for return of payment rendered for an illegal or immoral purpose);
- ***the condictio sine causa*** (action for return of a payment which the defender has no legal basis for retaining against the pursuer).

These Latin phrases were employed in the Scottish cases of repetition and restitution to explain which enrichments should or should not be reversed. In cases of recompense, however, there was no reference to the *condictiones*. Instead recompense appeared to cover cases of enrichment not falling within the categories of repetition and restitution, but where none the less it was held that there should be recovery. Examples included the provision of services such as improvements to another's property or other cases where exact return of the enrichment transferred was not possible but a benefit which ought to be paid for had clearly occurred.

A new approach

The approach outlined above was much criticised. Was there any reason for distinguishing **8–03** between repetition and restitution? What, if any, were the limits of recompense, and how did it relate to the other actions? Was it a subsidiary general action picking up those cases of enrichment which the other actions did not reach? Would it not be better and more in accordance with the principled nature of Scots law to start by defining the subject from the events which triggered liability—unjustified enrichments—rather than with the available remedial responses? The Scottish Law Commission brought enrichment law under detailed consideration in the 1990s. After this began, however, the courts started to move away from the approach outlined above, and to adopt a more general yet systematic way of looking at the subject, based on the idea of an obligation to restore or pay for unjustified enrichment at another's expense. The key cases are *Morgan Guaranty Trust Co. of New York v Lothian Regional Council* [6] and, in particular, *Shilliday v Smith.*[7] The facts and decision of these cases will be discussed later in the Chapter, but here we focus on the general approach to enrichment established by the judgements in them. In *Morgan Guaranty* Lord President Hope emphasised the need for a unified approach to the subject in a decision abolishing the exclusion of error in law as a ground for the recovery of a payment to another (see further below, para.8–19).

Morgan Guaranty Trust Co. of New York v Lothian Regional Council

1995 S.C. 151

Per Lord President Hope (at 155): "The important point is that these actions [of repetition, restitution and recompense] are all means to the same end, which is to redress an unjustified enrichment upon the broad equitable principle *nemo debet locupletari aliena jactura*. Thus the action of repetition, to take this as an example, may be based upon the *condictio causa data causa non secuta*, the *condictio sine causa* or the *condictio indebiti* depending upon which of these grounds of action fits the circumstances which give rise to the claim. The nature of the benefit received by the defender and the circumstances on which the pursuer relies for his claim ought, in

[6] 1995 S.C. 151.

[7] 1998 S.C. 725.

a properly organised structure for this branch of the law, to provide all that is needed for the selection of the appropriate remedy. The selection is distorted if there is introduced into the structure a rule [the error of law rule] which is essentially one of expediency rather than of equity between the parties ... It becomes wholly disorganised if that rule is applied to one of the remedies within the system and not to others, with the result that a pursuer is driven to seeking another less appropriate remedy to escape from it."

Shilliday is most important for the general approach to the whole subject outlined by the Lord President, Lord Rodger of Earlsferry. This was also approved by Lord Hope of Craighead in the subsequent House of Lords case, *Dollar Land (Cumbernauld) Ltd v CIN Properties Ltd.*[8]

Shilliday v Smith

1998 S.C. 725

Per Lord President Rodger (at 727, 728): "A person may be said to be unjustly enriched at another's expense when he has obtained a benefit from the other's actings or expenditure, without there being a legal ground which would justify him in retaining that benefit. The significance of one person being unjustly enriched at the expense of another is that in general terms it constitutes an event which triggers a right in that other person to have the enrichment reversed.

As the law has developed, it has identified various situations where persons are to be regarded as having been unjustly enriched at another's expense and where the person may accordingly seek to have the enrichment reversed. The authorities show that some of these situations fall into recognisable groups or categories. Since these situations correspond, if only somewhat loosely, to situations where remedies were granted in Roman law, in referring to the relevant categories our law tends to use the terminology which is found in the Digest and Code. The terms include *condictio indebiti*, *condictio causa data causa non secuta*, and, to a lesser extent, *condictio sine causa* ...

Once he has satisfied himself that he has a relevant case, anyone contemplating bringing an action must then determine how the court is to reverse the defender's enrichment if it decides in the pursuer's favour. This will depend on the particular circumstances. The person framing the pleadings must consider how the defender's enrichment has come about and then search among the usual range of remedies to find a remedy or combination of remedies which will achieve his purpose of having that enrichment reversed.

Elementary examples make this clear. For instance, if A has been unjustly enriched because he has received a sum of money from B, the enrichment can be reversed by ordering A to repay the money to B. B's remedy will be repetition of the sum of money from A. On the other hand, if the unjust enrichment arises out of the transfer of moveable property, the enrichment can be reversed by ordering A to transfer the property back to B. An action of restitution of the property will be appropriate ... If A is unjustly enriched by having had the benefit of B's services, the enrichment can be reversed by ordering A to pay B a sum representing the value of the benefit which A has enjoyed. An action of recompense will be appropriate. So repetition, restitution ... and recompense are simply examples of remedies which the courts grant to reverse an unjust enrichment, depending on the way in which the particular enrichment has arisen."

8 1998 S.C. (H.L.) 90 at 98.

Dollar Land (Cumbernauld) Ltd v CIN Properties Ltd
1998 S.C. (H.L.) 90

Per Lord Hope (at 98): "These actions [of repetition, restitution and recompense] were all means to the same end, which is to address an unjustified enrichment ... For my part I see no harm in the continued use of these expressions to describe the various remedies, so long as it is understood that they are being used merely to describe the nature of the remedy which the court is being asked to provide in order to redress the enrichment. The event which gives rise to the granting of the remedy is the enrichment. In general terms it may be said that the remedy is available where the enrichment lacks a legal ground to justify the retention of the benefit. In such circumstances it is held to be unjust."

As a result of these cases, Scots law has now reached a position where in principle an enrichment is said to be unjustified and one which should be reversed if its retention is supported by no legal ground. Examples of "legal grounds" or justifications for enrichments include receipt under a gift or in performance of a valid contract, as well as gain through lawful competition in the market place, already mentioned above. On the other side of the coin, the *condictiones* should be seen as descriptions of situations in which an enrichment of any kind would be seen as unjustified, while repetition (repayment of money), restitution (restoration of property) and recompense (payment for the service or other enrichment rendered) are remedies which the court can grant once it has decided that an enrichment is unjustified. But neither the *condictiones* nor the ground covered in the past by the traditional remedies exhaust the ways in which the courts may find or reverse unjustified enrichment: this is the significance of accepting the general principle requiring the reversal of unjustified enrichment.

Scots law on this subject is therefore still in a state of development and, consequently, some uncertainty, although the Scottish Law Commission has decided that, in the light of the 1990s cases, reforming legislation is no longer necessary, and that the law can be left for development by the courts and textbook writers. A broad framework for approaching enrichment has been indicated by the courts, but the full implications of this reorientation for the existing case law and the shaping of future decisions are at this stage still a matter on which textbook writers must speculate to some degree. There has however been a growing consensus amongst legal writers as to the underlying principles of the law and the approach which needs to be taken, and this Chapter seeks to reflect something of that consensus. It is structured around the three basic concepts of the defender's enrichment, at the expense of the pursuer, and the factors making this situation unjustified and in need of remedy. The Chapter then briefly considers the defences available to the enriched person, and the remedies which can be granted by the court. However, the reader should be warned that it can only amount to a provisional statement of the law, that will be subject to change and correction in the light of further decisions and analysis. Much is already to be learned from considering the experience of other European legal systems, and also that of South Africa, like Scotland a mixed jurisdiction. Developments in the rather different law of England may give us some insights as to problems likely to arise also in Scotland.

ENRICHMENT

What constitutes enrichment?

Enrichment is the receipt or acquisition of a benefit of economic worth, leading either to an increase in the person's wealth or to the avoidance of loss of wealth. This can arise from: **8–04**

- addition of a new asset to a person's wealth;
- adding value to a person's already existing asset;

- preserving another's asset which would otherwise have been lost or reduced in value, saving that other the expense involved;
- performing an obligation lying upon another, saving that other the expense of performance.

Receipt or acquisition of money

8–05 The classic case of such a benefit is the *receipt or acquisition of money*, and most of the cases in enrichment law are about that subject. See, for example:

Royal Bank of Scotland v Watt

1991 S.C. 48

W was a window-cleaner who had a bank account with RBS. W met T in a pub. T possessed a cheque drawn on the account of a well-known firm of solicitors, apparently for the amount of £18,631. T wanted to cash the cheque but told W he lacked a bank account with which to do this. W offered to help T. The cheque was paid into W's account at the RBS, and he then withdrew the cash equivalent from the bank and gave it to T. W never saw T again, and it turned out that the cheque, originally for only £631, had been fraudulently altered. W had thus received cash from RBS, *i.e.* he was enriched at the bank's expense (since it could not enforce the cheque against the solicitors). W was found liable to repay the full amount.

Morgan Guaranty Trust Co. of New York v Lothian Regional Council

1995 S.C. 151

LRC was a local authority and MG a merchant bank. The parties had entered into a contract under which MG made payments to LRC which would be repaid in certain market conditions. It turned out that the contract was void. LRC had money from MG without any legal basis for its retention, *i.e.* the authority was enriched at the bank's expense, and it was found liable to repay the bank.

Receipt or acquisition of other property

8–06 The benefit may also be other forms of property, such as *goods or corporeal moveables* (the most common case after money), land, or some incorporeal property right. See, for example:

Findlay v Monro

(1698) Mor. 1767

F sent an ox to Macfarlane, but by mistake it was delivered to M. M thought that the ox was a gift from a friend, killed the beast and salted the carcase for consumption. It was held that M was enriched by receipt of the animal and was liable for that. (See further below, para.8–34, on the remedy.)

Receipt or acquisition of intangible benefits

8–07 Enrichment can also arise through the *receipt or acquisition of intangible benefits*, like the provision of a service which leaves no end product as such with the recipient (for example, the oral provision of advice, cleaning windows or polishing shoes).

ELCAP v Milne's Executor

1999 S.L.T. 58

M was an NHS patient receiving free care in a hospital when it was taken over by a charitable company (E) and became a nursing home. In-patients not requiring continuing medical care were supposed thereafter to pay a charge to E. M was discharged as not requiring continuing medical care but continued to be cared for by E until his death three years later, although his *curator bonis* refused to pay the charges claimed by E. E's claim for recompense from M's estate for services rendered was held to be relevant (a case on implied contract was rejected, however).

Improvement of property

Sometimes enrichment arises because the recipient's *property is improved* in some way by another—for example, a building is repaired or renovated, either increasing the property's market value, or saving the owner having to spend money on doing the work if the repairs were necessary ones. But the improvement may go beyond repair and maintenance, and extend to enhancement (sometimes termed "meliorations" in the cases), as for example erecting completely new buildings, or draining and cultivating land. However, improvements which are merely the provision of luxuries—for example, putting statues up in somebody else's garden—are not treated as enrichments.[9] Although land is the usual kind of property involved in the reported improvement cases, there is no reason why the subject-matter may not be corporeal moveables or, indeed, incorporeals. **8–08**

See, for example:

Newton v Newton

1925 S.C. 715

H bought a house in the name of his prospective wife (W), in which the parties lived after their marriage. H, who honestly believed that he was the owner of the house, spent £400 on improving and repairing it. After the marriage broke down and it had been found that W, as owner, was entitled to continue to live in the house and exclude H from it, W was found to be enriched by having the benefit of H's improvements.

Shilliday v Smith

1998 S.C. 725

M and W began to live together in M's cottage in 1988, and became engaged in August 1990. They never married. In 1988, M had bought a house in a state of disrepair, and from about 1990 M and W began to improve this property, into which they moved together in 1991. The works were completed by Christmas 1992, when M ejected W from the house. W had spent about £9,600 on the works: approximately £7,000 direct to tradesmen whom she had instructed; £1,880 to M to pay for materials and work on the house, and £756 on items for the garden, left behind after her ejection. M was found to be enriched by W's payments to him and the workmen, which had led to the renovation of his property, and by the items she had left in the garden.

---

9 See Bankton, *Institutions*, 1.9.42.

York Buildings Company v Mackenzie
(1795) 3 Pat. 378; (1797) 3 Pat. 579

YBC's estates were sold under court authority to M, who erected a mansionhouse, sank coal-mines and laid out plantations and policies on the ground. Eleven years later, YBC successfully reduced the sale. *Held* that YBC was enriched by M's operations.

Edinburgh Life Assurance Co. v Balderston
(1909) 2 S.L.T. 323

A life assurance policy was kept in force by payment of premiums by assignees under an invalid assignation from the assured. *Held* that the assignees had maintained another's property in good faith, thereby creating a benefit for that other.

Nortje en'n Ander v Pool
1966 (3) S.A. 96 (A.)

In this South African case, a landowner (E) and a prospector (I) entered into a written agreement to the effect that I would be allowed to prospect for, and mine if found, kaolin on E's land. As a result of I's prospecting activities, which cost him R800, considerable quantities of kaolin were found on the land; but before mining could begin, the written agreement was found to be void, and E turned I off the ground. The land was now worth R15,000 more than it was before the discovery of the kaolin. Was E enriched? The South African court held not, but the general principle against unjustified enrichment in Scots law might suggest that the prospector I should have a claim. The case might be stronger if: (i) immediately after the discovery of the kaolin but before finding that the agreement with I was void, E sold the land to T, realising the enhancement of its value; or if (ii) E commenced mining operations and began to make large profits from the sale of kaolin; or if (iii) E, having commenced profitable mining operations, then sold the land and the mining business, realising large profits.

Unauthorised use of another's property

8–09 Again, there can be enrichment arising from the *unauthorised use of someone else's property*. Here again the enrichment is by way of a saving, in not having had to pay for that use hitherto. Thus in the leading case of *Earl of Fife v Wilson*[10] W had possession of land under a lease which was found to be invalid against F, the heir of entail in the land; W was held to be enriched by his possession. In more recent cases, tenants who stayed on after the lease had been lawfully terminated before its full term had expired were similarly found liable to the landlord for their unauthorised use.[11]

GTW Holdings Ltd v Toet
1994 S.L.T. (Sh. Ct) 16

T occupied land owned by GTW for five years, without any title to do so and without the owners knowing of the occupation. T was held to be enriched to the extent of the annual worth of the land over the period.

---

[10] (1867) 3 M. 323.

[11] *Glasgow District Council v Morrison McChlery & Co*, 1985 S.C. 52 (compulsory purchase of leased property); *HMV Fields Properties Ltd v Skirt' n' Slack Centre of London Ltd*, 1987 S.L.T. 2 (lease irritated).

There may also be enrichment in cases where the owner allows another to occupy land, but the circumstances show that the occupation was not intended to be gratuitous.

Glen v Roy

(1882) 10 R. 239

A father consented to his son's possession of a house without putting a formal lease in place, but the son was found liable to pay for the enrichment arising from his occupation, having failed to show any intention of the father to make a gift to him, and it being presumed that a person who occupies another's land does so as tenant.

Shetland Islands Council v BP Petroleum Development Ltd

1990 S.L.T. 82

S Council allowed BP to occupy land which it owned, in order to construct an oil terminal (Sullum Voe). For several years the parties negotiated a lease of the land, while BP conducted operations from the site, but the negotiations were unsuccessful. *Held* that BP could in these circumstances be made liable to the extent of the annual worth of the land.

Rochester Poster Services Ltd v A G Barr plc

1994 S.L.T. (Sh. Ct) 2

AGB leased an advertising board site in Glasgow from RPS. The lease expired at the end of 1992 and negotiations for its renewal were unsuccessful; but AGB continued to advertise at the site for 17 months after the expiry of the lease. AGB was held to be enriched to the extent of the annual worth of the site over the 17-month period.

This enrichment by use of another's property can extend beyond land to *moveables.*[12] With moveables, the types of enriching use can be quite varied. Thus, for example, the possessor may make a profit by reselling the moveable to a third party.[13] Or, the possessor may consume or otherwise destroy the moveable,[14] or through action with it, involving the property doctrines of accession, commixtion, confusion or specification, either gain ownership himself or confer it on a third party.[15] The following cases illustrate the types of situation which can arise, although the varying answers which they give on how much is recoverable by the pursuer will also be discussed later in this Chapter (see below, para.8–35).

Jarvis v Manson

1954 S.L.T. (Sh. Ct) 93

Jewellers bought for £3, renovated, polished (at a cost of £1.50), and resold for £10 a five-stone diamond half-hoop ring. The ring, which was worth £30, had been stolen. *Held* that the jewellers, being in good faith, were liable to the true owner to the extent of their enrichment from the resale (£5.50).

---

12 See, *e.g. Chisholm v Alexander* (1882) 19 S.L.R. 835.

13 *Scot v Low* (1704) Mor. 9123; *Jarvis v Manson*, 1954 S.L.T. (Sh. Ct) 93.

14 *Findlay v Monro* (1698) Mor. 1767; *Walker v Spence and Carfrae* (1765) Mor. 12802; *Faulds v Townsend* (1861) 23 D. 437.

15 *Oliver & Boyd v Marr Typefounding Co.* (1901) 9 S.L.T. 170; *International Banking Corporation v Ferguson, Shaw & Sons*, 1910 S.C. 182.

Faulds v Townsend

(1861) 23 D. 437

A manufacturing chemist bought for 12/- (60p), around midnight but in the course of its business, a horse, which was immediately killed and boiled up for use in manufacture, producing a profit of about 10/- (50p). The horse, it turned out, had previously been stolen and was worth £10. *Held* that the chemist was liable to the true owner for the full value of the horse. Although not in bad faith, there had been fault and lack of due care in checking the antecedents of the horse.

Oliver & Boyd v The Marr Typefounding Co. Ltd

(1901) 9 S.L.T. 170

OB employees stole type from their employers, and by various subsequent transactions the type ended up with MT, who were in good faith. MT melted down the type (this being held to amount to specification, the creation from earlier materials of a new subject, which is owned by the specificator) and resold it. *Held* that MT were liable to OB for the full value of the type.

International Banking Corporation v Ferguson, Shaw & Sons

1910 S.C. 182

FS bought refined cotton seed oil in good faith, and turned it into lard, which was then resold at a profit. But the party from whom the oil had been purchased had not had good title, and IBC, the true owners, sued FS as specificators for the full value of the oil. *Held* FS were liable for the full value of the oil.

North-West Securities Ltd v Barrhead Coachworks Ltd

1976 S.C. 68

NWS, a finance company, let a car to R on hire purchase. Before completing payment of all instalments due to NWS, R, although not the owner, sold the car to a motor dealer (BC), which then sold on to a private purchaser. Under s.27 of the Hire Purchase Act 1964, the private purchaser became owner as a result of this transaction, and NWS was deprived of its rights in the car. *Held* that BC were only liable to NWS to the extent that they had made a profit on the resale of the car to the private purchaser.

Lastly on enrichment from the use of another's property, there are cases about the *misappropriation of someone else's funds*.

Bennett v Carse

1990 S.L.T. 454

B was negotiating to buy a pub from X. Although the contract was not yet finalised, B agreed to take entry on February 2, 1987, to make certain payments to X for stock and discharge of debts, and to be responsible for payment of rates on the premises; he also installed C as manager of the pub. B then went abroad for two months. On his return, he discovered that X was no longer willing to sell, but only to lease, the pub, and that he had in fact leased it to C. Further, C had paid the rates on the premises by drawing a cheque on B's account. *Held* that C was enriched by his actions with B's funds, and was therefore liable to reimburse B.

Performance of another's obligation

8–10 Another, more complex enrichment situation is where a *party (P) pays or performs to a creditor (C) the debt or obligation owed to C by a debtor (D), without P having the authority of D to do so.* If D's obligation to C is discharged by P's action, then D is enriched by the saving in no longer having to pay or perform to C. This enrichment is at P's expense: P thus has an enrichment claim against D.

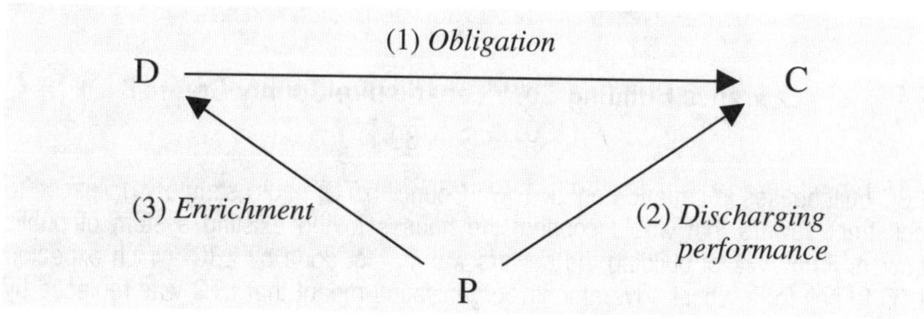

Scots law is, however, still unclear about when unauthorised third party performances discharge D's obligations, although the authorities seem to favour that result.[16] D on his own cannot stop C accepting *payment of money* from P to discharge the debt,[17] and it seems that where P is acting to protect his own legitimate interests—for example, to anticipate and prevent C doing diligence against P for D's debt—he may compel C to accept the payment.[18]

There is more difficulty in the case where *P performs a non-money obligation—e.g.* to build a wall—which D was ready and willing to perform, perhaps at a profit to himself; why should he be deprived of that opportunity by the actions of P as accepted by C, and moreover be subjected to an enrichment claim from P? If P acted despite knowing of D's readiness and willingness to perform, then he may lack a legitimate interest to discharge D's obligation in his own protection, and C will be liable to D for failure to accept his performance; indeed, D may also have a claim against P for inducing C to break a contract. If C enlisted P to get the benefit of a cheaper performance than that offered by D, then P will look to and rely upon C for payment, and it is suggested that his performance can only discharge his own obligations (the issue becomes acute only if C becomes insolvent or otherwise unable to pay his debts before paying P). Moreover, if C pays P for his work, P is not impoverished, even if D is in some sense enriched. P's performance of a non-money obligation may be refused by C if he has a specific interest in personal performance by D (*delectus personae*),[19] and obviously there will be no discharge if C does not accept the performance.

See for example:

Reid v Lord Ruthven

(1918) 55 S.L.R. 616

Lord R was indebted to a bank. The debts were guaranteed by K, whose own debts were in turn guaranteed by Mr R. On K's death, the bank found that his assets were not enough to cover Lord R's debt. Mr R paid the balance to the bank, which as a result treated Lord R's debt as discharged. Lord R was therefore enriched because he was no longer liable to pay the bank, *i.e.* he had made a saving, but at Mr R's expense. Lord R was found liable to pay Mr R the amount of the saving.

---

16 For the authorities on this subject, see Gloag and Henderson *The Law of Scotland* (11th ed., 2001), §15.02.

17 Bankton, *Institutions*, 1.24.1 ("he cannot hinder the creditor to take his payment where he can get it").

18 Bell, *Principles*, §557.

19 Bell, *Principles*, §557. The classic example would be an obligation to paint a portrait.

Duncan v Motherwell Bridge & Engineering Co. Ltd
1952 S.C. 131

D was employed by M to work for a period in Kuwait, the contract providing that outward and homeward travel fares at the beginning and end of the contract would be paid by M. During the contract period, D went on strike and was repatriated at his own request. Although not obliged to do so, M paid D's return fare. *Held* that D was enriched by the payment of his fare by M.

Lawrence Building Co. v Lanarkshire County Council
1978 S.C. 30

LBC built houses in Lanark. Lanark Town Council (LTC) had a statutory obligation to construct sewers that would connect the houses to the existing system of public sewers. The work of building the sewers was in fact done by LBC, which expected LTC to pay for it. Local government reorganisation meant that LTC was replaced by LCC, which refused to pay for the sewers. LCC was found to be enriched by the saving which it had made, in not having to construct the sewers despite the statutory obligation to do so; thus LBC had a relevant claim

Note that this last case involves performance of another's non-money obligation, but does not raise the issues about that topic discussed in the text above, because, the obligation being statutory, the creditor is the public paying local government taxes in Lanarkshire, and the debtor (LCC) is not a profit-making organisation. Contrast this decision with the very similar, earlier case of *Varney (Scotland) Ltd v Burgh of Lanark*,[20] where recompense was not allowed; the parties had been in dispute about liability to construct the sewers, and the contractors should have brought an action against the council for implement of its statutory duty, rather than proceeding to build the sewers.

Enrichment generally: transfer, imposition and taking

8–11 All these examples of enrichment help us to understand why different remedies may be required in enrichment law. In some cases restoration of the specific thing will be appropriate: money, for example (although, since money is fungible, the money repaid need not be exactly the same notes and coins that were originally received), or goods. But improvements, services, and use of property can never be restored; instead they will have to be valued and paid for. Similarly, with cases where the recipient of goods has consumed them, passed them on to others, or otherwise created a situation where they cannot be returned as they were received. Where a debt or obligation has been paid or performed by a third party, it too cannot be returned as such, although at least the amount of the money debt discharged can be precisely fixed.[21]

A very important distinction lies in the way enrichment comes about, and is caught in the phrase "receipt or acquisition" used at the beginning of the first paragraph of this section. A person may be enriched in a relatively passive way, by merely receiving and accepting the enrichment from someone else: that is, another person acts to make the enrichment, for example, by paying over a sum of money, or handing over goods. The enrichment is *transferred to* the enriched person by someone else. Again, in some other cases, the enrichment is *imposed upon* the enriched person by someone else, *e.g.* by carrying out improvements to another person's property or paying someone else's debt. In both cases the enriched party receives enrichment in a relatively passive way: the difference between the transfer and the imposition cases is that there is no need for the beneficiary to cooperate or consent in the latter; he has the enrichment regardless. This of course

[20] 1974 S.C. 245.
[21] See further para.8–36 below.

gives rise to issues about how to distinguish between the cases where such imposed enrichment must be paid for, and when the law should rather protect the recipient from unsought interventions in their affairs (see further below, para.8–25).

On the other hand, a person may take active steps to acquire an enrichment, typically by making use in some way of another person's property, rights, or money. The enrichment is *taken*, or achieved by way of *encroachment upon, interference with, or invasion of, another's rights*. Henceforth these actions will be generically described as "takings", although they encompass a wide range of actions by the enriched person. Improving someone else's property or paying their debts is not such taking to acquire enrichment, because the active person (the improver or the payer) confers, rather than gains, enrichment in these situations. Note, however, that the taking must be unauthorised, so that if the owner of the right consents to it, no enrichment claim will arise on this ground. As the discussion of property use cases above showed, however, there are examples in Scots law of enrichment being found to arise from use of property to which the owner consented, but it was apparent from the circumstances that this was not done gratuitously. Such cases may often be ones of contract rather than enrichment;[22] but insofar as they are to be located within enrichment law, they are best seen as transfer rather than taking cases.

Key Concepts

Enrichments by transfer, imposition, and taking:

- **Enrichment by TRANSFER**—impoverished person (P) delivers enriching subject-matter (money, corporeal property) to enriched person (D); D consents by receiving rather than refusing transfer.
- **IMPOSED enrichment**—P enriches D by an act other than transfer of an enriching subject-matter and without D's consent or authorisation to do so (e.g. improves D's property, pays D's debt to a third party).
- **Enrichment by TAKING / encroachment upon / interference with / invasion of another's property / rights**—D enriches himself by way of use of P's property or other rights without P's consent or authorisation.

Another important dimension of the property use cases, is that all types of property—land, corporeal moveables, and money—appear to be covered. Can the law go further and recognise taking of or interference with rights in general as a form of enrichment? The law of fiduciary obligations may provide an important example.[23] Fiduciaries such as trustees, agents, partners and company directors are liable to hand over to those to whom their duties are owed, any gain which they make as a result of abusing their fiduciary position. This is because fiduciaries are supposed to act only in the interests of these creditors (the trust beneficiaries, the principal, the other partners, or the company, as the case may be), and not in their own interest. In the Scottish case of *Teacher v Calder*,[24] T loaned £15,000 to C for investment in the latter's timber business, in return for interest and a half-share in the net profits of that business. In breach of contract, C used the money for other purposes, making a substantial profit as a result; but he was able to repay T with the interest and the half-share of the timber profits over the period of the advance. The House of Lords held that T was not entitled to claim the gain which C had made from the breach of contract; their relationship was not fiduciary. But this decision must now be seen in light of another decision

22 See, *e.g. Shetland Islands Council v BP Petroleum Development Ltd*, 1990 S.L.T. 82.
23 On fiduciary obligations in general see Gloag and Henderson, *The Law of Scotland* (11th ed., 2001), §4.16.
24 (1899) 1 F. (H.L.) 39.

of the House of Lords, in the English case of *Attorney-General v Blake*.[25] B was a member of the British intelligence service who betrayed his country and fled to the then Soviet Union. His memoirs were subsequently published in the UK and made a substantial profit. The Government sought to prevent these profits being transferred to B, and succeeded in doing so on the basis that the publication was a breach of B's lifelong contractual obligation to keep secret his activities as a spy. This, however, was not a fiduciary obligation. It remains to be seen how far this decision affects *Teacher v Calder*, to which the speeches of the Law Lords in *Blake* make no reference, and whether it has created a general right to recover enrichment arising from breach of contract regardless of whether economically measurable loss has occurred. See further below, para.8–26.

The distinctions between enrichment by transfer, imposition and taking help to tell us at whose expense the enrichment is acquired—the transferor, the imposer, or the owner/holder of the right taken, respectively—but its greatest importance is in determining which factors should be used to establish whether the enrichment is unjustified and should be restored or paid for. See further below, paras 8–17 to 8–26.

AT ANOTHER'S EXPENSE (LOSS AND CAUSATION)

Loss

8–12 To be returnable, an enrichment must be gained at the expense of another; that is to say, usually another person must have suffered a loss, a diminution or reduction in wealth which is in some sense the result or consequence of the other's enrichment.[26] In *transfer* cases, this is usually a relatively straightforward matter, because the transferee's gain has a mirror image in the transferor's loss of the amount transferred. Where enrichment arises from *takings*, the loss can usually be seen as the inability of that other to make, or bargain for the, use of its own property or rights. In cases of *imposed enrichment*, such as improvements to another's property or payment of another's debt, loss can be readily identified in the cost of carrying out the improvements or making the payment. But in improvement cases, the loss may be much greater than the enrichment on the other side, as where expensive works are carried out but lead to a much lesser increase in the value of the property concerned. So, it is important to emphasise that the role of the loss in enrichment cases is primarily to help in identifying those cases where there is a right to recover at all, and who has that right. Equally, though, a small expenditure on improvements may result in a much larger increase in the value of the property,[27] and here, it would seem, the amount of the loss is the limit of what can be recovered in any enrichment action; pursuers are not to make a profit out of enrichment claims.[28]

No loss: incidental benefits

8–13 The enrichment must generally not be an incidental or chance outcome of the pursuer's expenditure. If somebody does something for his own benefit which also incidentally confers a benefit on another, the former probably suffers no relevant loss; the latter's benefit did not cause him any extra expenditure. As noted in *Exchange Telegraph Co. Ltd v Giulianotti*,[29] a case of

[25] [2001] 1 A.C. 268. See also *Esso Petroleum Co. Ltd v Niad Ltd* [2001] All E.R. (D) 324; *WWF-World Wide Fund for Nature v World Wrestling Foundation* [2002] F.S.R. 32; *AB Corporation v CD Company (The Sine Nomine)* [2002] 1 Lloyd's Rep. 805; *Experience Hendrix LLC v PPX Enterprises Inc.* [2003] E.W.C.A. Civ. 323.

[26] See further para.8–16 below, however, for cases where "at the expense of'' is not necessarily equiparated with a direct economic loss to the pursuer.

[27] See the South African case of *Nortje en 'n Ander v Pool* 1966 (3) S.A. 96 (A.) (above, para.8–08), where expenditure of R800 enhanced the value of the defendant's property by R15,000. This type of situation has led to the comment that the easiest way to ruin somebody is to enrich him.

[28] Hume, *Lectures*, Vol.3, pp.166–7.

[29] 1959 S.C. 19.

unauthorised use of a subscription sports news service, "the fact that the defender by obtaining the news service from other subscribers incidentally benefited did not involve the pursuers in any extra expenditure".[30] A famous illustration was given by Lord President Dunedin in *Edinburgh and District Tramways Co. Ltd v Courtenay*:[31] "One man heats his house, and his neighbour gets a great deal of benefit. It is absurd to suppose that the person who has heated his house can go to his neighbour and say, 'Give me so much for my coal bill, because you have been warmed by what I have done, and I did not intend to give you a present of it.'"[32]

Edinburgh and District Tramways Co. Ltd v Courtenay

1909 S.C. 99

EDT ran trams in Edinburgh. C contracted with EDT to provide fittings on the trams, from which boards would be hung to carry advertisements. EDT acquired new trams which already had boards attached, to improve safety and "decency" (*i.e.* not expose the legs of the passengers, female ones especially, to onlookers). C thus no longer had to incur the expense of providing the fittings, but continued to charge EDT the same rate for its services. EDT argued that C, by making a saving in this way, was enriched. It was held that C were only incidentally benefited by expenditure which EDT had engaged upon with their own purposes—safety, decency, attraction of passengers—in mind, and that no claim lay.

Selfish or mixed motives

However, it cannot be said that the mere fact that the pursuer carried out expenditure with a view only of his own interests always precludes recovery altogether. Thus, for example, if I improve land in the honest but mistaken belief that it is mine, or if I perform another's obligations to protect my own interests, I am acting for my own benefit; but this will not prevent me recovering for the enrichment of the true owner.[33] Similarly, recovery has been allowed in cases of mixed motives, where the pursuer acted partly in her own interest, partly in that of the defender.[34] The purpose of the expenditure must therefore be seen as merely a factor which can—but need not—be relevant in considering whether or not resultant enrichment is at the expense of the pursuer. After all, if the expenditure was intended to benefit the pursuer, that may point as much to gift as to unjustified enrichment. As the cases of improving another's property or paying another's debt show, a more important factor than purpose is likely to be the *directness* with which the enrichment is created for the defender by the pursuer's activities. This also holds good for the takings cases, where the defender enriches himself by using the pursuer's property specifically.[35] **8–14**

Indirect enrichment

A difficult group of cases is concerned with what is known as "*indirect enrichment*", where three or more parties are involved in what is sometimes called an enrichment "chain" or "triangle" or "constellation". **8–15**

[30] At 26, *per* Lord Guest.
[31] 1909 S.C. 99.
[32] At 105.
[33] See, *e.g.* *Newton v Newton*, 1925 S.C. 715; *Lawrence Building Co. v Lanarkshire County Council*, 1978 S.C. 30.
[34] See, *e.g.* *Fernie v Robertson* (1871) 9 M. 437.
[35] See the cases listed above, para.8–09.

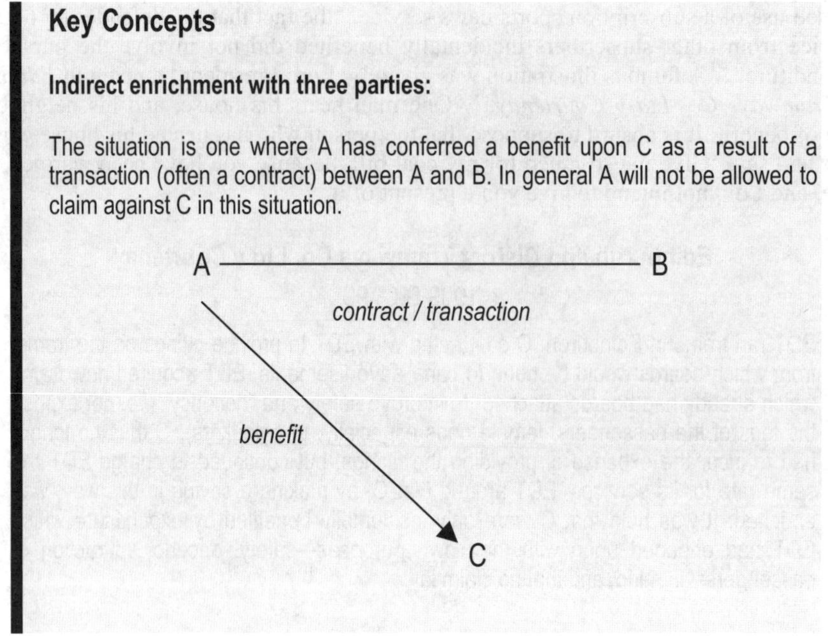

Key Concepts
Indirect enrichment with three parties:
The situation is one where A has conferred a benefit upon C as a result of a transaction (often a contract) between A and B. In general A will not be allowed to claim against C in this situation.
A
B
contract / transaction
benefit
C

So, for example, if A is a building sub-contractor who performs work under the sub-contract with B, thereby benefiting C, the building owner, but A is not paid by B because B has become insolvent, A does not have an enrichment claim against C for the work done.[36] This is because the law holds that A in entering the sub-contract relied only on the credit of the other contracting party, and therefore bears the risk of B's insolvency and is limited to its contractual claim against B. The same result occurs in what are often known as the "garage repair" cases, where A is the repairer of C's damaged car but is actually performing the repair under contract with C's insurers, B. If B becomes insolvent before paying A, the latter has no claim against C for the enrichment arising from the repair.[37]

However, in some cases of indirect enrichment recovery will be allowed, because the policy factors in favour of recovery outweigh those against it described above.[38]

---

[36] See for this example *J B Mackenzie (Edinburgh) Ltd v Lord Advocate*, 1972 S.C. 231 (where the unsuccessful claim was made in delict).

[37] *Kirklands Garage (Kinross) Ltd v Clark*, 1967 S.L.T. (Sh. Ct) 60; *Express Coach Finishers v Caulfield*, 1968 S.L.T. (Sh. Ct) 11. Contrast the South African cases of *ABSA Bank v Stander* 1998 (1) S.A. 939 (C.) and *McCarthy Retail Ltd v Shortdistance Carriers CC* 2001 (3) S.A. 482 (S.C.A.).

[38] In addition to the cases described below, see *Extruded Welding Wire (Sales) Ltd v McLachlan & Brown*, 1986 S.L.T. 314.

M&I Instrument Engineers Ltd v Varsada and Beattie

1991 S.L.T. 106

V defrauded M&I of £50,000 cash by falsely telling the company's directors that he represented a Saudi sheikh setting up a catering consultancy, and persuading them to invest in this new business. The next day V used £41,240 of the cash to buy a house at Shawhead, Dumfries, in the name of his mistress B.

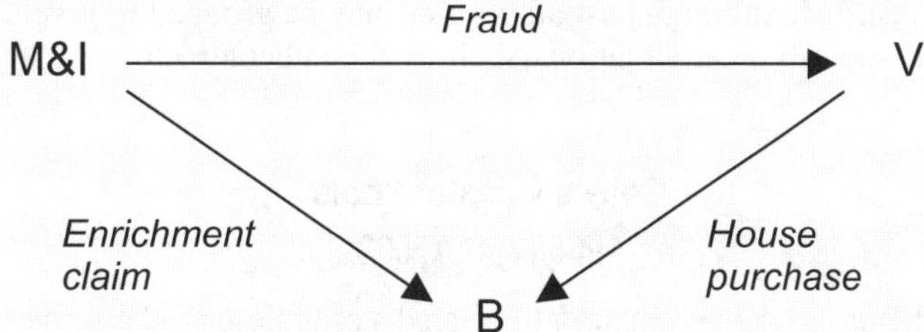

V was arrested, convicted and jailed for the fraud, but M&I were unable to recover the £50,000 from him. On release from prison, V lived with B in the Shawhead house. M&I sought restitution of £41,240 from B. *Held* that although B was only an indirect beneficiary of the fraudulent transaction between M&I and V, no person should be entitled to profit from the fraud of another, and she should repay the sum sought to M&I.

Mercedes-Benz Finance Ltd v Clydesdale Bank plc

1997 S.L.T. 905

MB supplied cars to GH for sale by the latter. GH paid the proceeds of such sales to its bank, CB, and MB claimed the payments due to it for the cars by way of a direct debit on GH's account with CB.

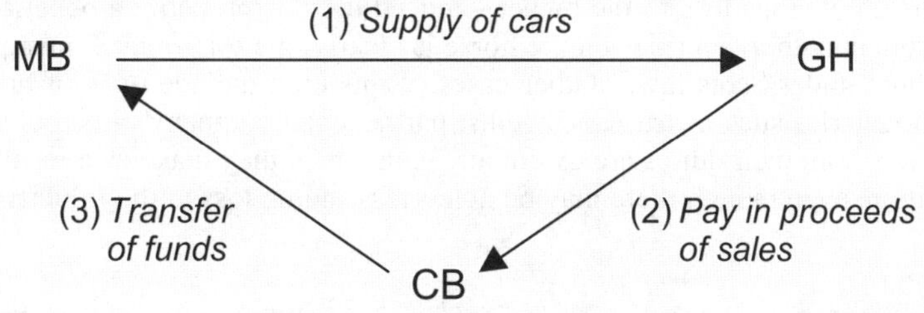

GH was heavily indebted to CB in other respects, and for that reason CB decided not to make a payment under the arrangements with MB. GH then became insolvent. *Held*, with hesitation, that MB had a relevant enrichment claim against CB because the bank knew about the purpose of GH's payments to it, which would not have been made but for the agreement of the bank that they would be applied for the benefit of MB.

It seems impossible to lay down general rules as to when an indirect enrichment claim will or will not be allowed, although typical situations can be identified and may yield up rules for those situations. While the main trend of Scottish authority is against recovery of indirect enrichment,[39] there is no absolute bar; and the modern recognition of the general principle against unjustified enrichment may mean that some of the existing cases of non-recovery—*e.g.* the "garage repair" cases—will come under review in future. As has been said by one author:

> "[T]hree-party situations are just too varied and complex for simple, hard-and-fast rules to be able to provide adequately for their solution … the best we can do in three-party situations is to lay down the general pattern along which a solution should proceed."[40]

That general pattern is to be found in the conventional analysis of enrichment at the expense of another which is not justified, although past authorities may be grouped to give us some indicators of likely outcomes in some typical situations such as the subcontractor and garage repair cases mentioned above.

Gouws v Jester Pools

1968 (3) S.A. 563

In this South African case a contractor (I) entered a contract to build a swimming pool for T on land which I understood to belong to T. In fact E was the owner of the land. I built the swimming pool and sought payment from T. But T disappeared without paying, and it emerged that E was the true owner of the land and therefore, by the doctrine of accession, of the pool. Could I recover the value of the pool from E? The South African court thought not; I had relied only on T to be paid. This would seem also to cover the case where T did not pay because he became insolvent. Perhaps the answer would have been different if E, after discovering the existence of the pool, had sold the land at a higher price than it would have commanded without the pool.

Enrichment recovery although no loss

8–16 Finally in this section, cases where there is enrichment recovery without any economic loss to the pursuer require brief discussion. This occurs principally (if not exclusively) in the category of takings cases. Suppose, for example, that as an enthusiastic rider I see in a small field a horse belonging to another but being left unexercised and in consequence deteriorating in condition. Without the owner's authority, I take the horse for regular rides, thereby enhancing its fitness and value. There is no obvious loss to the owner—indeed there is probably a benefit—but the benefit which I get from unauthorised rides on the horse is clearly one for which I must pay by way of an enrichment claim under Scots law.[41] Other cases of this kind include ones of breach of fiduciary duty, where fiduciaries such as trustees, agents, partners and company directors are liable to hand over to those to whom their duties are owed, any gain which they make as a result of abusing their fiduciary position, even though there may be no corresponding loss to the fiduciary creditors.

UNJUSTIFIED (WHEN ENRICHMENT IS TO BE REVERSED OR PAID FOR)

8–17 Before an enrichment can be reversed or paid for, its retention by the enriched person has to be unjustified. The general starting point is that enrichments will remain where they are unless a reason can be shown for their reversal. It is however helpful to remember, not only those circumstances where an enrichment will be considered to be unjustified, but also those where,

[39] See most recently *G W Tait & Sons v Taylor*, 2002 S.L.T. 1285.

[40] D. P. Visser, "Searches for silver bullets: enrichment in three-party situations", in D. Johnston and R. Zimmermann (eds), *Unjustified Enrichment: Key Issues in Comparative Perspective* (2002), Chap.19.

[41] Example adapted from *Watson, Laidlaw & Co. Ltd v Pott, Cassels and Williamson*, 1914 S.C. (H.L.) 18 at 31, *per* Lord Shaw of Dunfermline.

because the enrichment is justified, the enriched person will be entitled to retain it. In the language of the modern cases, enrichment is justified where there is a legal ground for the retention of the enrichment. The two major examples of such grounds in Scots law are where the enrichment was the result of an unconditional *gift or donation*, or of the performance of a *valid and subsisting contract* (see further below, paras 8–37 to 8–39).

From this starting point, Scots law could simply say that, unless the enrichment is justified by a legal ground such as a valid contract or gift, it falls to be reversed. That is the approach of some other legal systems (*e.g.* Germany).[42] But Scots law has not yet committed itself quite so far. Such an approach could throw much of the burden of the law upon the enriched person, who would have to show affirmative reasons why the enrichment should be kept. Considerations such as protecting possession and the security of transactions so that, once carried through, the law will need weighty reasons to undo them, have pointed in an opposite direction: it is for the person who wants to reclaim an enrichment to show reasons why that should be allowed.

This section returns to the distinction, outlined above (para.8–11), between different ways in which enrichment can arise: (1) through a *transfer* by the impoverished person to the enriched one; (2) through the *imposition* of an enrichment upon the enriched person by the activity of the impoverished one; and (3) through the *taking* of an enrichment by the enriched person by way of use of, or interference with, the property or rights of the impoverished one. This allows differences in the way these types of enrichment are treated in the law to be made clear.

Transfers

We begin with the situation where enrichment arises through transfer of an asset such as money or goods from the impoverished to the enriched person. As Lord President Rodger said in *Shilliday v Smith*,[43] the cases where recovery has been allowed can be put into groups or categories which often correspond with the typology of the Roman law *condictiones*. The approach in this section follows the model proposed in *Shilliday*, taking the *condictiones* as the basis for identifying when enrichments are unjustified. But it is important to remember that here the *condictiones* fall to be treated in their modern or Scots law guise; that some of the *condictiones* found in Roman law have not really been much discussed in Scots law and are therefore not treated in any detail or touched upon at all here; and that the principle against unjustified enrichment means that the law, now and in its future development, is not confined to the situations defined by the *condictiones*. **8–18**

Enrichment by transfer may be reversed in the following situations:

Condictio indebiti

"*Condictio indebiti*" means "action for the recovery of an undue (*indebitum*) transfer". The transfer falls to be reversed because it was not legally due to be made in the first place. But the law has restricted the breadth of this concept because, taken literally, it would mean, *e.g.*, that all gifts were reversible enrichments of the donee, which cannot be right. Instead the donee can retain the gift because gift or donation is a recognised legal ground for this (see below, para.8–38). The typical *condictio indebiti* case in Scots law is where the transferor has made the undue transfer in question as the result of an error that it *was* due by the transferor because of some legal obligation owed to the transferee/recipient. It is often said that such error is an essential element in making a transfer undue and so reversible. **8–19**

The courts have taken a reasonably wide approach to what may be an error of this type, although they have not gone so far as to say that any error which causes a transfer to be made[44] permits a claim for its recovery. Thus if A transfers money or goods to B meaning to pay or

[42] On German enrichment law, which has been influential in much writing on Scots law, see R. Zimmermann and J. du Plessis, "Basic features of the German law of unjustified enrichment" [1994] 2 *Restitution Law Review* 14.

[43] See above, para.8–03.

[44] The approach of the English courts: see *Barclays Bank v Simms* [1980] Q.B. 677.

transfer to C, or supplies to B more than he owes to B, the latter is liable to restore the money or goods to A because A was in error as to his liability towards B. The error may be in *fact* (*e.g.* the identity of the person to whom A is making the transfer, the quantity due to be transferred under a contract) *or in law* (*e.g.* the power of a local authority to borrow money under local government legislation[45]). Errors as to states of fact or law should be distinguished from mispredictions as to events in the future, *e.g.* it is an *error* if I think I am married, when I am not because, for example, my partner is party to an earlier and still undissolved marriage; while it is a *misprediction* if I say today that I am going to marry a person to whom I am engaged and therefore make a transfer to that person, who then breaks off the engagement the next day.

If mispredictions give rise to any claim for the reversal of enrichment, it is under other heads, such as the *condictio causa data causa non secuta* (see further below, para.8–22). Knowledge that a transfer is not due precludes the *condictio indebiti*. Error should probably also be distinguished from *doubt* as to whether or not a transfer is due; although doubt excludes knowledge that the transfer is due, it also does not manifest belief that the transfer is due, the basic requirement for recovery under the principle of the *condictio indebiti*.[46]

It is possible, but not necessary, for the error to be shared by the transferee; where the transferee also erroneously thought the transfer was due, the case for restoration is however strengthened.[47] The error may arise from the transferee's misrepresentation.[48] Fraud, it has been said, is not an error for the purposes of the *condictio indebiti*.[49] The transferor's error need not be excusable, although that may be a factor to be weighed in considering the overall equities of a given case (see further below, para.8–29): that is, if an error is excusable, that favours restoration to the pursuer, while if it is inexcusable, denial of recovery is more likely.

Credit Lyonnais v George Stevenson & Co. Ltd
(1901) 9 S.L.T. 93

(paying the wrong person)

CL, a bank in Paris, remitted certain moneys to the account of GS, merchants in Dundee. This was in error, CL having intended to pay a company of a similar name in Glasgow. The error was discovered 11 months later. GS argued that they had received the money in good faith, believing the money to have been transferred to them through CL by their Paris agent, and had made use of the money on that basis. *Held* that GS were liable to repay CL, having been negligent in the way they dealt with the payment when it arrived, and not having really altered their position with regard to it since.

---

[45] See *Morgan Guaranty Co. of New York v Lothian Regional Council,* 1995 S.C. 151. The equivalent case in England is *Kleinwort Benson v Lincoln City Council* [1999] 2 A.C. 349, in which the House of Lords discusses the conundrum arising where the error of law is the result of a judicial decision post-dating the payment in question. If the decision is merely declaratory so that previous understandings of the law were wrong (the view of the majority in *Kleinwort*), then the payment was indeed made under mistake; but if the decision *changes* the law (the minority view), then there was no mistake at the time of payment, but only a misprediction as to the law. This debate may suggest that mistake is not the best way of approaching the problem; a better analysis may be through the absence of a legal ground for retaining the payment, subject to a defence that the payer knew that it was not liable to pay (see S. Meier and R. Zimmermann, (1999) 115 L.Q.R. 556). See also from a Scottish point of view the speech of Lord Hope of Craighead in the *Kleinwort* case.

[46] See *Balfour v Smith & Logan* (1877) 4 R. 454; J. du Plessis and H. E. Wicke, 1993 S.L.T. (News) 303; Scot. Law Com. DP No.99 (1996), §4.27; *Kleinwort Benson v Lincoln City Council* [1999] 2 A.C. at 410, *per* Lord Hope of Craighead.

[47] *Hamilton v Western Bank* (1861) 23 D. 1033.

[48] *Balfour v Smith & Logan* (1877) 4 R. 454.

[49] *G M Scott (Willowbank Cooperage) Ltd v York Trailer Co. Ltd,* 1969 S.L.T. 87 at 88, *per* Lord President Clyde. On appeal, the pursuer was allowed to amend his averments from fraud to error (1970 S.L.T. 15).

Bank of New York v North British Steel Group
1992 S.L.T. 613
(paying the wrong person)

BNY were instructed by customer A to transfer money to another bank to the account of B, but, as the result of a slip entering the account numbers on a computer, erroneously transferred it to the account of NBSG. NBSG were already owed money by A and, when BNY claimed repayment, remitted only the balance beyond the debt they claimed from A. *Held* that for BNY to recover they would have to show how they had come to make the error, and its excusability would be a factor for the court to consider before reaching a decision.

British Hydro-Carbon Chemicals and British Transport Commission, Petitioners
1961 S.L.T. 280
(over-payment)

BHCC made payments to BTC under a contract, not realising that under the same contract it was entitled to a rebate on the sums paid. *Held* that BHCC was entitled to repayment of the amount of the rebate.

Peter Walker & Sons (Edinburgh) Ltd v Leith Glazing Co. Ltd
1980 S.L.T. (Sh. Ct) 104
(payment not due under contract)

PWS were contractors under a building contract, and LG were sub-contractors. The PWS chargehand authorised LG to perform extra work under the sub-contract, for which LG were paid by PWS. It was then found that under the sub-contract the chargehand had had no authority to authorise the work. PWS were *held* entitled to recover the payment which had been made under the error that it was contractually due to LG.

Morgan Guaranty v Lothian Regional Council
1995 S.C. 151
(payment made under void contract not due)

For the facts, see above, para.8–05. Here the error was an error in law (both parties believed, erroneously, that their transaction was valid under local government legislation, and that payments and repayments under the contract were therefore legally due).

Example(s) of non-liability errors:

(1) A bank in the exercise of its mandate pays its customer's creditor in the erroneous belief that cheques previously paid into the customer's account represented cleared funds sufficient to cover the transfer. Here the bank's error is not about its liability to make payment, but about whether funds are available meet the liability. The bank should not be able to recover from the customer's creditor (although it may have an action against its customer if the latter's debt is now discharged).[50]
(2) *Scanlon v Scanlon*, 1990 G.W.D. 12–598: W paid instalments towards the purchase of a car under a hire purchase agreement in which her male partner (M) was purchaser. She knew

[50] Based on the English case of *Lloyds Bank plc v Independent Insurance Co. Ltd* [2000] Q.B. 110.

that she was not liable under the contract, but mistakenly believed that the car would be jointly owned by her and M. *Held* that the error, not being as to liability, did not support recovery of the payments from the seller by W.[51]

(3) *G.M. Scott (Willowbank Cooperage) Ltd v York Trailer Co. Ltd*, 1970 S.L.T. 15: GMS ordered a York trailer from the local representative (Nichol) of YTC. N advised that he could acquire a trailer from a local garage and requested GMS to give him a cheque made out to that garage to enable him to pay them. N used the cheque to pay his own debt to the garage. GMS cancelled the order for the trailer and obtained one from another source; they then claimed repayment of the value of the cheque from YTC (as N's employers) and the garage under the *condictio indebiti*. A proof before answer was allowed. *Per* Lord Walker (dissenting, at 21):

> "Since the reclaiming motion was enrolled, the pursuers have been allowed to amend to the effect that they made the payment to the second defenders in the mistaken belief that they would receive in exchange a trailer supplied by the second defenders. That is not, I think, an averment they were presently due that sum to the second defenders. It is no doubt true that they drew the cheque in favour of the second defenders but their averment is that they did so at the request of Nichol in order that he might in future obtain a trailer from them. That is a different thing from a mistaken belief that they had contracted to purchase a trailer from the second defenders and so were liable to pay the price. In order to found a *condictio indebiti* it is, I think, essential that the mistake should be in believing a debt to be due when in truth it is not."

There may be other cases where payments or other transfers are made when not due, but without a liability error being the reason the transfer occurs. Nevertheless enrichment recovery is allowed. If the condictio indebiti is confined to cases of liability error, then some other condictio must explain recovery where no such error exists. Here are some examples:

Compulsion

8–20 The Scottish courts have recognised that transfers made under unlawful compulsion from the transferee may give rise to claims for reversal of those transfers. Such transfers will not however be made under errors as to liability; the transferor may well be very clear about not being liable, but nonetheless is compelled to carry the transaction through.

British Oxygen Co. v South of Scotland Electricity Board

1959 S.C. (H.L.) 17

SSEB, which was a statutory monopoly supplier of electricity, supplied BO with electricity at a high voltage. The supply cost less to provide than a low voltage one, but, in breach of the relevant statute, the tariff of charges applied by SSEB did not differentiate properly between high and low voltage customers. So, BO ended up paying too much, but was under no error about it. It protested but was told by SSEB that if it did not pay its electricity supply would be cut. In claiming recovery of overpayments, BO argued successfully that to remain operative it had had no choice but to pay too much, since SSEB was the only available electricity supplier. BO was therefore paying under compulsion and could recover.

It follows that if error is the only ground for the *condictio indebiti*, the cases allowing recovery for compulsion must be treated under some other head to be consistent with the approach in *Shilliday*. Candidates amongst the *condictiones* are the *condictio ob turpem vel injustam causam* (action for

[51] Although she did succeed against M, presumably on the basis of *causa data causa non secuta* (see further below, paras 8–22 *et seq.*).

recovery of a transfer made for an illegal or immoral purpose, *i.e.* in this case, to relieve the pressure resulting from improper compulsion) and the *condictio sine causa* (action for recovery of a transfer retained without legal justification, *i.e.* a transfer made subject to unlawful compulsion cannot be upheld because the transferee has no legal ground, that is, no valid indebtedness of the transferor, on which to retain it). If however the *condictio indebiti* was not confined to error cases, but was applied in cases where for whatever reason the transfer was not legally due, without regard to the subjective intention of the transferring party, then the law would certainly be simpler.

Payments subject to protests and reservations

A party may pay another while thinking that he is not liable to do so, and therefore making clear protests against the payments and reserving legal rights in the matter. What is happening in such cases is that, for various reasons, the party making the payment wishes to sue for recovery rather than to be subjected to an action for payment. Again, if the *condictio indebiti* is restricted to cases of error, some other basis is going to have to be found for recovery. Scots law seems to be to the effect that mere protest is not enough to justify recovery of the payment: the recipient must be made aware of a definite reservation of rights.[52] **8–21**

Nurdin & Peacock plc v Ramsden & Co. Ltd

[1999] 1 W.L.R. 1249

P paid D despite doubts as to liability to do so, and also assuming, wrongly, that in law he could recover if the liability did not exist. D knew that P paid under reservation of a right to recover. *Held* P could recover for mistake of law. In Scotland, because P's mistake was probably not a liability mistake, he would have had difficulty recovering under the error-based *condictio indebiti*. D's awareness that P was reserving his rights would probably have meant that the *condictio sine causa* was the appropriate basis of any recovery.

It may be that, where a payment is made to a public body acting under statutory powers, the mere fact that the legislation does not justify the payment or the demand for it suffices for recovery.[53]

Woolwich Building Society v Inland Revenue

[1993] A.C. 70

W made three payments totalling £57 million to the IR in response to a tax demand made under the Income Tax (Building Societies) Regulations 1986. W disputed the validity of the Regulations but made the payments because it feared penalties and adverse publicity if it did not. In subsequent litigation it was first found that the Regulations were indeed invalid. In a second case the House of Lords held (by a majority of 3–2, with the Scottish Law Lords forming the minority) that W was entitled to restitution of its payments, plus interest running from the dates of payment, since the money had been paid as the result of an *ultra vires* demand. From a Scottish point of view, the case is important because W were never under any error as to whether the payment was due; they always thought it was not. If this means that the *condictio indebiti* does not lie in Scotland, the case would have to be dealt with as one for either the *condictio ob turpem vel injustam causam* (W was improperly compelled by an ultra vires demand to pay IR) or the *condictio sine causa* (being ultra vires, IR

---

[52] Gloag, *Contract* (2nd ed., 1929), p.63. For a critique of the English case of *Nurdin* summarised below, see G. Virgo, [1999] *Cambridge Law Journal* 478.

[53] See also *Stonehaven Magistrates v Kincardine County Council*, 1939 S.C. 760; *Haggarty v Scottish TGWU*, 1955 S.C. 109.

had no legal justification for retaining the money). But if the *condictio indebiti* was not limited to cases of error, then, since the payments by W were not due to the IR, they would be recoverable on that ground alone.

Condictio causa data causa non secuta

8–22 This second ground on which an enrichment by transfer may be reversed (henceforth CCDCNS) can be translated as the action for the recovery of something transferred for a future purpose which failed to materialise. The underlying idea is that the transferor made a payment or other transfer on the basis of some anticipated return which is now not going to occur. Accordingly the transferee has no legal justification for retaining the money or other property transferred. The classic case referred to in the Institutional Writers is the engagement rings given to each other by the parties to the engagement; if the engagement is broken off and the marriage does not take place, then the rings must be returned, as the reason for the gift (the parties' wedding) will not now take place.[54] The same would apply to wedding presents purchased in advance, which are clearly a conditional gift.

Many modern cases on the CCDCNS have arisen, not out of engagements to marry, but from arrangements between men and women cohabiting and planning, with more or less enthusiasm on each side, to marry.

Shilliday v Smith

1998 S.C. 725

M and W began to live together in M's cottage in 1988, and became engaged in August 1990. They never married. In 1988, M had bought a house in a state of disrepair, and from about 1990 M and W began to improve this property, into which they moved together in 1991. The works were completed by Christmas 1992, when M ejected W from the house. W had spent about £9,600 on the works: approximately £7,000 direct to tradesmen, £1,880 to M to pay for materials and work on the house, and £756 on items for the garden, left behind after her ejection. It was held that W was entitled to repetition of the £1,880 she had paid to M on the basis of CCDCNS; she had made her payments in contemplation of a marriage which did not take place. On the same principle she was entitled to recompense for what she had expended on tradesmen and other items, the benefit of which was now being enjoyed by M.

Compare:

Grieve v Morrison

1993 S.L.T. 852

G and M decided to live together on the understanding that they would marry when G's first marriage was terminated by divorce. M bought a flat in which the parties lived, and the loan for which was paid by her. Later this flat was sold and another purchased, on the same basis as the first; G contributed work and money to the cost of renovations. The parties fixed their wedding for August 1984, and in October 1983 jointly purchased another flat, with a joint loan and the free proceeds of the sale of M's previous flat. G had always had considerable, but unexpressed, reservations about the wedding, but he only told M about this one month after they had moved into the new flat; he then left the property. G subsequently brought an action for division or sale of the flat. M argued on the basis of the CCDCNS that she was entitled to G's share of the property (rather than to any part of the free proceeds of the sale of the property), because the arrangements had been made on the basis that the parties

[54] Stair, *Institutions*, 1.7.7; Bankton, *Institutions*, 1.8.21; Erskine, *Institute*, 3.1.9, 10.

would marry. The court held that M had no such claim to G's share and that, for her to have any claim even to the proceeds of the sale of the property beyond her half, she would have to show (1) that the arrangements had been made on the basis of a mutually agreed understanding that was either express or to be implied from the circumstances; and (2) that she had made a contribution to the pursuer's share of the price of the property.

While *Grieve* seems to be correctly decided, the comments about the need to show an express or implied, mutually agreed understanding, that the transfer to be reversed was made on the basis of some future event occurring, must be read in the light of dicta of Lord President Rodger in *Shilliday*, explaining that it was not necessary for the transfer to be conditional in any technical sense upon the happening of the future event:

> "The important thing to notice is that ... the duty to restore is said to be based not on agreement (paction), but on a natural ground, i.e. it is a duty imposed by law. This is a useful reminder that ... the basis of liability to reverse unjust enrichment is not contractual but rests on this separate duty imposed by law. Counsel was therefore correct to argue that there was no need for the pursuer to point to any kind of contract between the parties under which the pursuer paid the various sums on condition that they married."[55]

The question in CCDCNS cases is—what was the cause of, or reason for, the transaction from the point of view of the transferor?—not whether both parties had agreed, or understood, that the transfer would fall to be reversed if a particular future event did not occur. All that mattered in *Shilliday* was that "the defender knew that the pursuer was expending money on his house which the parties had agreed would be their matrimonial home, and ... all that she did was done in contemplation of the parties' marriage".[56]

Shilliday thus shows that the purpose (*causa*) of the transfer need not be contractual in nature, or based upon the express or implied agreement of transferor and transferee. But a number of other CCDCNS cases do have a contractual dimension. This may be a special feature of the way in which Scots law has developed the original Roman law idea of the CCDCNS, which did not apply at all to contracts. The starting point for the modern development of Scots law on contractual situations and the CCDCNS was *Watson v Shankland*,[57] a shipping case about recovery of a payment made in advance of freight for the carriage of goods by sea, where the ship in question had sunk during its voyage, without fault on the part of the master and crew. Lord President Inglis, holding the advance to be recoverable, said:

> "There is no rule of the civil law, as adopted into all modern municipal codes and systems, better understood than this—that if money is advanced by one party to a mutual contract, on the condition and stipulation that something shall be afterwards paid or performed by the other party, and the latter party fails in performing his part of the contract, the former is entitled to repayment of his advance, on the ground of failure of consideration. In the Roman system the demand for repayment took the form of a *condictio causa data causa non secuta*, or a *condictio sine causa*, or a *condictio indebiti*, according to the particular circumstances. In our own practice these remedies are represented by the action of restitution and the action of repetition."[58]

This approach to recovery of advance payments after the full performance of contracts was frustrated by supervening events was taken much further by the House of Lords in the leading case of *Cantiere San Rocco v Clyde Shipbuilding Co.*[59]

---

55 1998 S.C. 725 at 730.

56 1998 S.C. 725 at 730.

57 (1871) 10 M. 142, affirmed (1873) 11 M. (H.L.) 51.

58 (1871) 10 M. 142 at 152.

59 1923 S.C. (H.L.) 105. It has been suggested that *Cantiere* is not a case of *causa non secuta*, but rather one for the *condictio ob causam finitam* (*i.e.* one where an existing state of affairs—here, the contract—provided the reason for the

Cantiere San Rocco v Clyde Shipbuilding Co. Ltd
1923 S.C. (H.L.) 105

In May 1914, Cantiere, an Austrian company, ordered marine engines for a price of £11,550 from Clyde, and made an initial payment of £2,310. In August 1914, before Clyde could do much significant work on the order, war broke out, and the contract was frustrated by the supervening illegality arising from Cantiere now being an enemy alien company. After the war ended in 1918, Cantiere, now an Italian company, successfully sought repayment of the advance payment on the grounds that the performance had not been met by any counter-performance from Clyde. This was held to be an instance of CCDCNS. Lord Dunedin explained:

"... the very short point on which, in my view, the whole case turns. Was the £2,310 paid in respect of the signing of the contract? If it were, then it cannot be said that there was a *causa non secuta*. In other words, if the £2,310 had been conditioned to be paid *for* signing the contract, my opinion would have been different. But it is not so. It is to be paid *on* signing the contract. It had, indeed, no separate existence. It is only an instalment of the total price which is the consideration for the whole engine. There is no splitting of the consideration."

Recovery was not prevented merely because Cantiere had made its payment as the result of a contractual obligation valid at the time of payment; the payment had not met with the anticipated counter-performance by Clyde (construction of the engines), and now never would be; therefore the payment fell to be returned.

Cantiere extends the Inglis dictum in *Watson v Shankland* because the payment in the former case was not an advance, but was rather an instalment of the full price due under the contract. The House of Lords was, however, quite clear that the CCDCNS principle was not limited to advances, but applied to all cases where a contractual performance had not been met by its corresponding counter-performance from the other party. This makes it very important to analyse the relationship between the two sides of the contract in such cases. If the party now seeking to recover its performance has actually received the counter-performance, the CCDCNS will not lie.

Connelly v Simpson
1993 S.C. 391

C paid £16,000 to S for one-third of the shares in S's company, but the parties agreed to defer delivery, enabling C to minimise the value of his estate during his divorce proceedings, which were also under way at this time. Over the next two years, the company did badly: S first issued more shares to raise capital, thereby diluting the value of C's holding, and then put the company into voluntary liquidation. The liquidator offered C £400, the value of his shares now. C claimed his £16,000 back from S under the CCDCNS. His action failed, Lord Brand dissenting. The majority judges differ as to the reasons for the outcome. One was of the view that C had received what he paid for, *viz*, a right to delivery of shares on demand. Another thought that the CCDCNS applied only in cases of frustration, which this was not, and otherwise could not be used in contract cases. The judges were clearly reluctant to allow C to escape the consequences of what had turned out to be a bad bargain in a market necessarily involving risk. If the case is rightly decided, it is probably on the basis that the purpose of C's payment had been fulfilled, probably at the time he made it, and so S could not be made liable to repay.

payment but it came to an end). There are references to this *condictio* in the development of Scots law (see, *e.g.* Craig, *Jus Feudale*, 3.5.23; Stair, *Institutions*, 1.7.7), but if received, it has not been developed.

Condictio sine causa

Transfers which cannot be brought within the scope of the *condictio indebiti* or the CCDCNS may nonetheless be reversible under the *condictio sine causa* (discussed above, para.8–20, in connection with compulsion; see also below, para.8–27). Examples of this are rare in Scots law, but it seems likely to provide the correct principle with which to deal with a common problem, readily illustrated from cases in other jurisdictions: *the position of a bank which pays on a cheque despite having previously received a countermand from the relevant customer/drawer of the cheque.*[60] **8–23**

The starting point is that the bank cannot debit the customer's account for the cheque. If the bank is not to suffer loss, it must effect recovery from the cheque payee. Assuming that the payee is enriched,[61] it would seem nevertheless that the *condictio indebiti* is inapt to the situation. Although the bank transferred funds to the payee, it did not do so in satisfaction of any liability it had to the payee, but acted rather in discharge of its obligation to its customer. There was no liability and no liability-error on the part of the bank. However, the payee has no legal ground on which it can retain the cheque proceeds against the bank, and recovery can therefore be made under the *condictio sine causa*.

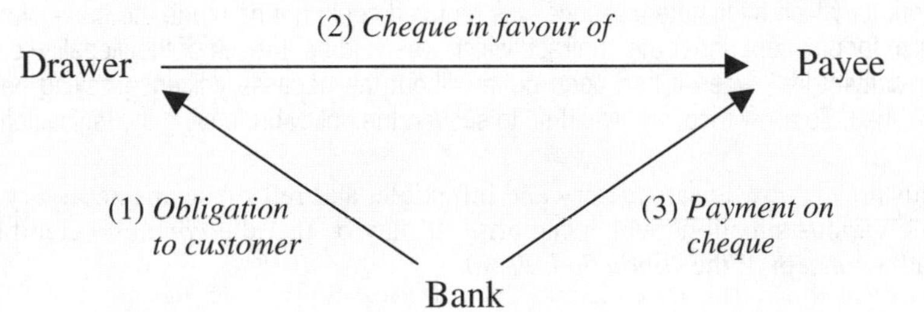

Similar reasoning can be applied to other cases of payments made in error by banks. In *Royal Bank of Scotland v Watt*,[62] (see above, para.8–05, for the full facts), the bank paid out on a fraudulently altered cheque, but could not debit its customer's account because of the fraud (see Bills of Exchange Act 1882, s.64); however, as already stated, there could be recovery from the person to whom payment had been made. Again, since the bank had acted in discharge of an apparent obligation to its customer, its error was not about liability to the recipient of the payment, and the recovery may therefore have been based upon the *condictio sine causa*. But in cases where a bank pays out on a cheque with forged endorsement of the payee's signature, the amount can be deducted from its customer's account as a result of the protection provided by s.60 of the Bills of Exchange Act, and the bank needs no enrichment claim against the payee; the impoverished person is rather the bank's customer.[63]

Condictio ob turpem vel injustam causam

The *condictio ob turpem vel injustam causam* was received in Scots law,[64] and enabled the recovery of a transfer made for an illegal or immoral purpose. Recovery was however not allowed where the parties to the transfer were equally responsible for the illegality; then the position of the possessor was stronger (*in pari delicto potior est conditio possidentis*). This allowed a relatively flexible evaluation of whether or not there should be recovery. The question of whether a transfer **8–24**

[60] See *Barclays Bank v Simms* [1980] 1 Q.B. 677 (England); *Govender v Standard Bank of South Africa* 1984 (4) S.A. 392 (C.); *B & H Engineering v First National Bank of South Africa Ltd* 1995 (2) S.A. 279 (A.).

[61] A conclusion not reached in the *B & H Engineering* case, because the payee's debt to the customer was discharged and he had lost any claim he might have in that direction; but accepted in *Simms* and *Govender*.

[62] 1991 S.C. 48.

[63] See *Alexander Beith Ltd v Allan*, 1961 S.L.T. (Notes) 80.

[64] See Stair, *Institutions*, 1.7.8; Bankton, *Institute*, 1.8.22.

of value was illegal was distinct from the one whether any underlying contract was void or unenforceable as a result of the illegality.

Cuthbertson v Lowes

(1870) 8 M. 1073

Statute declared void contracts of sale using customary rather than Imperial weights and measures, but the court held that the purchaser in a bargain for the sale of potatoes by the "Scotch acre", while not liable for the contract price, was nonetheless bound to account for the value of the potatoes he had acquired. The statute did not make the transfer of potatoes for value unlawful.

In the modern development of the law, however, the presence of illegality in a transfer has tended to be seen, not as a possible ground of, but as a near absolute barrier to recovery.

Jamieson v Watt's Trustee

1950 S.C. 265

Work for which by statute a licence was required could not be made the basis of any claim for payment under the contract, which was void as a result of the illegality, or in enrichment law, when it had been done without the necessary licence having been obtained. To allow recovery would be to subvert the policy underlying the legislation.

The law in this area is now unsatisfactory and inflexible, and reform seems necessary to deal more justly with the various situations which can arise. It may be that the *condictio* could be subsumed within a broader concept of the *condictio indebiti*.

Impositions

8–25 The *condictio indebiti*, the CCDCNS, and the other *condictiones* generally do not apply to imposed enrichments such as the unauthorised improvement of another's property or performance of another's obligation. This no doubt goes some way to explaining why such cases were characteristically dealt with under the heading of recompense in the law before the 1990s. It is possible for improvements to be made as undue transfers—*e.g.*, if I am a contractor carrying out repairs or enhancements under a void contract[65]—or for a purpose that fails—for example, if I improve my cohabitant's house in anticipation of a marriage that in the end does not take place[66]—and for the beneficiary to be liable as a result. If I pay C the amount of D's debt because I mistakenly think that I am bound to do so, the transfer which is undue is that to C, from whom I can recover on the principle of *condictio indebiti*; but there is no claim against D on that footing. Again, if I pay C because I think that he will then treat D's debt as discharged, but he does not and the debt is indeed not discharged, there might be a claim on the basis of CCDCNS; but again that claim is against C rather than D. Any claim I might have against D will have to be laid on some other basis.

If a general basis of recovery for enrichment imposed without authority is sought, is it provided by the general principle of unjustified enrichment? The enriched person—the one whose property has been improved or obligation discharged—has no legal ground for retaining that enrichment. However, at least in the cases of *unauthorised improvements to another's property*, this still seems too wide. So, for example, if I was a building contractor, I could use this principle to go around my home town looking for houses in need of repair, carry out the repairs when the owners were away, and then insist on a right to be paid for the enrichment which I had imposed upon them because

[65] See, *e.g. Rutherglen Magistrates v Cullen* (1773) 2 Pat. 305 and *Middleton v Newton Display Group Ltd*, 1990, G.W.D. 40–2305 (Glasgow Sheriff Court).

[66] *Shilliday v Smith*, 1998 S.C. 725.

they had no legal ground to retain it. Scots law has therefore created a number of further conditions to be satisfied before an enrichment claim for improvements will be successful.

These are as follows:

- The impoverished person must have been in *good faith possession* of the property while carrying out the improvement, that is, without knowledge of his lack of right to have possession; if the possession is in bad faith, there is no recovery except perhaps for *necessary* repairs and maintenance.[67]

Barbour v Halliday

(1840) 2 D. 1279

H owned land. On going to America, he left the title deeds with his brother (H2). H2 gave the deeds to B in security of a debt owed to B by M, and B then "sold" the ground to G, who carried out improvements. G returned the ground to B, who reimbursed him for his expenditure. H returned from America and, as owner, reclaimed the land with its improvements. B sought reimbursement for the improvements, but was denied because his possession had been in bad faith.

- The impoverished person must usually have worked under *error*, usually that the property being improved belonged to him.[68] It used to be thought that the owner had to have some sort of apparent title to the property as a basis for this error,[69] but since *Newton v Newton*[70] (above, para.8–08) this has not been essential so long as the error was in good faith. Improvers possessing on a limited title (for example, as tenants under a lease, or occupying as liferenters) cannot recover,[71] unless such a person erroneously believes him or herself to be an owner.[72]
- In some cases, the improver's error may be that a third party whom he wishes to benefit is, or will become, the owner of, or entitled to, the property.

Duff, Ross & Co. v Kippen

(1871) 8 S.L.R. 299

A partner (A) in a firm (AB) spent £234 improving its business premises, believing that they belonged to AB. In fact they belonged to someone else, and the other partner in the firm (B) was merely a tenant under a lease of the premises. *Held* the owner was liable to reimburse £234 to A.

McDowel v McDowel

(1906) 14 S.L.T. 125

Captain M granted his wife (Mrs M) a 99 year lease over property of which he was heir of entail, and then carried out expensive improvements. The captain's intention in all this was to make provision for his wife after his death. When he died, the lease was found to be invalid. *Held* that the captain's son, now owner of the property, was bound to reimburse the deceased captain's estate as represented by his executrix (Mrs M).

---

[67] *Barbour v Holliday* (1840) 2 D. 1279, over-ruling Stair, *Institutions*, 1.8.6.

[68] Note that cases of improvement where error was not required may well be treatable under another branch of the law, *e.g. Lawrence Building Co. v Lanarkshire County Council*, 1978 S.C. 30 is a case of performance of another's obligation.

[69] Note that since the replacement of the Sasine with the modern Land Register a recorded title to land is always a complete and valid one, so that it is no longer possible to possess on a colourable but actually defective recorded title.

[70] 1925 S.C. 715.

[71] *Wallace v Braid* (1900) 2 F. 754.

[72] *Morrison v Allan* (1886) 13 R. 1156.

- Insofar as it is a case of imposed enrichment, *Shilliday v Smith*[73] (see above, para.8–22) illustrates that there may be *recovery without error if some other ground making the enrichment unjustified is present*—in that case, *causa data causa non secuta*. There are a number of cases where improvers who knew that their titles were defective or non-existent have nevertheless been able to recover.[74]

There are still some difficult precedents where the good faith improver did not recover, but which, in the light of *Shilliday v Smith*, might be decided differently today:

Rankin v Wither

(1886) 13 R. 903

H rebuilt W's house at his own expense, W's intention being to leave H the house if he survived her. But W died before she could execute the necessary settlement on H. *Held* that H could not recover for his improvements. The case is confused: H attempted to prove donation, so that he could bring into play the rule that donations between spouses are revocable, but this failed, on the basis that the expenditure was for his own benefit ultimately and made in the knowledge that he had no title.

Error does not seem to play anything like as important a role in cases of enrichment by unauthorised performance of another's obligation, especially where the performance is *payment of money*. The payer can still recover from the debtor even though he paid the creditor deliberately and with full knowledge of all the relevant facts.[75] What matters is whether or not the debt is discharged; and if the creditor treats the payment as doing so, as he generally will, then the debtor is liable. He would have had to pay anyway, under the now discharged obligation; the fact that he is having to pay someone else under a new enrichment obligation makes little or no difference to his basic position. So there is no real need in that case to add in protections for the debtor against unwanted intervention in his affairs, especially if he can take against the payer those defences which he would have had against the creditor, such as a right of retention in respect of breach of contract by the creditor.

If the obligation was not a money one, however, the position is more difficult, as can be seen from this hypothetical example:

> C and D have a contract under which D is to build a wall for C. The price is £500. The job will cost D £450, so his profit on the contract is £50. P arranges with C that he will build the same wall for £400, leaving himself a profit of £40, and manages to do the job before D is due to start his operation. C refuses to let D start on building the wall, since he no longer needs it.

If P can now claim from D the latter's saving in not having to build C's wall—£450—then the former's total profit from his wall operation will be £490, while D will be down by £450 and will also not have his profit of £50 from the contract with C. D is, however, only enriched if P has discharged his obligation, and as discussed above at para.8–10, that may well not be the case. Moreover, if C has paid P, the latter is not impoverished and any enrichment of D is therefore not at P's expense. But the picture becomes more difficult if C is insolvent or otherwise unable to pay P. If D's obligation is discharged, he may be able to offset against any claim by P any costs already incurred in preparing to perform to C; in other words, to demonstrate that there is no enrichment at least to that extent. D's rights against C, in respect of the latter's breach of contract, might also be put in the balance as a matter of the overall equities, even if C was insolvent; setting

---

[73] 1998 S.C. 725. The case is also one where, like *Newton v Newton* (above, para.8–08), the improver had no apparent title to the property improved.

[74] *e.g. Paterson v Greig* (1862) 24 D. 1370; *Fernie v Robertson* (1871) 9 M. 437; *Nelson v Gordon* (1874) 1 R. 1093; *Reedie v Yeaman* (1875) 12 S.L. Rep. 625; *Yellowlees v Alexander* (1882) 9 R. 765.

[75] But note that P's knowledge that he does not owe C means that, if the payment does *not* discharge D's debt, P will not be able to use the *condictio indebiti* to recover the money from C (see para.8–19 above).

off against P D's claim for damages for breach by C would cover at least the lost profit, and might also extend to wasted expenditure.[76]

Takings

Like the imposed enrichment cases discussed in the previous section, takings cases were commonly treated under the heading of recompense under pre–1990s enrichment law.[77] Two grounds for holding enrichment by taking to be unjustified have been proposed. One is that *the enriched person has committed, or benefited from, a wrong* of some kind: not necessarily a crime or a delict, but an act which for the purposes of enrichment law is characterised as a wrong (*e.g.* breach of a fiduciary obligation or, possibly (after the *Blake* case, above, para.8–11), a contract). The second ground is based, not upon wrong but upon *the support and protection of property rights*, and is expressed as follows by the Scottish Law Commission (emphasis supplied): **8–26**

> "The right of property or ownership carries with it the *exclusive* rights of use, consumption and disposal (*jus utendi, fruendi, abutendi*): the objective of the law in attributing the ownership of a thing to any individual is to allow him the *exclusive* exercise and enjoyment of these rights. Any enrichment which any other person acquires by exercising these rights without the owner's authority is therefore, in principle, unjustified. It follows that that person must restore to the owner the value which he would have had to pay if he had bargained for the benefits in question. *In such a case the defender's enrichment is unjustified because it contradicts the objectives pursued by the law of property.*"[78]

It is certainly true that all the leading cases in this area show the owner of the taken property as the successful pursuer (see above, para.8–09), but there are some other cases where it is not clear that property rights form the basis for holding the enrichment to be unjustified. In particular here may be mentioned the enrichment arising from fiduciary obligations, in which the person to whom the obligation is owed is not usually the owner of the subject-matter from which the fiduciary derives enrichment, and also cases of enrichment from breach of contract after the *Blake* case,[79] where it is only in a very strained sense that the other contracting party's property may be said to have been taken by the contract-breaker.[80]

Wrongdoing which is neither criminal nor delictual but in nature, but is nonetheless identified as such by the law, may explain why the consequential enrichments are recoverable. Or, it may be that these instances of reversing enrichment are to be linked to a policy of ensuring high standards of probity amongst fiduciaries (where it is certainly necessary, given the basic principle that the obligation is to pursue the interests of others and not to promote one's own), and amongst certain types of contracting parties, such as members of the intelligence services, where there is a clear public interest in preventing abuse of position for personal gain, rather than to general concepts of unjustified enrichment as such. Further, given *Teacher v Calder*,[81] the decision in *Blake* may not be part of the general Scots law of either enrichment or contract; and fiduciary obligations may be a distinct chapter of the law in some ways similar to, but nevertheless separate from, both unjustified enrichment and contract. But until these propositions are made clear by decided cases, caution suggests that enrichment by taking should be seen as unjustified, not only when it arises from misuse of another's property, but also when it results from wrongdoing of a kind recognised by other branches of the law such as contract and fiduciary obligations.

---

[76] See MacQueen and Thomson, *Contract Law in Scotland* (2000), pp.229–234.
[77] Although note that restitution could be used in some cases: see above, para.8–09, and below, para.8–35.
[78] Scot. Law Com. DP No.95, § 3.115.
[79] *Attorney General v Blake* [2001] 1 A.C. 268.
[80] See above, para.8–11.
[81] (1899) 1 F. (H.L.) 39; and see above, para.8–11.

Unjustified enrichments outside transfers, impositions and takings?

8–27 There are some cases where the Scottish courts have allowed enrichment recovery but the facts are difficult to fit into the structure of transfer, imposition and taking outlined in the preceding paragraphs. Most, perhaps all, of these are three-party or indirect enrichment cases. The most notable examples in the cases already discussed in this chapter are *M&I Instrument Engineers Ltd v Varsada*[82] and *Mercedes-Benz Finance Ltd v Clydesdale Bank plc.*[83] For their facts, see above, para.8–15. In neither case can the enriched person be seen as a transferee, or as someone who has been imposed upon. There might be analogies with the cases of one who has taken something from another: in *Varsada*, B could be seen as one who had used another's property, but the money which V fraudulently obtained was probably his at the time he gave it to B; while in the *Mercedes* case, the bank was in possession of funds legitimately transferred to it by a third person, and its enrichment lay in *withholding* money due to be transferred on again under the direct debit arrangement with the impoverished person. In both cases, however, it is reasonably clear that the defenders had no legal ground for retaining the money against the enrichment claim of the pursuers (*i.e.* the enrichment was *sine causa*). This underlines the importance of the basic enrichment principle stated by the Scottish courts in the 1990s. The starting point is whether enrichment may be retained on legal grounds; and this leaves open the possibility of recognising new types of claim not necessarily readily fitting the established patterns of liability, and, indeed, of accepting that former exclusions from liability must now be overturned.

DEFENCES

8–28 There has been much less discussion of defences in enrichment actions than of the grounds on which enrichment will be found unjustified. In part, this is because some defences are implicit within the discussion of the grounds: whether or not there is enrichment, whether it is "at the expense of' the pursuer", whether or not it is "indirect", whether or not there is a legal ground such as gift or contract to justify the retention of the enrichment, whether or not a transferor knew that the transfer was undue, and so on. But the recognition that a general principle against unjustified enrichment underlies the whole subject does imply a need to consider whether there are also distinct defences arising after the grounds of action are established, the substance of which can be defined in their own right; and how far these defences are general for all unjustified enrichments.

Equity

8–29 It has long been stated in Scots law that enrichment remedies are equitable in nature,[84] meaning, not that they supplement the ordinary law in the English sense, but rather that the court may take account of, and balance, all factors affecting the relationship between the parties before deciding to order the restoration of or payment for enrichment. In other words, the overall equities of the case may mean that the enrichment stays where it is, even though all the positive requirements for recovery are met.[85] Thus, for example, in the case of *Varney v Burgh of Lanark*[86] (above, para.8–10), it was inequitable to allow the builder to recover for the sewers it had installed instead of the local authority, because the parties had been in dispute about liability to perform this act and the builder had had available at the time a remedy—an action for implement of a statutory duty—by

[82] 1991 S.L.T. 106.
[83] 1997 S.L.T. 905.
[84] See, *e.g. Bell v Thomson* (1867) 6 M. 64 at 69; *Lawrence Building Co. v Lanarkshire County Council*, 1978 S.C. 30 at 41–2.
[85] See *Morgan Guaranty Trust Co. of New York v Lothian Regional Council*, 1995 S.C. 151 at 165–6, *per* Lord President Hope.
[86] 1974 S.C. 245.

which the dispute could have been resolved. Again, in cases about unauthorised payment of another's debt, equity might allow the debtor to plead against the recovery-seeking payer the defences that would have been available against the creditor or the creditor's assignee.[87] Some former defences, such as the inexcusability of the impoverished person's error, have now been subsumed within the wider concept of equity, becoming merely factors in the balancing process.[88] On the other hand, a number of more specific concepts have emerged from the cases and writings on the subject, although often these cannot yet be seen as highly refined and worked out specific defences. The main example is change of position, sometimes also known as loss of enrichment.

Change of position/loss of enrichment

A party who has spent, consumed or otherwise disposed of an enrichment, and is therefore no **8–30** longer enriched, may be able to escape liability to restore or pay for it, in whole or in part. The approach to be taken is outlined by Lord Kyllachy in *Credit Lyonnais v George Stevenson & Co. Ltd*[89]:

> "[T]he defenders, in order to establish such a defence, would require to show (1) that they had reasonable grounds for believing that the money was theirs; and (2) that having that reasonable belief, they acted upon it so as to alter their position in such manner as to make repetition unjust."

Such a defence has been recognised in older *condictio indebiti* and CCDCNS cases. It also explains why in takings cases where a recipient of moveable property has transferred it to a third party the former's liability to the true owner is normally limited to his profit on the transaction, unless he has acted in bad faith or is at fault (see above, para.8–09, and below, para.8–35). Where the enrichment is by way of a saving, it can never be lost, so the defence does not apply in such cases.

See also the hard but salutary case of :

Royal Bank of Scotland v Watt

1991 S.C. 48

For the facts, see above, para.8–05. In defence to RBS's claim for repayment, W argued that he no longer had the money, having given it to the rogue. The court rejected the defence, as W had been negligent, and therefore an order for repetition was not unjust.

Bona fide perception and consumption

This is a defence of some importance in all cases where enrichment arises from possession of **8–31** property, whether by transfer or taking. The bona fide and enriched possessor[90] is generally liable to restore, not only the thing possessed, but also its fruits and accessions during his possession; but the identification and exploitation of such fruits and accessions during that time will usually avoid this liability.

[87] See above, para.8–25.
[88] See above, para.8–19, and note the case of *Bank of New York v North British Steel Group*, 1992 S.L.T. 613.
[89] (1901) 9 S.L.T. 93 at 95.
[90] This does not include the improver in bona fide possession of another's property, since he is impoverished and is the pursuer, not the enriched defender; but the improver's enrichment claim will be offset by the fruits and accessions he has perceived and consumed during his possession.

Other defences[91]

8–32 Examples of other defences include personal bar, prescription,[92] and compensation in the sense of set-off of the enriched person's claims against the impoverished person's enrichment claim (*e.g.* damages in some contract cases,[93] counter-enrichment claims[94]). When parties compromise or settle a dispute between themselves in order to avoid litigation, each surrendering some aspect of the rights they claim, resultant transfers cannot be later unseated as undue.

REMEDIES AND MEASURES OF RECOVERY

8–33 In *Shilliday v Smith*,[95] Lord President Rodger emphasised the characterisation of the "three R's" of Scots enrichment law—repetition, restitution, and recompense—as remedies, and earlier in this Chapter (above, para.8–11) it was shown how these fitted together with the various forms of enrichment. Repetition is the remedy for the return of money, restitution that for the return of corporeal property, and recompense that for other forms of enrichment. *Shilliday* shows how the remedies may be drawn together in a single case: recompense for the materials and work which the pursuer paid for, repetition for the money which she paid directly to the defender.

It is again useful to turn to the distinction between enrichments by transfer, imposition, and taking.

Transfer

8–34 In repetition cases, generally the amount of money received must be returned, with interest running from the date of the initial transfer, while in restitution of property the thing transferred must be returned with fruits and accessions (subject to the defence of bona fide perception and consumption—above, para.8–31). In *Findlay v Monro*,[96] a person who consumed goods delivered to him in error was found liable to restore their value. Recompense may be payable where the transfer is by way of services rendered or expenditure on the defender's interests, and the amount will be the value of the increase of assets or of the loss avoided for the defender.

Taking

8–35 Use of another's property attracts liability to pay a reasonable sum, which may be measured by, for example, market rents, the annual worth of the land, or the expenditure saved by the user through having the use in question. The taker may also be liable in repetition, repaying an amount taken. Where a thing cannot be returned because the defender has consumed, destroyed or sold it in good faith and acting with due care, generally the remedy is recompense and the defender is liable to the extent of his enrichment; bad faith or fault will make the defender liable for the full value of the thing, however, when the remedy is usually known as restitution. In cases where the defender so used the pursuer's property as to cause himself or a third party to gain title to it by

---

91 See generally Scot. Law Com. DP No.95, Vol.2, pp.63–95.

92 See Prescription and Limitation (Scotland) Act 1973, Sch.1, para.1(b)—obligation to redress unjustified enrichment prescribes five years after it became enforceable. See *NV Devos Gebroeder v Sunderland Sportswear Ltd*, 1990 S.C. 291.

93 See further below, para.8–39.

94 See for the court ordering the payer-pursuer to restore benefits received from the defender-payee as a condition of obtaining repetition, *e.g. North British and Mercantile Insurance Co. v Stewart* (1871) 9 M. 534; *Haggarty v Scottish TGWU*, 1955 S.C. 109 at 114, 115.

95 1998 S.C. 725; see above, para.8–03.

96 1698 Mor. 1707; see above, para.8–06.

original acquisition (*e.g.* by specification), the pursuer will recover the value of the property he has lost, not the defender's enrichment or the value of the new property.

Imposition

The remedy is recompense in property improvement cases, and the measure of recovery is the amount by which the defender is enriched, limited by the amount the improver has spent. The amount of the enrichment will be the enhanced permanent value of the property arising from the improvements carried out during the good faith possession, as determined at the date the good faith ceases or the true owner resumes possession. **8–36**

In cases of payment of another's debt, the amount due is the amount of the debt discharged with interest from the date of the payment, while in performance of another's non-money obligation the amount of the enrichment is due.

FLOWCHART OF UNJUSTIFIED ENRICHMENT IN TWO-PARTY CASES*

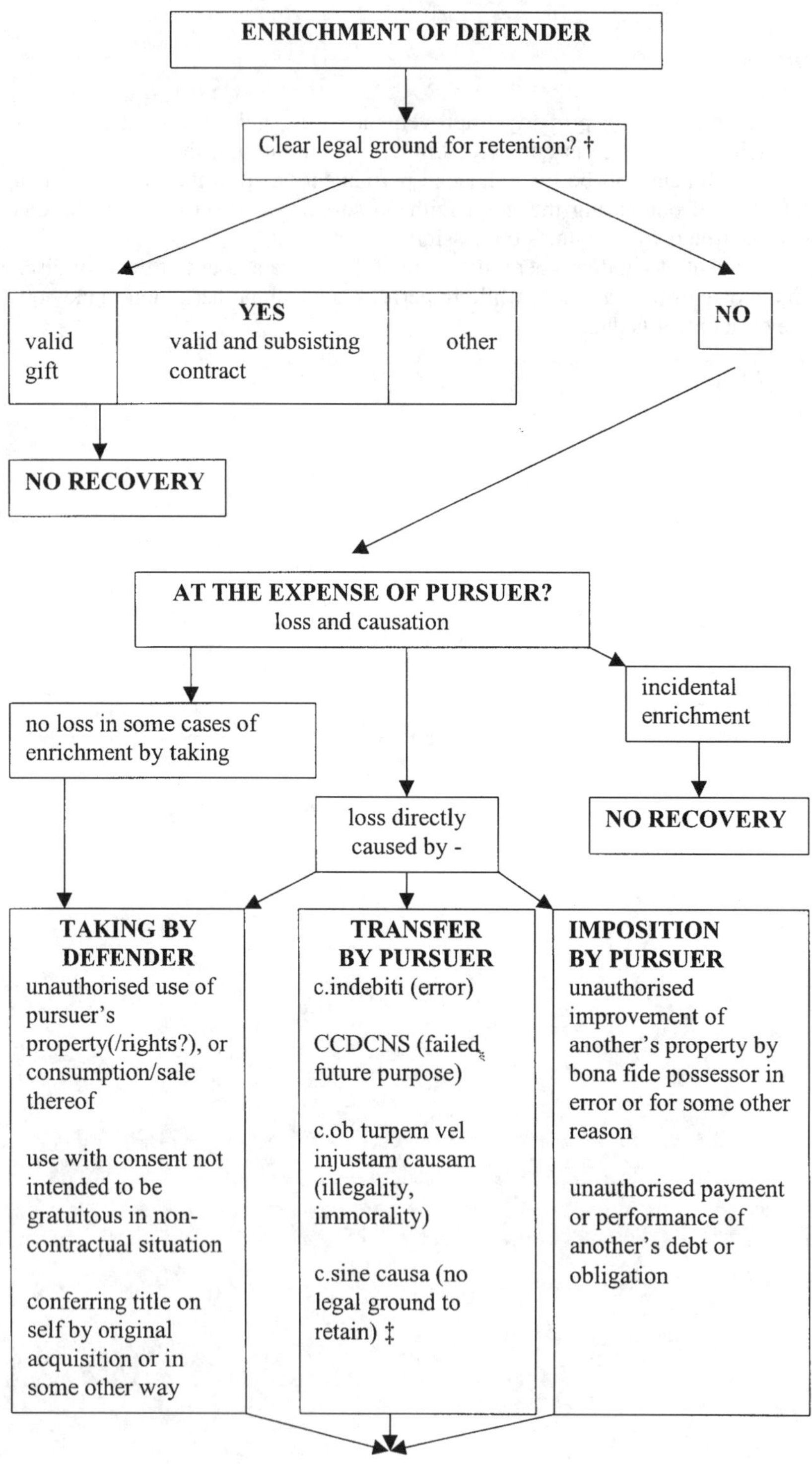

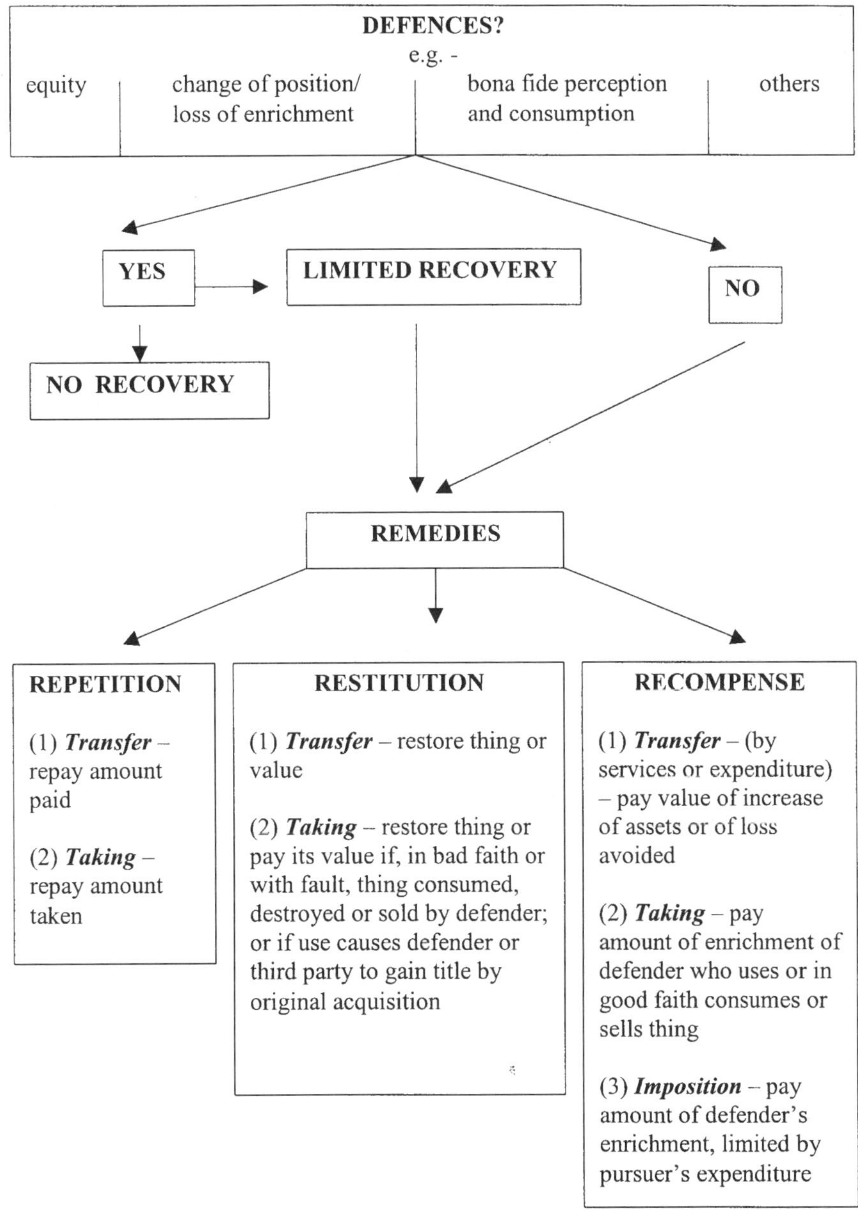

* *This flowchart would become very tangled were it to include the topic of 'indirect' or multi-party enrichment, which is accordingly excluded.*

† *This aspect could equally well appear amongst the defences.*

‡ *Note this is the second appearance of 'without legal ground' in this flowchart, illustrating the still incomplete analysis of Scots law on this issue.*

UNJUSTIFIED ENRICHMENT AND OTHER BRANCHES OF THE LAW

8–37 This Chapter has indicated several times the key principle that a person who is enriched can only retain it if the benefit is justified by some legal ground such as a gift or a contract. This section explores the principle further by considering these legal grounds for retention of enrichment in more detail. Unjustified enrichment can only be understood in relation to these other branches of law, and this may explain the concept of the "subsidiarity" of enrichment law, only to be used when no other rules apply.[97]

Gift

8–38 Few cases illustrate the justification of an enrichment as an unconditional gift. But the negative version of the proposition, namely, that an enrichment was conferred without intention to donate and is therefore reversible, is frequently found in the Institutional Writers and judicial dicta.[98] This has been particularly important in cases about use of and improvements to another's property, and about performance of another's obligation. The presumption against donation in Scots law is also relevant here. Conditional gifts (*e.g.* wedding presents) are, it is conceived, returnable if the condition fails (see further below).

A controversial case where a gift was found not to be returnable as an unjustified enrichment is *Masters and Seamen of Dundee v Cockerill.*[99]

Fraternity of Masters and Seamen of Dundee v Cockerill

(1869) 8 M. 278

The FMSD was a charitable organisation, the members of which subscribed an annual fee, in return for which they and their dependents were entitled to certain payments if the member died or fell into financial difficulties. C, a member, went on a voyage from Dundee and was not heard of for 16 years. During that time, when it was believed that C was dead, his wife received support from FMSD in accordance with the rules of the organisation, and also the sum of 13 shillings (65p) in addition. When C returned, it was held that the support given under the rules, having been made under an error of fact (that C was dead—see further below), should be repaid; but not the 13 shillings, since although it had been paid under the same mistake, it was a gift which FMSD had no legal obligation to make.

This case is controversial because arguably the FMSD's mistake about C's death was as much an invalidation of the gift as it was of the payment under the rules. Gifts may be contracts, and the factors which invalidate contracts may often also invalidate gifts. In the *Dundee* case, the judges said that the FMSD would not have been able to recover the 13 shillings if, *e.g.*, C's wife had unexpectedly become rich after the donation. But that situation, it is suggested, would not have involved an error of the kind required to trigger an enrichment claim for restoration of the gift, but was rather one of a misprediction as to uncertain future events, quite different in kind from the question of whether or not C was alive at the time of the donation (see further below). The result would certainly have been different if the 13 shillings had been paid conditionally, made for example on the basis that, if C returned, or if his wife remarried, it would be repayable; this would mean that the money was returnable upon the fulfilment of the condition.

---

[97] See in particular *Stair Memorial Encyclopaedia*, Vol.15, paras 68–71.

[98] Stair, *Institutions*, 1.8.2, 6; Bankton, *Institutions*, 1.9.1, 41; Bell, *Principles*, §538; *Lawrence Building Co. v Lanarkshire County Councill,* 1978 S.C. 30 at 41, *per* Lord President Emslie.

[99] (1869) 8 M. 278.

Contract

An enrichment, whether a saving or a gain, is justified if it arises through the performance of a valid and subsisting contract: legal grounds exist for the retention of such enrichment. The law of unjustified enrichment does not enable inquiries into whether too much or too little was paid for goods or services or any other performance supplied under a contract. **8–39**

Dollar Land (Cumbernauld) Ltd v CIN Properties Ltd

1998 S.C. (H.L.) 90

Complex arrangements for the development of a shopping centre involved the establishment of a 125-year lease, between DLC as landlords and CIN as tenants for a nominal rent of £1 per year if asked, and a 99 year sub-lease back from CIN to DLC. The rent payable by DLC was a 77.5 per cent proportion of the rents payable to them by the "occupational" sub-tenants of the shopping centre. DLC and their predecessors in title had made a contribution to the capital costs of developing the centre. CIN terminated the sub-lease for non-payment of rent by DLC. The sub-lease provided that on such termination CIN was entitled to enter on the premises and use, possess and enjoy the same free of all claims by DLC as tenants, as if the sub-lease had never been granted. This meant that CIN became entitled to 100 per cent of the occupational sub-tenant rents, while under the head lease DLC was only entitled to £1 per year. DLC claimed that CIN was in the circumstances unjustifiably enriched, the losses to DLC being wholly disproportionate to their breach of contract, and involving deprivation of any return on their capital investment. *Held* that DLC had no enrichment claim. Lord Hope of Craighead said (at p.94): "An obligation in unjustified enrichment is owed where the enrichment cannot be justified on some legal basis arising from the circumstances in which the defender was enriched. There can be no better justification for an enrichment than that it was obtained and is being retained in the exercise of a contractual right against the party who seeks to invoke the remedy. ... The benefit which has enriched CIN is one which was provided for them expressly in the contract of sublease."

But despite this general principle, there are a number of cases closely connected to the performance of contracts where enrichment law does become relevant.

The most obvious example is with regard to performances where a contract is null (or void); that is to say, although there appears to be a contract, it never had any existence in law as a result of some flaw in its formation, such as the lack of capacity, or an error, of one or more of the parties, or the use by one party against the other of overwhelming force or duress, or its illegality. If, despite the nullity, performance is rendered, then it may be reversed or paid for under the law of enrichment, typically as an undue performance (see further para.8–19 above on the *condictio indebiti*).

Wilson v Marquis of Breadalbane

(1859) 21 D. 957

(contract void for dissensus on price)

Bullocks were delivered by A to B, but the parties could not agree on the price to be paid. It was held that there was no contract but that B, being unable to restore the cattle, had to pay their market value.

Morgan Guaranty v Lothian Regional Council

1995 S.C. 151

(contract void for lack of capacity)

For the facts, see above, para.8–05. Payments made in error under the void contract fell to be restored. Lord President Hope said (at p.156): "[T]he payments were made in implement of a supposed obligation under a contract which was discovered not to exist, and the recipients of the payment were enriched because the payment was of money to which they were not entitled. Leaving aside any equitable considerations which might suggest that the defenders should keep the money, I would regard this as a clear case for a remedy on the ground of unjustified enrichment."

The position is, however, different where the contract is merely annullable (or voidable). Here the contract does take and retain legal effect until such time as it is annulled, or reduced, by court process. Therefore performances rendered under it before its reduction are valid contractual performances and cannot be seen as undue for the purposes of the *condictio indebiti* (see above, para.8–19). One of the conditions on which annulment will be allowed is that *restitutio in integrum* (restoration of the parties to their pre-contractual position) may be effected. Although this requirement of restoration looks like reversing or paying for enrichments, it is not viewed as a remedy for enrichment, but is rather a condition of annulment or reduction, and in working out what must be done, enrichment principles are not applied.

As discussed earlier in this Chapter (above, para.8–22), where a contract is discharged by frustration, and is therefore no longer subsisting, Scots law allows enrichment principles and remedies to govern what is to happen with regard to performances rendered under the contract which have not been met by the anticipated counter-performance as a result of the frustrating event. This is seen as a major instance of the CCDCNS, the classic case being *Cantiere San Rocco v Clyde Shipbuilding Co. Ltd.*[1]

Similar issues can arise in cases where the contract is terminated prematurely because the material breach of one of the parties enables the other to exercise the contractual remedy of rescission. In many such cases, one result of rescission is mutual restitution: in sale of goods, for example, where the seller does not give good title to the goods, or where the seller supplies goods which are defective, the buyer is entitled to get the price back, while the goods fall to be returned to the seller (or to the true owner, where appropriate). It is not clear whether this restitution after material breach should be treated as governed by enrichment principles such as CCDCNS, or is rather something like *restitutio in integrum*, a contractual remedy with some similarity to enrichment ones.[2] The latter seems the better view at present. It seems that restitution cannot be claimed from the contract-breaker's assignee because, while an assignee is subject to the *defences* available against the cedent, *counterclaims* available against the cedent cannot be made against the assignee.[3] Finally, at present a contract-breaker is not generally liable to account to the other contracting party for gains made as a result of the breach of contract[4]; but the English decision of *Attorney General v Blake*[5] has thrown this doctrine into doubt. A gain-based remedy for breach of contract might provide a just solution in cases like *Ruxley Engineering v Forsyth*,[6] where a builder saved money by constructing a swimming pool disconform to the contractual specifications but

1 1923 S.C. (H.L.) 105; see above, para.8–22.

2 As in South Africa: *Baker v Probert* 1985 (3) S.A. 429 (A.).

3 *Compagnie Commerciale Andre SA v Artibell Shipping Co. Ltd*, 2001 S.C. 653, following the English House of Lords decision, *Pan Ocean Shipping Ltd v Creditcorp Ltd (The Trident Beauty)* [1994] 1 W.L.R. 161; see also the Sheriff Court cases, *Binstock Miller & Co. v Coia & Co*, 1957 S.L.T. (Sh. Ct) 47, and *Alex Lawrie (Factors) Ltd v Mitchell Engineering Ltd*, 2001 S.L.T. (Sh. Ct) 93. Compare the South African case, *LTA Engineering Co. Ltd v Seacat Investments (Pty) Ltd* 1974 (1) S.A. 747 (A.), under which the assignee must "defend" the cedent if the assignation was made in bad faith to defeat the debtor's counter-claim (see also Digest 3.3.34).

4 *Teacher v Calder* (1899) 1 F. (H.L.) 39.

5 [2001] 1 A.C. 268; see above, para.8–11.

6 [1996] A.C. 344.

was liable for only nominal damages because the client had suffered no significant loss as a result of the breach.

On the other side of the coin, a group of cases shows that in some situations a party who has broken a contract and is, as a result of the doctrine of mutuality of contract, unable to raise an action under the contract for payment in respect of contractual performances rendered, may be able to make an enrichment claim instead; typically, again, by way of the principle of the CCDCNS.[7] It seems that a pre-condition of use of the enrichment remedy is that the contract has been terminated as a result of the breach; the claim is also subject, of course, to the other party's counterclaim of damages for breach of contract.[8] The classic case is, again, that of the builder who fails to complete or completes defectively, but this time viewed from a different angle[9]:

Steel v Young

1907 S.C. 360

A builder deviated from its contract to build a house by using milled lime rather than the contractually specified cement mortar. The client refused to pay the whole contract price, although the difference in value between a house with cement mortar and one with milled lime was only £5, but the cost of repairing the defect, which would have entailed pulling the house down and rebuilding it, exceeded the original contract price. The client was occupying the house. The court held that the builder, being in material breach, had no claim for the contract price, but could use an alternative approach, based upon the client's enrichment at his expense.

Thomson v Archibald

1990 G.W.D. 26–1438 (Edinburgh Sheriff Court)

A builder abandoned its contract with the work only 45 per cent done, and the employer, having terminated the contract, had the work completed by a second contractor. The builder sued the employer successfully on the grounds that the latter was enriched by having 45 per cent of the work done without being contractually bound to pay for it.

The doctrine is not applicable only in building cases, however[10]:

Graham v United Turkey Red Co.

1922 S.C. 533

G was an agent acting for UTR and paid by commission upon sales he made for the company. In July 1916 G went into breach of the UTR contract by starting to sell also the goods of a rival company. Upon discovery of this, UTR dismissed G, who sued for unpaid commission. It was held that, while he could not recover the contractual commission for sales made after July 1916, G had an enrichment claim in respect of such sales.

---

7 See H. L. MacQueen, "Unjustified enrichment and breach of contract" 1994 *Juridical Review* 137 at 149–66.

8 Where the breach is non-material, the contract-breaker will usually be able to sue for the price of the work done with a deduction for the cost of repairing the breach. See also *Wiltshier Construction (Scotland) Ltd v Drumchapel Housing Co-operative Ltd*, 2003 S.L.T. 443.

9 See in addition to the cases described below, *Ramsay v Brand* (1898) 25 R. 1212; *Forrest v Scottish County Investment Co. Ltd*, 1915 S.C. 115, affirmed 1916 S.C. (H.L.) 28; and note the South African cases of *Hauman v Nortje* 1914 A.D. 293 and *BK Tooling (Edms) Bpk v Scope Precision Engineering (Edms) Bpk* 1979 (1) S.A. 391 (A.).

10 See in addition to the cases described below *NV Devos Gebroeder v Sunderland Sportswear Ltd*, 1990 S.C. 291; *Dollar Land (Cumbernauld) Ltd v CIN Properties Ltd*, 1998 S.C. (H.L.) 90.

PEC Barr Printers Ltd v Forth Print Ltd

1980 S.L.T. (Sh. Ct) 118

B and F had a contract for typesetting. B delivered half the work, but F terminated the contract because B would be unable to complete the remainder in time. B claimed successfully for the value of the work delivered.

Zemhunt Holdings Ltd v Control Securities plc

1992 S.C. 58

Land was sold at an auction, with a condition being payment by the purchasers of a deposit of 10 per cent of the purchase price. The purchasers duly paid the deposit, but failed to come up with the balance of the price on the due date. The vendors terminated the contract on the ground of the purchasers' material breach. The purchasers then claimed repayment of the deposit under the CCDCNS. In the Outer House, Lord Marnoch held that the deposit was an advance part-payment, and was not therefore forfeited as a result of the breach; but, further, that the CCDCNS could not be invoked by a party in breach and so responsible for the failure of overall performance. In the Second Division, Lord Marnoch was reversed on the deposit point, which made it unnecessary to determine whether or not a purchaser in breach was entitled to restoration of his advance payment. In an important *obiter dictum*, however, Lord Morison indicated that he saw such a claim as legitimate, given the ability of the payee to counterclaim for damages for breach of contract.

Two other situations closely connected to contracts should be mentioned. One is where parties are negotiating but have not yet formed a contract. In practice negotiating parties often commence performance of the transaction without having reached the contractual stage, anticipating a successful outcome of their dealing. If however the contract is never concluded, then return of and payment for the performances rendered during the abortive negotiations will generally be a matter for enrichment law. This might be on the basis of either the *condictio indebiti* or the CCDCNS, or through use of another's property not intended to be gratuitous.[11] A second situation is what may be called over-performance of a contract—paying more than the contract price, or paying twice; supplying more than the required number of goods, or supplying what is meant to be the same consignment more than once; doing more work than is required under a contract. Enrichment law can be used to provide a fair answer to these types of situation, since the over-performance was not due: for example, by enabling the return of the over-payment or the extra goods.[12] Sometimes, especially where the recipient has used or taken the benefit of the over-supply, there could be an enrichment by taking or use of another's property; but the situation may be better analysed as one of implied contract.[13]

The two situations mentioned in the previous paragraph can coalesce in the case where parties reach the end of a long-term contract such as a lease while negotiating its renewal, and, pending that renewal, allow the relationship to continue. In the event that the negotiations are unsuccessful, so that no new contract is ever formed, then performances rendered during the post-contract period may be restored or paid for under enrichment law.[14]

---

11 See, *e.g. Microwave Systems (Scotland) Ltd v Electro-Physiological Instruments Ltd*, 1971 S.C. 140; *Site Preparations Ltd v Secretary of State for Scotland*, 1975 S.L.T. (Notes) 41 (both claims unsuccessful); *Shetland Islands Council v BP Petroleum Development Ltd*, 1990 S.L.T. 82 (relevant claim; see above, para.8–09, for possibility that this was an implied contract case).

12 See *Chisholm v Alexander* (1882) 19 S.L.R. 835.

13 Note also Sale of Goods Act 1979, s.30 (if recipient does not reject the over-supply of goods, the seller may charge him at the contract rate).

14 See *Rochester Poster Services Ltd v A G Barr plc*, 1994 S.L.T. (Sh. Ct) 2 (above, para.8–09).

NEGOTIORUM GESTIO (UNAUTHORISED MANAGEMENT OF ANOTHER'S AFFAIRS)

As is apparent from its Latin name meaning "management (or administration) of affairs", this part of the law of obligations also originated in Roman law.[15] By comparison with enrichment or contract, however, *negotiorum gestio* is of rather narrow scope, and there is little case law to elaborate the statements of principle found in the Institutional Writers and subsequent literature.[16] **8–40**

The situation envisaged is one where the manager (the *gestor*) steps in, without authority, to manage the affairs (*negotia*) of another (the *dominus*) when the latter is unable (through absence, ignorance, or incapacity such as mental disability) to deal with them himself or to authorise others to do so. This can range from the preservation of property, such as putting a lost or abandoned car in a garage,[17] or putting goods in danger in a war-zone into a place of safety,[18] or repairing or improving a house,[19] to the payment of the debts of the *dominus*[20]; but Scots law has yet to apply the concept to the preservation of the life, health or well-being of the *dominus*.

Paterson v Greig

(1862) 24 D. 1370

A mother improved the heritable property of her eldest son, a pupil child with no father or tutor. She was held to be a *gestor* for the boy.

Fernie v Robertson

(1871) 9 M. 437

A daughter improved the heritable property of her senile mother. She was held to be a *gestor* for the old lady.

SMT Sales and Services Co. Ltd v Motor and General Finance Co. Ltd

1954 S.L.T. (Sh. Ct) 107

MGF let a car to W on hire purchase. The police found the car abandoned. W, who was behind on his instalment payments, said the car was stolen but did no more. The police, as required by statute, ordered SMT to remove the vehicle to its garage. SMT could not get W to collect and pay for the service and sued MGF as owners. *Held* SMT was a *gestor* entitled to claim expenses from the owner of the car.

If the *dominus* is aware of the situation with which the manager is trying to deal, and has never the less chosen not to act, the manager has no claim under the principles of *negotiorum gestio* and must make any claim under the law of enrichment. See for example:

---

15 See Digest 3.5; Code 2.18(19).

16 Stair, *Institutions*, 1.8.3–5; Bankton, *Institutions*, 1.9.22–27; Erskine, *Institute*, 3.3.52–53; Hume, *Lectures*, Vol.3, pp.175–7; Bell, *Principles*, §§540–1.

17 *SMT Sales and Services Co. Ltd v Motor and General Finance Co. Ltd*, 1954 S.L.T. (Sh. Ct) 107.

18 *Kolbin v Kinnear*, 1931 S.C. (H.L.) 128.

19 *Paterson v Greig* (1862) 24 D. 1370; *Fernie v Robertson* (1871) 9 M. 437.

20 *Reid v Lord Ruthven* (1918) 55 S.L.R. 616.

Garriock v Walker

(1873) 1 R. 100

The master of a ship saved a putrefying cargo of whale blubber and whale heads by having it unloaded from the ship, cleaned and put into casks, creating a profit for the owner who had refused to accept responsibility in the situation. The master's claim lay in enrichment (the owner's saving) rather than *negotiorum gestio*.

North British Railway Company v Tod

(1893) 9 Sh. Ct Rep. 326

T's horse was injured and the pursuer railway company incurred veterinary and livery charges in dealing with the animal, the owner having refused to accept responsibility for it. The railway company's claim lay in enrichment (the owner's saving) rather than in *negotiorum gestio*.

As a result of the absence or inability of the *dominus*, the actions of the manager cannot be based upon a contract between the parties, nor has the intervention been otherwise authorised by the *dominus*. Despite this lack of consent or authority, the *dominus* is liable for the expenses and outlays incurred by the manager in the course of the management. Note, then, that this is essentially a claim for loss rather than for any enrichment which the *dominus* might have as a result of the manager's intervention in his affairs.

To have a claim, however, the manager must intend the management to be of benefit to the *dominus* and, probably, to claim his expenses in achieving this. If the manager also intended some benefit to himself, he may still recover his expenses; but if he was acting entirely in his own interests, the claim of *negotiorum gestio* is generally excluded. If the manager intended to donate his services to the *dominus*, again there is no *negotiorum gestio*. Given that there is a presumption against donation in Scots law, it would probably be for the *dominus* to prove that a gift was intended, and otherwise it would be assumed that the manager had not intended to act gratuitously.

Kolbin v Kinnear

1931 S.C. (H.L.) 128

K2 transported K1's goods from Archangel to England in 1919, rescuing them from the Red Army then closing in on the city. K2 were interested in the safety and eventual resale of the goods because they had had possession as K1's export agents and had already incurred charges in respect of them. *Held* K2's mixed motives did not prevent them from claiming in *negotiorum gestio*.

The manager's intervention must be of at least initial utility to the *dominus*. This does not mean that the situation must be one of emergency or necessity,[21] but rather that the manager's intervention is useful to the *dominus* at the time of the intervention.

The classic illustration of *negotiorum gestio* is where you find my house burning down while I am away on holiday. Your attempt to put out the fire is unauthorised but is probably a justified effort to protect my interests. You may also have been motivated by a desire to stop the fire spreading to your house next door, but that does not stop the situation being one of *negotiorum gestio*. Nor does the failure of your intervention; even if my house is completely destroyed, you will still be entitled to claim your fire-fighting expenses. On the other hand, if you negligently used inappropriate means of tackling the fire and made the situation worse, I might have a delictual action against you to compensate me for the loss you have caused me.[22] There is also a

[21] *Negotiorum gestio* should not be confused with agency of necessity.

[22] See *Kolbin v Kinnear*, 1931 S.C. (H.L.) 128.

link with unjustified enrichment in that if you make a profit from your intervention, you must account to me for it.

The law of *negotiorum gestio* deals with situations very similar to those treated under the heading of enrichments by imposition (above, paras 8–11, 8–25). Key differences would include the following:

- In cases of improvements to another's property, the manager need not be labouring under any error as to ownership or any other ground making the other person's enrichment unjustified before a claim can be made; nor need the management enrich the other person.
- In cases of payment of another's debt, the payer who intends to discharge the other's obligation can use *negotiorum gestio* as the basis of recovery if the payment achieves its objective, the claim being for the cost of doing so (which, in money cases, is exactly the same as the amount of the debtor's enrichment).[23] But if the debtor is not absent, ignorant or incapable, or if the payer acted entirely to protect its own interests, then in principle only the enrichment claim is available to that party.

Given the idea that enrichment claims are "subsidiary", only for use where there is no other legal remedy (above, para.8–37), it would seem that a claim should be made in *negotiorum gestio* first if possible.

Not every legal system recognises the obligation of *negotiorum gestio*. The obvious problem is the encouragement which it may give to those who meddle without authority in other people's business. It is a perfectly tenable view that in general such interference should not impose legally enforceable obligations upon the recipient. On the other hand, it would be a poor kind of society in which people helped each other only when specifically asked or authorised to do so, particularly when the person in difficulty was unable to help him or herself for some reason. The rules of *negotiorum gestio* are intended to distinguish the deserving intervener from the unworthy busybody, and seem to have done so successfully since Roman times.

[23] See, *e.g. Reid v Lord Ruthven* (1918) 55 S.L.R. 616.

Quick Quiz

Unjustified enrichment

- How may enrichment by transfer, enrichment by taking, and imposed enrichment be distinguished from each other? Why do these distinctions matter?
- What is (i) indirect; (ii) incidental enrichment? In what circumstances is recovery for each (i) allowed; (ii) disallowed?
- Which of the Roman law *condictiones* is recognised in the modern Scots law of unjustified enrichment, and what role do they now play? Explain the differences between the main recognised *condictiones*.
- How may the remedies of repetition, restitution and recompense be related to the different kinds of enrichment?
- On what legal grounds may an enrichment be justified?
- When will the law allow a claim for unauthorised intervention in another's affairs?

Further Reading

On the *history of enrichment law in Scotland*, see H. L. MacQueen and W. D. H. Sellar, "Unjust enrichment in Scots law" in ***Unjust Enrichment: The Comparative Legal History of the Law of Restitution*** (E. J. H. Schrage ed., 1995); and R. Evans-Jones, "Unjustified enrichment" in ***History of Private Law in Scotland*** (**K. G. C. Reid and R. Zimmermann** eds, 2000), Vol.2. This should be seen against the *general Roman law and European background*, for which see **R. Zimmermann, *The Law of Obligations: Roman Foundations of the Civil Law Tradition*** (1990), Chap.26.

For valuable *detailed accounts of Scots law pre-Shilliday*, see ***The Laws of Scotland: Stair Memorial Encyclopaedia*** (1996) Vol.15, paras 10–86, and **W. J. Stewart, *The Law of Restitution in Scotland*** (1992, with supplement 1996). See **Gloag and Henderson, *The Law of Scotland*** (11th ed., 2001), Chap.28, for a lightly revised version of an account originally written by Lord Rodger of Earlsferry before *Shilliday* (Chap.29, 10th ed., 1995). The discussion of *law reform* by the Scottish Law Commission, in its Discussion Papers Nos 95 (1993), 99 and 100 (1996) and the resulting Report on Unjustified Enrichment: Error of Law and Public Authority Receipts and Disbursements (Scot. Law Com. No.169, February 1999), contains much influential analysis of the pre-*Shilliday* authorities. For *assessment of the impact of Shilliday* (along with *Morgan Guaranty* and *Dollar Land*) see, *e.g.* P. Hellwege, "Rationalising the Scottish law of unjustified enrichment" (2000) 11 *Stellenbosch Law Review* 50; M. A. Hogg, "Lowlands to Low Countries: perspectives on the Scottish and Dutch law of unjustified enrichment", Ius Commune Lectures in European Private Law, No.3 (2001); W. D. H. Sellar, "*Shilliday v Smith*: unjustified enrichment through the looking glass" (2001) 5 *Edinburgh Law Review* 80, and two articles by N. R. Whitty: "The

Scottish enrichment revolution" (2001) 6 *Scottish Law & Practice Quarterly* 167, and "Rationality, nationality, and the taxonomy of unjustified enrichment", in ***Unjustified Enrichment: Key Issues in Comparative Perspective*** (**D. Johnston and R. Zimmermann** eds, 2002), Chap.23.

See on *indirect enrichment*, N. R. Whitty, "Indirect enrichment in Scots law" 1994 *Juridical Review* 200 and 239 (2 parts); D. P. Visser and S. Miller, "Between principle and policy: indirect enrichment in subcontractor and 'garage repair' cases" (2000) 117 *South African Law Journal* 594, and D. P. Visser, "Searches for silver bullets: enrichment in three-party situations", in Johnston and Zimmermann (above), Chap.19.

On *the condictiones in Scots law*, see two articles by R. Evans-Jones: "From 'undue transfer' to 'retention without a legal basis' (the *condictio indebiti* and *condictio ob turpem vel injustam causam*)", in ***The Civil Law Tradition in Scotland*** (Stair Society supp., Vol.2, 1995), and "The claim to recover what was transferred for a lawful purpose outwith contract (the *condictio causa data causa non secuta*)" [1997] *Acta Juridica* 139. Note also D. R. Macdonald, "Mistaken payments in Scots law", 1989 *Juridical Review* 49. For *enrichment by takings*, see K. G. C. Reid, "Unjustified enrichment and property law" 1994 *Juridical Review* 167; A. J. M. Steven, "Recompense for interference in Scots law" 1996 *Juridical Review* 50; and J. W. G. Blackie, "Enrichment, wrongs and invasion of rights in Scots law" [1997] *Acta Juridica* 284.

On *unauthorised improvements*, see J. Wolffe, "Enrichment by improvements in Scots law", in Johnston and Zimmermann (above), Chap.15, while for *unauthorised performance of another's obligations*, see H. L. MacQueen, "Payment of another's debt", also in Johnston and Zimmermann (above), Chap.17. On the defence of *change of position*, see G. C. Borland, "Change of position in Scots law" 1996 S.L.T. (News) 139; and P. Hellwege, "The scope of application of change of position in the law of unjust enrichment: a comparative study" [1999] 7 *Restitution Law Review* 92.

On *enrichment and contract* in general, see H. L. MacQueen, "Contract, unjustified enrichment and concurrent liability: a Scots perspective" [1997] *Acta Juridica* 176; on void contracts note further A. Rodger, "Recovering payments under void contracts in Scots law", in ***The Search for Principle: Essays in Honour of Lord Goff of Chieveley*** (**W. J. Swadling and G. Jones** eds, 2000); while on breach of contract, see H. L. MacQueen, "Unjustified enrichment and breach of contract" 1994 *Juridical Review* 139; and J. A. Dieckmann and R. Evans-Jones, "The dark side of *Connelly v Simpson*" 1995 *Juridical Review* 90.

For *comparative perspectives on enrichment and contract*, see **E. J. H. Schrage (ed.), *Unjust Enrichment and Contract*** (2002). A more *general comparative overview* is P. Schlechtriem, C. Coen and R. Hornung, "Restitution and unjust enrichment in Europe" (2001) 9 *European Review of Private Law* 377. For *South African law*, see **W. A. Joubert (ed.), *The Law of South Africa***, Vol.9. The most accessible detailed account of *English law* is **A. Burrows, *The Law of Restitution*** (2nd ed., 2002); contrast **S. Hedley, *A Critical Introduction to Restitution*** (2001). Hedley also runs an invaluable restitution website including Scots law and other comparative materials: *www.law.cam.ac.uk/restitution*. An English journal offering a wide comparative perspective, and again including Scots law, is the ***Restitution Law Review***.

On *negotiorum gestio*, see ***The Laws of Scotland: Stair Memorial Encyclopaedia***, (1996) Vol.15, paras 87–143. Again, for the general Roman law and European background, see **Zimmermann, *Law of Obligations*** (above), Chap.14.

Chapter 9

DELICT

Dr Douglas Brodie[1]

THE LAW OF NEGLIGENCE—INTRODUCTION

The most important branch of the law of delict is the law of negligence. The law of negligence will sometimes, but not always, require a defender who has behaved carelessly to pay damages to a pursuer who has suffered loss as a result of that carelessness. What then are the requirements of a successful negligence action? **9–01**

> **Key Concepts**
>
> For a successful negligence action, in essence the defender must have owed the pursuer a **duty of care** and have **breached that duty** (the standard of care question). Moreover, the breach of duty must have caused the loss which has arisen (the **causation** question).

DUTY OF CARE

It has been clear for many years that you can be careless to your heart's content if you do not owe a duty of care. Lord Dunedin in *Clelland v Robb*[2] said that "Negligence ***per se*** will not make liability unless there is first of all a duty which there has been failure to perform through that neglect."[3] Again, Lord MacMillan in *Donoghue v Stevenson*[4] accepted that there will be no liability for negligent behaviour unless a duty of care had been owed. **9–02**

It is self evident that a motorist owes a duty to take reasonable care for the safety of other drivers and pedestrians, etc., that an employer owes a duty to take reasonable care for his/her staff. Likewise, a doctor to his patients and so on. When one moves away from such obvious cases a test to determine the existence of a duty is required. The most famous test is that set down by Lord Atkin in:

---

1 Reader in Law, University of Edinburgh.
2 1911 S.C. 253.
3 1911 S.C. 253 at 256.
4 [1932] A.C. 562 at 618.

Donoghue v Stevenson

[1932] A.C. 562

"The rule that you are to love your neighbour becomes, in law, you must not injure your neighbour, and the lawyer's question, who is my neighbour, receives a restricted reply. You must take care to avoid acts or omissions which you can reasonably foresee would be likely to injure your neighbour. Who then in law is my neighbour? The answer seems to be—persons who are so closely and directly affected by my act that I ought reasonably to have them in contemplation as being so affected when I am directing my mind to the acts or omissions called in question."

In *Home Office v Dorset Yacht*[5] and *Anns v Merton LBC*[6] the Atkin dictum was approached in a distinctly pro-pursuer fashion. In the latter case Lord Wilberforce said:

> "First one has to ask whether, as between the alleged wrongdoer and the person who has suffered damage, there is sufficient relationship of proximity or neighbourhood such that, in the reasonable contemplation of the former, carelessness on his part may be likely to cause damage to the latter—in which case a *prima facie* duty of care arises. Secondly, if the first question is answered affirmatively, it is necessary to ask whether there are any considerations which ought to negative, or to reduce or limit the scope of the duty or the class of person to whom it is owed."

Lord Reid's approach was itself amplified by Lord Wilberforce in *Anns v Merton LBC* where the latter put forward his two stage test for duty of care.[7] A prima facie duty would arise where the harm to the pursuer was within the reasonable contemplation of the defender. However, there might well be further considerations which required that prima facie duty to be restricted or negatived. Lord Wilberforce built on Lord Reid's judgment and articulated with commendable clarity that one is not necessarily simply choosing between duty and immunity from liability but that a duty may arise only if factor(s) over and above reasonable contemplation are present.

From the mid-1980s onwards the House of Lords began to take a more restrictive approach to duty of care questions. This led to the approach in *Anns* being departed from.

Caparo Industries plc v Dickman

[1990] 2 A.C. 605

The current approach was set out as follows: "... in addition to the foreseeability of damage, necessary ingredients in any situation giving rise to a duty of care are there that there should exist between the party owing the duty and the party to whom it is owed a relationship characterised by the law as one of 'proximity' or 'neighbourhood' and that the situation should be one in which the court considers it fair, just and reasonable that the law should impose a duty of a given scope upon the one party for the benefit of the other."[8]

Moreover, the following dictum of Brennan J. in *Sutherland Shire Council v Heyman* was approved: "It is preferable in my view, that the law should develop novel categories of negligence incrementally and by analogy with established categories, rather than by a massive extension of a prima facie duty of care restrained only by indefinable considerations which ought to negative, or to reduce or limit the scope of the duty or the class of person to whom it is owed."[9]

---

[5] [1970] A.C. 1004.
[6] [1978] A.C. 728.
[7] [1978] A.C. 728 at 751–752.
[8] [1990] 2 A.C. 605 at 617–618.
[9] (1985) 60 A.L.R. 1.

More recently in *Marc Rich v Bishop Rock* the House of Lords approved the following dictum of Saville J.:

> "... whatever the nature of the harm sustained by the plaintiff, it is necessary to consider the matter not only by inquiring about foreseeability but also by considering the nature of the relationship between the parties; and to be satisfied that in all the circumstances it is fair, just and reasonable to impose a duty of care. Of course ... these three matters overlap with each other and are really facets of the same thing. For example, the relationship between the parties may be such that it is obvious that a lack of care will create a risk of harm and that as a matter of common sense and justice a duty should be imposed ... Again in most cases of the direct infliction of physical loss or injury through carelessness, it is self-evident that a civilised system of law should hold that a duty of care has been broken, whereas the infliction of financial harm may well pose a more difficult problem. Thus the three so-called requirements for a duty of care are not to be treated as wholly separate and distinct requirements but rather as convenient and helpful approaches to the pragmatic question whether a duty should be imposed in any given case. In the end whether the law does impose a duty in any particular circumstances depends upon these circumstances ..."[10]

In many situations existing case law will indicate whether a duty of care is owed. However, in situations which have not yet been tested in the courts the *Caparo* formula will be applied to determine the existence of the duty which is alleged to exist. There are a number of situations where because of, for instance, the nature of the loss or the identity of the defender the concept of duty of care will often result in a denial that a duty is owed by the defender to the pursuer. Alternatively a duty might be owed but only if requirements other than reasonable foreseeability are met. In such situations the courts will determine what constitutes sufficient proximity to allow a finding that a duty is owed. For example, in a case of negligent misrepresentation (see below) the question of whether reliance was placed upon the words used by the defender will be very important. Moreover, in any event public policy considerations may play a part. The courts will not impose a duty if it would not be fair, just and reasonable to do so. It should also be said that situations where the loss suffered is purely economic or where there is nervous shock are likely to be problematic. Again should the defender be a public body further considerations come into play. It is proposed now to illustrate the operation of the *Caparo* duty by examining a number of situations where recovery can be problematic.

Key Concepts

Negligence *per se* will not make liability unless there is first of all a **duty** which there has been **failure to perform** through that neglect.

In many situations existing case law will indicate whether a **duty of care** is owed. However, in situations which have not yet been tested in the courts the *Caparo* formula will be applied to determine the existence of the duty which is alleged to exist.

Pure economic loss

Pure economic loss is incurred where the pursuer suffers a financial loss which is not the consequence of physical damage to either his person or his property. It may, of course, be the case that the person or property of someone else has been damaged. For instance, the defender may have damaged property which the pursuer does not own but upon which he nevertheless depends. The classic example is perhaps that of the severance of the power supply. **9–03**

[10] [1996] 1 A.C. 211.

Spartan Steel Ltd v Martin & Co. Ltd

[1972] 3 All E.R. 557

Contractors severed electricity supply to the plaintiff's factory.[11] The cables were not owned by the plaintiff but he, nevertheless, suffered harm because the loss of power supply caused physical damage to molten metal in a furnace. The plaintiff was allowed to recover for the damage to the melt and consequent loss of profit. However, during the time the power was off the plaintiff would have been able to process four more melts. Recovery for the profits that would have resulted was not permitted as there had been no physical damage.

On similar principles, in general, you cannot recover if you suffer financial loss when someone else is injured.

Reavis v Clan Line Steamers

1925 S.C. 725

The owner of an orchestra raised an action when a boat was sunk and several members of the orchestra were drowned and others were injured. It was held that an employer has no right of action for damages caused to him through the death or injury of an employee occasioned by the fault of a third party.

The courts also tend to hold that you should look to contractual remedies where you suffer loss because property is defective. Thus, in:

Murphy v Brentwood District Council

[1990] 2 All E.R. 908

The plaintiff discovered cracks in the walls of his house which had been caused by defective foundations. He sued the council who had approved the plans for the house. He also alleged that the defects posed a risk to his health and safety. The House of Lords held that the council did not owe a duty of care.

Lord Bridge stated that "[i]f a dangerous defect in a chattel is discovered before it causes any personal injury or damage to property, because the danger is now known and the chattel cannot be safely used unless the defect is repaired , the defect becomes merely a defect in quality. The chattel is either capable of repair at economic cost or it is worthless and must be scrapped. In either case the loss sustained by the owner or hirer of the chattel is purely economic ... it is not recoverable in tort in the absence of a special relationship of proximity imposing on the tortfeasor a duty to safeguard the plaintiff from economic loss. There is no such special relationship between the manufacture of a chattel and a remote owner or hirer."[12]

One area where the courts are likely to allow recovery for pure economic loss is where the loss has been caused by a direct misrepresentation.

Hedley Byrne v Heller & Partners Ltd

[1964] A.C. 465

In this case the question arose as to whether a duty of care was owed in respect of a banker's reference. The answer was held to be yes but, on the facts, there was no liability because of an exemption clause. Lord Reid stated that a duty not to make a negligent misrepresentation would arise in all relationships where "... it is plain that

---

[11] See also *Dynamco Ltd v Holland and Hannen & Cubitts (S) Ltd*, 1971 S.C. 257.

[12] [1990] 2 All E.R. 908 at 925.

> the party seeking information or advice was trusting the other the other to exercise such a degree of care as the circumstances required, where it was reasonable for him to do that, and where the other gave the information or advice when he knew or ought to have known that the inquirer was relying on him."[13]
>
> Lord Morris put it rather differently: "... it should now be regarded as settled that if someone possessed of a special skill undertakes, quite irrespective of contract, to apply that skill for the assistance of another person who relies on such skill a duty of care will arise."[14]

The statement in *Hedley Byrne* was made directly by the defendant to the plaintiff (or, at least, it was treated as having been so made). However, where you rely on a statement which is in general circulation it is unlikely a duty of care will be owed.

Caparo Industries plc v Dickman

[1990] 2 A.C. 605

> The plaintiff owned shares in a company and on the strength of the accounts bought more and subsequently mounted a successful take-over bid. It was then discovered that the accounts were inaccurate and should have showed a loss rather than a profit. To whom did the auditors owe a duty of care? It was held that there was no duty owed to a member of the public who bought shares on the strength of the accounts. It was held further that existing investors were not in a better position. Lord Bridge notes that putting a statement into general circulation will not give rise to a duty of care unless "... the defendant knew that his statement would be communicated to the plaintiff, either as an individual or as a member of an identifiable class, specifically in connection with a particular transaction or transactions of a particular kind (*e.g.* in a prospectus inviting investment) and that the plaintiff would be very likely to rely on it for the purpose of deciding whether or not to enter on that transaction or on a transaction of that kind."[15] What though of existing shareholders who would be entitled to receive the accounts ? It was held that there was no proximity because they did not receive the accounts "... for the purposes of individual speculation with a view to profit."[16] On the other hand, while "[i]t is unnecessary to decide the point on this appeal. I can see more force in the contention that one purpose of providing the statutory information might be to enable the recipient to exercise whatever rights he has in relation to his proprietary interest by virtue of which he receives it, by way, for instance, of disposing of that interest."[17]

However, a duty may be owed where a statement is made to one party in the knowledge it will be passed on to a third party. In *Smith v Bush* the defendants were surveyors but the plaintiffs were not in a contractual relationship with them. The case involved the everyday situation of a plaintiff buying a house with the aid of a building society mortgage and the society instructing the surveyor. The plaintiff paid for the report and the surveyors knew it would be shown to her. It was held that a duty of care was owed. The case was made more complicated by the existence of exemption clauses. In holding that a duty of care was owed Lord Templeman said that:

> "... the valuer who values a house for the purpose of a mortgage, knowing that the mortgagee will rely and the mortgagor will probably rely on the valuation, knowing that the purchaser mortgagor has in effect paid for the valuation, is under a duty to exercise reasonable care and skill and that duty is owed to both parties to the mortgage for which the valuation is made."[18]

---

13 [1964] A.C. 465 at 486.
14 *ibid.* at 502–503.
15 *ibid.* at 576.
16 *per* Lord Oliver at 601.
17 *ibid.*, see also Lord Bridge at 580–581.
18 *ibid.* at 523.

The House of Lords have also held that an employer giving a reference to a prospective employer in respect of an ex-employee owes a duty of care to take reasonable care in the compliation of the reference. Lord Goff's judgment viewed the situation in terms of *Hedley Byrne*: "… when such a reference is provided by an employer, it is plain that the employee relies upon him to exercise due skill and care in the preparation of the reference before making it available to third parties."[19]

A duty of care may also be owed by the defender where he has assumed a responsibility to protect the pursuer from suffering pure economic loss. In a 3-2 decision the House of Lords upheld the Court of Appeal in *White v Jones*.[20] As a result, a solicitor will a duty not just to his client but to the potential beneficiary under the will. The case is very much an exercise in "creative jurisprudence":

> "… there is a lucana in the law, in the sense that practical justice requires that the disappointed beneficiary should have a remedy against the testator's solicitor in circumstances in which neither the testator nor his estate has in law suffered a loss."

The basis for the decision, according to Lord Goff, is to:

> "… extend to the intended beneficiary a remedy under the *Hedley Byrne* principle by holding that the assumption of responsibility by the solicitor towards his client should be held in law to extend to the intended beneficiary who (as the solicitor can reasonably foresee) may, as a result of the solicitor's negligence, be deprived of his intended legacy in circumstances in which neither the testator nor his estate will have a remedy against the solicitor."

That assumption of responsibility by the solicitor towards the disappointed beneficiary was described in the following terms by Lord Nolan:

> "… a professional man or an artisan who undertakes to provide his skill in a manner which, to his knowledge, may cause loss to others if carelessly performed, may thereby implicitly assume a legal responsibility towards them. The fact that he is doing so in pursuance of a contractual duty or a statutory function cannot of itself exclude that responsibility."[21]

Key Concepts

Pure economic loss is incurred where the pursuer suffers a financial loss which is not the consequence of physical damage to either his person or his property.

In general, you cannot recover if you suffer **financial loss** when someone else is injured.

Public authority defenders

9–04 At first glance a pursuer who alleges that a public authority[22] has been negligent should be in a position no different to anyone else seeking to recover damages.[23] Nevertheless, it has been the case for a long time that this is a particularly difficult area of negligence law.[24] Since the decision of the House of Lords in *Dorset Yacht v Home Office*[25] it has seemed that difficulties may flow from the mere fact that the defender is a public authority. A more long-standing source of difficulty has been the question of when the exercise of statutory duties/powers will give rise to a

19 *ibid.* at 370.
20 [1995] 1 All E.R. 691.
21 *ibid.* at 735.
22 Defining the term is not free of difficulty, see *e.g.* Harlow (1980) M.L.R. 241 at 253–254.
23 See, for example, Arrowsmith, *Civil Liability and Public Authorities*, Chap.6.
24 Friedman (1945) M.L.R. 31. It has perhaps not attracted the same degree of attention as say recovery for pure economic loss or nervous shock.
25 [1970] A.C. 1004.

common law duty of care. It is well established that such a duty may arise (*e.g.*, see *Geddis v Proprietors of Bann Reservoir*[26]) but it has been equally clear that there are occasions when one will not.[27] Predicting the outcome in any given situation has been less than easy. Certainly, it will be very difficult to establish that a duty of care was owed when a public authority was exercising a discretion under statute:

> "[M]ost statutes which impose a statutory duty on local authorities confer on the authority a discretion as to the extent to which, and the methods by which, such statutory duty is to be performed. It is clear both in principle and from the decided cases that the local authority cannot be liable in damages for doing that which Parliament has authorised. Therefore if the decisions complained of fall within the ambit of such statutory discretion they cannot be actionable in common law."[28]

However, where no issue of statutory discretion arises, the nature of the harm which has been suffered will be crucial. If , due to carelessness on the part of a public authority, you have suffered personal injury a duty of care may well be held to exist. In *Perrett v Collins*, the plaintiff suffered personal injuries when the plane in which he was flying crashed. There were a number of defendants to the action including the Popular Flying Association (PFA). It is the involvement of the latter that gives rise to interest since the PFA performs delegated statutory functions on behalf of the Civil Aviation Authority (CAA). Under the framework of the Civil Aviation Act 1982 the plane could not have taken off without a certificate of airworthiness issued by a PFA inspector. The plaintiff alleged that had the PFA exercised reasonable care in carrying out their inspection functions they would have refused to issue a certificate of airworthiness. The PFA is not a public authority but a limited company. Nevertheless, since the PFA exercised statutory powers on behalf of the CAA the decision is important from the perspective of public authority liability.

In holding for the plaintiff, the crucial consideration for the court was the nature of the harm suffered. It is more important to protect health than wealth. Despite this, the PFA had sought to deny responsibility for the infliction of personal injury. Nevertheless, given that the plaintiff sought to impose a common law duty of care in the context of the operation of a regulatory framework imposed by statute the defendant's prospects of success must have seemed reasonable. What is undoubtedly surprising is thc vchemence with which the PFA's stance was rejected. It represented

> "a fundamental attack upon the principle of tortious liability for negligent conduct which had caused foreseeable personal injury to others. That such a point should be considered even arguable shows how far some of the fundamental principles of the law of negligence have come to be eroded."

Indeed, the prima facie case for the plaintiff was overwhelming:

> "The denial of a duty of care owed by such a person in relation to the safety of the aircraft towards those who may suffer personal injuries, whereas as passengers in the aircraft or upon the ground, would leave a gap in the law of tort notwithstanding that a plaintiff had suffered foreseeable personal injury as a result of the unsafety of the aircraft and the unreasonable and careless conduct of the defendant. It would be remarkable if that were the law."

The key to the decision in favour of the plaintiff is the nature of the harm. The precise form the unreasonable behaviour of the defendant takes is neither here nor there. A careless statement by a public authority being no different to say dangerous roadworks set up by them. Further evidence of the importance of the element of personal injury is furnished by the Outer House decision in:

---

[26] 3 App. Cas. 430. There it was said (at 455–456) that "... it is now thoroughly well established that no action will lie for doing that which the legislature has authorised, if it is done without negligence, although it does occasion damage to anyone; but an action does lie for doing that which the legislature has authorised, if it be done negligently."

[27] *Geddis* was not always followed; *e.g. Wodehouse v Levy* [1940] 2 K.B. 561, *Lyus v Stepney BC* [1941] 1 K.B. 134. The latter two cases show that the fact that the defender was operating under a statutory power resulted in the negativing of the common law duty alleged.

[28] *op cit.* at 170.

Gibson v Chief Constable of Strathclyde

1999 S.C. 420

A bridge had collapsed due to flooding. The fire service informed the police as to the condition of the bridge. Two constables had then proceeded to the north side of the bridge and positioned their Land Rover on that side with its blue light flashing and headlights illuminated so as to be visible and give warning to any persons approaching from the south side. They remained with their vehicle so positioned until some time between 4.10pm and 4.20pm that afternoon when they withdrew with their vehicle. At the time they did so they had received no information to confirm that any barrier or warning was in place on the south side of the bridge. Within a few minutes of their departure the car in which the pursuer was travelling made is approach from the south aside and fell into the river. In holding that a duty of care was owed the actual practice of policing (and perhaps the expectations induced thereby) was important: the key background factor which pointed towards a finding that proximity existed was that "it is within common experience, at least in Scotland, that police officers, in emergencies and otherwise, take control of traffic or other road safety situations with a view better to safeguarding life and property. Such action is no sense dependent on any crime having been committed or on any crime being apprehended. It is a civil function in respect of which constables have authority, with attendant responsibility." Once the police had taken control of a hazardous road traffic situation they had put themselves into " ... a sufficiently proximate relationship with road users likely to be immediately and directly affected by the hazard as is sufficient for the purposes of the existence of a duty of care to such road users. That duty may extend not only to the manner of the exercise of that control but... to the relinquishment of it."

A point left unexplored by *Gibson* is what would have happened if the emergency services had nothing at all. In *Gibson* the defender had placed considerable reliance upon *Hill v Chief Constable.*[29] The latter was distinguished as arising out of the exercise of police functions in the investigation and suppression of crime. The policy factors listed in that case did not impact on the "... function of performing civil operational tasks concerned with human safety on the public roads".

Where the loss suffered is purely economic the task facing the pursuer is likely to remain arduous. *Harris v Evans* dealt with the actions of a health and safety inspector who, in the course of his duties, gave advice to certain local authorities about the safety of a mobile crane used by the plaintiff for the purpose of bunjee jumping.[30] This resulted in the business being shut down for a period of time with consequent loss of profit. Did the inspector owe a duty of care as to the content of his advice? The answer given was no. At the same time, the court in *Harris* offered some encouragement to would-be pursuers. It was recognised that there might come a point when a public authority came under a duty:

> "it could be that a particular requirements imposed by an inspector, whether expressed in an improvement notice or prohibition notice ... might introduce a new risk or danger not present in the business activity as previously conducted. The new risk or danger might materialise and result in economic damage to the business itself as well as physical damage to the person or property. We do not need to decide the point but I would not be prepared to rule out the possibility that damage thus caused could be recover by means of a negligence action."

One might argue that there is an element of arbitrariness here in the emphasis on the introduction of a new risk. What of the inspector in *Harris* itself who had not introduced a new risk but had caused loss by carelessly closing the operation down? If the degree of negligence had been gross should that not have led to recovery?

[29] [1989] A.C. 53.

[30] [1998] 3 All E.R. 522.

Psychiatric harm

A pursuer who alleges that a duty of care was owed to them in respect of psychiatric harm may well encounter difficulties. This type of harm is sometimes referred to as nervous shock. In *Simpson v ICI* Lord Robertson said that the pursuer must suffer "not merely grief, distress or any other normal emotion, but a positive psychiatric illness." Should such harm be suffered the pursuer will be owed a duty if the conditions set out below are satisfied. It is convenient to divide the cases up depending upon whether they concern imperilment. **9–05**

Imperilment cases

A pursuer may suffer psychiatric illness as a result of his own imperilment or reasonable fear of danger to himself. In the alternative, he may suffer such harm as a result of the physical injury or imperilment of a third party (or parties) which has been caused by the defender. In such cases, recovery will only be allowed where the psychiatric harm involves the sudden appreciation by sight or sound of a horrifying event, which violently agitates the mind. It does not include psychiatric illness caused by the accumulation over a period of time of more gradual assaults on the nervous system. Thus the stress and strain of caring for an injured person over a prolonged period, even if it caused psychiatric harm, would not give rise to a claim in damages. Moreover, the requirements of a successful action very much depend on whether the pursuer can be classified as a primary or a secondary victim. The law looks much more favourably on the former. **9–06**

Primary victims

In *Page v Smith*[31] the plaintiff had been involved in a relatively minor motor accident but was not physically hurt. It was alleged that the accident had aggravated the plaintiff's ME. The Court of Appeal denied recovery on the basis that injury by nervous shock was not reasonably foreseeable. However, the House of Lords tell us that in a nervous shock case the initial question is to classify the plaintiff as being either a primary or secondary victim. The former are participants in the incident *i.e.* someone who was "... directly involved in the accident, and well within the range of foreseeable physical injury." The latter are those "... in the position of a spectator or bystander." In the case of primary victims, it will suffice to show that some sort of personal injury was reasonably foreseeable. Thus if physical injury is reasonably foreseeable so is nervous shock. One result of this simplification of the law is that primary victims will not have to meet the requirement that foreseeability of shock to someone of normal fortitude existed. **9–07**

Would a rescuer be a primary victim?

White v Chief Constable of South Yorkshire

[1999] 2 A.C. 455

Claims had been brought by a number of police officers who had suffered nervous shock in consequence of the scenes they had witnessed at Hillsborough. Whilst the officers in question had not been in physical danger they were "... more than mere by-standers. They were all on duty at the stadium. They were all involved in assisting in the course of their duties in the aftermath of terrible events. And they have all suffered debilitating psychiatric harm". The case for the plaintiffs was based both on their status as employees (see below) and as rescuers. The plaintiffs' attempt to recover upon the basis that they were rescuers failed. They had been classified as rescuers by the Court of Appeal because of their activity in the aftermath of the tragedy. However, the real question is whether or not a pursuer is a primary victim. In

[31] [1995] 2 W.L.R. 644.

approaching this question no allowance should be made for the fact that the pursuer might be depicted as a rescuer. Here the plaintiffs were not primary victims since "it is common ground that none of the officers were at any time exposed to personal danger and none thought that they were so exposed." For a rescuer to be so viewed "the plaintiff must at least satisfy the threshold requirement that he objectively exposed himself to danger or reasonably believed that he was doing so."

Secondary victims

9–08 In *McLoughlin v O'Brian*[32] the plaintiff's husband and four children were involved in a road accident when their car was in collision with a lorry. The plaintiff, who was at home two miles away at the time, was told of the accident, about two hours later, by a neighbour, who took her to hospital to see her family. There she learned that her youngest daughter had been killed and saw her husband and the other children and witnessed the nature and extent of their injuries. She alleged that the impact of what she heard and saw caused her severe shock resulting in psychiatric illness. The critical question to be decided was whether a person in the position of the appellant, *i.e.* one who was not present at the scene of grievous injuries to her family but who comes upon those injuries at an interval of time and space, can recover damages for nervous shock. It was held that a plaintiff was entitled to recover damages for negligence in respect of nervous shock caused by seeing or hearing an injury to a close relative or by experiencing its immediate aftermath; that one could have expected nothing else of the plaintiff than that she should have gone to the hospital where her family had been taken; and that, accordingly, she had been within the scope of the immediate aftermath of the accident and was entitled to recover.

Lord Wilberforce summarised the authorities as follows:

"2. A plaintiff may recover damages for 'nervous shock' brought on by injury caused not to him or herself but to a near relative, or by the fear of injury. So far (subject to 5 below), the cases do not extend beyond the spouse or children of the plaintiff … 3. Subject to the next paragraph, there is no English case in which a plaintiff has been able to recover nervous shock damages where the injury to the near relative occurred out of sight and earshot of the plaintiff … 4. An exception from, or I would prefer to call it an extension of, the latter case, has been made where the plaintiff does not see or hear the incident but comes upon its immediate aftermath."

In *McLoughlin* itself, recovery was regarded as involving a modest extension of bullet point 4:

"She was not present at the accident, but she came very soon after upon its aftermath. If, from a distance of some 100 yards, she had found her family by the roadside, she would have come within principle 4 above. Can it make any difference that she comes upon them in an ambulance, or, as here in a nearby hospital, when, as the evidence shows, they were in the same condition, covered with oil and mud, and distraught with pain?"

Lord Wilberforce also took the opportunity to set out the rules for secondary victim cases:

"It is necessary to consider three elements inherent in any claim: the class of persons whose claims should be recognised; the proximity of such persons to the accident; and the means by which the shock is caused. As regards the class of persons, the possible range is between the closest of family ties—of parent and child, or husband and wife—and the ordinary bystander. Existing law recognises the claims of the first: it denies that of the second, either on the basis that such persons must be assumed to be possessed of fortitude sufficient to enable them to endure the calamities of modern life, or that defendants cannot be expected to compensate the world at large. In my opinion, these positions are justifiable, and since the present case falls within the first class, it is strictly unnecessary to say more. I think, however, that it should

[32] [1983] A.C. 410.

follow that other cases involving less close relationships must be very carefully scrutinised. I cannot say that they should never be admitted. The closer the tie (not merely in relationship, but in care) the greater the claim for consideration. The claim, in any case, has to be judged in the light of the other factors, such as proximity to the scene in time and place, and the nature of the accident. As regards proximity to the accident, it is obvious that this must be close in both time and space. It is, after all, the fact and consequence of the defendant's negligence that must be proved to have caused the 'nervous shock.' Experience has shown that to insist on direct and immediate sight or hearing would be impractical and unjust and that under what may be called the 'aftermath' doctrine one who, from close proximity, comes very soon upon the scene should not be excluded. Lastly, as regards communication, there is no case in which the law has compensated shock brought about by communication by a third party. In *Hambrook v. Stokes Brothers* [1925] 1 K.B. 141, indeed, it was said that liability would not arise in such a case and this is surely right. It was so decided in *Abramzik v. Brenner* (1967) 65 D.L.R. (2d) 651. The shock must come through sight or hearing of the event or of its immediate aftermath. Whether some equivalent of sight or hearing, *e.g.* through simultaneous television, would suffice may have to be considered."

In the subsequent House of Lords case of the *Alcock v Chief Constable*[33] it was said that recovery on the basis of relationship between pursuer and primary victim was not limited to particular relationships such as husband and wife. The key is the existence of "close ties of love and affection". Lord Keith said that "the closeness of the tie would, however, require to be proved by a plaintiff, though no doubt being capable of being presumed in appropriate cases".[34] Moreover, there may be circumstances where the element of direct visual perception may be provided by witnessing the actual injury to the primary victim on simultaneous TV.

Non-imperilment cases

Even where the harm arises in a situation which does not involve imperilment, a duty of care may be owed to protect the pursuer from suffering psychiatric harm. In such cases the defender has neither imperiled nor caused physical injury to anyone. One example is: **9–09**

Walker v Northumberland CC

[1995] 1 All E.R. 737

The plaintiff suffered a psychiatric illness caused by stress at work. Colman J. held that he was entitled to recover damages by reason of his employer's failure to provide him with a safe system of work.

The key to such cases is to be able to say that the defender has assumed responsibility to the pursuer. In *Walker* the fact of the employer–employee relationship demonstrated that such responsibility had been assumed. The case tells us that the employer's duty to take reasonable care for the health and safety of employees extends to protection against psychological harm it is surely unexceptional.

Returning to the case of *White*, it will be recalled that no duty was owed even though the victims were employees. The explanation for this is that the case was an imperilment one. The House of Lords decided that, in such cases, employees must satisfy the standard rules on primary and secondary victims. Lord Hoffmann took the stance that the modern control mechanisms which limit recovery for secondary victims "... were plainly never intended to apply to all cases of psychiatric injury. They contemplate that the injury has been caused in consequence of death or injury suffered (or apprehended to have been suffered or as likely to be suffered) by someone else." However, where these control mechanisms are applicable you are not in a better position in

[33] [1991] 4 All E.R. 907.
[34] *ibid.*

the eyes of the law of negligence by being injured in the course of your employment. Lord Hoffmann regards it as doubtful "whether the authorities have gone so far as to recognise duty to guard employees against psychiatric injury suffered as a result of injury to others ..." Where the harm arises in a different way then, on Lord Hoffmann's reasoning, there is nothing to prevent the employer's duty to the employee encompassing protection against psychological harm.

Key Concepts

A pursuer who alleges that a duty of care was owed to them in respect of psychiatric harm may well encounter difficulties. This type of harm is sometimes referred to as **nervous shock**.

A plaintiff may recover damages for "**nervous shock**" brought on by injury caused not to him- or herself but to a near relative, or by the fear of injury.

Even where the harm arises in a situation which does not involve imperilment, a duty of care may be owed to protect the pursuer from suffering **psychiatric harm**.

STANDARD OF CARE

9–10 If we assume that a duty was owed to the pursuer it must be stressed that recovery will only take place should that duty be breached. This is sometimes referred to as the standard of care question. A defender will be in breach of duty if they fall below the standards of the reasonable man. The reasonable man test was put forward in the famous case of:

Muir v Glasgow Corporation

[1943] A.C. 448

"The standard of foresight of the reasonable man is, in one sense, an impersonal test. It eliminates the personal equation and is independent of the idiosyncrasies of the particular person whose conduct is in question. Some persons are by nature unduly timorous and imagine every path beset with lions. Others, of more robust temperament, fail to foresee or nonchalantly disregard even the most obvious dangers. The reasonable man is presumed to be free both from over-apprehension and from over-confidence, but there is a sense in which the standard of care of the reasonable man involves in its application a subjective element. It is still left to the judge to decide what, in the circumstances of the particular case, the reasonable man would have had in contemplation, and what, accordingly, the party sought to be made liable ought to have foreseen."[35]

The test is an objective one. It is irrelevant that the defender could not have done any better if the reasonable man could have done. What is the reasonable man expected to do? He should not take unreasonable risks:

> "Whether the act or omission in question is one which a reasonable person would recognise as posing an unreasonable risk must be determined by balancing the magnitude of the risk, in the light of the likelihood of an accident happening and the possible seriousness of its consequences, against the difficulty, expense or any other disadvantage of desisting from the venture or taking a particular precaution."[36]

---

[35] [1943] A.C. 448 at 457.
[36] Fleming, *Law of Torts* (9th ed.), p.127.

Much depends on what the defender knew, or should have known, and hence should have foreseen. Thus, in *Walker* the employer was liable in respect of the second nervous breakdown but not the first. Prior to the first breakdown there was nothing to alert the employer to the employee's vulnerability; the very fact of the first nervous breakdown altered what the employer was expected to know.

Key Concepts

If we assume that a duty is owed to the pursuer, recovery will only take place should that duty be breached. This is sometimes referred to as the **standard of care question**.

A defender will be in breach of duty if they fall below the standards of the **reasonable man**.

CAUSATION

Even where the defender has breached a duty of care he will only be liable if the breach has been **9–11**
the cause of the pursuer's loss. The test deployed is the "but for" test. The defender is only responsible if the harm would not have arisen *but for* his careless behaviour. This is illustrated by:

Barnett v Chelsea & Kensington Hospital Management Committee

[1969] 1 Q.B. 429

At a hospital casualty department, three fellow night-watchmen presented themselves, complaining to a nurse on duty that they had been vomiting for three hours after drinking tea. The nurse reported their complaints by telephone to the duty medical casualty officer, who thereupon instructed her to tell the men to go home to bed and call in their own doctors. That she did. The men then left, and, about five hours later, one of them died from poisoning by arsenic which had been introduced into the tea; he might have died from the poisoning even if he had been admitted to the hospital wards and treated with all care five hours before his death. It was held that since he must have died of the poisoning even if he had been admitted to the wards five hours before his death and treated with all care, the plaintiff had failed to establish on the balance of probabilities that the defendants' negligence had caused the death; and that, therefore, the claim failed.

Key Concepts

Even where the defender has breached a duty of care he will only be liable if the breach has been the cause of the pursuer's loss.

The defender is only responsible if the harm would not have arisen **but for** his careless behaviour.

Quick Quiz

Delict

- Which three elements are essential for a successful negligence action?
- In addition to the foreseeability of damages, which other ingredients are necessary to give rise to a duty of care?
- When is pure economic loss incurred?
- What were the facts of the *Gibson v Chief Constable of Strathclyde* case?
- Could a rescuer ever be a primary victim?
- What is the reasonable man test?
- What is the test deployed in establishing causation?

Further Reading

Books

For broader, more in-depth coverage see the relevant chapters of ***The Laws of Scotland: Stair Memorial Encyclopaedia*** (Butterworths, 1996), Vol. 15, **W.J. Stewart, *Delict*** (3rd ed., W.Green, 1998), and **Thomson, *Delictual Liability*** (2nd ed., Butterworths, 1999). See also **W.J. Stewart, *A Casebook on Delict*** (2nd ed., W.Green, 1997), and for an easy to use study and revision guide of the law of delict see **Cameron, *Delict LawBasics*** (W.Green, 2002).

Internet sources

For full cases and details of new articles see:

- Westlaw UK: *www.westlaw.co.uk*

Chapter 10

PROPERTY

David Brand[1]

INTRODUCTION

Property is a large topic in Scots law, as in all legal systems. It covers rights and obligations in relation to land, moveable items and intangible items such as intellectual property. The right of peaceful enjoyment of property subject to certain controls in the public interest is recognised in human rights legislation.[2] This Chapter provides a general overview of Scottish property law. It does not cover in any detail the transmission of property rights which is the subject of conveyancing. **10–01**

The two main sources of Scottish property law are Roman law and feudal law. Roman law remains the foundation of much of the modern law, particularly the law on moveable property. The influence of feudal law has waned over the centuries and the remaining feudal remnants are about to be finally abolished. Scottish property law is substantially different from English property law.

When the Scottish Parliament was established after devolution, the first Scottish Executive chose land law reform and the abolition of the feudal system in particular, as one of its key reforms to symbolise a new, modern Scotland. Accordingly, an extensive programme of land reform legislation is currently in progress. At the time of writing, certain statutes have been

---

[1] Senior Lecturer in Law, University of Dundee.

[2] European Convention on Human Rights, Protocol 1, Art.1.

enacted,[3] other Bills have just completed their progress through the Scottish Parliament[4] and future legislation is intended. Scottish land law will change substantially over the next few years.

GENERAL CONCEPTS

Property and ownership

10–02 The term "property" can be used to mean two different things. It can be used to signify the right of ownership of something or it can be used to mean the actual thing which is owned. Property in the first sense is equivalent to ownership. Property in the first sense was known as *dominium* in Roman Law. Property in the second sense of the thing owned was known as a *res*[5] in Roman Law. In other words, property can signify the right of ownership itself or the thing which is subject to the right of ownership.

Property rights can exist in property a person owns and can also exist in a property owned by another. The former are known as *iura in re propria* and the latter as *iura in re aliena.* Examples of the latter include:

- rights of tenants in leased property
- rights of a creditor where the property has been used as a security
- servitude rights such as a right of way over a neighbour's property
- the rights of beneficiaries under a trust.

It is possible, therefore, for more than one property right to exist in a thing. Someone will own the thing but others may have a property right different from ownership in that thing.

The classic definition of property in the sense of ownership in Scots law is "the right of using and disposing of a subject as our own, except in so far as we are restrained by law or paction (*i.e.* agreement)".[6] The first part of this definition states what most people understand as property. The subject or thing is owned by a person to do with as they please. The second part qualifies this by making it clear that this right is not absolute. The law imposes restrictions on the exercise of the right of ownership and the owner may agree to restrict the right. For instance, an owner cannot use the subject in a way which causes a nuisance to neighbours or for a purpose which requires planning permission. These are restrictions on absolute ownership which the common law or specific statutes impose on an owner. In addition, an owner may agree to a restriction on the absolute use of the subject, for instance by granting a neighbour a servitude right of access over the subject.[7]

Classification of property

10–03 Property can be classified in various ways:

- heritable and moveable
- corporeal and incorporeal
- fungible and non-fungible.

Classification is important because various property rules relating to transfer, rights in security and succession depend on how a property is classified. There are different rules on these matters for different types of property.

---

[3] Notably the Abolition of Feudal Tenure etc. (Scotland) Act 2000 although most of the provisions will not come into force until November 28, 2004.

[4] Title Conditions (Scotland) Act 2003, Land Reform (Scotland) Act 2003, Agricultural Holdings (Scotland) Act 2003.

[5] *Res* is the source of the word real used in real rights and real property.

[6] Erskine II, ii, 1.

[7] Restrictions on landownership, below.

Heritable and moveable[8]

The most important classification is whether a property is heritable or moveable. Most heritable property is classified as heritable because of its nature and broadly covers land and buildings or anything attached to the land. Rights connected with land and buildings, such as servitudes and leases, are also heritable. All other property is moveable, which is by its nature capable of being moved, such as furniture and cars. Rights connected with moveables such as a right to sue under contract or delict are also moveable rights. **10–04**

This classification of property into heritable or moveable derives from the old law of intestate succession in Scots law which had different rules on who would succeed to the property of a deceased where there was no will. Under the principle of *primogeniture* the land, *i.e.* heritable property went to the heir-at-law who was the eldest son. This was abolished by the Succession (Scotland) Act 1964, although the distinction between heritable and moveable property is still important in relation to legal rights.[9]

Some types of property are clearly heritable or moveable. Land and buildings are obviously heritable, as are trees. When trees are cut down as timber, the timber is clearly moveable. Cows grazing in a field are obviously moveable. The grass on which the cows are grazing is growing out of the ground and is acceding to, or attached to, the soil. Natural fruits of the land which require no constant cultivation including grass are regarded as heritable by nature and remain so until severed from the land.[10] An exception to this rule is made of industrial growing crops which are classified as moveable although physically growing from the soil and acceding to the land. These crops, such as barley, wheat, and potatoes require cultivation and are classified as moveable.[11]

This principle of property where something growing accedes to where it is growing is known as accession by fruits. The principle also applies to growing in moveables and young unborn animals accede to their mothers.[12]

This classification is not completely straightforward, however, as property may become heritable, not by its nature but by accession or by destination. Accession is where moveable property converts to heritable property by attachment to the land. Destination is where certain moveable property is treated as heritable in cases of succession.

Accession will occur in such circumstances as where a substantial summerhouse is erected on land and becomes part of that land[13] or where a fireplace is built into a room in a building on land. What was originally moveable converts to heritable under the principle of accession. The question of whether a moveable item has converted to become a heritable item can be a difficult one and is a problem area in the sale and purchase of houses and other properties. It is generally known as the law of fixtures and is discussed more fully below.

In succession, there is the possibility that certain moveable property may be classified as heritable by destination. This means that certain moveable items are regarded as heritable because that was the implied intention of the deceased. This has limited operation. In one case[14] a person died during the construction of a building and the materials to be used in the construction were regarded as heritable for the purpose of succession to the deceased's estate.

Corporeal and incorporeal

Property is corporeal if it is tangible and can be seen or touched such as furniture or jewellery. **10–05**
Incorporeal property is intangible such as shares in a company or an insurance policy. A share certificate or insurance policy document is tangible and corporeal but the right itself is intangible

[8] In England the terms are real and personal property which are almost synonymous with heritable and moveable property.
[9] See Chapter 12.
[10] Erskine II, ii, 3.
[11] Erskine II, ii, 4.
[12] *Lamb v Grant* (1874) 11 S.L.R. 672.
[13] *Christie v Smith's Exr.*, 1949 S.C. 572.
[14] *Malloch v McLean* (1867) 5 M. 335.

and incorporeal. These examples are moveable but both heritable and moveable property can be either corporeal or incorporeal. Land is corporeal heritable property and rights relating to land such as a lease or a servitude are incorporeal heritable property.

Fungible and non-fungible

10–06 A fungible property is property which disappears when used but can be replaced by a similar property, such as milk or money. A non-fungible property is one which cannot be replaced readily and has an inherent value such as a work of art. In other words, fungible property is non-specific whereas is non-fungible is specific.

Ownership and possession

10–07 Possession is an important concept in both heritable and moveable property. One of the incidents of unrestricted ownership is the right to exclusive possession and the ability to prevent others from interfering with it. An owner of land is entitled to be free from persons trespassing or encroaching on the land.[15] In the law of heritable property the operation of prescription, whereby land held on a good title for the appropriate period of time, usually 10 years, is free from challenge by anyone claiming title to that land, is fundamental.[16] Possession is also important in moveable property. There is a presumption that the possessor of goods is the owner, in the absence of evidence to the contrary.[17] This gives some weight to the popular phrase, "possession is nine tenths of the law". Possession can be either natural or civil.[18] Natural possession is where the possessor actually occupies the land or retains the goods personally. Civil is where the possession is by another on behalf of the owner. For instance, if a person owns a house and actually lives there this is natural possession by the owner but if the owner leases the house to a tenant and the tenant lives there this is civil possession by the tenant.

What constitutes possession itself may not be straightforward. The classic definition states "there must be an act of the body which is the detention and holding; and an act of the mind which is the inclination or affection to make use of the thing obtained".[19] This means that there are two elements which are an act of body, which means there must be a physical element of actual retention and holding the property and an act of mind, which means the mental intention to possess property for oneself.[20] It is possible to have one element without the other. A person can have actual physical retention of the property without intending to keep it as his or her own. The property may be held on behalf of someone else such as a friend or employer and in this case there is no legal possession, only custody. It is also possible to have possession of a property without a legal right, as where a thief is in possession of stolen goods intending to keep them and satisfies both elements of possession.

Real rights and personal rights

10–08 There is an important fundamental distinction in property rights between real rights and personal rights. A real right is enforceable against anyone at all whereas a personal right is enforceable only against a particular person or persons. Personal rights are created by an agreement or contract between parties. Many types of personal rights and corresponding obligations can arise from the contract. These will be enforceable by the parties to the contract against each other but not against

---

[15] See Incidents of landownership, below.
[16] See Prescription, below.
[17] Stair II, i, 42, *Prangnell-O'Neill v Skiffington*, 1984 S.L.T. 282.
[18] Erskine Inst. II, ii, 22.
[19] Stair II, i, 17.
[20] This concept is known as *animus possidendi*.

third parties. A real right is enforceable against third parties. To take the example of a sale of a house, when houses are sold and transferred to the seller, the first stage is usually the missives. These are letters which constitute the contract for the sale and purchase of the house. When the missives are completed there are several steps required before the house transfers to the seller and the seller becomes the owner but there is a completed enforceable contract. At this stage, the purchaser remains the owner. The seller could sell to someone else and transfer ownership to that person. The purchaser would then have to sue the seller for breach of contract. This would be on the basis of the personal right under the missives. Once all the steps to transfer ownership have been completed, and the document transferring the title to the purchaser has been registered in the appropriate Register, the purchaser becomes the new owner and obtains a real right to defend that right of ownership against anyone.

Real rights are created in different ways for different types of property. Normally this involves two stages. The first stage will be an agreement or contract between the parties. In the case of the house as heritable property this is the missives stage when the contract for the sale and purchase is concluded. This gives rise to a personal right only. The next stage is a public act by registering the document of transfer of title in the appropriate public property register, either the General Register of Sasines or the Land Register. This second stage of recording in the public property register creates the real right.[21]

There is normally a two stage process with moveable property also. In the transfer of corporeal moveables the first stage is the agreement or contract between the parties and the second stage which creates the real right is the delivery of the moveables.[22]

Co-ownership

Both heritable and moveable property can be owned by more than one person. There is a distinction between: **10–09**

- joint property
- common property
- common interest.

Joint property

This is where two or more persons own a property as an individual whole. This is known as *pro indiviso* or undivided ownership and the property is said to vest in the owners *pro indiviso*. The joint owner cannot dispose of the right during lifetime or on death by a will and when the ownership is surrendered or the person dies, that right of ownership accresces, or is added to, the other joint owner or owners. Examples of this type of ownership include an unincorporated association such as a club where the members of the club own the club's property jointly and a club member will be a joint owner but will cease to be so on ceasing to be a member, or trust property where the trustees own trust property jointly.[23] **10–10**

Common property

Common property is much more widespread than joint property. This is where two or more persons own a property and each owner has an individual share of the property. This can be disposed of during the co-owner's lifetime or under a will or according to the rules of intestate **10–11**

[21] See Registration, below.
[22] See Corporeal moveable property, below.
[23] See Chapter 12.

succession on death.[24] A co-owner can also divide their share or grant a security over it. If a co-owner wishes to dispose of their share and the other co-owner or co-owners refuse, it is open to apply to the court under an action of division and sale to have the court order the whole property sold and the proceeds divided amongst the co-owners.[25]

The usual example of co-ownership is a husband and wife owning their home as common property. It is usually said that their title is in joint names but this does not mean that the property is joint property. If one spouse wished to sell and the other does not there are protection provisions in actions of sale and division.[26]

The general rule for management of common property is that all co-owners must consent to the management of the property. This includes any alterations, improvements or repairs to the property.[27] Accordingly, one co-owner can veto the proposals of all the others. In the case of essential repairs, it is possible for one co-owner to instruct these and recover the appropriate share of the cost from the other co-owners.[28]

Common interest

10–12 Common interest is a right which an owner of property has in respect of property owned by another by implication of law. This right acts as a restriction on what the owner of the property can do with the property as certain actions may affect the property of the other person. In a tenement building, in the absence of provision in the title deeds, a ground floor flat owner will own the section of the external gable wall enclosing the flat.[29] An upper-floor flat owner will have a right of common interest in that section of the gable wall as the wall supports the upper flat. The ground- floor flat owner cannot do anything which adversely affects the right of common interest of support such as putting in a new window which destabilises the gable wall.

Common interest occurs mainly in the law of tenement which is discussed below but can occur in other situations as where owners of a river have a common interest in the water of the river.[30]

Liferents

10–13 A liferent is a special type of property right. It is the right to the use of or income from a property during the lifetime of the person who has the right, known as the liferenter, or some other period set out in the deed constituting the liferent. It applies to both heritable and moveable property. The liferenter is not entitled to the capital of the property, known as the fee, which belongs to the person known as the fiar. The fiar is the owner of the property but will not have complete ownership of the property until the liferent comes to an end. During the liferent, the liferenter must not do anything to the detriment of the capital of the liferented subjects. Liferents are classed as either proper or improper liferents and alimentary liferents are an important type of improper liferent. Liferents are covered in more detail in the Chapter on Trusts.

---

[24] Unless there is a survivorship destination—see Chapter 12.
[25] *Upper Crathes Fishings Ltd v Bailey's Exrs.*, 1991 S.L.T. 747.
[26] Matrimonial Homes (Family Protection) (Scotland) Act 1981, s.19.
[27] *Rafique v Amin*, 1997 S.L.T. 1385.
[28] *Deans v Woolfson*, 1922 S.C. 221.
[29] See Law of the tenement, below.
[30] See Water rights, below.

Key Concepts

"**Property**" can be used to mean two different things. It can be used to signify the right of ownership of something or it can be used to mean the actual thing which is owned.

Property can be **classified** in various ways:

- heritable and moveable
- corporeal and incorporeal
- fungible and non-fungible.

Most **heritable** property is classified as heritable because of its nature and broadly covers land and buildings or anything attached to the land. All other property is **moveable**, which is by its nature capable of being moved.

Corporeal property is tangible and can be seen or touched. **Incorporeal** property is intangible.

Fungible property is non-specific. It can be replaced by similar property. **Non-fungible** property is specific. It cannot readily be replaced and has an inherent value.

The right to exclusive **possession** is an incident of unrestricted ownership. In heritable property, prescription, whereby land is held on a good title for a certain period, is fundamental. In moveable property there is a presumption that the possessor of goods is the owner.

A **real right** is enforceable against anyone at all whereas a **personal right** is enforceable only against a particular person or persons.

In **co-ownership** there is an important distinction between:

- joint property
- common property
- common interest.

CORPOREAL MOVEABLE PROPERTY

Acquisition

Corporeal moveable property can be acquired independent of the ownership of another person. This is known as original acquisition. In this case the property right of ownership comes into being without reference to the previous owner or may not have been previously owned at all. Where acquisition is by transfer from one owner to a new owner this is known as derivative acquisition. **10–14**

Original acquisition can be divided into four categories:

- occupation
- accession
- specification
- confusion and commixtion.

Occupation

10–15 Moveable property which has never been owned by anyone becomes the property of the person who acquires it with the intention of becoming the owner.[31] Such property is known as *res nullius*. The most obvious example of such property is wild animals or birds or fish which can be acquired by the first person to take possession or control of them. Certain wild creatures cannot be acquired in this way, such as salmon and royal birds which belong to the Crown or protected species, such as ospreys or badgers.[32]

Once such property is in the control of a person, that person remains the owner and the property cannot be legally removed. In the case of wild creatures, however, if the creature escapes then it returns to its wild ownerless state. Domestic animals and creatures with a homing instinct such as bees and pigeons cannot be acquired by occupation.[33]

Similarly, property which has been owned by someone cannot be acquired by occupation. Ownership will remain with that person even if that owner has lost possession. Lost or abandoned property cannot be acquired by occupation. If the owner of lost property retains the intention of keeping the property, ownership will be retained. If property is abandoned or long lost with the owner resigned to the loss, the property belongs to the Crown as part of the royal prerogative.[34] This includes treasure trove which does not belong to the finder.[35] The finder of lost or abandoned property is under a statutory duty to take reasonable care of the property and report the finding or deliver the property to the police within a reasonable time of finding.[36] The Chief Constable has a discretion to give the property to the finder.[37]

Lord Advocate v University of Aberdeen

1963 S.C. 533

A team of students from Aberdeen University were on a field trip to St Ninian's Isle in Shetland and discovered eighth century treasure hidden underground. The University appropriated the treasure and took it to its museum in Aberdeen. The Lord Advocate on behalf of the Crown sued for delivery of the treasure. The University argued that the treasure was governed by udal law, which is a relict of the time when Shetland and Orkney belonged to Norway and part of which law still applies in Shetland and Orkney. Under udal law the finder of treasure would keep part of it. The Inner Division of the Court of Session held that Scots law applied, not udal law, and the Crown owned the treasure.

Accession

10–16 Accession is more common where moveable property accedes to heritable property and converts from being moveable to being heritable by attachment.[38] However, it is possible for there to be accession of moveables to moveables. This can occur naturally as when animals have offspring. The owner of the animal becomes the owner of the offspring.[39] It can also take place with incorporeal moveable property, as when interest accumulates on a bank account. The owner of the bank account is entitled to the interest on the account.

---

[31] Stair II, i.33. Stair refers to the Roman Law principle *quod nullius est, fit primi occupantis*.
[32] Wildlife and Countryside Act 1981; Badgers (Protection) Act 1992.
[33] Stair II.i.33.
[34] Erskine Inst.II.i,12.
[35] *Lord Advocate v University of Aberdeen*, 1963 S.C. 533, the "St Ninian's Isle Treasure Case".
[36] Civic Government (Scotland) Act 1982, Pt VI.
[37] s.70(i)(b).
[38] See Fixtures, below.
[39] *Lamb v Grant* (1874) 11 S.L.R. 672.

Specification

Specification concerns property which is newly created from component materials and cannot revert back to its original components. When grapes are made into wine or corn into flour it is not possible to turn the wine back into grapes or the flour back to corn. When such a new entity is created, the person who creates the new entity will become the owner of the new entity provided the creator has acted in good faith. This applies whether or not the creator provided the component materials.[40] **10–17**

It is essential that a new entity comes into existence and the component parts cannot be separated back to their original state.[41] If they can, the component parts will belong to their original owners. In one case, where the front part of one car and the rear part of another had been welded together, it was held that specification could not take place because the two parts could be separated again.[42] It is also essential that the creator acted in good faith because the doctrine is an equitable one.[43]

The owner or owners of the original component materials may be entitled to compensation for the cost of the materials.[44]

International Banking Corporation v Ferguson, Shaw & Sons
1910 S.C. 182

A company bought oil in good faith from another company who had no right to sell as it belonged to a different company. The purchasing company paid for and received the oil and manufactured lard which the company sold. The true owners succeeded in an action to recover the cost of the oil.

Confusion and commixtion

Confusion and commixtion occur when materials of the same kind are mixed together. Confusion applies to liquids and commixtion to solids. If the constituent liquids or solids are not the same and a new liquid or solid is created which cannot be separated, the principle of specification will apply. Where the constituents are of the same kind, the liquid or solid is owned in common in shares corresponding to the amount and value of the contribution to the whole.[45] **10–18**

Derivative acquisition or transfer

Derivative acquisition is transfer of ownership to a new owner from an existing owner. Corporeal moveable property can be transferred in various situations such as gift, exchange, sale or loan. The rules on security for a loan are examined later.[46] There are two basic essentials for derivative acquisition to operate—intention and delivery. Erskine states: **10–19**

> "Two things are … required to the conveyance in this matter: First, the intention or consent of the former owner to transfer it upon some just or proper title of alienation, as sole gift, exchange, etc: Secondly, the actual delivery of it, in pursuance of that intention."[47]

---

[40] Stair, Inst.II, i,41.
[41] *North-West Securites Ltd v Barrhead Coachworks Ltd*, 1976 S.C. 68 *per* Lord McDonald at 72.
[42] *McDonald v Provan (of Scotland Street) Ltd*, 1960 S.L.T. 231.
[43] Bell Princ. 1298.
[44] *International Banking Corporation v Ferguson, Shaw & Sons*, 1910 S.C. 182.
[45] Stair, Inst. II, i.37.
[46] See Rights in security over moveable property, below.
[47] Erskine Inst. II, I, 18.

As previously noted,[48] the first stage of intention set out in an agreement only creates a personal right. The second stage of delivery is required to create a real right of ownership enforceable against the world.[49] It is generally not possible for someone other than the owner to transfer a good title to a property by mere delivery without the owner consenting to or intending to transfer the property.[50] Similarly, owners cannot transfer a more extensive right than their own.[51]

It is important to note here that in the field of sale of goods, these general rules have been modified by statute under the Sale of Goods Act 1979. It is also possible for a contract to provide that title is reserved to a seller notwithstanding delivery of goods to the purchaser until the price has been fully paid.

The intention to transfer will usually be set out in writing in a form of agreement. Delivery can be actual, constructive or symbolic. Actual delivery is where the property is physically handed over to the acquirer or the agent of the acquirer or physical control is handed over, for instance by means of a key.[52] Constructive delivery occurs when a third party is holding property on behalf of the original owner and is instructed by the original owner to hold the property on behalf of the acquirer.[53] Symbolic delivery occurs when the property or control of the property cannot be physically handed over and a symbol of this is handed over instead. The main example of this is a bill of lading which is a document of title to goods which are in transit by ship.[54]

Inglis v Robertson & Baxter

(1898) 25 R. (H.L.) 70

Goldsmith owned whisky in a bonded warehouse in Glasgow. The warehouse held this on behalf of him or his assignees and Goldsmith had a warrant to this effect. Goldsmith borrowed money from Inglis and endorsed and delivered the warrant to Inglis. This was not intimated to the warehouse keepers. In a dispute between Inglis and creditors of Goldsmith it was held that as there had been no intimation to the third party holding the whisky, the real right to the whisky remained with Goldsmith.

Key Concepts

Original acquisition is where ownership is acquired independent of the ownership of another. It can be divided into four categories:

- occupation
- accession
- specification
- confusion and commixtion.

Derivative acquisition is transfer of ownership to a new owner from an existing owner. The two basic essentials of derivative acquisition are intention and delivery.

48 See Real and personal rights, above.
49 Lord President Inglis in *Clark v West Calder Oil Co* (1882) 9 R. 1017 at 1024.
50 This principle is known as *nemo dat quod non habet*.
51 *The Scottish Widows Fund v Buist* (1876) 3 R. 1078 dealing with incorporeal moveable property.
52 *West Lothian Oil Co Ltd v Mair* (1892) 20 R. 64.
53 *Inglis v Robertson & Baxter* (1898) 25 R. (H.L.) 70.
54 *Hayman v McLintock*, 1907 S.C. 936.

INCORPOREAL MOVEABLE PROPERTY

Incorporeal moveable property is property which is the subject of commercial and mercantile law such as shares in a company or insurance policies and the creation of such property rights is governed by mercantile law. In addition, there are special laws in relation to rights arising from original and creative works in cultural, scientific or business areas, known as "intellectual property". **10–20**

As with corporeal moveable property the general rule is that there are two requirements for the transfer of incorporeal moveable property. Unlike corporeal moveable property, incorporeal moveable property is intangible and cannot be physically delivered to transfer ownership. The two requirements to transfer are assignation and intimation. Certain incorporeal moveable property cannot be transferred at all. Rights which are personal to a particular person, under the doctrine known as *delectus persona*, cannot be transferred, for instance a contract of employment.

An assignation is the transfer of ownership from the assignor to the assignee. Technically, an assignation need not be in writing[55] but, in practice, it usually is. Some types of assignation, for instance policies of assurance, need to have a certain form as laid down by statute.

Delivery of the assignation gives the assignee an effective personal right but the assignee will not obtain a real right against third parties unless there is intimation. There are various forms of intimation set out by statute[56] and various equivalents of intimation, for instance the debtor acknowledging the assignee's right.

The effect of assignation is that the assignee takes the place of the assigner and succeeds to all the rights and obligations of the assigner. The assignee will have no greater right than the assigner and if there is a defect in the rights of the assigner this defect will pass to the assignee.[57] There is one exception to this rule. If there is a latent trust of which the assigner is unaware and the assignee takes in good faith and for valuc, the assignee will not be affected by the latent trust.[58]

Intellectual property rights

Intellectual property rights are incorporeal moveable rights which relate to original and creative works in cultural, scientific or business areas. This is a complex and expanding area of law. The main types of intellectual property are: **10–21**

- patents
- copyright
- trade marks
- designs.

Patents give the creator of an invention a monopoly in respect of the manufacture and use of the invention. The main statutory provision is the Patents Act 1977.

Copyright can exist in certain types of literary, dramatic, musical or artistic work and covers visual, aural and written forms. Copyright gives an exclusive right to make copies and reproduce the work of the author. The main statutory provision is the Copyright, Designs and Patents Act 1988.

Trade marks are graphical signs which distinguish the goods or services of one undertaking from another. They enable the public to identify a particular business with the trade mark. Protection of trade marks is achieved by registration. The main statutory provision is the Trade Marks Act 1994.

---

[55] The Requirements of Writing (Scotland) Act 1995, s.11.
[56] Moveable Property (Scotland) Act 1862.
[57] *Scottish Widows' Fund v Buist* (1876) 3 R. 1078.
[58] *Redfearn v Somervail* (1830) 1 Dow 50.

Designs are similar to copyright and are shapes which can be either functional or aesthetic. Certain designs may be registered. The main statutory provision is the Copyright, Designs and Patents Act 1988.

Key Concepts

Incorporeal moveable property is property which is the subject of commercial and mercantile law, such as shares in a company or insurance policies.

Rights arising from original and creative works in cultural, scientific or business areas are known as **intellectual property** rights, and include:

- patents
- copyright
- trade marks
- designs.

RIGHTS IN SECURITY OVER MOVEABLE PROPERTY

10–22 One of the uses of property is to use it as security to obtain something else, usually a loan of money. Both heritable and moveable property can be used for this purpose. It is common place when a house is purchased for a bank or building society loan to be obtained to help finance the purchase and the house itself is used as a heritable security. Jewellery or other valuable moveable property can be taken to a pawn shop and handed over in exchange for a loan of money. In such cases the property acts as security for the debt and gives the holder, the creditor, a preferential right over an unsecured creditor in the secured property. In the event of the granter of the security, the debtor, becoming insolvent a secured creditor generally has a right to sell the secured property and be paid before the unsecured creditors.

If properly constituted, the right is a real right in security enforceable against the world.[59] A right in security is only an accessory right to secure the performance of an obligation, usually repayment of a loan, and once the obligation has been performed the creditor must return the secured property to the debtor or grant an appropriate discharge. The right in security is redeemable and must be redeemed on performance of the obligation.

Rights in security can arise by agreement or by operation of law. Some rights are governed by common law and some by statute. There are different rules for the constitution of rights in security over different types of property. Generally, security rights over moveable property require delivery.[60]

Securities over corporeal moveable property

10–23 Securities over corporeal moveable property which require delivery can arise by agreement known as pledge or by operation of law known as liens. Securities which do not require delivery are hypothecs and floating charges.

[59] Contrast cautionary obligations.

[60] The Roman maxim *traditionibus non nudis pactis dominium rerum transferuntur* applies.

Pledge

A pledge is a simple contractual form of security. The owner of the corporeal moveables, the pledger, agrees with the lender, the pledgee, usually to borrow a sum of money. In exchange for the money the pledger deliveries the property to the pledgee. On repayment of the debt the pledgee is bound to return the property to the pledger. Pawnbroking is a good example of a pledge although there are special rules for pawnbroking under the Consumer Credit Act 1974.[61] **10–24**

Delivery is an essential element in pledge. Delivery may be actual, constructive or symbolic.[62]

Liens

A lien is a security right which arises by operation of law and results from the creditor being in possession of the property belonging to the debtor. A lien can be special or general. A special lien is the right of a creditor to retain a specific item of property until the debt incurred in relation to that property has been repaid. This will often occur when something is handed over for repair. Until the repair bill is paid the item will not be handed back and the special lien exercised. **10–25**

A general lien is the right of a creditor to retain property of the debtor in possession of the lender until all the general debts due by the debtor have been settled, whether relating to that property or not. These liens relate to particular trades and four are generally recognised. A factor has a general lien over all goods, bills, money or documents of the principal which have come into the factor's possession during the employment of the factor.[63] This includes advances made to the principal, salary and commission and any liabilities incurred on behalf of the principal.[64] The banker has a general lien over all negotiable instruments belonging to customers which have come into possession of the bank in business transactions as opposed to mere deposit.[65] An innkeeper has a general lien over luggage of a guest for the amount of the hotel bill.[66] Certain items, such as clothes, are excluded.[67] A solicitor has a general lien over all papers belonging to a client, including title deeds, wills and share certificates, for unpaid bills and expenses made in the ordinary course of business.[68]

Hypothecs

Hypothecs give a creditor a right in security without delivery to the creditor in certain situations. The hypothec may be conventional or legal. A conventional hypothec arises by agreement. They are rare and are confined to maritime law.[69] A legal hypothec arises by operation of law. There are certain maritime hypothecs which give a right in security over a ship, including a right to seamen in respect of unpaid wages and the master in respect of properly incurred wages.[70] A solicitor has a hypothec over costs or property recovered in a court action for expenses incurred in the court action.[71] A landlord has a hypothec over certain property of a tenant for rent.[72] **10–26**

---

61 ss.114–122.

62 See Derivative acquisition or transfer, above.

63 Bell Princ. 456.

64 *Glendinning v Hope*, 1911 S.C. (H.L.) 73.

65 Bell Princ. 1451.

66 Bell Princ.1428.

67 *Sunbolf v Alford* (1838) 2 M. & W. 248.

68 Bell Princ. 1438.

69 Bell Princ. 456.

70 Merchant Shipping Act 1995, ss.39 and 40.

71 Solicitors (Scotland) Act 1980, s.62.

72 See Leases, below.

Floating charges

10–27 Floating charges were introduced in Scotland in 1961[73] and can be created over heritable or moveable property.[74] They can only be used by companies. The charge does not attach to a company's assets until an event such as the winding-up of the company causes the charge to crystallise and attach to all the assets of the company.

Securities over incorporeal moveable property

10–28 The rules for creation of a security over incorporeal moveables which cannot be delivered follow those for transfer of incorporeal moveables and require assignation in security and intimation. In relation to company shares a valid right in security requires a share transfer form and registration of this form with the company, subject to the right to transfer back to the debtor when the debt is repaid.

> **Key Concepts**
>
> A **right in security** is only an accessory right to secure the performance of an obligation; once the obligation has been performed, the creditor must return the secured property to the debtor or grant an appropriate **discharge**.
>
> Securities over corporeal moveable property which require delivery can arise by agreement known as **pledge** (a simple contractual form of security) or by operation of law known as **liens** (special or general). Securities which do not require delivery are **hypothecs** (conventional or legal) and **floating charges** (in the case of companies).

LANDOWNERSHIP

Historical background

10–29 The two key features of landownership in Scotland throughout the centuries have been the feudal system and registration in a public land register. The feudal system in Scotland dates back to the twelfth century and a public land register was first introduced in 1617.[75] Registration is discussed in the next section. As noted in the introduction to this Chapter, abolition of the feudal system was chosen as a symbolic major reform by the first Scottish Executive following devolution in 1999 and was welcomed by the new Scottish Parliament without opposition. At the time of writing, the Abolition of Feudal Tenure etc. (Scotland) Act 2000 is not yet fully in force but the days of the feudal system are numbered.[76]

Feudalism was introduced into Scotland as a social, political and economic system.[77] The fundamental principle of feudalism is that all land derives from the Crown as ultimate feudal superior. Originally, the King granted land to his nobles in the return for services to the King. These services were originally military service in the far off days of constant warfare. Land was

---

[73] Under the Companies (Floating Charges) (Scotland) Act 1961.
[74] For heritable property, see below.
[75] Registration Act 1617.
[76] The appointed day for the main provisions to be introduced is November 28, 2004.
[77] See generally Reid, *The Law of Property in Scotland* (1996), paras 41–113 (written by Professor G. Gretton); Gordon, *Scottish Land Law* (1999), Chaps 2 and 3.

not granted to the nobles outright but was feued or transferred to them on a tenure, a type of holding of land, in return for the services, known as a *reddendo*. The nobles in turn were able to grant land to lesser mortals who actually worked on the land by subfeuing the land to them, again on a tenure in return for a *reddendo*, which might be agricultural services. The person who granted or feued the land was known as the superior and the person who received the land was known as the vassal.

The superior retained a right of ownership in the land as it was not granted outright and this right enabled the superior to claim and receive the *reddendo*. This right of ownership is known as *dominium directum*. The right of ownership of the vassal who received the land to use but without outright ownership is known as *dominium utile*. This meant that every time there was a grant of land and land was feued, or more correctly subfeued, there was a new link in a chain of ownership stretching back to the Crown as ultimate feudal superior. This ultimate ownership of the Crown is known as *dominium eminens*. Therefore, from the Crown down to the person actually occupying and using the land was a feudal chain of ownership with a person being at the same time the vassal of the superior who had subfeued to them, and the superior of the vassal to whom they, in turn, had subfeued.

Originally, under the feudal system there were different types of tenure and *reddendo* but by the twentieth century there was virtually only one type of tenure, feu farm, and *reddendo*, feu duty or payment of money. Over the centuries substantial reform has taken place. The feudal system which is about to be abolished is very different from the original one and many of the features of feudalism have long since gone. In particular, since the mid-eighteenth century it has been possible to transfer land not by subfeuing but by substitution without the consent of the superior.[78] This is where a vassal transfers land, not by subfeuing whereby the vassal will become the superior of the vassal who is granted the land, but instead by stepping out of the feudal chain with the person granted the land becoming the new vassal of the original vassal's superior. Thus, instead of creating an additional new link in the feudal chain, the link is replaced by a substitute link.

Two further features of the feudal system were that it was commonplace for a superior to insert feuing conditions, usually known as real burdens, in the title of the vassal when granting the land. These related to such matters as restrictions on the use that vassals could make of the land to protect the amenity of the neighbouring land.[79] If such conditions were properly constituted, a superior would retain the right to enforce these conditions against the vassal. This could be done on the basis of simply being the superior even if the superior had no other connection with the land. To back up enforcement, it was usual to insert in the title of a vassal a right of irritancy which gave the ultimate power to a superior to take back the land if the vassal failed to observe the feuing conditions.

A major reform of the feudal system took place when the Land Tenure Reform (Scotland) Act 1974 abolished the right to create new feuduties.[80] The Act also introduced provisions for most feuduties to be redeemed, or paid off automatically, when land was sold and for vassals to voluntarily redeem their feuduty.[81] Both these cases involved the vassal making a one off capital payment to the superior.[82] Since 1974, the number of feuduties in existence rapidly diminished and it was estimated prior to the 2000 Act that less than ten per cent of land in Scotland was subject to payment of feuduty.[83]

Under the Abolition of Feudal Tenure etc. (Scotland) Act 2000, when the appointed day which will trigger the abolition provisions arrives, the feudal system will be abolished.[84] All superiorities will be abolished and *dominium utile* will become full *dominium* or outright ownership.[85] All feuduties will be extinguished[86] and there are provisions for payment of compensation to superiors,

---

78 Tenures Abolition Act 1746.
79 See Restrictions on landownership, below.
80 1974 Act, s.1.
81 ss.4–6.
82 This was under a complicated formula linked to the value of certain British Government stock. See s.5(4).
83 Scottish Law Commission Report on Abolition of the Feudal System, No.168, 1999, 3.7.
84 2000 Act, s.1.
85 2000 Act, s.2.
86 s.7.

which must be claimed and is not paid automatically.[87] Other provisions in the Act deal with a former superior's rights to enforce feuing conditions and are examined in the section on Restrictions on landownership, below. Irritancies have already been abolished and certain other provisions of the Act are also already in force.[88]

> **Key Concepts**
>
> The two key features of landownership are the **feudal system** and **registration** in a public land register.
>
> The feudal system is about to be finally abolished by the Abolition of Feudal Tenure etc. (Scotland) Act 2000. There are two public land registers in Scotland. The Register of Sasines dates back to 1617 and the new Land Register was introduced in 1979.

Registration

10–30 The key feature of landownership in Scotland along with the feudal system has been the need for registration in a public property register to complete a good title to land. Since 1617, a system of registration has existed in Scotland and the registration of a title to land has been necessary to complete a real right in the land. Most rights in land whether they be outright ownership of land or a more restrictive property right such as a right in security require the title to such right to be in writing and the title deed to be registered.[89] The Register of Sasines[90] was introduced in 1617[91] and was the basis of the system of land registration in Scotland for well over 300 years. Although the system was not perfect it did work remarkably well. By the latter half of the twentieth century, however, it was felt that the system was becoming outmoded and a new system of land registration was introduced in 1979 with a new register, the Land Register. Over a long period of time all land in Scotland will be registered in the Land Register with the advantages that register brings.

The system of registration introduced in 1617 with the Register of Sasines is a system in which the register is a register of deeds only, not a register of title. The title to land does not flow from the register itself but from the deed. The deed acts as a public notice that the person has registered a particular title deed but if that title deed is faulty the register does not cure the defect. In contrast, the Land Register is a register of title where the title flows from the register itself and the Land Register does guarantee title. Once a title deed has been registered in the Land Register and the Keeper of the Register issues a land certificate, the land certificate is a guarantee that the holder has title to the land and this is backed up with a state guarantee so that the holder will be indemnified against any adverse action against the title.

On the face of it, the Register of Sasines was seen to be a poor system of registration as a person cannot get a title which is free from challenge after registration. The system is fortified, however, by the operation of positive prescription. This is examined in the next section. The basic principle is that if a person has a title to land which is not obviously defective and possesses the land for the appropriate prescriptive period, then the title becomes free from challenge. This system of registration in the Register of Sasines plus the operation of positive prescription lasted until the introduction of the Land Register in 1979. As it will be many years before the new system of land registration applies to all land in Scotland it is the way certain land in Scotland is still held.

---

[87] s.8.

[88] s.53.

[89] On the requirements of writing in deeds relating to interests in land see generally the Requirements of Writing (Scotland) Act 1995.

[90] Sasine means the act of giving and taking possession of land.

[91] The Registration Act 1617.

One other drawback to the system of registration in the Register of Sasines, apart from the lack of a guarantee of title, is inadequate description of the land in the register. There are various formal requirements for a title deed before it will be accepted in the Register of Sasines. These include the need for a description of the subjects. Many sasine title deeds do not contain plans of the subjects.[92] Those that do are often inaccurate. The subjects are also described in words in the deed. These words are all too often vague or ambiguous. For instance, it maybe impossible to tell where the physical boundaries are. The operation of positive prescription may help[93] but all too often the position is unsatisfactory. The requirement for an accurate plan of the subjects would be a distinct improvement. This was one of the reasons for introducing a new system of land registration in 1979.

The Land Registration (Scotland) Act 1979 introduced a new system of land registration which will be gradually extended throughout Scotland. Land in Scotland was divided into operational areas[94] and the provisions in the Act were introduced to these areas between 1979 and 2003.[95] However, land is only registered in the new Land Register on a sale, not for instance where it is gifted or subject to a security, and it will be some time in the future before all land in Scotland is registered in the Land Register.

When land is first registered in the Land Register, the Keeper examines the title deeds to be satisfied that the person registering the title is the owner of the specified land. Once satisfied, the title is registered and a land certificate is issued which will have a plan attached. This will be an ordinance survey plan and will accurately delineate the boundaries of the land.

The certificate has four sections:

- property section, detailing the property and referring to the plan
- proprietorship section, stating who the owner is
- charges section, detailing any securities over the property
- burdens section, setting out the burdens which affect the property.

The effect of registration of title is that the title is guaranteed and indemnity will be paid if a subsequent problem arises with the title.[96] If the Keeper anticipates a potential problem as there is some doubt as to certain aspects of the title of the person seeking to register, for instance a doubt as to whether a piece of land forms part of the subjects actually owned by the person seeking to register, it is open to the Keeper to exclude indemnity from part of the title.[97]

It is also open to the Keeper to rectify the Land Register by altering the register in certain circumstances.[98] This is a problem area, as the purpose of the Land Register is to guarantee title and the guarantee will be undermined if the register can be altered after a title has been registered and a land certificate issued.[99]

A further problem with registration generally has arisen recently following the case of *Sharp v Thomson.* Prior to that case it was accepted that registration in the appropriate register was essential to create a real right and that any earlier stage, such as the delivery of the title deed by a seller to a purchaser, would not create a right greater than a personal right.

---

92 No record of plans attached to deeds was kept at Register House prior to 1924 and plans were only automatically recorded from 1933.
93 See Prescription, below.
94 1979 Act, s.30.
95 The final areas in the Highlands and Islands were declared operational from April 2003.
96 s.12.
97 s.12 (2).
98 1979 Act, s.9.
99 See generally the series of cases leading to *Short's Trs v Chung*, 1999 S.L.T. 751.

Sharp v Thomson
1997 S.C. (H.L.) 66

The Thomsons purchased a flat from a company, Albyn Construction Ltd. The first stage of a contract for the sale, the missives was concluded. The company had a floating charge over its whole property including the house sold to the Thomsons. Due to a departure from normal conveyancing practice the document transferring the title to the Thomsons, the disposition, was delivered late and then not registered straight away. Before the disposition was registered, the company went into receivership and the floating charge "crystallised" over the assets. The question was who received the house? Scottish land law is clear that the receivership should take precedence over the Thomsons as the disposition was not recorded and that was the decision of the Inner House of the Court of Session. The House of Lords, however, reversed this on the ground that the result was manifestly unjust with the actual reason for the decision not being entirely clear. This decision seems to go against a fundamental principle of Scottish land law and has been subject to much criticism.[1]

Subsequent to *Sharp v Thomson* it was thought that this deviation from the principle that registration is essential to create a real right would only apply to situations involving a receivership. However, there has been an attempt to extend this to a situation similar to that in *Sharp v Thomson* except involving a trustee in sequestration as opposed to a receivership in the case of *Burnett's Trustees v Grainger.*[2] In this case a house was purchased, missives concluded, the disposition delivered but not registered by the purchaser, the seller was sequestrated and the trustee in sequestration of the seller registered his title before the disposition was belatedly registered by the purchaser. The Sheriff Principal held that the House of Lords decision in *Sharp v Thomson*[3] also applied to a sequestration. His decision was overturned by the Inner House of the Court of Session who ruled that the decision in *Sharp v Thomson* did not apply to a trustee in sequestration situation and the case is under appeal to the House of Lords at the time of writing.

The problems of the case of *Sharp v Thomson* and registration of title generally are currently under review and change in this important area of law is likely.[4]

Key Concepts

The **Register of Sasines** is a register of deeds only, not a register of title and title is not guaranteed. The **Land Register** is a register of title where the title flows from the register itself and the Land Register does guarantee title.

Prescription

10–31 Prescription may be positive or negative. The function of positive prescription is to create rights in land or render existing rights unchallengeable. The function of negative prescription is to extinguish rights which have not been exercised. Both types of prescription have existed under the common law and there was a statute on prescription as early as 1617.[5] The main statute dealing with the modern law of prescription dates from 1973.[6] The most important changes over the years have been to the length of the various prescriptive periods.

---

1 See for example—"Jam today: Sharp in the House of Lords" 1997 S.L.T. (News) 79.
2 2002 S.L.T. 699.
3 1997 S.C. (H.L.) 66.
4 The Scottish Law Commission have published a discussion paper on *Sharp v Thomson*, Discussion Paper No.114, July 2001 and the Scottish Law Commission are reviewing the operation of the 1979 Act as a medium term project.
5 Prescription Act 1617.
6 Prescription and Limitation (Scotland) Act 1973.

The two main periods of negative prescription set out in the 1973 Act are known as the short negative prescription and the long negative prescription. The former is a period of five years[7] and the Act sets out various rights such as the right to receive payment of rent under a lease which will be extinguished if not exercised during the period.[8] The latter is a period of 20 years[9] and includes such rights as a servitude right of way which will be similarly extinguished if not exercised during the period.

Positive prescription operates to create a right or to fortify an existing right. The operation of positive prescription alongside the system of registration of a deed in the Register of Sasines ensures that the registration system functioned effectively for many years. For positive prescription to operate a person must have a suitable title to an interest in land and have had suitable possession of that interest for the appropriate prescriptive period. The 1973 Act sets out the nature of the title and possession which is required.[10] Positive prescription usually applies to the right of ownership of land but also applies to other rights such as servitudes,[11] recorded leases[12] and salmon fishings.[13]

The title must be *ex facie* valid and not forged.[14] It need not be in good faith and it is possible to record what is known as an *a non domino* deed which means the person recording the deed is not the owner.

The possession must be for the appropriate period and openly, peaceably and without judicial interruption.[15] Openly, simply means that the right has been possessed in an obvious and unsecretive way. Peaceably, simply means that there has been no dispute over the possession and without judicial interruption means that the possession has not been challenged by some court or similar action.[16]

The appropriate period is 10 years for most interests including the right of ownership,[17] 20 years for rights in respect of the foreshore and salmon fishings[18] and also in respect of recorded leases[19] and positive servitudes and public rights of way.[20]

Key Concepts

The function of **positive prescription** is to create rights in land or render existing rights unchallengeable. The function of **negative prescription** is to extinguish rights which have not been exercised.

Extent of landownership

If a person owns heritable property or land, various questions arise as to the extent of that landownership. What exactly is the physical extent of the landownership? What are the actual property rights that go with ownership of the land? To what extent is an owner of land restricted in the use and enjoyment of the land? The first two questions are now dealt with under the headings *Physical extent of landownership* and *Incidents of landownership* and the third under the following section *Restrictions on landownership*. **10–32**

7 s.6.
8 Sch.1.
9 s.7.
10 s.1.
11 s.3.
12 s.2.
13 s.1(2).
14 s.1(i).
15 s.1(i)(a).
16 The appropriate actions are set out in s.4.
17 s.1(i)(a).
18 s.1(4).
19 s.2.
20 s.3.

Physical extent of landownership

10–33 The physical boundaries of land with neighbouring land will be determined by the title deeds. In an ideal world, all titles to land will have an accurate plan attached which clearly sets out where the physical boundaries are. This is one of the aims of the Land Register introduced in 1979 whereby all title deeds of all land in Scotland will have an ordinance survey plan showing the physical boundaries. This will not happen for some considerable time however.[21] Meantime, many title deeds registered in the Register of Sasines do not have accurate plans or have no plans at all.[22] The question of where the boundaries are must be determined by a construction of the wording in the title deeds. All too often the wording is vague or ambiguous in such titles and boundary disputes are not uncommon.

Where the description in the title deeds is referred to as a "bounding" description this will normally contain specific details of the boundaries and will be sufficient to accurately identify the actual boundaries.[23] Where there is an ambiguity then prescription may establish the extent of the land and where the boundaries are. If a landowner has a recorded title which on the face of it could be interpreted as including the boundary the landowner claims is the true boundary and the landowner possesses the land contained by that boundary peaceable, openly and without judicial interruption for the prescriptive period of 10 years,[24] that boundary will normally become the legal boundary. The position is not straightforward, however, and this whole area is a problem one for conveyancers.

Landownership is theoretically from "the heavens to the centre of the earth".[25] This means that a landowner owns the airspace above the land and the ground strata below. This allows a landowner to prevent encroachment into the airspace by such things as overhanging branches of a neighbours' tree[26] or a tower crane.[27] This right is subject to limitations. A landowner cannot prevent aeroplanes flying overhead. There is statutory provision to allow aeroplanes to fly over property at a reasonable height.[28] Further upwards, there are statutes dealing with space exploration and outer space.[29] Below the ground there are also restrictions. Certain precious metals belong to the Crown under a statute dating back to 1424[30] as do petroleum and natural gas.[31] The coal and the right to mine for it vests in the British Coal Corporation.[32] Other minerals are included with landownership but the right of ownership to these can be severed.

Halkerston v Wedderburn

(1781) Mor. 10495

Wedderburn's garden in Inverness had elm trees in it. The branches of the elm trees grew to overhang his neighbour, Halkerston's property. Halkerston was annoyed and went to court. The court decided that Wedderburn was bound to prune his trees so that they would not overhang Halkerston's property. Although not actually decided in the case itself, this case is usually taken as authority for a neighbour's right to remove an encroachment of branches of trees.

---

[21] See Registration, above.

[22] No record of plans attached to deeds was kept at Register House prior to 1924 and plans were only automatically recorded from 1933.

[23] See further McDonald, *Conveyancing Manual* (6th ed., 1997), Chap.8.

[24] Prescription and Limitation (Scotland) Act 1973, s.1; see Prescription, above.

[25] The latin maxim is *a coelo usque ad centrum.*

[26] *Halkerston v Wedderburn* (1781) Mor. 10495.

[27] *Brown v Lee Construction Ltd*, 1977 S.L.T. (Notes) 61.

[28] Civil Aviation Act 1982.

[29] For example, the Outer Space Act 1986.

[30] Royal Mines Act 1424.

[31] Petroleum Production Act 1934 and subsequent Acts.

[32] Coal Industry Act 1994.

In a tenement, in the absence of provisions in the title deeds, ownership extends vertically to the mid-point of the joist separating upper and lower individual flats.[33] Ownership of the air space above the roof belongs to the ground floor flat owner.[34]

Fixtures

Ownership of land includes ownership of any buildings on the land under the principle of accession. When moveable items are attached to a building or land these items may convert to become heritable and part of the building or land by accession. The law on this is known as the law of fixtures. **10–34**

Prior to 1876, Scots law on fixtures seemed simple and straightforward but a case decided in that year has complicated the position.[35]

Brand's Trustees v Brand's Trustees

(1876) E.R. (H.L.) 16

Mining machinery was introduced onto land leased by a tenant for use in the tenant's business. The tenant died and the question was who owned the mining machinery? Prior to this case it was generally understood that the position in Scots law was that if moveables were introduced onto land and were removable, they did not become a fixture and that the intention of the parties was a relevant factor. The machinery in dispute was removable. The case was decided by the House of Lords with three English judges sitting. These judges assumed that the law on fixtures was the same in Scotland and England and applied English law in their decision. English Law was different. It provided that mining machinery was a trade fixture which belonged to the landlord on the tenant's death unless previously removed. Accordingly, they decided that the machinery belonged to the landlord. The intention of the parties was irrelevant.

It appears that there are usually three essentials before an item of moveable property will acceed to heritable property. These are:

- physical attachment
- functional subordination
- a degree of permanency.

There must be some degree of physical attachment. The greater the physical attachment the more likely accession has taken place. For instance, wallpaper attached to a wall will accede but a picture loosely attached by a picture hook will not. In between these extremes a painting on a panel which could be removed without damage but which exposed a bare wall was held to remain moveable.[36] The weight of an item may make it a fixture, as with a two ton summer house.[37]

Functional subordination is where the use of the moveable item is subordinated to the use of the heritable property. For instance, if storage heaters are attached to a heritable property the function of these is to heat the heritable property and they become fixtures, even though they are relatively easy to remove.[38]

There must be some degree of permanency before a moveable item becomes a fixture. This will vary according to circumstances but the attachment must be more than temporarily. If any change

---

[33] *Houston v Barr*, 1911 S.C. 134.
[34] *Watt v Burgess' Trs* (1891) 18 R. 766. See Law of the tenement, below.
[35] *Brand's Trs v Brand's Trs* (1876) E.R. (H.L.) 16.
[36] *Cochrane v Stevenson* (1891) 18 R. 1208.
[37] *Christie v Smith's Ex.*, 1949 S.C. 572.
[38] *Assessor of Fife v Hodgson*, 1966 S.C. 30.

is made to the item to make it fit in a building or if the building is adapted to take the item such as laying special foundations, this will be a strong indication of permanency.[39]

In addition to these three essentials, there are other factors which may be relevant. Whether an item can be removed without destruction of the item itself or damage to the land or building may be important. If it can, it is more likely to be regarded as moveable, but if it cannot, then it may well be a fixture.[40]

The intention of the parties would seem to be a relevant factor but the case of *Brand's Trs v Brand's Trs* in 1876 ruled that it is not. However, a later case appears to allow some room for the deemed intention of the parties to be relevant.[41]

Even though the item has become a fixture by accession there may be a right to remove the fixture in certain circumstances. This right to remove applies to certain trade fixtures which the tenant has introduced for business use,[42] certain ornamental fixtures[43] and certain agricultural fixtures in agricultural holdings.[44]

Crown rights

10–35 Various rights of property vest in the Crown as sovereign. These Crown rights are known as *regalia. Regalia* are divided into two types, *regalia majora* and *regalia minora.* The former are held by the Crown in trust for the public and cannot be sold. This means that such rights are, in practice, public rights. The latter originally belonged to the Crown but could be disposed of by the Crown by sale or other means and are now under the control of the Crown Estate Commissioners.

The *regalia majora* are:

- the sea and seabed within territorial waters
- the foreshore[45] in respect of navigation, fishing and moorings
- tidal navigable rivers.

The *regalia minora* are:

- certain precious metals[46]
- the foreshore
- treasure and lost property[47]
- salmon fishings.

Law of the tenement

10–36 A tenement is a building of several storeys where different parts are owned by different persons. It is a widespread type of building in Scotland and rules regarding the ownership of different parts of a tenement have developed at common law. These rules regarding the ownership of the different parts of tenement are subject to the overriding common interest in the whole tenement of all the owners. The individual titles of flats in many tenements contain specific provisions in relation to the common parts of a tenement but in the absence of provisions or where the provisions are unclear or not comprehensive the common law of the tenement will apply.[48]

---

39 *Scottish Discount Co v Blin*, 1985 S.C. 216.
40 *Dowall v Miln* (1874) 1 R. 1180.
41 *Scottish Discount Co. v Blin*, above.
42 *Syme v Harvey* (1861) 24 D. 202.
43 *Spyer v Phillipson* (1931) 2 Ch. 183.
44 Agricultural Holdings (Scotland) Act 1991, s.18.
45 The section of the beach lying between the high and low water marks of the spring tide.
46 Royal Mines Act 1424.
47 *Lord Advocate v University of Aberdeen*, 1963 S.C. 533.
48 *Rafique v Amin*, 1997 S.L.T. 1385.

Rafique v Amin
1997 S.L.T. 1385

There were provisions in the title deed of flats in a tenement property which purported to alter the common law of the tenement in respect of common property. It appears that the drafting did not achieve all that was intended. There was a dispute as to the rights of the proprietors of the flats. It was held that one proprietor had an absolute right of veto to prevent alterations to the common property.

Lord Justice-Clerk Ross (at p.1387f): "It is somewhat ironical that if, instead of making these elaborate provisions regarding common property, the granter had allowed the more usual law of the tenement to prevail, many of these difficulties [in this case] would not have arisen."

The *solum,* the ground on which the tenement is built, and adjacent ground belongs to the owner of the ground or basement flat, or where more than one, the *solum* below the individual flat and adjacent ground.[49] The internal walls in flats are owned by the individual flat-owners, external walls are owned in sections by the flat owners whose flat they enclose and walls dividing flats are owned to the mid-point.[50] Similarly, floors/ceilings are owned to the centre line of the joist.[51] The roof and roof space within the roof is owned by the top floor flat owner, or where more than one, the section above the individual flat.[52] The airspace above the roof belongs to the owner of the *solum*, following the principle that ownership extends from the centre of the earth to the heavens.[53] Accordingly, it is an encroachment to build into the airspace, as with a dormer window,[54] although if this takes place without initial objection the owner of the *solum* may be personally barred from objecting later.[55]

The common passage and stair is owned by all the owners in the tenement to whose flat they give access, probably in equal shares.[56] This includes the portion of the *solum* and roof below and above the common passage and stair.

The right of common interest includes a right of support in the walls and a right of shelter from the roof. If any actual damage is caused by failure of a part of a tenement building, for instance the fracture of an iron support beam, an action for damages will only succeed if negligence can be proved.[57]

Repairs to the common parts of a tenement are a problem area under the common law. Decisions on whether repairs are necessary require the consent of all the flat owners. If a repair is essential it may be the position that one owner may instruct the repair and recover from the others.[58] In some cases the local authority may issue a repairs notice in respect of such repairs.[59]

The Scottish Law Commission has issued a report on reform of the law of the tenement[60] which is likely to be enacted in due course. This recommends that where there is no provision in the title deeds relating to repairs, the simpler of two management schemes for tenements will apply which provides that a simple majority of flat owners will be entitled to instruct repairs. Other proposed reforms include a clarification of the rules of ownership of various parts of a tenement which covers modern additions to tenements such as entry phone systems.

---

49 *Johnston v White* (1877) 4 R. 721.
50 Bell Princ. 1086.
51 *Girdwood v Paterson* (1873) 11 M. 647.
52 *Taylor v Dunlop* (1872) 11 M. 25.
53 See Physical Extent of Landownership above.
54 *Watt v Burgess's Trs* (1891) 18 R. 766.
55 *Brown v Baty*, 1957 S.L.T. 336.
56 *WVS Office Premises Ltd. v Currie*, 1969 S.L.T. 254.
57 *Thomson v St Cuthbert's Co-op Association*, 1959 S.L.T. 54.
58 *Deans v Woolson*, 1922 S.C. 221.
59 Housing (Scotland) Act 1987, s.108.
60 Report No.162, 1998.

Key Concepts

Physical boundaries of land with neighbouring land will be determined by the title deeds. Landownership is theoretically from "the heavens to the centre of the earth".

When moveable items are attached to a building or land these items may convert to become heritable and part of the building or land by accession under the law of **fixtures**. For this to happen there must be:

- physical attachment
- functional subordination
- a degree of permanency.

Various rights of property vest in the Crown as sovereign. These **Crown rights** are known as *regalia majora* and *regalia minora*.

The individual titles of flats in many tenements contain specific provisions in relation to the common parts of a tenement but in the absence of provisions or where the provisions are unclear or not comprehensive the **law of the tenement** will apply.

Incidents of landownership

10–37 Landownership includes the right to exclusive possession of the land and to use and enjoy the land. Exclusive possession includes the right to prevent trespass and encroachment. The right to use and enjoy the land includes the right of support, certain rights in water, certain game and fishing rights and the right to be free from nuisance. These are sometimes collectively known as incidents of landownership.

Exclusive possession

10–38 A landowner has the right of exclusive possession of the land and can exclude others from the land. This possession will be natural possession where the landowner physically occupies the land personally. It is open to the landowner to give the right of actual physical possession to someone else, *e.g.*, a tenant under a lease. Where this happens the possession by the tenant will be civil possession of behalf of the landlord landowner.

This right of exclusive possession is subject to various statutory restrictions whereby certain people are given the right to enter land in the public interest, for instance, gas board officials under the Gas Act 1995 and health and safety inspectors under the Health and Safety at Work etc. Act 1974.

It follows that a landowner can prevent trespass or encroachment on the land.

Trespass and encroachment

10–39 Trespass is where a landowner's right of exclusive possession is encroached by the temporary intrusion of someone on the land. However, trespass is not by itself recognised as a crime in Scotland.[61] There is very little a landowner can do against a single act of trespass. The landowner

[61] See generally Gordon, *Criminal Law* (3rd ed., 2001) 15.43.

can ask the trespasser to leave but cannot use force unless the trespasser threatens violence to person or property.[62] Trespass by itself is not a civil wrong either but if damage is caused the trespasser may be sued. It may be possible to obtain an interdict against trespass but this may not be granted if the trespass is trivial[63] or if repetition of the trespass is not expected.[64]

A landowner can endeavour to prevent trespass by notices, alarms or barbed wire but a duty of care is owed in delict to trespassers which would prevent the use of such things as booby-traps.[65]

It is not trespass to enter on land in an emergency such as a fire, pursuit of a criminal or to avoid danger.[66]

Encroachment is where a landowner's right of exclusive possession of the land including the airspace above the land is interfered with. Encroachment into airspace has already been noted.[67] Encroachment can also take place on or below ground. If roots from a neighbour's tree grow into land this is an encroachment on that land. If the owner of minerals under a landowner's land extracts these without permission or express title to do so, this will also be an encroachment.

Like trespass, the usual remedy against encroachment is interdict.

Right of support

Land would collapse if it was not supported. Support is necessary from below and also from surrounding land to prevent collapse or subsidence. It is a natural right of a landowner to receive such support and any operations beneath the land or on neighbouring land which cause surface damage will lead to a claim for damages. It is not necessary to prove negligence.[68] Such a right of support arises automatically by law. In other situations a right of support may be implied in all the circumstances. An automatic right of support only arises in respect of the land itself and not buildings on the land but such a right may be implied. This question usually arises when minerals are excavated under the land. **10–40**

Angus v National Coal Board
1955 S.C. 175

This case concerned an action of damages brought after an agricultural worker died due to subsidence in a field where he was working and under which a colliery company had formerly worked coal.

Lord Justice-Clerk Thomson (at p.181): "The right of support is an incident of property ... The owner, in virtue of his ownership, has the right to have his land left in its natural state and he enjoys that right *qua* owner. If the owner's right of support is breached, he becomes entitled to damages for surface damage without requiring to establish negligence."

The right to work minerals may be reserved by a previous owner, usually the superior. In such cases a right of support of buildings will be implied where the buildings were already on the land at the time of reservation,[69] where there was an obligation imposed in the title to erect buildings when the reservation was made[70] or where the erection of buildings was clearly foreseen at the time of reservation.[71]

---

[62] *Wood v North British Railway Co* (1899) 2 F. 1.
[63] As with a straying pet lamb in *Winans v Macrae* (1885) 12 R. 1051.
[64] *Hay's Trs v Young* (1877) 4 R. 398.
[65] Occupiers' Liability (Scotland) Act 1960, s.1(1).
[66] Bell Princ. 956.
[67] See Physical extent of landownership, above.
[68] *Angus v National Coal Board*, 1955 S.C. 175 at 181.
[69] *Caledonian Railway Co v Sprot* (1856) 2 Macq. 449.
[70] *North British Railway Co v Turners Ltd* (1904) 6 F. 900.
[71] *Neill's Trs v William Dixon Ltd* (1880) 7 R. 741.

If buildings are damaged as a result of operations by a neighbouring landowner this may constitute a nuisance.[72]

Various statutes make provision for loss of support or damage. For instance, the Coal Mining Subsidence Act 1991 provides for remedial work to be paid by British Coal where subsidence to land or buildings is caused by the loss of support due to their mining operations.

Water rights

10–41 The Crown has extensive rights in water, particularly the sea, sea lochs and tidal rivers as part of the Crown *regalia*.[73] This section deals with landowners who have water as part of the land they own. Water can be running water such as rivers and streams or still water such as a loch or a bog.[74] Still water which lies on the surface of land or water which percolates through the ground belongs to the owner of the land. This can be extracted by a well and can be used for manufacturing purposes even if it would otherwise flow to a stream.[75] Such water can be discharged onto a lower landowner's land if it naturally flows that way, but not in a polluted state.[76]

Lochs are either sea lochs or fresh water lochs. A sea loch is equated to the sea and belongs to the Crown.[77] For other lochs, if the loch is completely surrounded by a landowner's own property the landowner has full rights of ownership in the loch. Where a loch is surrounded by land belonging to different landowners, these landowners own the loch in common. The bed of the loch, the *alveus*, is owned by each landowner adjacent to their land up to the centre of the loch.

The rights in rivers and streams depends on whether they are navigable or non-navigable. If a navigable river is tidal the Crown owns the *alveus*[78] but the public have a right to navigate and fish the river and to moor boats temporarily on the river.[79] If the navigable river is non-tidal the banks and the *alveus* to the mid-point of the river are owned by the riparian owners, that is those owning land up to the banks of the river. This is subject to the public's right of navigation and the question of whether a river is navigable and the extent of the right of navigation can be a matter of dispute.[80] The riparian owners must not interfere with the public right of navigation.[81]

Orr Ewing & Co. v Colquhoun's Trustees

(1873) 4 R. (H.L.) 116

The owner of land on both banks of a river constructed a bridge across the river. Two of the piers were built in the water. From time immemorial, small vessels had used the river to get from the River Clyde to Loch Lomond. Objection was taken to this artificial structure in the river. The Inner House of the Court of Session held that the river was a public navigable river and no one had a right to erect structures on the bed of the river. The House of Lords reversed this decision and held that, while the public may have a right of navigation in a non-tidal navigable river, the proprietors of the *alveus* are entitled to erect structures on it unless the structure so erected would actually interfere with and obstruct navigation.

---

[72] *Lord Advocate v The Reo Stakis Organisation Ltd*, 1982 S.L.T. 140.

[73] See Crown rights, above.

[74] Stair states "running waters are common to all men, because they have no bounds; but water standing, and capable of bounds, is appropriated" Inst II.i.5.

[75] *Milton v Glen-Moray Glenlivet Distillery Co* (1898) 1 F. 135.

[76] *Montgomerie v Buchanan's Trs* (1853) 15 D. 853.

[77] See Crown rights, above.

[78] See Crown rights, above.

[79] *Crown Estates Commissioners v Fairlie Yacht Slip Ltd*, 1979 S.C. 156.

[80] See, *e.g. Wills' Trs v Cairngorm Canoeing & Sailing School Ltd*, 1976 S.C. (H.L.) 30. It was held that a one-way right of navigation existed where logs had been floated down a river to the sea from time in memorial.

[81] *Orr Ewing & Co v Colquhoun's Trs* (1877) 4 R. (H.L.) 116.

Where a river is non-navigable, the riparian owners own the banks, the *alveus* and the surface of the river. Where there is more than one owner each riparian owner owns the river adjacent to his or her land up to the mid-point of the river. These riparian owners have a common interest in the flow of the water and one owner cannot interfere with the character or quality of the water or increase or diminish the flow of water.[82] Each owner can take water from the river for drinking or washing even if this diminishes the flow, but not for any commercial purpose, unless there is no change to the flow or quality of the water.

Fishing and game rights

The right of ownership includes the right to fish in lochs, streams and rivers belonging to the landowner. This right does not extend to sea lochs or tidal rivers which belong to the Crown.[83] If there is more than one owner of a river or stream each riparian owner has the right to fish to the centre line. The right to fish does not include salmon as salmon fishing forms part of the *regalia* of the Crown.[84] **10–42**

A landowner has a right to kill game on the land although it is possible and common to lease shooting rights. Certain wildlife is protected by statutes and is excluded from the right to kill game.[85]

Freedom from nuisance

A landowner is entitled to be free from actions and behaviour by other landowners which interferes with the enjoyment of the land. Such conduct may constitute a nuisance under the common law and is considered in the next section on Restrictions on landownership. **10–43**

Key Concepts

Landownership includes various **incidental rights** which are:

- exclusive possession and the right to be free from trespass and encroachment
- water rights
- support
- fishing and game rights
- freedom from nuisance.

Restrictions on landownership

Although theoretically an owner of land is unrestricted in the use and enjoyment of the land there are various restrictions on this use. These restrictions are imposed for the benefit of other landowners and for the public generally. They exist to limit the activities of a landowner which may be detrimental to neighbours or the public generally, to regulate property which may be owned or used in common and to give landowners certain rights to another's land. These restrictions may be imposed by law or may be agreed by the owner. When agreed by the owner they are usually inserted in the owner's title as title conditions and are generally known as real **10–44**

---

[82] *Young & Co v Bankier Distillery Co* (1893) 20 R. (H.L.) 76.
[83] See Crown rights, above.
[84] See Crown rights, above.
[85] Wildlife & Countryside Act 1981 and other Acts.

burdens and servitudes. As noted in the introduction to this chapter, title conditions are under review at the time of writing as the Title Conditions (Scotland) Act 2003 has just completed its way through the Scottish Parliament. Once the new legislation is in force it will compliment certain provisions of the Abolition of Feudal Tenure etc. (Scotland) Act 2000 in relation to real burdens and substantially alter the existing law. Although the new law will affect the validity of certain existing real burdens and the enforcement of existing real burdens, it will not affect the constitution of existing real burdens and both the existing law and the position under the new legislation generally are examined in this section.

Restrictions at common law and by statute

10–45 There are restrictions imposed by law on the use and enjoyment of land. This is both under the common law and extensively by statute. The restrictions under the common law are sometimes referred to as the law of neighbourhood as the underlying principle is that a landowner cannot use land in such a way as to interfere with a neighbour's use and enjoyment of their land. If such interference is regarded as unlawful, it amounts to a nuisance which is a delictual wrong. A nuisance can be caused to the public generally as well as to neighbours.

Nuisance is defined as:

> "Whatever obstructs the public means of commerce and intercourse… Whatever is noxious or unsafe, or renders life uncomfortable to the public generally, or to the neighbourhood; whatever is intolerably offensive to individuals, in their dwelling houses, or inconsistent with the comfort of life…"[86]

Various factors are taken into account to ascertain whether or not a nuisance has been committed, including the nature of the harm suffered and the nature of the conduct causing the harm. There are not many recent cases on nuisance, probably as there are many statutory provisions which deal with conduct which may also be a common law nuisance.[87]

Webster v Lord Advocate

1984 S.L.T. 13

The owner of a flat adjacent to and overlooking Edinburgh Castle esplanade sought an interdict against nuisance by noise caused by the erection of scaffolding for the Edinburgh Military Tattoo and the Tattoo itself. It was held that the Tattoo itself was not a nuisance but the noise from the erection of steel scaffolding was, although the interdict was postponed for six months to allow the Tattoo to proceed and allow a system of scaffolding erection to be considered which did not involve a nuisance.

The usual remedy against a nuisance is an interdict. If damage has been caused it will be necessary to establish *culpa* or blame before damages can be recovered.[88]

Another common law restriction which is rarely but sometimes established is where the conduct of a land owner is regarded as spiteful[89] and is for no other purpose than to cause harm to neighbours. Older cases deal with such matters as erecting a wall on a boundary to block out a neighbour's light[90] but in a relatively recent case, shutting off a water pipe which supplied the pursuer and ran through the defender's garden was held to be within the doctrine.[91]

Many statutes impose restrictions on the use of land in various ways. These include legislation on town and country planning, building control, the countryside, public health, housing and civic

---

86 Bell Princ. 974.
87 One recent case is *Webster v Lord Advocate*, 1984 S.L.T. 13.
88 *RHM Bakeries (Scotland) Ltd v Strathclyde Regional Council*, 1985 S.L.T. 214.
89 The Latin term is *aemulatio vicini.*
90 *e.g. Ross v Baird* (1827) 7 S. 361.
91 *More v Boyle*, 1967 S.L.T. (Sh. Ct) 38.

government, health and safety at work and environmental matters.[92] In all these statutes in these areas and many more there is some restriction on the use a landowner can make of land.

Real burdens

A real burden is defined in the Title Conditions (Scotland) Act 2003 as: **10–46**

> "An encumbrance on land constituted in favour of the owner of other land in that person's capacity as owner of that other land."[93]

It is an obligation in respect of the land which is inserted in the title to that land for the benefit of another landowner. If it is properly constituted, it will be enforceable against the owner of the burdened land for the time being by the owner of the other land for the time being and is said to "run with the land". Often these burdens have been inserted long ago but they remain enforceable against the burdened proprietor by the benefited proprietor.

Feudal and non-feudal real burdens

Under the feudal system, it was usual for the superior to insert real burdens in the title of the vassal **10–47** to restrict the use of the land by the vassal. This originally served a useful purpose in the days before there were any statutes dealing with such matters as planning restrictions, development control and pollution. These burdens acted as a social control on land which would otherwise be uncontrolled. If a superior retained other land in the vicinity it was in the superior's interest that land in the community was properly regulated. In the modern era, this type of burden, which is sometimes termed a community burden,[94] still serves a useful purpose, particularly in housing estates, tenements or other areas where neighbouring landowners have a communal interest. It is possible that other landowners in the community may have the right to enforce such real burdens.[95] So far as superiors are concerned however, whilst they originally had an interest to ensure the burdens were observed, after all the land in the area has been feued they have no connection with the land other than the fact of being the superior, yet at present are still able to enforce the real burdens.

Real burdens can also be inserted in transfers of land which are not feudal transfers by subinfeudation but non-feudal transfers by substitution. In addition to community burdens, another type of real burden is frequently used known as a neighbour burden which one owner can enforce against another with the purpose of the burden being to preserve the amenity of the land.

Under the Abolition of Feudal Tenure etc. (Scotland) Act 2000, feudal burdens will be abolished. Superiors and vassals will disappear and the right to enforce a real burden simply by being a superior will also disappear.[96] Not all feudal burdens will disappear however and certain ones which still have a useful purpose can be saved by converting into a different type of burden.[97]

Constitution of real burdens

Real burdens are inserted in the title of the burdened proprietor by the benefited proprietor, usually **10–48** when the land is being transferred for the first time, or can appear in a separate deed of conditions.[98] The leading case of *Tailors of Aberdeen v Coutts*[99] sets out the requirements of a real burden. These are:

---

[92] See further, McDonald, *op.cit.*, Chap.19.
[93] s.1(1).
[94] See Scottish Law Commission Report on Real Burdens, No.181, 2000, Pt 7.
[95] See Enforcement of real burdens, below.
[96] s.17(1).
[97] See Saving existing feudal burdens, below.
[98] Land Registration (Scotland) Act 1979, s.17.
[99] (1840) 1 Rob. App. 296.

- clear intention to burden the land not the person
- acceptable purpose
- expressed in clear terms
- registered in the Register of Sasines (or Land Register).

Tailors of Aberdeen v Coutts

(1840) 1 Rob. App. 296

This dispute involved a disposition by the Tailors of Aberdeen to George Nicol of part of Bon Accord Square in Aberdeen. Nicol undertook a number of obligations including in particular an obligation to build houses and to pay two thirds of the cost of forming and enclosing the central square. Nicol then became insolvent and the subjects were sold and conveyed to Coutts. The essential question was whether the obligations imposed on Nicol in the disposition were enforceable against Coutts. The court's judgement sets out in detail the requirements for the constitution of real burdens.

The purpose of a real burden is to impose an obligation on land, not the person who owns the land. No matter who happens to be the owner of the land, the real burden will be enforceable against that person simply because he or she is the owner.

A real burden must be for an acceptable purpose. It must not be contrary to law, otherwise the landowner would be committing a crime, or public policy such as endeavouring to create a perpetual commercial monopoly.[1] It must not be useless or vexatious such as compelling someone to permanently fly the saltire flag from a roof. It must not be inconsistent with the nature of the property[2] such as removing a landowner's right to lease the land.

A real burden must be expressed in clear and unambiguous terms. There is a presumption that landownership is free from restriction and therefore any restriction is strictly construed *contra proferentem*, that is against the person wishing to apply the restriction. Examples of wording rejected as too vague and ambiguous by the courts include a restriction against any building "of an unseemly description"[3] and a prohibition against any operations the superior "may deem objectionable".[4]

Anderson v Dickie

1915 S.C. (H.L.) 74

A purported real burden was inserted in a title deed to impose conditions on part of the ground attached to a mansion house. The wording referred to "the ground occupied as the lawn". This was held to be too imprecise wording for the constitution of a real burden.

A real burden must be registered in the Register of Sasines or the Land Register. If it is not, the burden will only be personally binding on the original parties and will not become real and run with the land.[5] The requirement for registration of a real burden only applies to the burdened proprietor's land. There is no requirement to register the real burden in the title of the benefited proprietor's land. In its report on real burdens, the Scottish Law Commission recommended this should change and the real burden be registered in both titles.[6] This recommendation is included in

---

1 *Aberdeen Varieties v James F Donald (Aberdeen Cinemas) Ltd*, 1939 S.C. 788.
2 *Beckett v Bissett*, 1921 S.L.T. 33.
3 *Murray's Trs v St Margaret's Convent Trs*, 1907 S.C. (H.L.) 8.
4 *Meriton Ltd v Winning*, 1995 S.L.T. 76 although the court did consider that the wording may be appropriate in certain circumstances.
5 *Wallace v Simmers*, 1960 S.C. 255.
6 SLC Report on Real Burdens, 3.3–3.10.

the Title Conditions (Scotland) Act 2003[7] and will help overcome one of the criticisms of the current law on real burdens, namely, a lack of transparency.

In addition to the need to register a real burden in the title of both the benefited and burdened land, the Title Conditions (Scotland) Act 2003 provides that the word "real burden" must be used in the title.[8]

Enforcement of real burdens

Under the existing law, a person wishing to enforce a real burden must have both a title and interest to do so. **10–49**

The owner of the benefited land for the time being must have a title to enforce a real burden. The person who originally inserted the real burden in the title and the successors to the title of that person will have such a title. This applies to both feudal burdens where the benefited proprietor is the superior and to non-feudal burdens.[9] In addition, the owner of the benefited land must have an interest to enforce the real burden. This interest is implied in the case of a superior.[10] Other owners must demonstrate a praedial interest, which means that there would be a material detrimental effect to their land if the real burden was not enforced.[11]

Earl of Zetland v Hislop

(1882) 9 R. (H.L.) 40

In 1814, land in Grangemouth was feued under certain restrictions. In 1880 the superior sought to enforce a restriction which was breached.

Lord Watson (at p.47): "*Prima facie*, the vassal in consenting to be bound by the restriction concedes the interest of the superior; and, therefore, it appears to me, that the onus is upon the vassal who is pleading a release from his contract to allege and prove that, owing to some change of circumstances, any legitimate interest which the superior may originally have had in maintaining the restriction has ceased to exist."

It is possible for a superior or other owner of benefited land to lose an interest to enforce. This can be due to a change of circumstances or to acquiescence. Any change in circumstances has to be substantial before the interest will be lost. In one case which concerned a restriction allowing properties to be used as houses only and one third of the houses in the relevant street were no longer used as houses, the superior was held not to have lost an interest to enforce.[12] Acquiescence will operate where breaches of a real burden are allowed, provided that the person entitled to enforce is aware of the breach and deliberately allows it to happen.[13]

In certain cases, a title and interest to enforce a real burden can be shown by a third party who is neither the owner of the burdened nor benefited land. This right to enforce is known as a *ius quaesitum tertio*. This is where neighbouring landowners are affected by the real burden. This right may be created expressly, usually in a deed of conditions setting out mutual restrictions and enforcement rights for a neighbourhood such as a housing estate, or by implication. The existing law was developed in the leading case of *Hislop v MacRitchie's Trs*[14] and subsequent cases[15] but the position is complex and not entirely clear. If the title creating the real burden is one of a number of titles granted by the same person and all of these titles have the same real burdens,

[7] ss.4 and 108.
[8] s.4(2)(a) and (3).
[9] *Nicolson v Glasgow Blind Asylum*, 1911 S.C. 391.
[10] *Earl of Zetland v Hislop* (1882) 9 R. (H.L.) 40.
[11] *Maguire v Burges*, 1909 S.C. 1283.
[12] *Howard De Walden Estates Ltd v Bowmaker*, 1965 S.C. 163.
[13] *Ben Challum Ltd. v Buchanan*, 1955 S.C. 348.
[14] (1881) 8 R. (H.L.) 95.
[15] Especially *J A Mactaggart & Co v Harrower* (1906) 8 F. 1101.

known as a common scheme, and there is clear reference to a common scheme, then each landowner will be able to enforce the real burdens against each other. To establish a *ius quaesitum tertio* a landowner must also show a praedial interest to enforce, which can be lost by change of circumstances or acquiescence. A right of a landowner with an *ius quaesitum tertio* to enforce is a separate right from the right of the benefited landowner and acquiescence by the latter will not prevent the former from enforcing.[16]

Hislop v MacRitchie's Trustees

(1881) 8 R. (H.L.) 95

One side of a square was feued in separate feus for the erection of detached villas. There were conditions in each of the separate title deeds which were similar but there was no uniformity, other than the distance back from the street and the conditions were adapted to suit each house. There was no reference to a common feuing plan. The House of Lords held that this did not constitute any right in a third party to enforce the feuing conditions.

Lord Watson (at p.102): "The fact of the same condition appearing in feu charters derived from a common superior, coupled with a substantial interest in its observance does not appear to me to be sufficient to give each feuar a title to enforce it. No single feuar can, in my opinion, be subjected in liability to his co-feuars, unless it appears from the titles under which he holds his feu that such similarity of conditions and mutuality of interest among the feuars either had been or was meant to be established."

Under the new legislation, implied third party rights to enforce real burdens will be simplified. The starting point is that all implied rights to enforce are abolished.[17] For all new burdens created after the Act is in force it will be necessary to nominate and identify the benefited and burdened proprietor. For existing burdens, if they relate to a common scheme affecting both benefited and burdened proprietors or to a common facility or the provision of a service, rules for enforcement are set out. For existing other burdens which are neighbour type burdens, these will cease to be enforceable after 10 years from the commencement of the Act unless a notice of preservation procedure is followed.[18] Where a real burden regulates a common facility or the provision of a service, it will be enforceable by the owner of any property which the facility benefits or to which the notice is provided.[19] Where real burdens are imposed in a common scheme there are provisions to deal with different types of common scheme. An owner of a flat in a tenement can enforce the burden against any other owner of a flat in the tenement.[20] An owner of a unit in a shelter housing complex can enforce the burden against any other owner of a unit in the complex.[21] In any other type of common scheme an owner of property in the scheme can enforce the burden against an owner of any other property in the scheme.[22]

Saving existing feudal burdens

10–50 When the feudal system is abolished by the Abolition of Feudal Tenure etc. (Scotland) Act 2000, feudal burdens will be abolished. There is provision in the Act to save certain feudal burdens. These fall into four categories:

---

16 *Lawrence v Scott*, 1965 S.L.T. 390.
17 Title Conditions (Scotland) Act 2003, s.45.
18 s.46.
19 s.51.
20 s.49.
21 s.50.
22 s.48.

- re-allotted neighbour burdens
- conservation burdens
- maritime burdens
- facility and service burdens.

Re-allotted neighbour burdens are where the superior owns the *dominium utile* of other land as a vassal, which will convert to outright ownership, and nominates that land to be the new benefited land by registering a notice. That land must have a permanent building used as a place of human habitation or resort within a hundred metres of the burdened land.[23]

Where the superior is a designated conservation body and the burden is to preserve or protect architectural, historical or other characteristics of land for the benefit of the public, the burden can be converted to a conservation burden enforceable by the conservation body.[24]

Any feudal burden which affects the seabed or foreshore and where the Crown is the superior is automatically preserved as a maritime burden enforceable by the Crown.[25]

Feudal burdens which regulate the provision of facilities or services which were only enforceable by a superior are automatically enforceable by the owners of land benefited by the facilities or which receive the service.[26]

In some cases, a superior may be entitled to compensation for the loss of the right to enforce a real burden if there is a loss of development value.[27]

Extinction of real burdens

It is a feature of a real burden that it runs with the land, theoretically forever, unless formally discharged, although the right to enforce it may be lost. Many existing real burdens were created a considerable time ago and are of no relevance today. To remedy this, the new legislation will introduce what is known as the "sunset rule".[28] If a real burden is more than 100 years old, the burdened proprietor known as "the terminator"[29] can intimate an intention to register a notice of termination on the benefited proprietor. If the benefited proprietor does nothing the notice can be registered and the burden discharged. If the benefited proprietor wishes to have the burden renewed and continued there must be an application to the Lands Tribunal which will decide whether to renew or discharge.[30] **10–51**

Servitudes

A servitude is defined as: **10–52**

> "burden on land or houses, imposed by agreement—express or implied—in favour of owners of other [land]".[31]

It is similar to a real burden but a real burden is only enforceable against the burdened proprietor for the time being whereas servitudes are enforceable against anyone. In addition, a real burden must appear in the title of the land whereas a servitude may be express in the title or implied. The benefited proprietor in servitudes is usually referred to as the owner of the dominant tenement[32] and the burdened proprietor is referred to as the owner of the servient tenement. Servitudes can be

---

23 s.18.
24 2000 Act, ss.26–32.
25 s.60.
26 s.23.
27 s.33.
28 2003 Act, ss.19–23.
29 s.19(2).
30 s.81(1)(b).
31 Bell Princ. 979.
32 Tenement in this sense means an interest in property not a block of flatted property.

positive which permit the owner of the dominant tenement to do something such as exercise access over the servient tenement or negative which allows the owner of the dominant tenement to prevent the owner of the servient tenement from doing something.

There is very little difference between a negative servitude and a real burden and the proposed new legislation will prohibit the creation of new negative servitudes and convert existing ones into real burdens.[33]

There are several essentials before servitude can be created. There must be two different tenements or interests in land owned by two different persons.[34] The land concerned must be neighbouring or reasonably adjacent if not actually contiguous. As with real burdens, the benefit must be for the land itself and the person who is the owner of that land for the time being and not the owner personally. The servitude must be a known servitude or analogous to an existing servitude as it is generally thought that it is not possible to create a new type of servitude.[35] There is no such requirement to be an existing servitude under the new legislation.[36]

Creation of servitudes

10–53 Servitudes can be created in three ways:

- express grant or reservation
- implied grant or reservation
- prescription.

A servitude may be expressly created by either granting to another when the title to that land is given or reserving to oneself when the title is given. In the former case the benefit of the servitude is for the grantee and in the latter it is for the granter. In either case the servitude is created by agreement. It is also possible to have a separate agreement constituting the servitude. It is not necessary for the deed in which the servitude appears to be recorded. No precise form of wording is required[37] and use of the word "servitude" is not required.[38]

Under the new legislation a positive servitude must be in writing and registered in the title of both the benefited and burdened properties.[39]

A servitude may be implied either as a grant or a reservation if the title deed omitted to include a servitude expressly and the servitude is necessary for the reasonable enjoyment of the property. For instance, if part of an owner's land has been sold and a servitude of access over the land sold is not reserved and the remaining land cannot be accessed and is "landlocked" a servitude right of access may be implied.[40] There have been various cases on what is necessary for reasonable enjoyment.[41]

Ewart v Cochrane

(1869) 4 Macq. 117

The implied servitude sought in this case was a right to use a certain drain leading from the Cochranes' tanyard to a cesspool on land belonging to Ewart. The House of Lords held that an implied servitude was essential to the enjoyment of the property.

---

[33] Titles Conditions (Scotland) Act 2003, ss.70 and 71.

[34] Therefore a public right of way is not a servitude. See *Ayr Burgh Council v British Transport Commission*, 1955 S.L.T. 219.

[35] *Neill v Scobbie*, 1993 G.W.D. 13–887.

[36] 2003 Act, s.76.

[37] *Axis West Developments Ltd v Chartwell Land Investments Ltd*, 1999 S.L.T. 1416.

[38] *Moss Bros Group plc v Scottish Mutual Assurance plc*, 2001 S.L.T. 641.

[39] 2003 Act, s.75.

[40] Although whether this implied right of access is strictly a servitude has been questioned recently. See *Bowers v Kennedy*, 2000 S.L.T. 1006.

[41] Contrast *Ewart v Cochrane* (1869) 4 Macq. 117 and *Murray v Medley*, 1973 S.L.T. (Sh. Ct) 75.

Murray v Medley

1973 S.L.T. (Sh. Ct) 75

The implied servitude sought in this case was a right to use a water pipe which ran under a building and piece of land sold by Murray to Medley and serving both Medley's property and property retained by Murray. The Sheriff held there was no implied servitude right.

A servitude can be created by prescription by use continually for 20 years openly, peaceably and without judicial interruption under statute.[42]

Extinction of servitudes

Servitudes can be extinguished by express discharge or renunciation, *confusio* where the two separate tenements come into ownership of one person, negative prescription after twenty years where the servitude has not been exercised,[43] acquiescence where, for instance, an access has been blocked for some time, a change of circumstances where, for instance, a particular building which was the subject of the servitude has been demolished or by the Lands Tribunal. **10–54**

Extinction, variation and discharge of title conditions

Title conditions generally can be extinguished in one of five ways: **10–55**

- express discharge
- prescription
- consolidation
- compulsory purchase
- variation or discharge by the Lands Tribunal.

Express discharge is where the parties agree to discharge the condition in some form of agreement. The long negative prescription will operate to extinguish a servitude which has not been exercised for 20 years.[44] Consolidation is where the ownership of the burdened and benefited land comes into single ownership. Compulsory purchase has the legal effect of extinguishing conditions in the title. In addition to extinction on these four grounds, it has been possible since 1970 to apply to the Lands Tribunal for Scotland to either vary or discharge a title condition.

Variation and discharge

Prior to 1970, unless a benefited proprietor lost an interest to enforce a title condition it was impossible for a burdened proprietor to have a title condition varied or discharged without the consent of the benefited proprietor. There was no action a benefited proprietor could take unilaterally. The usual way to get a condition in the title varied was to ask the benefited proprietor for a minute of waiver which the benefited proprietor may or may not have granted. If granted it was usually done so in exchange for a payment.[45] In 1970, the Lands Tribunal for Scotland was set up and one of its functions is to adjudicate on applications to vary or discharge title conditions which are referred to as land obligations in the Act.[46] **10–56**

[42] Prescription and Limitation (Scotland) Act 1973, s.3.
[43] Prescription and Limitation (Scotland) Act 1973, s.7.
[44] See Prescription and servitudes, above.
[45] The original method of changing title conditions was by a charter of novodamus.
[46] Conveyancing and Feudal Reform (Scotland) Act 1970, s.1(2).

The Lands Tribunal can hear an application by a burdened proprietor to vary or discharge an obligation which is enforceable by a benefited proprietor. Land obligations include such title conditions as real burdens, servitudes and leasehold conditions in recorded leases. Certain types of obligations are specifically excluded from the operation of the provisions of the Act such as feuduty and mineral obligations.[47] Obligations created within two years of the application are also excluded.[48] There are three grounds on which a variation or discharge can be made[49]:

- a change in the character of the land rendering the obligation unreasonable or inappropriate
- the obligation is unduly burdensome compared with any benefit resulting
- the existence of the obligation impedes some reasonable use of the land.

These grounds are not mutually exclusive and an application can be made on one or more ground. In practice, the third ground is most often used. In this ground, when assessing whether a proposed use if reasonable, the fact that planning permission or a liquor licence has been obtained for the use will be persuasive but not conclusive.[50] Under the Title Conditions (Scotland) Act 2003, the three grounds are merged and the Lands Tribunal is directed to consider seven factors in determining applications.[51]

The Lands Tribunal has power to add or substitute any provision which appears to be reasonable as a result of the variation or discharge of an obligation.[52] In this event, the applicant can either accept this or opt for the status quo. There are provisions for awarding compensation to the benefited proprietor for either substantial loss or disadvantage resulting from the variation or discharge or to make up for any reduction in the consideration paid to the benefited proprietor due to the existence of the obligation.

Key Concepts

Restrictions on landownership are imposed for the benefit of other landowners and the public generally. These are:

- restrictions at common law and by statute
- real burdens
- servitudes.

Under the common law unlawful interference with a neighbour's use and enjoyment of land is a **nuisance** which is a delictual wrong. Many statutes impose restrictions on the use of land in various ways.

A **real burden** is an encumbrance on land constituted in favour of an owner of other land as owner. Real burdens can be feudal or non-feudal. Non-feudal burdens will be abolished under the Abolition of Feudal Tenure etc. (Scotland) Act 2000 although some may be converted into a different type of burden.

The requirements of a real burden are:

- clear intention to burden the land not the person
- acceptable purpose
- expressed in clear terms
- registered in the Register of Sasines or Land Register.

---

47 Sch.1.

48 s.2(5).

49 s.1(3)(a), (b) and (c).

50 *Anderson v Trotter*, 1999 S.L.T. 442.

51 2003 Act, s.100.

52 1970 Act, s.1(5).

Under the Title Conditions (Scotland) Act 2003 the words "real burden" must be used and the real burden must be registered in the title of both the benefited and burdened land.

A person wishing to enforce a real burden must have a title and an interest to enforce. A third party may have an implied right to enforce if there is a *ius quaesitum tertio*. Implied rights are reformed under the Title Conditions (Scotland) Act 2003.

It will be possible to terminate a real burden which is more than 100 years old.

A **servitude** is a burden on land imposed by express or implied agreement in favour of owners of other land. They are enforceable against anyone.

Servitudes can be negative or positive and can be created by:

- express grant or reservation
- implied grant or reservation
- prescription.

Title conditions generally can be varied or discharged in various ways, including application to the Lands Tribunal.

LEASES

A lease is a contract between a landlord, usually the owner, and a tenant to use or possess land or other heritable subjects for a certain period in return for a rent, usually money. It is an ancient legal concept and old statutes as far back as the fifteenth century are still in force. 10–57

Key Concepts

There are three distinct **types of leases**:

- residential leases
- commercial and industrial leases
- agricultural leases and crofts.

Residential leases can be in either the public or private sector and there is considerable legislation controlling this area including right to buy legislation under which certain tenants in the public sector can purchase their rented property.[53] Similarly, agricultural leases and crofts are subject to considerable statutory controls which are under review at the time of writing.[54] Commercial and industrial leases, however, are largely free from specific statutory control[55] and depend on the contractual terms of the lease. In all types of lease, the common law and general statutes on leases applies in the absence of specific legislation.

53 See particularly the Housing (Scotland) Acts 1987, 1988 and 2001.

54 Agricultural Holdings (Scotland) Act 1991, Agricultural Holdings (Scotland) Act 2003 and Crofters (Scotland) Act 1993.

55 Exceptions are the Tenancy of Shops (Scotland) Act 1949 and 1964.

With the exception of leases for less than one year, a lease must be in writing.[56] Until 2000 there was no limit on the length of the lease. Since 2000, a lease cannot be longer than 175 years.[57]

Essentials of a lease

10–58

Key Concepts

There are four **essentials** for a contract of lease:

- two separate parties
- heritable subjects
- a period
- a rent.

As a lease is a contract the parties must agree on its terms and these parties must be two separate legal persons. It is not possible for a legal person to be both landlord and tenant.[58]

The subjects must be heritable, otherwise the contract will be for hire not a lease. The subjects must be properly identified in the lease. It is possible to lease fishing rights or rights to shoot game separate from the land where the fish and game are situated.

The period of the lease, known as a term or ish, must be definite or ascertainable. It cannot be for a period more than 175 years.[59] Where there is agreement between the parties on all the essentials of a lease but no period has been specified the law will imply a period of one year or a shorter period if consistent with the other terms of the lease.[60]

There must be a rent, which will normally be a sum of money paid periodically throughout the term of the lease. If there is no rent, there will be no lease but only a licence to occupy.

Real rights in leases

10–59 As a lease is a contract, at common law it is only personally binding and will not bind the successors of a landlord, rendering the tenant vulnerable to ejection by a successor of the landlord. To remedy this defect, the Leases Act 1449 was introduced and is still on the statute book today. If the requirements of the Act are satisfied the tenant in a lease has a real right which is enforceable against the landlord and the landlord's successors. The requirements of the Act are:

- if the lease is for more than a year it must be in writing
- the subjects must be land, thus excluding leases of fishing or shooting game
- a rent
- an ish
- the tenant must occupy personally
- the landlord's title must be registered.

It is also possible to acquire a real right in a lease if the lease is registerable and has been registered in the Register of Sasines or Land Register.[61]

---

[56] Requirements of Writing (Scotland) Act 1995, ss.1 and 2.
[57] Abolition of Feudal Tenure etc. (Scotland) Act 2000, s.67.
[58] *Kildrummy Estates (Jersey) Ltd v Inland Revenue Commissioners*, 1991 S.C. 1.
[59] Abolition of Feudal Tenure etc. (Scotland) Act 2000, s.67.
[60] *Shetland Islands Council v BP Petroleum Development Ltd*, 1990 S.L.T. 82.
[61] Registration of Leases (Scotland) Act 1857 as amended by the Land Tenure Reform (Scotland) Act 1974.

Security of tenure

10–60 The protection of obtaining a real right under the Leases Act 1449 or by registration of a lease ensures that a tenant will not be forced to vacate the subjects before the end of the term of the lease. In certain types of leases there are statutory provisions to give tenants security of tenure beyond the end of the period of the lease.[62] In addition, if no notice to quit is served by a landlord on a tenant before the end of the period of lease, the lease will renew for a period of one year or a shorter period if the original period was shorter under the principle of tacit relocation.

Assignation and subletting

10–61 The general principle is that a tenant cannot assign a lease to a new tenant without the consent of the landlord due to the operation of the doctrine *delectus persona,* meaning the landlord personally knows and accepts the particular tenant. The right to assign with consent is often inserted in a lease, but unless this is worded to say that consent will not be unreasonably withheld, a landlord will retain the right to accept or reject a particular new tenant.[63]

If an assignation does take place, the assignee is substituted for the original tenant and when the assignation is intimated to the landlord the original tenant ceases to have any rights or liabilities in respect of the lease.

Similarly, subletting is not possible unless the landlord agrees. Where it take place the original lease remains in force with all the rights and liabilities of the landlord and tenant intact and a new lease between the original tenant and the subtenant is created. There is no contractual relationship between the landlord and the subtenant unless the landlord is a party to the sublease.

Obligations of a landlord

10–62

Key Concepts

A **landlord** must:

- give full and undisturbed possession to the tenant for the full period of the lease
- provide the subjects in reasonable condition for their use
- keep the subjects in repair.

Once the tenant is in possession the landlord must not take any action to prejudice the tenant's possession[64] but the obligation is only in respect of deliberate actings.[65]

Golden Sea Produce Ltd v Scottish Nuclear plc

1992 S.L.T. 942

Owners of a fish hatchery business leased a site at Hunterston A Power Station for their business. The lease included a right to use the waste heated cooling water from the power station. A large stock of fish died from pollution by chlorine in the water pumped from the power station and used by the tenants. It was held that the landlords were under an implied obligation not to do anything which adversely affected the tenants' operations under the lease.

---

[62] *e.g.* under the Housing (Scotland) Acts 1987, 1988 and 2001 and the Agricultural Holdings (Scotland) Act 1991.

[63] *Lousada & Co Ltd v J E Lessel (Properties) Ltd*, 1990 S.C. 178.

[64] *Golden Sea Produce Ltd v Scottish Nuclear plc*, 1992 S.L.T. 942.

[65] *Chevron Petroleum (UK) Ltd v Post Office*, 1987 S.L.T. 588.

The subjects must be provided in a suitable condition for their use[66] but if let for commercial purposes it is the responsibility of the tenant to ensure that the proposed use is permitted under planning legislation.[67]

Under the common law, if a lease is an urban as opposed to a rural lease, that is one which is not for agricultural purposes, a landlord must keep the subjects in a tenantable and habitable condition throughout the period. They must be kept wind and water tight. A landlord must be aware of the need for repair before there will be a liability.

Key Concepts

A **tenant** must:

- enter into occupation and occupy and use the subjects
- use the subjects only for the purposes for which they are let
- take reasonable care of the subjects
- pay the rent when due
- plenish the subjects to secure the rent.

It is in the landlord's interest that the tenant actually occupies and uses the subjects for the period of the lease. If a tenant does not, a landlord may recind the lease for breach of contract.[68] In commercial leases it is usual to insert what are known as "keep open" or "keep trading" clauses to ensure that the tenant continues to occupy and trade from the commercial premises and such clauses will be enforceable by the courts.[69]

A tenant cannot use the subjects for a different purpose than that agreed in the lease.[70]

A tenant must take reasonable care of the subjects and this obligation continues until the lease comes to an end.[71]

A tenant must pay the rent on time and plenish the subjects to secure the rent which means that a tenant is obliged to stock the subjects with sufficient moveable property to be available as security for the rent.

Remedies for breach of terms of a lease

10–63 As a lease is a contract, both the landlord and tenant will have the usual contractual remedies available to them for breach of contract. These are interdict, specific implement, recission and damages. In addition, both the landlord and tenant have further remedies.

A landlord will have the usual remedies of a creditor for recovery of debt if the tenant fails to pay the rent, including summary diligence. A landlord also has a hypothec over most moveable property in the leased subjects. The hypothec excludes money and clothing but includes moveable property on the leased subjects which do not belong to the tenant.[72] The hypothec enables the landlord to sell these items to recover the rent but only the current year's rent and not arrears.

A landlord may be able to irritate the lease. An irritancy means that the lease comes to a premature end and the tenant's rights are extinguished. An irritancy can be legal or conventional. A legal irritancy is implied by law and occurs at common law if a tenant does not pay rent for two

---

[66] *Kippen v Oppenheim* (1847) 10 D. 242.
[67] *Ballantyne v Meoni*, 1997 G.W.D. 29–1489.
[68] *Blair Trust Co v Gilbert*, 1940 S.L.T. 322.
[69] *Retail Parks Investment Ltd v Royal Bank of Scotland*, 1996 S.L.T. 669 and subsequent cases.
[70] *Bayley v Addison* (1801) 8 S.L.T. 379.
[71] *Fry's Metals Ltd v Durastic Ltd*, 1991 S.L.T. 689.
[72] *Dundee Corporation v Marr*, 1971 S.C. 96.

years. There are also legal irritancies in legislation on agricultural holdings and crofts.[73] A conventional irritancy is where the lease has a specific term allowing this to happen. There are statutory controls on conventional irritancies.[74]

A landlord cannot physically eject a tenant even if in breach of the lease and must raise an action of removing.

In addition to the normal contractual remedies, a tenant may be entitled to a reduction in rent or abandon the lease where there is a material breach. There is little authority for this and the terms of a lease usually exclude these remedies.

Termination and tacit relocation

A lease will terminate in the following circumstances: 10–64

- at the end of the period
- on irritancy
- on recission by the landlord or tenant
- on renunciation by both parties
- on the total destruction of the subjects
- on the death of the tenant if granted for the tenant's lifetime.[75]

A lease will not terminate at the end of the period unless a notice to quit as been given by the landlord to the tenant before the end of the period. The period of notice may be agreed in the lease but there are minimum periods laid down by statute for particular types of lease.[76]

If a landlord fails to give notice to quit, the lease will be renewed under the principle of tacit relocation for a further period of one year or if the original period was less than one year, the same period.

Key Concepts

A **lease** is a contract between a landlord and a tenant to use or possess land or other heritable subjects for a certain period in return for a rent.

If a lease is for more than a year it must be in **writing.**

A tenant can acquire a **real right** under the Leases Act 1449 or by registering the lease if it is registrable.

It is a general principle that a tenant cannot **assign** or **sublet** without the consent of the landlord.

A **breach of terms** of a lease gives both the landlord and tenant the usual contractual remedies. In addition, a landlord may **irritate** the lease and bring it to a premature end. A landlord cannot physically **eject** a tenant but must raise an action of removing.

A lease will continue by **tacit relocation** if no notice to quit is given.

---

[73] Agricultural Holdings (Scotland) Act 1991, s.20 and Crofters (Scotland) Act 1993, s.5.
[74] Law Reform (Miscellaneous Provisions) (Scotland) Act 1985, ss.4–7.
[75] For succession to leases see Chapter 12.
[76] For example, Sheriff Courts (Scotland) Act 1907.

SECURITIES OVER HERITABLE PROPERTY

Standard securities

10–65 A security over heritable property which is registered in the Register of Sasines or Land Register gives the creditor a real right in security over the heritable subjects. In an ordinary debt the creditor has a personal obligation owed by the debtor. If the debtor grants the creditor a heritable security and defaults, the personal right under the debt is fortified by the real right under the security which, in essence, will normally allow the creditor to sell the security subjects to recover the debt.

Since 1970, a heritable security must be in the form of a standard security.[77] A standard security can be granted over any interest in land which is capable of being owned or held as a separate interest and to which a title can be registered in the Register of Sasines or the Land Register.[78] A standard security can be used to secure obligations to pay money or *ad factum praestandum,* that is to do something.[79] The debt may be a present, future or contingent debt.[80] A standard security can be granted by the debtor or a third party. A standard security is registered in the Register of Sasines or the Land Register. A standard security by a company must also be registered in the Companies Charges Register within 21 days of creation.[81]

Form

10–66 A standard condition can be in one of two forms, either A or B.[82] In form A, the debtor's personal obligation is included in the standard security and in form B the personal obligation is constituted in a separate deed. The 1970 Act sets out a number of standard conditions which are automatically incorporated into every standard security.[83] These deal with the debtor's rights and obligations and the powers of the creditor. With the exception of the power of sale and foreclosure, these can be varied by agreement between the debtor and creditor.[84]

Ranking

10–67 If there is more than one security over the same heritable property, the question of ranking is relevant. The general common law rule is that ranking depends on the date of registration of the security. A security registered earlier in time has prior ranking. If an earlier security secures future borrowing, a later security which is registered and intimated to the earlier security holder will limit the prior ranking to the amount advanced as at the date of intimation.[85] The creditors and the debtor can adjust the ranking by agreement in a ranking agreement.[86]

Assignation and transmission, restriction and discharge

10–68 A standard security may be assigned in whole or in part.[87] Both the creditor and debtor can assign.

On the death of the debtor, the liability is heritable in succession but if the security subjects when realised do not pay off the debt, the balance must be paid from the remainder of the estate.

On the death of the creditor, a standard security is moveable except for the calculation of legal rights.

---

[77] Conveyancing and Feudal Reform (Scotland) Act 1970, s.9.
[78] 1970 Act, s.9(8)(b), Land Registration (Scotland) Act 1979, s.29(1).
[79] 1970 Act, s.9(8)(c).
[80] s.9(8)(c).
[81] Companies Act 1985, s.410.
[82] 1970 Act, s.9(2) and Sch.2.
[83] Sch.3.
[84] s.11(3).
[85] *Union Bank of Scotland v National Bank of Scotland* (1886) 14 R. (H.L.) 1.
[86] s.13(3)(b).
[87] s.14 and Sch.4.

If the debtor is sequestrated, the heritable subjects vest in the permanent trustee,[88] but the trustee can only sell with the consent of the creditor unless sufficient money is obtained to settle all debts secured by heritable securities.[89]

A part of the security subjects may be released from the heritable security.[90] If there is a part payment, a form of partial discharge and deed of restriction is used. If there is no payment, a deed of restriction only is used.[91] A standard security is extinguished by payment of the debt in full or performance of the obligation secured. It is normal for the security to be formally discharged by registering a discharge in the Register of Sasines or Land Register.[92]

Default

A creditor has various remedies available when the debtor is in default. The creditor is in default in three situations: **10–69**

- where a calling up notice has been served but not complied with[93]
- where the debtor has failed to comply with other requirements[94]
- where the proprietor of the security subjects is insolvent.[95]

In the first situation the creditor will be able to exercise all the remedies available. In the second situation the creditor can follow a default notice procedure and then exercise all the remedies available except foreclosure. In the third situation and in the second situation where appropriate, the creditor can apply to the court to obtain all the remedies available.[96] The creditor's remedies are[97]:

- sale
- entering into possession
- carrying out repairs
- foreclosure.

In addition there are little used common law remedies:

- adjudication
- poinding of the ground.

In a sale the creditor must advertise the sale which may be by private bargain or public roup and has a duty to obtain the best price which can be reasonably obtained.[98] Under the Mortgage Rights (Scotland) Act 2001, once the creditor has set in motion the procedures that will give the creditor the remedy of sale, it is open to the debtor or proprietor of the security subjects or certain persons living with the debtor or proprietor to apply to the court to suspend the creditor's rights to such extent, for such period and subject to such conditions as the court thinks fit.[99] The purpose of this is
to allow the debtor to have more time to make arrangements to repay the loan in suitable circumstances where it is reasonable to do so.

---

88 Bankruptcy (Scotland) Act 1985, s.31(1).
89 1985 Act, s.39(4).
90 1970 Act, s.15.
91 Sch.4.
92 s.17, Sch.4.
93 Sch.3, 9(1)(a).
94 Sch.3, 9(1)(b).
95 Sch.3, 9(1)(c).
96 s.24.
97 Under Standard Condition 10 in Sch.3.
98 s.25.
99 s.2(1)(a).

If a creditor enters into possession the creditor may uplift rents or lease the subjects but may be subject to certain liabilities.[1]

Foreclosure is where a creditor has been unable to sell at a price sufficient to satisfy the debt and the court grants a decree to enable the creditor to take title to the security subjects.[2]

Floating charges

10–70 A floating charge is a security which can be created over heritable or moveable property by companies. It is an English concept which was introduced into Scotland in 1961.[3] It is not a fixed charge when created but becomes a fixed charge when it "crystallises" and attaches to the company's assets. Until it attaches the company is free to dispose of its assets without the consent of the holder of the floating charge. A floating charge attaches when the company goes into liquidation[4] or a receiver is appointed under the floating charge.[5] A floating charge does not attach to all company assets.[6]

A floating charge must be in writing and must be registered in the Companies Charges Register within 21 days of creation.[7] It is not registered in the Register of Sasines or the Land Register.

Floating charges usually contain ranking clauses prohibiting subsequent securities of any type in which case the floating charge will rank prior to any subsequent charge. Fixed charges created before the crystallisation of a floating charge rank prior to the floating charge. Where there is more than one floating charge ranking is determined by order of registration.

Floating charges are extinguished when the debt is paid in full.

Key Concepts

A **heritable security** which is registered in the Register of Sasines or Land Register gives the creditor a **real right** in security over the heritable subjects.

A heritable security must be in the form of a **standard security**. There are two types of standard security which are **Form A** which includes a personal obligation and **Form B** where the personal obligation is in a separate deed. Certain **standard conditions** are automatically incorporated into all standard securities.

Ranking of securities depends on the date of registration of the security.

A creditor has various **remedies** available when the debtor is in **default** including sale, entering into possession, carrying out repairs and foreclosure.

A **floating charge** is a security which can be created over heritable or moveable property by companies. It must be in writing, and it must be registered in the Companies Charges Register within 21 days. It only becomes a fixed charge when it "crystallises" and attaches to the company's assets.

1 See *David Watson Property Management Ltd v Woolwich Equitable Building Society*, 1992 S.L.T. 430.
2 1970 Act, s.28.
3 Companies (Floating Charges) (Scotland) Act 1961.
4 Companies Act 1985, s.461(1).
5 Insolvency Act 1986, ss.53(7) and 54(6).
6 See *Sharp v Thomson*, above.
7 Companies Act 1985, ss.410 and 420.

Quick Quiz

Property law

- What is the classic definition of "property"?
- Against whom is a real right enforceable?
- Why is possession important in heritable and moveable property?
- What is common interest?
- Original acquisition can be divided into which four categories?
- Is the feudal system still operating?
- What is the difference between the Register of Sasines and the Land Register?
- Who owns the air space above the roof of a tenement?
- State the four requirements of a real burden and the changes under the Title Conditions (Scotland) Act 2003.
- Who can enforce a real burden?
- What is the difference between a real burden and a servitude?
- What are the four essentials of a lease?
- What is the effect of the Mortgage Rights (Scotland) Act 2001?

Further Reading

The following titles would be of assistance:

Carey Miller, *Corporeal Moveables in Scots Law* (W. Green, 1991)

D.J. Cusine and R. Rennie, *Standard Securities* (2nd ed., W. Green, 2002)

D.J. Cusine and R. Rennie, *Missives* (2nd ed., Butterworths/Law Society of Scotland, 1999)

W. Gordon, *Scottish Land Law* (2nd ed., W. Green, 1999)

G. Gretton and K. Reid, *Conveyancing* (2nd ed., W. Green, 1999)

J. Halliday, *Conveyancing Law and Practice* (2nd ed., W. Green, Vol.1 1996, Vol.2 1997)

A. McAllister, *Scottish Law of Leases* (3rd ed., Butterworths, 2002)

A.J. McDonald, *Conveyancing Manual* (6th ed., T. & T. Clark, 1997)

R. Paisley, *Land Law* (W. Green, 2000)

K.G.C. Reid, *The Law of Property in Scotland* (Butterworths/Law Society of Scotland, 1996)

P. Robson and A. McCowan, *Property Law* (2nd ed., W. Green, 1998)

P. Robson and S. Halliday, *Residential Tenancies* (2nd ed., W. Green, 1998)

J.H. Sinclair, *Handbook of Conveyancing Practice* (4th ed., Butterworths/Law Society of Scotland, 2002)

Chapter 11

TRUSTS

James Chalmers[1]

THE TRUST CONCEPT

A trust may be most easily understood as a tripartite relationship, involving three roles: **11–01**

- the truster (the person who creates the trust and is the owner of the trust property before its creation);
- the trustee (who is the owner of the trust property after the trust is created and is responsible for administering the trust); and
- the beneficiary (the person for whose benefit the trust property is held by the trustee).

[1] Lecturer in Law, University of Aberdeen.

In other words, a trust is created when one person (the truster) transfers property to a second person (the trustee) who is then under an obligation to apply the property for the benefit of a third person (the beneficiary).

It is possible for there to be more than one truster, trustee or beneficiary, and it is possible for one person to hold more than one of those roles (except that a sole trustee cannot be a sole beneficiary).

Trust property is owned by the trustee.[2] However, if the trustee becomes insolvent, the trust property is not available to satisfy the claims of his creditors.[3] Nor is it available to satisfy the claims of the truster's creditors. In this fashion, it forms a separate "patrimony" from the property which the trustee owns personally.[4] This "insolvency effect" is the most important—and often the most useful—feature of the trust.[5] The trust can *itself* become insolvent and be sequestrated, however.[6]

Consequences of a trust

11–02 The trust is a versatile device and its use is not restricted to any one particular context. Seven useful features of the trust may be noted:

- it can divorce the right to benefit from property from the right of ownership of that property;
- it can divorce the right to benefit from property from the control and administration of that property;
- it can split the right to benefit from property between two or more individuals;
- it can place restrictions on the right to benefit from trust property, or lay down conditions which must be fulfilled before an individual is entitled to become owner of that property;
- it can be used to postpone a decision on who is to benefit from that property;
- it can be used to place property in the hands of persons who are regarded as more appropriate to administer it than the truster—perhaps because they are better qualified to do so, or are able to devote more time to the role; and
- as noted earlier, trust property is protected from the insolvency of either the truster or the trustee.

Why create a trust?

11–03 Trusts may be created for any number of reasons. Some of the more common are as follows:

- *Protection of the incompetent or the vulnerable.* A truster may wish to set up a trust for a beneficiary who is legally incapable of managing property, or whom the truster believes would not manage the property sensibly.
- *Trusts for the benefit of the public.* A truster may set up a trust fund to be applied to specified public purposes.
- *Collective investment purposes.* Trusts provide a convenient means of administering collective investment schemes (such as pension funds), which allow for professional management and diversification of investment to a degree which would not normally be available to individual investors.

---

2 See *Sharp v Thomson*, 1995 S.C. 455, *per* the Lord President (Hope) at 474–475 (decision reversed on other grounds at 1997 S.C. (H.L.) 66).

3 *Heritable Reversionary Co. Ltd v Millar* (1892) 19 R. (H.L.) 43.

4 For the "patrimony" theory, see K. G. C. Reid, "Patrimony not Equity: the trust in Scotland" (2000) 8 E.R.P.L. 427; G. L. Gretton, "Trusts Without Equity" (2000) 49 I.C.L.Q. 599.

5 See G. L. Gretton, "Constructive Trusts" (1997) 1 E. L. R. 281, 287–288.

6 *Bain, Petr* (1901) 9 S.L.T. 14.

- *Tax efficiency.* Manipulation of ownership and control by means of the trust device may be used by a truster in order to minimise liability to taxation.[7]
- *Executors.* The executors in a deceased's estate are (for most purposes) trustees on the estate.[8]

Classifications of trusts

Trusts are frequently classified in various ways. The following are the most important classifications: **11–04**

Public and private trusts

The distinction between public and private trusts is of considerable importance. It has been summarised as follows: **11–05**

> "A private trust is a trust designed to benefit a specified individual or a specified group of individuals … A public trust on the other hand is one that is set up for the benefit of the public in general, or of a specified class of the public in general."[9]

A number of consequences flow from this distinction. The most important consequence relates to the power of the Court of Session to sanction variation of trust purposes, as the relevant law is entirely different depending on whether the trust is private or public.[10] In addition, the courts generally adopt an approach of "benignant construction" towards public trusts,[11] accepting relatively vague statements of purpose as sufficient to create a valid trust,[12] and stepping in to provide machinery to give effect to those purposes where the truster has failed to do so.[13] The Lord Advocate also has the power to take court action in the public interest to enforce the purposes of a public trust.[14]

Inter vivos and mortis causa trusts

An *inter vivos* trust takes effect during the truster's lifetime; a *mortis causa* (or "testamentary") trust takes effect on the truster's death. A person who is appointed executor under a will may therefore be regarded as a trustee for most purposes.[15] **11–06**

Charitable trusts

Charity law is not part of the law of trusts, but many charities take the form of trusts. If a trust has been granted "recognised body" status by the Commissioners of Inland Revenue—meaning that it is entitled to relief from tax—it is subject to a regulatory framework which is contained in the Law Reform (Miscellaneous Provisions) (Scotland) Act 1990. The provisions of the 1990 Act impose certain duties on charities, particularly with regard to the keeping of accounting records, and gives **11–07**

---

7 For a useful summary of the relevant law, see R. A. Pearce and J. Stevens, *The Law of Trusts and Equitable Obligations* (2nd ed., 1998), 140–145.

8 See further W.A. Wilson and A.G.M. Duncan, *Trusts, Trustees and Executors* (2nd ed., 1995), paras 31–08 *et seq.*

9 K.McK. Norrie and E.M. Scobbie, *Trusts* (1991), 17–18. The distinction is not always easy to draw: see *Glentanar v Scottish Industrial Musical Association*, 1925 S.C. 226.

10 See below, paras 11–66 *et seq.*

11 See generally W.A. Wilson and A.G.M. Duncan, *Trusts, Trustees and Executors* (2nd ed., 1995), paras 14–47 *et seq.*

12 See below, para.11–19.

13 See J. Chalmers, *Trusts Cases and Materials* (2002), paras 12–10 to 12–12.

14 *Aitken's Trs v Aitken*, 1927 S.C. 374, *per* Lord Ashmore at 387.

15 For further discussion, see W.A. Wilson and A.G.M. Duncan, *Trusts, Trustees and Executors* (2nd ed., 1995), Chap.31.

the Lord Advocate a supervisory role over Scottish charities.[16] The law relating to charities in Scotland was recently reviewed by the Scottish Charity Law Commission, whose recommendations were under consideration by the Scottish Executive at the time of writing.[17]

Discretionary trusts

11–08 It is commonly said that Scots law does not recognise a special category of "discretionary trusts".[18] Nevertheless, a truster is entitled to confer discretion upon his trustees as to exactly who should benefit from a trust (*e.g.*, by creating a trust for "charitable purposes" and leaving his trustees to decide exactly which charities should benefit). There are limits, however, to how wide a discretion a truster may confer upon his trustees in such cases. This question is discussed further below.[19]

Trusts created voluntarily and those created by legal implication

11–09 Trusts are normally created voluntarily by the truster, and it is this type of trust with which this Chapter is primarily concerned. It is possible, however, for trusts to be created by implication of law. Both forms of creation are discussed in the next section.

> **Key Concepts**
>
> A **trust** is created when one person (the truster) transfers property to a second person (the trustee) who is then under an obligation to apply the property for the benefit of a third person (the beneficiary).
>
> It is possible for there to be more than one truster, trustee or beneficiary.
>
> The trustee is the owner of trust property.
>
> Trust property is protected from the insolvency of either the truster or the trustee.
>
> Trusts may be either **private trusts** (for the benefit of individuals or a specified group of individuals) or **public trusts** (for the benefit of the general public or a specified class of the public).
>
> Trusts may be also be either ***inter vivos*** (taking effect during the truster's lifetime) or ***mortis causa*** (taking effect on the death of the truster).
>
> While trusts are normally created **voluntarily**, they may also be created **by implication of law**.

---

[16] For further detail, see J. Chalmers, *Trusts: Cases and Materials* (2002), Chap.11, and C.R. Barker (ed.), *Charity Law in Scotland* (1996).

[17] *Charity Scotland: The Report of the Scottish Charity Law Review Commission* (2001). See also J. McFadden, "The Modernisation of Charity Law in Scotland: The Report of the Scottish Charity Law Commission" (2001) 6 S.L.P.Q. 215.

[18] See, *e.g.* K. McK Norrie and E. M. Scobbie, *Trusts* (1991), p.23.

[19] See below, para.11–19.

CREATION OF A TRUST

Who can create a trust?

The law does not place any specific restrictions on the type of person who may create a trust. The general rules of legal capacity apply, and therefore children under 16—who normally have no legal capacity to enter into any transaction—cannot normally be trusters.[20] Where a truster is insolvent at the time of the trust's creation, or was rendered insolvent by its creation, the trust may be challenged as a gratuitous alienation[21]—but this is an issue of insolvency law and is not specific to the law of trusts in any way. **11–10**

What property can be subject to a trust?

Again, there are no specific restrictions on the type of property which may be subject to a trust. It is, therefore, commonly said that "any property which can be alienated can be the subject of a trust".[22] Even that statement may be too restrictive—it has been held in England that where a person holds property which he is legally incapable of alienating (perhaps because he is bound by contract not to do so), he can nevertheless declare *himself* to be trustee of that property.[23] There would seem to be no good reason why the Scottish courts would not take the same view.[24] **11–11**

How to create a trust

Trusts may be divided into two types—those created voluntarily and those created by legal implication. There are different rules governing the creation of each type of trust (and, indeed, a number of different types of legally implied trust, each of which is created in a different way). The following section deals with the creation of voluntary trusts; legally implied trusts are dealt with later in this Chapter.[25] **11–12**

How to create a trust: voluntarily created trusts

Two requirements must be satisfied for the creation of a voluntary trust. There must be (a) a declaration of trust and (b) a transfer of property from the truster to the trustee. **11–13**

Declaration of trust

In order to create a trust, A must transfer property to B accompanied by a declaration that B is to apply the property for specified purposes. No "special or technical" form of words is required.[26] **11–14**

The crucial question is this: did A (i) intend to make an outright gift of the property to B coupled with a recommendation as to how the property should be applied, but ultimately leaving it up to B as to what he chose to do with the property—in which case no trust is created—or (ii)

---

20 Age of Legal Capacity (Scotland) Act 1991, ss.1(1)(a) and 2(1).

21 See generally Bankruptcy (Scotland) Act 1985, s.34; Insolvency Act 1986, s.242; D.W. McKenzie Skene, *Insolvency Law in Scotland* (1999), Chap.30.

22 W.A. Wilson and A.G.M. Duncan, *Trusts, Trustees and Executors* (2nd ed., 1995), para.2–18. See also A. Mackenzie Stuart, *The Law of Trusts* (1932), p.65.

23 *Don King Productions Inc. v Warren* [1999] 3 W.L.R. 276; *Swift v Dairywise Farms* [2000] 1 W.L.R. 1117.

24 See further D. Cabrelli, "Can Scots Lawyers Trust Don King? Trusts in the Commercial Context" (2001) 6 S.L.P.Q. 103; J. Chalmers, *Trusts: Cases and Materials* (2002), paras 3.07–3.09.

25 See below, paras 11–25 *et seq.*

26 *Macpherson v Macpherson's CB* (1894) 21 R. 386, *per* Lord McLaren at 387.

intend to bind B to apply the property to specified purposes, thus creating a trust? The following two cases illustrate the distinction:

Barclay's Exr. v McLeod

(1880) 7 R. 477

Mr Barclay died, leaving all his property to his wife. His will stated that it was his "anxious desire" that "as soon after my death as is convenient", his wife should execute a will dividing one-half of her property at the time of her death amongst certain relatives specified by Mr Barclay. His wife later died without ever having executed any will.

It was argued that, because Mr Barclay had transferred property to Mrs Barclay while specifying certain purposes to which that property was to be applied, she held that property in trust and her executor was therefore required to distribute that property in accordance with Mr Barclay's wishes. This argument was rejected. Mr Barclay's "anxious desire" was no more than a recommendation.

Macpherson v Macpherson's CB

(1894) 21 R. 386

Robina Young died in 1893, leaving money "to Katherine Alexandrina Macpherson, for the benefit of herself and her sister Jane Macpherson". (Jane Macpherson was mentally incapable and reliant on others for her care). There was some doubt about the meaning of this provision in Miss Young's will, and a special case was presented to the Court of Session.

It was held that the words "for the benefit of" were quite clear—this was not an absolute gift to Katherine, but instead a gift to Katherine in trust for the benefit of herself and her sister.

While words such as "in trust" or "on behalf of" will normally be sufficient to create a trust, they will only have that effect "if the circumstances of the case are consistent with that interpretation".[27]

No special formalities are required for the declaration of trust—and so, therefore, the declaration may be verbal—except in the following three cases, where a written document subscribed by the truster is required[28]:

- "a trust whereby a person declares himself to be sole trustee of his own property or any property which he may require",[29]
- a trust of an interest in land (except where created by court decree, statute or rule of law),[30]
- a *mortis causa* trust (*i.e.* one created by a will).[31]

---

[27] *Style Financial Services Ltd v Bank of Scotland (No.2)*, 1998 S.L.T. 851, *per* Lord Gill at 865. See also *Gillespie v City of Glasgow Bank* (1879) 6 R. (H.L.) 104, *per* Lord Cairns LC at 107 (there is no magic about the word "trust").

[28] See Requirements of Writing (Scotland) Act 1995, s.2(1). Witnessing is not essential for validity, but it is desirable because a properly witnessed document will have "self-proving" status (*i.e.* it will be presumed to have been signed by the granter). See the 1995 Act, s.3 for the relevant formalities.

[29] Requirements of Writing (Scotland) Act 1995, s.2(a)(iii).

[30] Requirements of Writing (Scotland) Act 1995, s.2(b).

[31] Requirements of Writing (Scotland) Act 1995, s.2(c).

Transfer of property

A trust will not be effective until the trust property is transferred to the trustee. It has been observed that the requirement of a transfer of property is necessary to prevent fraudulent misuse of the trust device: 11–15

Allan's Trs v Inland Revenue
1971 S.L.T. 62

Lord Reid: "I reject the argument ... that a mere proved intention to make a trust coupled with the execution of a declaration of trust can suffice. If that were so it would be easy to execute such a declaration, keep it in reserve, use it in case of bankruptcy to defeat the claims of creditors, but if all went well and the trustee desired to regain control of the fund simply suppress the declaration of trust."

While the property may be transferred to the trustee by physical delivery, that is not essential. First, some types of property (heritable and incorporeal property) cannot, for obvious reasons, be transferred in this way. Secondly, it is possible to transfer ownership in corporeal moveable property without actually moving the property—in *Milligan v Ross*,[32] a woman executed a deed of trust in which she transferred furnishings and household goods to trustees for the benefit of herself, her husband and her daughter. The trust deed was delivered to the trustees and registered in the Books of Council and Session. Mrs Milligan remained in possession of the property. It was held that these actions were sufficient for delivery and that a valid trust had been created.

The law relating to the transfer of property is not specific to the law of trusts, but is of general application and is discussed elsewhere in this book.[33]

Problem of the truster as trustee

It is possible for a truster to declare himself to be sole trustee of his own property. In such a case, there can obviously be no question of delivery between the truster and the trustee. As an alternative to the transfer of property, therefore, intimation to the beneficiaries of their rights under the trust is required for the trust's creation.[34] Intimation to an agent (such as a solicitor or accountant) or to a parent (where the beneficiary is a child) will normally be sufficient.[35] 11–16

Where there are multiple beneficiaries under a trust, intimation to one of the beneficiaries will suffice.[36] Such a course should only be followed with caution, however: in *Clark's Trs v Inland Revenue*,[37] C took out seven assurance policies which he purported to hold for seven different beneficiaries. There was one single proposal form and the initial premiums were paid by one single cheque. Despite this, it was held that these were seven separate trusts and intimation to one of the beneficiaries was insufficient to bring the other six trusts into effect.

The intimation must take place simultaneously with, or subsequent to, the execution of the declaration of trust.[38] If it takes place before the declaration of trust, it is merely an expression of an intention to create a trust and is not legally effective. Furthermore, a declaration of trust cannot be made unless there is actually a trust fund in existence:

---

32 1994 S.C.L.R. 430.
33 See above, Chapter 10.
34 *Allan's Trs v Inland Revenue*, 1971 S.L.T. 62.
35 *Kerr's Trs v Inland Revenue*, 1974 S.L.T. 193, *per* Lord Fraser at 201.
36 *Allan's Trs v Inland Revenue*, 1971 S.L.T. 62.
37 1972 S.L.T. 190.
38 *Kerr's Trs v Inland Revenue*, 1974 S.L.T. 193.

Clark Taylor & Co. Ltd v Quality Site Development (Edinburgh) Ltd[39]

1981 S.C. 111

C sold bricks to Q under a contract which stated that if Q resold or otherwise disposed of the bricks before Q had paid C for them, Q would hold the proceeds of the disposal in trust for C until payment had been made. It was held that this contract could not in itself create a trust, as there was no trust fund in existence at the time the contract was made—the proceeds of disposal were not received until a later date.

Validity of the trust purposes

11–17 The declaration of trust must specify the purposes of the trust in order to be effective. Trust purposes may be invalid for three reasons. First, they may be void from uncertainty. Secondly, they may be overly wide and therefore ineffective. Thirdly, they may be illegal. Each of these categories will be dealt with in turn.

Purposes void from uncertainty

11–18 Purposes will be void from uncertainty if it is impossible to establish their meaning. An example is provided by the following case:

Hardie v Morison

(1899) 7 S.L.T. 42

David Hardie's will directed his trustees to use his estate for the purposes of establishing "a shop in which one of the objects is the sale of books dealing with the subject of free thought."

Lord Kincairney: "I think that a bequest for the promotion of free thought is void from uncertainty, from want of any recognised or determinate meaning of that term ... In carrying out this trust it would not be possible to determine what class of books was intended."

By contrast, in *McLean v Henderson's Trs,*[40] it was held that a bequest "for the advancement and diffusion of the science of phrenology" was valid. It was observed that "the expression phrenology denotes a known, although not a flourishing, branch of science".

Overly wide purposes

11–19 It is not essential (and in many cases it would not be possible) for a truster to specify down to the last detail how his trustees should distribute or apply his property. He may confer a degree of discretion on his trustees to make that decision:

Crichton v Grierson

(1828) 3 W. & S. 329

Lord Lyndhurst LC: "a party may, in the disposition of his property, select particular classes of individuals and objects, and then give to some particular individual a power, after his death, of appropriating the property, or applying any part of his property, to any particular individuals among that class whom that person may select and describe in his will."

---

[39] For further discussion of the issues arising from this case, see G. L. Gretton, "Using Trusts as Commercial Securities" (1988) 33 J.L.S.S. 53; W. A. Wilson, "Romalpa and Trust" 1983 S.L.T. (News) 106.

[40] (1880) 7 R. 601.

(Although Lord Lyndhurst is dealing here with *mortis causa* trusts—those created on death—the same principle is applicable to *inter vivos* trusts.)

Two issues arise from Lord Lyndhurst's statement of principle. First, there must be a selection of a "particular individual" (or individuals) as trustee(s). Secondly, the truster must select a "particular class" of individuals and objects. The trustees must then exercise their discretion as to who (or what) within that "particular class" is to benefit from the trust.

The first issue—the selection of a "particular individual" is unproblematic in *inter vivos* trusts, as it is impossible to create such a trust without appointing trustees. It may be problematic, however, in *mortis causa* trusts. In such cases, the trustees named in the testator's will may have died before the testator or may decline office—or the testator may simply fail to name an executor in his will. While in such cases, the courts may appoint an executor-dative or judicial factor to administer the deceased's estate, these persons are not entitled to exercise discretion in carrying out trust purposes.[41] In such cases, therefore, the trust purposes will be invalid as being overly wide, and the trust will fail. This is illustrated by the following case:

Angus's Exrx. v Batchan's Trs

1949 S.C. 335

Anne Angus's will directed that, after certain specific legacies had been paid, the residue of her estate should be given to charity. She did not nominate a trustee or executor. It was held that this bequest was, therefore, invalid:

Lord President (Cooper): "No encroachment has yet been tolerated on the basic requirement that a testator must make his own will, and that, when he makes it by designating a class and a person to choose within that class, the designation of both must be his own act, express or plainly implied. To allow a testator to confine himself to designating the class, while deliberately leaving the choice of the individual beneficiaries to anyone who may anyhow acquire a title to administer the estate is, in my opinion, to authorise that testator to delegate the power to test ... A *mortis causa* declaration of charitable benevolence is not a will."

Secondly, the "particular class" must be specified by the trustee. The test for this is "whether or not the [trustee] has described the class he means to benefit with sufficient accuracy as to enable a reasonable man to know who the persons are that he meant to benefit, leaving it only to the trustees to select among those who form that class the particular recipients of his bounty."[42]

It has been held, therefore, that it is insufficient to give property to trustees "to be disposed of ... in such manner as they may think proper"[43] or "in such way or ways as my trustees shall deem best".[44] By contrast, a direction that the residue of a testator's estate should be disposed of "among any poor relations, friends or acquaintances of mine" was held to be valid.[45]

A more difficult question arises where a truster uses a vague form of words such as "public purposes" or "charitable purposes".[46] A special status is given to the words "charitable purposes", which are valid without any further specification.[47] "Educational purposes" is probably sufficiently specific.[48] By contrast, "benevolent purposes" and "public purposes" are not.[49] "Religious purposes" is not sufficiently specific unless the relevant religion is specified.[50]

---

41 *Angus's Exrs v Batchan's Trs*, 1949 S.C. 335; *Vollar's J.F. v Boyd*, 1952 S.L.T. (Notes) 84. The authorities are not entirely clear, however: see further, J. Chalmers, *Trusts: Cases and Materials* (2002), paras 5.11–5.13.

42 *Salvesen's Trs v Wye*, 1954 S.C. 440, *per* Lord Carmont at 444.

43 *Sutherland's Trs v Sutherland's Tr.* (1893) 20 R. 925.

44 *Allan and Others (Shaw's Trs)* (1893) 1 S.L.T. 308.

45 *Salvesen's Trs v Wye*, 1954 S.C. 440.

46 As to the even more difficult situation which arises where such terms are combined (*e.g.* a bequest to "charitable and religious purposes"), see W. A. Wilson and A. G. M. Duncan, *Trusts, Trustees and Executors* (2nd ed., 1995), paras 14–100 to 14–117.

47 *Turnbull's Trs v Lord Advocate*, 1918 S.C. (H.L.) 88; A. Mackenzie Stuart, *The Law of Trusts* (1932), 112.

48 *Brough v Brough's Trs*, 1950 S.L.T. 117. *cf. Harper's Trs v Jacobs*, 1929 S.C. 345.

Illegal purposes

11–20 There are four types of purpose which will be held invalid due to illegality, which are as follows[51]:

- criminal purposes;
- directly prohibited purposes;
- purposes which are *contra bonos mores*; and
- purposes which are contrary to public policy.

Each of these will be dealt with in turn.

(i) Criminal purposes

11–21 There is an almost total absence of authority on this issue, and it is doubtful that it is of much practical importance. It is clear, however, that a trust for criminal purposes is void. The following English case illustrates the point:

Bowman v Secular Society Ltd
[1917] A.C. 406

Charles Bowman left the residue of his estate to the Secular Society Limited, the principal purpose of which was "to promote ... the principle that human conduct should be based upon natural knowledge, and not upon super-natural belief." It was argued that these purposes would necessarily involve committing the criminal offence of blasphemy and that the bequest to the Society was therefore void. The House of Lords held that such conduct was not necessarily blasphemous, and that the bequest was therefore valid. It was accepted that if carrying out the purposes of the Society did amount to blasphemy, the bequest would have been for a criminal purpose and therefore unenforceable.

(ii) Directly prohibited purposes

11–22 There are three forms of trust purpose which are directly prohibited by statute, as follows:

(a) *Entails.*[52] An entail is a device which was historically used to keep heritable property in the same family indefinitely. The owner would normally be obliged to pass the property to his eldest son on his death, and the son on to his eldest son, and so on. This device came to be seen as economically and socially disadvantageous and was gradually restricted by statute. The creation of entails was finally prohibited in 1914.[53] Any existing entails will cease to exist when the Abolition of Feudal Tenure etc. (Scotland) Act 2000 is brought into force.[54]

(b) *Successive liferents.*[55] Successive liferents are similar to entails but can be used in relation to moveable property. A truster might, for example, direct that the trustee is to receive a liferent of the property and hold the fee in trust for his (the trustee's) eldest son, who is then to receive a liferent of the property and hold the fee in trust for his eldest son, and so on. While successive liferents can still be created, their duration is now restricted by statute. If

---

[49] *Caldwell's Trs v Caldwell*, 1920 S.C. 700, *per* Lord Skerrington at 702 ("benevolent purposes"); *Blair v Duncan* (1901) 4 F. (H.L.) 1 ("public purposes").

[50] *Grimond v Grimond's Trs* (1905) 7 F. (H.L.) 90; *Bannerman's Trs v Bannerman*, 1915 S.C. 398.

[51] *Bowman v Secular Society Ltd* [1917] A.C. 406, *per* Lord Dunedin at 434.

[52] See generally Scottish Law Commission, *Report on Abolition of the Feudal System* (Scot. Law Com. No.168, 1998), paras 9.8–9.17.

[53] Entail (Scotland) Act 1914.

[54] See ss.50–52 of that Act.

[55] On the concept of liferent and fee generally, see Chapter 10.

a person, who was not alive or *in utero* (conceived but unborn) at the time the deed was executed becomes entitled to a liferent interest under the deed, they become the absolute owner of the property.[56] This applies unless they are not yet of full age, in which case they will become the absolute owner upon reaching that age.[57]

(c) *Excessive accumulations of income*. A truster may not create a trust where the trust income is simply added to the trust fund and not spent for longer than certain periods of time. The applicable period of time is generally 21 years, but there are a number of other possibilities depending on the applicability of certain rather complex statutory provisions.[58]

(iii) Purposes which are *contra bonos mores*

Trust purposes may be invalid as being *contra bonos mores* (described by Lord Dunedin in *Bowman v Secular Society Ltd* as "offence against what may be termed the natural moral sense"[59]). This head of invalidity has most commonly been used to hold that conditions attached to bequests in wills are invalid. The cases may be divided into three categories, as follows: **11–23**

(a) *Conditions relating to living arrangements*. In *Fraser v Rose*,[60] a testator left money to his (adult) daughter on the condition that she should leave her mother within four weeks of his death and never live with her again. It was held that the condition was invalid and that the daughter should take the bequest free of the condition.
(b) *Conditions relating to marriage*. A condition that a person may only take a benefit under a trust if they remain unmarried is generally thought to be invalid.[61] However, it is competent to establish a trust to provide financial support for a person for as long as they remain unmarried, and so in *Sturrock v Rankin's Trs*, a provision which was "not a condition in restraint of marriage, but simply a provision for unmarried daughters who, in the view of the testator, had no other means of support"[62] was held to be valid. The distinction is a narrow one.
(c) *Conditions relating to religion*. A truster may provide that a person may only benefit under a trust if he adheres (or refrains from adhering) to a particular religion.[63] However, a condition that a beneficiary must promise to maintain a particular faith for the rest of his life before taking a benefit would probably be invalid as being *contra bonos mores*.[64]

Where a condition is held invalid, the beneficiary will normally take the benefit without being required to comply with the condition.[65]

(iv) Purposes which are contrary to public policy

While "public policy" is a recognised ground of invalidity, the term is a misleading one. In this context, it refers to a very narrow doctrine, which is that if trust purposes "are unreasonable as conferring neither a patrimonial benefit upon anybody nor a benefit upon the public or any section thereof, the directions are invalid."[66] The following two cases provide examples of such invalidity: **11–24**

---

[56] Law Reform (Miscellaneous Provisions) (Scotland) Act 1968, s.18.
[57] "Full age" for these purposes is the age of 18: Age of Majority (Scotland) Act 1969, s.1.
[58] Trusts (Scotland) Act 1961, s.5 and the Law Reform (Miscellaneous Provisions) (Scotland) Act 1966, s.6. See generally, W. A. Wilson and A. G. M. Duncan, *Trusts, Trustees and Executors* (2nd ed., 1995), Chap.9.
[59] [1917] A.C. 406, at 434.
[60] (1849) 11 D. 1466. See also *Grant's Trs v Grant* (1898) 25 R. 929.
[61] *Aird's Exrs v Aird*, 1949 S.C. 154. A condition that the beneficiary should not marry a specified individual appears to be valid: *Forbes v Forbes's Trs* (1882) 9 R. 675.
[62] (1875) 2 R. 850, *per* Lord Gifford at 854.
[63] *Blathwayt v Baron Cawley* [1976] A.C. 397.
[64] *Innes's Trs v Innes*, 1963 S.L.T. 353, *per* Lord Carmont at 358.
[65] There are conflicting statements on this point in the textbooks, however. For discussion, see J. Chalmers, *Trusts: Cases and Materials* (2002), paras 5.29–5.30.
[66] *Aitken's Trs v Aitken*, 1927 S.C. 374, *per* Lord Sands at 381.

McCaig's Trs v Kirk-Session of United Free Church of Lismore

1915 S.C. 426

In her will, Catherine McCaig directed that her trustees should convert the McCaig Tower in Oban into a private enclosure, and should erect bronze statues within the tower of members of her family, each of which was to cost not less than £1,000. The trustees were to be bound in all time coming not to sell the tower and statutes. It was held that these purposes were invalid as conferring no benefit on any person: the incidental benefit which might be received by workmen in constructing the enclosure was insufficient.

Sutherland's Tr. v Verschoyle

1968 S.L.T. 43

A testatrix directed in her will that her trustees should purchase a house "of a certain size and dignity" in St Andrews to exhibit and preserve for perpetuity her "valuable art collection". In actual fact, the "collection" was unlikely to attract any scholarly or public interest, and many of the items were simply copies. It was held that her directions were invalid, as they conferred no benefit either on particular individuals or the general public.

There are two exceptional cases, however, where trust purposes may be valid despite the fact that they do not confer any benefit upon particular individuals or the general public. These are trusts for memorials (provided they are not unreasonable or extravagant),[67] and trusts for the maintenance of particular animals.[68] Trusts for the benefit of a class of animals or the prevention of cruelty to animals are regarded as conferring a benefit upon the general public.[69]

How to create a trust: legally implied trusts

Resulting trusts

11–25 A resulting trust will arise where the purposes of an existing trust fail to dispose of all the trust property. In such a case, the trustees will be deemed to be holding the trust property in a resulting trust for the benefit of the truster or his representatives. This is probably not, strictly speaking, a special form of trust, but simply a "term implied by law into all [voluntarily created] trusts".[70] However, it arises in special circumstances and for that reason is normally treated separately in the textbooks.

A resulting trust may arise in two principal types of case. Firstly, the trust purposes may be void or impossible to fulfil.[71] Secondly, the trust purposes may not exhaust the full trust estate,[72] as in the following case:

[67] *Lindsay's Exr. v Forsyth*, 1940 S.C. 568, *per* the Lord Justice-Clerk (Aitchison) at 572.

[68] *Flockhart's Trs v Bourlet*, 1934 S.N. 23. See further K. McK Norrie, "Trusts for Animals" (1987) 32 J.L.S.S. 386.

[69] *Aitken's Trs v Aitken*, 1927 S.C. 374, *per* Lord Sands at 381; A. Mackenzie Stuart, *The Law of Trusts* (1932), pp.69–71.

[70] G. L. Gretton, "Constructive Trusts" (1997) 1 Edin. L.R. 281, at 309.

[71] See, *e.g. Templeton v Burgh of Ayr*, 1910 2 S.L.T. 12. Or, exceptionally, unascertainable: see *Thomas v Tennent's Trs* (1868) 7 M. 114.

[72] This application of the doctrine can pose particular problems with regard to public subscriptions (fundraising). See further J. Chalmers, *Trusts: Cases and Materials* (2002), paras 2.34–2.36.

Anderson v Smoke

(1898) 25 R. 493

Mr Anderson created a trust for the benefit of his son, to be administered by his two daughters as trustees. Upon the death of the son, only half of the fund had been spent. It was held that the trustees were not entitled to keep the money for themselves, but should return it to Mr Anderson's heirs.

Fiduciary fees

A fiduciary fee is a special kind of trust created where A purports to transfer property to B in liferent and to B's children in fee despite B having no children at the time.[73] Such a transfer cannot be effective in its own terms, as it would leave the fee in an "ownerless" state. To avoid this problem, B will be deemed in such cases to hold the property as a kind of trustee, for himself in liferent and his children in fee.[74] This device is now largely obsolete, although still technically competent.[75] If such an arrangement were desired nowadays, it would be normal to explicitly create a trust rather than rely upon this doctrine. **11–26**

Constructive trusts

Scots law (in stark contrast to English law) only recognises constructive trusts to a very limited extent—if, indeed, these are recognised at all. It is commonly thought that a constructive trust will be created in two situations, as follows[76]: **11–27**

(a) *Where a person in a fiduciary position gains an advantage by virtue of that position.* An example is provided by the following case:

Cherry's Trs v Patrick

1911 2 S.L.T. 313

Mr Patrick, a wholesaler, supplied goods to Mr Cherry's business. Upon Mr Cherry's death, he was appointed a trustee on Mr Cherry's estate. The trustees continued to run the business and Mr Patrick continued to supply goods to it. It was held that this amounted to Mr Patrick taking a benefit from his fiduciary position, and that he was therefore obliged to return the benefit received to the trust.

It is commonly asserted that Mr Patrick held the benefit received from his dealings on a constructive trust,[77] although the court does not explicitly refer to the concept of "constructive trust" at any point.[78]

---

[73] On liferent and fee generally, see Chapter 10.

[74] Trusts (Scotland) Act 1921, s.8.

[75] For discussion, see G. L. Gretton, "Trusts", in *A History of Private Law in Scotland* (Reid and Zimmerman, eds., 2000), Vol.1, 481, at 513; W. A. Wilson and A. G. M. Duncan, *Trusts, Trustees and Executors* (2nd ed., 1995), paras 6–01 to 6–21.

[76] The classification is from W. A. Wilson and A. G. M. Duncan, *Trusts, Trustees and Executors* (2nd ed., 1995), para. 6–61.

[77] See, *e.g.* K. McK Norrie and E. M. Scobbie, *Trusts* (1991), p.55.

[78] G. L. Gretton, "Constructive Trusts" (1997) 1 Edin. L.R. 281, at 294.

(b) *Where a person who is a stranger to an existing trust is to his knowledge in possession of property belonging to the trust.* Although the existence of this type of constructive trust in Scots law has been asserted on a number of occasions,[79] supporting authority is slim if not non-existent.[80]

There is no doubt that a person in position (a) or (b) is under an obligation to repay the benefit received. However, it has been argued that this has nothing to do with any doctrine of constructive trust.[81] The question of whether or not a trust has been created would only be of importance if the alleged "constructive trustee" had become insolvent, as the existence of a trust would protect the trust funds from the claims of his other creditors.[82] In cases not involving insolvency, the result is the same, whether or not it is reached by the creation of a constructive trust.

Key Concepts

There are no specific restrictions on the persons who may create a trust or the type of property which may be subject to a trust. The general rules of property and legal capacity apply.

A **voluntarily created trust** is created by (a) a **declaration of trust** accompanied by (b) a **transfer of property** from the truster to the trustee.

Where the truster and the trustee are the same person, there can be no transfer of property. In such cases, **intimation to the beneficiaries** of their rights under the trust is required for the creation of the trust.

Trust purposes may be **invalid** for the following reasons:

- they may be too uncertain (*i.e.* the truster's meaning cannot be ascertained);
- they may be overly wide;
- they may be illegal as being:
  - contrary to the criminal law;
  - directly prohibited (entails, accumulations of income and successive liferents);
  - *contra bonos mores* (an offence against the "natural moral sense"); or
  - contrary to public policy (if they confer no benefit upon any person).

A **resulting trust** is a type of legally implied trust. It will arise where the purposes of an existing trust fail to dispose of all the trust property. In such a case, the trustees will hold the remaining property in trust for the original truster or his representatives.

---

79 W. A. Wilson and A. G. M. Duncan, *Trusts, Trustees and Executors* (2nd ed., 1995), paras 6–65 to 6–68; K. McK Norrie and E. M. Scobbie, *Trusts* (1991), p.54.

80 *cf. Huisman v Soepboer*, 1994 S.L.T. 682, discussed by G. L. Gretton, "Constructive Trusts" (1997) 1 Edin. L.R. 281, at 300.

81 G. L. Gretton, "Constructive Trusts" (1997) 1 Edin. L.R. 281.

82 *cf. Sutnam International Inc v Herbage*, Outer House, August 2, 1991, unreported (excerpted in J. Chalmers, *Trusts: Cases and Materials* (2002), para.2.43), and see G. L. Gretton, "Constructive Trusts and Insolvency" (2000) 8 E.R.P.L. 463. On this "insolvency effect", see above, para.11–01.

> A **constructive trust** will be created where:
>
> - a person in a fiduciary position gains an advantage by virtue of that position; or
> - a person who is a stranger to a trust is to his knowledge in possession of property belonging to the trust.
>
> In such cases, the constructive trustee will be required to communicate the relevant property to the trust estate. There is some doubt as to whether this is, strictly speaking, actually a form of trust.

OFFICE OF TRUSTEE

Who can be a trustee?

The law does not generally place any specific restrictions on the type of person who may act as trustees. The general rules of legal capacity apply, and therefore children under 16—who normally have no legal capacity to enter into any transaction—cannot normally be trustees.[83] Bankruptcy or insolvency is not normally a barrier to acting as a trustee.[84] A person may be both truster and trustee. **11–28**

There are, however, specific statutory restrictions on the type of person who may act as a trustee in certain types of trust, particularly charitable trusts.[85]

Appointment and acceptance of the original trustees

Trustees will generally be appointed in the trust deed. They may be named as individuals, or identified *ex officio* (as the holder of an office). For example, the trust deed in *Parish Council of Kilmarnock v Ossington's Trs*[86] stated that one of the trustees would be "the chairman of the Parochial Board of the parish of Kilmarnock". Essentially, any description which is sufficient to identify the relevant individual is enough—in *Martin v Ferguson's Trs,*[87] a testator's will stated that "I wish my estate to be managed by the same trustees as my brother", and that was held to be sufficient. **11–29**

The trustee must accept office. No trustee can be forced to accept office against his will.[88] No particular form of acceptance is required—and, indeed, acceptance need not necessarily be express but can be inferred from actions, as the following case demonstrates:

---

83 Age of Legal Capacity (Scotland) Act 1991, s.9(f).

84 See A. J. P. Menzies, *The Law of Scotland Affecting Trustees* (2nd ed., 1913), paras 77 and 913 and cases cited there.

85 Law Reform (Miscellaneous Provisions) (Scotland) Act 1990, s.8. See also Pensions Act 1995, ss.3–6 and 29–30 (pension trusts); Finance Act 1989, Sch.5, para.3(3)(c) (employee share ownership trusts) and the Inheritance Tax Act 1984, Sch.4, para.2(ii).

86 (1896) 23 R. 833.

87 (1892) 19 R. 474.

88 *Vestry of St Silas Church v Trs of St Silas Church*, 1945 S.C. 110, *per* the Lord Justice-Clerk (Cooper) at 121 (referring to *ex officio* trustees, but the point is of general application).

Ker v City of Glasgow Bank
(1879) 6 R. (H.L.) 52

Ker was named as trustee in a deed. He never formally accepted office, and never attended a meeting of trustees. However, he did sign a transfer of railway stock in favour of the trust "as trustee". It was held that this was sufficient to amount to an implied acceptance of office.

Appointment or assumption of new trustees

11–30 Trustees always have a power to assume additional trustees unless this is excluded by the terms of the trust deed.[89] In a private trust, if there is no remaining trustee(s) (perhaps because all the original trustees have resigned or died), the truster has a "radical right" to appoint new trustees.[90] It is possible for a trust deed to be drafted so as to confer a wider power upon the truster to appoint new trustees, or even to confer such a right upon third parties.[91]

The court has a statutory power to appoint trustees where there is no power to assume additional trustees under the trust deed, or where a sole trustee is or has become insane or incapable, or has been absent from the UK for six months or has disappeared for that period.[92] The court may also appoint new trustees at common law in exceptional cases. This power has been used where two trustees were unable to work together and the appointment of a third was required to resolve the deadlock.[93]

Resignation of trustees

11–31 Trustees always have a power to resign office unless the trust deed provides otherwise.[94] However, a sole trustee is not entitled to resign unless new trustees[95] are appointed, and a trustee who has accepted any legacy, bequest or annuity given on condition of accepting the office of trustee is not entitled to resign unless he is explicitly given the power to do so by the trust deed. Alternatively, he may apply to the court for authority to resign. If the court grants such authority, it may impose conditions relating to the repayment of the legacy accepted by the trustee.[96]

Removal of trustees

11–32 The court has a statutory power to remove a trustee in the following cases[97]:

- where the trustee is insane;
- where the trustee is "incapable of acting by reason of physical or mental disability";
- where the trustee has been absent from the UK continuously for at least six months; and
- where the trustee has disappeared for at least six months.

---

[89] Trusts (Scotland) Act 1921, s.3. In relation to charitable trusts, see also the Law Reform (Miscellaneous Provisions) (Scotland) Act 1990, s.13(1).
[90] *Lindsay v Lindsay* (1847) 9 D. 1297.
[91] See, *e.g. Morison, Petr* (1834) 12 S. 307 and 547.
[92] Trusts (Scotland) Act 1921, s.22.
[93] *Aikman, Petr* (1881) 9 R. 213; *Taylor, Petr*, 1932 S.C. 1.
[94] Trusts (Scotland) Act 1921, s.3(a).
[95] *cf. Kennedy, Petr*, 1983 S.L.T. (Sh. Ct) 10 (holding that it is sufficient to appoint a single trustee).
[96] For these restrictions, see the Trusts (Scotland) Act 1921, s.3.
[97] Trusts (Scotland) Act 1921, s.23.

In the first two of these cases, the court is obliged to remove the trustee.[98] In the last two cases, it has a discretion as to whether or not to do so.

The court also has a common law power to remove a trustee for misconduct in office, as in the following case:

Stewart v Chalmers

(1904) 7 F. 163

Thomas Chalmers and Robert Stewart were both trustees under Peter Stewart's will. Stewart was also law-agent to the trust. A third trustee resigned, leaving Chalmers and Stewart as the only trustees. Stewart wrote to Chalmers regarding the investment of the trust funds, and Chalmers replied: "As your position and mine as trustees are now equal, I am to insist on half fees for all business to be done by you for this trust. On hearing that you agree to this condition, I will consider the question of investing the trust funds."

The beneficiaries petitioned the Court of Session to remove Thomas Chalmers from his position as trustee. The court held that Chalmers' conduct had been "quite indefensible", and granted the petition.

Death of a trustee

Where one of several trustees dies, his share in the trust property passes automatically to the other trustees.[99] The position is more complex where a sole trustee dies. In such cases, the title remains with the sole trustee "and has to be taken out of him by process of conveyancing."[1] **11–33**

Key Concepts

Trustees may be **appointed** by any description which is sufficient to identify the relevant individual. They must **accept** office; they cannot be forced to do so. Acceptance may be either express or implied.

Trustees always have the power to **assume additional trustees** unless this is excluded by the terms of the trust deed. The court has the power to **appoint additional trustees** in certain cases.

Trustees always have a power to **resign office** unless the trust deed provides otherwise.

The court has the power to **remove** trustees who are insane, incapable, have been absent from the UK or who have disappeared for at least six months, or who have misconducted themselves in office.

---

98 This is clear from the language of the statute: see also *Tod v Marshall* (1895) 23 R. 36.

99 *Gordon's Trs v Eglinton* (1851) 13 D. 1381.

1 A. J. P. Menzies, *The Law of Scotland Affecting Trustees* (2nd ed., 1913), para.153. For the procedure required, see W. A. Wilson and A. G. M. Duncan, *Trusts, Trustees and Executors* (2nd ed., 1995), paras 20–09 *et seq* and 22–05 *et seq*.

DECISION-MAKING BY TRUSTEES

11–34 As a general rule, trust decisions may validly be made by a majority of trustees.[2] There are two exceptions to this rule:

- The trust deed may state that the appointment of the trustees is "joint". In this case, decisions must be taken unanimously to be effective.
- The truster may appoint a *sine qua non* trustee. Without the consent of this trustee, "no act of administration shall be effectual".[3]

Importance of a quorum

11–35 The "quorum" is both:

- the minimum number of trustees who must participate in trust decision-making for any decisions taken to be valid; and
- the minimum number of trustees who must participate in a trust action (*e.g.* signing contracts on behalf of the trust) for such actions to validly bind the trust, unless the trustees have appointed an agent (who may be one of their own number) with the authority to bind the trust.

Unless the trust deed provides otherwise, the quorum is a "majority of the trustees accepting and surviving".[4] It should be noted that a trustee who dissents from a decision is nevertheless obliged to take any steps which are necessary to give effect to that decision,[5] and a trustee who does not participate in a contract made by the trust may nevertheless be personally liable on that contract.[6] If a dissenting trustee believes that the decision of the majority is in breach of trust, it is open to him to take an action for interdict or declarator accordingly. Alternatively, he can resign as a trustee, assuming that he has power to do so under the trust deed.

All trustees have a right to be consulted in trust decision-making. A failure to consult a trustee will render a decision taken by the remaining trustees void.[7] Third parties are, however, protected in such a situation by two factors: (a) the personal liability of trustees who make contracts on behalf of the trust[8] and (b) s.7 of the Trusts (Scotland) Act 1921, which states that a deed which bears to be granted by trustees but is "in fact executed by a quorum of such trustees in favour of any person other than a beneficiary or co-trustee" shall not normally be challengeable for lack of consultation or other irregularity of procedure.[9]

A trustee may lose his right to be consulted, as in the following case:

Malcolm v Goldie

(1895) 22 R. 968

One of five surviving trustees left Scotland to reside in Australia. The remaining trustees, acting on the basis that the emigrant trustee "is now resident in Australia and has ceased to act", assumed two new trustees. The proposal to assume the two

---

[2] *McCulloch v Wallace* (1846) 9 D. 32. One-half of the body of trustees is insufficient: *Neilson v Mossend Iron Co.* (1885) 12 R. 499.

[3] John McLaren, *The Law of Wills and Succession as Administered in Scotland* (3rd ed., 1894), para.1656.

[4] Trusts (Scotland) Act 1921, s.3(c).

[5] *Lynedoch v Ouchterlony* (1827) 5 S. 358.

[6] *Cuninghame v City of Glasgow Bank* (1879) 6 R. (H.L.) 98. On the personal liability of trustees under contract generally, see below, para.11–64.

[7] *Wyse v Abbott* (1881) 8 R. 983.

[8] See below, para.11–64.

[9] The effect of this section on transactions involving heritable property is not entirely clear and it is best practice to insist that all trustees sign any relevant deeds: see G. L. Gretton, "Problems in Partnership Conveyancing" (1991) 36 J.L.S.S. 232, 235.

new trustees was not intimated to the emigrant trustees. The validity of this assumption was later challenged.

It was held that, if the remaining trustees knew that the emigrant trustee was resident in Australia, and did not intend to come back, "to give notice of the meeting would be a mere futile formality", and that the failure to do so did not render the assumption invalid.

Modern advances in communications might mean that this case would be decided differently today.

Can the courts interfere in the trustees' exercise of discretion?

The courts will not normally interfere with decisions taken by trustees except in very limited circumstances: **11–36**

Board of Management for Dundee General Hospital v Bell's Trs
1952 S.C. (H.L.) 78

Lord Reid: "If it can be shown that the trustees considered the wrong question, or that, although they purported to consider the right question, they did not really apply their minds to it or perversely shut their eyes to the facts or that they did not act honestly or in good faith, then there is no true decision and the Court will intervene."

Trustees who are given a discretion to act must exercise it. They cannot simply refuse to apply their minds to the issue,[10] and the court will not exercise the discretion for them.[11] Trustees are not obliged to give reasons for their decisions.[12]

Key Concepts

Trust decisions may validly be made by a **majority** of trustees.

A **quorum** is a majority of the trustees unless the trust deed provides otherwise. This is the minimum number of trustees who must participate in decision-making for any decisions taken to be valid, and the minimum number of trustees who must participate in a trust action (such as signing contracts) for such actions to validly bind the trust.

All trustees have a **right to be consulted** in trust decision-making. A failure to consult a trustee may render a decision void.

The courts will not **interfere with decisions taken by trustees** unless it can be shown that they have not properly applied themselves to their duties, or have not acted honestly or in good faith.

---

[10] *Train v Buchanan's Trs*, 1907 S.C. 517, *per* the Lord President (Dunedin) at 524–525.
[11] *Earl of Stair's Trs* (1896) 23 R. 1070, *per* Lord McLaren at 1074.
[12] *Scott v National Trust* [1998] 2 All E.R. 705. See also *Board of Management for Dundee General Hospital v Bell's Trs*, 1952 S.C. (H.L.) 78, *per* Lord Normand at 85.

DUTIES OF A TRUSTEE

General duty of care

11–37 Trustees must, in all cases, exercise due care in their dealings with the trust estate. The standard of care required in that of the "ordinary prudent man".[13] This is an objective standard, and a trustee who fails to live up to this standard will be liable for any loss caused by this breach of the duty of care even if he has acted in good faith and to the best of his abilities.

Where a person is appointed as a remunerated trustee on the basis that they have held themselves out as being particularly skilled in some way (perhaps skill in relation to investment matters), they may be liable for failing to exercise the higher standard of care which this skill would suggest.[14]

Duty not to delegate the trust

11–38 Trustees must take responsibility for trust decision-making themselves and cannot delegate this responsibility to a third party.[15] This does not mean, however, that they are bound to undertake every act of trust administration personally. Instead, they are entitled to employ agents when a person of reasonable prudence would do so.[16] Trustees are not liable for losses caused by the negligence of fraud of an agent whom they legitimately appoint,[17] unless they have failed to exercise due care in the selection or supervision of the agent.[18]

Duty to secure trust property

11–39 A trustee is responsible for ingathering and securing trust property:

> "It is the duty of a trustee to take possession of the estate, and to have it transferred into the name of the trustees to the extent that no individual trustee or third party can use it for other than trust purposes. If he allows trust estate to remain in the hands of a third party, or of the law agent, without reducing it into the possession of the trust, he incurs the risk of personal liability if it should be lost."[19]

Investment duties

11–40 When trustees hold the trust estate for any period of time, they must consider investing the estate to protect its value.

> **Melville v Noble's Trs**
>
> (1896) 24 R. 243
>
> Trustees left a substantial trust fund on deposit-receipt with a bank for 19 years without considering the question of investment. If it had been invested properly, a return of 3 per cent per annum could have been received. It was held that they were liable to make up this 3 per cent return personally.

---

13 *Raes v Meek* (1889) 16 R. (H.L.) 31.

14 See the English case of *Bartlett v Barclays Bank Trust Co. Ltd (No.1)* [1980] Ch. 515. For further discussion, see J. Chalmers, *Trusts: Cases and Materials* (2002), paras 9.05–9.08.

15 *Scott v Occidental Petroleum (Caledonia) Ltd*, 1990 S.L.T. 882.

16 *Hay v Binny* (1861) 23 D. 594, and see Trusts (Scotland) Act 1921, s.4(1)(f) (power to appoint factors and law agents normally implied in all trust deeds).

17 *Thomson v Campbell* (1838) 16 S. 560.

18 *Carruthers v Carruthers* (1896) 23 R. (H.L.) 55.

19 A. Mackenzie Stuart, *The Law of Trusts* (1932), 200. See also *Forman v Burns* (1853) 15 D. 362.

If the trustees in *Melville* had addressed their minds to the question of investment, and concluded honestly and reasonably that leaving the money on deposit-receipt was the best course, they could not have been liable for any loss.[20]

Any investment must meet two criteria:

- it must be "authorised"; and
- it must be "proper".

"Authorised" means that the investment is of a type which the trustees have power to make under the terms of the trust deed or the Trustee Investments Act 1961. The 1961 Act lists at length the types of investments which trustees are entitled to make (unless the trust deed provides for narrower or wider powers of investment).

The investments which are permitted under the 1961 Act are divided into two categories: "wider-range" (higher risk) and "narrower-range" (lower risk) investments. "Narrower-range" investments are generally very safe investments such as national savings certificates, government securities and building society deposits. "Wider-range" investments are slightly riskier investments such as shares in UK companies which meet certain criteria and units in unit trust schemes. If there is no provision in the trust deed to the contrary, trustees are not permitted to invest more than three quarters of the trust fund in "wider-range" investments.[21] The 1961 Act is generally felt to be rather outdated and restrictive,[22] and no longer applies in England.[23] Legislative reform has been recommended,[24] and the matter was understood to be under consideration by the Scottish Executive at the time of writing.

Investments must not only be "authorised", but also "proper". This means that the trustees must exercise reasonable care in their selection of investment and not take undue risks. If they do take excessive risk in investment decisions, and this causes loss to the trust, they may be liable to make up the loss personally.[25]

Trustees should normally take professional advice before making investment decisions (unless they are themselves appropriately qualified). This duty exists both under statute in relation to certain types of investment,[26] and more generally at common law.[27]

Problem of "ethical" investment

In taking investment decisions, trustees must act in the best interests of the trust beneficiaries. They are not entitled to disregard those interests in favour of other considerations, as the following case demonstrates: **11–41**

Cowan v Scargill
[1985] Ch. 270

A mineworkers' pension scheme was established under statute. There were ten trustees, five of which were appointed by the National Union of Mineworkers. The NUM trustees objected to the investment plan on the basis that it involved investment overseas and investment in energies in competition with coal, both of which conflicted with NUM policy. The other trustees sought a declaration that the NUM trustees were

20 See *Manners v Strong's J.F.* (1902) 4 F. 829.
21 Trustee Investments (Division of Trust Fund) Order 1996 (SI 1996/845).
22 See Law Commission and the Scottish Law Commission, *Trustees' Powers and Duties* (Law Com. No.260; Scot. Law Com. No.172, 1999), paras 2.16–2.18.
23 Trustee Act 2000, ss.3–7.
24 See the Scottish Law Commission's report cited above, and also *CharityScotland: The Report of the Scottish Charity Law Review Commission* (2001), para.2.20.
25 Liability may be, in practice, difficult to establish: see G. Watt and M. Staunch, "Is There Liability For Imprudent Trustee Investment?" [1998] Conv. 352.
26 Trustee Investments Act 1961, s.6.
27 *Crabbe v Whyte* (1891) 18 R. 1065.

in breach of their duties as trustees by demanding that investment decisions be made in accordance with NUM policy. The declaration was granted.

This decision does not necessarily prevent trustees from taking into account what might be termed "ethical" considerations in making investment decisions. Given the wide range of investments which are often open to trustees, if a trustee has a choice between investment A and investment B, which appear to be equally good investments from the point of view of maximising the funds available for distribution to the beneficiaries, he cannot be criticised for choosing to select investment A over investment B on the basis of ethical factors.[28] What he may not do is to subordinate the interests of the beneficiaries to those ethical factors (unless, of course, the trust deed empowers him to do so).

Duty to take advice

11–42 It was noted earlier that trustees must administer the trust-estate to (at least) the standard that a man of ordinary prudence would exercise in the management of his own affairs. The man of ordinary prudence, of course, recognises that he is not an expert in all matters and must seek professional advice in appropriate cases.[29] The following case demonstrates the importance of this duty:

Martin v City of Edinburgh District Council

1988 S.L.T. 329

Edinburgh City Council was responsible for the administration of 58 trusts. In 1984, the Labour Party won a majority of seats on the council and put into effect a policy of withdrawing, for ethical reasons, investments held by those trusts in South Africa. A councillor brought an action for declarator that the council had acted in breach of its duty as a trustee.

Lord Murray: "I conclude that the pursuer has proved a breach of trust by the council in pursuing a policy of disinvesting in South Africa without considering expressly whether it was in the best interests of the beneficiaries and without obtaining professional advice on this matter ... the trustees acting on behalf of the council misdirected themselves in failing to comply with a prime duty of trustees, namely, to consider and seek advice as to the best interests of the beneficiaries, and so they are in breach of trust."

Although trustees must take advice, they are not obliged to follow it (provided that they have concluded it is in the best interests of the beneficiaries not to do so). To simply rubber-stamp the advice of professional advisers would be to improperly delegate the trust.[30] This duty is most important in relation to investment matters but is not confined to such issues.

Duties regarding existing debts and obligations

11–43 While it is unusual for an *inter vivos* trust to have existing debts and obligations, these will exist as a matter of course in *mortis causa* trusts. In such cases, trustees are required to pay off the debts of

---

[28] See *Harries v Church Commissioners for England* [1992] 1 W.L.R. 1241, *per* Nicholls V.C. at 1247–1248.

[29] This duty is statutory in relation to certain types of investment: Trustee Investments Act 1961, s.6(2).

[30] *Martin v City of Edinburgh District Council*, 1988 S.L.T. 329, *per* Lord Murray at 334.

the deceased, but are not personally liable for those debts. If the deceased's liabilities exceed his assets, then his estate may be sequestrated.[31]

An trustee on a *mortis causa* trust (normally an executor) cannot be compelled to pay an ordinary debt until six months have expired from the date of death.[32] This rule prevents one creditor obtaining an advantage over another by taking acting immediately upon a debtor's death before other creditors become aware of the fact.[33] If an executor pays any debts (or legacies) before the expiry of the six month period, he does so at his own risk and may be liable to make up the shortfall if the estate proves to be insolvent.[34]

Duties regarding new debts and obligations

In most cases, in order to discharge their duties, trustees will have to enter into contracts with third parties. The general rule is that they incur personal liability in respect of any such contracts, unless they explicitly contract out of such liability.[35] They are, of course, entitled to be reimbursed from the trust-estate for such expenses as they properly incur in the discharge of their duties as trustees.[36] **11–44**

Duty to keep accounts

Trustees must keep accounts which detail their dealings with the trust estate.[37] Where a trustee has failed to keep proper accounts, he is theoretically liable to a "strict accounting": "that is, he is given the benefit only of such items as the beneficiaries care to admit".[38] A beneficiary has a right to see the trust accounts and supporting documentation.[39] **11–45**

Exceptionally, the truster may be regarded as having excluded any duty to keep accounts, as in the following case:

Leitch v Leitch
1927 S.C. 823

The defender's father-in-law made over the whole stock on a small farm to her as her sole and exclusive property for behoof of herself and her family. Some years later, the pursuer—the defender's daughter—took an action of accounting against her mother, claiming £1,000 in lieu of production of accounts.

Lord Sands: "In the circumstances of the present case I think it extremely improbably that, when the arrangement was entered into, there was any thought in anybody's mind of division among the children in equal shares, or anything of that kind. The defender was left with a large young family to struggle through with ... The idea that it was contemplated that she should keep trust accounts appears to me to be fantastic."

It was held that the action was ill-conceived and should be dismissed.

---

31 Bankruptcy (Scotland) Act 1985, s.5.
32 Act of Sederunt, February 28, 1662. Certain debts such as funeral expenses are regarded as "privileged" and can be paid immediately.
33 See *Sanderson v Lockhart-Mure*, 1946 S.C. 298, *per* Lord Patrick at 300.
34 See, *e.g. Murray's Trs v Murray* (1903) 13 S.L.T. 274.
35 See below, para.11–64.
36 See below, para.11–48.
37 *Ross v Ross* (1896) 23 R. (H.L.) 67. The duty exists at common law but is recognised in statute: Prescription and Limitation (Scotland) Act 1973, Sch.3, para.e(i).
38 *Polland v Sturrock's Exrs*, 1975 S.L.T. (Notes) 76, *per* Lord Guthrie at 76 (quoting A. Mackenzie Stuart, *The Law of Trusts* (1932), 220).
39 *Murray v Cameron*, 1969 S.L.T. (Notes) 76; *Nouillan v Nouillan's Exrs*, 1991 S.L.T. 270.

Duty to pay the correct beneficiaries

11–46 A trustee must pay out funds to the correct beneficiaries. If a trustee pays out funds to the wrong beneficiaries, "he is held in law still to have the money"[40] and is obliged to make payment to the correct beneficiary out of his own funds. A trustee is protected from liability for improper distribution in a number of specific cases, as follows:

- theft or embezzlement of the trust estate (provided the trustee is not himself at fault)[41];
- a true beneficiary may be personally barred from bringing a claim against the trustees if he is himself at fault at causing the trustees to pay out to the wrong party[42]; and
- trustees who wrongly distribute property because they are unaware of the existence of an illegitimate child are protected by statute.[43]

There is some doubt as to whether trustees who wrongly distribute the estate due to an honest and reasonable error are liable for improper distribution.[44] However, a trustee in this position is entitled to apply to the court to be relieved from liability for breach of trust,[45] which may render this question somewhat academic.

Where the trustees distribute trust property in error, they may be entitled to recover the property by means of the *condictio indebiti*.[46]

Key Concepts

Trustees have the following duties:

- The duty to **exercise due care** in their dealings with the trust estate. The standard of care required is that of the "ordinary prudent man".
- The duty **not to delegate the trust** and to take responsibility for trust decision-making themselves.
- The duty to **secure trust property**.
- The duty to **invest the trust estate** if they hold it for any period of time. Investments entered into by trustees must be both **authorised** (permitted under the trust deed or by statute) and **proper** (not exposing the trust deed to excessive risk).
- The duty to **take advice** where it is prudent to do so, particularly in relation to investment matters.
- The duty to **meet trust debts and obligations**.
- The duty to **keep accounts**.
- The duty to **pay the correct beneficiaries**.

---

40 A. Mackenzie Stuart, *The Law of Trusts* (1932), 221.
41 *Jobson v Palmer* [1893] 1 Ch. 71.
42 *Buttercase & Geddie's Tr. v Geddie* (1897) 24 R. 1128, *per* Lord Kinnear at 1134.
43 Law Reform (Miscellaneous Provisions) (Scotland) Act 1968, s.7 (as amended by the Law Reform (Parent and Child) (Scotland) Act 1986).
44 See J. Chalmers, *Trusts: Cases and Materials* (2002), para.6.27.
45 Trusts (Scotland) Act 1921, s.32. See below, para.11–61.
46 *Armour v Glasgow Royal Infirmary*, 1909 S.C. 916. See J. Chalmers, *Trusts: Cases and Materials* (2002), paras 6.28–6.29. On the *condictio* generally, see Chapter 8.

RULE AGAINST *AUCTOR IN REM SUAM*

Auctor in rem suam may be translated as "actor in his own cause". This rule prohibits a trustee from placing himself in a position where his interests as trustee and his interests as an individual conflict. 11–47

The consequences of breaching the rule are severe. If a trustee enters into a transaction in breach of the rule, the transaction is voidable regardless of whether he was acting in good faith or whether or not the transaction was a fair one.[47] If he profits from a breach of the rule, he must hand over those profits to the trust-estate regardless of whether the trust-estate has in fact suffered any loss.[48]

The rule has three main consequences[49]:

- Trustees may not enter into transactions with the trust estate.[50]
- Trustees may not use their position to obtain a personal advantage (*e.g.* if a trustee is given a discretion, he may not exercise it in his favour).[51]
- Trustees may not charge fees for work done for the trust.[52]

A trustee, may, however, be *auctor in rem suam* where this is sanctioned in the trust deed. So, for example, it is not unusual for trust deeds to provide that a trustee may provide professional services (such as legal services) to the trust and be appropriately remunerated for this. The sanction should normally be express, but may be implied, as in the following case:

Sarris v Clark

1995 S.L.T. 44

James Clark executed a will in November 1985 bequeathing his whole property equally among his wife and his three children. His wife was named as one of his executors under his will. In December 1985, he entered into a contract of copartnery in his wife regarding their business as farmers. Upon his death, his wife was placed in a position whereby, as one of the executors, she was involved in negotiations to give up the tenancies of the holdings in exchange for payment. It was argued that the eventual agreement was voidable because she had acted in breach of the *auctor in rem suam* principle. The court held that, in the circumstances, Mr Clark could be regarded as having impliedly sanctioned his wife being *auctor in rem suam*, as this was an inevitable consequence of the arrangements he had entered into.

A trustee may also be *auctor in rem suam* if this is sanctioned by the beneficiaries.[53]

Where a trustee enters into a transaction in breach of the *auctor rem suam*, this is voidable and may be challenged by the beneficiaries.[54] The beneficiaries may elect either to have the transaction reduced (if the parties can be restored to their original position),[55] or to require the trustee to communicate any benefit received from the transaction to the trust.[56]

---

47 *Aberdeen Railway Co. v Blaikie Bros* (1854) 1 Macq. 461.
48 *Hamilton v Wright* (1842) 1 Bell 574.
49 See K. McK Norrie and E. M. Scobbie, *Trusts* (1991), 128–133.
50 *University of Aberdeen v Town Council of Aberdeen* (1876) 3 R. 1087.
51 *Inglis v Inglis*, 1983 S.C. 8.
52 *Home v Pringle* (1841) 2 Rob. 384.
53 *Bruckner v Jopp's Trs* (1887) 14 R. 1006.
54 *Fraser v Hankey & Co.* (1847) 9 D. 415. As to the situation where a *former* trustee enters into such a transaction, see J. Chalmers, *Trusts: Cases and Materials* (2002), para.8.32.
55 See *Sarris v Clark*, 1995 S.L.T. 44, *per* the Lord Justice-Clerk (Ross) at 49.
56 See, *e.g. Hamilton v Wright* (1842) 1 Bell 574.

Key Concepts

A trustee may not be ***auctor in rem suam***. This means that he may not place himself in a position where his interests as trustee and interests as an individual conflict.

The rule has three main consequences:

- trustees may not enter into transactions with the trust estate;
- trustees may not use their position to obtain a personal advantage; and
- trustees may not charge fees for work done for the trust.

A trustee may, however, be *auctor in rem suam* if this is **sanctioned** in the trust deed or by the beneficiaries.

A transaction entered into in breach of this principle is **voidable** and may be challenged by the beneficiaries.

TRUSTEE'S RIGHT TO REIMBURSEMENT

11–48 It is implicit in every trust deed that the trustee is entitled to "receive out of the trust estate all the proper charges and expenses incurred by him in the execution of the trust."[57] Trustees are, of course, entitled to apply the trust funds directly to payments which are necessary for the trust—they are not required to pay such expenses out of their pocket and claim reimbursement later.[58]

Much of the case law concerning the right to reimbursement is concerned with the issue of whether trustees who initiate or defend court actions are entitled to be reimbursed for their expenses from the trust estate.[59] As a general rule, they are entitled to be reimbursed unless they have "acted unreasonably or recklessly, or otherwise than in accordance with their duty."[60] Where the court action is lost by the trust, trustees will generally be personally liable for the other party's expenses,[61] but will be entitled to pay those expenses out of the trust estate unless they have acted improperly in bringing or defending the action.

Key Concept

A trustee is entitled to be **reimbursed** for any expenses properly incurred in administering the trust.

POWERS OF A TRUSTEE

11–49 Trustees may not do any act in furtherance of the trust purposes unless they have the power to perform such an act (*e.g.* a power to sell the trust estate; a power to pay debts, etc.) Trustees' powers may be divided into three categories, as follows:

---

57 A. Mackenzie Stuart, *The Law of Trusts* (1932), p.358.
58 *Cunningham v Montgomerie* (1879) 6 R. 1333.
59 For a review of the case law, see J. Chalmers, *Trusts: Cases and Materials* (2002), paras 10.12–10.19.
60 *Gibson v Caddall's Trs* (1895) 22 R. 899, *per* the Lord President (Robertson) at 892.
61 *Mulholland v Macfarlane's Trs,* 1928 S.L.T. 251; *Jeffrey v Brown* (1842) 2 Shaw 349.

- powers granted in the trust deed;
- powers conferred by statutory provisions; and
- common law powers which may be granted upon an application to the court.

Powers granted in the trust deed

It has been said that the trust deed "is the foundation and the measure of the powers of the trustees."[62] The trust deed may confer powers upon the trustees either explicitly or implicitly. 11–50

It was formerly common to list the powers of the trustees at length in the trust deed, but that is now normally unnecessary due to s.4 of the Trusts (Scotland) Act 1921,[63] under which certain general powers are implied in all trust-deeds. Nevertheless, the trust-deed must be examined in all instances to determine which powers it confers upon trustees (and also whether it excludes any of the powers which are otherwise implied under s.4 of the 1921 Act).

Powers conferred by statutory provisions

Section 4 of the Trusts (Scotland) Act 1921 contains a list of seventeen general powers which all trustees have unless to so act would be "at variance with the terms or purposes of the trust."[64] The principal powers conferred by this section are as follows: 11–51

- to sell the trust estate or any part thereof;
- to grant leases of the trust estate or any part thereof;
- to acquire with trust funds any interest in residential accommodation "reasonably required to enable the trustees to provide a suitable residence for occupation by any of the beneficiaries";
- to appoint factors and law agents and pay them suitable remuneration;
- to uplift, discharge, or assign debts due to the trust estate;
- to grant all deeds necessary for carrying into effect the powers vested in the trustees; and
- to pay trust debts without requiring the creditors to constitute such debts.

It should be noted that there is no general power to purchase heritable property under the statute.

Trustees may, of course, only exercise these powers if to do so would further the purposes of the trust.

Occasionally, some of these powers may be specifically excluded by the trust deed. In such cases, the trustees may petition the court under s.5 of the 1921 Act for power to do the relevant act. The court may grant the power if it is "satisfied that such act is in all the circumstances expedient for the execution of the trust." Section 5 was applied in the following case:

Tod's Trs, Petrs

1999 S.L.T. 308

Under a 1929 trust deed, the trustees held property including a large country house ("Tirinie House") in trust for the purpose of providing professional persons with rest and a change of air. It was initially successful but began to run at a loss during the 1990s and was closed. At the time of the court case, the house was in a deteriorating condition and the trustees had limited funds available to maintain it. The trustees, on the view that the trust had failed, sought permission to sell the house so that the value of the trust estate could be preserved while it was determined what should be done with the trust estate. In the "very unusual" circumstances, the court granted the power.

---

[62] *Goodsir v Carruthers* (1858) 20 D. 1141, *per* Lord Ardmillan at 1145.
[63] See below, para.11–51.
[64] For the meaning of this phrase, see *Marquess of Lothian's C.B.*, 1927 S.C. 579, *per* Lord Blackburn at 587–588.

Certain special trustees (such as trustees in bankruptcy) have additional powers which are granted under statute.[65]

Common law powers with court application

11–52 Aside from s.5 of the 1921 Act, the court cannot normally grant additional powers to trustees.[66] In exceptional cases, however, where it would be impossible to fulfil the trust purposes without additional powers being granted, the court may be able to intervene,[67] as in the following case:

Anderson's Trs
1921 S.C. 315

Mr Anderson was a farm tenant. In his will, desiring that his nephew should carry on the farm, he directed his trustees to hold the lease of the farm and the stock in trust for his nephew until he attained the age of 21, whereupon the whole residue of the estate (including the lease and stock) should be conveyed to his nephew. After Mr Anderson's death, the landlord decided to sell the farm, but gave the trustees the option of purchasing it. The trust-deed did not, however, confer upon the trustees any power to purchase heritage. The trustees petitioned the *nobile officium* of the court for authority to purchase the farm. It was held that, in the exceptional circumstances of the case, where the trust purposes would be wholly frustrated unless the power was granted, authority to purchase the farm should be given.

Key Concepts

The trust deed is the principal source of trustees' powers, although **there are a number of powers which are conferred by statute upon all trustees** unless they are "at variance with the terms or purposes of the trust". The principal statutory powers are as follows:

- to sell the trust estate or any part thereof;
- to grant leases of the trust estate or any part thereof;
- to acquire with trust funds any interest in residential accommodation "reasonably required to enable the trustees to provide a suitable residence for occupation by any of the beneficiaries";
- to appoint factors and law agents and pay them suitable remuneration;
- to uplift, discharge, or assign debts due to the trust estate;
- to grant all deeds necessary for carrying into effect the powers vested in the trustees; and
- to pay trust debts without requiring the creditors to constitute such debts.

There is **no implied power** under statute to **purchase heritable property**.

---

[65] See generally the Bankruptcy (Scotland) Act 1985. See also the Married Women's Policies of Assurance (Scotland) (Amendment) Act 1980, s.2(2), and the Judicial Factors Act 1849, s.7.

[66] *Berwick* (1874) 2 R. 90, *per* the Lord President (Inglis) at 92; *Scott's Hospital Trs*, 1913 S.C. 289, *per* the Lord Justice Clerk (Macdonald) at 290–291.

[67] See A. Mackenzie Stuart, "The *Nobile Officium* and Trust Administration" 1935 S.L.T. (News) 1.

If one of these powers is excluded by the trust deed, the trustees may **petition the court** for authority to exercise it.

In exceptional cases, the court may be able to grant **further powers** to trustees if this is necessary in order to avoid an **impossibility** in fulfilling the trust purposes.

LIABILITIES OF A TRUSTEE

Liability to beneficiaries

Where a trustee has committed or appears likely to commit a breach of trust, various remedies may be open to the beneficiary, as follows: **11–53**

Remedies for breach of trust

The principal remedies for breach of trust are court actions for: (a) interdict; (b) damages and (c) accounting. Depending on the circumstances, it may also be appropriate to petition the court for the removal of an offending trustee,[68] or even to report the matter to authorities such as the police. **11–54**

(a) Interdict

Where a trustee proposes to do something which a beneficiary believes to be a breach of trust, the beneficiary is entitled to seek an interdict. An interdict is a court order prohibiting a person from doing a specified act. If the breach of trust has already taken place, interdict is useless and will not be granted. **11–55**

(b) Damages

Where a breach of trust has caused a loss to the trust estate, a beneficiary may take a court action to require the offending trustee to make up the loss in damages.[69] It is a defence for the trustee(s) to show that the loss would have occurred even if the breach had not taken place, as in the following case: **11–56**

Millar's Trs v Polson

(1897) 24 R. 1038

A trustee became aware that his co-trustee, Elliot, had not banked £150 which belonged to the trust. Over a period of months, he took no action to recover the money, and Elliot eventually became insolvent. In his defence, he argued that Elliot had always been incapable of repaying the money and that court action would have been fruitless. The court accepted his evidence on this point and held that he was not liable to make good the loss of £150.

Where a trustee has committed multiple breaches of trust, some profitable and others not, he may not set off the profit on one breach against the loss on another in order to minimise his liability in

[68] See above, para.11–32.
[69] As to whether the terminology of "damages" is appropriate, *cf. Tibbert v McColl*, 1994 S.L.T 1227.

damages.[70] Set off may, however, be allowed if the multiple breaches are part of a single scheme—as in the English case of *Bartlett v Barclays Bank Trust Co. Ltd (No.1)*,[71] where trustees improperly made two speculative property investments, one of which made a profit and the other of which made a loss.[72]

(c) Accounting (count, reckoning and payment)

11–57 A beneficiary may also bring an action of "count, reckoning and payment" (commonly referred to as an action for accounting), calling upon the trustee to produce trust accounts and to make up any shortfall.[73] This should generally have the same practical result as an action for damages. However, it has two advantages in appropriate cases. First, it may provide a means of ascertaining the amount of any loss where this cannot be otherwise done. Secondly, it may remain available where an action for damages is barred by prescription.[74]

Protecting trustees from liability

11–58 Trustees may receive some protection from liability for breach of trust through an immunity clause in the trust deed or one of the statutory provisions contained in ss.30–32 of the Trusts (Scotland) Act 1921.

(a) Immunity clauses

11–59 An attempt is sometimes made to protect trustees from liability for breach of trust by inserting an immunity clause into the trust deed stating (for example) that they will not be liable for errors or neglect of management. It has traditionally been said that such clauses will protect trustees from liability for negligence, but not for liability from gross negligence.[75] However, this view has been thrown into doubt by a recent English case:[76]

Armitage v Nurse

[1998] Ch. 241

A trust-deed provided that trustees would not be liable for any errors short of "actual fraud". It was argued that this clause could not be effective. Millet L.J. held that the clause was effective. He concluded the earlier Scottish cases which suggested that such clauses did not exclude liability for gross negligence were simply interpretations of the particular clauses under consideration in those cases, and did not lay down any rule that it was impossible to exclude liability for gross negligence. Where the language of a clause clearly did exclude liability for anything short of actual fraud, there was no reason not to give effect to it. Any change in the law—which might well be desirable—had to be a matter for Parliament.

---

[70] A. Mackenzie Stuart, *The Law of Trusts* (1932), 375.

[71] [1980] Ch. 515.

[72] For an argument that this decision should not be followed in Scotland, see K. McK Norrie and E. M. Scobbie, *Trusts* (1991), 144. For a counter-argument, see J. Chalmers, *Trusts: Cases and Materials* (2002), para.9.18.

[73] On the duty to keep accounts, see above, para.11–45.

[74] See *Hobday v Kirkpatrick's Trs*, 1985 S.L.T. 197. *cf. Ross v Davy*, 1996 S.C.L.R. 369.

[75] *Lutea Trs Ltd v Orbis Trs Guernsey Ltd*, 1997 S.C.L.R. 735; K. McK Norrie and E. M. Scobbie, *Trusts* (1991), p.148. This does, of course, raise the question of whether it is actually possible to distinguish between these two forms of negligence.

[76] See further G. McCormack, "The Liability of Trustees for Gross Negligence" [1998] Conv. 100.

(b) Statutory protections

There are three principal statutory protections from liability under the Trusts (Scotland) Act 1921. **11–60**

(i) Trustees who have acted "honestly and reasonably"

The main statutory protection is found in s.32, which allows the court to relieve a trustee from personal liability for a breach of trust if he "has acted honestly and reasonably" and "ought fairly to be excused". It must be noted that a trustee who has acted honestly and reasonably is not *automatically* entitled to be relieved of the consequences—this is a matter which is in the discretion of the court, which may be faced with the awkward task of apportioning a loss between two blameless parties. **11–61**

However, where a trustee has acted honestly and reasonably, it will normally be assumed that it is fair to grant relief.[77] The fact that the trustee has acted on legal advice is relevant but will not automatically result in relief being granted.[78] The court may grant partial rather than full relief if this is felt appropriate.[79] It has been suggested that a non-gratuitous (remunerated) trustee is never entitled to claim relief under this section,[80] but this is probably incorrect, although the court will be less willing to grant relief to such a trustee.[81]

(ii) Trustees who have committed a breach of trust with the beneficiary's consent

Under s.31 of the 1921 Act, if a trustee has committed a breach of trust at the instigation or request or with the written consent of a beneficiary, the court is entitled to apply or of any part of that beneficiary's interest in the trust estate to indemnify the trustee. **11–62**

For s.31 to operate, the beneficiary must have been aware of the facts which made the proposed action a breach of trust, although it is not necessary for the beneficiary to know that it was legally a breach of trust.[82] A beneficiary who has instigated or consented to a breach of trust may be personally barred from bringing any action against the trustee, but s.31 may still be important in such cases by affording some protection to the trustee if another beneficiary brings an action.

(iii) Trustees who have lent money on security of heritable property

Section 30 of the 1921 Act states that a trustee shall not be liable for breach of trust by reason of having made a loan on the security of property provided that: (a) a proper valuation was obtained; and (b) the amount of the loan did not exceed two-thirds of the valuation. This protection would have been of considerable importance historically, because loans on the security of heritable property in Scotland were one of the very few implied powers of investment which trustees had at common law. It is unlikely to be of much practical importance today. **11–63**

Liability to third parties

Trustees will commonly, in order to discharge their responsibilities as trustees, enter into contracts with third parties. As a general rule, they are personally liable on such contracts "unless there is an agreement express or implied that the trust estate only is to be held bound."[83] **11–64**

---

[77] *Perrins v Bellamy* [1898] 2 Ch. 521, *per* Kekewich J at 528; affirmed [1899] 1 Ch. 797.
[78] *Marsden v Evans* [1954] 1 W.L.R. 423.
[79] See, *e.g. Re Evans* [1999] 2 All E.R. 777.
[80] A. Mackenzie Stuart, *The Law of Trusts* (1932), 382–383.
[81] See J. Chalmers, *Trusts: Cases and Materials* (2002), para.9.31.
[82] See *Cathcart's Trs v Cathcart* (1907) 15 S.L.T. 646; *Henderson v Henderson's Trs* (1900) 2 F. 1295; *Re Somerset* [1894] 1 Ch. 321.
[83] A. Mackenzie Stuart, *The Law of Trusts* (1932), 358. See *Brown v Sutherland* (1875) 2 R. 615.

This point is generally only of importance if the trust fund is or becomes insolvent. Consequently, many of the reported cases on personal liability arose in the context of the disastrous collapse of the City of Glasgow Bank in 1878. It appears that many trust funds included stock in the bank, which was subject to heavy calls. (For example, the trust fund in *Cunningham v Montgomerie*[84] included £1,000 of stock, on which calls of £27,500 were made). In these cases, the trust estate was frequently insufficient to meet the calls, leaving the trustees personally liable for the shortfall.

The rationale for the personal liability rule is that the trustees are supposed to know the state of the trust estate and are warranting its sufficiency to persons with whom they make contracts.[85] For this reason, trustees will generally not be personally liable on a contract with the solicitors to the trust or with a co-trustee, because such persons themselves know the state of the trust.[86]

In order to exclude personal liability, it is not sufficient to show that the third party knew that he was contracting with a trustee.[87] There must be an agreement that the trustee is not to be personally liable. Where a person signs a contract "as trustee", this will generally be taken as indicating such an agreement.[88] The mere use of the word "trustee" is not sufficient, as this may be intended only to describe or identify the signatory.[89]

Third parties who acquire trust property

11–65 Where a trustee, acting in breach of trust, sells trust property to a third party, that third party will acquire a good title to the property provided that he purchased the property in good faith and for value.[90] Where a third party acquires trust property in bad faith or gratuitously, his title may be reduced.[91]

Third parties also receive further protection by way of s.2 of the Trusts (Scotland) Act 1961.[92] Under this provision, where a trustee enters into a transaction which purports to be an exercise of any of the first six general powers of trustees which are implied by s.4 of the 1921 Act, the validity of that transaction may not be challenged by any person on the ground that the act was at variance with the terms or purposes of the trust.[93] This protection is very strong, because such a transaction cannot be challenged on the ground of bad faith. It is intended to limit any need for trustees to seek court approval before entering into a transaction involving the exercise of one of those implied powers.[94]

Key Concepts

Where a trustee has committed or appears likely to commit a breach of trust, the following remedies may be open to the beneficiaries:

- interdict (a court order preventing the trustee from doing a particular act);
- an action for damages; and
- an action for accounting (a combination of an action to produce accounts and for payment of any shortfall in the trust funds).

---

[84] (1879) 6 R. 1333.

[85] *Cullen v Baillie* (1846) 8 D. 511, *per* Lord Fullerton at 522.

[86] *Ferme, Ferme and Williamson v Stephenson's Tr.* (1905) 7 F. 902 (solicitors); *Cullen v Baillie* (1846) 8 D. 511 (co-trustee).

[87] *Mackenzie v Neill* (1899) 37 S.L.R. 666, *per* Lord Kincairney at 667.

[88] *Gordon v Campbell* (1842) 1 Bell 428.

[89] *Thomson v McLachlan's Trs* (1829) 7 S. 787; *Lumsden v Buchanan* (1865) 3 M. (H.L.) 89.

[90] Hume, *Lectures* (1821–1822) (G. C. H. Paton ed., Stair Society, Vol.17, 1952), Vol.IV, 315.

[91] *Macgowan v Robb* (1864) 2 M. 943; *Thomson v Clydesdale Bank* (1893) 20 R. 50.

[92] Note also the Succession (Scotland) Act 1964, s.17 (protection of persons acquiring title via an executor).

[93] The relevant powers are the powers to sell, feu, lease, excamb (swap) or borrow money on the security of the trust estate (or any part thereof), or to acquire an interest in residential accommodation for occupation by the beneficiaries. See Trusts (Scotland) Act 1921, s.4(1)(a)–(ee) (as amended).

[94] See J. Chalmers, "In Defence of the Trusting Conveyancer", 2002 S.L.T. (News) 231, at 234.

Trustees may be protected from liability by **immunity clauses** in the trust deed providing that they are not to be liable for negligence.

Trustees who commit a breach of trust but who have acted **honestly and reasonably** may apply to the court to be relieved from the consequences of their breach of trust.

Trustees who commit a breach of trust at the request of or with the consent of a beneficiary may apply to the court to be **indemnified** by that beneficiary's interest in the trust estate.

Trustees will be **personally liable to third parties** on contracts which they make on behalf of the trust unless they have contracted out of such liability.

Third parties who acquire trust property **in good faith and for value** will receive a good title to the property even if the trustee was acting in breach of trust.

VARIATION OF TRUST PURPOSES

A trust, by its very nature, severely limits the manner in which the property which is subject to it may be held and applied. The relevant limitations have, of course, been selected by the truster, and doubtless because, when establishing the trust, he considered that they would represent the most appropriate and expedient set of rules for governing the trust. **11–66**

Circumstances change, however, and what appears appropriate when the trust is established may cease to be appropriate with the passage of time. For example:

- Changes in the law of taxation or in the investment climate may mean that the trust property is no longer being managed in the most effective way possible.
- A public trust may be established for a purpose which is subsequently satisfied by government action without the expenditure of the trust funds, or which the trustees manage to fulfil without expending all of the trust capital. Alternatively, there may be insufficient funds to give effect to the trust purposes.
- A testator may, in a will, have left money to an institution which no longer exists or never existed.
- Some or all of the beneficiaries in a private trust may decide amongst themselves that they would prefer the trust to be administered differently.

It is not, of course, open to the truster (unless the trust is revocable)[95] to amend the terms of the trust in such cases. That would be to defeat the very essence of the trust, which is that the truster has alienated his property and put it beyond his control. So what scope exists for varying the terms of the trust?

The answer differs according to whether the trust is private or public.[96] Each type of trust will be dealt with in turn.

Private trusts

At common law, variation of the terms a private trust was competent if all the beneficiaries consented to the variation.[97] The obvious practical problem with this approach is that not all the **11–67**

---

[95] See below, para.11–73.
[96] On this distinction generally, see above, para.11–05.
[97] See A. Mackenzie Stuart, *The Law of Trusts* (1932), p.346.

beneficiaries may be capable of consenting. For example, the beneficiaries may include children, or the trust deed may even make provision for persons who have not yet been born (and who may never be). A second problem is that if the trust includes an alimentary liferent, the alimentary beneficiary cannot lawfully renounce that liferent.

The Court of Session did have a very limited jurisdiction at common law to authorise variation (or termination) without all the necessary consents being obtained, such as where the trust would become unworkable without additional powers being granted or where the trustees were only prevented from obtaining the consent of all the beneficiaries by virtue of the fact that unborn children who were, in fact, unlikely ever to be born, would be entitled to benefit under the trust.[98] This inflexibility gave rise to some concern,[99] and was eventually addressed by the Trusts (Scotland) Act 1961.[1]

Section 1 of the 1961 Act enables the court to give consent to a variation on behalf of:

(a) any person who is incapable of consenting by reason of nonage or other disability;
(b) any person who is not currently a beneficiary but may become one on the happening of a future event or on a particular date, unless that person is currently ascertained and is capable of assenting; or
(c) any unborn person.

The court is not entitled to approve the arrangement on behalf of any person "unless it is of the opinion that the carrying out thereof would not be prejudicial to that person."[2] As to what amounts to prejudice, see the following case[3]:

Pollok-Morris, Petrs
1969 S.L.T. (Notes) 60

P established a trust for the benefit of his wife, lawful issue, mother and two sisters. It proved to be unlikely that there would be any children of his existing marriage and he and his wife adopted a child. Approval was sought for a variation so that adoptive children and their issue would fall within the class of beneficiaries. The court refused to approve the proposed variation on behalf of any unborn children.

Lord President (Clyde): "If the group of persons among whom the estate may be divided is increased to include some other person not originally in it, that does, in my view, constitute a possible prejudice to those in the group and makes it impossible for this Court to hold that the carrying out of this arrangement would not be prejudicial… "

It does not follow that, simply because a proposed variation is shown not to be prejudicial, that the court will necessarily grant approval.[4] Instead, the court has a discretion as to whether or not to grant consent and will take into account the intention of the truster (although this is not conclusive),[5] and all other relevant circumstances including the relative benefits which the various parties would gain from the variation. The question of whether those benefits are fairly distributed is clearly relevant.[6]

---

98 See A. Mackenzie Stuart, *The Law of Trusts* (1932), pp.254–259 and pp.349–353; *Coles*, 1951 S.C. 608; *McPherson's Trs v Hill* (1902) 4 F. 921.
99 See Law Reform Committee for Scotland, *Ninth Report: The powers of trustees to sell, purchase or otherwise deal with heritable property; and the variation of trust purposes* (Cmnd.1102, 1960).
1 See generally Colin Tyre, *Variation of Trusts in Scotland* (1997) 3 Priv. Client Bus. 184; J. W. Harris, *Variation of Trusts* (1975) (a study of the equivalent English legislation).
2 Trusts (Scotland) Act 1961, s.1(1).
3 For further discussion, see J. Chalmers, *Trusts: Cases and Materials* (2002), para.12.06.
4 *Lobnitz, Petr*, 1966 S.L.T. (Notes) 81.
5 *Goulding v James* [1997] 2 All E.R. 239. *cf. Re Steed's Will Trusts* [1960] Ch. 407.
6 See *Lobnitz, Petr*, 1966 S.L.T. (Notes) 81.

It was formerly thought that the court could not grant consent to a variation which extended the trustees powers of investment beyond those sanctioned by the trust deed and the Trustee Investment Act 1961.[7] However, such a variation would probably now be regarded as competent.[8]

Public trusts

There are two mechanisms available for varying the terms of a public trust. These are first, the common law *cy-près* jurisdiction, and secondly, variation under s.9(1) of the Law Reform (Miscellaneous Provisions) (Scotland) Act 1990. Variation under s.9(1) of the 1990 Act is only possible where the trust has already taken effect in some form; it is not possible where it is impossible to give any effect to the terms of the trust (but in such cases, *cy-près* will be available).[9] *Cy-près* is available whether or not the trust has taken effect, but much stricter criteria must be met for the *cy-près* jurisdiction to be available. **11–68**

The criteria which must be satisfied in order for the court to sanction variation are therefore different depending on whether we are concerned with a case of "initial failure" (where it was never possible to give effect to the trust) or "subsequent failure" (where the trust was initially given effect to but later failed).[10]

Initial failure

Variation in such cases must be under the *cy-près* jurisdiction. In such cases, two factors must be established for variation to be permissible: **11–69**

- a "general charitable intention" on the part of the truster; and
- failure of the trust purposes (impossibility).

In determining whether the truster had a "general charitable intention", the court must ask whether his object was "to establish a charity for the benefit of a certain class with a particular mode of doing it? Or was the mode of application such an essential part of the gift that it is not possible to distinguish any general purpose of charity?"[11] The distinction is illustrated by the following case:

Hay's J.F. v Hay's Trs

1952 S.C. (H.L.) 29

A testatrix directed in her will that her trustees should maintain a mansion-house "under the style and designation of 'The Hay Memorial'" as a hospital on Shetland. The funds available under the trust-deed were insufficient to maintain the house for this purpose. The trustees applied to the court for a variation of the trust purposes under the *cy-près* jurisdiction. Held, that *cy-près* was not available as no general charitable intention existed. It was clear that the use of the house as the "Hay Memorial" was an essential part of the testatrix's intention. If this was not possible, there was no general purpose of charity to fall back on.

---

7 *Inglis, Petr*, 1965 S.L.T. 326. On the 1961 Act, see above, para.11–40.

8 See *Henderson, Petr*, 1981 S.L.T. (Notes) 40; *University of Glasgow, Petrs*, 1991 S.L.T. 604, *per* the Lord President (Hope) at 606.

9 See J. Chalmers, *Trusts: Cases and Materials* (2002), para.12.18.

10 For cases on the distinction, see *Davidson's Trs v Arnott*, 1951 S.C. 42; *Lindsay's Trs v Lindsay*, 1948 S.L.T. (Notes) 81; *Cuthbert's Trs v Cuthbert*, 1958 S.L.T. 315.

11 *Burgess' Trs v Crawford*, 1912 S.C. 387, *per* Lord Mackenzie at 398.

(If, as in *Hay's J.F.*, the purpose of a testamentary trust proves impossible to fulfil but *cy-près* is unavailable, the relevant part of the testamentary estate will normally fall into intestacy and the relevant rules of intestate succession will apply.)[12]

Where a testator leaves money to a supposed charitable organisation which never in fact existed, the court will normally find a general charitable intention.[13] Where the institution did in fact exist but is now defunct, the court will normally not find such an intention,[14] although this distinction has been criticised.[15]

Impossibility may be established by, for example, showing that there are insufficient funds available in the trust estate to carry out the trust purposes,[16] or where property has been left to an organisation for a specific purpose, that the specified organisation is unwilling to accept the property.[17] The fact that the trust purposes cannot be given effect to immediately does not amount to impossibility,[18] nor does the fact that they may be attended with some difficulty.[19]

Subsequent failure

11–70 In cases of subsequent failure, it is not necessary to establish a general charitable intention on the part of the truster. It is only necessary to establish impossibility (in which case the *cy-près* jurisdiction may be invoked) or one of the statutory grounds under s.9(1) of the Law Reform (Miscellaneous Provisions) (Scotland) Act 1990, which are as follows:

"(a) that the purposes of the trust, whether in whole or in part—
 (i) have been fulfilled as far as it is possible to do so; or
 (ii) can no longer be given effect to, whether in accordance with the directions or spirit of the trust deed or other document constituting the trust or otherwise;
(b) that the purposes of the trust provide a use for only part of the property available under the trust;
(c) that the purposes of the trust were expressed by reference to—
 (i) an area which has, since the trust was constituted, ceased to have effect for the purpose described expressly or by implication in the trust deed or other document constituting the trust; or
 (ii) a class of persons or area which has ceased to be suitable or appropriate, having regard to the spirit of the trust deed or other document constituting the trust, or as regards which it has ceased to be practicable to administer the property available under the trust; or
(d) that the purpose of the trust, whether in whole or in part, have, since the trust was constituted—
 (i) been adequately provided for by other means; or
 (ii) ceased to be such as would enable the trust to become a recognised body [a charity]; or
 (iii) ceased in any other way to provide a suitable and effective method of using the property available under the trust, having regard to the spirit of the trust deed or other document constituting the trust."

In cases involving small public trusts (those having an annual income not exceeding £5,000) where one of these conditions is satisfied, the trustees may vary the purposes of such a trust,

---

[12] On those rules, see Chapter 12.
[13] See, *e.g. Tod's Trs v The Sailors' and Firemen's Orphans' and Widows' Society*, 1953 S.L.T. (Notes) 72 ("The Society for Old and Infirm Officers of the Mercantile Marine").
[14] See, *e.g. Laing's Trs v Perth Model Lodging House*, 1954 S.L.T. (Notes) 13.
[15] K. McK Norrie and E. M. Scobbie, *Trusts* (1991), 180–182. See also J. M. Thomson, "A Question of Identity—The Problem of Bequests to Non-Existent Institutions in Scots Law" 1973 J.R. 281.
[16] See, *e.g. Tait's J.F. v Lillie*, 1940 S.C. 542.
[17] See, *e.g. National Bible Society of Scotland v Church of Scotland*, 1946 S.L.T. (Notes) 26.
[18] *cf. Templeton v Burgh of Ayr*, 1910 2 S.L.T. 12.
[19] *Scotstown Moor Children's Camp*, 1948 S.C. 630.

transfer its assets to another public trust, or amalgamate it with one or more public trusts without the necessity of court application, by following procedures laid down in statute and regulations,[20] provided that the Lord Advocate does not object.

It may also be possible to use the *cy-près* jurisdiction to amalgamate two or more trusts on the grounds of expediency, without any need to show impossibility.[21]

What can the court do once the variation jurisdiction is triggered?

Once the criteria for variation have been met, the court may approve a scheme for the variation of **11–71** the trust. In doing so, the court will adhere to the "principle of approximation". This means that the objects of the varied trust must "approximate as closely as may be" to those which were originally selected by the truster.[22] See the following case:

Glasgow Royal Infirmary v Magistrates of Glasgow
(1888) 15 R. 264

A society raised funds to provide a fever hospital in Glasgow. The local authority later established a fever hospital without use of those funds. The trustees sought approval for a *cy-près* scheme. It was suggested by the Infirmary that the funds should be used to provide a home for nurses, while other parties to the case suggested that it should be used to provide warm clothing for fever convalescents on leaving the hospital. The court approved the latter suggestion, holding that this was closest to the original purposes of the trust.

Where the trust purposes were originally confined to a particular locality, the court will seek to maintain this connection.[23] The court will not sanction a variation whereby the trust funds will be used to provide services or facilities which government agencies are obliged to provide.[24]

As part of variation, the court may transfer trust funds to another body,[25] widen the class of persons who are entitled to benefit from the trust,[26] or extend the powers of the trustees.[27] It has been held that the court is not entitled to extend the investment powers of the trustees beyond those permitted by the Trustee Investments Act 1961,[28] but the courts would probably not take the same view today.[29]

Key Concepts

In some cases, it may be desirable to **vary the purposes** of a trust.

In **private trusts**, the basic principle is that variation is possible with the consent of all the beneficiaries. Where a person who is or may be a beneficiary is unable to consent to a variation, the court may consent on their behalf provided that it is satisfied the variation would not be **prejudicial** to that person.

---

20 Law Reform (Miscellaneous Provisions) (Scotland) Act 1990, s.10; Public Trusts (Reorganisation) (Scotland) (No.2) Regulations 1993 (SI 1993/2036).
21 See *Mining Institute of Scotland Benevolent Fund, Petrs*, 1994 S.L.T. 785; *Clutterbuck, Petr*, 1961 S.L.T. 427; J. Chalmers, *Trusts: Cases and Materials* (2002), para.12.38.
22 *Stranraer Original Secession Corporation*, 1923 S.C. 722, *per* the Lord President (Clyde) at 725.
23 *Glasgow Royal Infirmary v Magistrates of Glasgow* (1888) 15 R. 264.
24 *Governors of Jonathan Anderson Trust* (1896) 23 R. 592. This does not apply to services provided at governmental discretion: *Campbell Endowment Trust*, 1928 S.C. 171.
25 See, *e.g. Clyde Industrial Training Ship Association*, 1925 S.C. 676.
26 See, *e.g. Trs of Carnegie Park Orphanage* (1892) 19 R. 605.
27 *McCrie's Trs*, 1927 S.C. 556.
28 *Mitchell Bequest Trs*, 1959 S.C. 395.
29 See J. Chalmers, *Trusts: Cases and Materials* (2002), para.12.42.

Where it has never been possible to give effect to the terms of a **public trust** (**initial failure**), the court may apply ***cy-près*** to vary the terms of the trust provided that a **general charitable intention** on the part of the truster can be shown and that it is **impossible** to give effect to the trust purposes.

Where it has been possible initially to give effect to the terms of a public trust (cases of **subsequent failure**), ***cy-près*** may be applied if it has become **impossible** to give effect to the trust purposes. It is not necessary to show a general charitable intention in such cases. Variation may also be possible under s.9 of the Law Reform (Miscellaneous Provisions) (Scotland) Act 1990 if the trust purposes have become in some way inappropriate—s.9 lays down criteria which must be satisfied for variation under this section.

Where grounds for variation of a public trust have been established, the court may **vary the purposes** of the trust, **transfer trust funds** to another body, or **extend the powers** of the trustees.

TERMINATION OF A TRUST

11–72 This section considers the circumstances in which a trust may be brought to an end. There are three principal ways in which this may happen:

- revocation by the truster;
- termination by the trustees; and
- termination by the beneficiaries.

Revocation by the truster

11–73 Because a *mortis causa* trust is not effective until the testator's death, it is always open to the testator to revoke his will and prevent the trust from even taking effect.[30] It is possible, however, for a person to contractually bind themselves to include certain provisions in their will, in which case they will be barred from revoking those provisions.[31]

An *inter vivos* trust is only irrevocable if the following conditions are satisfied:

- there must be an ascertained beneficiary (if the only ascertained beneficiary is the truster himself, the trust remains revocable)[32]; and
- the beneficiary must have a *jus quaesitium* (an "immediate beneficial interest"[33]). If the truster only intended to confer a testamentary benefit on the beneficiary (*i.e.* a benefit in the event of the truster's death), then this is a testamentary provision and is revocable.[34] If the beneficiary's interest is contingent on a particular event taking place, then the trust is revocable,[35] unless all that is required is that the beneficiary survive to a specified date.[36]

If these conditions are not satisfied, the truster is entitled to revoke the trust. The question may arise indirectly—*e.g.*, if the truster becomes insolvent, his creditors may seek to have the trust revoked so that the trust property can be applied to payment of his debts, or if the trustee dies, a

[30] C. de B. Murray, *The Law of Wills in Scotland* (1945) 45.
[31] *Paterson v Paterson* (1893) 20 R. 484.
[32] *Bertram's Trs v Bertram*, 1909 S.C. 1238.
[33] W. A. Wilson and A. G. M. Duncan, *Trusts, Trustees and Executors* (2nd ed., 1995), para.11–03.
[34] *Bertram's Trs v Bertram*, 1909 S.C. 1238.
[35] *Bulkeley-Gavin's Trs v Bulkeley-Gavin's Trs*, 1971 S.C. 209 (benefit contingent on the wholesale nationalisation of land).
[36] *Robertson v Robertson's Trs* (1892) 19 R. 849.

question may arise as to whether the trust property formed part of his estate at the time of his death.

If the truster was insolvent at the time of the trust's creation, or was rendered insolvent by its creation, the creation of the trust may be challengeable by his creditors as a gratuitous alienation.[37]

Termination by the trustees

The trustees may bring the trust to an end by fulfilling the trust purposes and distributing the trust estate. Trustees are entitled to receive a discharge before leaving office, which should generally be granted by the person entitled to the residue of the trust estate.[38] **11–74**

Termination by the beneficiaries

There are two relevant principles here, as follows: **11–75**

- all the beneficiaries in a private trust may, acting together, compel the termination of a trust; and
- a beneficiary who has acquired a right in fee to property is entitled to insist that the trustees pass the property to him absolutely (the *Miller's Trustees* principle).

Termination by consent of all the beneficiaries

If all the beneficiaries in a private trust consent to the termination of a trust, the trustees must comply, unless the trust includes any alimentary rights (because these cannot be renounced except with the permission of the court),[39] or where termination would prejudice the proper administration of the trust, as in the following case: **11–76**

De Robeck v Inland Revenue

1928 S.C. (H.L.) 34

In his will, D's husband left his estate to trustees for certain purposes. The heritable estates were found to be heavily mortgaged, and considerable death duties applied. To avoid a forced sale, the trustees elected to pay these duties by 16 half-yearly instalments. At a later date, a question arose as to whether, for taxation purposes, D was to be treated as to owner of the estate—which she would have been if she was entitled to insist that the trust be terminated. It was held that, while the payments were ongoing, D was not entitled to insist on termination because that would have prejudiced the legitimate arrangement which the trustees had entered into regarding payment of death duties.

The Miller's Trustees *principle*

According to the case of *Miller's Trs v Miller*,[40] a beneficiary who has acquired a right in fee to property is entitled to insist that the trustees transfer the property to him absolutely, even if they have instructions to the contrary. **11–77**

---

[37] On gratuitous alienations generally, see D. W. McKenzie Skene, *Insolvency Law in Scotland* (1999), Chap.30.
[38] On discharges generally, see J. Chalmers, *Trusts: Cases and Materials* (2002), paras 13.29–13.37.
[39] See the Trusts (Scotland) Act 1961, s.1(4).
[40] (1890) 18 R. 301.

Miller's Trs v Miller

(1890) 18 R. 301

In his will, Sir William Miller directed his trustees to manage certain property for the benefit of his son John Miller. He directed that the property was to vest in him once he reached the age of 25, or upon marriage if he married between the ages of 21 and 25. The trustees were to pass the property to him once he reached the age of 25.

John Miller married after reaching the age of 21 and requested that the trustees pass the trust property to him. The Court of Session held that the trustees were obliged to pass it to him notwithstanding the directions in his father's will.

It should be noted that, if the trust deed had simply stated that the estate would not vest in the beneficiary until he attained the age of 25, he would not have been entitled to lay claim to it until he reached that age. If the trustees were to pay it over to him before the property had vested in him, they would be acting to the potential prejudice of whoever was to become entitled to the estate if he had died without reaching that age.

The trustees may be entitled to refuse to transfer the property if this would prejudice the proper administration of the trust (as in *De Robeck v Inland Revenue*, discussed above), or if it would prejudice other trust purposes—as in *Graham's Trs v Graham,*[41] where the trustees might have required to use the capital which was being claimed by one beneficiary in order to make annual payments to other beneficiaries.

Key Concepts

Trusts may be **terminated** in a number of ways.

By the **truster**:

- Because a ***mortis causa*** trust does not take effect until the testator's death, it is normally open to the testator to revoke his will at any time before his death and prevent the trust ever taking effect.
- An ***inter vivos*** trust may be revoked by the truster unless (a) there is an ascertained beneficiary (other than the truster himself) and (b) that beneficiary has an "immediate beneficial interest".

By the **trustees**: the **trustees** may terminate a trust by fulfilling the trust purposes and distributing the trust estate.

By the **beneficiaries**:

- In a private trust, all the beneficiaries acting together may compel the termination of a trust.
- A beneficiary who has acquired a right in fee to property is normally entitled to insist that the trustees pass the property to him absolutely.

[41] (1899) 2 F. 232.

Quick Quiz

Basic concepts and the creation of a trust

- What is a trust? How may trusts be classified?
- Who owns trust property?
- How is a voluntary trust created?
- What types of legally implied trust are recognised by Scots law?
- What restrictions does Scots law place on the validity of trust purposes?

Trustees and trust management

- On what grounds may a trustee be removed from office by the court?
- When will the court interfere in the discretion of trustees?
- Must trust decisions be taken unanimously?
- What general duties does the law impose on trustees?
- What are the obligations of trustees in relation to investment matters?
- What is meant by the rule against auctor in rem suam?
- What are the sources of trustees' powers?

Trustees' liabilities

- When a trustee has been in breach of trust, what remedies are open to the beneficiaries?
- How may trustees be protected from liability for breach of trust?
- Are trustees personally liable on trust contracts?

Variation of trust purposes

- What requirements must be satisfied before the terms of a private trust can be varied? To what extent is the court involved in this process?
- In what circumstances may the terms of a public trust be varied?

Termination of a trust

- In what ways may a trust be terminated?

Further Reading

The leading textbook on the Scottish law of trusts is **W.A. Wilson and A.G.M. Duncan's *Trusts, Trustees and Executors*** (2nd ed., 1995). It is a detailed reference work but is generally unsuitable for someone who is approaching the subject for the first time. Reference is sometimes also made to a number of older textbooks, particularly **A. Mackenzie Stuart's *The Law of Trusts*** (1932). Mackenzie Stuart's book is brief and readable but must be treated with some caution given developments in the law of trusts since it was published.

There are relatively few student textbooks on the subject. The most recent is a cases and materials book: **J. Chalmers, *Trusts: Cases and Materials*** (2002), on which this Chapter draws heavily. There is one textbook: **K.McK. Norrie and E.M. Scobbie, *Trusts*** (1991). Although it is now over 10 years old, there have been few major developments in the law of trusts over that period and it is still a very useful introduction to the subject. **R.R.M. Paisley, *Trusts LawBasics*** (1999) is a very brief introduction to the subject.

Reference may also be made to **J. McLaren, *The Law of Wills and Succession as Administered in Scotland, Including Trusts, Entails, Powers and Executry*** (3rd ed., 1894) and **A.J.P. Menzies, *The Law of Scotland Affecting Trustees*** (2nd ed., 1913). These are very detailed works which may be of use for researching particular points, but are too dated to be relied upon in themselves.

Two recent articles which provide useful analyses of the theory of the trust in Scots law should be specifically mentioned: **K.G.C. Reid, "Patrimony not Equity: the trust in Scotland"** (2000) 8 E.R.P.L. 427; and **G.L. Gretton, "Trusts Without Equity"** (2000) 49 I.C.L.Q. 599.

Chapter 12

SUCCESSION

David Brand[1]

INTRODUCTION

The law of succession governs the distribution of property belonging to a person who has died. **12–01** Accordingly, with the exception of those few people who die leaving nothing, the law of succession affects everyone. The law deals with a range of matters. It deals with who is entitled to succeed to the property of the deceased person who has made no provision which expresses his or her wishes as to who is to inherit. This is known as the law of intestate succession. It deals with the situation where the deceased has left a will or some other testamentary writing or evidence of intention as to who he or she wishes to inherit his or her property. This is known as testate succession and the person leaving the will is known as the testator. Testate succession deals with

[1] Senior Lecturer in Law, University of Dundee.

such matters as the formal requirements for the validity of a will or other testamentary writing, whether the testator had the requisite legal capacity to make a will and the limitations on the testamentary freedom of testators to leave property as they wish. The law of succession also requires to deal with the administrative process of transferring the property of the deceased to those entitled to inherit, known as the beneficiaries. This is carried out by the executor of the deceased and the administration of a deceased's estate is known as an executry.

Scots law on succession was radically altered by the Succession (Scotland) Act 1964, particularly in relation to intestate succession. Prior to this Act, intestate succession to heritable and moveable property was different. The Act changed this and for most purposes the same rules apply to both heritable and moveable property. The Act also introduced prior rights for surviving spouses on intestacy and altered the rules for the administration of a deceased's estate.

Subsequent to the 1964 Act, the Scottish Law Commission examined the law of succession in some detail in the latter half of the 1980s and issued a report in 1990[2] recommending a range of reforms.[3] None of these reforms has been implemented yet and, with limited exception, there is no sign that this is likely to change in the foreseeable future.

In this Chapter the following matters are considered:

- proof of death and survivorship
- legal rights
- intestate succession
- testate succession
- revocation of wills
- will substitutes
- interpretation of wills
- legacies
- vesting and accretion
- executry administration
- reform.

PRIVATE INTERNATIONAL LAW

12–02 Private international law is important in relation to questions of succession. Private international law governs situations where the laws of more than one country may apply to particular circumstances, in order to determine which is the appropriate law to apply. For instance, if an English person who lived in Scotland dies leaving a house in France, does the succession law of England, Scotland or France apply to determine who inherits the house? The rules relating to such matters are complicated.[4]

The basic position in Scotland is that if a person dies domiciled in Scotland, Scots law of succession will apply to that person's moveable property wherever it is situated. Scots law will also apply to any immoveable property situated in Scotland, as the general rule in private international law is that the law of the country where immoveable property is situated applies to that property. It follows that if a person who is not domiciled in Scotland dies leaving immoveable property in Scotland, Scots law applies to that property.

Domicile, therefore, has an important effect in private international law. Domicile, however, is a difficult concept. A person will have a domicile of origin and may acquire a domicile of choice. "The central idea is that it is the place where [he] has made his home."[5] Simple residence in a place is not sufficient to establish domicile, however.[6]

---

[2] Report on Succession, Scot. Law Com. No.124, 1990.
[3] See Reform, below.
[4] See Anton and Beaumont, *Private International Law* (2nd ed.).
[5] Anton and Beaumont, *op.cit.*, p.125.
[6] Anton and Beaumont, *op.cit.*, p.124.

The classification of a property as moveable or immoveable also has an important effect in private international law and the law which determines how a particular property is classified is governed by the country where the property is situated.[7] It should be noted that the concept of heritable and moveable in Scots law is not exactly the same as that of immoveable and moveable.[8]

> **Key Concepts**
>
> If a person dies **domiciled** in Scotland, Scots law of succession will apply to that person's moveable property wherever it is situated.
>
> If a person who is **not domiciled** in Scotland dies leaving immoveable property in Scotland, Scots law applies to that property.

PROOF OF DEATH AND SURVIVORSHIP

Proof of death

In most cases, the fact of death and the date and time of death can be readily ascertained, although modern medical ethics can produce difficulties in relation to brain death as opposed to physical death. There can be no inheritance unless death is proved and an executor must state the precise date and place of death to enable an estate to be administered. If this is challenged the executor must prove this.[9] **12–03**

Death is usually evidenced by an extract from the Register of Deaths and such an extract is deemed "sufficient evidence of the death" under the Registration of Births, Deaths and Marriages (Scotland) Act 1965[10] although not conclusive. Problems can occur with deaths in foreign countries where foreign registration procedures are inadequate. Problems can also occur where no body is found, as a death certificate cannot be issued without a doctor viewing the deceased's body.[11]

Presumption of death

At common law there was no provision for presuming a person to be dead after disappearance for a certain period of time. The common law presumed that a person lived to an extreme old age[12] in the absence of proof of death. Such proof required to be beyond reasonable doubt to rebut the presumption.[13] **12–04**

Since 1881,[14] there has been statutory provision on presumption of death. The current law is set out in the Presumption of Death (Scotland) Act 1977. Under this Act any person having an interest can raise an action to have a person declared legally dead. This applies in two main situations:

- where a person is thought to have died, *e.g.*, in a plane crash
- where a person has not been known to be alive for seven years, *e.g.*, a person disappearing without any contact with anyone.

---

7 *MacDonald v MacDonald,* 1932 S.C. (H.L.) 79.
8 See Chapter on Property.
9 Currie, *Confirmation of Executors* (4th ed., 1995), 7.10–7.12.
10 s.41(3).
11 s.24.
12 Stair states 80 or 100 years—Inst. VI xlv 17.
13 See, *e.g. Secretary of State for Scotland v Sutherland,* 1944 S.C. 79.
14 Presumption of Life Limitation (Scotland) Act 1881.

Proof is on the balance of probabilities. In the first situation the date of death will be either the actual date of death if proved or the end of a period of time within which it is not certain when the person died. In the second situation it will be at the end of the day seven years after the person was known to have been alive.[15]

The court can decide any question relating to any interest in property resulting from the death.[16] The court decree dissolves the missing person's marriage, if married, but the estate will be divided as if the person were married.

If a missing person reappears or is proved to have died at a different date from that in the decree, any person with an interest can apply to have the decree varied or recalled by a variation order.[17] In order to protect those who have acquired rights by the original court decree, a variation order does not automatically affect any property rights acquired under the decree. If such a variation order is made within five years of the decree, the court can make an order which it "considers fair and reasonable in all the circumstances" which includes restitution in cash or kind.[18] A variation order cannot affect any income already received or the title of a third party acquiring in good faith and for value.[19]

Proof of survivorship

12–05 A beneficiary must survive the deceased in order to inherit. This must be proved on the balance of probabilities.[20] "Survivance is in every case a matter of proof, and … when a claimant whose claim depends on proof of survivorship is unable to establish the fact of survivorship, his claim necessarily fails."[21] There is no period of time required and a few seconds of survivorship is sufficient. In practice, to avoid difficulties where a person dies and a beneficiary of that person, for example, a spouse, dies at the same time or within a short time thereafter, it is usual in wills to specify a period of time for survivorship. 30 days is the most common period specified.

Where more than one person died and it was impossible to determine who had died first, there were no presumptions under the common law to assist. This could have unfortunate results in such common calamities.

Ross's Judicial Factor v Martin

1955 S.C. (H.L.) 56

Two sisters left identical wills leaving everything to each other, whom failing a charity. They died together in their home due to a gas leak and it was not clear who had died first. Neither could be proved to have survived the other and the whom failing part of the will could not be applied. Their estates went to their relatives under the law of intestacy instead of the charity which they wished to benefit.[22]

The Succession (Scotland) Act 1964 reformed the law. The general rule is that where two persons have died in circumstances indicating that they died simultaneously or that it is uncertain who survived whom, it is presumed that the younger survived the elder.[23] There are two exceptions. Firstly, where the persons were husband and wife, it is presumed that neither survived the other thus retaining the common law position.[24] Secondly, where the elder left a legacy to the younger

---

15 1977 Act, s.2.
16 1977 Act, s.3(1).
17 1977 Act, s.4(1).
18 1977 Act, s.5(3).
19 1977 Act, s.5(2).
20 *Lamb v Lord Advocate*, 1976 S.L.T. 151.
21 Lord Justice-Clerk Cooper in *Drummond's Judicial Factor v Lord Advocate*, 1944 S.C. 298 at 302.
22 See also *Mitchell's Executrix v Gordon*, 1953 S.C. 176.
23 1964 Act, s.31(1)(b).
24 1964 Act, s.31(1)(a).

whom failing a third party and the younger dies without a will, the elder is presumed to have survived for the purpose of that legacy only.[25]

Under inheritance tax law, parties to a common calamity are deemed to die simultaneously which avoids a double charge to tax.[26]

Postumous children

Where a deceased person has left a child conceived but not born, such a child may be treated as having been born and having survived the deceased for the purposes of succession.[27] Two conditions must be satisfied. First, the child must be born alive and not stillborn. Secondly, the rule cannot be invoked to benefit a third party, as with a trust, but only the child directly.[28] **12–06**

Entitlement to inherit

A person who would otherwise inherit in an estate may be debarred from doing so on certain grounds. These grounds do not include incapacity, as a person who is incapax due to mental incapacity or is under the age of sixteen is entitled to inherit and the property concerned will normally be held by a curator or guardian of the incapax or the parent or guardian of a child. **12–07**

The relevant situations where a person may not inherit are:

- the unworthy heir
- illegitimate children
- adopted children,

although the former discrimination against illegitimate and adopted children in favour of legitimate blood relations has been largely abolished.

The unworthy heir

An unworthy heir is the term usually applied to a beneficiary who has unlawfully killed the deceased. The rule in Scots law which prevents an unworthy heir inheriting appears to derive from both statute and the common law and seems to be based on principles of public policy. **12–08**

An old statute, the Patricide Act 1594 deals with the killing of parents and grandparents but the scope of the Act is not clear and it has never been used to disinherit someone in any reported case.

The rule applies to both murder and culpable homicide[29] but a criminal conviction is not essential. The unworthy heir is not regarded as predeceasing the deceased but is simply ignored in the distribution of the deceased's estate.[30]

Burns v Secretary of State for Social Services
1985 S.L.T. 351

A woman was provoked by her husband's violence. She had been assaulted by him over a period of years and she had suffered numerous injuries. She stabbed him and he died. She pled guilty to culpable homicide. Her claim for a widow's allowance was disallowed as she had deliberately killed her husband.

---

25 1964 Act, s.31(2).
26 Inheritance Tax 1984, s.4(2).
27 The latin maxim is *qui in utero est, pro iam nato habetur, Cox's Trs v Cox*, 1950 S.C. 117.
28 *Elliot v Joicey*, 1935 S.C. (H.L.) 57.
29 *Burns v Secretary of State for Social Services*, 1985 S.L.T. 351.
30 *Hunter's Exrs, Petitioners*, 1992 S.L.T. 1141.

The Forfeiture Act 1982 enables the court to modify this "forfeiture rule" in appropriate circumstances but is given no power to modify the effects of the 1594 Act. The court can modify the rule where it is satisfied that it is just to do so, having regard to the conduct of the offender and the deceased and other relevant circumstances.[31] A court can only modify and not completely exclude the rule but the modification can be virtually a complete exclusion. In one case, the killer of the deceased in extenuating circumstances received 100 per cent of the heritable estate and 99 per cent of the moveable estate.[32]

Illegitimate children

12–09 At common law an illegitimate child was regarded as *filius nullius*, nobody's child, and had no right to inherit from anyone.[33] Various statutory reforms dating from 1926 gradually reduced this discrimination.[34] The current law is set out in the Law Reform (Parent and Child) (Scotland) Act 1986.

The 1986 Act provides that the fact "that a person's parents are not or have not been married to one another shall be left out of account in establishing the legal relationship between the person and any other person".[35] The effect of this is that for virtually all purposes there is no difference between legitimate and illegitimate persons in succession. However, the Act does not apply to titles, coats of arms or honours[36] or deaths or wills executed before December 8, 1986.

Adopted children

12–10 Prior to 1964, adoption did not affect the succession rights of adopted children. They retained a right of inheritance in the natural parents' estates but not in the adopted parents' estates. This position was reversed under the Succession (Scotland) Act 1964.[37] The change does not apply to titles, coats of arms or honours[38] or to deaths before September 10, 1964. There are special rules relating to the relationship of the adopted person with brothers and sisters and their descendents.[39]

Key Concepts

Death is usually evidenced by an extract from the Register of Deaths.

Statutory provisions on **presumption of death** provide that a person can be declared legally dead in two situations:

- where a person is thought to have died
- where a person has not been known to be alive for 7 years.

A beneficiary must **survive** the deceased in order to inherit. No period of time is necessary. This must be proved on the balance of probabilities.

The relevant situations where a person **may not inherit** are:

---

31 s.2(2).
32 *Cross, Petitioner*, 1987 S.L.T. 384.
33 Erskine Inst. III. x. 8, *Clarke v Carfin Coal Co* (1891) 18 R. (H.L.) 63.
34 Starting with the Legitimacy Act 1926.
35 s.1(1).
36 s.9(1)(c).
37 s.23(1).
38 ss.23(4) and 37(1).
39 ss.24(1) and 24(1A).

- the unworthy heir
- illegitimate children
- adopted children.

The former discrimination against illegitimate and adopted children has been largely abolished.

LEGAL RIGHTS

Legal rights have existed in Scots law for several centuries to protect spouses and children from disinheritance. It is not possible to completely exclude a spouse and children from inheritance by making a will which omits them. Legal rights apply in both testate and intestate succession. Strictly speaking, legal rights are not rights of succession but are debts due by the deceased estate.[40] If claimed, they are paid out of the net moveable estate after deduction of debts and funeral expenses and also after deduction of prior rights in an intestate estate.[41] **12–11**

Legal rights can be claimed only by spouses and children. Cohabitees have no such rights and neither do stepchildren. Illegitimate and adopted children can claim legal rights.[42] Where a child has predeceased the deceased, the children or remoter descendents of that child can claim under the doctrine of representation.[43]

Legal rights are not paid out automatically in the administration of a testate estate; they must be claimed. The right to claim is extinguished after 20 years by the long negative prescription.[44] They are paid out of the moveable estate only but there is no right to claim specific assets as part of the right. An estate, therefore, must be divided into heritage and moveables for the purpose of calculating legal rights. It follows that it is possible for a person to reduce or defeat a potential legal rights claim by converting assets from moveables to heritage in their lifetime although this has practical limitations.[45]

Legal rights fall into two categories:

- *ius relicti* or *ius relictae*
- legitim.

Ius relicti is the right of a widower and *ius relictae* is the right of a widow. Legitim is the right of children, sometimes known as "bairns' part". The amount of the right depends on who has survived the deceased:

- where both a spouse and children (or remoter issue) survive, *ius relicti* or *relictae* is one third of the moveable estate, legitim is one third and the remaining one third is the free estate, sometimes known as "dead's part" which is distributed according to the provisions of the will or rules of intestate succession
- where a spouse only survives, the *ius relicti* or *relictae* is one half and the other half is free estate
- where children (or remoter issue) only survive, legitim is one half and the other half is free estate.

---

[40] Lord Watson in *Naismith v Boyes* (1899) 1 F. (H.L.) 79 at 81.
[41] See Prior Rights below.
[42] See Illegitimate Children and Adopted Children above.
[43] See below.
[44] Prescription and Limitation (Scotland) Act 1973, s.7 and Sch.1, para.2(f).
[45] Another device would be to use up assets to purchase an annuity which would cease on death. Trusts can also be used to limit legal rights claims.

Election

12–12 It is not possible to take both a provision under a will and claim legal rights. A spouse or child must choose between accepting what is left to them in a will or rejecting this and claiming legal rights, presumably on the basis that more will be received. This is known as the doctrine of approbate and reprobate in Scots law.

Representation

12–13 Prior to 1964, if a child predeceased the deceased and left children, these grandchildren had no right to legitim. The 1964 Act altered this by providing for representation.[46] If a deceased has a child who predeceases him or her leaving grandchildren or remoter issue, such issue have the same right to legitim as the child would have had by surviving the deceased.

Where there is more than one person claiming legitim there are rules as to how the legitim fund is divided. If all those claiming are related in the same degree to the deceased, division is *per capita,* or by head. For instance, if there are four grandchildren they will each receive one quarter of the legitim. If all those claiming are not related in the same degree to the deceased, the division is *per stirpes,* or by branch. For instance, if there is one child living and another child who predeceased leaving two children, *i.e.* grandchildren, the child of the deceased will receive one half of the legitim and the grandchildren will receive one half between them, *i.e.* one quarter each.

Collation

12–14 If a person wishes to claim legitim and has received advances of moveable property during the lifetime of the deceased, the doctrine of collation *inter liberos* applies. Collation is the adding back of the advances to the legitim fund which is then divided *inter liberos*, amongst the children. The purpose of this doctrine is to treat children equally in the division. It only applies in legitim. There must be more than one person claiming legitim before the doctrine operates.[47] Where the claimant is representing a predeceasing child, advances made to both the claimant and the predeceasing child must be collated.

Not all advances require to be collated. The following advances are excluded:

- an advance made which is clearly intended by the deceased to be in addition to a claim to legitim
- a loan to a child, which is a debt due to the deceased's estate
- remuneration for services rendered
- money used for the education and maintenance of a child.[48]

Discharge of legal rights

12–15 Legal rights can be formally discharged either during the lifetime of the deceased or after the death. *Ius relicti* and *ius relictae* can be discharged unilaterally or by a bilateral agreement which was common at one time but is now rare. A discharge of legitim requires the consent of the child or remoter issue concerned.[49]

Where the discharge is during the deceased's lifetime, the granter of the discharge is treated as dead which increases the proportional share of any other legitim claimants. Where the discharge is

46 1964 Act, s.11.
47 *Coats' Trs v Coats*, 1914 S.C. 744.
48 Ersk. Inst. III, xi, 24.
49 1964 Act, s.12.

after the death, the share affected by the discharge falls into the free estate and the share of any other legitim claimant is unaffected.

> **Key Concepts**
>
> **Legal rights** protect spouses and children from disinheritance. They apply in testate and intestate succession. They are paid out of the net moveable estate only.
>
> ***Ius relicti*** is the right of a widower and ***ius relictae*** is the right of a widow. **Legitim** is the right of children.
>
> They amount to one third of the net moveable estate for each category if both spouse and children survive or one half if either the spouse only or children only survive. Grandchildren or remoter issue can represent a child who predeceases the testator.
>
> Legal rights can be discharged during the lifetime of the testator or after the death.

INTESTATE SUCCESSION

Intestacy occurs where there is no will or other testamentary provision relating to a deceased's estate. Intestacy can be total or partial where part of the estate is not disposed of. Partial intestacy may be deliberate although this is unusual or as a result of a failure of part of a will. If a will fails in part or completely this is known as artificial intestacy. In practice, most intestacies occur where the deceased died without leaving a will. This is an unfortunate but frequent occurrence as many people do not bother to make wills. The rules of intestacy attempt to set out how society generally would expect someone to dispose of his or her estate which may or may not be what the deceased would have wanted. **12–16**

The rules of intestate succession were radically reformed by the Succession (Scotland) Act 1964. Prior to this Act there were different rules for heritable and moveable property, with heritable property going exclusively to the oldest male heir under the principle known as *primogeniture*. The 1964 Act applies to most property but not to titles, coats of arms and honours. There is now no distinction between entitlement to heritable and moveable property, although the distinction remains important in relation to legal rights. The 1964 Act improved the position on intestacy for spouses with the introduction of prior rights which are paid first out of the net intestate estate. The 1964 Act also altered the order in which relatives of the deceased are entitled to succeed.

The order of succession in the 1964 Act sets out six stages to be followed in distributing an intestate estate. These are:

- payment of debts[50]
- prior rights—right to dwelling house[51]
- prior rights—furniture and plenishings[52]
- prior rights—cash right[53]
- legal rights
- free estate.[54]

---

[50] See Assets and debts, below.
[51] 1964 Act, s.8(1).
[52] 1964 Act, s.8(3).
[53] 1964 Act, s.9.

Prior rights

12–17 Prior rights are only payable on intestacy, either total or partial. If an intestacy is partial, they are only payable out of the intestate part of the estate. A surviving spouse is the only person entitled to prior rights: cohabitees and children are not. Prior rights are extinguished after 20 years under the long negative prescription.[55] The value for calculating prior rights is the value as the date of death.[56]

Dwelling house

12–18 A surviving spouse has a right to the deceased's dwelling house, or one of them if more than one, or a cash equivalent depending on the value of the house. A dwelling house includes a part of a building occupied as a separate house and any garden or amenity ground attached.[57]

This prior right applies to a house owned by the deceased or tenanted by the deceased.[58] Tenancies covered by the Rent Acts are excluded as are tenancies which terminate on the death of the deceased.[59] Also excluded are a house which forms part only of a single tenancy[60] and a house which is used for a business where the value of the whole estate would be likely to be substantially diminished by disposing of the house separate from the business.[61]

The surviving spouse must have been ordinarily resident in the house for the prior right to operate.[62] It is not relevant whether or not the deceased was ordinarily resident in that house. If the surviving spouse was ordinarily resident in more than one house, a choice must be made within six months of the date of death as to which one is taken as a prior right.[63]

The upper value for a house which can be taken as a prior right was set at £15,000 under the 1964 Act and has been increased periodically by statutory instrument. The current figure is £130,000.[64] If the house is valued at over £130,000 the surviving spouse will receive a cash equivalent of £130,000.[65] In practice, where this happens it is usual for the surviving spouse to make up the difference to enable the house to be taken. The value of the house is taken after deduction of any heritable debts such as a mortgage over the house. Any disagreement as to the value is determined by arbitration.[66]

Furniture and plenishings

12–19 The surviving spouse has a right to the furniture and plenishings of a dwelling house where normally resident at the date of death. Furniture and plenishings include "garden effects, domestic animals, plate, plated articles, linen, china, glass, books, pictures, prints, articles of household use and consumable stores"[67] but this list is not exhaustive. Articles and animals used for business purposes, money, securities and heirlooms are all excluded.[68]

---

[54] 1964 Act, s.2.
[55] Prescription and Limitation (Scotland) Act 1973, s.7, and Sch.1, para.2 (f).
[56] 1964 Act, s.9A.
[57] 1964 Act, s.8(6)(a).
[58] 1964 Act, s.8(6)(d).
[59] 1964 Act, s.36(2).
[60] 1964 Act, s.8(2)(a).
[61] 1964 Act, s.8(2)(b).
[62] 1964 Act, s.8(4).
[63] 1964 Act, s.8(1).
[64] SI 1999/445.
[65] 1964 Act, s.8(1)(b).
[66] 1964 Act, s.8(5).
[67] 1964 Act, s.8(6)(b).
[68] 1964 Act, s.8(6)(b).

The current upper limit is £22,000.[69] A surviving spouse is entitled to furniture and plenishings up to that value. If the total value exceeds £22,000, items up to that value must be chosen. The furniture and plenishings must come from one house only. If there is more than one house in which the surviving spouse was normally resident at the date of death, the spouse must choose within six months of the date of death from which house they will be taken.[70] The furniture and plenishings need not be taken from the same house which was chosen for the right to the dwelling house.

Cash right

A surviving spouse has a right to a sum of cash in addition to the right to the house and furniture and plenishings but this cash right only arises after the other two rights have been satisfied. The sum is currently a maximum of £35,000 if the deceased is survived by children or remoter issue or £58,000 if the deceased is not.[71] The cash right is paid out proportionately from the heritable and moveable estate.[72] Interest is payable on the cash sum from the date of death until payment[73] at a rate fixed by the Secretary of State from time to time. It is currently 7 per cent.[74] **12–20**

If the intestacy is partial only and the spouse has been left a legacy in the testate part of the estate other than a legacy of a dwelling house or of furniture and plenishings taken as prior rights, the value of that legacy as at the date of death must be set off against the cash right and will reduce it accordingly.[75]

Free estate

Prior rights will exhaust the whole estate in many cases. If not, legal rights are calculated and satisfied next. If there is any estate left after satisfaction of prior rights and legal rights this is known as the free estate and is divided under the rules set out in the 1964 Act. The Act lays out the following order of succession[76]: **12–21**

- children
- parents and brothers and sisters provided there is at least one from each class—each class taking one half
- brothers and sisters where there is no surviving parent
- parents where there is no surviving brothers or sisters
- spouse
- uncles and aunts, both paternal and maternal
- grandparents, both paternal and maternal
- brothers and sisters of grandparents
- remoter ancestors
- the Crown as *ultimus haeres*, ultimate heir.[77]

Each successive class of relatives is examined until there is someone entitled to inherit and succession stops at that class. Each class must be exhausted before the next class is examined. Representation is applied in all classes except parents and spouses.[78] Issue includes issue however remote with no distinction between legitimate and illegitimate relationships.[79]

---

69 SI 1999/445.
70 1964 Act, s.8(3).
71 SI 1999/445.
72 1964 Act, s.9(3).
73 1964 Act, s.9(1).
74 Interest on Prior Rights (Scotland) Order 1981 (SI 1981/805).
75 1964 Act, ss.9(1) and 9(6)(b).
76 1964 Act, s.2.
77 1964 Act, s.7.
78 1964 Act, s.5.
79 See Illegitimate children, above.

Where there is more than one person with a right of succession the division is *per capita*, by head, if they are related in the same degree to the deceased or *per stirpes*, by branch, if they are not related in the same degree to the deceased.

Collaterals of the whole blood who have two parents in common exclude collaterals of the half blood who have only one parent in common. The former distinction between collaterals of the half blood *consanguinean,* half brothers and half sisters who have the same father, and collaterals of the half blood *uterine,* half brothers and half sisters who have the same mother, no longer applies.

As prior rights are satisfied before legal rights, a surviving spouse may be better off if an estate is intestate where the estate has been left to the surviving spouse under a will and children claim legal rights.[80]

Kerr, Petitioner

1968 S.L.T. (Sh. Ct) 61

Mr Kerr died leaving all his estate to his wife in a will. He had a daughter who claimed her legal rights. Mrs Kerr renounced her rights under the will and Mr Kerr's estate fell into intestacy. Prior rights were payable first and Mrs Kerr was better off than she would have been under the will because legitim of one third of the moveable estate would have been deducted. The court held she was entitled to do this.

Key Concepts

Intestacy occurs where there is no will or other testamentary provision relating to a deceased's estate.

Prior rights are only payable on intestacy, either total or partial. A surviving spouse is the only person entitled to prior rights.

There are three types of prior rights which are satisfied in the following order:

- dwelling house up to a value of £130,00
- furniture and plenishings up to the value of £22,000
- cash up to £58,000 if the deceased left no children or £35,000 if the deceased left children.

Prior rights will exhaust the whole estate in many cases. If not, **legal rights** are calculated and satisfied next. If there is any estate left after satisfaction of prior rights and legal rights this is known as the **free estate** and is divided under the rules set out in the 1964 Act.

TESTATE SUCCESSION

12–22 The law of testate succession governs situations where the deceased has left a will or other testamentary writing. If a will is valid and disposes of all of the estate of a deceased it will be given effect and the rules of intestate succession will not apply. As already noted,[81] it is not possible to avoid claims for legal rights by making a will. If a will disposes of part only of a deceased's estate that part of the estate will be distributed according to the will and the remaining estate will fall into intestacy and be distributed accordingly.

[80] *Kerr, Petitioner*, 1968 S.L.T. (Sh. Ct) 61.

[81] See Legal Rights above.

A testamentary writing is one which is intended to dispose of a person's estate after his or her death.[82] They are usually, but not always, in the form of a formal will. Testamentary intention can also be established in other writings. It is sensible, however, to have a formal will drawn up by a solicitor who is qualified and experienced in such matters. Some people endeavour to make homemade wills and there are various will forms available for such do-it-yourself wills. These can cause problems if not completed correctly, which practice indicates is often the case.

There can be more than one testamentary writing which taken together form the complete testamentary position. Formal additions or alterations to wills are known as codicils. Where a will has trust provisions, such as leaving property to beneficiaries who are under age and therefore the property is to be held by trustees until they reach a certain age, it is sometimes known as a trust disposition and settlement.

The validity of wills and other testamentary writings depends on a number of factors which are usual grouped together under the headings of essential and formal validity but fall into three areas:

- intention to test
- capacity
- formal validity.

Intention to test

A will does not require to have a set form of words but it must be clear that the person making the will, known as the testator, has the intention to test, that is to make a testamentary writing. If it is intended as instructions[83] or notes[84] for a future will it will be ineffective. This may not be entirely clear, especially if there is an indication in an informal writing that the writer intends to make a formal will in the future. In such cases the wording must be examined to establish whether there is testamentary intention in the current writing.[85] **12–23**

Capacity

A person must be aged 12 or older to have capacity to make a will.[86] A person must also be of sound mind to make a will. This means that a person must know the nature and effect of the will. If a person suffers from a mental illness which normally prevents this but has lucid intervals and it can be shown that the will was made during such a lucid interval the will will be valid.[87] Conversely, a normally sane person can temporarily become of unsound mind due, for instance, to alcohol or drugs which will render the person incapable of making a will.[88] **12–24**

Nisbet's Trs v Nisbet

(1871) 9 M. 937

Major Nisbet was resident in a mental institution for many years before he died. Two months before he died he made a will. There was medical evidence that he was in a lucid interval at the time the will was made. It was held that he "had become of a sound and disposing mind to the effect of being able to execute the deed".

---

[82] It derives from the Latin *testare* which means to verify.

[83] *Munro v Coutts* (1813) 1 Dow 437.

[84] *Colvin v Hutchison* (1885) 12 R. 947.

[85] *Rhodes v Peterson*, 1971 S.C. 56.

[86] Age of Legal Capacity (Scotland) Act 1991, s.2(2). Interestingly, a person must be aged 16 or over to act as a witness under ss.2(1) and 9 of the same Act. In England, with limited exceptions, the age is 18.

[87] *Nisbet's Trs v Nisbet* (1871) 9 M. 937.

[88] *Laidlaw v Laidlaw*, (1870) 8 M. 882.

If a person is partially insane, for instance, is suffering from certain delusions and these delusions have influenced the person in making the will, the will may be invalid.[89] "If the testator is not generally insane, the will must be shown to have been the outcome of the special delusion … The delusion must be shown to have been an actual and compelling influence."[90]

Eccentricity is different from mental incapacity and if a will is challenged it must be proved that the testator has no mental capacity to make a will before it will be set aside.[91] This was clearly shown in a somewhat bizarre case.

Morrison v Maclean's Trs

(1862) 24 D. 625

Colonel Alexander Maclean died aged 80. He left a will and two codicils which directed that his estate was to be invested to pay an annuity to his housekeeper and to educate poor boys named Maclean. He left nothing to his relatives. His nearest relative raised an action to have the will reduced on the ground that Maclean was insane. There was evidence that he was given to obscene and rambling conversations and claimed to have no relatives. He said that he had been fed when young from an eagle's nest. (There was, in fact, evidence to support this.) The court held there was no proof of insanity, even if the will might have been morally objectionable to some people, particularly the testator's relatives.

A will made by a person who is not of sound mind is void and has no effect. A will which has been made in circumstances which amount to either facility and circumvention or undue influence is voidable. This means that the will is valid but if challenged may be set aside.

Facility and circumvention

12–25 Facility is where a person has a weakness of mind which does not amount to insanity. This is usually due to illness or old age. Where such a facile person makes a will due to circumvention, which is pressure by someone seeking to influence the terms of the will, such a will may be successfully challenged. Both elements of facility and circumvention must be present. They have been described as being present where "a person is in such a mental state that he is unable to resist pressure, and… someone else can mould and fashion his conduct as he pleases".[92]

It is a matter of degree whether a person is sane, facile or insane. Facility can take a number of forms. "A man may be weak and facile from want of judgement or reason… [or] from mere nervousness and incapacity to resist solicitation."[93] Other forms include illness and bereavement[94] and alcoholism.[95] Similarly, circumvention can occur in different circumstances such as taking a facile person to a solicitor's office where she will simply sign what she is asked to sign[96] or where a facile person is afraid of a relative.[97]

[89] *Sivewright v Sivewright's Trs*, 1920 S.C. (H.L.) 63.
[90] Viscount Haldane in *Sivewright v Sivewright's Trs*, 1920 S.C. (H.L.) 63 at 64.
[91] *Morrison v Maclean's Trs* (1862) 24 D. 625.
[92] Lord Justice-Clerk Alness in *Gibson's Ex. v Anderson*, 1925 S.C. 744 at 790.
[93] Lord Justice-Clerk Inglis in *Morrison v MacLean's Trs* (1862) 24 D. 625 at 635.
[94] *Munro v Strain* (1874) 1 R. 522.
[95] *Pascoe-Watson v Brock's Ex.*, 1998 S.L.T. 40.
[96] *Wheelans v Wheelans*, 1986 S.L.T. 164.
[97] *Cairns v Marianski* (1850) 12 D. 1286.

Pascoe-Watson v Brock's Ex
1998 S.L.T. 40

Mrs Brock died of cancer and alcohol abuse in 1994. She left a will made in 1993 in which most of her estate was left to a Mrs Ritchie. Mrs Brock's cousin, Mrs Pascoe-Watson, was left £5,000 but was the main beneficiary in an earlier will which was revoked by the 1993 will. Mrs Pascoe-Watson was unhappy and raised an action to have the will reduced on the ground that Mrs Brock was facile due to dependence on alcohol and Mrs Ritchie had used circumvention to make her change her will. She argued that Mrs Ritchie has dominated Mrs Brock and turned her against her family and friends and that Mrs Brock became dependent on Mrs Ritchie to supply her with whisky after her housekeeper refused to do so. It was held that the deceased's state of mind was facile due to the dependence on alcohol and influence of Mrs Brock and there were sufficient circumstances to infer circumvention.

Undue influence

Undue influence is where a person has abused a position of trust for personal benefit. A will made in such circumstances may be successfully challenged. The difference between undue influence and facility and circumvention is that the former does not require some weakness of mind in the testator.[98] **12–26**

There are various relationships in which the doctrine may apply. The most obvious are a parent and child,[99] solicitor and client[1] and doctor and patient.[2] Other less obvious relationships such as an art dealer and customer have been included[3] and the list is not closed.

In some cases both facility and circumvention and undue influence are present[4] or at least pleaded[5] and the distinction between the two is becoming blurred.

Honeyman's Exrs v Sharp
1978 S.C. 223

A widow gifted four valuable paintings to an art dealer. She had known him for seven years and it was alleged that she had been unduly influenced by him. When the gift was challenged it was argued that undue influence was irrelevant in such circumstances. It was held that where there is a relationship of adviser and advised and the advised places trust and confidence in the adviser, breach of trust for the benefit of the person in whom the trust is confided can constitute undue influence.

Formal validity

It is obvious that a will or testamentary writing must have some formal requirements to prevent any possibility of fraud because of the importance of the consequences of a will. All legal documents have certain requirements to fulfil to ensure their validity which may vary depending on the type of legal document. If a will does not comply with these formalities it will be invalid.[6] **12–27**

---

[98] Lord President Clyde in *Ross v Gosselin's Exrs*, 1926 S.C. 325 at 334.
[99] This can operate both ways—parent influencing child, *e.g. Allan v Allan*, 1961 S.C. 200 or child influencing parent, *e.g. Grant's Exrs v Grant*, 1999 G.W.D. 36–1772.
[1] *Stewart v MacLaren*, 1920 S.C. (H.L.) 148.
[2] *Radcliffe v Price* (1902) 18 T.L.R. 466.
[3] *Honeyman's Exrs v Sharp*, 1978 S.C. 223.
[4] *Ross v Gosselin's Exrs*, 1926 S.C. 325.
[5] *Boyle v Boyle's Ex.*, 1999 S.C. 479; *Gaul v Deerey*, 2000 S.C.L.R. 407.
[6] *Williamson v Williamson*, 1997 S.L.T. 1044.

A will must be in writing[7] and the formal requirements are different for wills made before and after August 1, 1995 when the Requirements of Writing (Scotland) Act 1995 came into force. A verbal agreement cannot affect the terms of a will.[8]

Williamson v Williamson

1997 S.L.T. 1044

Mrs Williamson made a will in 1988. One of the witnesses to her signature on her will was a solicitor, David Carment Reid Wilson. Instead of signing his normal signature, "David C R Wilson", Mr Wilson signed, "David C R Williamson". The will was held to be invalid as it had not been witnessed properly. If the will had been signed and witnessed after August 1, 1995 when the 1995 Act came into force, the will would have been valid although not probative.

Prior to 1995

12–28 A will executed before 1995 was valid if in one of two forms:

- formally attested
- holograph.

Formally attested wills

12–29 A formally attested will is a will which is signed by the testator and witnessed. Various requirements for signing, also referred to as execution, have existed over the years and the most recent changes prior to 1995 were made in 1970.[9] Three elements were required to formally attest a will. First, the will had to be subscribed, or signed at the bottom, on every page by the testator. Second, two witnesses had to see the testator sign or acknowledge an already made signature.[10] Third, the witnesses had to sign on the last page and the witnesses had to be designed, or described sufficiently to identify them. It was usual for the date and place of signing to be added, normally in the clause at the end called the testing clause, but this was not essential.

The witnesses needed to be aged 16 or over, have legal capacity and know the testator, although an introduction from a reliable person was sufficient. It did not invalidate the process if the witness was a beneficiary in the will, although this was not advisable. The witnesses were required to sign without any delay and if they signed after the testator died, the will was invalid.[11]

Walker v Whitwell

1916 S.C. (H.L.) 75

Shortly before she died, Mrs Walker made a new will which she dictated to her son, a doctor, who wrote it out for her. She signed this will in front of her son and a nurse. The nurse then signed as a witness. The son did not sign as he mistakenly thought he could not act as a witness since he was a beneficiary under the will. Mrs Walker died on July 1. After she had died her solicitor sent the will to the son to sign as a witness and he signed on July 25. The will was held to be invalid.

---

[7] Requirements of Writing (Scotland) 1995 Act, s.1(2)(c).
[8] *McEleveen v McQuillan's Executrix*, 1999 S.L.T. (Sh. Ct) 46.
[9] Conveyancing and Feudal Reform (Scotland) Act 1970, s.44.
[10] *Lindsay v Milne's Ex.*, 1995 S.L.T. 487.
[11] *Walker v Whitwell*, 1916 S.C. (H.L.) 75.

There were various rules covering such matters as alterations to the will before signature and signature on behalf of a blind person or someone unable to write, known as notarial execution.[12] Certain minor defects in the execution could be cured by a statutory process.[13]

The advantage of a formally attested will was that it was probative, or self proving. This means that there was no other requirement to establish the validity of the will.

Holograph wills

A holograph will was valid if it was either in the testator's own handwriting and signed at the end of the last page, or written by some other person or typed or printed and the testator wrote in his or her own handwriting the words "adopted as holograph" followed by his or her signature.[14] Witnesses were not required. However, such a will was not probative. To enable an estate to be wound up by the process of confirmation[15] the will had to proved to be the will of the testator. This was done by obtaining affidavit evidence that the writing and signature on the will were those of the testator.[16] **12–30**

Form of signature

The signature of the testator was the surname and a Christian name, abbreviated Christian name or the initial of the Christian name. In certain circumstances, as in correspondence with family or friends, a shortened name such as "Connie"[17] or "Mum"[18] was sufficient. An incomplete signature was invalid.[19] The testator must have actually signed. It would invalidate a signature and a will if the testator's hand was guided, as opposed to supported above the wrist.[20] **12–31**

Rhodes v Peterson

1972 S.L.T. 98

Mrs Rhodes died in 1969. She left a will made in 1965 and had written a holograph letter to her daughter in 1966 which read, "I want you to have 63 Merchiston and all the contents, the furniture, linen, silver and all my treasures etc. ... " She had signed it, "lots of love, Mum". It was held that the letter expressed testamentary intention and was sufficiently signed.

Post 1995

Under the Requirements of Writing (Scotland) Act 1995 a will must be in writing.[21] It will be formally valid if subscribed by the testator.[22] It is no longer necessary to sign a will on every page or have the signature witnessed to be valid. It must be signed on every sheet, however, which **12–32**

---

[12] Conveyancing (Scotland) Act 1924, s.18.
[13] Conveyancing (Scotland) Act 1874, s.39.
[14] In an unusual case a will was upheld as valid where the words "adopted as holograph" were typed—*McBeath's Trs v McBeath's Trs*, 1935 S.C. 471.
[15] See Executry administration, below.
[16] Succession (Scotland) 1964, s.21.
[17] *Draper v Thomason*, 1954 S.C. 136.
[18] *Rhodes v Peterson*, 1972 S.L.T. 98.
[19] *Donald v McGregor*, 1926 S.L.T. 103.
[20] *Noble v Noble*, (1875) 3 R. 74.
[21] 1995 Act, s.1(2)(c).
[22] 1995 Act, s.2.

could be folded up into, say, four pages.[23] The rules relating to holograph documents including wills are specifically abolished by the Act.[24]

A will which complies with these formalities will be valid but will not be probative or self proving. As already noted, however, an estate cannot be wound up by the process of confirmation[25] if the will is not probative without an additional court process. In such cases after 1995, it is necessary to apply to the court for a decree or certificate that the subscription of the testator is self proving on production of affidavit evidence relating to the handwriting.[26] It is much easier, therefore, to ensure the will is self-proving at the time it is made. This is the normal practice of solicitors in preparing wills.

A will is self-proving after 1995 if it is signed by the testator on every page and is witnessed by one witness[27] who signs on the last page.[28] The rules regarding signature and the process of witnessing are very similar to those prior to 1995.[29] There are similar provisions for signature on behalf of a person who is blind or unable to write.[30]

Mutual wills

12–33 A mutual will is a will by more than one person in one will document which is executed by both parties. They were popular at one time, particularly with married couples who wanted to leave a will in identical terms, but they are not popular now. There is a general presumption that a mutual will is simply two different wills in one document but there can be problems in relation to the revocability or otherwise of such wills.[31] They are not recommended.

Informal writings

12–34 Formal wills often include a provision that future informal writings may be incorporated as part of the will. Such provisions normally refer to future informal testamentary writings subscribed by the testator. Such provisions need to be carefully worded and the informal writing needs to be properly linked to the will.[32] Similarly, but less frequently, later writings may adopt earlier writings.[33] Such informal writings can cause difficulties and are not recommended. It is much better to make a formal codicil where minor changes to a will are required.

Key Concepts

The law of **testate** succession governs situations where the deceased has left a will or other testamentary writing.

The **validity** of wills and other testamentary writings depends on a number of factors which fall into three areas:

- intention to test
- capacity
- formal validity.

---

[23] See *Baird's Trs v Baird*, 1955 S.C. 286.
[24] 1995 Act, s.1(3)(b).
[25] See Executry administration, below.
[26] 1995 Act, s.4.
[27] After 1995 two witnesses are no longer required.
[28] 1995 Act, ss.3(1)(a) and 3(2).
[29] 1995 Act, s.7.
[30] 1995 Act, s.9.
[31] See Revocation of wills, below.
[32] *Waterson's Trs v St. Giles Club*, 1943 S.C. 369.
[33] *Craik's Exrs v Samson*, 1929 S.L.T. 592.

> A person must be aged 12 or older to have **capacity** to make a will and must be of sound mind. A will may be challenged where it has been made under circumstances amounting to **facility** and **circumvention** or undue influence.
>
> A will must be in **writing**.
>
> A will executed **before 1995** was valid if in one of two forms:
>
> - formally attested
> - holograph.
>
> A will executed **after 1995** need not be signed on every page or witnessed. It must be signed on every sheet. It must be signed on every page and witnessed by one witness to be self-proving.

REVOCATION OF WILLS

A will is not effective until the testator dies. A person can, and some people do, change a will as often as they wish. Even if a will states that it is irrevocable this cannot bind the testator and the will can be revoked. If a person contracts with someone that they will leave a will in certain terms, the position is different. As this is a contract the testator will be bound.[34] There would be nothing to prevent the testator disposing of the assets covered by the contract during their lifetime, however, as the contract would only take effect on death. In a mutual will,[35] there may be a contractual term not to revoke the will without the consent of the other party to the will.[36] **12–35**

Revocation of a will may be express or implied.

Express revocation

A will may be expressly revoked in two ways. These are: **12–36**

- making a new will
- destruction of the will.

A new will

If a testator makes a new will, the will usually contains a clause revoking all previous wills and testamentary writings. If properly worded, revocation will take place but care is required in the wording. The term "testamentary writings" is wider than "wills" and where a later will contained a clause revoking "all wills previously executed by me" this did not revoke a valid bequest of a stamp collection which was not in a will.[37] If there is more than one earlier will, care is required to correctly identify which will is being revoked.[38] **12–37**

Destruction of a will

If a testator physically destroys a will or instructs an agent to do so and this is done, the will no longer exists and is revoked by the express action of the testator. The testator must deliberately intend to destroy the will and destruction while insane, drunk or in a fit of rage is insufficient for **12–38**

---

[34] *Paterson v Paterson* (1893) 20 R. 484.
[35] See Mutual wills, above.
[36] *Dewar v Dewar's Trs*, 1950 S.L.T. 191.
[37] *Clark's Exs v Clark*, 1943 S.C. 216.
[38] *Gordon's Exs v MacQueen*, 1907 S.C. 373.

revocation.[39] The destruction may not be complete destruction but some symbolic act such as cutting off a seal[40] or cutting out clauses on a copy of a will with a written explanation.[41] There must be express instruction to an agent to destroy and instructing a solicitor to make a new will does not imply an instruction to destroy an earlier will.[42]

Bruce's Judicial Factor v Lord Advocate

1969 S.C. 296

Mr Bruce made a will in 1945. In 1949 he instructed his solicitors to make a new will which disposed of all his estate and revoked all previous testamentary writings. He did not expressly instruct his solicitors to destroy the 1945 will. When he died the solicitors were still holding the 1945 will but the 1949 will could not be found. It was held that the 1949 will was presumed to have been intentionally destroyed by Mr Bruce and the 1945 will regulated the disposal of his estate.

If a will is accidentally destroyed or lost, an action known as proving the tenor is required to allow the will's provisions to be proved and the will to be given effect. The onus is on the party wishing the will to be reinstated to prove that the testator did not intend to destroy it and what the terms of the will were.[43]

Where part of a will has been destroyed by the testator deleting part of it, proof is required that there was no intention to revoke the deleted words,[44] as where a married woman deleted her married name in her will as she was reverting to her maiden name.[45]

Implied revocation

12–39 A will may be impliedly revoked in two ways. These are:

- making a new will
- birth of children to the testator in certain circumstances.

A new will

12–40 Where a new will does not contain an express revocation of previous wills and testamentary writings, an earlier will may be revoked by implication. The general rule is that in such a case both wills must be read together to establish the intention of the testator.[46]

The position has been clearly stated that "it is a well established principle of the law of Scotland that where a person deceased has left various writings, probative in themselves, for disposing of his or her property, they are to be understood as constituting one testamentary settlement in so far as they have not been revoked and are not inconsistent with each other."[47]

If the terms are inconsistent the later will may revoke the earlier, as where the later will deals with the whole estate.[48] The onus of proof is on the person seeking to establish implied revocation.[49]

---

[39] *Laing v Bruce* (1838) 1 D. 59.
[40] *Nasmyth v Hare's Trs*, (1821) 1 Sh. App. 65.
[41] *Thomson's Trs v Bowhill Baptist Church*, 1956 S.L.T. 302.
[42] *Bruce's Judicial Factor v Lord Advocate*, 1969 S.C. 296.
[43] *Morrison v Morrison*, 1992 G.W.D. 23–1350.
[44] *Pattison's Trs v University of Edinburgh* (1888) 16 R. 73.
[45] *Fotheringham's Trs v Reid*, 1936 S.C. 831.
[46] *Duthie's Ex. v Taylor*, 1986 S.L.T. 142.
[47] *Stoddart v Grant* (1852) 1 Macq. 163.
[48] *Cadger v Ronald's Trs*, 1946 S.L.T. (Notes) 24.
[49] *Mitchell's Administratrix v Edinburgh Royal Infirmary*, 1928 S.C. 47.

Birth of children to the testator

If a testator has a child subsequent to making a will, the will may be impliedly revoked on the principle that it is presumed that the testator would not want to omit the child from the testamentary provision. This principle is known as the *conditio si testator sine liberis decesserit.* The principle does not apply automatically but is a rebuttable presumption. The only person who can rely on the presumption is a child born after the will.[50] The presumption can be rebutted by proof that the testator deliberately intended to omit to benefit the child.[51] **12–41**

It should be noted that a will is not impliedly revoked on the marriage or divorce of the testator.[52]

Revival of revoked wills

If a later will which revoked an earlier will is revoked in turn, there is a possibility that the earlier will may revive. The case law is divided on this issue with some cases in favour of revival[53] and others against.[54] If the earlier will has been destroyed, revival is impossible and a clause which revokes previous wills should also authorise their destruction. **12–42**

> **Key Concepts**
>
> A will is not **effective** until the testator dies. A person can **change** a will as often as he or she wishes.
>
> A will may be **expressly revoked** by making a new will or by destruction of the will.
>
> A will may be **impliedly revoked** by the making of a new will or by birth of children to the testator in certain circumstances.

WILL SUBSTITUTES

The usual way to leave all or part of an estate to beneficiaries and avoid the rules of intestate succession applying is to make a will or other testamentary writing. There are other methods to achieve this which are recognised under Scots law. These are generally known as will substitutes or quasi-wills. These are: **12–43**

- special destinations
- life assurance policies
- nominations
- gifts in contemplation of death
- rearrangements after death.

---

[50] *Stevenson's Trs v Stevenson*, 1932 S.C. 657.
[51] *Stuart-Gordon v Stuart-Gordon* (1899) 1 F. 1005.
[52] Unlike the position in England.
[53] *Scott's Judicial Factor v Johnston*, 1971 S.L.T. (Notes) 41.
[54] *Elder's Trs v Elder* (1895) 22 R. 505.

Special destinations

12–44 Special destinations take two forms, known as a destination-over or a survivorship destination. Destinations-over, where property is left to one person whom failing another, are now rare.[55] Survivorship destinations, where property is left to two (or more) persons and the survivor (or survivors) remain common. They are mainly used in heritable property. The way they operate is that if such a survivorship destination is placed in the title of the property, on the death of the first person the property automatically passes to the survivor without the need for any formal procedures. The usual situation for their use is when a house is bought by a husband and wife and the title to the house is placed in their joint names and to the survivor.[56]

The revocability of survivorship destinations is a problem area. It is clear that a party to the destination can evacuate or revoke the destination by disposing of his or her share during his or her lifetime.[57] On death, whether or not the destination can be revoked depends on whether or not the destination is regarded as contractual. Normally this depends on who paid for the property. Where one party contributed the whole price, that party will be entitled to revoke the destination by a will.[58] Where both parties contributed to the price, or the property was gifted, the destination will be regarded as contractual and a will cannot revoke the destination.[59]

If a destination is revocable on death, it must be properly revoked by "a specific reference to the destination and the declared intention on the part of the testator to evacuate it".[60] This is strictly construed.[61] Property which passes under a contractual destination on death is subject to the debts of the deceased.[62]

The operation of survivorship destinations can cause difficulties and unintended results.[63] If a will is made at the time the property is purchased there is no need for the destination and potential problems will be avoided.

Gardner's Exrs v Raeburn

1996 S.L.T. 745

Mr and Mrs Gardner bought a house together and the title was put in their joint names with a survivorship destination. They later separated and divorced. As part of the divorce settlement, Mr Gardner paid Mrs Gardiner £40,000 and Mrs Gardner conveyed her one half share of the house to Mr Gardner. When Mr Gardner died his ex-wife claimed that his original one half share of the house passed to her under the survivorship destination. This claim succeeded despite the fact that she had received £40,000. To evacuate the destination in the transfer of the property at the time of the divorce settlement Mr and Mrs Gardner should have jointly conveyed the whole house to Mr Gardner.

Life assurance policies

12–45 It is possible for a person to take out a life policy on his or her own life for the benefit of someone else. On death the proceeds of the policy will be paid direct to the other person and will not form part of the deceased's estate. Certain policies under the Married Women's Policies of Assurance (Scotland) Act 1880 operate in this way.[64]

---

[55] Except in wills—see Destinations-over, below.
[56] Although the property is said to be in joint names, it is common property—see Chapter 10.
[57] *Steele v Caldwell*, 1979 S.L.T. 228.
[58] *Brown's Trs v Brown*, 1944 S.L.T. 215.
[59] *Perrett's Trs v Perrett*, 1909 S.C. 522.
[60] 1964 Act, s.30.
[61] *Marshall v Marshall's Ex.*, 1987 S.L.T. 49.
[62] *Fleming's Tr. v Fleming*, 2000 S.L.T. 406 overruling *Barclay's Bank v McGreish*, 1983 S.L.T. 344.
[63] See, *e.g. Gardner's Exrs v Raeburn*, 1996 S.L.T. 745 and *Redfern's Exrs v Redfern*, 1996 S.L.T. 900.
[64] s.4 as amended by the Married Women's Policies of Assurance (Amendment) (Scotland) Act 1980.

Nominations

Nominations relate to money deposited with certain small savings institutions. On death the money is paid to the person nominated by the deceased. Nominations are of limited scope with a maximum sum allowed of £5,000.[65] **12–46**

Gifts in contemplation of death

These gifts, known as *donationes mortis causa*, are made during the lifetime of the granter to a person on condition that the person survives the granter.[66] The gift can be revoked by the granter at any time before he or she dies. Such gifts are rare. **12–47**

Rearrangements on death

It is possible for the beneficiaries under a will to rearrange the division of an estate after the death.[67] No one can be compelled to take what is due to them under a will or on intestacy. A rearrangement is sometimes effected formally for tax purposes under what is known as a deed of family arrangement. To be effective for such tax purposes, which may include a reduction of inheritance tax, the deed must be made within two years of the date of death and intimation made to the Capital Taxes Office within six months of the date of the deed.[68] **12–48**

Key Concepts

Other legally recognised methods of avoiding the rules of intestate succession are known as **will substitutes** or **quasi-wills**. They are:

- special destinations (destinations-over or survivorship destinations)
- life assurance policies (taken out for the benefit of someone else)
- nominations (to a maximum of £5,000)
- gifts in contemplation of death (*donationes mortis causa*)
- rearrangements after death.

INTERPRETATION OF WILLS

How a will is interpreted or construed is obviously important in testate succession. The fundamental principle is that the intention of the testator must be interpreted from what has actually been written.[69] Normally extrinsic evidence will not be allowed to ascertain the intention, but it may be in certain circumstances. There are a number of rules of interpretation which can be applied to wills generally but they are only applied to aid interpretation. The terms of the will itself is the primary means of interpretation. **12–49**

---

65 Administration of Estates (Small Payments) Act 1965, ss.2 and 6, Administration of Estates (Small Payments) (Increase of Limit) Order 1984 (SI 1984/539).
66 *Morris v Riddick* (1867) 5 M. 1036.
67 *Gray v Gray's Trs* (1877) 4 R. 378.
68 Inheritance Tax Act 1984, s.142.
69 *e.g. Fortunato's Judicial Factor v Fortunato*, 1981 S.L.T. 277.

> "We must find all the intention of the testatrix within the four corners of the deed which she has legally executed … It is only if the terms of the deed appear to be in themselves doubtful in their import or legal construction, that it is either necessary or legitimate to affect or explain them by extraneous circumstances."[70]

There are three rules to aid interpretation. These are:

- the will should be read as a whole
- the will should be interpreted to avoid intestacy
- words should be given their ordinary meaning.

The will should be read as a whole

12–50 A will should be read as a whole including later or ancillary codicils or other testamentary writings to establish the testator's whole intention. Any apparently conflicting intentions should be reconciled as far as possible. Where a later deed refers to a bequest in an earlier deed which contains no such bequest, the bequest will be given effect.[71] If a later deed conflicts with an earlier one, such as in the amount of a legacy, the later one will be given effect.[72]

Forbes Trs v Forbes

(1893) 20 R. 248

In an ante nuptial contract of marriage a husband bound himself to pay his wife a yearly annuity of £100 after he died. In a later will he referred to this contract as providing for payment of a yearly annuity of £150. It was held that the widow was entitled to an annuity of £150.

The will should be construed to avoid intestacy

12–51 A court will do its best to avoid an intestacy where there is a will, on the grounds that intestacy is not what a testator intends. To do otherwise has been referred to as a "counsel of despair".[73] Accordingly, an interpretation which avoids intestacy may be given, even if the usual rules of interpretation are not strictly followed.[74]

Magistrates of Dundee v Morris

(1858) 3 Macq. 134

Trustees were directed in a will to set up a school. No sum was stated for this purpose but the will did specify the size of the school and the size of the legacy necessary could be worked out. The legacy was held to be valid and not void from uncertainty. The school was built and is now Morgan Academy in Dundee.

Words should be given their ordinary meaning

12–52 Words are interpreted to have their ordinary meaning.[75] Where words are used which have a technical legal meaning, that technical meaning will normally be applied because they are used in a will.[76]

---

70 Lord Justice-Clerk Moncrieff in *Blair v Blair* (1849) 12 D. 97 at 107.
71 *Grant v Grant* (1851) 13 D. 805.
72 *Forbes Trs v Forbes* (1893) 20 R. 248.
73 Lord McLaren in *MacDuff v Spence's Trs*, 1909 S.C. 178 at 184.
74 *e.g. McGinn's Executix v McGinn*, 1994 S.L.T. 2, and *Magistrates of Dundee v Morris* (1858) 3 Macq. 134.
75 *Young v Robertson* (1862) 4 Macq. 314.
76 *Macdonald's Trs v Macdonald*, 1974 S.L.T. 87.

If the estate or part of the estate is left to a class, such as children or nieces and nephews, the question arises as to when the class is established. The normal rule is that the class is established and identified as at the date of death.[77] Therefore a legacy left to the nephews and nieces of the testator will include a nephew or niece born after the will was made but before the testator died. Care is required in properly identifying a class and some words, such as "dependants", have no precise meaning and a legacy to dependants will be void due to uncertainty.[78]

Robertson's Judicial Factor v Robertson

1968 S.L.T. 32

In a holograph will Miss Robertson made a provision for her nephew and niece "and their dependants". Lord President Clyde stated "In our system of law the word ... is ... too vague a description ... to ascertain what class of persons was intended to be benefited there by." He held the bequest to dependants was void from uncertainty.

Use of extrinsic evidence

Extrinsic evidence can be admitted for a number of purposes: **12–53**

- to translate a will in a foreign language
- to establish whether a deed is a will
- to interpret words differently from their ordinary meaning
- to rebut the presumption against double provision
- to prove what the testator knew about the property
- to identify the subject or object of a legacy.

It is obvious that extrinsic evidence in the form of a translation is required to translate a will in a foreign language. Similarly, if a will is in the form of a code, this will be allowed.[79]

Extrinsic evidence may be required to show that a deed is not a will but intended as a draft or has been revoked.[80] It may also show that the testator lacked capacity or has been subject to facility and circumvention or undue influence.[81]

Where a word has an ordinary meaning and a possible secondary meaning, extrinsic evidence may be allowed to show that the secondary meaning was intended by the testator. This has been used to interpret the word children as including grandchildren.[82]

There is a presumption that two identical legacies in a will is a mistake and only one is payable. This can be rebutted by extrinsic evidence.

If there is a question as to whether or not the testator knew that he or she owned property bequeathed in his or her will, extrinsic evidence may be allowed. If a person bequeaths property which is not owned, this is known as a *legatum rei alienae*, a legacy of a thing belonging to another. The normal rule is that this was a mistake and the legacy falls. Extrinsic evidence, however, may show that the testator knew the correct position and deliberately made the legacy. In such a case, the executor must try to acquire the object of the legacy and give it to the legatee. If this is not possible, the value of the object must be paid to the legatee.[83]

If there is an ambiguity as to the subject or object of a legacy, extrinsic evidence may be allowed. This may be used where there is a minor error in identifying the beneficiaries.[84]

---

[77] *Gregory's Trs v Alison* (1889) 16 R. (H.L.) 10.
[78] *Robertson's Judicial Factor v Robertson*, 1968 S.L.T. 32.
[79] *Goblet v Beechey* (1829) 3 Sim. 24.
[80] See Revocation of wills, above.
[81] See Capacity, above.
[82] *Yule's Trs*, 1981 S.L.T. 250.
[83] *Meeres v Dowell's Ex.*, 1923 S.L.T. 184.
[84] *Keiller v Thomson's Trs* (1824) 3 S. 279.

Keiller v Thomson's Trs

(1824) 3 S. 279

Mr Thomson died, leaving a legacy to "Janet Keiller or Williamson, confectioner in Dundee". There was no such person but there was an Agnes Keiller or Wedderspoon who was married to a confectioner in Dundee. There was also a sister Janet Keiller married to a seaman named Whitton. The court allowed extrinsic evidence which showed that Mr Thomson had intended the legacy to go to Agnes Keiller.

Mr Thomson was not very good with names and had also left a legacy to "William Keiller, confectioner in Dundee". No such person existed. There was a William Keiller who was a confectioner in Montrose and a James Keiller who was a confectioner in Dundee. The court again allowed extrinsic evidence which showed that Mr Thomson had intended the legacy to go to James Keiller.[85]

Key Concepts

The terms of the will itself is the primary means of **interpretation**. The three rules to aid interpretation are:

- the will should be read as a whole
- the will should be interpreted to avoid intestacy
- words should be given their ordinary meaning.

Extrinsic evidence can also be admitted for a number of purposes.

LEGACIES

12–54 Legacies fall into three main categories. These are:

- specific or special legacies
- general legacies
- residue.

A specific legacy is a legacy of a specific, identifiable object such as a house or a car. If the object of the legacy no longer exists or no longer belongs to the testator, the legacy will fall under the principle of ademption.[86]

Ogilvie-Forbes' Trs v Ogilvie-Forbes

1955 S.C. 405

Sir George Ogilvie-Forbes made a will in 1952 which gave his daughter a liferent of his mansion house and other land. Before he died, he transferred the mansion house and other land to a company in which he retained a controlling interest. It was held that the transfer to the company meant he no longer owned the mansion house and other land at the time he died and the legacy had adeemed. The daughter did not receive the liferent.

85 *Keiller v Thomson's Trs* (1826) 4 S. 730.
86 *Ogilvie-Forbes' Trs v Ogilvie-Forbes*, 1955 S.C. 405.

If a specific legacy indicates the source of a particular object, for instance, a sum of money from a certain bank account, this is known as a demonstrative legacy. If there is insufficient money to pay that sum in that bank account at the date of death, the legatee will have a claim against the residue of the estate.

A general legacy is a legacy of a subject which is no different from any other subjects of the same kind and has no specific, individual characteristics. A legacy of a sum of money, also known as a pecuniary legacy, is a typical general legacy.

A legacy of the residue is a legacy of all of the estate that remains after everything else has been deducted. These deductions cover all debts and other expenses, taxes, claims for legal rights and other legacies. Any legacies which have lapsed or failed will form part of the residue. If there is no legacy of the residue, the residue will fall into intestacy and be divided accordingly.

Cumulative and substitutional legacies

If there is more than one legacy to the same person, the legacies may be cumulative when both will be paid or substitutional when only one will be paid. The intention of the testator may be clearly expressed, but if the intention is not clear, certain presumptions are applied. If a deed contains identical legacies, they are presumed to be substitutional and only one will be paid on the ground that the testator is presumed to have repeated the legacy through forgetfulness. This is a presumption only which can be rebutted.[87] If the legacies in the same deed are different they will be presumed to be cumulative and both will be paid. If there are more than one legacy in more than one deed they will be presumed to be cumulative whether they are identical or not.[88] **12–55**

Destinations–over

A destination-over is a provision in a will in favour of one person with the possibility of another taking the legacy after or instead of that person. The wording is in the form of a legacy to "X whom failing Y". X is the primary legatee and is known as the institute. Y is known either as a conditional institute or alternative legatee, or as a substitute or second successive legatee. If X dies and does not inherit, in both cases Y will inherit in his or her place. If X does survive and inherit, if Y is a conditional institute he or she will have no further right. If Y is a substitute, however, he or she will take the legacy in turn on surviving the death of X, provided X has not disposed of the subject of the legacy during lifetime or under his or her will. **12–56**

Whether Y is a conditional institute or substitute depends on the terms of the will[89] or on certain presumptions if the will is not specific. Where the legacy is of heritable property the presumption is for conditional institution and where it is of moveable property the presumption is for substitution.[90]

Division of legacies

Where a legacy is left to a number of legatees it is presumed that all the legatees will take an equal share, if the will does not provide to the contrary. This is known as division *per capita*, by head. The alternative division is *per stirpes,* by branch, which may be important in relation to certain categories of legatees. For instance, if a testator leaves a legacy to the children of a brother and sister, the brother may have two children and the sister have three children. If the division is *per capita* each of the five children will get one-fifth but if the division is *per stirpes* each of the brothers' children will get one-half of one-half, *i.e.* one-quarter, and each of the sisters' children **12–57**

[87] *Gillies v Glasgow Royal Infirmary*, 1960 S.C. 438, although the facts were unusual and unusually interpreted.
[88] *Edinburgh Royal Infirmary v Muir's Trs* (1881) 9 R. 352.
[89] *Simpson's Trs v Simpson* (1889) 17 R. 248.
[90] *Crumpton's Judicial Factor v Barnardo's Homes*, 1917 S.C. 713.

will get one-third of one-half, *i.e.* one-sixth. It is important, therefore, to specifically provide for *per stirpes* division in the will if this is intended, because the presumption is for *per capita* division.

Children of a legatee

12–58 Where a legacy is made to someone who dies before the testator, that legacy will normally lapse. There is an exception to this rule in certain circumstances under the doctrine known as *conditio si institutus sine liberis decesserit.* This presumes that there is an implied gift to the children of a predeceasing legatee. The doctrine only applies to certain close relatives. It applies to the testator's own children and remoter descendants including grandchildren[91] and even more remote descendants,[92] It also applies to nephews and nieces on the basis that the testator is *in loco parentis* to his or her nephews or nieces, which means a parent figure to them. This will be presumed unless it can be shown that the testator was not *in loco parentis.*[93]

Where the *conditio* applies it will take precedence over any conditional institute in a destination-over.[94] As the *conditio* is only a presumption it can rebutted, for instance where there is separate provision for the children of the legatee.[95]

Conditions attached to legacies

12–59 A will may attach conditions to a legacy. These conditions must be satisfied before the legatee can take the legacy. Certain conditions may be ineffective and, if so, the condition is ignored and the legacy is unconditional. A condition will be ineffective where it is impossible to perform, unlawful or against public policy, such as attempting to prevent marriage or cohabitation by the legatee.[96] If the condition is inconsistent with the legacy, it will also be ineffective under the doctrine of repugnancy.[97]

There are three types of conditions:

- potestative
- suspensive
- resolutive.

Potestative conditions are those which require the legatee to do something before the legacy can be taken, such as moving to live with the testator.

A suspensive condition is one where the making over of payment of the legacy is postponed until the condition is fulfilled, such as attaining a certain age. If the condition is not met the legacy will fall.

A resolutive condition is one where the legacy may lapse if a certain event takes place, for instance if the legatee remarries.

Interest and abatement

12–60 Interest is payable on a legacy from the date of death until payment. There is no fixed rate of interest and the rate paid should be equivalent to what the estate earned or should have earned

[91] *Mowbray v Scougall* (1834) 12 S. 910.
[92] *Grant v Brooke* (1882) 10 R. 92.
[93] *Knox's Ex. v Knox,* 1941 S.C. 532.
[94] *MacGregor's Trs v Gray,* 1969 S.L.T. 355.
[95] *Greig v Malcolm* (1835) 13 S. 607.
[96] *Aird's Ex. v Aird,* 1949 S.C. 154.
[97] *Miller's Trs v Miller* (1890) 18 R. 301.

during the administration if it was properly administered.[98] It is open to the testator to provide that a legacy is paid without interest.

If there is insufficient estate to pay all the debts and other expenses, any tax, and all the legacies, the legacies must be reduced under the doctrine of abatement. The order in which legacies are abated is:

- residuary legacies
- general legacies equally
- demonstrative legacies do not abate until the specified fund is exhausted but then abate like general legacies
- specific legacies.

If the legacies are numbered in a will this will not alter this priority.[99]

Key Concepts

Legacies fall into three main categories. A **specific legacy** is a legacy of a specific, identifiable object. A **general legacy** is a legacy of a subject which is no different from any other subject of the same kind and has no specific, individual characteristics. A legacy of the **residue** is a legacy of all of the estate that remains after everything else has been deducted.

The doctrine known as ***conditio si institutus sine liberis decesserit*** presumes that there is an implied gift to the children of a predeceasing legatee, but applies only to certain close relatives.

A will may attach **conditions** to a legacy (potestative, suspensive or resolutive). These conditions must be satisfied before the legatee can take the legacy.

Interest is payable on a legacy from the date of death until payment.

If there is insufficient estate to pay all the legacies, the legacies must be reduced under the doctrine of **abatement**.

VESTING AND ACCRETION

Vesting

Vesting takes place in two situations. These are vesting in an executor and vesting in a beneficiary. **12–61**
Vesting in an executor is where the whole estate passes to the executor for the purpose of administration of the estate.[1] It gives the executor the title to administer the property which comprises the estate.[2] Vesting in a beneficiary is a more difficult concept.

A legacy or a share in the testate estate vests in the beneficiary when the beneficiary obtains a completed right to it. Vesting is different from actual receipt or payment. A beneficiary may have a vested right in the benefit of a legacy or share of the intestate estate before receiving possession or payment of the benefit. This enables the beneficiary to dispose of the benefit as part of his or her property either during lifetime or in a will.

There are various rules which apply in vesting. These are:

---

98 *Kearon v Thomson's Trs*, 1949 S.C. 654.
99 *McConnel v McConnel's Trs*, 1939 S.N. 31.
1 Succession (Scotland) Act 1964, s.14 (1).
2 See Executry administration, below.

- the intention of the testator is paramount
- early vesting is presumed
- suspensive conditions postpone vesting.

The intention of the testator is, as always, paramount and a will may expressly provide for vesting.

Where the intention is not clear, an interpretation which produces an earlier date of vesting will be presumed. A legacy without any conditions and a share of the intestate estate vest in the beneficiary at the earliest possible date, which is the date of death of the testator.

A suspensive condition in any legacy, which means that the legatee will not get the legacy until the condition is met, postpones vesting. Conversely, a resolutive condition does not postpone vesting, but is said to vest subject to defeasance because the legacy may lapse on the happening of a certain event.

Accretion

12–62 Where there is a legacy in favour of more than one person, each of the legatees will take a proportionate share of the legacy by surviving the testator. A problem arises if one or more of the legatees die before the testator. The question is whether the share of a predeceasing legatee forms part of his or her estate or whether it passes to the surviving legatee or legatees under the principle of accretion. This depends on whether the legacy is joint or several. If it is joint, the legacy remains individual and accresses or passes to the surviving legatee or legatees by accretion. If it is several, it will not accress.

The will may make express provision for this and in the simple case of a legacy to "X and Y" this will be joint and accretion will apply. Conversely, a destination-over will exclude accretion. Accretion will also be excluded if there are what are known as words of severance such as "equally among them" or "in equal shares".[3] Words of severance do not exclude accretion in relation to class gifts.

> **Key Concepts**
>
> **Vesting** takes place in two situations. These are vesting in an executor and vesting in a beneficiary. The estate of the deceased vests in the executor for the purpose of administering the estate. Vesting in a beneficiary is different from receipt or payment and is when the beneficiary obtains a completed right. Vesting in a beneficiary may be at the date of death or postponed.
>
> **Accretion** may apply where there is a legacy in favour of more than one person and one person dies before the testator.

EXECUTRY ADMINISTRATION

12–63 When a person dies, the process of winding up the deceased's estate is known as executry administration. The first stage is ascertaining the assets and debts or liabilities of the deceased. Then the assets must be ingathered, debts and any tax due paid and the estate distributed to the beneficiaries. The person responsible for this is the deceased's executor. Under the Succession (Scotland) Act 1964, the estate of a deceased vests in the executor by the process of confirmation for the purpose of administering the estate.[4]

---

3 *Paxton's Trs v Cowie* (1886) 13 R. 1191.

4 s.14(1).

Executors

An executor may be appointed by a will, known as an executor-nominate or by the Sheriff Court, known as an executor-dative. An executor is not entitled to payment for acting as executor unless there is a provision in the will for this. A beneficiary may be an executor but cannot derive any personal benefit at the expense of the estate.[5] There is no limit on the number of executors. A majority of the executors is a quorum unless the will provides to the contrary.[6] The executor is only liable for his or her own acts or omissions. If an executor deals with the estate without obtaining confirmation, he or she may be liable for all the debts of the deceased by being what is known as a vitious intromittor. **12–64**

An executor-nominate is appointed in the testator's will. If the testator fails to appoint an executor or the executor has died or is otherwise unable to act, an executor-dative will be appointed by the Sheriff Court. A petition is lodged in the Sheriff Court with a bond of caution from an insurance company guaranteeing that the executor-dative will perform his or her duties honestly.[7] There is a set order for who may be appointed an executor-dative as follows:

- general disponees, universal legatees or residuary legatees
- the deceased's spouse where prior rights exhaust the whole estate
- the person who is entitled to inherit the free estate[8]
- the deceased's creditors.

Assets and debts

Assets

The estate of the deceased includes all property belonging to the deceased and certain personal obligations as at the date of death. The property of the deceased extends to all types of property, including the deceased's *pro indiviso* share of property held in common with others.[9] Where there is a special destination, the deceased's share of the property held under the destination forms part of the estate and is taxable but passes automatically under the destination.[10] It does not vest in the executor and confirmation is not required to transfer this asset to the survivor in the destination. **12–65**

Certain property rights which belong to the deceased, however, will be extinguished on his or her death. A liferent in the sole name of the deceased will come to an end.[11] Occupancy rights under matrimonial homes legislation will also come to an end.[12] A benefit payable on death under an insurance policy on the life of the deceased may not be payable if the deceased committed suicide and there is express or implied provision in the policy to this effect.

Property rights in leases form part of the deceased's estate and vest in the executor on confirmation.[13] Whether the lease comes to an end or not depends on whether it is the landlord or tenant who has died and the terms of the lease. On the death if the landlord the position is straightforward. The landlord owns the property and it forms part of the estate. The tenant will have the right to continue as tenant.[14] If the tenant dies and the lease expressly prohibits transfer on death, the lease will come to an end unless the landlord consents otherwise. If there is no express

---

5 *Clark v Clark's Exs*, 1989 S.L.T. 665.
6 Trusts (Scotland) Act 1921, s.3(c).
7 A bond of caution is not necessary where the executor-dative is a spouse and prior rights exhaust the estate. A bond of caution is not necessary for an executor-nominate.
8 Under the 1964 Act, s.2.
9 See Chapter 10.
10 See Will substitutes, above.
11 See Chapter 11.
12 See Chapter 13.
13 1964 Act, ss.14(1) and 36(2).
14 Leases Act 1449, see Chapter 10.

prohibition on transfer, the executor will transfer the lease to the legatee if the estate is testate or to the person entitled to succeed if the estate is intestate.[15]

A deceased's claim in delict or for patrimonial loss, which is financial loss by damage to earning capacity or property, forms part of the deceased's estate. A deceased's claim for *solatium*, which is pain and suffering, provided it relates to the period between an injury and death, also forms part of the estate.

A deceased's contractual rights will also form part of the estate, unless they are regarded as personal to the deceased, such as a contract of employment.

Debts

12–66 When a person dies, his or her estate is liable for his or her debts. Inheritance to the estate only takes place after payment of debts, funeral expenses and the expenses of winding up the estate. After an executor obtains confirmation, he or she is liable for the debts of the deceased up to the value of the estate. If the estate is insolvent, he or she must proceed to have a judicial factor or trustee in bankruptcy appointed.[16]

Debts intimated to the executor within six months of the death rank equally, with the exception of certain limited privileged debts such as funeral expenses which can be paid immediately. If an executor pays out debts or legacies before six months after the death, he or she will be personally liable to a creditor who appears within this six month period. Conversely, if he or she pays out after six months in good faith and a creditor subsequently appears, he or she is not liable.[17]

The order of ranking for debts is:

- expenses of sequestration
- deathbed and funeral expenses
- secured debts, such as a standard security over a house
- preferred debts, such as tax and social security contributions due in the twelve months before death and employees' wages for four months before death
- ordinary debts.

Moveable debts are paid out of moveable property and heritable debts out of heritable property. Where a debt is secured over a particular asset, such as a loan over a house, the person who inherits the house will take the house subject to the debt, unless the will provides otherwise.

Inheritance tax

12–67 Inheritance tax is a debt on the estate. It is chargeable on the value of the deceased's estate at the time of death, after deduction of debts and funeral expenses.[18] The executors and beneficiaries are liable to account for the tax to the estate confirmed or inherited, although the executor is liable first, as confirmation cannot be obtained until the executor has accounted to the Capital Taxes Office for inheritance tax. Inheritance tax is paid out of residue unless there is a direction in a will to pay a legacy subject to deduction of inheritance tax.

Confirmation

12–68 Confirmation is the process whereby the commissary court confirms the appointment of the executor and authorises administration of the estate as detailed in the inventory of assets prepared by the executor. In most cases an executor must produce confirmation issued by the commissary

[15] 1964 Act, s.16.
[16] Bankruptcy (Scotland) Act 1985, s.8(4).
[17] *Beith v Mackenzie* (1875) 3 R. 185.
[18] Inheritance Tax Act 1984, s.1.

court to uplift the assets of the deceased in the UK. The procedures for uplifting assets of the deceased situated abroad can be complicated and depend on the law on administration of estates in the foreign country. An executor must apply for confirmation within six months of assuming possession and management of an estate. Commissary courts form part of most Sheriff Courts. Applications for confirmation must be made by a solicitor or licensed executry practitioner.

Confirmation is not required where there is a survivorship destination or in respect of certain small sums. Where property is held under a survivorship destination it will pass automatically under the destination.[19] Payment of certain small sums not exceeding £5,000 may be made without production of confirmation in respect of certain savings bank accounts and financial savings certificates, building society deposits and government stock.[20] If an estate is a small estate where the gross amount does not exceed £25,000,[21] a simplified procedure can be adopted in which it is not necessary to employ a solicitor to obtain confirmation and assistance in winding up the estate is given by the commissary court.

Distribution of the estate

Once the executor has obtained confirmation, the confirmation is exhibited to all the holders of the assets such as banks, insurance companies and company registrars to enable the executor to ingather all the assets. Once all the assets have been ingathered the executor distributes the estate. The order of distribution is: **12–69**

- debts and funeral expenses and the expenses of administering the estate
- inheritance tax
- prior rights if the estate is intestate
- legal rights
- legacies
- residue.

Once the estate has been wound up the executor is formally discharged.

Key Concepts

When a person dies, the process of winding up the deceased's estate is known as **executry administration**. The person responsible for this is the deceased's **executor**.

The estate of a deceased vests in the executor by the process of **confirmation** for the purpose of administering the estate. The following steps take place:

- the assets and debts or liabilities of the deceased are ascertained
- the executor obtains confirmation from the commissary court
- the assets are ingathered
- the debts and any tax due are paid
- the estate is distributed to the beneficiaries.

[19] See Special destinations, above.

[20] Administration of Estates (Small Payments) Act 1965; Administration of Estates (Small Payments) (Increase of Limit) Order 1984 (SI 1984/539).

[21] Confirmation to Small Estates (Scotland) Act 1979, s,1(3).

REFORM

12–70 In 1990 the Scottish Law Commission published its Report on Succession,[22] after extensive consultation on the operation of the 1964 Act and changing social values. There are many recommendations for reform in the Report. The most substantial relate to intestate succession.

The report proposes that prior rights should be abolished. Where the deceased is survived by a spouse and no children (or remoter issue) the spouse will take the whole estate, unlike the present position. In the reverse situation where the deceased is survived by children and no spouse, the children will take the whole estate, which is the same as the current position. Where both a spouse and children survive the spouse will take the first £100,000 and half any excess over that amount with the children taking the other half of any excess.

The other main recommendation in the Report relates to legal rights. It is proposed that legal rights continue in a new form known as legal share. This is payable from both heritable and moveable property and must be claimed within two years of the death. A surviving spouse is entitled to 30 per cent of the first £200,000 and 10 per cent of the excess. The same goes to children if there is no spouse and 15 per cent of the first £200,000 and 5 per cent of the excess if there is. The Commission considered and rejected a system similar to the English system of discretionary payment on application to a court instead of a fixed payment. The Commission also rejected any fixed or discretionary payment for cohabitees.

Since the report was published there has been no move to implement its recommendations and it appears unlikely that this will happen in the foreseeable future. The only possible reform that is likely is in relation to cohabitees. After deciding not to recommend that cohabitees have any entitlement to a share in an estate in its Report on Succession in 1990, the Scottish Law Commission changed its mind and in its Report on Family Law in 1992 recommended that cohabitees should be entitled to apply to a court for a discretionary share from the deceased's estate.[23] The Scottish Executive in its White Paper on Scottish family law has indicated that this will be implemented in due course.[24]

---

[22] Scot. Law Com. No.124, 1990.
[23] Scot. Law Com. No.135, 1992 16.31–16.36.
[24] *Parents and Children* (2000), Chap.7.

Quick Quiz

Succession

- When can a person be declared legally dead?
- What presumptions apply when two people die simultaneously?
- Who can claim legal rights and when can they be claim?
- What are the conditions for the prior right to a dwelling house to apply?
- What is known as the "free estate"?
- The validity of a testamentary writing depends on which three factors?
- What are the essentials for a will to be self-proving after 1995?
- When is a will impliedly revoked?
- Should a survivorship destination be used instead of a will?
- What is the primary means of interpreting a will?
- Legacies fall into which three main categories?
- How is an executor appointed?
- What is the order of distribution of an estate?

Further Reading

Macdonald, *Succession* (3rd ed., W. Green, 2002)

Hiram, *The Scots Law of Succession* (Butterworths, 2002)

Meston, *The Succession (Scotland) Act 1964* (5th ed., W. Green, 2002)

***Stair Memorial Encyclopaedia—Wills and Succession*, Vol.25** (Butterworths, 1989)

Chapter 13

FAMILY

Dr Anne Griffiths[1]

FAMILIES AND MARRIAGE

Families take many forms in Scotland today. They include lone-parent households, cohabiting heterosexual and same sex couples with or without children, as well as marital relationships. Individuals may enter into a number of these forms in their lifetime as they move from marriage to lone-parenthood on to a cohabiting relationship, or from cohabitation to marriage. The changing dynamics of family life create a challenge for Scots family law in its approach to the recognition and enforcement of legal rights and duties among family members. What constitutes a "family" for legal purposes may be at odds with social perceptions of what makes a family unit. **13–01**

Some data on contemporary families

- Forty three per cent of live births were to unmarried parents but over 60 per cent of these were jointly registered by parents living at the same address.[2] **13–02**

---

[1] Reader in Law, University of Edinburgh.
[2] Registrar General for Scotland (RGS), Annual Report 2001, p.31.

- There were 30,367 marriages in Scotland in 2000, of these nearly 30 per cent represented people who had previously been married.[3]
- There were 11,143 divorces in Scotland in 2000.[4]
- 49 per cent of children adopted in Scotland in 2000 were adopted by a step-parent or relative of the child.[5]
- Cohabiting unions have grown at the expense of marriage, almost 4 in 10 non-married women aged between 25 and 29 were cohabiting in 1998, and over one-third of those aged 30 to 34. The proportion was still over one-quarter for women in their early 40s. The picture is broadly similar for men, although, age for age, the proportions are generally slightly higher.[6]
- On separation or divorce, mothers with children experience on average a 20 per cent drop in income.[7]
- The presence of dependent children in the family still has a major effect on the economic activity of women. About 44 per cent of women of working age had dependent children in Spring 2001. Only 18 per cent of women whose youngest child was under five worked full time, but this proportion rose with the age of the youngest child so that for those whose youngest child was aged 16–18 it reached 44 per cent. Only five percentage points lower than for women with no dependent children. Among women with pre-school children, most were either working part-time (36 per cent) or were economically inactive and looking after family and home (38 per cent).[8]

Changing approaches to defining families in terms of marriage

13–03 Traditionally, marriage has had a central role in family law, but growing recognition and acceptance of other types of non-marital family units has led to changes in the way that law deals with them. Thus, Scots law no longer discriminates against children on the basis of whether or not their parents were married.[9] In *Fitzpatrick v Sterling Housing Association*,[10] the House of Lords held in an English case, that a same sex partner was capable of being a member of the original tenant's "family" for the purposes of succeeding to his deceased partner's tenancy.[11] Statutory provision for this interpretation to take effect in Scotland has been made under s.108 of the Housing (Scotland) Act 2001.[12] Scots law is sensitive to developments taking place in the broader European and International community of which it forms part, including international conventions such as the United Nations Convention on the Rights of the Child and the European Convention on Human Rights and Fundamental Freedoms, to which the UK is a signatory. The latter has now been partially incorporated into UK law by the Human Rights Act 1998 and has brought about

---

[3] RGS, p.133.
[4] RGS, p.143.
[5] RGS, p.151.
[6] *Population Trends* 103, Spring 2001, p.13.
[7] *Poverty,* Issue 11, Winter 2002, p.3.
[8] *Social Trends* No.3, 2001, p.75.
[9] Law Reform (Parent and Child) (Scotland) Act 1986, s.1(1).
[10] [1999] 4 All E.R. 705 (H.L.). The majority noted that such a person would have to establish the characteristics of "family" namely "a mutual degree of inter-dependence, of the sharing of lives, of caring and love, and commitment and support" (at 714).
[11] Note that in the Court of Appeal [1997] 4 All E.R. 991 (whose judgment was overturned by the House of Lords), Lord Justice Ward, who dissented from the majority opinion, was prepared to go even further and view the surviving partner as a "spouse" of the deceased based on the functions he fulfilled (at 1022). The House of Lords, however, rejected this interpretation on appeal. However, in *Ghaidan v Godin-Mendoza* [2002] 4 All E.R. 1162 the Court of Appeal held that in order to render the Rent Act 1977 compatible with the Human Rights Act 1998 and Art.8, the words "as his or her wife" were to be read to mean "as if they were his or her wife or husband". This new construction would enable a same sex partner to be treated as if he or she were a spouse and thus entitled to succeed to the tenancy.
[12] For a an overview of the way in which same sex couples are treated in Scots law see B. Dempsey, "Same-Sex Couples in Scots Law—Part 1" (2002) SCOLAG No.300, 181 and "Same-Sex Couples in Scots Law—Part 2" (2002) SCOLAG No.301, 201.

change through decisions of the European Court of Human Rights (ECHR) at Strasbourg, which now, through incorporation, may be directly founded upon by UK citizens along with rights under the Convention.

Human Rights Act 1998

The Human Rights Act does not provide in a straightforward way that the Convention shall have effect as part of UK law, but seeks instead to give effect to what it defines as "the Convention Rights",[13] in a number of different ways. First, it establishes a "rule of interpretation". Legislation is to be "read and given effect" in a away which is compatible with "Convention rights"[14]; and the Act provides that courts must, in determining questions relating to such rights "take into account" the jurisprudence established by the Strasbourg Commission and Court.[15] This is so even where the decision would be at odd with an earlier decision of a UK court. Secondly, the Act provides that it is unlawful for a "public authority" to act in a way which is incompatible with a Convention right[16]; and s.7 gives "victims" of any such unlawful act the right either to rely on the Convention right in any legal proceedings or to institute legal proceedings against the relevant authority. Thirdly, the Act, whilst recognising the ultimate sovereignty of the Westminster Parliament, provides in s.4 a controversial procedure whereby a court may make a declaration that a statutory provision is incompatible with a Convention right. If it does so, a Minster may (provided that he considers such action to be necessary to remove the incompatibility and that there are "compelling reasons" for adopting the special procedure laid down by the Act—rather than bringing new legislation before Parliament in the usual way) make an order effecting the necessary changes.[17] **13–04**

Of key interest in family law are: Art.8 dealing with the right to respect for private and family life[18]; Art.12, dealing with the right to marry; Art.14, dealing with the right not to be discriminated against; and Art.6 dealing with the rights to a fair and public hearing in proceedings determining an individual's civil rights and obligations. Over the years the ECHR has expanded the concept of what constitutes a "family" together with the range of persons that fall within its ambit and the rights accorded to them. In *Marckx v Belgium*,[19] the European Court held that the notion of family life under Art.8 is not confined to marriage-based relationships but may encompass other *de facto* ties[20] such as those between an unmarried mother and her child. In the *Goodwin v UK*,[21] the Court held that the failure to allow a transsexual to marry a person of the sex opposite to their re-assigned gender was not only a breach of Art.12, but a failure to respect the applicant's right to private life in breach of Art.8. In *Salqueiro da Silva Mouta v Portugal*,[22] the court held that there had been discrimination in violation of Art.14 as well as a breach of Art.8 where a Portugese court recalled an order granting parental responsibility, including residence, in favour of a father, on the

---

13 s.1.

14 s.3.

15 s.2.

16 s.6.

17 s.10. Note discussion of this declaration of incompatibility in *S v Miller (No.2) (1st Div)*, 2001 S.L.T. 1304, where the court declined to make such a finding on the basis that it was now agreed that Scottish Ministers had power under existing legislation to make regulations to provide for representation before a children's hearing.

18 Immigration is an area where recent cases have alleged human rights violations under Art.8. See *Ahmed v SS for Home Department*, 2002 S.L.T.S. 1347 (O.H.); *Akhtar v SS for Home* Department, 2002 S.L.T. 1239 (O.H.); *Saini v SS for Home* Department, 2001 S.C. 951 (O.H.).

19 (1979–80) 2 E.H.R.R. 330.

20 See also *X, Y and Z v UK* and *Application No.25680/94 I v UK*, European Commission on Human Rights, Information Note No.129.6 where the Commission found the UK in violation of Art.8, in respect of family life, where the Registrar General refused to allow a post-operative female-to-male transsexual in a stable relationship to be registered as the father of a child born as a result of artificial insemination because only a biological man could be regarded as the father for the purposes of registration.

21 (28957/95) [2002] I.R.L.R. 664. Note that while no judgment of the ECHR has yet found that homosexual partners had a right to marry under Art.12 as this matter falls within the "margin of appreciation" of member state in *S v UK* (1986) 47 D. & R. 271 the Commission held that even though a stable homosexual cohabiting relationship did not fall within the definition of "family life" such a relationship might still be a matter affecting *private life*.

22 2001 Fam. L.R. 2; (2001) 31 E.H.R.R.47.

basis of his sexual orientation as a gay person.[23] In *P, C and S v UK*,[24] the court held that a mother's rights under Arts 8 and 6 had been breached by the removal of her son straight after birth, without providing her with relevant and sufficient reasons for their action and without affording her the opportunity to have legal representation.[25]

In some cases, however, discrimination in relation to substantive rights contained in the Convention, including the right to respect for family life, may be permitted where a state can show that it has a legitimate aim, and there is a reasonable relationship of proportionality between the legitimate aim and the means employed to achieve it. So, for example, in *McMichael v UK*[26] an unmarried father took his case to the European Court on the basis that he had no domestic legal right to obtain custody of his son or to participate in care and adoption proceedings before a children's hearing involving him. He argued that this infringed his right to respect for "family life" under Art.8 in a discriminatory manner that was contrary to Art.14. His action was unsuccessful. While the European Court in *Marcks v Belgium*[27] held that family life is not confined to marriage-based relationship but may encompass other de fact ties it ruled that there had been no violation of Arts 8 and 14 in *McMichael's* case. This was because the government was able to appeal to the proviso contained in Art.8(2) which requires any interference with family life to be justified on the basis that it is in accordance with the law and necessary to achieve a legitimate aim in a democratic society. In taking account of this the European Court has allowed a margin of appreciation to Member States, taking on board the political climate at the given time.

The court accepted the Government's explanation that the aim of the relevant legislation was to provide a mechanism for identifying "meritorious" fathers who might be accorded parental rights, thereby protecting the interests of the child and the mother. For discrimination to occur under Art.14 it must have "no objective and reasonable justification", that is if it does not pursue a "legitimate aim" or there is not a "reasonable relationship of proportionality between the means employed and the aim sought to be realised".[28] The court ruled that in this case the Government's aim was legitimate and that the conditions imposed on natural fathers for obtaining recognition of their parental role respected the principle of proportionality. There was thus an objective and reasonable justification for the difference of treatment complained of.[29] More recently, in *B v UK*[30] the court revisited the issue of whether unmarried fathers are discriminated against in the protection given to their relationship with their children by comparison with the protection given to married fathers under English law. It reached the conclusion that the Children Act 1989 did not violate an unmarried father's rights, as, following on from *McMichael*, "there exists an objective and reasonable justification for the difference in treatment between married and unmarried fathers with regard to the automatic acquisition of parental rights."[31]

Marriage

13–05 It is clear that families and marriage need not go together. At one time, under the common law, marriage had substantial consequences for spouses but a series of statutes has limited its legal consequences. Nonetheless, marriage still has important legal consequences for family members,

---

[23] The extent to which this case can be used by members of same sex couples to access other family law rights and liabilities in Scots and English law is explored in K. Norrie "Constitutional Challenges to Sexual Orientation Discrimination" (2000) 49 I.C.L.Q. 755.

[24] 2002 Fam.L.B. 59.

[25] In this case the mother had a previous conviction in America for harming one of her children and had been diagnosed with Munchausen's syndrome by proxy. The local authority found out her prior history and took out an order allowing them to remove her son hours after his birth. A care order followed and within a year the child had been freed for adoption. See also *S v Miller*, 2001 S.L.T. 531 on childrens' rights to legal representation before a children's hearing.

[26] (1995) 20 E.H.R.R 205.

[27] (1979–80) 2 E.H.R.R. 330.

[28] See *Marckx v Belgium* (1979–80) 2 E.H.R.R. 330 at para.33.

[29] *McMichael v UK* (1995) 20 E.H.R.R. 205 at para.98.

[30] [2000] 1 F.L.R. 1.

[31] *B v UK* [2000] 1 F.L.R. 1 at 5.

e.g. concerning rights to property and support, parenthood, financial provisions on the termination of a relationship and for rights to intestate succession on the death of one of the spouses.

Who can marry?

The law dealing with marriage is set out in the Marriage (Scotland) Act 1977 (as amended by the Marriage (Prohibited Degrees of Relationship) Act 1986). It provides that parties are free to marry provided they do not fall within the legal impediments to marriage set out in s.5(4) of the 1977 Act. The following constitute a legal impediment to a marriage, where: **13–06**

- the parties fall within the forbidden degrees of relationship[32];
- one of the parties is, or both are, married[33];
- one or both parties will be under the age of 16 on the date of the solemnisation of the intended marriage[34];
- one of the parties is or are incapable of understanding the nature of a marriage ceremony or of consenting to marriage[35];
- both parties are of the same sex[36]; or
- one or both of the parties is, or are, not domiciled in Scotland and the marriage would be void according to the law of the domicile of the party or parties.[37]

Some contentious issues

Position of transexuals and same sex couples

One of the fundamental requirements for marriage is that it takes place between a man and a woman. Under s.5(4)(b) of the 1977 Act there is a legal impediment to marriage where parties are of the same sex. Legal challenges to the exclusion of same sex marriages have mainly taken the form of cases concerning transsexuals. The leading case in this area is *Corbett v Corbett* which established that the criteria for identifying a person's sex are determined at birth according to certain immutable biological features: **13–07**

Corbett v Corbett

[1971] P. 83

One of the parties, who was born a male at birth, underwent sexual realignment surgery and thereafter lived as a women known as April Ashley. April, who had a passport issued in that name and who was accepted as a woman for national insurance purposes, took part in a marriage ceremony with a man. The relationship

---

32 1977 Act, s.5(4)(a). These are relationships based on consanguinity and affinity as set out in s.2 and Sch.1 of the 1977 Act.

33 1977 Act, s.5(4)(b).

34 1977 Act, s.5(4)(c). Note that where such a marriage takes place (which is most unlikely given the fact that birth certificates must be submitted to the registrar) it will be void under s.1.

35 1977 Act, s.5(4)(d). Lack of capacity to understand or consent to marriage may involve, mental incapacity, error (but only as to the identity of the person or the nature of the ceremony and not as to its effects), fraud (but only in so far as it produces the appearance without the reality of consent), marriages entered into under force and fear or duress, and sham marriages (discussed below).

36 1977 Act, s.5(4)(e).

37 1977 Act, s.5(4)(f). For more detailed information on marriage see Edwards and Grifiths, *Family Law* (1997) pp.246–262.

did not work out and the man raised an action to have the marriage annulled on the basis that April was not a woman for the purposes of marriage.[38]

The judge set out four main criteria for determination of sex, including:

- chromosomal make up;
- presence of absence of gonads (ovaries or testicles);
- structure of the genitals;
- person's psychological orientation.

The first three criteria, which carried the greatest weight, were to be assessed according to the position at birth.

While attempts have been made to challenge the criteria for the determination of sexual identity, these have not, as yet, been successful.[39] In *Bellinger v Bellinger*[40] the Court of Appeal recently upheld the biological criteria set down for determining sex in *Corbett*. Where, however, someone is born whose sex is indeterminate at birth, so that he or she is intersex, then a choice must be made taking into account not only the preponderance of biological criteria but that person's medical history and development.[41] If later developments, including psychological factors, suggest that the original assessment of the child's sex was wrong, then it can be changed.[42] An entry in the Register of Births may also be altered if it can be established that a genuine error was made in registering the sex of a person at birth.[43] In all other cases, when all the biological criteria are congruent at birth, a child's sex is established and it cannot be changed. Thus the sex recorded on a person's birth certificate is the sex attributed to him or her for the purpose of marriage.[44]

Human rights challenges

13–08 Attempts have been made to challenge UK law on same sex marriage on another front, on the basis that it discriminates against Art.8 (right to respect for private and family life) and Art.12 (right to marry).[45]

---

38 He alternatively sought to have the marriage annulled on the basis of willful non-consummation.

39 *Re P and G (Transexuals)* [1996] 2 F.L.R. 90 attempted to challenge Corbett on the basis of advances made in scientific thinking on the subject. While the applicants were unsuccessful in getting their entries in the Register of Births, altered, the court's judgment indicates that the registrar's decision could have been set aside if he had used indicators of sexual identity which had clearly been superseded by scientific advances of which he ought to have been aware. See also *B v B (Validity of Marriage: Transexual)* [2001] 1 F.L.R. 389 where the court accepted that recent research in the field of Gender Identity Disorder was leading to the view that the criteria for designating a person as male or female were complex and probably not simply an outcome of the first three criteria laid down in *Corbett*, but that such research had not yet gained sufficient recognition to amount to an advance in medical science that would overturn the ruling in *Corbett*.

40 [2002] 1 All E.R. 311.

41 *W v W (Gender: Nullity)* [2001] 1 F.L.R. 324. In this case the woman had been registered as a boy by her parents and she had been brought up as such by her adoptive parents. However, it would appear that while the woman's chromosomal and gonadal sex was male, the appearance of her external genitalia was ambiguous so that she was neither a normal man nor woman, and her general appearance from early teens, plus her gender orientation was female. The court held that the biological test in *Corbett* was not satisfied, that there had been an error in registering the respondent as a boy, and that she was a female for the purposes of marriage.

42 *W v W (Gender: Nullity)* [2001] 1 F.L.R. 324.

43 *X, Petitioner*, 1957 S.L.T. (Sh. Ct) 61.

44 This means that a post-operative transsexual does not have the right to have the change of sex registered or to acquire a birth certificate showing the new gender, see *Rees v UK* (1987) 9 E.H.R.R. 56; *Cossey v UK* (1991) 13 E.H.R.R. 622; *Sheffield v UK* [1998] 2 F.L.R. 928.

45 See *Rees v UK* (1987) 9 E.H.R.R. 56; *Cossey v UK* (1991) 13 E.H.R.R. 622; *Sheffield v UK* [1998] 2 F.L.R. 928 where the challenges were unsuccessful but note the most recent judgment of the ECHR in *Goodwin v UK* (above).

Sheffield v UK

[1998] 2 F.L.R. 928

In this case the ECHR once again held that the UK was not in violation of Arts 8 or 12.[46] This meant the UK was not obliged to change the birth certificates of post-operative transsexuals to reflect new sexual identities. It reached this decision in view of the lack of any shared approach among Contracting States towards the complex issues raised by transsexualism and on the basis that individual States were entitled to rely on a margin of appreciation to defend a refusal to grant new legal gender status to post-operative transsexuals. While observing that the Commission took the view that appropriate ways could be found to provide for transsexuals to be given prospective legal recognition of their gender reassignment, without destroying the historical nature of the register of births, the court found that legislative trends were not sufficient to establish the existence of any common European approach to the problems created by the recognition in law of post-operative gender status, especially with regard to areas of the law dealing with marriage, filiation, privacy and data protection. However, it did note that the UK had not kept the need for appropriate legal measures in this area under review and reiterated that all the Contracting States should do so.

However, the position has changed and in the recent case of:

Goodwin v UK

(28957/95) [2002] I.R.L.R. 664

The court held that the UK was in breach of Arts 8 and 12. It argued that while the court should not depart from precedents laid down in previous cases, without good reason, since the Convention is first and foremost a system for the protection of human rights, the court must have regard to the changing conditions within the respondent state and within Contracting States generally, and respond to any evolving convergence as to the standards to be achieved. It found the current position of transsexuals in the UK to be unsatisfactory[47] and unsustainable. It found that the right of transsexuals under Art.8, to personal development and to physical and moral security in the full sense enjoyed by others in society could no longer be regarded as a matter of controversy requiring the lapse of time to cast clearer light on the issues involved. It rejected the government's claim that the matter fell within their margin on appreciation (except with respect to the appropriate means of achieving recognition of the right protected under the Convention) and found that there were no significant factors of public interest to weigh against the interest of the applicant in obtaining legal recognition of her gender re-assignment.

With regard to Art.12, the court considered whether the allocation of sex in national law to that registered at birth was a limitation impairing the very essence of the right to marry in this case. It found that it was artificial to assert that post-operative transsexuals have not been deprived of the right to marry, as according to law, they remain able to marry a person of their former opposite sex. The court observed that while fewer countries permit the marriage of transsexuals in their assigned gender than recognise the change of gender itself,[48] it was not persuaded that this supported an argument for leaving the matter entirely to the Contracting States as being within

[46] See *Rees v UK* (1987) 9 E.H.R.R. 56; *Cossey v UK* (1991) 13 E.H.R.R. 622.

[47] This was acknowledged by the court in *Bellinger v Bellinger* [2002] 1 All E.R. 311.

[48] The Court noted that 54% of Contracting States, including Austria, Belgium, Denmark, Finland and the Netherlands, permit post-operative transsexuals to marry a person of sex opposite to their acquired gender.

their margin of appreciation, because this would be tantamount to finding that the range of options open to a Contracting State included an effective bar on any exercise of the right to marry. The margin of appreciation could not extend so far and barring a transsexual from enjoying the rights to marry under any circumstances amounted to a breach of Art.12 in the present case.

The Government is currently reviewing the law in this area. The ruling does not, however, affect the position of same sex couples who continue to be excluded from marriage. While most European countries, with the exception of the Netherlands and Belgium, do not yet permit same sex marriages many of them do allow same sex partners to enter into registered partnerships, or legally enforceable cohabitation contracts. While a number of local authorities in the UK allow for such registration,[49] this does not yet carry with it any legal rights, although the Government has indicated that it plans to introduce legislation dealing with this issue in the near future.

Sham marriages

13–09 Where parties establish that, although they went through a form of marriage ceremony, they never truly consented to marriage, they can apply to the court to have the marriage declared null and void. In "sham" marriages the claim is that *both* parties (rather than one) are withholding matrimonial consent. They may go through a marriage ceremony to achieve a certain end (*e.g.* for immigration purposes), so that there is a serious purpose underlying their actions, but it does not include assuming the relationship of husband and wife or the normal features associated with marital life. In English law, such "limited purpose" marriages are considered valid and cannot be set aside.[50] In Scots law, however, such marriages may be set aside on the basis that true matrimonial consent was not exchanged, as illustrated by the following leading case:

Orlandi v Castelli

1961 S.C. 113

In this case, the parties went through a civil marriage ceremony to enable the man, who as an Italian national, to remain in Scotland after his residence permit expired. Both parties were Catholics who, it was argued, did not regard the civil ceremony as a marriage. There was no cohabitation or sexual intercourse after the marriage and the man soon returned to Italy. Three years later, the woman raised an action of declarator of nullity on the basis of no true consent. The court granted the declarator on the basis that the formal consent which they exchanged was not with a view to marriage but to inducing the Home Office to allow the man to remain in Scotland. Thus it is "*consent* and not the *form* in which consent is given or evidenced that makes marriage".[51]

Subsequent cases, such as *Mahmud v Mahmud*,[52] *Akram v Akram*,[53] and *Ebrahem v Ebrahem*,[54] have endorsed this position. It is important to stress that in these cases parties must establish that they did not consent to marriage *at all*. If, on the evidence available, it can be established that the parties considered themselves married for a limited purpose only, then consent will have been exchanged, and the marriage will stand.

---

49 Such local councils include London, Leeds, Bournemouth, Manchester, Swansea, Liverpool, Brighton and Hove, Devon and Somerset.

50 *Silver v Silver* [1955] 2 All E.R. 614.

51 1961 S.C. 113 at 115.

52 1977 S.L.T. (Notes) 17.

53 1979 S.L.T. (Notes) 87.

54 1989 S.L.T. 808.

Given the tenuous nature of the distinction which requires to be drawn between consent, consent for a limited purpose, and no consent at all, it is not surprising that the Scottish Law Commission have recommended that tacit mental reservation should not render a marriage invalid.[55] The Scottish Executive have endorsed their recommendation in their proposals for legislative change.[56] It will still be competent, however, to have a marriage set aside on the grounds of non consent where duress is established.[57]

Constitution of regular marriage

Marriage (Scotland) Act 1977 (as amended by the Marriage (Scotland) Act 2002)

A regular marriage may be either a religious or a civil marriage.[58] In either case each party to the marriage must submit to the registrar of the district in which the marriage is to be solemnised, a notice of intention to marry, accompanied by a birth certificate, and where either party has previously been married, evidence of the dissolution of the previous marriage.[59] There are special provisions where a party to a marriage intended to be solemnised in Scotland is residing in another part of the UK or is not domiciled in any part of the UK and also for marriages outside Scotland where a party resides in Scotland.[60] After receipt of the notice, the registrar, if satisfied that there is no legal impediment, or if so informed by the Registrar General issues a marriage schedule which is the authority for the solemnisation of the marriage.[61] The schedule may not, however, be issued before the expiry of 14 days from receipt of the notice unless on the written request of a party to the marriage and with the authority of the Registrar General.[62] **13–10**

Civil marriage

The marriage must be conducted by an authorised registrar[63] and is normally conducted at the registrar's office,[64] although there is now provision for Scottish Ministers to make regulations extending the range of places where civil marriages may be solemnised with the approval of local authorities.[65] Both parties must be present together with two witnesses who profess to be aged 16 or over.[66] There is no prescribed form of ceremony laid down by the Act but it generally follows a certain procedure which involves the registrar explaining the nature of marriage in Scots law and asking the parties to declare if they know of any legal impediment to their marriage. The parties are then asked to take each other as husband and wife and to exchange consent to marriage. After they had done so, the registrar declares them to be married and the marriage schedule is then signed by both parties, the witnesses and the registrar. The marriage is then registered. **13–11**

---

55 See *Report on FamilyLaw* (1992) para.8.20.

56 See *Parents and Children: A White Paper on Scottish Family Law* (2000), para.6.4.17, which provides that a marriage may be invalid "because of mental incapacity, error or duress, either party did not effectively consent to the marriage but, without prejudice to the law on error or duress, will not be invalid merely because one or both parties went through the ceremony of marriage with a tacit mental reservation to the effect that notwithstanding the nature and form of the ceremony no legal marriage would result from it".

57 See *Mahmood v Mahmood*, 1993 S.L.T. 589 and *Mahmud v Mahmud*, 1994 S.L.T. 599.

58 1977 Act, s.8.

59 1977 Act, s.3(1).

60 1977 Act, s.3(4), (5) and (7).

61 1977 Act, s.6.

62 1977 Act, s.6(4).

63 This is a district or assistant district registrar appointed in term of s.17 of the 1977 Act.

64 In exceptional cases, *e.g.* where a person is seriously ill or suffering from serious bodily injury and is unable to attend and there is good reason why the marriage cannot be delayed, a registrar may give special dispensation for it to be solemnised elsewhere, *e.g.* in a hospital. See s.18(4)(b).

65 1977 Act, s.18A, added by the Marriage (Scotland) Act 2002.

66 1977 Act, s.19(2).

Religious marriage

13–12 A religious marriage may be solemnised by a minister of the Church of Scotland, a minister, clergyman, pastor or priest of a religious body prescribed by the regulations, or other approved celebrant.[67] The marriage schedule must be produced to the celebrant and the parties to the marriage and two witnesses (professing to be aged 16 or over) must be present. Where the celebrant belongs to the Church of Scotland or a prescribed religious body, the marriage must be in accordance with a form recognised as sufficient by the church or body to which the celebrant belongs.[68] In any other case, the statutory requirement is that the form of solemnisation must include a declaration by the parties, in the presence of each other, the celebrant and the witnesses, that they accept each other as husband and wife and a declaration thereafter that they are husband and wife.[69] After the ceremony, the marriage schedule is signed by both parties, the witnesses and the celebrant. It must then be returned to the district registrar for registration within three days of the ceremony.[70]

Unauthorised celebrant and validity of marriage

13–13 It is an offence for anyone, who is not within the classes of person authorised under the Act to solemnise marriages, to conduct a marriage ceremony in such a way as to lead the parties to believe that he or she is solemnising a valid marriage, or for the celebrant of a religious marriage to solemnise it without at the time having the marriage schedule, or for either the celebrant of a religious marriage or an authorised registrar to solemnise a marriage without both parties being present.[71] Provided both parties were present at the marriage ceremony *and* the marriage has been registered, its validity is not to be questioned in any legal proceedings on the ground of failure to comply with a requirement or restriction imposed by the Act.[72] This provision does not save a marriage that has never been registered and where no marriage schedule was ever issued.[73] In such a case the marriage is null and void.

Impediments to marriage

13–14 At any time before the solemnisation of a marriage any person may submit an objection in writing to the registrar.[74] Where the objection relates to a matter of misdescription or inaccuracy the registrar may, with the approval of the Registrar General, make any necessary correction. In any other case he or she must, pending consideration of the objection by the Registrar General, suspend the completion or issue of the marriage schedule or, if a marriage schedule has already been issued for a religious marriage, notify the celebrant of the objection and advise him not to solemnise the marriage.[75] If the Registrar General is satisfied that, on consideration of an objection, there is a legal impediment to the marriage as set out in s.5(4) of the 1977 Act he must direct the registrar to take all reasonable steps to ensure that the marriage does not take place. If on the other hand he is satisfied that there is no legal impediment, he must inform the registrar and the marriage schedule may then be completed and issued, if that has not already been done, so that the marriage may proceed.[76]

---

[67] 1977 Act, s.8(1). See also Marriage (Prescription of Religious Bodies) (Scotland) Regulations 1977 (SI 1977/1670).
[68] 1977 Act, s.14(a).
[69] 1977 Act, ss.14(b) and 9(3).
[70] 1977 Act, s.15(2).
[71] 1977 Act, s.24.
[72] 1977 Act, s.23A, as inserted by the Law Reform (Miscellaneous Provisions) (Scotland) Act 1980, s.22(1)(d).
[73] *Saleh v Saleh*, 1987 S.L.T. 633.
[74] 1977 Act, s.5(1).
[75] 1977 Act, s.5(2).
[76] 1977 Act, ss.5(3) and 6(1).

Defects and invalidity: effect on marriage

A marriage will be treated as void, that is as a nullity, where either party is under the age of 16,[77] or falls within the prohibited degrees of relationship.[78] It will also be treated as void where it falls within the statutory legal impediments to marriage under s.5(4) which include in addition to the foregoing, the existence of a prior subsisting marriage, incapacity with regard to understanding or consent, and the fact that both parties are of the same sex. Section 5(4)(f) also contemplates the existence of an impediment under a foreign domicile law of one or both parties. In addition, a marriage may be rendered voidable, that is it remains valid up until the point at which it is challenged, on the ground of impotency.[79] In the past, the consequences of declaring a marriage void were severe. Each party lost their status as married and, with it, any legal claims to support or property which they might have had arising from the marriage. In addition, the status of any children of the relationship was altered from legitimate to illegitimate, with all the legal consequences that this entailed. The only exception to this rule related to the children of putative marriages, that is, void marriages where one or both parties believed in good faith that the marriage was valid. Over time, the unfortunate consequences attached to nullity have been modified. When it comes to the parties themselves, a court,[80] on granting declarator of nullity, has the same powers to award financial provision in respect of a void or voidable marriage as it has on granting a decree of divorce.[81] **13–15**

Irrregular marriage

Under common law only one form of irregular marriage is now recognised by Scots law and that is marriage by cohabitation with habit and repute.[82] This form of marriage arises where a couple set up home together without going through *any* form of ceremony. It operates on the presumption that *tacit* consent to marriage is constituted by the cohabitation, as man and wife,[83] in Scotland,[84] of a couple free to marry, who are generally reputed to be husband and wife. The presumption is rebuttable. There are two major hurdles to be overcome in establishing a marriage of this kind, namely (a) satisfying the requirement that the cohabitation must be for a considerable period,[85] and (b) fulfilling the requirements of habit and repute.[86] It has now been established that there is no minimum period required for cohabitation.[87] To meet the second requirement, not only must the parties behave towards one another as husband and wife but they must also be reputed to be such by third parties. According to *Low v Gorman* [88] "although repute need not be universal it must be general, substantially unvarying and consistent and not divided". The opinion of others comes into **13–16**

---

77 1977 Act, s.1.
78 1977 Act, s.2.
79 The SLC has recommended the abolition of impotency as a voidable ground of marriage in its *Report on Family Law*, Scot. Law Com. No.135 (1992) recommendations 49 and 50. The Scottish Executive, however have declined their recommendation on the basis that it "provides a facility that would not otherwise be available to a limited number of couples in extreme circumstances", see *Parents and Children: A White Paper on Scottish Family Law* (2000), para.10.10.
80 At present only the Court of Session has power to award a declarator of nullity of marriage. However, the Scottish Executive following up on the SLC's recommendations in their 1992 Report are proposing to extend jurisdiction to the Sheriff Courts. See *Parents and Children: A White Paper on Scottish Family Law* (2000) paras 6.4.8 and 6.4.9.
81 Family Law (Scotland) Act 1985, s.17(1).
82 The other two were declaration *de praesenti* and promise *subsequent copula* both of which were abolished by s.5 of the Marriage (Scotland) Act 1939.
83 Note that it is not cohabitation *per se* that gives rise to the presumption but cohabitation as husband and wife.
84 See Lord Watson's dicta to this effect in the *Dysart Peerage Case* (1881) L.R. 6 App. Cas. 489 at pp.537–538.
85 *Campbell v Campbell* (1866) 4 M. 867.
86 See *Ackerman v Logan's Executors*, 2002 S.L.T. 37, IH where the court held that the evidence fell far short of establishing the pursuer's averments of general repute.
87 See *Kamperman v MacIver*, 1994 S.L.T. 763 where the court held that a period of cohabitation lasting six and a half months after an impediment to marriage was removed was not insufficient.
88 1970 S.L.T. 356 at 395.

play and the weight attached to their opinions varies.[89] It is clear that if parties openly admit that they are not married then marriage on the basis of cohabitation with habit and repute can never be established. The issue of admissions to certain third parties is, however, less clear cut. In *Mackenzie v Scott*[90] the court refused to grant a declarator of marriage on the basis that as several friends know that the couple were not in fact married and that they had discussed getting married on several occasions, all they had was a *future* intention to marry and that they did not regard themselves as married. This case may be contrasted with that of *Shaw v Henderson*[91] where the court granted a declarator in circumstances very similar to those of *MacKenzie v Scott* adopting the view that while relatives knew that the couple had never gone through *any* form of ceremony this did not mean that they did not regard themselves as being husband and wife. This approach was criticised in *Kamperman v McIver*[92] but followed in *Dewar v Dewar*.[93]

The fact that there was a legal impediment to marriage when the cohabitation began does not preclude the constitution of marriage by continuance of the cohabitation with repute after the parties become free to marry,[94] though circumstances after the removal of the impediment must be sufficient in themselves to establish the inference of tacit consent.[95] Consent to marriage may be proved by cohabitation with habit and repute where spouses have previously been married to one another and divorced.[96] A declarator of marriage must be sought from the Court of Session before the legal rights and obligation that attach to marriage will apply to a marriage constituted by consent following relevant cohabitation with habit and repute.[97] The Scottish Law Commission have recommended that, given the uncertain status of habit and repute marriage (until a judicial ruling confirms the position) such marriages should now be abolished.[98] However, after consultation, the Scottish Executive have declined to implement this recommendation on the basis that they did not "wish to penalise those who wish to benefit from this form of marriage, however irregular it may be."[99]

Key Concepts

Scots law no longer discriminates against **children** on the basis of **whether or not** their parents are **married**.

Marriage still has **important legal consequences** for family members, *e.g.* concerning rights to property and support, parenthood, financial provisions on the termination of a relationship and for rights to intestate succession on the death of one of the spouses.

Parties are free to marry provided they do not fall within the **legal impediments** to marriage set out in s.5(4) of the 1977 Act.

---

[89] See *Petrie v Petrie*, 1911 S.C. 360 where the court placed greater weight on the evidence of the man's professional colleagues and relatives, who considered him unmarried, compared with the views of persons such as the cleaner and the postman. See also *Ackerman v Logan's Executors*, 2002 S.L.T. 37, where the parties were considered married by neighbours, customers of the pursuer's shop and members of the various organisations with which the deceased was involved but not by close family members of the deceased. In weighing the evidence the views of the latter prevailed.

[90] 1980 S.L.T. (Notes) 9.

[91] 1982 S.L.T. 211.

[92] 1993 S.L.T. 732.

[93] 1995 S.L.T. 467.

[94] *Campbell v Campbell* (1867) 5 M. (H.L.) 115.

[95] *Low v Gorman*, 1970 S.L.T. 356.

[96] *Mullen v Mullen*, 1991 S.L.T. 205.

[97] Where such a declarator is granted the court must, under s.21 of the 1977 Act, state the date on which the marriage was constituted and forward it to the Registrar General for registration.

[98] See *Report on Family Law* (1992), para.7.9.

[99] See *Parents and Children: A White Paper on Scottish Family Law* (2000), para.10.5.

One of the fundamental requirements for **marriage** is that it takes place between a **man** and a **woman**.

The sex recorded on a person's birth certificate is the sex attributed to him or her for the purpose of **marriage**.

While a number of local authorities in the UK allow for registration of **partnerships**, this does **not yet** carry with it any **legal rights**.

In "**sham**" marriages the claim is that **both** parties (rather than one) are withholding matrimonial consent.

A **regular marriage** may be either a religious or a civil marriage. A **civil** marriage must be conducted by an authorised registrar – **no prescribed form of ceremony** is laid down by the Act. A **religious** marriage may be solemnised by a minister of the Church of Scotland, a minister, clergyman, pastor or priest of a religious body prescribed by the regulations, or other approved celebrant.

Under common law only one form of **irregular marriage** is now recognised by Scots law and that is **marriage by cohabitation with habit and repute**.

PARENTS AND CHILDREN

Who is a parent?

A child's first legal relationship is with his or her parents. An essential starting point in the law relating to children and parents is the determination of who is a parent in law as this has important legal consequences. These primarily revolve round parentage as a key prerequisite to establishing parental responsibilities and rights and the principle that a parent is responsible for his or her children's financial support. In regulating this area the law has to deal with genetic and social parenthood and the complications that arise from advances in reproductive technology where a distinction can now be drawn between "natural" parents who can conceive without the use of medical assistance or technology and "artificial" or "assisted" parenthood, in which the link between genetic parenthood and social or gestational parenthood may be broken. **13–17**

Presumptions of paternity and related provisions

At common law, a woman who gives birth is regarded as the legal mother of the child regardless of whether she is married to the child's father. Where fatherhood is concerned, the Law Reform (Parent and Child) (Scotland) Act 1986 now provides that a man is presumed to be the father of a child "if he was married to the mother of the child at any time beginning with the conception and ending with the birth of the child"[1] even if the marriage is invalid or irregular.[2] Where the presumption arising from marriage does not apply, a man is presumed to be the father of a child if both he and the mother have acknowledged his paternity and he has been registered as the father in any register of birth kept under statutory authority in any part of the UK.[3] These statutory presumptions of paternity are rebuttable by proof on a balance of probabilities[4] without **13–18**

---

1 1986 Act, s.5(1)(a).
2 s.5(2).
3 s.5(1)(b).
4 s.5(4).

corroboration.[5] Where assisted reproduction has taken place, Human Fertilisation and Embryology Act 1990 provides rules to establish parentage in law. Unless a child is adopted, the mother is the women who is carrying or has carried a child as a result of the placing in her of an embryo or of sperm and eggs.[6] Where pregnancy of a married woman results from the foregoing but her husband is not the genetic father of the child, he will nevertheless be treated as the father unless it is shown that he did not consent to the procedure.[7] Similar provisions apply where treatment is provided to an unmarried couple together.[8] These statutory rules regarding paternity do not apply, however, where by virtue of another enactment or rule of law the child is to be treated as the child of parties to a marriage,[9] or where the child is subsequently adopted.[10] Where a child is the genetic child of one or both of the parties to a marriage but was carried by a woman other than the wife, and certain other statutory requirements are fulfilled, a court may make a "parental order", declaring that the child is the child of the married couple.[11] A challenge to any of these presumptions or statutory rules may be taken in an action for declarator of parentage or non-parentage raised in either the Sheriff Court or the Court of Session.[12] A party to such proceedings can be requested to provide a sample or blood or other fluid, or body tissue for testing; if such a request is refused, the court has a discretion to draw such inference, if any, as seems appropriate (including an adverse inference) taking into account the subject-matter of the proceedings.[13] Where a child lacks capacity to consent this may be provided by any person having parental responsibility for a child under 16, or care and control of such a child.[14] Where such a person refuses to consent on the child's behalf, the court may request them to do so and may draw an adverse inference where s/he refuses.

Parental responsibilities and parental rights

13–19 However, acquiring the status of parentage does not automatically accord parental responsibilities and rights to a parent. Such responsibilities and rights (PRRs) are now codified in the Children (Scotland) Act 1995. They supersede any such PRRs under common law.[15] Under the 1995 Act parents are now entrusted with statutory responsibilities towards children, and parental rights are given only to enable them to discharge those parental responsibilities. The general statutory responsibilities are:

- to safeguard and promote the child's health, development and welfare[16];
- to provide direction and guidance in a manner appropriate to the stage of development of the child[17];
- if the child is not living with the parent, to maintain personal relations and direct contact with the child on a regular basis[18];
- to act as the child's legal representative, but only in so far as compliance if practicable and in the interests of the child.[19]

A parent's corresponding rights are:

---

5 Civil Evidence (Scotland) Act 1988, s.1(1).
6 1990 Act, s.27.
7 s.28(1) and (2).
8 s.28(3).
9 s.28(5)(b).
10 s.28(5).
11 s.30.
12 1986 Act, s.7.
13 s.70(2).
14 1986 Act, s.6(2).
15 ss.1(4) and 2(5).
16 s.1(1)(a).
17 s.1(1)(b).
18 s.1(1)(c).
19 s.1(1)(d).

- to have the child living with him or otherwise to regulate the child's residence[20];
- to control, direct or guide, in a manner appropriate to the stage of development of the child, the child's upbringing[21];
- if the child is not living with him, to maintain personal relations and direct contact with the child on a regular basis[22]; and
- to act as the child's legal representative.[23]

When a child reaches the age of 16 parental responsibilities and rights cease under this Act, with the exception of the responsibility to give guidance which subsists until the children reaches 18.[24]

Acquisition of PRRs—mother

A mother automatically has statutory PRRs in relation to her child whether or not she is, or has been, married to the father.[25] **13–20**

Acquisition of PRRs—father

In contrast, a father only aquires PRRs under the Act: **13–21**

- If he is married to the mother at the time of the child's conception or subsequently.[26]
- If he is unmarried, where he and the mother have reached agreement and registered it in the Books of Council and Session under s.4 of the 1995 Act. Note that in this case the mother must not have been deprived of any parental rights by the courts. Once registered, such an agreement can only be revoked by the court.
- If he has applied for a court order under s.11 of the 1995 Act.

As a result, some unmarried fathers find themselves without PRRs. Such discrimination on the basis of a parent's sex has been upheld notwithstanding the incorporation of Arts 8 and 14 of the European Convention of Human Rights into domestic law.[27] However, under growing pressure to remedy this situation, the Scottish Executive has proposed that unmarried fathers should have full, automatic PRRs where they have registered the child's birth together with the mother.[28] It has also proposed potentially extending such rights to step-parents where they enter into step-parents' parental responsibilities and rights agreements.[29] The 1995 Act also allows persons who do not have PRRs but who have care and control of a child under 16 "to do what is reasonable in all the circumstances to safeguard the child's health, development and welfare, including consent to medical treatment and related procedures where the child is incapable of giving consent and it is not known that the parent would refuse such consent."[30]

Where PRRs are held by more than one person, each person may exercise them separately without the consent of the other, unless a court decree or deed provides otherwise.[31] However, there is still a duty to consult under s.6(1). Also, where both parents are exercising parental rights, the consent of both of them is required before the child can be removed from or retained outside Scotland.[32] Indeed, there is a specific prohibition on removal from or retention outwith the UK of a

---

20 s.2(1)(a).
21 s.2(1)(b).
22 s.2(1)(c).
23 s.2(1)(d).
24 ss.1(2) and 2(7).
25 s.3(1)(a).
26 s.3(1)(b).
27 *McMichael v United Kingdom* (1995) 20 E.H.R.R. 205; *B v UK* [2001] 1 F.L.R. 1.
28 *Parents and Children: A White Paper on Scottish Family Law* (2000), paras 2.12–2.14.
29 *Parents and Children: A White Paper on Scottish Family Law* (2000), para.2.45
30 s.5(1).
31 s.2(2).
32 s.2(3) and (6).

child habitually resident in Scotland without the consent of a person who has and is exercising a right of residence or contact to that child.[33]

Views of the child

13–22 In an attempt to comply with Art.12 of the UN Convention on the Rights of the Child, where any major decision arises, those exercising PRRs or entrusted with the care and control of children, must have regard to the child's views (if s/he wishes to express them) so far as is practicable.[34] Account must be taken of the age and maturity of the particular child, but there is a rebuttable presumption that a child of 12 or older is of sufficient age and maturity to form such views under s.11(10). This does not preclude a child who is younger, but deemed sufficiently mature, from expressing such views. The 1995 Act also requires that children are given the opportunity of having their views considered in court proceedings affecting them[35] (discussed in greater detail below).

Guardianship

13–23 A guardian is a person *other than* a parent who takes on that role in certain circumstances. Under the 1995 Act a parent may appoint a "testamentary" guardian or guardians to act in the event of his or her death. As such an appointment is a "major decision" a mature child should be consulted before such an appointment is made. An appointment must be in writing and signed by a parent entitled to act as the child's legal representative.[36] A guardian may also be appointed the court,[37] or by a testamentary guardian with a view to replacing him/her in the event of his/her death.[38] If the appointment is accepted, a guardian acquires full PRRs in respect of the child.[39] Once established, the appointment of a guardian can only be terminated on the death of the child or guardian, by court order (*e.g.* for bad administration), or on the child reaching 18 (unless the deed provides for earlier termination).[40] Where there is more than one guardian, each may act independently of the others, unless the decree or deed of appointment provides otherwise.[41] Where disputes arise between guardians these have to be resolved by the court under a s.11 application (discussed below). The same holds good for disputes between a surviving parent and a guardian.

Court orders relating to PRRs

13–24 Under s.11 of the 1995 Act the Court of Session or the Sheriff Court may make an order relating to PRRs, guardianship or administration of a child's property. Such an order includes, but is not limited to:

- a *residence* order, which regulates the arrangements as to the person with whom a child is to love, or the persons with s/he is to live alternatively or periodically[42];
- a *contact* order, which regulates the arrangements for maintaining personal relations and direct contact between a child and a person with whom s/he is not, or will not be, living[43];

---

33 s.2(3) and (6).
34 s.6(1).
35 ss.11(7) and 16(2).
36 s.7(1).
37 s.11(2)(h).
38 s.7(2).
39 s.7(2).
40 s.8(5).
41 ss.7(5) and 2(2).
42 s.11(2)(c).
43 s.11(2)(d).

- a *specific issue order*, which regulates any specific question which has arisen or may arise in connection with PRRs or guardianship or the administration of a child's property[44];
- an interdict prohibiting the taking of any step specified therein in the fulfilment of PRRs relating to a child or in the administration of a child's property[45];
- an order appointing a judicial factor to manage a child's property or remitting that matter to the Accountant of Court[46];
- an order appointing or removing a person as guardian of the child.[47]

All these orders can be made on a temporary basis and varied and discharged by the court.

Who can apply?

Not only are the court's powers extensive but they can be invoked by a wide range of people. These include persons who already have PRRs,[48] persons who have had, but no longer have, PRRs (with four exceptions),[49] and any person who despite never having had PRRs in respect of the child claims an "interest".[50] Persons in the last category are very broadly construed and include unmarried fathers, grandparents, step-parents, siblings or other relatives and any anyone else with a connection to or legitimate concern for the welfare of the child, *e.g.* foster carers. It is also open to a child to make an application.[51] Even without a formal application by any of those qualified the court can make an order on its own behalf, or on request where this forms part of competent proceedings.[52] Note that where two parents have PRRs, and the court grants any of the specified orders this will only inhibit the exercise of those PRRs to the extent provided for in the order.[53] All other rights may continue to be exercised by either parent without the consent of the other, subject to the exception noted above that deals with the removal or rentention of a child habitually resident in Scotland where both parents must consent. **13–25**

Overriding principles for making an order

A child's welfare prevails over PRRs so that a court can only grant an order if the requirements of s.11(7) are met. These are that: **13–26**

- the welfare of the child throughout his or her childhood shall be [the court's] paramount consideration[54];
- children must be given the opportunity to express their views and have them taken into account where sufficiently mature.[55] There is a presumption in favour of children aged 12 or over having such maturity[56];
- there should be minimum intervention, that is, a court should only make an order if it is better for the child to make such an order than to make no order at all.[57]

It is now clear that under the 1995 Act, the welfare principle does not of itself place any onus on the party seeking a PRR order to establish that this is in the child's best interest. The recent case of

---

44 s.11(2)(e).
45 s.11(2)(f).
46 s.11(2)(g).
47 s.11(2)(h)
48 s.11(3)(a)(iii).
49 s.11(4).
50 s.11(3)(a)(i).
51 s.11(5).
52 s.11(3)(b).
53 ss.3(4) and 11(11).
54 s.11(7)(a).
55 s.11(7)(b).
56 s.11(10).
57 s.11(7)(a).

White v White[58] has settled the matter by holding that the "court must consider all the relevant material and decide what would be conducive to the child's welfare."[59] There is no exhaustive list of factors relevant to welfare, which is deemed to cover a child's physical, emotional, spiritual and material needs. The factors that operated in earlier cases concerned with custody and access continue to feature in residence and contact cases. Among the most influential are, the maintenance of the status quo in the child's life,[60] the desirability of maintaining contact with both parents[61] and with other family members,[62] and the need to understand one's racial or ethnic origin.[63] In applying the welfare principle courts must be careful to comply with the European Convention on Human Rights. Thus, refusal of a PRR application on the basis of a parent's religious affiliation may amount to a breach of the Convention.[64] Similarly, courts must be careful not to discriminate against an applicant on the basis of sexual orientation. In *T Petr*[65] the court held that sexual orientation was only relevant if it directly affects the child's welfare. The European Court has held that discrimination on the grounds of sexual orientation is a breach of Art.14.[66]

In reaching their decisions courts are explicitly instructed to have regard to the views of the child. This requires intimation to the child in "child friendly" language.[67] Courts may dispense with intimation, on application, where a child is considered too young to present views. However dispensation does not relieve the court of its ongoing duty to provide a child with an opportunity to express his views where this is practicable.[68] However these views must always be weighed against the child's welfare which prevails. The views of a sufficiently mature child are likely to prevail if they are reasonable and coincide with his or her best interests.[69] However, where a child is subject to undue influence less significance may be attached to his or her views.[70]

Aspects of children's legal capacity

13–27 Parental rights exist to enable parents to fulfil their parental responsibilities towards children. As children mature Scots law empowers them to make decisions on their own behalf before they become adults at 18.[71] The Age of Legal Capacity (Scotland) Act 1991 provides under s.1(1) that, as a general rule, children under 16 have no legal capacity to enter into any transaction unlike those aged 16 or over who acquire full legal capacity. Transaction is broadly defined to include unilateral transactions, the exercise of testamentary capacity or of a power of appointment, the giving of any consent having legal effect and the taking of any step in civil proceedings. There are, however, four important exceptions to the general rule that a child under 16 has no legal capacity and that any transaction entered into by such a child is void and unenforceable. These are contained in s.2 and cover:

- Children under 16 who have legal capacity to enter transactions "of a kind commonly entered into by persons of his age and circumstances" so long as the terms of the transaction are "not unreasonable".[72] The aim of the provision is to recognise the validity of

[58] 2001 S.L.T. 485.
[59] At 491G–H.
[60] *Brixey v Lynas*, 1994 S.L.T. 847; *Breingan v Jamieson*, 1993 S.L.T. 186; *Whitecross v Whitecross*, 1977 S.L.T. 225; *J v C* [1970] A.C. 668.
[61] *Sanderson v McManus*, 1997 S.C. (H.L.) 55.
[62] *Early v Early*, 1989 S.L.T. 114; 1990 S.L.T. 221.
[63] *Perendes v Sim*, 1998 S.L.T. 1382 at 1384; *Osborne v Matthan*, 1998 S.L.T. 1264.
[64] *Hoffman v Austria* (1994) 17 E.H.R.R. 293.
[65] 1997 S.L.T. 724.
[66] *Salgueiro da Silva Mouta v Portugal*, 2001 Fam. L.R. 2. *cf X v Y*, 2002 Fam. L.R. 58.
[67] This is done by mean of an F9 form under rules of court made under the 1995 Act.
[68] *Shields v Shields*, 2002 S.L.T. 579.Where a child is initially too young to express views, in long drawn out proceedings the court will remain under a continuing duty to check that the child has not developed views since the start of the case, or changed their mind where they have expressed views in earlier proceedings.
[69] *Fourman v Fourman*, 1998 Fam. L.R. 98.
[70] *Perendes v Sim*, 1998 S.L.T. 1382.
[71] Age of Majority (Scotland) Act 1969.
[72] s.2(5).

everyday, common transactions of children of differing ages and circumstances. The transaction, however, may still be invalid if its terms are unreasonable.

- Children aged 12 or over who can make a valid will[73] and whose consent to adoption or to an order freeing him or her for adoption must be obtained.[74]
- Children under 16 who can consent on their own behalf to any surgical, medical or dental procedure where, in the opinion of a qualified medical practitioner, they are capable of understanding the nature and possible consequences of the procedure of treatment.[75] Note that the doctor is not required to acquire parental consent or to establish that the treatment is in the child's best interests. Where a child has sufficient maturity and understanding a question arises as to whether parents can consent to such treatment where the child refuses it. Section 15(5)(b) of the Children (Scotland) Act 1995 provides that a parent can *only* act as a legal representative "where the child is incapable of so acting or so consenting on his own behalf". However, where a child is under 16, the court has powers to make a specific issue order under s.11 of that Act, that can cover treatment where that is in the child's best interests. In that case an application may be made by a medical practitioner. Where children area not deemed competent to consent those with PRRs or who have care and control over them[76] may consent on their behalf.

Legal representation

Children under 16 have legal capacity to instruct a solicitor and to sue or defend any civil matter in their own name, where they have a "general understanding of what it means to do so".[77] There is a presumption that a person aged 12 or over is sufficiently mature to have such understanding[78] although this does not preclude a younger child from having such capacity if sufficiently mature. This right is made more effective by the fact that the Legal Aid board now accept that a 12-year-old child or older now instructing a solicitor without parental assistance, may apply for civil legal and or legal advice and assistance conditional only on the solicitor enclosing a letter confirming that the child meets the s.2(4A) test. The same procedure is followed for a child under 12 except the Board reserves the right to query such a letter.[79] Parents may still represent children under 16 who meet the s.2(4A) test so long as the child consents to such representation.[80] Note that where a child fails the s.2(4A) test s/he must be represented by parents or other persons qualified to act as legal representatives who entirely control the case, unless there is no such representative, or that representative has adverse interests or refuses to act.[81] In such cases the court can appoint a *curator ad litem* to conduct the case. Children 16 and over can bring and defend any court proceedings except those involving variation of trusts where s/he must be over 18. **13–28**

Children aged 16 or over

Children aged 16 or over have full legal capacity. Some protection against transaction to their detriment is afforded to children aged 16 or 17 which allows them to apply to court to have a prejudicial transaction set aside until they reach the age of 21.[82] A transaction is prejudicial if an **13–29**

[73] s.2(2).
[74] s.2(3).
[75] s.2(4). This provision essentially embodies the decision reached by the House of Lords in *Gillick v West Norfolk and Wisbech Area Health Authority* which provided that children under 16 could consent to medical treatment without parental approval provided they had reached a certain degree of maturity and understanding.
[76] s.5.
[77] s.2(4A) inserted by s.105(4) of the 1995 Act and Sch.4.
[78] s.2(4B).
[79] Scottish Legal Aid Board Guidance 1996 J.L.S.S. 83.
[80] s.15(6).
[81] s.1(3)(f)(iii).
[82] s.3(1).

adult exercising reasonable prudence would not have entered into it and if it has caused or is likely to cause substantial prejudice to the young person.[83] Certain types of transaction are excluded from this provision. Testamentary acts, consent to an adoption order or to medical treatment, initiating, defending or taking steps in civil proceedings, transactions entered into in the course of the young person's trade or business, or induced by his fraudulent misrepresentation as to his age or other material fact, and transactions ratified by the young person or the court cannot be set aside.[84] Ratification by the court is available only in respect of proposed transactions by persons of 16 or 17 and will not be granted if it appears that an adult exercising reasonable prudence would not enter into the transaction.[85] Ratification must be sought in the Sheriff Court and the sheriff's decision is final.[86]

Areas not covered by the 1991 Act

13–30 The Act does not affect the delictual or criminal responsibility of any person.[87] Neither does it affect statutory age limits for particular purposes,[88] *e.g.* voting at 18[89] or the capacity of persons under 16 to receive or hold any right, title or interest.[90]

Children as witnesses in court

13–31 There is no fixed age at which a child acquites capacity to be a witness in either civil or criminal proceedings. *Rees v Lowe*[91] established that a child becomes a competent witness when a judge is satisfied that the child knows the difference between truth and lies and appreciates the duty to tell the truth. In civil proceeding any statement made by a person, which might be written or recorded, is admissible as direct oral evidence given in court by the same witness on the same matter.[92] The interpretation of this provision in *T v T*[93] now allows for the admissibility of hearsay evidence without the need to establish the competency of the witness.[94] However, where children give *direct* evidence in court they will still have to meet the *Rees* test.

In criminal proceedings a hearsay statement can be introduced as evidence if the maker of the statement cannot give evidence, because, by reason of his bodily or mental condition, he is unable to give evidence in a competent manner.[95] While the court still has to establish that the child would have been a competent witness at the date the statement was made[96] there appears to be no reason why this cannot be done by the use of extrinsic evidence, *e.g.* from the child's teacher or G.P. However, where a child gives *direct* evidence in criminal proceedings the *Rees* test still applies.

---

83 s.3(2).
84 s.3(3).
85 s.4(1) and (2).
86 s.4(3).
87 s.1(3).
88 s.1(3)(d).
89 Representation of the People Act 1983, s.1(1).
90 s.1(3)(e).
91 [1989] S.C.C.R. 664.
92 Civil Evidence Act 1988, s.2(1).
93 2000 S.L.T. 144.
94 This resolves the problems raised in *F v Kennedy (No.1)* where a three-year-old boy who had given evidence of sexual abuse to social workers refused to say anything at all when questioned by the sheriff in his attempt to establish the boy's competency as a witness. As a result the sheriff held that the boy's previous statements were inadmissible as hearsay because the *Rees* test had not been met.
95 s.259 Criminal Procedure (Scotland) Act 1995.
96 s.259(1).

Key Concepts

An essential starting point in the law relating to **children and parents** is the determination of who is a parent in law as this has important legal consequences.

A woman who gives birth is regarded as the **legal mother** of the child regardless of whether she is married to the child's father.

Acquiring the status of parentage does not automatically accord **parental responsibilities and rights** to a parent except where that parent is the mother. Such responsibilities and rights are now codified in the **Children (Scotland) Act 1995**.

Where any major decision arises, those exercising **PRRs** or entrusted with the **care and control of children**, must have regard to the **child's views** (if s/he wishes to express them) so far as is practicable.

A parent may appoint a "testamentary" **guardian** or guardians to act in the event of his or her death.

A child's **welfare** prevails over **PRRs**.

As a general rule (there are four important exceptions), **children under 16** have no **legal capacity** to enter into any transaction.

PROPERTY DURING MARRIAGE AND NON-MARITAL RELATIONSHIPS

Property for couples in Scotland today not only includes traditional forms of wealth such as heritage and capital but also forms of "new property" that include wages from employment and benefits associated with such labour, or purchased by it, such as pensions and insurance rights as well as social security benefits. **13–32**

Marriage and the "separate property" rule

Where parties marry or form a non-marital relationship the law upholds legal rights and duties, most notably the duty of parents to support their children. Property, however is generally subject to the separate property rule that provides that marriage shall not of itself affect the property rights of the spouses.[97] Nor does it affect their legal capacity.[98] This means that neither spouse acquires a right to own or administer the property of the other on marriage (except by express agreement). Similarly, unmarried couples are treated as separate individuals and ordinary property rules apply. **13–33**

For most families, the most important asset they possess is the home in which they live. The family home may be owned privately, or occupied under a public or private sector tenancy. Public sector tenancies are regulated principally by the Housing (Scotland) Act 1987 and private sector tenancies by the Housing (Scotland) Act 1988 and Rents (Scotland) Act 1984. In the case of private ownership, title to heritable property is conferred by a document known as the disposition which must be recorded in the Register of Sasines, or registered in the Land Register of Scotland. Most couples buying a home take title in joint names, but where they do not, it is only the person whose name is recorded in the disposition who is treated as the owner in law. Where the home is

---

[97] Family Law (Scotland) Act 1985, s.24.
[98] s.24(1)(b).

rented, title to occupy is conferred on the tenant by way of a lease, which lays down the terms and conditions under which the tenancy is held, including the duration of the lease as well as the period of notice which must be given on either side to terminate the tenancy. It is only the persons named in the lease who are treated as legal tenants although various protections are extended to family members in certain circumstances (see below).

Exceptions to "separate property" rule

13–34 There are however certain exceptions to the general rule that marriage does not affect the spouses' property rights. These include:

- a spouse's right to aliment[99];
- provisions under the Matrimonial Homes (Family Protection) (Scotland) Act 1981[1];
- spousal presumption of equal shares in household goods[2];
- spousal presumption of equal shares in money and property derived from any housekeeping allowance[3];
- exception to requirement of delivery where insurance policy in favour of spouse and/or children[4];
- right to retain possession of tenancy where spouse who is tenant leaves matrimonial home[5];
- right to succeed to private tenancy on spouse's death as statutory tenant[6];
- right to succeed to public sector secure tenancy on death of spouse[7]; and
- right to financial provision on divorce where matrimonial property is subject to fair sharing between the spouses regardless of who holds title to it.[8]

Aliment

13–35 Under s.1(1)(a) of the Family Law (Scotland) Act 1985 spouses are obliged to aliment one another. The obligation is to provide such support as is reasonable in the circumstances having regard to the needs and resources of the parties,[9] their earning capacities, and all the circumstances of the case.[10] Tax relief is not longer effectively available to those paying aliment it is more appropriate when computing parties resources' to consider their income net of tax. Among the circumstances of which the court may, if it thinks fit, take account is any support, financial or otherwise, which the payer gives, whether or not under an alimentary obligation, to a person whom

---

99 1985 Act, s.1(1)(a).

1 Discussed in paras 13–53 to 13–62.

2 1985 Act, s.25. This provision only covers spouses although the SLC have recommended that a modified version be extended to cohabiting couples in *Parents and Children: A White Paper on Scottish Family Law* (2000), para.7(4)(a).

3 s.26. This provision only covers spouses although the SLC have recommended that a modified version be extended to cohabiting couples in *Parents and Children: A White Paper on Scottish Family Law* (2000), para.7(4)(d).

4 Married Women's Policies of Assurance (Scotland) Act 1880, s.2. In this case the policy vests in the spouse and his or her representatives as soon as the policy is effected, without delivery.

5 1981 Act, s.2(8).

6 Rent (Scotland) Act 1984, Sch.1, para.2. Also protected under para.3 is "a person who was a member of the original tenant's family residing with him". After the House of Lords decision in *Fitzpatrick v Sterling Housing Association* [1999] 4 All E.R. 705 a member of the tenant's family may now be interpreted to include a tenant's same sex cohabitee.

7 Housing (Scotland) Act 1987, s.52(1). Protection is also extended under s.52(2) to a member of the tenant's family. S.108 of the Housing (Scotland) Act 2001 extends this definition to include same sex couples but note that where it is a secure tenancy, the property must have been the person's only or principal home throughout the period of six months ending with the tenant's death, a condition which does not apply to married cohabitants.

8 1985 Act, s.10.

9 Defined in s.27 of the Act as including "present and foreseeable" needs and resources. The provision of benefits in kind by an employer amounts to a resource to the employee, but not to a cash sum equivalent *Semple v Semple*, 1995 S.C.L.R. 569.

10 s.1(2) and 4.

he maintains as a dependant in his household.[11] In calculating aliment conduct is to be left out of account unless it would be "manifestly inequitable to leave it out of account".[12]

Proceedings for aliment may be brought by a spouse in the Court of Session or in the Sheriff Court.[13] They may stand alone or form part of other proceedings such as divorce, separation or declarator of marriage or of nullity, or relating to orders for financial provision or concerning parental responsibilities or parental rights[14] guardianship, parentage, legitimacy or in any other proceedings where the court considers it appropriate to include a claim for aliment.[15] Where any claim for aliment is made, the court also has power to award interim aliment, that is aliment pending the outcome of a court case.[16] There is no fixed scale for aliment and courts generally assess need relative to the lifestyle enjoyed by the parties during the marriage. An action may be raised even where the claimant is living in the same household as the defender.[17] However, it is a defence that the defender has made an offer, which it is reasonable to expect the payee to accept, to receive that person into his household and to fulfil the obligation of aliment.[18] When assessing the reasonableness of an offer the court is to have regard to any conduct, decree or other circumstances which appear to be relevant but an agreement by husband and wife to live apart is not of itself to be regarded as making it unreasonable to expect an offer to be accepted.[19]

Where an award is granted, the court will usually order the making of periodical payments, for a definite or indefinite period.[20] Note that it is also competent for the court to make alimentary payments of an occasional or special nature if the court sees fit.[21] Under the 1985 Act an award of aliment may now be backdated to the date of bringing the action or even earlier on special cause shown.[22] However, backdating provisions do not apply to awards for interim aliment.[23] A decree for aliment may be varied or recalled if there has been a material change of circumstances.[24] The change must be one which affects the resources of either party, *e.g.* an increase or decrease in the earning or means of either party, such as where one spouse inherits property,[25] takes up employment[26] or loses his or her job.[27] The making of a maintenance assessment under the Child Support Act 1991 is specifically designated as a material change of circumstances justifying variation of aliment paid to a spouse as well as to a child.[28] Variations of awards may be backdated, but the power to backdate variations does not extend to the variation of an agreement[29] nor to the variation of awards of interim aliment.[30] Where parties reach their own agreement as to aliment, any provision which purports to exclude liability for future aliment or to restrict the right to claim aliment is of no effect unless it was fair and reasonable in all the circumstances of the agreement when it was entered into.[31]

---

11 s.4(3)(a).
12 s.4(3)(b).
13 s.2(1).
14 But note that the opportunity to resolve all such issues in one actions is now restricted by the provisions of the Child Support Act 1991, see paras 13–47 to 13–51, below.
15 s.2(2).
16 s.6(1).
17 s.2(6).
18 s.2(8)
19 s.2(9).
20 s.3(1)(a).
21 s.3(1)(b), *e.g.* for inlaying expenses associated with the birth of a child or where a child incurs expenses associated with disability.
22 s.3(1)(c).
23 *McColl v McColl*, 1993 S.C. 276.
24 s.5(1).
25 *Donald v Donald* (1862) 24 D. 499.
26 *Doswell v Doswell*, 1943 S.C. 23.
27 *Brotherstone v Brotherstone* (1938) 54 Sh. Ct Rep. 218.
28 s.5(1A).
29 *Ellerby v Ellerby*, 1991 S.C.L.R. 608.
30 See *McColl*, above.
31 s.7(1).

The obligation to aliment a spouse, which only arises during the subsistence of a marriage, terminates on death[32] or divorce. However, an ex-spouse may still be able to claim support in the form of a periodical allowance as part of an award of financial provision on divorce in certain limited circumstances.[33]

Social security and income-related state benefits

13–36 Where couples cohabit but are unmarried they are under no obligation to aliment one another as the right to aliment only arises through marriage. In such cases, where individuals are in need they will have to turn to the state for support under public law.[34] This may also be true for married couples where they are on very low incomes. However, eligibility for state benefits is dependent upon meeting certain criteria which may prove hard to establish. Each benefit has its own qualifying conditions but benefits are in general divided into those that are contributory and those that are non-contributory. Certain social security benefits are only payable to individuals who have paid sufficient National Insurance contributions through deductions from their earnings which entitle them to make a claim. All other benefits are "non-contributory" since they do not depend on the claimant satisfying a given level of National Insurance contributions. The main income-related benefits are jobseeker's allowance, working families tax credit, housing benefit, council tax benefit and in some cases income support.

Jobseeker's allowance

13–37 Jobseeker's allowance has two distinct components: a time limited period of support based on past national insurance contributions for unemployed persons seeking work and an income-based benefit for the unemployed. Persons seeking this allowance must have signed a jobseeker's agreement[35] and be actively seeking employment. The two components have separate rules of entitlement.[36]

Working Tax Credit[37]

13–38
- *Working Tax Credit*: Paid to those in low-paid work.
- *Child Tax Credit*: Paid to people with children, whether they are in, or out of, work.

The new system of Working Tax Credit and Child Tax Credit which replaces working families' tax credit will only come into force in full for people on income support/income-based jobseeker's allowance from April 2004. Under the new system adults will be entitled to claim either working tax credit or wage replacement benefits (adult-related allowance only). Child Tax Credit will be paid for children *in addition* to child benefit. A family element in Child Tax Credit will replace the family premium in income support/income-based jobseeker's allowance. Child dependency increases paid with some social security benefits will continue to be made, but will generally be taken into account as income when calculating tax credit entitlement. Child Tax Credit and child benefit, will, therefore, become the main source of financial support for children. These new payments challenge existing provision based on social insurance: they rely on a means-tested

---

32 But a widow has an independent claim against her husband's estate for temporary aliment after his death.

33 s.13, 1985 Act.

34 Benefits are now administered by the Department for Work and Pensions. The basic legislative framework for benefits is contained in The Social Security Contributions and Pensions Act 1992 and the Social Security Administration Act 1992.

35 Jobseeker's Act 1995, s.1(2)(b).

36 Jobseeker's Act 1995, ss.2 and 3.

37 This has replaced working families' tax credit which was abolished in April 2003, together with child tax credit. See Tax Credits Act 2002, the Working Tax Credit (Entitlement and Maximum Rate) Regulations 2002 (SI 2002/2005) and the Child Tax Credit Regulations 2002 (SI 2002/2007).

system to deliver the most help to families on the lowest incomes; and they separate benefits for adults and children. These tax credits will be administered by the Inland Revenue.

(1) *What is Working Tax Credit?*

To qualify a person must be in low-paid work and be:

- over 16, have a child and work at least 16 hours a week; or
- over 16, be disabled and work at least 16 hours a week; or
- over 25 and work at least 30 hours a week; or
- 50 or more, work at least 16 hours a week and be receiving certain benefits.

(2) *What is Child Tax Credit?*

To qualify a person must be at least 16 and be responsible for a child (*i.e.* be the main carer). It is paid in addition to child benefit. A child includes a young person under 19 in full-time, non-advanced education.[38]

Housing Benefit and Council Tax Benefit

Housing Benefit (HB)[39] and Council Tax Benefit (CTB)[40] are means-tested benefits which are administered by the local authority for claimants who have a low income to help them meet their rent liability or Council Tax liability for the place where they live. It is available to claimants where or not they are working full-time and can be claimed in addition to any other benefit. There are, however, some circumstances where HB cannot be claimed regardless of a claimant's income and the fact that he has to pay rent.[41] The rules relating to CTB are exactly the same as those for HB, apart from the liability to pay rent being replaced by a liability to pay council tax. **13–39**

Income support

Income support[42] is a means-tested benefit and provides a weekly cash sum to up a claimant's income to a minimum level as prescribed each year by the Secretary of State. It is available to those who are not in full-time work and are not required to sign on as available for work, *e.g.* people aged over 60 or who are incapable of work through sickness or disability, people bring up children on their own and people who are unable to work because they are caring for a disabled person. **13–40**

Aggregation of resources—what is a family?

These benefits are all "income-related", in the sense that they are assessed on the basis of the resources available to the individual claimant. Under the Social Security Contributions and Benefits Act 1992, these resources include the resources of the claimant's family. The Act provides: **13–41**

> "Where a person claiming an income-related benefit is a member of a family, the income and capital of any member of that family shall, except in prescribed circumstances, be treated as the income and capital of that person."[43]

[38] For more detailed information see Child Poverty Action Group, *Welfare Benefits and Tax Credits Handbook 2003/2004*, pp.1239–1371.
[39] Housing Benefit (General) Regulations 1987 (SI 1987/1971).
[40] Council Tax Benefit (General) Regulations 1992 (SI 1992/1814).
[41] Council Tax Benefit (General) Regulations 1992 (SI 1992/1814), reg.7.
[42] Income support (General) Regulations 1987 (SI 1987/1967).
[43] s.136(1).

For these purposes "family" is broadly defined to include both married and unmarried couples, with or without children, as well as single parent families including a child or young person.[44] Under s.137(1) of the 1992 Act, a "married couple" is defined as "a man and a woman who are married to each other and who are members of the same household". An "unmarried couple" is defined as "a man and a woman who are living together as husband and wife".[45] Where individuals fall within this definition of family both entitlement and the amount payable in respect of all benefits are determined by aggregating the claimants capital and income together with that of family members which may well bring him or her above the cut-off point for benefit. The underlying rationale is that the state should not have to support the claimant if sufficient resources are being brought into the household by another member of the family (even if the claimant does not in fact benefit from them). For this reason the "family" is broadly defined under social security legislation to cover unmarried couples (but not same sex partners). Such persons are expected to mutually support one another, rather than rely on the state for support, even although they have no obligations to aliment each other under private law.

Recovery from liable relatives

13–42 Where benefit is paid to individuals the state reserves he right to recover the cost of an award from those who fall within the category of "liable relatives".[46] Under s.78(6) of the 1992 Act, spouses are liable to maintain each other and a parent is liable to maintain his or her children. A "child" in this context covers not only a person who is under the age of 16, but one who is 16 or more but under the age of 19 and in respect of whom either parent, or some other person acting in place of either parent, is receiving income support.[47] Note that an ex-spouse is not a liable relative as the duty to aliment a spouse ends on divorce. Where liable relatives fail to meet their alimentary obligations, the Secretary of State is empowered to recover costs. An application may be made to the sheriff who, having regard to all the circumstances, including the defender's resources, may order the defender to pay whatever sum is considered appropriate, on a weekly, monthly or other basis.[48]

Aliment for children

13–43 Children have a right to financial support from both parents, whether or not the parents are or have been married to one another and whether or not they live together or apart. The Family Law (Scotland) Act sets out the principles for determining what support is owed by parents to their children known as aliment. In practice, however, the provisions of the 1985 Act are rarely invoked where parents share a household with each other and the child, and in cases where the parents live apart the 1985 Act rules on aliment have largely been eclipsed by the Child Support Act 1991 which has introduced wide-ranging changes throughout the UK in relation to the child's right to support.

Who is liable for aliment?

13–44 The 1985 Act provides that aliment is owed:

---

[44] s.137(1).
[45] s.137(1). For general discussion of complexities in claiming for the family see K. Tonge, *Tolley's Social Security and State Benefits: A Practical Guide* (2001).
[46] s.106, 1992 Act.
[47] s.78(6)(d).
[48] s.106(2).

- by a father or mother to his or her child[49]; and
- by any person to a child who has been "accepted" as part of their family, except where the child has been boarded out as a foster child by the local authority or voluntary organisation.[50]

Under the Act a child is generally defined as a person aged under 18 but may also include a person over the age of 18 but under the age of 25 who is "reasonably and appropriately undergoing instruction at an educational establishment, or training for employment or for a trade, profession or vocation".[51] Under this Act alimentary liability extends beyond the biological, nuclear family to include liability for step-parents, grandparents and others in contrast with the 1991 Act where liability is restricted to parents having a duty to support their *legal* children.[52] Where aliment is owed to a child it is generally the person with care of the child who receives any money that is payable to the child. This is because children have limited legal capacity which means that a parent or other adult will be required to administer the child's aliment.

Amount

Unlike the 1991 Act, there is no fixed amount for aliment. As with spouses, the obligation is to **13–45** provide such support as is reasonable in the circumstances,[53] having regard to the factors which the courts use to determine the amount of aliment, *i.e.* the needs and resources of the parties, their earning capacities and generally all the circumstances of the case.[54] Where two or more parties own an obligation of aliment to a child, while there is no order of liability, the court, in deciding how much, if any, aliment to award against those persons, must have regard to the obligation of aliment owed to the child by any other person.[55] Where a child is under 16 the court may also include an amount for the reasonable expenses of the person having care of the child where these are incurred in looking after the child.[56]

Who may raise an action?

A claim for aliment may be brought by: **13–46**

- The child himself.[57] A child has full legal capacity aged 16 or over. If under 16 the child will have legal capacity to pursue the action if the child has capacity to instruct a solicitor,[58] if 18 or over, the child *must* pursue the action as it is no longer competent for a parent to raise the action on the child's behalf.[59]
- A child's parent or guardian.[60]
- By anyone with whom he lives or who is seeking a residence order in respect of him.[61]
- His or her *curator bonis* if incapax.[62]

---

[49] s.1(1)(c).
[50] s.1(1)(d). A child whom a father once treated as his own child but subsequently discovered to have been fathered by another man has not been "accepted" by him as a child of the family: *Watson v Watson*, 1994 S.C.L.R. 1097.
[51] s.1(5).
[52] Parents in this context include genetic and adoptive parents and persons who are to be treated for all purposes as parents under the Human Fertilisation and Embryology Act 1990.
[53] s.1(2).
[54] s.4(1).
[55] s.4(2). In *Inglis v Inglis*, 1987 S.C.L.R. 608 the court took into account the fact that the uncle and aunt owed an obligation to aliment the child in their action against the father of the child for aliment.
[56] s.4(4), added by the Child Support Act 1991, Sch.5, para.5.
[57] s.2(4)(a).
[58] See s.2(4A) and (4B) of the Age of Legal Capacity (Scotland) Act 1991.
[59] *Hay v Hay*, 2000 S.L.T. (Sh. Ct) 95.
[60] s.2(4)(c)(i).
[61] s.2(4)(c)(iii).
[62] s.2(4)(b).

A woman, whether married or not, may bring an action in respect of her unborn child but no such action can be heard or disposed of until the child is born.[63] An order may be made for the making of alimentary payments of an occasional or special nature, including payments in respect of inlying, funeral or educational expenses.[64] Where the person to be alimented is living in the same house as the defender it is a defence to the action for aliment that the defender is thereby fulfilling his alimentary obligation and intends to continue doing so,[65] and it is also a defence that the defender is making an offer, which it is reasonable to expect the person concerned to accept, to receive that person into his household and thereby fulfil his obligation of aliment.[66] However, that defence is not open in the case of aliment for a child under 16. This is because the question of where a child should live is *prima facie* an issue in proceedings for a residence order where the child's welfare will be the paramount consideration. Where a child is over 16, the defence stands if the defender had offered a home to the child which it was reasonable to expect the child to accept.[67] In determining whether it was reasonable for the child to accept such an offer, the defender's conduct will be taken into account.[68]

A claim for aliment may be brought in the Court of Session or the Sheriff Court and, unless the court considers it inappropriate, may be raised as an ancillary matter in various proceedings, *e.g.* divorce, declarator of parentage, actions in relation to parental responsibilities and rights.[69] It takes the form of periodical payments, whether for a definite or indefinite period or until the happening of a specified event.[70] However, the court can order alimentary payments of an occasional or special nature to meet special needs which it would be unreasonable to expect the claimant to meet out of a periodical allowance.[71] As noted above it can be backdated to the date of the bringing of the action and, on special cause shown, to a date prior to the bringing of the action.[72] It can also be varied or recalled on the basis of a material change of circumstances since the date of decree.[73] But note that an application to vary can only be made while the obligation to aliment exists, it cannot be varied retrospectively when the child has become an adult.[74] When a variation is backdated, any sums paid under the order before variation can be ordered to be repaid.[75] While an interim award of aliment can be varied or recalled, there is no power to backdate the variation.[76]

Child Support Act 1991

Definition of child and parent

13–47 The Child Support Act 1991[77] creates a new administrative scheme, administered by the Child Support Agency, for assessing and enforcing maintenance owed by a parent to a "qualifying" child.[78] A child[79] is defined as a person:

63 s.2(5).
64 s.3(1)(b).
65 s.2(7).
66 s.2(8).
67 s.2(8).
68 s.2(9).
69 s.2(1) and (2).
70 s.3(1)(a).
71 s.3(1)(b).
72 s.3(1)(c).
73 s.5(1). An increase in the cost of maintaining a child as the child grows older amounts to a material change of circumstances, *Skinner v Skinner*, 1996 S.C.L.R. 334.
74 *Paterson v Paterson*, 2002 S.L.T. (Sh. Ct) 65.
75 s.5(4).
76 *McColl v McColl*, 1993 S.L.T. 617.
77 As amended by the Child Support Act 1995 and by the Child Support Pensions and Social Security Act 2000.
78 s.3.
79 s.55.

- under 16;
- under 19 and in full-time, non advanced education[80]; or
- under 18 and registered for work or youth training while a parent is still claiming child benefit in respect of the child.

Persons who are or have been married do not fall within the definition.[81] A qualifying child is one where one or both parents are non-resident parents,[82] *i.e.* they do not live with the child. A non-resident parent is a parent not living in the same household as the child, where the child is living with a person with care.[83] A person with care is a person with whom the child has his home, who provides day to day care of the child and who does not fall within certain prescribed categories.[84] A person with care does not require to be an individual, so that a parent can be found liable to contribute to the maintenance of a child in the care of a voluntary agency, although no assessment can be levied against an agency.[85]

Under the Act each parent of a qualifying child is responsible for that child's maintenance. It is important to note that the definition of parent is limited to "any person who is in law the mother or father of the child".[86] Thus, natural and adoptive parents are covered but not step-parents who have no liability under the Act. It is also important to note that maintenance under the Act is only the responsibility of the non-resident parent. The person with day-to-day care of the child in effect meets his or her responsibility to maintain by looking after the child, and need make no payments to, or for the benefit of, the child. A child is generally cared for by one of his or her natural parents ("the person with care"), who is separated from the other ("the non-resident parent"). However, this is not always the case and where the person with care is not a parent, both parents will qualify as non-resident parents under the Act.

Who can apply for a maintenance calculation?

Voluntary application

A maintenance calculation[87] in respect of a child may arise either voluntarily[88] or compulsorily.[89] **13–48**
Section 4 of the 1991 Act provides a voluntary procedure that may be initiated by either the person with care, or the non-resident parent, of a qualifying child. These persons may not only authorise the Secretary of Sate to make a maintenance calculation but also to enforce and collect it. They may also withdraw their authority to act. However, a s.4 application is not competent where there is a compulsory maintenance calculation in force under s.6. A qualifying child, aged 12 or over, who is habitually resident in Scotland may also apply for a maintenance calculation in his or her own right,[90] provided no application has already been made under s.4 and provided that the Secretary of State has not taken any action under s.6.

---

80 Full-time education covers those attending school or a further education college but not universities or similar institutions. See Sch.1 to SI 1999/1813.
81 s.55(2).
82 The term non-resident replaces the original term "absent" parent: Child support Pensions and Social Security Act 2000, Sch.3, para.11(2).
83 s.3, 1991 Act.
84 s.3(3). The categories are prescribed in SI 1992/1813, reg.51 and cover local authorities and their carers.
85 s.44(2).
86 s.54.
87 The term "maintenance assessement" under the original 1991 Act has been replaced by the term "maintenance calculation": s.1(2), 2000 Act.
88 s.4.
89 s.6.
90 s.7.

Compulsory application

13–49 Section 6 deals with benefit cases. It provides that a *parent* with care is to be treated as having applied for a maintenance calculation and authorised the Secretary of State to take action to recover child support maintenance from the non-resident parent, if the parent with care is claiming a qualifying benefit. Such benefit includes means tested benefits such as income support or income-based jobseeker's allowance. Under the new rules that are not yet in force, the claim itself is the authorisation and no separate maintenance application form is needed. A parent must opt out if they wish to prevent the Child Support Agency pursuing the other parent. If they do opt out their benefit will be paid at a reduced rate unless the Department of Work and Pensions agree that there is a risk of harm or undue distress. Where the claimant opts out there is a four week cooling off period. In considering whether or not to make a reduced benefit direction the Department must consider whether the welfare of the child would be adversely affected by the making of the direction. Where a direction is made benefit may be cut by up to 40 per cent for a three-year period.

Once a maintenance calculation has been made,[91] the non-resident parent comes under a duty to make payments of the amounts specified in the calculation. The Secretary of State has power to arrange for the collection and enforcement of maintenance in the case of all compulsory calculations made under s.6, and those voluntary calculations under ss.4 and 7 where the Secretary of State has been authorised to collect and enforce the amounts due. Payments may be made in a variety of ways but the Secretary of State has two important powers. The first is to make a deduction from earnings order[92] which enables an employer to deduct maintenance from earnings at source and remit them to the Secretary of State. The second is to apply for a liability order[93] which enables diligence to be carried out, but this may be done only where there are arrears, and either a deduction from earnings order would be inappropriate, or has been tried already and proved ineffective. A defaulter may, ultimately, be sent to prison.[94] Where arrears remain outstanding there is provision for imposing a financial penalty.[95] Decisions of the Child Support Agency may be appealed to appeal tribunals.[96]

New formula for maintenance calculation

13–50 The new rules, that have not yet come into force, simplify the formula applied to maintenance calculations.[97] They provide that the basic rate of child support maintenance is calculated as a percentage of the non-resident parent's net weekly income[98]:

- 15 per cent if one qualifying child;
- 20 per cent if 2 qualifying children;
- 25 per cent if 3 or more qualifying children.

The basic rate applies provided the non-resident parent's income is £200 a week or more. The maximum net income is deemed to be £2,000 a week. Net weekly income is gross income *less* income tax, National Insurance and all payments into approved pension schemes. Housing and travel to work costs are ignored as is the income of any new partner. The scheme also ignores the income of the person with care and that of the qualifying child. The amount will be reduced if the non-resident parent has one or more qualifying children living in his household. These include step-children as well as children conceived with the new partner. Note that where the non-resident

---

91 Under ss.4, 6 or 7.
92 ss.31 and 32.
93 s.33.
94 s.40A (added by s.17 of the CSPSSA 2000).
95 s.18 of the CSPSSA 2000 (replacing s.41 of the 1991 Act).
96 s.20 (as substituted by s.10 of the CSPSSA 2000).
97 ss.1 and 2 of the CSPSSA 2000.
98 Sch.1 of the 1991 Act (as substituted by Sch.1 to the CSPSSA 2000).

parent's weekly income is less than £200 a reduced rate is payable, and that where this income is £100 or less, this is further reduced to a flat rate of £5 per week. In order to encourage parents with care to support the system there is a maintenance disregard on the first £10 where they are receiving income support or income-based jobseeker's allowance. When the non-resident parent pays the flat rate, the person with care will be paid the £5 per week without any reduction of benefit.

Variation

The non-resident parent can only apply for a variation of the maintenance calculation in very **13–51**
limited circumstances. These include taking account of "special expenses" that may be incurred,[99] *e.g.* where costs of maintaining contact with the child are high or where the non-resident parent has made a transfer of property or capital to the person with care in a divorce settlement pre-April 1993 that he or she wishes to have taken into account. A parent with care can also seek variation on the ground that the non-resident parent's declared income does not truly reflect his or her ability to pay.

Relationship between courts and Child Support Agency

The courts' powers to award aliment to qualifying children have largely been replaced by the **13–52**
powers of the Child Support Agency to make maintenance calculations.[1] Thus it is not competent for a court to make any order which has the effect of awarding aliment in cases where a child support calculation may be made under ss.4 or 7 of the 1991 Act, or where the Secretary of State can take action under s.6.[2] This means that the courts have no jurisdiction to award aliment under the Family Law (Scotland) Act 1985 if the Child Support Agency has jurisdiction under the 1991 Act. However, they may still make awards in the following cases where the 1991 Act does not apply:

- where a child over 18 is undergoing education or training[3];
- where a claim is made against a step-parent or any other person who has "accepted" the claimant as part of the family;
- where the non-resident parent is not habitually resident in the UK[4];
- where a child seeks aliment from the person with care (because a maintenance calculation cannot be made in respect of such a person).

In those cases where there are existing court maintenance orders or pre-1993 agreements for aliment the courts retain power to vary them.[5]

There are three exceptions to the general principle that courts do not have the power to award aliment in cases where a maintenance calculation could be made. These are:

- where the award represents a "top up".[6] This occurs where the non-resident parent has more than enough assessable income to met the maximum child maintenance allowance under the 1991 Act and the court is satisfied that the circumstances of the case make it appropriate for an award to be made under the 1985 Act;

---

99 ss.28A–28F of the 1991 Act (added by the Child Support Act 1995, ss.1–6, and substituted and amended by the CSPSSA 2000, s.5).

1 ss.11 and 13 of the 1991 Act.

2 s.8 of the 1991 Act. Note that there is no need for a calculation to have been made for the court's jurisdiction to be ousted.

3 *Park v Park*, 2000 S.L.T. (Sh. Ct) 65; *Macdonald v Macdonald*, 1998 Fam. L.B. 31–4.

4 1991 Act, s.44(1). Note that Crown servants and ex-patriots working abroad for UK companies are now within the scope of the 1991 Act through s.44(2A) (added by s.22 of the CSPSSA 2000).

5 ss.8(3A) and 4(10), 1991 Act.

6 s.8(6).

- where the award is made solely for the purpose of meeting some or all of the expenses incurred by a child in receiving instruction at an educational establishment or undergoing teaching for a trade, profession or vocation[7];
- where the child is disabled and the order is made solely for the purpose of meeting some or all of the expenses due to the disability[8];
- where parties seek to convert an agreement into a court order.[9]

Key Concepts

Property is generally subject to the **separate property rule** that provides that marriage shall not of itself affect the property rights of the spouses.

Most couples buying a **home** take title in **joint names**, but where they do not, it is only the person whose name is **recorded in the disposition** who is treated as the owner in law.

Spouses are obliged to **aliment** one another, to provide such support as is **reasonable in the circumstances** having regard to the needs and resources of the parties, their earning capacities, and all the circumstances of the case.

Children have a right to **financial support** from **both parents**, whether or not the parents are or have been married to one another and whether or not they live together or apart.

The **Child Support Act 1991** creates a new administrative scheme for assessing and enforcing **maintenance** owed by a parent to a "qualifying" child.

A **maintenance calculation** in respect of a child may arise either **voluntarily** or **compulsorily**.

DOMESTIC VIOLENCE AND THE FAMILY HOME

13–53 One exception to the general principle that marriage has no effect on the property rights of the spouses is provided by the Matrimonial Homes (Family Protection) (Scotland) Act 1981. Only the person who own property or holds title to it is entitled to possess it, occupy it and alienate it by sale or gift. Thus, in principle the person who owns the family home has the power to evict any other occupants and to interdict them from returning to the premises.[10] Clearly these kind of rights can cause hardship in the domestic sphere. Particular concern arose in the 1970s after a number of studies showed that domestic violence was a prevalent and increasing problem. Domestic violence continues to concern the Scottish Executive today who have targeted it as a key area for action following on from the Zero Tolerance Campaign that was launched throughout Scotland in 1994.

Studies documenting violence and abuse identified a number of key areas for concern.[11]

---

7 s.8(7)

8 s.8(8).

9 s.8(5). *Otto v Otto*, 2002 Fam. L.R. 95. Note that existence of court order prevents later application to Child Support Agency.

10 In *Millar v Millar*, 1940 S.C. 56 a wife who let property gave her husband notice to quit and the court upheld her action. In *Maclure v Maclure*, 1911 S.C. 200 a husband who was the sole tenant of the family home was granted an interdict to exclude his drunken wife from the premises.

11 *Report from the Select Committee on Violence in Marriage* (1974–75 H.C. 533) and the *Observations* on that report (Cmnd.6690 (1976)).

- If a violent partner was the sole owner of the home (and most perpetrators of such violence are male) than he had the sole right to occupy and thus to eject all other inhabitants of the house is he pleased, *e.g.* as a reprisal for calling out police because of assault. If the victim left the house she would have no right to re-enter the family home against his will.

This had implications for women, namely:

- that they might be rendered homeless, or forced to accept sub-standard accommodation for themselves and their children; and
- that for this reason many women put up with abuse or violence because they did not have anywhere suitable to go.

These findings made a great impression on both English and Scottish Law Commissions and led to immediate legislation drafted to deal with the situation. In Scotland this took the form of the Matrimonial Homes (Family Protection) (Scotland) Act 1981. The Act has two main aims:

(1) to provide a spouse who has no legal right to live in the home with that right (and to extend this to a limited extent to cohabitees); and
(2) to provide increased protection for spouse and children (and to a limited extent a cohabitee) who is at risk from domestic violence or abuse.

To achieve these ends, the Act is framed around rights to occupy and to exclude a violent party from the family home. It confers occupancy rights together with various subsidiary and ancillary rights and remedies[12] on a spouse who is not the owner or tenant of the matrimonial home, referred to as a "non-entitled spouse" (NES).[13] The spouse who owns, is the tenant of, or who is permitted by a third party to occupy the property, is the "entitled spouse" (ES).[14] What counts as a matrimonial home is broadly defined to include:

> "Any house, caravan, household or other structure which has been provided or made available by one or both spouse as a family residence (or which, having been provided or made available by one or both of the spouses, has become a family residence)."[15]

Under this definition, parties may have more than one matrimonial home. It does not apply, however, where parties are separated and one spouse has bought the property for the other to live in.[16]

Occupancy rights of non-entitled spouse

A NES has the right (a) if in occupation, to continue to occupy the matrimonial home, and (b) a right, if not in occupation to enter into and occupy the matrimonial home. The rights arise through marriage and need not be applied for and they may be exercised together with any child of the family. A child is defined as "any child or grandchild of either spouse, and any person who has been brought up treated by either spouse as if he or she were a child of that spouse".[17] This definition covers step-children and has no age restriction so that it covers adult children. **13–54**

In order to uphold or enforce these rights an NES must apply to the court. An NES who has been refused entry to the matrimonial home may exercise the right to enter and occupy the home only with the leave of the court.[18] Either spouse may apply to the court for an order declaring, enforcing or restricting occupancy rights or regulating their exercise or protecting the rights of the applicant spouse in relation to the other spouse.[19] The court must make an order declaring the

---

[12] Some of these affect a spouse's ability to enter into property transactions, see s.2 of the 1981 Act.
[13] s.1(1).
[14] s.1(2).
[15] s.22.
[16] s.22.
[17] s.22
[18] s.3(1).
[19] s.3(1).

rights of the applicant spouse if the application relates to a matrimonial home. Otherwise, the court has discretion to make such orders as it considers just and reasonable.[20] In reaching its decision it is directed to have regard to all circumstances of the case including the conduct of the spouses, their respective needs and financial resources, the needs of any child of the family, the use of the matrimonial home in relation to any trade, business or profession of either spouse, and whether the entitled spouse has offered suitable alternative accommodation to the NES.[21] The court can grant interim orders pending a decision on regulation of occupancy rights.[22] It also has the power to grant an NES the possession or use of furniture and plenishings in the matrimonial home where these are owned or hired by the ES.[23]

In order to protect these occupancy rights, the NES is also granted various subsidiary rights under the Act. These include a right to make payment of outgoings,[24] *e.g.* rent, rates, mortgage payments, and to perform obligations incumbent on the ES (other than non-essential repairs and improvements),[25] to enforce performance of an obligation given by a third party to the ES,[26] to carry out essential repairs and to take other steps to protect his or her occupancy rights.[27] An NES who wishes to carry out non-essential repairs or improvements must seek authorisation from the court.[28] The court has power to apportion expenditure between the spouses on anything relating to the matrimonial home.[29] The court also has power to enable non-essential repairs to be carried out and to apportion expenditure where both spouses are entitled.[30]

While the court has a whole range of powers to enforce, restrict and protect the occupancy rights of the NES it may not make an order that would have the effect of excluding the non-applicant spouse from the matrimonial home. This is because this would be a derogation from the common law rights of the proprietor to occupy his or her own property, which requires a special statutory exclusion order as provided for under s.4 of the 1981 Act.

Exclusion orders

13–55 Section 4 of the 1981 Act gives the court power to exclude a spouse whether ES or NES from the matrimonial home. Thus either spouse, whether or not in occupation, may apply to the court for an exclusion order suspending the occupancy rights of the other spouse.[31] Under s.4(2) the court must make an order:

> "If it appears to the court that the making of the order is *necessary* for the protection of the applicant or of any child of the family from any conduct *or threatened or reasonably apprehended conduct* of the non-applicant spouse which is *or would be* injurious to the physical *or* mental health of the applicant or child." [Emphasis added.]

However, it is also directed under s.4(3)(a) that it shall *not* make such an order if it would be unjustified or unreasonable having regard to all the circumstances including the s.3(3) factors set out above. In the particular case of a matrimonial home which is, or forms part of, an agricultural holding,[32] or is a tied house,[33] there are further reasons given why a court should not make an exclusion order.

---

20 s.3(3).
21 s.3(3)(a)–(e). Conduct relates to the spouses' conduct in occupying the matrimonial home: *Berry v Berry*, 1988 S.L.T. 650.
22 s.3(4).
23 s.3(5).
24 s.2(1)(a).
25 s.2(1)(b) and (2).
26 s.2(1) and (2).
27 s.2(1)(d) and (f).
28 s.2(1)(e).
29 s.2(3). In doing so the court must have regard to the respective financial circumstances of the parties.
30 s.2(4). This extends the common law right of co-owners to carry out only essential repairs without the other party's consent.
31 s.4(1).
32 Defined in Agricultural Holdings (Scotland) Act 1991.

In reaching a decision about whether to grant an exclusion order, the court has been directed to consider four questions:

- What is the nature and quality of the alleged conduct?
- Is the court satisfied that the conduct is likely to be repeated if cohabitation continues?
- Has the conduct been or, if repeated, would it be injurious to the physical or mental health of the applicant or to any child of the family?
- If so, is the order sought *necessary* for the future protection of the physical or mental health of the applicant or child.[34]

There is provision for interim suspension of occupancy rights pending the making of an exclusion order, subject to the opportunity being afforded to the non-applicant spouse to contest the application.[35] Initially the courts took a very restrictive view of s.4[36] but subsequent case law has overridden the earlier decisions[37] However, the court must still consider whether the lesser protection of an interdict regulating the conduct of the non-applicant spouse towards the applicant spouse would be insufficient or inappropriate when deciding whether or not to make an order.[38] The role of the court under the 1981 Act is not to act as arbiter over the spouses' arrangements for sharing the matrimonial home, nor to provide relief to one spouse who no longer wishes to live with the other; but rather to provide protection where one spouse is genuinely causing, or in danger of causing, injury of some kind to the other spouse or child of the family. The injury complained of should therefore derive directly from the acts of the defender spouse, and not just be stress or unhappiness generally induced by the breakdown of the marriage.[39]

Other orders

Where the court grants an exclusion order it *must* grant the following orders: **13–56**

(a) a warrant for the summary ejection of the non-applicant spouse;
(b) an interdict prohibiting the excluded spouse from entering the matrimonial home without the express permission of the applicant; and
(c) an interdict prohibiting the non-applicant spouse from recovering any furniture or plenishings from the house except with the consent of the other spouse or by further order of the court.

In the case of (a) and (c) however the defender spouse can plead that the order is unnecessary. In addition, the court *may* grant certain other orders,[40] including importantly, an interdict prohibiting the other spouse "from entering or remaining in a specified area in the vicinity of the matrimonial home".[41] This may be particularly useful as the protection that can be afforded by s.4(4) alone is limited. Orders made under that section cannot prevent a husband entering a house bought or rented after separation which is not a matrimonial home, nor a refuge where a spouse is staying temporarily, nor a spouse's place of work, nor the school which the parties' children attend. These are all areas, as experience demonstrates, where couples are likely to come into contact and where one party me be vulnerable and put at risk. However the protection offered by a s.4(5) interdict may still prove inadequate as it all depends on the interpretation of what is "in the vicinity" of the matrimonial home.

---

33 s.4(3)(b)(ii).
34 These questions were set out in *McCafferty v McCafferty*, 1986 S.L.T. 650 at 656.
35 s.4(6).
36 *Bell v Bell*, 1983 S.L.T. 224; *Smith v Smith*, 1983 S.L.T. 275.
37 *Colagiacomo v Colagiacomo*, 1983 S.L.T. 559; *Brown v Brown*, 1985 S.L.T. 376 and see *McCafferty*, above.
38 *Roberton v Roberton*, 1999 S.L.T. 38.
39 *Matheson v Matheson*, 1986 S.L.T. (Sh. Ct) 2.
40 s.4(5).
41 s.4(5)(a).

Matrimonial interdicts and powers of arrest

13–57 The existing common law remedy of interdict has been strengthened by the introduction in the legislation of particular "matrimonial interdicts". The term is used in the Act to denote an interdict which under s.14(2):

(a) restrains or prohibits any conduct of one spouse towards the other spouse or a child of the family; or
(b) prohibits a spouse from entering or remaining in a matrimonial home or n a specified area in the vicinity of the matrimonial home.[42]

Section 14(2)(b) cannot be used as a method of removing a spouse from the matrimonial home which can be achieved only by an exclusion order.[43] The Act requires a power of arrest to be attached to matrimonial interdicts where an application to attach such a power is made and where the non-applicant spouse has had an opportunity to contest it, unless it appears to the court that in all the circumstances of the case such a power is unnecessary.[44] There is no discretion to refuse to attach a power of arrest to any matrimonial interdict ancillary to an exclusion order.[45] Intimation of a power of arrest requires to be made to the police, after which any police officer may arrest the non applicant spouse without warrant on having reasonable cause to suspect a breach of the interdict.[46] A power of arrest continues to have effect until the marriage terminates.[47]

Third party dealings

13–58 The 1981 Act does not confer ownership of the matrimonial home on the NES. This means that an ES is free to sell the home. In order to protect the NES in this situation the Act provides that, as a general rule, the continued exercise by an NES of his occupancy rights is not to be prejudiced by reason only of any dealing by the ES relating to the home and a third party is not by reason of such dealings entitled to occupy the matrimonial home or any part of it.[48] Relevant dealings include the sale or lease of a home.[49] However, there are certain situations in which this general protection does not apply, where the ES occupies the home by the permission of a third party, or along with a third party,[50] or where the ES has consented to the dealing or renounced his or her occupancy rights.[51] The NES also loses protection where the ES sells to a third party who has acted in food faith *and* has either been presented with an affidavit by the seller declaring that the property is not a matrimonial home,[52] *or* a renunciation of occupancy rights *or* consent to the dealing by the NES.[53]

---

[42] s.14(1) makes clear that the application can competently be made while the parties are living together as husband and wife.
[43] *Tattersall v* Tattersall, 1983 S.L.T. 506. But note that where a spouse is an ES he or she may apply to the court for an interdict under s.14(2)(b) with powers of arrest attached.
[44] s.15(1)(b).
[45] s.15(1)(a).
[46] s.15(3) and (4).
[47] s.15(2).
[48] s.6(1).
[49] s.6(2).
[50] s.6(2).
[51] s.6(3)(a). Note that the court also has power to dispense with the NES' consents, s.7(1).
[52] In such a case the NES may be entitled to "such compensation as the court in the circumstances considers just and reasonable" under s.3(7).
[53] s.6(3)(e).

Transfer of tenancy

Where a matrimonial home is occupied under a lease, the court has power, on application by the NES, to make an order transferring the tenancy of the matrimonial home to that spouse.[54] It may also provide for the payment of such compensation to the ES as seems just and reasonable in all the circumstances of the case.[55] Where an application is made under s.13 the court is directed to have regard to all the circumstances of the case including the suitability of the applicant to become tenant and the applicant's capacity to perform the obligations under the lease.[56] The landlord of the property must be given an opportunity to contest the application for transfer and will in any event be notified of any order made.[57] Where the court makes an order the tenancy vests immediately in the transferee and the transferee becomes subject to all the liabilities under the lease, except of arrears of rent, which remain the liability of the transferor.[58] While all other rights under the Act terminate when the marriage comes to an end, the court retains the power to transfer a tenancy under s.13, on decree of divorce[59] or nullity of marriage.[60] **13–59**

Cohabitees

The protections afforded to adults under the 1981 Act are dependant upon them having marital status. However domestic violence and abuse is not restricted to married couples. For this reason the Act provides certain more limited protections for cohabiting couples.[61] In order to qualify as a cohabiting couple the parties must be "a man and a woman who are living with each other as if they were man and wife".[62] In determining the issue the court is expressly directed to consider all the circumstances of the case, including the length of the cohabitation and whether there are any children of the relationship.[63] Unlike spouses, cohabitees do not have automatic occupancy rights but must apply to the court to have them declared. Where an application is made the court has no power to make an interim order.[64] This means that a cohabitee who wishes to exclude a violent partner under s.4 of the Act must first raise an action for full occupancy rights, which, due to the procedure involved, may take several months. Where the application is granted the court can only make an order for a limited period of up to six months, initially, that may be extended on application for further six month periods.[65] When it comes to a transfer of tenancy the court can only make such an order in favour of the non-entitled partner if that party has been granted occupancy rights by the court, or to either partner, if both are entitled to jointly occupy the home (*e.g.* as joint tenants).[66] A major oversight arises under the Act where a home shared by a cohabiting couple is owned or tenanted solely by one partner and it is the *entitled* partner who wishes to exclude the *non-entitled* partner from the home.[67] In such a case this will not be possible as s.18(4) expressly provides that only a non-entitled partner with occupancy rights or a jointly entitled partner can apply for a s.4 exclusion order. **13–60**

54 s.13.
55 s.13(1).
56 s.13(9).
57 s.13(4) and (6).
58 s.13(5).
59 s.13(2)(a).
60 s.13(2)(b).
61 Only ss.2–5(1), 13–18 and 22 apply to cohabiting couples. The provisions relating to dealing under s.6 do not apply.
62 s.18(1). Given this wording a same sex couple cannot come within the definition of a cohabiting couple.
63 s.18(2).
64 *Smith-Milne v Gammack*, 1995 S.C.L.R. 1085.
65 s.18(1).
66 ss.13 and 18(4).
67 See *Clarke v Hatten*, 1987 S.C.L.R. 527.

Termination of rights under the 1981 act

13–61 Rights under the 1981 Act will cease to exist where:

- the marriage comes to an end by death or divorce (except where a transfer of tenancy is concerned)[68];
- where the entitled spouse ceases to be entitled[69];
- where the NES consents to the dealing or renounces his or her occupancy rights[70];
- the NES's occupancy rights are protected under s.6 and he or she ceases to occupy the matrimonial home. The non-entitled spouse's rights under s.6 do not operate where the ES has permanently ceased to be entitled to occupy the home in question and for a continuous period of five years thereafter the NES has not occupied the home.[71]

Limitations of the 1981 Act

13–62 The 1981 Act is limited in dealing with violence because it only applies to married couples, and to a limited extent, heterosexual cohabiting couples. Its provisions do not apply to same sex couples, divorced spouses, non-cohabiting partners or other family members yet these persons may be just as much at risk from domestic abuse or violence. One of the advantages of having a matrimonial interdict with powers of arrest is that it enables the police to arrest the non-applicant spouse without warrant, where they have reasonable cause for suspecting that spouse of being in breach of the interdict.[72] This means that the police do not need to wait for a breach of the ordinary criminal law to have occurred, or be suspected, before the power of arrest can be exercised by a constable, as it will be sufficient for a constable to take immediate action removing the violent or abusive person from the scene where he or she forms the view that an actual or suspected breach of interdict has occurred.[73] This advantage is lost where a marriage ends because the interdict with its powers of arrest will fall. Concern about the inadequate protection afforded to individuals at risk of abuse from other individuals and a desire to give the police more powers to protect such individuals led to the passing of the Protection From Abuse (Scotland) Act 2001.

Protection From Abuse (Scotland) Act 2001

13–63 This Act extends the range of interdicts to which powers of arrest may be attached. Under its provisions, applicants no longer need to demonstrate any particular personal relationship to an alleged abuser. Instead the court simply has to find that granting the power of arrest is necessary to protect the applicant from the risk of abuse through a breach of interdict. Those currently excluded from using the 1981 Act, noted above, may now use the 2001 Act to have powers of arrest attached to an interdict that has been obtained or is being sought to provide protection from abuse. Such an order may be obtained from either the Court of Session or the Sheriff Court.[74] Abuse under the Act is widely defined to cover psychological as well as physical abuse. It includes conduct, which need not be active, and which covers a relatively wide category of behaviour including presence in a specified place or area.[75] Thus interdicts with powers of arrest may be granted in situations that are not presently covered by s.4(5) of the1981 Act dealing with an

---

68 ss.1(1) and 5(1)(a).
69 As the NES right's under the 1981 Act are derived from the ES's rights it follows that where the ES ceases to have such rights those of the NES must fall. However, s.6 proves an exception to this rule.
70 s.6(3)(i) and (ii) and s.6(3)(e).
71 s.6(3)(f). *Stevenson v Roy*, 2002 S.L.T. 445.
72 s.15(3).
73 s.15(3).
74 s.7.
75 s.7.

applicant's place of work, for example, or the children's school. Unlike the 1981 Act, power of arrest are limited and can only last for three years although an application for extension can be made.[76] The three year life span runs from the time of the power being granted and not from the time of the power having effect. Powers of arrest will also terminate on recall or variation of the interdict. Those individuals who already possess an interdict with powers of arrest under the 1981 cannot apply for an order under the 2001 Act. Similarly, the 1981 Act is out of bounds for those who have been granted a power of arrest under the 2001 Act.

Protection From Harassment Act 1997

Another way of regulating abusive or violent conduct is to utilise the provisions of the Protection **13–64**
From Harassment Act 1997. This Act makes it an offence to pursue a course of conduct amounting to harassment of a person. Where this occurs a civil delict is created in Scotland against which an order restraining harassment may be sought. In this context "conduct" is broadly defined to include speech[77] and that harassment includes "causing the person alarm or distress".[78] Where an application is made to the court it may award damages as well as granting an interdict or interim interdict. Damages may include damages for any anxiety caused by the harassment or any financial loss arsing from it. The court may also, if appropriate, issue a "non-harassment order". Where such an order is made and breached the party breaching it is guilty of an offence and may be liable to imprisonment, or to a fine, or both.

Key Concepts

One **exception** to the general principle that marriage has no effect on the property rights of the spouses is provided by the **Matrimonial Homes (Family Protection) (Scotland) Act 1981**. The Act is framed around **rights to occupy** and to exclude a violent party from the **family home**.

The **1981 Act** also provides limited protections for "cohabiting couples". In order to qualify as a **cohabiting couple** the parties must be "a man and a woman who are living with each other as if they were man and wife".

PROPERTY ON DIVORCE AND TERMINATION OF NON-MARITAL RELATIONSHIPS

Grounds for divorce

Under Scots law marriage cannot be terminated until death,[79] except by divorce. Where married **13–65**
couples wish to apply the provisions dealing with financial provision at the end of a relationship, under the Family Law (Scotland) Act 1985, they must get a divorce. This is now regulated by the Divorce (Scotland) Act 1976 that provides for divorce on the "irretrievable breakdown of

---

[76] s.2.

[77] s.8(3).

[78] s.8(3).

[79] On death a surviving spouse is entitled to prior rights under the Succession (Scotland) Act 1964 where a spouse dies without making a will. Where a deceased spouse makes a will, the surviving spouse may still claim legal rights if he or she is disinherited or decides to reject any testamentary provision under the 1964 Act. These provisions do not apply to unmarried cohabiting couples although the Scottish Executive has endorsed proposals by the Scottish Law Commission to provide some discretionary benefit in limited circumstances. See *Parents and Children: A White Paper on Scottish Family Law* (2000), para.7.4(i).

marriage".[80] This ground can only be established, however, if one of the five following conditions are met:

- the adultery of the defender[81];
- the behaviour of the defender is of such a kind that the pursuer cannot reasonably be expected to cohabit with him[82];
- desertion of the pursuer by the defender for a period of two years[83];
- non-cohabitation for a period of two years combined with the defender's consent to divorce,[84] and
- non-cohabitation for a period of five years.[85]

This means that a pursuer will be unable to obtain a divorce even where the marriage has in fact irretrievably broken down if he or she is unable to prove one of the facts above.[86] The court does have power to continue the action if it seems that there is a reasonable prospect of reconciliation[87] but this power is rarely, if ever, used. A divorce may be raised in either the Sheriff Court or the Court of Session,[88] provided the Scottish courts have jurisdiction: (a) under the Council Regulation on jurisdiction and the recognition and enforcement of judgments in matrimonial matters and in matters of parental responsibility for children of both spouses[89]; or (b) the action is an excluded action and either of the parties to the marriage is domiciled in Scotland on the date when the action is begun.[90] Proof is on a balance of probabilities.[91]

General scheme of financial provision on divorce

13–66 Financial provision on divorce is now governed by the Family Law (Scotland) Act 1985.[92] Orders for financial provision on divorce can generally[93] only be made by the court on granting decree of divorce or within a period specified by the court on granting decree of divorce.[94] The court is directed, where an application for financial provision has been made, to make such order, if any, as is: (a) justified by the principles set out in s.9 of the Act[95]; and (b) reasonable having regard to the parties' resources.[96] The five principles are:

---

80 s.1(1).
81 s.1(2)(a).
82 s.1(2)(b). The Scottish Executive has consulted on whether the grounds of adultery and unreasonable behavior should be merged in divorce reforms put forward by SLC, Consultation Paper, *Parents and Children: A White Paper on Scottish Family Law* (2000), paras 4.1–4.11.
83 s.1(2)(c). The SLC has recommended abolition of this ground, *Report on the Reform of the Ground for Divorce* (Scot. Law Com. No.116).
84 s.1(2)(d). The SLC has recommended reducing the period to one year, *ibid*.
85 s.1(2)(e). The SCL has recommended reducing this period to two years, see note 4, above.
86 For detailed discussion of the grounds of divorce see Edwards and Grifiths, *Family Law* (1997) pp.375–392.
87 s.2(1).
88 Divorce Jurisdiction, Court Fees and Legal Aid (Scotland) Act 1983, s.1.
89 Council Regulation 1347/2000/EC [2000] O.J. L160.
90 Domicile and Matrimonial Proceedings Act 1973 (DMPA), s.7(2A)(a) and (b) (as amended by the European Communities (Matrimonial Jurisdiction and Judgments) (Scotland) Regulations 2001 (SSI 2001/36), reg.2. Note that in the case of the Sheriff Court, either party must, in addition, be resident in the sheriffdom for a period of 40 days ending with that date or have been resident in the sheriffdom for a period of not less than 40 days ending not more than 40 days before the said date and have no known residence in Scotland at that date. DMPA 1973, s.8(2)(b).
91 s.1(6).
92 These provisions also apply to actions for declarator of nullity of marriage under s.17 of the 1985 Act.
93 There are two exceptions. Under s.13(1)(c) periodical allowance can be applied for after divorce where no order was made at the time and there has been a change of circumstances since the date of decree. Under s.14(10) and (3) dealing with incidental orders, 8 out of the 10 may be made before, on or after decree of divorce is granted to refused.
94 s.12(1).
95 s.8(2)(a).
96 s.8(2)(b).

- fair sharing of net value of matrimonial property[97];
- redressing imbalance of economic advantages and disadvantages[98];
- fair sharing of child care burden[99];
- adjustment for loss of support[1]; and
- relief of serious economic hardship.[2]

Fair sharing of matrimonial property

Matrimonial property is defined as: **13–67**

> "all the property belonging to the parties or either of them at the relevant date which was acquired by them or him (otherwise than by way of gift or succession from a third party)—
> (a) before the marriage for use by them as a family home or as furniture or plenishing for such a home; or
> (b) during the marriage but before the relevant date."

It is crucial to note that matrimonial property includes all property acquired during the relevant period by *either* or *both* spouses (subject to the stated exceptions), regardless of whether one or both parties had legal title to the property in question during the subsistence of the marriage. One of two dates may qualify as the "relevant date"; either the date on which the parties cased to cohabit,[3] or the date of service of the summons in the divorce action,[4] whichever one is the earlier.[5] Parties cease to cohabit only when they cease in fact to live together as man and wife.[6] The fact that parties live together in the same house does not necessarily mean that they are still "cohabiting" for the purposes of the Act.[7] The definition has been seen to include a claim for damages for personal injuries sustained during the marriage,[8] a potential claim against dismissal from employment[9] and a claim for criminal injuries compensation.[10] It also includes a refund of income tax paid by one party during the marriage if the refund is paid after the relevant date,[11] although a redundancy payment received after the relevant date will not be so classified.[12]

Pension and other rights

The 1985 Act expressly provides that rights to, or interest in, pension schemes or life policies and similar arrangements fall within the definition of matrimonial property.[13] The proportion of the pension rights which fall into matrimonial property at the relevant date is calculated according to a formula set out in reg.3 of the Divorce etc. (Pensions) (Scotland) Regulations 1966.[14] This involves an apportionment of the total value of the pensions rights over the time of the marriage, according to a formula: **13–68**

---

97 s.9(1)(a).
98 s.9(1)(b).
99 s.9(1)(c).
1 s.9(1)(d).
2 s.9(1)(e).
3 s.10(3)(a).
4 s.19(3)(b).
5 s.10(3).
6 s.27(2).
7 *Buczynska v Buczynski*, 1989 S.L.T. 558.
8 *Skarpaas v Skarpaas*, 1993 S.L.T. (Sh. Ct) 343.
9 *Louden v Louden*, 1994 A.L.T. 381.
10 *McGuire v McGuire's Curator Bonis*, 1991 S.L.T. (Sh. Ct) 76.
11 *MacRitchie v MacRitchie*, 1994 S.L.T. (Sh. Ct) 72.
12 *Smith v Smith*, 1989 S.L.T. 688.
13 s.10(5).
14 SI 1966/1901as amended by the Divorce etc. (Pensions) (Scotland) Amendment Regulations 1997 (SI 1997/745).

Key Concepts

Pension Apportionment

$$\frac{A \times B}{C}$$

Where: **A** is the value of the pension rights at the "relevant date"

B is the period during the marriage when the party is a member of the pension scheme

C is the total period of membership of the scheme before the relevant date

Valuation of pension and other rights is done according to the cash equivalent transfer value (CETV) at the relevant date.[15]

Under s.12A[16] the courts have power to "earmark" a proportion or fixed lump sum amount of the pension for the benefit of the non-members spouse, payable at the date when the pension matures. Such a "pension lump sum order"[17] can be ordered by the courts when making an order for a capital sum but is ordered against the trustees or managers of the pension scheme of the payee spouse, rather than against the spouse him- or herself. The court's power to make such an order only arises if it is making a capital sum order, not an order for a periodical allowance. Where made it *does not accelerate payment* so that the member and non-member spouses will receive payment only when the pension right becomes due, normally on the retirement or earlier death of the member spouse. However, it is now possible for the spouses to share a pension when it matures.[18] This is done by the parties reaching agreement (a qualifying agreement)[19] or by obtaining a pension sharing order under s.8(1)(baa) of the 1985 Act.[20] Where there is to be pension sharing the court cannot make a pension lump sum order under s.12A of the 1985 Act.[21] The advantage of these options is that they do not require any immediate payment out of available resources. The idea is that on divorce the transferor spouse's shareable rights in his or her pension arrangement are subject to a debit of the appropriate amount and the transferee spouse becomes entitled to a credit of that amount which is enforceable against he person responsible or running the pension scheme.[22] The pension credit can then be used to purchase rights in the pension arrangement in the transferee's own name. The pension will become payable when the transferee retires. Before a qualifying agreement is signed, the transferor must have intimated his intention to share his or her pension rights with the transferee to the managers of his or her pension fund. Such agreements must be registered in the Books of Council and Session and cannot be made after the parties have divorced. Alternatively, the court can make a pension sharing order which will specify the percentage value or the amount to be deducted from the transferor's pension rights.[23] On divorce, the spouses send the decree,[24] the qualifying agreement or pension order to the pension scheme managers so that pension sharing can be effected.

---

15 There was some doubt as to ether the court was obliged in terms of the earlier regulations to use the "cash equivalent" figure in valuing benefits at the relevant date for divorce proceedings raised between August 19, 1996 and December 1, 2000. The Divorce etc. (Pensions) (Scotland) Regulations 2000 (SSI 2000/112) now make it clear that for all divorce actions commencing after December 1, 2000 that it is the cash equivalent value that should be applied.

16 Added by s.167(3) of the Pensions Act 1995.

17 Welfare Reform and Pensions Act 1999 (WRPA), s.28(1)(f); Pensions on Divorce etc. (Pension Sharing) (Scotland) Regulations 2000 (SI 2000/1051), regs 3 and 5.

18 This does not apply to state pensions.

19 Welfare Reform and Pensions Act 1999 (WRPA), s.28(1)(f); Pensions on Divorce etc (Pension Sharing) (Scotland) Regulations 2000, S.I. 2000/1051, regs 3 and 5.

20 The order is defined in the 1985 Act, s.27 (as amended by WRPA 1999, s.20).

21 s.8(4), (5) and (6) of the 1985 Act (added by WRPA 1999,ss.28(6) and 84 and Sch.12, para.6.

22 WRPA 1999, s.29.

23 1985 Act, s.27 (as amended by WRPA 1999, s.20(3)).

24 Within two months of the extract decree.

Excluded from definition of matrimonial property

Property will not fall within the definition of matrimonial property where: **13–69**

- Property is acquired *before* marriage,[25] except (a) where it is acquired for use as a family home,[26] or (b) where property acquired before marriage changes its original form, *e.g.* is sold and thus through acquiring a new form becomes matrimonial property.[27]
- Property is inherited or a gift (unless to both parties), unless it changes its original form, in which case it will become matrimonial property.[28]
- It represents an increase or decrease in value of the matrimonial property since the relevant date.[29] The rule applies whether or not the property is owned by one spouse or both of them jointly and does not amount to a "special circumstance" justifying a departure from the norm of fair sharing.[30] Where property is jointly owned the court may make an order for division and sale so that any increase in value after the relevant date can be divided equally between the parties as joint owners.[31]

Net value

It is the *net* value of the matrimonial property that is to be divided so that any debts incurred during the marriage (or before marriage where these relate to matrimonial property) that are still outstanding at the relevant date, *e.g.* mortgage, must be deducted. After the net value of the property has been calculated it is to be shared fairly, that is equally between the parties.[32] **13–70**

Special circumstances[33]

However, there are special circumstances[34] where the court may depart from the norm of equal sharing. The following are listed in the Act but are not exhaustive[35]: **13–71**

- the terms of any agreement on ownership or sale[36];
- the source of funds or assets used to acquire the property if not derived from the income or efforts of the parties during the marriage[37];
- any destruction, dissipation or alienation of property by either party[38];
- the nature of the property and the use made of it and the extent to which it is reasonable to expect it to be realised or divided or used as security[39]; and
- actual or prospective liability for expenses of valuation or transfer in connection with the divorce.[40]

---

25 *MacLellan v MacLellan*, 1988 S.C.L.R. 399.
26 s.10(4).
27 *Davidson v Davidson*, 1994 S.L.T. 506. See also *Jacques v Jacques*, 1997 S.L.T. 963. But note that in some cases it may be subject to departure from the norm of equal sharing, s.10(6).
28 *Whittome v Whittome (No.1)*, 1994 S.L.T. 114.
29 In *Wallis v Wallis*, 1993 S.C. (H.L.) 49, the House of Lords held that any increase or decrease in the value of matrimonial property between the relevant date and the date of divorce must be left out of account in determining what amounts to fair sharing of the property.
30 *Wallis v Wallis*, 1993 S.C. (H.L.) 49.
31 *Jacques v Jacques*, 1997 S.C. (H.L.) 20.
32 s.10(1).
33 s.10(6)(e).
34 s.10(6).
35 *Cunniff v Cunniff*, 1999 S.C. 537 at 540.
36 s.10(6)(a).
37 s.10(6)(b).
38 s.10(6)(c).
39 s.10(6)(d).

It is important to note that although these circumstances might justify departure from equal sharing, they cannot *require* it: where the circumstances cited are of negligible significance, or opposing special circumstances counterbalance each other, then equal division may be allowed to stand.[41]

In reaching a decision as to whether or not special circumstances apply to divert from equal sharing in any particular case, the court is expressly directed to ignore the issue of conduct on the part of either spouse unless it has adversely affected relevant financial sources.[42] Amoral behaviour is not relevant as "special circumstances" per se but the financial consequences of that behaviour are, *e.g.* where spouse has gambled away the assets of the marriage.

Economic advantage and disadvantage and contributions

13–72 This principle is designed to deal with the situation where one spouse (the "homemaker" spouse) has given up or reduced his or her career prospects to care for the other spouse and, possibly the children of the family, the other spouse (the "wage-earner" spouse) has continued to work and benefited from this arrangement in terms of earnings and career advancement. In these circumstances a capital settlement based on equal sharing of the matrimonial property may not be sufficient to compensate for the long-term economic disadvantage the homemaker spouse may have suffered in terms of career prospects, earnings level, and associated benefits, such as occupational pension rights. For this reason the 1985 Act provides that, in addition to the principle of fair sharing under s.9(1)(a), the court must also consider:

> "Fair account should be taken of any economic advantage derived by either party from contributions by the other, and of any economic disadvantage suffered by either party in the interests of the other party or of the family."[43]

"Economic advantage" extends to include any advantage gained before or during the marriage, and includes gains in capital, income and earning capacity, while "economic disadvantage" is defined as the converse.[44] "Contributions" are defined to include any contributions made before or after the marriage[45] and expressly cover indirect and non-financial contribution, in particular, any such contributions made by looking after the family home or caring for the family.[46]

However, in practice, the courts have tended to be reluctant to make awards under this section. This is because they are instructed when applying s.9(1)(b) to take into account the extent to which:

(a) the economic advantages or disadvantages sustained by either party have been balanced by the economic advantages or disadvantages sustained by the other party; and
(b) any resulting imbalance has been or will be corrected by a sharing of the matrimonial property or otherwise.[47]

It is often successfully argued that either the advantages and disadvantages suffered or gained by the spouses have balanced themselves out,[48] or that any imbalance has been sufficiently accommodated through the equal sharing of matrimonial property under s.9(1)(a). The most significant application of this principle has been the award of £100,000 to a wife in addition to a capital sum based on the equal division of matrimonial property.[49]

---

40 s.10(6)(e).
41 *Jacques v Jacques*, 1997 S.C. (H.L.) 20, *per* Lord Clyde at p.24.
42 s.11(7)(a).
43 s.9(1)(b).
44 s.9(2).
45 s.9(2).
46 s.9(2).
47 s.11(2).
48 *Adams v Adams (No.1)*, 1997 S.L.T. 144.
49 See *Wilson v Wilson*, 1999 S.L.L.T. 249 where a farmer's wife obtained a capital sum in respect of her contribution to running a farm which was not matrimonial property and not therefore subject to the rules of fair sharing.

Fair sharing of child care burden

Section 9(1)(c) was intended to ensure that the economic burden of child care is shared fairly between the parties. In practice, this meant that the parent who looked after children aged under 16 received additional financial provision in recognition of the economic burden of child care. Since the Child Support Act 1991 has come into effect the scope and importance of the principle has been reduced, because where maintenance is paid in terms of the formula this includes an element for support of the parent who cares for the child, but it may still be used to justify and additional capital sum payment[50] or transfer of property order.[51] **13–73**

Adjustment from loss of support

Section 9(1)(d) provides that a spouse who has been financially dependent on the other spouse to a substantial degree should be awarded such financial provision as is reasonable to allow him or her to adjust to the loss of that support on divorce, over a period of not more than three years from the date of divorce. What the Act clearly envisages is that for many homemaker spouses the three-year period will provide a transitional stage during which they can retrain or re-enter the labour market with a view to reacquiring financial independence. Section 11(4) lists various factors the court should consider when making an award, including the age, health, earning capacity and level of dependence of the party making the claim, together with any intention he or she has to undergo a course of education or training and the needs and resources of the parties. **13–74**

Relief of serious economic hardship

Section 9(1)(e) requires the court to award such financial provision as is reasonable to relieve a party of serious financial hardship where that is a likely consequence of divorce. Although the hardship must stem from the divorce itself and not any other factor such as illness, it does *not* apparently require (like s.9(1)(d)) that the claimant spouse be financially dependent on the other spouse. In assessing what amounts to "serious" financial hardship, the applicant spouse's access to sources of support other than the spouse including state benefits, must be considered.[52] It is only in very exceptional circumstances that this principle will be relevant. **13–75**

Although conduct is generally ignored it is relevant to s.9(1)(d) and (e) not only where it has affected the financial resources of the marriage, but also where it would be manifestly inequitable to leave it out of account.[53]

Financial orders

Section 8(1) of the Act entitles either party to apply for one or more of the following orders: **13–76**

- an order for the payment of a capital sum[54];
- an order for the transfer of property[55];
- an order for a periodical allowance[56];
- a pension sharing order[57];
- an "earmaking order" under s.12A(2) or (3) of the Act[58]; and

---

[50] *MacLachlan v MacLachlan*, 1998 S.L.T. 693.
[51] See *Cuniff v Cuniff*, 1999 S.C. 537.
[52] s.11(5)(a)and (d).
[53] s.11(7)(b).
[54] s.8(1)(a).
[55] s.8(1)(aa) inserted by the Law Reform (Miscellaneous Provisions) (Scotland) Act 1990, Sch.8, para.34.
[56] s.8(1)(b).
[57] s.8(1)(baa), inserted by the WRPA 1999, s.20

- an incidental order within the meaning of s.14(2) of the Act[59];
- anti-avoidance orders under s.18; and
- enforcement orders under ss.19 and 20.

In dealing with an application for financial provision the court is directed to make such order, if any, as is: (a) justified by the principles set out in s.9 of the Act[60]; and (b) as is reasonable having regard to the parties' resources.[61]

Given that the sole ground for divorce is now irretrievable breakdown of marriage, the principle philosophy underlying the Act is that divorce should be as far as possible a "clean break" between the parties: that is, the former spouses should be free to lead separate lives after divorce, unrestricted by continuing financial obligations to each other. Marriage is seen as a partnership "wound up" by divorce, and ideally, the assets of that partnership should be distributed once and for all on its termination to the former partners in the form of capital, or by a transfer of property. Accordingly, the 1985 Act restricts the making of a periodical allowance award, requiring one spouse to continue to maintain the other after divorce, to occasions where a capital or property transfer award is insufficient to meet the objectives of the Act.[62] Furthermore, the court is given a wide range of powers to make it easier for it to award am equitable clean break settlement, including the power to award capital by instalments[63] and make a property transfer order.[64]

It is important to note that ex-spouses cannot expect any clean break from any *children* of the marriage. While divorce may end the legal relationship between spouses, that between parent and child persists, and the divorce court where it has jurisdiction still to do so since the advent of the Child Support Act 1991, will make such award of aliment of children of the marriage as is justified in the circumstances, before turning to any question of financial provision.[65]

The courts may make an order for periodical allowance only where it can be justified under s.9(1)(c),(d) or (e), and only where a capital sum or property transfer order would be inappropriate or insufficient to meet the demands of s.9 principles, given the resources available to the parties.[66] It is an order for ongoing support not intended to be used as a method of dividing the parties' capital. It may be awarded for a definite or indefinite period,[67] but in any event ceases to have effect on the death or remarriage of the payee.[68] The order may be varied or recalled on a material change of circumstances since the date it was made.[69] While the death or remarriage of the payer does not terminate the award, the former at least is likely to constitute a material change of circumstances justifying a variation.[70] In many marriages it is difficult to order a capital "clean break" settlement because there are few or no liquid assets available at the date of divorce. However, a spouse who has no current access to capital may nonetheless have an expectation of acquiring some at a future date, *e.g.* under an insurance policy, pension scheme or other investment. Alternatively, the paying spouse may have a high enough salary to be able to pay off a capital sum by instalments out of income. The courts are therefore given the power to defer the date of payment of the capital sum,[71] and to order payment of capital by instalments.[72] Otherwise, a capital sum is due and enforceable on decree of divorce being extracted. It is important to note that an order for payment of capital by instalments is quite different from an order for payment of a

---

58 s.8(1)(ba), inserted by the Pensions Act 1995, s.167(1).
59 s.8(1)(c).
60 s.8(2)(a).
61 s.8(2)(b).
62 s.13(2)(a) and (b).
63 s.12(3).
64 s.12(1).
65 See paras 13–47 to 13–51 for discussion of child support and aliment.
66 s.13(2).
67 s.13(3).
68 s.13(7).
69 s.13(4).
70 s.13(7)(a).
71 s.12(4). There is an exception to the rule against variation where they payer is sequestrated within five years of the order, Bankruptcy (Scotland) Act 1985, s.35.
72 s.12(3).

periodical allowance, because although both may be paid out of recurrent income, the amount payable under a capital sum order cannot be varied once made. The courts are, however, empowered to vary the date or method of payment on a material change of circumstances,[73] *e.g.* if an expected pay-out from an investment fails to materialise or if a job is lost or pay-cut imposed.

An order directing the trustees of a pension scheme to pay all or part of a lump sum due to the member, known as an "earmarking order", can only be made by the court on making a capital sum award and will satisfy, at least in part the amount so ordered.[74] In divorce proceedings initiated on or after December 7, 2000, a pension sharing order can provide that one spouse's rights under a specified pension arrangement or state scheme shall be subject to pension sharing for the benefit of the other spouse and will specify the percentage value, or the amount to be transferred.[75] Unlike an earmarking order, pension sharing can be activated by the parties themselves if they enter into a formal agreement in the prescribed form and give intimation to the trustees or managers of the scheme after decree of divorce.[76] Another option open to the courts, and in keeping with the philosophy of a clean break, is to make a property transfer order. The transfer may be stipulated to take place at the date of divorce or at a future specified date,[77] *e.g.* when a child of the marriage reaches 16.

The court has the power to make one or more incidental orders to assist it in implementing its decision under the s.9 principles.[78] Among the court's powers under s.14(2) are the power to:

- order the sale or valuation of property[79];
- to regulate the occupation of the matrimonial home after divorce[80];
- to declare the property rights of the spouse[81];
- to allocate liability for household outgoings after the divorce[82]; and
- to order that security be given in respect of any financial provision ordered.[83]

In general, the court can make any ancillary order which it feels necessary in order to give effect to the s.9 principles.[84] Any incidental order made must be justified under the s.9 principles and be reasonable having regard to the resources of the parties. An incidental order of interest[85] is frequently sought where there is a lapse in time between the date at which payment of a capital sum or transfer of property is ordered, usually the date of divorce, and the date at which the capital is actually paid or the property transferred.

Sometimes a spouse seeks to reduce his or her potential liability to make financial payments to the other spouse on divorce, by giving away property or selling assets at below market value, with the intention of reducing the total value of the matrimonial property or reducing his or her resources at the date of divorce. In order to prevent such fraudulent behaviour, the court may, under s.18, set aside or vary the terms of any transaction or transfer of property which had the effect of defeating a claim for financial provision.[86] The court may in addition make such order in relation to property as it sees fit.[87] Application may be made under s.18 up to a year after the date of divorce.[88] However, transactions or transfers can only be reduced or varied if they have occurred

---

[73] s.12(4).
[74] s.12A(2).
[75] s.27(1) as inserted by the WRPA 1999.
[76] s.28(1)(f), WRPA 1999. See also SI 2000/1051, regs 2 and 3.
[77] s.12(2).
[78] A spouse cannot apply for an incidental order under s.14(2) in isolation but only in connection with an order for financial provision: *MacClue v MacClue*, 1994 S.C.L.R. 933.
[79] s.14(2)(a) and (b).
[80] s.14(2)(d).
[81] s.14(2)(c).
[82] s.14(2)(e).
[83] s.14(2)(f).
[84] s.14(2)(k).
[85] s.14(2)(j).
[86] s.18(1).
[87] s.18(2).
[88] s.18(1).

within the previous five years.[89] When it comes to enforcement, the court has the power, on cause shown, to grant warrant for inhibition or arrestment on the dependence of the action in which a claim is made.[90] The court may also order that either spouse reveals details of their financial resources.[91] Finally, it should also be noted that until decree of divorce is granted, the court has power to award interim aliment to either spouse.[92]

It is important to realise that the s.9 principles, and the powers of the court, however skillfully manipulated, are not in themselves capable of preventing poverty on the termination of every relationship. In many marriages, there is simply no property to divide on divorce, although the 1985 Act does help by providing the possibility of the payment of a capital sum by instalments out of the income or future resources, and by contemplating the splitting of pension rights.[93]

Unmarried couples

13–77 Unmarried couples (whether heterosexual or same sex) or partners have no right to seek an award equivalent to that of financial provision on divorce on the breakdown of their relationship (except where marriage is reduced or declared null in a successful action for nullity[94]). The Scottish Law Commission has recommended that cohabiting couples be given a limited right to apply for financial provision under s.9(1)(b) only, within a year of cohabitation coming to an end.[95] This, however, would not extend to same sex couples who do not fall within the definition of a cohabiting couple as this requires "a man and a woman". Until Scotland legislates for the kind of statutory scheme dealing with property rights that many countries in Europe have adopted with respect to unmarried couples of whatever sexual orientation, such couples can only regulate the division of their assets on termination of their relationships by entering a separation or cohabitation contract.[96]

Where this is not done, a cohabitee may experience hardship, especially where she or he has made financial contributions towards a property he or she does not own, *e.g.* by paying towards the deposit on the purchase price of the family home, or by making contributions towards the mortgage payments, or by paying for improvements to the house. In these circumstances it may be possible to seek a remedy under unjustified enrichment. Under this heading the remedy sought may be one *repetition* (the repayment of money), *restitution* (the transfer of property) or *recompense* (the payment of a sum representing the value of the benefit which the enriched party has enjoyed.[97] Thus:

> "a person may be said to be unjustly enriched at another's expense when he has obtained a benefit from the other's actings or expenditure. Without there being a legal ground which would justify him in retaining that benefit"[98]

While the requisites are not wholly settled it seems necessary to establish that:

- the claimant spouse had no intention of donation;
- the claimant suffered loss, while the other spouse or cohabitee was enriched as a result;
- the claimant did not act so as to benefit herself, *i.e.* did not act *in suo*; and
- no other remedy is available, *e.g.* under a contractual agreement, or in delict.

---

89 s.18(1)(i).
90 s.18(3)(a).
91 s.20.
92 s.6.
93 See Robinson on termination of the relationship in *Social Security and Family Benefit Law* (Tolley, 2002), pp.206–231.
94 s.17(1).
95 *Report on Family Law,* Scot. Law Com. No.135 (1992), para.16.18. This proposal has been taken up by the Scottish Executive, White Paper on *Parents and Children: A White Paper on Scottish Family Law* (2000), para.7.4(e).
96 See para.13–86, below.
97 *Shilliday v Smith*, 1998 S.C. 725 at 728, per Lord President Rodger; *Morgan Guaranty Trust Company of New York v Lothian Regional Council*, 1995 S.C. 151 at 155, per Lord President Hope.
98 *Dollar Land (Cumbernauld) Ltd v CIN Properties Ltd*, 1996 S.C. 331, Lord Cullen at 348–349.

If the claim is proven, the party who benefits must compensate the other party to the extent of enrichment, so long as this is equitable in the circumstances.[99] In practice, it is very difficult to succeed in an action for unjustified enrichment in the domestic sphere because it is very hard to meet the requirement that the claimant did not act to his or her own benefit in some way.[1]

Under English common law, it is accepted that one party may have the "beneficial interest" in a piece of property while another party has the formal legal interest. In a number of English cases, claims have been made on behalf of both spouses and cohabitees, that although formal legal title to a property lies with the other spouse or cohabitee, the claimant has a beneficial or equitable interest in the property which the courts should recognise. These claims have been made on the basis of the law of trusts, in particular in terms of implied,[2] resulting or constructive trusts.[3] At one time it was thought that the scope of a constructive trust was limited because, as a result of the Blank Bonds and Trusts Act 1696, proof of the existence of the trust was restricted to the writ or oath of the alleged trustee. Although the 1696 Act has now been repealed,[4] there is no indication that the Scottish courts are going to develop the law of trusts in such a way as to benefit cohabitees.

Key Concepts

Under Scots law **marriage** cannot be terminated until death, except by **divorce**.

The Divorce (Scotland) Act 1976 provides for **divorce** on the **"irretrievable breakdown of marriage"**, where there has been:

- adultery;
- behaviour of such a kind that the other party cannot reasonably be expected to cohabit;
- desertion;
- non-cohabitation for a period of two years combined with consent to divorce; or
- non-cohabitation for a period of five years.

Matrimonial property includes all property acquired during the relevant period by **either** or **both** spouses (subject to the stated exceptions).

Unmarried couples (whether heterosexual or same sex) or partners have no right to seek an award equivalent to that of **financial provision on divorce** on the breakdown of their relationship (except where marriage is reduced or declared null in a successful action for nullity).

---

99 *Newton v Newton*, 1925 S.C. 715.

1 But see *Shilliday v Smith*, 1998 S.C. 725 where payments made, in contemplation of marriage, for repairs and for materials used in repairs to the defender's home and money paid to defender to carry out work on his home recoverable by pursuer. The court rejected the argument that pursuer benefited in *suo* (because she lived in the house for part of the period) on the basis that the critical factor in her ground of action was that she only acted as she did in contemplation of the parties' marriage, which did not take place. But see *Grieve v Morrison*, 1993 S.L.T. 852 where such a claim failed because the woman failed to establish that the transfer of property was made in consideration of their marriage taking place.

2 *Pettitt* [1970] A.C. 777; *Gissing v Gissing* [1971] A.C. 886; *Lloyds Bank v Rosset* [1991] 1 A.C. 107.

3 *Cooke v Head* [1972] 2 All E.R. 38; *Eves v Eves* [1975] 3 All E.R. 768; *Grant v Edwards* [1986] Ch. 638.

4 Requirements of Writing (Scotland) Act 1995, s.11(1) and Sch.5.

PRIVATE ORDERING

13–78 When it comes to dealing with family matters such as child care, aliment and the distribution of property on the termination of a relationship not all couples find themselves going to court to have their disputes resolved. Many prefer to reach their own agreements on these issues, and indeed, much of the emphasis behind the Children (Scotland) Act 1995 and the Family Law (Scotland) Act 1985 has been towards enabling parties to reach their own decisions with less intervention by the courts. In reaching these agreements parties may resort to mediation, involving an impartial third party, the mediator, who assists couples considering separation or divorce to meet and reach agreement on arrangements that need to be made for the future.[5] Among the benefits of parties reaching their own agreements are that they:

- save time and money; and
- may reduce the kind of hostility generated by full open court proceedings.[6]

Minutes of Agreement and Joint Minutes—married couples

13–79 Where such agreements are made during the marriage or on or after divorce they are formally referred to in law as Minutes of Agreement (MoA). Where entered into they are usually registered in the Books of Council and Session for preservation and execution, or, in the Sheriff Court books. The purpose of this is not only to maintain a record of agreement but to enable either party to enforce the terms of the deed when the other party is in default. Enforcement is a very important issue. Where an agreement is registered enforcement can be done by summary diligence which saves time and money. This is because a party can act immediately on the warrant in the document, without having to go to court to enforce the terms of the deed.

Sometimes parties will reach agreement only after the divorce is already underway in the courts. Disputes about financial provision often commence as defended actions in court, but end up being settled by agreement between the parties. In such cases, settlement can be reached in the form of a *Joint Minute of Agreement* (JMoA). It is usual to ask the court to interpone authority to a JMoA and to grant decree in terms of the arrangements in the agreement. This has the effect of transforming the parties' private agreement into a binding decree of the court.

Once reached, such agreements whether MoAs or JMoAs are binding and cannot be varied or reduced without the consent of both parties, except in certain limited circumstances.[7] This serves to prevent reappraisal and re-negotiation of matters that have already been dealt with and provides another type of "clean break". Thus parties are free to set their own terms, which may be quite different from the kind of settlement that would be reached under the 1985 Act. Once made agreements are binding and enforceable in law[8] (except possibly in the case of children).

---

[5] In Scotland mediators may be volunteers appointed by Family Mediation Scotland or lawyer-mediators who are jointly accredited by the Law Society of Scotland and CALM (Comprehensive Accredited Lawyer Mediators).

[6] Note that the courts in Scotland have power to compulsorily refer parties to mediation where they are involved in divorce or child-related disputes. See OCR 33.22 and RC 49.23.

[7] Where one of the parties is in material breach it may be open to the other party to rescind the agreement without the other's consent see *Morrison v Morrison*, 2000 Fam. L.B. (42) p.6.

[8] However, where parties make a separation agreement and then reconcile their actings may be held to be consistent with an intention to revoke the agreement and the principles of financial provision under the 1985 Act may be applied. See *Methven v Methven*, 1999 S.L.T. 117.

Circumstances allowing for variation or reduction

Children

Under s.12 of the Children (Scotland) Act 1995 the court is directed in any matrimonial proceeding concerning children under 16 to consider whether any s.11 order should be granted, such as a residence or contact order. Its paramount concern in so doing must be the welfare of the child.[9] Thus, agreements reached by parents concerning their children are not binding on the court and, indeed, any person may apply at any time for a s.11 order notwithstanding that an agreement has already been signed about residence or contact.[10] However, in practice where agreements about children have been reached the court does tend to rubber stamp them. **13–80**

Contractual grounds allowing for reduction or variation

Once made, variation is limited to the terms of the agreement itself, or to claims that consent was procured on the basis of fraud, misrepresentation, undue influence or force and fear.[11] The latter, however, require a very high standard of proof and very few contracts have been set aside on this basis. **13–81**

Variation of periodical allowance to ex-spouse or aliment for children

While there is some scope for varying contractual provisions on periodical allowance this is limited in the case of MoAs to cases where parties have made appropriate express provision[12] or in the case of JMoAs to where there has been a material change of circumstances.[13] However variation on the grounds of a material change in circumstances is only permissible where the agreement forms part of a court decree. It is also important to note that a material change in circumstances must be actual and not based on a deemed or hypothetical change of circumstances brought about, for example, by the granting of decree on the basis of erroneous information.[14] **13–82**

Statutory challenge under the Family Law (Scotland) Act 1985, s.16

Is it fair and reasonable?

Another statutory ground of challenge provides that an agreement may be set aside where it was not "fair and reasonable at the time it was entered into".[15] This will apply to any term of the agreement whether it relates to capital, income or transfer of property. The jurisdiction of the court to alter agreements under s.16 cannot be ousted and any term of the agreement purporting to do this will be void.[16] The power applies in respect of both MoAs and JMoAs.[17] The test of unfairness must be applies as at the time agreement was reached, and not at any other date. This means that **13–83**

---

[9] s.11(7)(a).

[10] *Horton v Horton*, 1992 S.L.T. (Sh. Ct) 37.

[11] Variation of the terms of a periodical allowance may also take place in certain circumstances where the payer becomes bankrupt. In this event the court may, on or after granting decree of divorce, make an order setting aside or varying any term of the agreement relating to periodical allowance under s.16(3).

[12] s.16(1)(a).

[13] s.13(4) in respect of periodical allowance and ss.5(1) and 7(2) in respect of aliment. See *Watson v Mclay*, 2002 G.W.D. 2–73.

[14] *Bye v Bye*, 1999 G.W.D. 33–1591.

[15] s.16(1)(b) of the 1985 Act.

[16] s.16(4).

[17] *Jongejan v Jongejan*, 1993 S.L.T. 595.

changes in the parties' circumstances *after* agreement has been reached cannot be taken into account, for example, if one spouse acquires unforeseen financial burdens in the shape of a new family after separation.[18]

Independent legal advice

13–84 One of the major issues the court will consider is whether the parties had independent legal advice when drawing up the agreement. If such advice was obtained then the courts will normally assume that each party was fully appraised of his or her legal rights and understood the consequences of entering the particular agreement. However, the presence of legal advice does not necessarily mean the agreement cannot be reduced:

McAfee v McAfee

1990 S.C.L.R. (Notes) 805 at 808

"[T]he extent of a party's professional qualifications and experience and the nature of any advice received from a professional source may well be important factors to bear in mind in the judgment of what is fair and reasonable. Nevertheless, they cannot in themselves be determinative of the issue where there are other circumstances, suggesting unfair advantage or unreasonable conduct by one party to influence the other in the signing of an agreement which in its terms expressly surrenders rights which that other party would have on divorce."

This approach was upheld in the following case:

Gillon v Gillon (No.1)

1994 S.L.T. 978

In this case, the principal issue was whether the quality of the legal advice had been substandard. The wife maintained that when she signed the agreement, it had not been made clear to her by her lawyers that she was entitled to a share of the value of the defender's pension rights, nor had these rights been valued. These were later found to be worth about £30,000. The court held it should consider all the circumstances surrounding the making of the agreement to see whether there was some unfair advantage taken by virtue of the relationship between the parties. If relevant information, such as the value of the pension, had been withheld, this should be taken into account even if (as here) the omission was accidental rather than fraudulent. What was to be disclosed should not be restricted to what would be required in a commercial context. Accordingly, a proof of the facts was allowed.

In *Gillon v Gillon (No.3)* the court attacked the merits of the case:

Gillon v Gillon (No.3)

1995 S.L.T. 678

The court held that notwithstanding the failure to value the pension, the agreement was fair and reasonable at the time it was entered into. Under the agreement, the wife was to purchase the husband's interest in the matrimonial home at a very substantial discount in return for renouncing any further claim on any of her husband's assets, including his pension. It was clear that the wife had been anxious to reach this

[18] See *Drummond v Drummond*, 1992 S.C.L.R. 473. See also *Gray v Gray*, 1999 G.W.D. 33–1590 where a husband unsuccessfully attempted to argue that an award of periodical allowance, made under s.5 of the Divorce (Scotland) Act 1976, should be subject to the principles contained in the 1985 Act and that account should be taken of the fact that his circumstances had changed since the divorce as he had remarried and retired from full employment.

> agreement for fear that if she waited until the case came to court, the house would rise in value, and she would be unable to buy him out. The evidence suggested this fear was well-founded and that the wife had not done badly out of the arrangement. Taking all the facts into consideration in this case, the court refused to vary the agreement.

A similar finding was made in *Inglis v Inglis*,[19] which endorsed the approach adopted in *Gillon (No.3)*, that the agreement had been entered into by the wife in the full knowledge that she had a potential claim in her husband's pension rights and she had renounced that claim in order to achieve what had appeared to her to be the immediate and significant advantage of the husband's departure from the matrimonial home.

The fact that both parties are advised by the same law agent does not automatically imply that the agreement drawn up was fair or reasonable because of the conflict of interest[20]:

Worth v Worth

1994 S.C.L.R. (Notes) 362

> In this case the parties drew up their own agreement and took it to the solicitor who had acted in their house purchase and was a mutual friend. They were advised that they should seek independent legal advice if they thought there might be a conflict of interest, but chose not to. Several years after the agreement had taken effect, the wife learned that she might have had a claim on her husband's pension under the 1985 Act, an issue never raised or mentioned in the original agreement. She sought to have the agreement set aside under s.16. The court found that the solicitor had not acted improperly as he had raised the issue of conflict of interest, and had attempted to act as an "honest broker" between the parties. However, the agreement might still be objectively unfair even though there had been no "concealment, trickery, or pressure". The court reluctantly found that the "agreement does not fairly reflect the actual value of the parties' property or the defender's fair entitlement to it, for the defender was in law, and this presumably in fairness, entitled to a share of the value of the pursuer's pension rights".[21] As a result a term of the agreement was reduced.

Unequal division of assets

The mere fact that there has been an unequal division of assets between the parties by agreement **13–85**
does not of itself give rise to an inference of unfairness or unreasonableness.[22] In some cases, an unequal division may be accepted by one party against their best interests because, as in *Gillon*, they prefer the certainty of knowing precisely what they are to receive on divorce, rather than the uncertainty of waiting to see what a court settlement might produce at a future date.

---

19 1999 S.L.T. (Sh. Ct) 59.

20 But note Patterson's observations on r.3 of the Solicitors (Scotland) Practice Rules dealing with professional responsibility in this matter, *Professional Responsibility: Student Manual* (2001) at p.110. See also Lord Nicholls observations in *Royal Bank of Scotland v Etridge (No.2)* [2001] 4 All E.R. 449 at 471 where he sets out the pros and cons of acquiring independent legal advice as set against the benefits of using the same law agent, such as, less expense.

21 Note this was also an issue in *Inglis v Inglis*, 1999 S.L.T. (Sh. Ct) 59 where the court held that the wife had been given the clearest warning that it would have been in her best interests to seek separate legal representation and advice but had declined to do so without any undue pressure from her husband.

22 *Gillon v Gillon (No.3)*, 1995 S.L.T. 678. In *Anderson v Anderson*, 1997 S.L.T. (Sh. Ct) 11 the husband in a fit of remorse at his conduct made a written gift of his whole share of the matrimonial property to his wife. The court held that even if this was an "agreement" under s.16(1)(b) which was dubious, it was fair and reasonable when entered into as the husband had acted voluntarily and in full knowledge of what he was doing.

An agreement can be reduced or varied under s.16 only either before decree of divorce is granted, or within such time thereafter as the court may specify.[23] Thus, in most cases, if the s.16 plea is not made at the time of divorce the agreement will stand. This can be invidious, given that divorce is often a time of turbulence and disruption, and that the full effect of an agreement negotiated under the pressure of this period (which are unlikely to constitute legal duress sufficient to allow reduction) may not become apparent until some time later when the action is barred. Further more, in many cases, full details as to the financial position, *e.g.*, the value of pension rights, may only emerge after the divorce. Even where the action is raised in time, as can be seen in cases like *Gillon* and *McAfee*, the courts are most reluctant to reopen a formal written agreement reached by the parties. This is because of the ordinary principle that parties, should be bound to contracts they have entered voluntarily, in the interests of certainty for both the parties themselves and third parties. It is submitted that this principle is not as compelling in relation to domestic relationships as commercial ones, something which s.16 already reflects, but perhaps not fully enough. There is something to be said for the concept of a "cooling-off" period within which a s.16 action could be brought by right *after* the divorce.

In the meantime it is strongly advisable to draft any agreement as comprehensively as possible, with provision built in for unforeseen material changes in either party's circumstances. Otherwise, problems may arise in connection with assets that have not been specifically dealt with in the agreement. In *Atkinson v Atkinson*,[24] for example, the agreement dealt with capital but made no mention of periodical allowance. The court found that it still had jurisdiction to make an order for a sum of periodical allowance.[25] For the avoidance of doubt, it should always be expressly provided that the agreement is to be in full settlement of all future financial claims between the parties arising out of the marriage. Given the limited scope for variation it is therefore essential that women and their partners get fully informed independent legal advice.[26]

Private ordering for cohabitees

13–86 The above discussion on minutes and joint minutes has focused on married couples. Unmarried couples, including same sex couples, may also wish to enter into agreements about finance and property. However, the legal status of such agreements is not as settled as those made by married couples,[27] nor is there the same right to have agreements reduced on the basis that they were not fair and reasonable at the time they were entered into, as s.16 of the 1985 Act only applies to married persons. Where such agreements are entered into and recognised by the court they will only be subject to reduction under the ordinary principles of contract law. Other jurisdictions provide for legally enforceable cohabitation contracts or registered partnerships outwith marriage.[28] There has been no legislation, yet, in the UK although two private members Bills dealing with domestic partnerships were introduced to Parliament in 2001, the Civil Partnerships Bill and the Relationship (Civil Registration) Bill.

---

[23] s.16(2)(b), see also *Jongejan v Jongejan*, 1993 S.L.T. 595.

[24] 1988 S.C.L.R. 396.

[25] But compare *Sochart v Sochart*, 1988 S.L.T. 449 where the parties agreed by joint minute that the husband should make the wife a periodical allowance, but said nothing about any capital sums. In this case, the terms of the minute were held impliedly to dispose of all financial claims between the parties, and so the husband was not allowed to seek a capital sum order from the court payable by the wife.

[26] Where this advice is negligent clients may sue their legal adviser see *Darrie v Duncan*, 2001 Fam. L. R. 14 and *Dible v The Morton Fraser Partnership*, 2001 Fam.L.R. 15.

[27] They may be subject to the claim that they are unenforceable on the basis of the "illegal purposes" doctrine in contract law although the Scottish Law Commission has recommended that there should be a statutory provision upholding such contracts made between cohabitants or prospective cohabitants and the Scottish Executive have endorsed their proposal, *Parents and Children: A White Paper on Scottish Family Law* (2000), para.7.4(j).

[28] These include Denmark (1989), Norway (1993), Sweden (1994), Iceland (1996) the Netherlands (1998), Belgium (1998) France (1999) and Germany (2001). For an overview of other jurisdictions' approaches see Wintermute and Andenas (eds.), *Legal Recognition of Same-Sex Partnerships* (Hart Publishing, 2001).

> **Key Concepts**
>
> Many prefer to make their **own agreements** as to child care, aliment and the distribution of property **on the termination of a relationship**.
>
> Where such agreements are made during the marriage or on or after divorce they are formally referred to in law as **Minutes of Agreement**.
>
> Once made agreements are **binding and enforceable in law** (except possibly in the case of **children**).
>
> **Variation** or **reduction** of such agreements may occur:
>
> - with regard to **children**;
> - where there are **contractual grounds** allowing for reduction or variation;
> - where variation of **periodical allowance to ex-spouse** or **aliment for children** is permitted; or
> - following a **statutory challenge** under s.16 of the Family Law (Scotland) Act 1985 (Was it fair and reasonable? Did the parties have independent legal advice?—the mere fact that there has been an **unequal division of assets** between the parties by agreement does not of itself give rise to an inference of **unfairness** or **unreasonableness**.)

STATE INTERVENTION IN THE LIVES OF CHILDREN: CARE AND PROTECTION

There are three main institutions in Scotland which are involved where children are in need of care and protection. These are: **13–87**

- the local authority, who has both duties and powers in relations to children, which are usually exercised by its social work department;
- the courts, who have a significant role in preventing the local authority from taking unfettered action and giving children and parents a right to judicial hearing; and
- the children's hearings system.

Local authority duties and powers

The Children (Scotland) Act 1995, Pt II, in conjunction with what remains of the Social Work (Scotland) Act 1968, attempts to set out a new framework to support children and their families in the community, emphasising partnership between parents and local authorities. The local authority is generally under a duty to promote social welfare by making available advice, guidance and assistance to persons in the area for which they are responsible.[29] This assistance can take the form of: **13–88**

- cash, but only in exceptional circumstances[30];
- assistance in kind[31];
- the provision of residential nursing accommodation,[32] home helps or laundry facilities.[33]

---

[29] s.12 of the 1968 Act.
[30] s.12(3) and (4).
[31] s.12(1).
[32] s.13A.
[33] s.14.

Assistance under s.12 is restricted to persons aged 18 or over.[34] This is because the 1995 Act now gives local authorities special duties in relation to children[35] in need. In particular, under s.22(1) of the 1995 Act, a local authority is under an obligation:

(a) to safeguard and promote the welfare of children in its area who are in need; and
(b) so far as is consistent with that duty, to promote the upbringing of such children by their families so that the children can be helped within their home environment.

Children "in need" are broadly defined[36] to include:

- children who are unlikely to achieve to maintain a reasonable standard of health or development without local authority assistance;
- children whose health or development is likely to be significantly impaired without such assistance;
- disabled children; and
- children affected by the disability of another member of the family.

In providing child care services, the local authority should, so far as is practicable, have regard to the child's religion, racial origin and linguistic background.[37] In keeping with the policy that children in need should be supported within their families, the Children (Scotland) Act 1995 requires local authorities to prepare and publish plans for the provision of relevant services within their areas.[38] They are also under a duty to co-operate with other agencies and authorities such as health boards.[39]

Voluntary care

13–89 A local authority *may* provide accommodation for any child within its area if it considers that it would safeguard or promote the child's welfare to do so.[40] However, a local authority *must* provide accommodation for any child,[41] residing or found in it area, if it appears to the local authority that the child requires accommodation because:

- no-one has parental responsibility for the child[42];
- the child is lost or abandoned;
- the person who has been caring for the child is prevented, whether or not permanently and for whatever reason, from providing the child with suitable accommodation or care.[43]

When providing a child with accommodation, the local authority, so far as practicable, must have regard to the child's views (if the child wishes to express them), taking account of the child's age and maturity.[44] In keeping with the Act's philosophy of keeping children at home, a local authority cannot provide accommodation for a child if any person with parental responsibilities and rights objects *and* is willing and able to provide accommodation for the child.[45] In addition, any such person may remove the child from local authority accommodation at any time. However, s.25(7) provides that if a child is in care *for a continuous period of six months,* a parent has no right to take him away without the consent of the local authority unless that parent has given *not less than 14 days' notice*. It is important to note that this duty to look after the child arises not only when the

[34] s.12(2) as amended by the 1995 Act, Sch.4, para.15(11).
[35] A child is a person under 18, s.93(2)(a) of the 1995 Act.
[36] s.93(4)(A).
[37] s.22(2).
[38] s.19.
[39] s.21.
[40] s.25(2).
[41] That is a person under 18.
[42] On parental responsibilities see paras 13–19 to 13–21.
[43] s.25(1).
[44] A child aged 12 or over is deemed to be of sufficient age and maturity to form a view although this does not preclude younger children from being consulted if they have sufficient maturity, s.25(5).
[45] s.25(6)(a).

child has been accommodated under s.25 of the 1995 Act but also when the child is in local authority accommodation as a result of a supervision requirement[46] or any order, warrant or authorisation made under the 1995 Act, as a result of which the local authority has responsibilities in respect of the child.

Children who are in s.25 accommodation are "looked after" children. A Local Authority has extensive duties to safeguard and promote the welfare of any child "looked after" by them under s.17. Such children include:

- children in s.25 accommodation;
- children taken from the family home under child protection or child assessment orders; and
- children under supervision order(s) made by the children's hearing.[47]

Before making any decision relating to a looked after child, a local authority must, so far as practicable, have regard to the views of the child and of parents or any person with parental rights and any other relevant person.[48]

Local authority powers

Under the 1995 Act, a local authority is empowered to apply to a sheriff court for a range of court **13–90** orders to help the local authority fulfil its obligations in respect of children. These include child protection orders, child assessment orders, exclusion orders and parental responsibilities orders.

Child protection orders (CPOs)

Situations can arise where it is necessary to act quickly to protect a child from serious ill-treatment **13–91** by removing the child[49] to a place of safety. Any person can apply to a sheriff for a child protection order (CPO), who *may* make an order if satisfied that:

> "(a) there are reasonable grounds to believe that a child—
> (i) is being so treated (or neglected) that he is suffering *significant harm*; or
> (ii) will suffer such harm if he is not removed to and kept in a place of safety, or if he does not remain in the place where he is then being accommodated (whether or not resident there); *and*
> (b) an order ... is necessary to protect that child from such harm (or such further harm)."[50]

Where the local authority applies special provisions apply to ensure that an order is only used where investigation of the child's welfare would otherwise be frustrated.[51] The application must identify the applicant and, where it is practicable, the child concerned. It must state the grounds for the application, supported by evidence.[52] Notice of the application must be given to the reporter and the relevant local authority, if the local authority is not the applicant. The effect of the order is to require any person in a position to do so to produce the child and to authorise the removal of the child to a place of safety[53] (or prevent the child being removed from the place the child is currently being accommodated).[54] It does not transfer parental responsibilities or rights but the sheriff can

---

46 See para.13–97, below.
47 For full definition see s.17(6).
48 s.17(4).
49 Child is defined as a person under 16 or between the ages of 16 and 18 where a supervision requirement is in force: s.93(2)(b).
50 s.57(1).
51 s.57(2).
52 s.57(3).
53 A place of safety is a residential or other establishment provided by a local authority, a community home, a police station, a hospital or surgery whose management is willing temporarily to receive the child, the dwelling house of a suitable parent or any other suitable place the occupier of which is willing to receive the child under s.93(1) (as amended by the Regulation of Care (Scotland) Act 2001, s.74).
54 s.57(4).

attach conditions and directions, *e,g.* regulating contact and the exercise of such rights.[55] This may include medical assessment and treatment[56] although the child's right to refuse such treatment is reserved.[57] The order can provide that the location of the place of safety should not be disclosed to any person in the order.[58] Under a CPO, an applicant's actions in respect of the child are restricted to those acts the applicant believes are necessary to safeguard or promote the welfare of the child.[59]

It is important to note that once the CPO is granted, it must be implemented within 24 hours or it will lapse.[60] If the parents do not successfully challenge the CPO at any earlier stage, the CPO must at latest come to an end on the eight working days after it was taken, when the hearing meets to decide whether grounds of referral exist.[61] However, they have an opportunity to challenge the CPO in the courts at two earlier stages.

Stage one challenge

13–92 After a CPO has been made by the sheriff under s.57(1) or (2), the application to a sheriff to set aside or vary the CPT (and/or directions made under s.58) is possible before the commencement of the "initial hearing".[62] Such an application must be determined within three working days. The reporter can arrange a hearing to give advice to the sheriff in relation to the CPO.[63] If the sheriff determines that the conditions for making the CPO are *not* satisfied, he or she must recall the order and cancel any directions under s.58.[64] If satisfied the condition for granting the CPO *are* met, the order and any directions granted under s.58 should be confirmed or varied, new directions can be granted, and the order continued in force until the full children's hearing on the eighth working day.[65]

If a stage one challenge is made, there is no "initial" hearing, and if the CPO is confirmed by the sheriff, the child will be kept in the place of safety with any directions made about contact, etc. maintained, until the eighth working day hearing.[66] At that stage, the normal procedure in relation to children's hearings comes into play.[67]

Stage two challenge

13–93 If *no* "stage one" challenge is made prior to the "initial" hearing then there is a second chance to make an application to recall the CPO within two working days of the "initial" hearing.[68] The options available to the sheriff are the same as in the stage one application for recall, except that an advice hearing need not be convened.[69] If the CPO is continued (with or without variation of the order and/or directions) a full hearing is held on the eighth working day from the implementation of the original CPO as above.[70]

A stage one or two challenge may be made by the child, a person with parental responsibilities or rights in relation to the child, a person who ordinarily has charge of the child, anyone who by

---

55 s.57(4).
56 s.58(5).
57 s.90.
58 s.57(4).
59 s.57(6).
60 s.60(1).
61 s.60(6)(e).
62 s.60(6)(e).
63 s.60(10).
64 s.60(13).
65 s.60(12).
66 s.60(12)(d).
67 See paras 13–98 to 13–101 below.
68 s.60(8)(b).
69 s.60(10).
70 s.65(2).

regulation was notified of the application for the order, and the applicant for the order.[71] There is no further appeal from the sheriff granting, refusing or continuing a CPO, to the sheriff principal or Inner House.[72] This is appropriate given the emergency and time-limited nature of the order. Given the highly complex procedure a flow chart is provided below.

FIGURE 1

Child Protection Orders Sections 57–62

Application to Sheriff by "any person" *s. 57(1)* / by local authority *s. 57(2)*

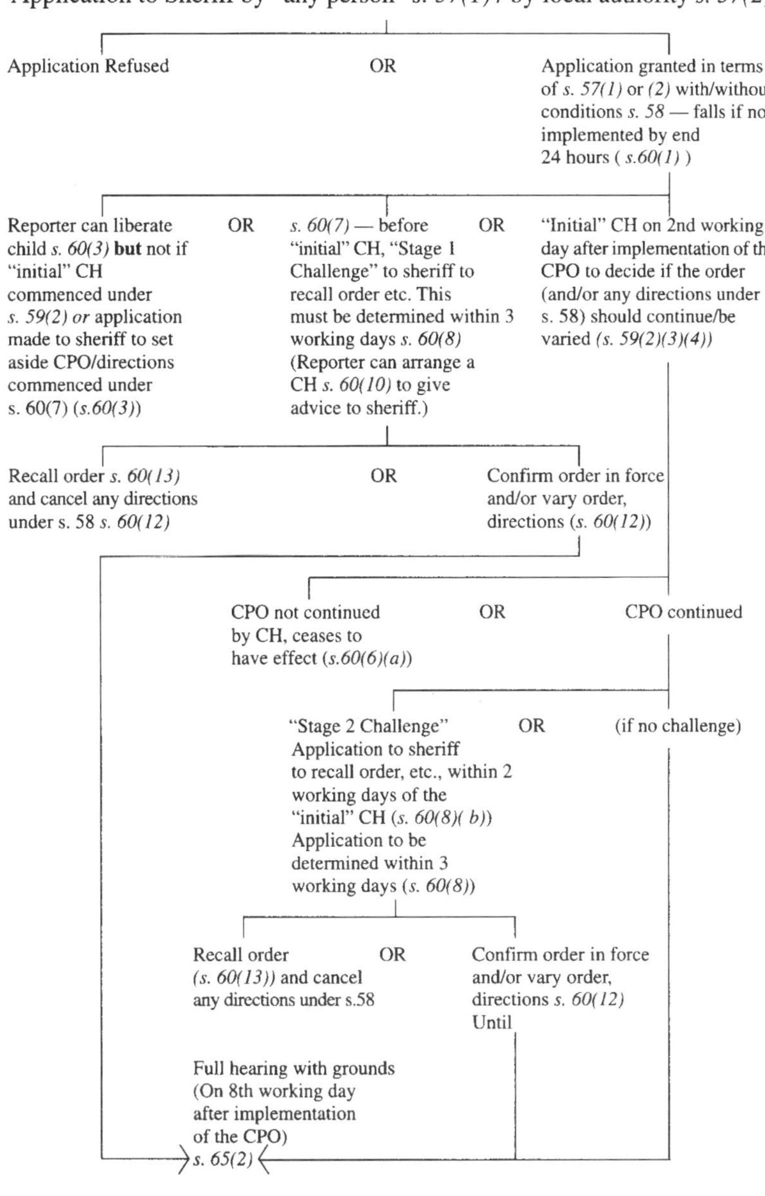

---

[71] s.60(7).

[72] s.51(15).

If it is not "practicable" to make an application to a sheriff for a CPO, emergency authorisation for removal can be made by a Justice of the Peace.[73]

Child assessment orders (CAOs)

13–94 In order to safeguard and promote the welfare of children, local authority social workers may require access to the child in order to make an assessment of the child's needs. If there is reason to suspect that a child is suffering from harm and the parents refuse to allow the child to be seen or examined, then a local authority can apply to a sheriff for a child assessment order (CAO).[74] This empowers the local authority to see and asses and to have the child examined by medical professionals, without the need to take the more extreme step of removing the child from the home.[75] The order lasts seven days. Note, however, that a local authority can be authorised to remove a child from his or her parents so as to carry out the assessment under the CAO.[76] The order lasts seven days.[77]

Exclusion orders

13–95 A local authority only has power to apply to a sheriff for an order excluding an alleged abuser, referred to as the "named person" from a child's[78] family home.[79] Such an order is in line with the tenet that the child's needs should take precedence over those of the adults involved. However, what the legislation attempts to do rather than provide the court with an unfettered discretion to exclude, is to require the sheriff to balance the interests of the child and adult involved using multiple tests. [80] The onus lies on the local authority to satisfy the court that the conditions set out in s.76(2) are met on proof of a balance of probabilities.[81] The grounds set out for exclusion in that section are almost identical to those required for a CPO, *i.e.* they involve "significant harm". In determining whether an exclusion order should be made, a sheriff has a duty to consult the child.[82] An exclusion order cannot be made unless the named person has been afforded an opportunity of being heard, or represented before the sheriff, and the sheriff has considered the views of any person on whom notice of the application has been served.[83]

Even where the conditions of s.76(2) are met a sheriff may not make an exclusion order if it appears unjustifiable or unreasonable to grant the order having regard to all circumstances of the case,[84] or if the named person satisfies the sheriff that it is unnecessary.[85] The factors to be taken into account are much the same as those under s.3(3) of the Matrimonial Homes (Family Protection) (Scotland) Act 1981.[86] Where the order is granted a sheriff may grant an interdict preventing the named person from entering the home and attach powers of arrest to it.[87] Where granted an exclusion order ceases to have effect six months after being made.[88]

---

73 s.61.
74 s.55(1).
75 s.55(5).
76 s.55(4).
77 s.55(3)(a) and (b).
78 A child is a person who is under 16 and also includes a person between 16 and 18 who is subject to a supervision requirement, s.93(2)(b).
79 s.76.
80 See ss.76–80.
81 *Russell v W*, 1998 Fam. L.R. 25.
82 s.16(2) and (4)(b)(i).
83 s.76(3). But if a sheriff is satisfied that the conditions in s.76(2) are met but that the conditions in s.76(3) are not fulfilled, *i.e.* the named person has not been heard, the sheriff may grant an interim order.
84 s.76(10).
85 s.77(4).
86 See para.13–54, above.
87 ss.77 and 78.
88 s.79(1).

Parental responsibilities orders (PROs)

A parental responsibilities order (PRO) will be sought by a local authority as part of long term planning to safeguard the future of a child when it seems that reintegration of that child into the family home is unlikely and undesirable. The effect of such an order is the transfer of parental responsibilities and rights over a child from the parents (or other person exercising such rights) to the local authority. Where granted the child will often be removed from home and the local authority will have the right to make the major decisions in relation to the upbringing of the child. In doing so, the local authority must act in accordance with the principles already discussed in the context of the provision of accommodation for children being looked after by the authority.[89] **13–96**

Under s.86(1) of the Children (Scotland) Act 1995 a local authority may apply to a sheriff for an order transferring the appropriate parental rights and responsibilities in respect of a child[90] from a relevant person to the local authority where the following conditions[91] are met, that is where the relevant person:

- freely consents[92];
- is not known, cannot be found, or is incapable of giving agreement[93];
- is withholding such agreement unreasonably[94];
- has persistently failed without reasonable cause to fulfil parental responsibilities[95];
- had seriously ill-treated the child *and* reintegration into a household with that person is unlikely because of the serious ill-treatment or for other reasons.[96]

A relevant person is defined as the child's parent or any person having parental rights in respect of the child.[97] When an order is being made or is in force, the child has the right to reasonable contact with a relevant person and any person who had a residence order in respect of the child immediately before the order was made.[98] Thus the child, the local authority or any person with an interest may apply to the sheriff for a contact order.[99] A sheriff may vary or discharge a PRO at any time on the application of the child, a relevant person immediately before the order was made, any person claiming an interest or the local authority.[1] However, while a PRO is in force, a parent has no title to sue for an order relating to parental responsibilities under s.11 of the 1995 Act.[2] Similarly, a local authority has no title to sue for parental responsibilities under s.11, as it is required to apply to the court for a PRO under s.86(2) and to meet the more stringent provisions laid down in that section. Where an order is granted it will terminate when a child reaches 18 or if he or she is adopted or freed for adoption.[3]

---

89 See para.13–89, above.
90 A child for these purposes is a person under 18, s.93(2)(a) of the 1995 Act.
91 These condition s are exactly the same as the grounds for dispensing with parental agreement in adoption proceedings under s.16(2) of the Adoption (Scotland) Act 1978.
92 s.86(2)(a).
93 s.86(2)(b)(i).
94 s.86(2)(b)(ii).
95 s.86(2)(b)(iii).
96 s.86(2)(b)(iv).
97 s.86(4).
98 s.88(2).
99 s.88(3).
1 s.86(5).
2 s.11(4)(d).
3 s.86(6)(a) and (b).

The children's hearings system—children who are in need of compulsory measures of supervision

13–97 Under the Children (Scotland) Act 1995[4] hearings comprised of children's panels exist to deal with children under 16 who are in need of compulsory measures of supervision.[5] State intervention in this context covers a wide range of circumstances[6] including the neglect and abuse of children, or the commission of offences by children, as well as dealing with children who are "beyond the control of a relevant person" or who fail "to attend school regularly without reasonable excuse". It is panel members who are public volunteers, whose services are unpaid, and who work on a part-time basis, who make decisions about whether or not children are in need of compulsory measures of supervision. Each panel consists of three members, one of whom must be male, one of whom must be female, and one of whom acts as chairman.[7] Members are appointed by the Secretary of State for Scotland on the advice of the Children's Panel Advisory Committee (CPAC) which exists in each of the 32 local authorities which form part of local government in Scotland. Each local authority has a children's panel made up of members, including a Chairman and a Deputy Chairman. Members receive training before they serve on a panel and are required to attend further in-service training sessions to extend their knowledge and skills.

Local Authorities play an important part in the hearings system in terms of administration, support, and in implementation of the hearings' decisions. However, cases are referred to a children's hearing by a reporter who draws up the grounds for referral and who is employed by the Scottish Children's Reporter Administration (SCRA)[8] a national body charged with the management and deployment of reporters throughout Scotland. Reporters (who act independently from local authorities) act as gatekeepers to the system investigating cases brought to their attention by agencies such as social work departments, schools, and police. After reviewing the situation the reporter decides whether to drop the matter, or to encourage a child and family to work with social services on a voluntary basis, or whether to proceed to a hearing. When a hearing is held it is the panel members who must decide whether or not to discharge the referral, or whether a child is in need of compulsory measures of supervision, and if so, what conditions if any should be imposed.[9] While panel members make decisions about whether or not a child is in need of compulsory supervision reporters play a central role in the operation of the hearing system for it is they who make the initial decision about whether or not a child should go before a hearing, who organise the timetable and necessary documentation for the hearings, and who have responsibility for ensuring that the legal requirements of the process are met.[10]

---

[4] Along with the Children's Hearings (Scotland) Rules 1996 (SI 1996/3261), hereafter referred to as the 1996 Rules and the Children's Hearings (Legal Representation) (Scotland) Rules 2002 (SSI 2002/63). The 1995 Act reflects the philosophy that underlies the recommendations made by the Kilbrandon Committee, *Report on Children and Young Persons, Scotland,* Cmnd.2306 (1964), that led to the implementation of the hearings system in Scotland under the Social Work (Scotland) Act 1968 which Pt II of the 1995 Act replaces.

[5] See s.56(6) and s.65(1). Children over 16 but under 18 in respect of whom a supervision requirement remains in force may also come before a hearing under s.93(2)(b) of the 1995 Act. Young persons under 18 who have been prosecuted for offences in the criminal courts may also be remitted to the hearing for disposal, rather than being sentenced by the court; the court may also simply seek the advice of the hearing relating to the disposal of such a case under s.49(1) of the Criminal Procedure (Scotland) Act 1995.

[6] Under s.52(2).

[7] s.39(3) and (5).

[8] Local Government etc. (Scotland) Act 1994, s.128(4) and (5). The term "reporter" means the Principal Reporter and any officer of SCRA to whom he has delegated any of his functions under s.131(1) of the 1994 Act.

[9] Under s.70 the hearing has a wide range of powers including the power to make a residential supervision requirement placing the child in a foster or local authority home, or even, in secure accommodation.

[10] Reporters may but need not be legally qualified. Some come from a background in social work or education.

Key features of the system

Although a legal forum, every effort is made to encourage children and families to participate in proceedings by dispensing with the kind of legal formalities associated with courts. Thus, in keeping with Kilbrandon's recommendations,[11] a determination of the facts is separated out from a disposal of the case by the requirement that no hearing can proceed unless the child and family accept the grounds for referral.[12] In this way the demands of formal legality—requiring determination of the facts with regard to due process—are kept distinct from a disposal of the case. The latter, which is concerned with the welfare and development of the child, is more appropriately placed within the jurisdiction of the panels.[13] In cases of dispute, the hearing can either discharge the referral or refer the matter to the Sheriff Court for a finding as to whether the disputed grounds are established.[14] **13–98**

This approach, premised on consensus as the starting point for discussion, seeks to avoid the adversarial nature of legal proceedings. It is one that minimises the role of lawyers so that children and families are not subject to confrontation with and intimidation by the kind of legal process that operates in ordinary law courts. In order to maintain confidentiality and protect the privacy of children and families hearings are conducted in private "with no person other than a person whose presence is necessary for the proper consideration of the case which is being heard" being present[15] except for those who have a right to attend,[16] or who fall within the category of persons whose attendance may be authorised by the chairman of the hearing.[17] Rules of evidence and procedure are much less stringent and while lawyers may be present at a hearing they do not act as advocates speaking on behalf of their clients. However, while not intended to operate like a court, the proceedings before children's hearings involve the determination of civil rights and obligations that are subject to the terms of Art.6(1) of the European Convention on Human Rights dealing with the right to a fair trial.[18]

S v Miller

2001 S.L.T. 531

The court held that the fact that a child was referred to a hearing on the ground of having committed an offence did not mean that the child was being charged with an offence and thus the mandatory protections of Art.6(3) did not apply. However, it also held that in every referral a child is entitled to a fair hearing under Art.6(1). This means that all documentary information used in the decision-making process must be distributed to all parties, including the child.[19] The right to a fair hearing also raised the issue of a right to legal representation. The court held that the hearings system failed to comply with Art.6 due to the statutory unavailability of funding for the legal

---

[11] See the first note to para.13–97, above.

[12] Under s.65(9) where a child is too young to understand the grounds for referral, or has not in fact understood them after an explanation has been given, the hearing can either discharge the referral or direct the reporter to apply to the sheriff for a finding as to whether the grounds of referral are established.

[13] Kilbarandon, para.72.

[14] s.65(7)(a).

[15] Under s.43(1) of the Children (Scotland) Act 1995.

[16] s.43(3).

[17] Children's Hearing (Scotland) Rules 1996, r.13.

[18] See *S v Miller*, 2001 S.L.T. 531. Article 6 provides that in determining civil rights and obligations or any criminal charge, everyone is entitled to a fair and public hearing within a reasonable time by an independent and impartial tribunal established by law. In addition, there are specific guarantees that are brought into play by Arts 6(2) and (3) where someone is charged with a criminal offence.

[19] Prior to the 1995 Act, in the interests of confidentiality, children and families were not entitled to copies of reports submitted to panel members by social workers and other professionals. The European Court in *McMichael v UK* (1995) 20 E.H.R.R. 205 held, that notwithstanding the chairman's obligation to reveal the substance of these reports at the beginning of the hearing, children's hearings were in breach of the European Convention on Human Rights. The rules were amended to provide adults entitled to be at hearings with copies of reports under r.5(3) of the 1996 Rules, but they did not extend to children.

representation of children at such hearings.[20] It acknowledged that legal representation would not be required in every case involving a referral but only those cases where a child was unable to represent him or herself properly and satisfactorily at the hearing.

The court did not set out all the circumstances where a child might require legal representation to enable him or her to participate effectively in a hearing but they include:

- cases involving deprivation of liberty, *e.g.* where secure accommodation might be imposed;
- cases involving particularly vulnerable groups of children, *e.g.* the very young or those with learning disabilities or special needs;
- hearings involving difficult issues of law or procedure, *e.g.* a defence of self-defence or provocation in an "offence" referral.

The new Children's Hearings (Legal Representation) (Scotland) Rules 2002[21] allow for legal representation to be provided, not by ordinary solicitors using civil legal aid funds, but by "legal representatives".[22] The tests for appointment of a legal representative are taken from *S v Miller*[23] namely, if it is required to allow the child to "effectively participate", or if there is a possibility that the child may be placed in secure accommodation.[24] The decision to appoint can be made prior to the hearing[25] or later by the children's panel itself.[26]

Where a hearing takes place three overriding principles apply. These are that:

(1) the welfare of the child is paramount[27];
(2) children must be able to express their views and have them taken account where sufficiently mature[28] with a presumption in favour of children aged 12 or over having such maturity[29];
(3) that there should be minimum intervention, that is, that a hearing should only make an order if it is better for the child to make such an order than to make no order at all.[30]

Right of attendance at hearing

Child

13–99 Where a case is referred by the reporter to a children's hearing, the child has the right to attend all stages of the hearing and is obliged to do so.[31] However the hearing with the reporter can meet at an earlier "business meeting" [32] to agree to release the child from the duty to attend on the grounds that his or her presence would be detrimental to his or her interests.[33] Where the child fails to attend as requested, a warrant may be issued for his or her apprehension.[34]

---

20 *S v Miller (No.2)*, 2001 S.L.T. 1304.
21 SSI 2002/63. These rules came into force on February 23, 2002 replacing an earlier version (SSI 2001/478).
22 These are to be drawn from the new panels of safeguarders and curators *ad litem* who must hold a current solicitor's practicing certificate, see r.5. Appointment of a "legal representative" will not preclude appointment of a safeguarder under s.41 of the 1995 Act.
23 2001 S.L.T. 531 and *(No.2)* 2001 S.L.T. 1304.
24 r.3(1), 2002 Rules.
25 At a s.64 business meeting, r.4, 2002 Rules.
26 r.4, 2002 Rules.
27 s.16(1) of the 1995 Act.
28 s.16(2).
29 s.11(10).
30 s.16(3).
31 s.45(1)(a) and (b).
32 s.64.
33 s.45(2).
34 s.45.

Relevant person

Where a child is brought before a hearing, a relevant person has the right to attend all stages of the hearing and is obliged to do so.[35] Relevant persons are defined to include: **13–100**

- persons with parental responsibilities and rights under Pt I of the 1995 Act; and
- any person who ordinarily has charge of or control over the child.[36]

Such persons normally include a married parent, cohabiting father and father (or other relative) who has gained a parental responsibility or parental responsibilities, *e.g.* through a contact order. It does not, however, include an unmarried father who no longer cohabits with the child's mother.[37] It is only relevant persons who have guaranteed right to attend the hearing of the child they are in charge of and thus who have the right to deny grounds of referral or appeal the disposal of the hearing. Unless invited by the child to attend as a friend or representative,[38] or permitted to attend at the discretion of the chair[39] an unmarried non-cohabiting father[40] will have no right to attend a hearing and express his views. While relevant persons have the right to attend a hearing they can be excluded so long as it is necessary in the interests of the child, where the hearing is satisfied that it must do so in order to obtain the child's views or because the presence of the relevant person is causing, or is likely to cause, significant distress to the child.[41] However, in order to maintain an "open" process, the chair must explain the substance of what has occurred during the excluded person's absence on his or her return.[42]

Review, appeal, termination

The child or relevant person may appeal to the sheriff against any decision of a children's hearing.[43] This includes both to the making of the supervision requirement itself as well as to any of the conditions attached to such a requirement. In reaching a decision the sheriff has a duty to consult the child.[44] Where a sheriff forms the view that the hearing's decision is not justified in all the circumstances he or she may: **13–101**

- remit the case with reasons for his decision to the children's hearing for reconsideration of their decision[45]; or
- discharge the child from any further hearing or other proceedings in relation to the grounds for the referral of the case[46]; or
- substitute for the disposal by the children's hearing any requirement which could be imposed by them under s.70 of the 1995 Act.[47]

Where an appeal is unsuccessful, the sheriff will confirm the decision of the children's hearing.[48] Where a supervision requirement is in force it should not continue any longer than is necessary in the interests of the child.[49] If a local authority takes the view that the requirement should cease to

---

35 s.45(8).
36 s.93(2)(b). Such persons include foster carers, see *S v N*, 2002 S.L.T. 589.
37 Note that where the child is already under a supervision requirement of the children's hearing he is barred from applying to the courts for rights under s.11, *D v Strathclyde Regional Council*, 1985 S.L.T. 114.
38 r.11 of the 1996 Rules.
39 r.13 of the 1996 Rules.
40 Without a s.4 agreement with the mother or a court order regulating parental responsibilities and rights.
41 s.46(1).
42 s.46(2).
43 s.51(1).
44 s.16(2) and (4)(c).
45 s.51(5)(c)(i).
46 s.51(5)(c)(ii).
47 s.51(5)(c) (iii).
48 s.51(4).
49 s.73(1).

have effect, it can refer the case to the reporter for review by a children's hearing who can terminate the requirement if it sees fit.[50] In any event, a supervision requirement cannot remain in force after a year unless it has been continued as a result of a review by a children's hearing.[51] The child and any relevant person have the right to a review of the requirement.[52] On review, a children's hearing may continue the requirement, vary it or terminate it. When a child reaches 18 any supervision requirement ceases to have effect.[53]

Key Concepts

The three main institutions in Scotland which are involved where **children** are in need of **care and protection** are the local authority, the courts and the children's hearing system.

Under the **Children (Scotland) Act 1995** a local authority is empowered to apply to a sheriff court for a range of court orders to help the local authority fulfil its obligations in respect of children. These include:

- **child protection** orders;
- **child assessment** orders;
- **exclusion** orders; and
- **parental responsibilities** orders.

Under the 1995 Act hearings comprised of children's panels exist to deal with children under 16 who are in need of compulsory measures of supervision.

[50] s.73(4)(a) and (8)(a)(i).
[51] s.73(2) and (9)(e).
[52] s.73(6).
[53] s.73(3).

Quick Quiz

Family law

- Who can marry?
- When is a man presumed to be the father of a child?
- Which exceptions are there to the "separate property" rule?
- What is aliment?
- Who may apply for Working Tax Credit?
- What is Child Tax Credit?
- When would a court make an exclusion order?
- Name the five conditions meeting the ground of "irretrievable breakdown of marriage"?
- Which Act is framed around the rights to occupy and to exclude a violent party from the family home?
- What are the benefits of private ordering?
- What is the effect of a CPO?

Further Reading

There are numerous sources for further information on Family Law in Scotland.

For more in depth analysis see the two Scottish Universities Law Institute's titles: **Wilkinson and Norrie, *The Law Relating to Parent and Child in Scotland*** (2nd ed. by K.McK. Norrie, W.Green/SULI, 1999); and **Clive, *The Law of Husband and Wife*** (4th ed., W.Green/SULI, 1997).

Numerous textbooks are also recommended, such as **Edwards and Griffiths, *Family Law*** (W.Green, 1997); **Sutherland, *Child and Family Law*** (Butterworths, 1999); and **Thomson, *Family Law in Scotland*** (4th ed., Butterworths, 2002).

For a pre-examination guide see **Sutherland, *Family Lawbasics*** (W.Green, 1999); and for a comprehensive collection of extracts see **Mays, *Child and Family Law: Cases and Materials*** (W.Green, 2001).

As well as the numerous current articles and cases which should be sourced via Westlaw UK (**www.westlaw.co.uk**) it is recommended that the following reports and white papers be referred to for discussion of the various contentious areas:

- Kilbrandon Committee, *Report on Children and Young Persons, Scotland* (1964) (Cmnd.2306).
- *Report on Family Law* (1992) (Scot. Law Com. No.135).
- *Parents and Children: A White Paper on Scottish Family Law* (2000).
- *Report on the Reform of the Ground for Divorce* (Scot. Law Com. No.116).

Chapter 14

CRIMINAL

James Chalmers[1]

THE NATURE OF CRIMINAL LAW

It has been said that criminal law "is a species of political and moral philosophy".[2] That is not to say that a philosophical training is required for the study of criminal law, but that the question which criminal law asks is in substance philosophical—what are the conditions under which persons may be held criminally responsible for their actions and therefore liable to be punished by the state? The study of criminal law is a study of those conditions. **14–01**

There are, of course, important underlying philosophical questions regarding the issue of why the state is entitled to hold people "criminally responsible". In other words, why is a state entitled

[1] Lecturer in Law, University of Aberdeen. I am indebted to Professor Christopher Gane and Fiona Leverick for their comments on an earlier draft of this Chapter, and also to Michael Christie and Professor Gane for devising the structure of the first year criminal law course at Aberdeen, on which the structure of this Chapter is based.

[2] George P. Fletcher, *Rethinking Criminal Law* (1978), xix.

to punish its citizens? However, a basic study of criminal law is not concerned with such issues.[3] Instead, the student approaching criminal law for the first time will (normally) be required to consider how criminal offences are defined, what must be proven in order to convict a person of a crime, and which defences may exonerate persons from criminal liability. It is these issues with which this chapter is concerned.

SOURCES OF SCOTS CRIMINAL LAW

14–02 Throughout the world, criminal law is normally codified law. Most systems—and certainly almost all Western systems—have a criminal (or "penal") code which lays out the definitions of offences and the conditions under which individuals can be held responsible for committing those offences.[4]

In this respect, however, Scots law is radically different. There is no Scottish criminal code, although a group of academics has been working for some years on an "unofficial draft" of what a Scottish criminal code might look like.[5] Instead, the predominant part of Scots criminal law is common law: *i.e.* constructed from judicial decisions in particular cases over the years. There is a great deal of statutory criminal law, particularly in "regulatory" areas such as road traffic and health and safety law, and also misuse of drugs legislation, but almost all major criminal offences have no statutory definition, which must instead be discerned from the decided cases.[6] In addition to case law, the Scottish courts often rely on a number of legal writers, particularly (Baron) David Hume, whose nineteenth-century work *Commentaries on the Law of Scotland, Respecting Crimes*[7] is generally considered an authoritative statement of the criminal law as it applied at the time, and is even now frequently relied upon by the courts in the process of ascertaining the modern criminal law.[8]

The case-based nature of Scots criminal law is generally thought to allow for greater flexibility in the development of the criminal law. Historically, the Scottish courts have asserted a power referred to as the "declaratory power"—that is, a power on the part of the High Court "competently to punish … every act which is obviously of a criminal nature; though it be such which in time past has never been the subject of prosecution."[9]

While this power to "create new crimes" has rarely been exercised explicitly[10]—at least in recent times—the courts have still drawn on the "flexible nature" of the criminal law in more modern cases to address what might be seen as "new problems". So, in *Khaliq v H.M. Advocate*,[11] the High Court felt able to declare that selling "glue-sniffing kits" to children was the offence of "causing real injury", on the basis that the sellers bore responsibility for any injury caused to the children from their substance abuse, and in *Carmichael v Black; Black v Carmichael*,[12] it was held that to "wheel-clamp" cars which had been improperly parked on private property and demand a fee for their release could be both theft and extortion at common law.

In this way, it has been judicially suggested, the courts have "helped to ensure that Scots criminal law… has not been subject to undue interference by overenthusiastic legislators".[13] Against that must be weighed two principled objections. The first principle is that of *legality*: criminal law should be known (or, at least, accessible). Citizens are entitled to know in advance whether or not any conduct on which they intend to embark is criminal—they should not have to

---

[3] For a modern discussion, see Nicola Lacey, *State Punishment* (1988), especially Chap.2.
[4] *cf.* George P. Fletcher, *Basic Concepts of Criminal Law* (1998), p.3.
[5] See Eric Clive, "Current codification projects in Scotland" (2000) 4 Edin.L.R. 341.
[6] English law is similar in approach, although a much greater part of the "common law" has been altered by or codified in statute in England than is the case in Scotland.
[7] David Hume, *Commentaries on the Law of Scotland, Respecting Crimes* (4th ed., 1844, by B.R. Bell) (hereafter cited as "Hume, *Commentaries*").
[8] See also the further reading notes section at the end of this Chapter.
[9] Hume, *Commentaries*, i, p.12.
[10] It has not been explicitly relied upon since *Bernard Greenhuff* (1838) 2 Swin. 236.
[11] 1984 J.C. 23.
[12] 1992 S.L.T. 897.
[13] *McLay v H.M. Advocate*, 1994 J.C. 159, *per* Lord McCluskey at 173. Compare, however, the comments by the same judge in *Lord Advocate's Reference (No.1 of 2001)*, 2002 S.L.T. 466.

wait for the courts to decide that question afterwards. The second principle is, quite simply, *democracy*: many would argue that it is fundamentally inappropriate for the courts to be acting as legislators, and that such questions must be for the Scottish or Westminster Parliaments to address. The question has been hotly debated with respect to the declaratory power in particular.[14]

It would be all but impossible for the declaratory power to be invoked today, due to the provisions of the Human Rights Act 1998 and the European Convention on Human Rights, Art.7 of which explicitly states that "no one shall be held guilty of any criminal offence on account of any act or omission which did not constitute a criminal offence under national or international law at the time when it was committed".[15] Some development of the criminal law through judicial decision is, however, probably inevitable and necessary, because it is never possible to anticipate in advance all the problems which the criminal courts might require to address. Provided that any development of the law by the courts is reasonably foreseeable, this will not violate the European Convention on Human Rights.[16]

Any study of criminal law will reveal numerous areas where the law is uncertain or unclear. While the resultant "grey area" may well be frustrating, it should be remembered that it may well be of limited importance in practice. Most cases of crime which are reported to the police and prosecution authorities will quite clearly fall within (or quite clearly fall outwith) the definition of a criminal offence. Similarly, while the exact boundary of a criminal offence may be unclear, it will normally still be clear how citizens are expected to behave if they do not wish to fall foul of the law. The lack of a clear boundary is not necessarily unfair, provided that it is not difficult to stay on the right side of the boundary. In that sense, the "grey area" may be more theoretical than real in many cases. That is not to say that the exact definitions of crimes are not important—far from it—simply that the ambiguities which exist may not present as many practical problems as might first appear.

GENERAL PRINCIPLES OF CRIMINAL LIABILITY

The anatomy of a crime

It is normal to regard a criminal offence as being made up of three elements, as follows: **14–03**

(1) *actus reus*
(2) *mens rea*
(3) the absence of a defence

The *actus reus* is probably best understood as the physical element of the crime. Despite the term "*actus*", it need not necessarily be an action—depending on the crime, it may be constituted by an omission to act or a "state of affairs" (such as being in possession of a controlled drug).

Mens rea is the fault element which is required for the crime, such as an intention to cause a particular result, knowledge that a particular circumstance exists, or recklessness as to the consequences of one's actions. For some statutory offences, a fault element may not actually be required. This is known as "strict liability", and is discussed further below.[17]

It is important to notice that the word "defence" is used here in a technical sense. In ordinary language, we refer to anything which might result in a person's acquittal as a defence—so in that sense, it is a defence to show (for example) that someone else committed the crime, that the complainer in a theft case consented to the appropriation of his property, or that an accused did not actually possess the *mens rea* required for the crime. These are simply denials that the prosecution have proved *actus reus* or *mens rea*.

---

[14] See most recently, Ian Willock, "The declaratory power—still indefensible", 1996 J.R. 99; Scott Styles, "The declaratory power: inevitable and desirable", 1999 J.R. 99.

[15] See further Christopher Gane, "The substantive criminal law" in *A Practical Guide to Human Rights Law in Scotland* (Reed ed., 2001), p.61.

[16] See *SW v United Kingdom* (1996) 21 E.H.R.R. 363.

[17] See below, para.14–10.

The word "defence" is used here to refer to those rules of law which may be pled as a *justification* or *excuse* for the accused's conduct where *actus reus* and *mens rea* have both been shown to exist. In this sense, defences include such concepts as self-defence, insanity or necessity. Defences are discussed in full at the end of this Chapter.[18]

It is important to note that an accused cannot normally be required to prove anything in a criminal trial. Even where an accused pleads a defence such as self-defence, the most they can be required to do by law is simply to produce *some* evidence to suggest that the defence might apply. The prosecution must then prove beyond a reasonable doubt that the defence does not apply, otherwise the accused is entitled to an acquittal.[19] The only exceptions to this rule at common law[20] are the defences of insanity[21] and diminished responsibility,[22] which must be proved by the accused on the balance of probabilities.[23]

Actus reus

14–04 All crimes require a physical element, referred to as an *actus reus*. The law does not punish a guilty mind alone. This physical element may include such factors as the conduct of the accused, the circumstances in which that conduct takes place, and the results of that conduct.

Normally, the *actus reus* will involve some sort of action by the accused—which is relatively unproblematic—but the criminal law also imposes liability for omissions in certain circumstances. This is more problematic, and requires further discussion.

Liability for omissions

14–05 Crimes of omission may be divided into two forms. The first category, sometimes referred to as "pure omissions", are crimes which consist simply of a failure to do something, such as a failure to report a road traffic accident where required by law to do so.[24] Virtually all examples of such crimes are statutory.

The second category may be referred to as crimes of "commission by omission". Omitting to act may amount to the *actus reus* of a result crime. Where a person is under a duty to act but fails to do so, and this has the effect of causing a particular legally prohibited result, the person may be guilty of that offence. The most obvious example is a person who fails to prevent a death when they are legally obliged to do so: such a person may be guilty of murder or culpable homicide. Duties to act are only imposed in exceptional cases: under Scots law, a person who walks past a stranger in peril and fails to assist may be morally guilty, but cannot be said to be legally guilty of anything.[25]

There is very little authority on the extent of crimes of commission by omission in Scots law, but it is generally thought that duties to act are recognised in the following circumstances:

(1) *Family relationships.* A parent has a duty to prevent harm coming to their child.[26] It is normally thought, however, that a child has no reciprocal duty towards a parent unless they have assumed responsibility for that person (see (3) below).

---

18 See below, paras 14–61 *et seq.*
19 *Lambie v H.M. Advocate*, 1973 J.C. 53.
20 Exceptions in statutory offences are extremely common: *cf.* Andrew Ashworth and Meredith Blake, "The presumption of innocence in English criminal law" [1996] Crim.L.R. 306.
21 See below, para.14–62.
22 See below, para.14–18.
23 *Lindsay v H.M. Advocate*, 1997 J.C. 19.
24 See Road Traffic Act 1988, s.170.
25 *H.M. Advocate v McClure and Bone,* unreported, September 2002, High Court at Stonehaven (observations of Lord Abernethy in his charge to the jury).
26 *H.M. Advocate v McClure and Bone,* unreported, September 2002, High Court at Stonehaven. See also *R. v Gibbins and Proctor* (1918) 13 Cr.App.R. 134; *cf. Paterson v Lees*, 1999 J.C. 159.

(2) *Assumption of responsibility.* A person who assumes responsibility towards another must prevent harm coming to that person. In the English case of *R. v Stone and Dobinson*,[27] a man and his partner allowed the man's sister to live with them. The sister, described as "eccentric in many ways", did not eat properly and largely confined herself to her room. Eventually, she became unwilling or unable to leave her bed. Stone and Dobinson made some ineffectual attempts to seek medical assistance but did nothing further, and the sister died. It was held that they had accepted responsibility for her by taking her in, and that their failure to summon medical assistance meant that they were guilty of manslaughter (the English equivalent of culpable homicide).

Responsibility may in such cases have been assumed by contract, although it should certainly not be thought that a contract is essential. In *William Hardie*,[28] it was held that a man employed as a poor inspector could in principle be held guilty of culpable homicide if it was shown that his failure to render assistance to a woman who had made an application for poor relief had caused her death.

(3) *Creation of a dangerous situation.* A person who has created a dangerous situation may be under an obligation to remedy the danger created, even if they were not initially at fault. In the English case of *R. v Miller*,[29] a tramp squatting in an unoccupied house fell asleep while smoking a cigarette, which set fire to his mattress. He then awoke, left the mattress smouldering and moved to another room instead. The house caught fire and he was charged with arson.[30] It was held that he could be held liable for arson on the basis that he had done nothing to remedy the danger caused by his initial act of falling asleep while smoking.

Causation

In crimes which require a particular result as an element of the *actus reus* (such as murder or culpable homicide, where the relevant result is the death of the victim), it must be shown that the accused's act (or omission) caused that result. Although much academic and philosophical work has been directed towards developing a theoretical account of causation,[31] the courts have tended to take the view that causation "is essentially a practical question of fact which can best be answered by ordinary common sense rather than by abstract metaphysical theory".[32] **14–06**

There are two well-recognised doctrines which require special attention, however. The first of this is the doctrine of *taking your victim as you find him* (also referred to as the "thin skull" rule). If A assaults B, and it transpires that B has a weak heart, or an egg-shell skull, and dies as a result, B's special susceptibility to injury is no reason to hold that A has not caused B's death.[33] In the English case of *R. v Blaue*,[34] Blaue stabbed a young woman who later refused a blood transfusion on the ground that she was a Jehovah's Witness and died as a result. While it was accepted that she would not have died had she accepted a blood transfusion, the Court of Appeal held that Blaue's actions were still to be regarded as the cause of her death—an assailant must take his victim as he finds him, religious beliefs and all.

The second doctrine is that of *novus actus interveniens* (a new intervening cause). If A assaults B, and B later dies, but something new and unforeseeable has happened between the two incidents which can be regarded as a new, supervening cause of B's death, A's assault will not be regarded as the cause of death. This might include extremely poor medical treatment (sometimes referred to as "malregimen"), a new act by a third party, or possibly even the actions of the victim himself. The need for such actions to be unforeseeable before they will break the chain of causation must

---

27 [1977] Q.B. 354.
28 (1847) Ark. 247.
29 [1983] 2 A.C. 161. See also the Scottish case of *Macphail v Clark*, 1983 S.L.T. (Sh. Ct) 37.
30 Scots law does not use the term "arson". The nearest equivalent offence is fireraising, on which see below, para.14–49.
31 See, in particular, H.L.A. Hart and T. Honoré, *Causation in the Law* (2nd ed., 1985).
32 *Alphacell Ltd v Woodward* [1972] A.C. 824, *per* Lord Salmon at 847.
33 *James Williamson* (1866) 5 Irv. 326; *Bird v H.M. Advocate*, 1952 J.C. 23.
34 [1975] 1 W.L.R. 1411.

be emphasised, however—where A supplies a harmful substance (such as glue or a controlled drug) to B knowing that B wishes to abuse that substance, B's actions in abusing the substance will not break the chain of causation between A's original act and any harm sustained by B as a result.[35]

Mens rea

14–07 For all common law crimes, the accused cannot be criminally liable on the basis of the *actus reus* alone. It is essential that the prosecution also prove *mens rea* (sometimes referred to as a "guilty mind").

The exact form of *mens rea* required will depend upon the definition of the particular offence. It is usually expressed in terms of intention, knowledge, or recklessness. Scots law has not paid much attention to how the first two of those terms might be defined, although it is not clear that attempts to define those terms would be particularly helpful. Recklessness is generally defined as an "utter disregard" for the consequences of one's actions,[36] although it is possible that different definitions may apply with respect to different criminal offences.[37]

The (ir)relevance of motive

14–08 It is commonly said that motive is irrelevant to culpability: "It is as firmly established in legal doctrine as any rule can be that motive is irrelevant to responsibility".[38] This is only true up to a point, however. Motive is, indeed, generally irrelevant to questions of *mens rea*. If A intends to hit B, he has the *mens rea* for assault (that is, an intention to attack B) regardless of his motives for doing so. Motivation can, however, be extremely relevant to the question of whether A has a valid justification or excuse for his conduct, such as the defence of self-defence.[39]

Error

14–09 An error as to the scope of the criminal law (*i.e.* a belief that a certain act is *not* criminal) is no defence to a criminal charge. Other errors of fact, however, may relieve a person from criminal liability. It is important to distinguish between three types of error in this respect.

First, errors may be irrelevant—for example, if A hits B, it is no defence for him to say that he thought he was hitting C.[40]

Secondly, an error of fact may show that the accused did not in fact have the *mens rea* required for the crime. For example, the *mens rea* required for the crime of rape is that the man knew that the woman was not consenting to sexual intercourse, or was reckless as to whether or not she was consenting. It has, therefore, been held that a man who has sexual intercourse with a woman in the belief that she is consenting is not guilty of the offence of rape, however unreasonable that belief may be.[41] Where the accused lacks the *mens rea* for a crime because of an error of fact, it matters not how unreasonable it is—he is still entitled to be acquitted.[42]

Thirdly, errors of fact may provide a foundation for a justificatory or excusatory defence. For example, if A believes (wrongly) that he has grounds for acting in self-defence, and does so, he may be entitled to plead the defence of self-defence.[43] His belief must be reasonable, however.[44]

---

[35] *Khaliq v H.M. Advocate*, 1984 J.C. 23; *Lord Advocate's Reference (No.1 of 1994)*, 1996 J.C. 76.
[36] *Cameron v Maguire*, 1999 J.C. 63; *Quinn v Cunningham*, 1956 J.C. 22.
[37] *cf. Allan v Patterson*, 1980 J.C. 57.
[38] A. Norrie, *Crime, Reason and History* (2nd ed., 2001), p.36.
[39] On the requirements of this defence, see below, para.14–65.
[40] *cf. Roberts v Hamilton*, 1989 S.L.T. 399.
[41] *Jamieson v H.M. Advocate*, 1994 J.C. 88; *Meek v H.M. Advocate*, 1983 S.L.T. 280. See further below, para.14–32.
[42] *cf.*, however, *Dewar v H.M. Advocate*, 1945 J.C. 5.
[43] See further below, para.14–65.

Strict liability

Although no person can be convicted of a common law offence without proof of *mens rea*, this is not always the case with statutory offences. Some statutory offences may not require proof of any *mens rea* for conviction. These are referred to as "strict liability" offences. **14–10**

The question of whether or not an offence requires proof of *mens rea* for conviction is one of statutory interpretation. It is always presumed that an offence requires *mens rea* unless the terms of the statute imply otherwise.[45] The statute may make it clear that *mens rea* is required, by the use of terms such as "knowingly" or "wilfully". In many cases, however, a statutory offence will make no explicit provision as regards *mens rea*, and the courts must therefore apply various criteria in order to determine whether the offence is one of strict liability. These criteria were set out in the following case:

Gammon Ltd v Attorney-General of Hong Kong
[1985] A.C. 1

Lord Scarman: "(1) there is a presumption of law that mens rea is required before a person can be held guilty of a criminal offence; (2) the presumption is particularly strong where the offence is 'truly criminal' in character; (3) the presumption applies to statutory offences, and can be displaced only if this is clearly or by necessary implication the effect of the statute; (4) the only situation in which the presumption can be displaced is where the statute is concerned with an issue of social concern, and public safety is such an issue; (5) even where a statute is concerned with such an issue, the presumption of mens rea stands unless it can also be shown that the creation of strict liability will be effective to promote the objects of the statute by encouraging greater vigilance to prevent the commission of the prohibited act."

The fact that an offence is punishable by imprisonment is no bar to it being held to be one of strict liability.[46]

Corporate liability[47]

While it is clearly competent to prosecute a corporation for a criminal offence,[48] the extent to which corporations may be held guilty of criminal offences under Scots law remains unclear. In the first major case on the issue, *Dean v John Menzies (Holdings) Ltd*,[49] it was held that a company could not be guilty of the offence of shameless indecency,[50] because shamelessness was a uniquely human characteristic which could not be possessed by a company. This decision, however, must be read against the background of concern about the widespread use of shameless indecency charges at the time,[51] and it has been suggested that the decision might not be followed if the issue were to arise again now.[52] **14–11**

In *Purcell Meats (Scotland) Ltd v McLeod*,[53] the only other major case which deals with the point, it was held that a company could, in principle, be found guilty of the offence of attempted

[44] *Owens v H.M. Advocate*, 1946 J.C. 119. See, however, Fiona Leverick, "Mistake in self-defence after *Drury*", 2002 J.R. 35.
[45] *Duguid v Fraser*, 1942 J.C. 1; *Sweet v Parsley* [1970] A.C. 132.
[46] *Gammon Ltd v Attorney-General of Hong Kong* [1985] A.C. 1, *per* Lord Scarman at 17.
[47] See generally Richard Mays, "The criminal liability of corporations and Scots law: learning the lessons of Anglo-American jurisprudence" (2000) 4 Edin.L.R. 46.
[48] Criminal Procedure (Scotland) Act 1995, ss.70 and 143.
[49] 1981 J.C. 23.
[50] On which see below, para.14–36.
[51] See, *e.g.* Ian Willock, "Shameless indecency—how far the Crown Office has reached" (1981) 52 SCOLAG 199.
[52] G.H. Gordon, *Criminal Law* (3rd ed., 2000, by M.G.A. Christie), Vol.I, p. 393.
[53] 1987 S.L.T. 528.

fraud. This suggests that corporations could be found guilty of most offences under Scots law, except those which require specifically human conduct—such as, for example, rape, although even in those cases there might be no barrier to holding a corporation art and part guilty of the crime (*i.e.* as an "accessory").[54]

The problem in such cases is likely to be proving *mens rea* on the part of an organisation, because a corporation is not a person and does not have "states of mind". If *mens rea* on the part of persons who are sufficiently senior to be regarded as the "controlling mind" of the company can be proven, it seems that will be sufficient.[55]

Defences

14–12 Even where both *actus reus* and *mens rea* can be proven, an accused may be able to argue that his conduct is in some way justified or excused. Such a claim will only result in an acquittal if it can be framed in terms of one of the several general defences (such as self-defence or necessity) which are recognised by Scots law. These are discussed in full at the end of this Chapter.

Key Concepts

A **criminal offence** is constructed from three elements: (1) the *actus reus* (the physical element); (2) *mens rea* (the fault element) and (3) the absence of a defence.

There is **generally no liability for omissions** in the criminal law unless (a) this is explicitly provided for by statute or (b) a person is under a duty to act. Duties to act may arise from family relationships, the assumption of responsibility or the creation of a dangerous situation.

Where the *actus reus* of a crime requires a particular result, it must be shown that the accused caused that result: this is the requirement of **causation**.

Mens rea requirements are usually defined in terms of **intention, knowledge or recklessness**.

Some statutory crimes do not require *mens rea*: this is known as **strict liability**.

Corporations can be liable for most offences under Scots law.

HOMICIDE

14–13 Scots law distinguishes between two forms of homicide: murder and culpable homicide.[56] (There is also a statutory offence of causing death by dangerous driving).[57] The *actus reus* of both types of homicide is the destruction of a self-existent human life,[58] although the *mens rea* differs (the definitions of *mens rea* which apply to each form of homicide are explained below).

[54] On art and part liability, see below, para.14–60.

[55] *Purcell Meats (Scotland) Ltd v McLeod*, 1987 S.L.T. 528.

[56] Note also the relevant crimes against international law which are recognised by the International Criminal Court (Scotland) Act 2001, s.1.

[57] Road Traffic Act 1988, s.1, as amended. Such conduct can, of course, be charged as either murder or culpable homicide if the requirements of those crimes are met: see, *e.g. McDowall v H.M. Advocate*, 1998 J.C. 194.

[58] Macdonald, *Criminal Law* (5th ed., 1948), p.87.

The destruction of an unborn child is not homicide under Scots law, because such a child does not have an independent existence.[59] It may, however, be the crime of abortion.[60] The situation is different, however, where injuries are inflicted on an unborn child who is born alive but subsequently dies as a result of those injuries. Such circumstances are generally thought to be sufficient for the *actus reus* of homicide.[61]

Culpable homicide is a lesser crime than murder: while murder carries a mandatory sentence of life imprisonment,[62] there is no fixed sentence for culpable homicide and it is not unknown for persons convicted of culpable homicide to walk free from court in some cases.[63] It is, however, competent to pass a sentence of life imprisonment on a conviction for culpable homicide in appropriate cases.[64]

Murder

The classic definition of murder is that offered by Macdonald: **14–14**

> "Murder is constituted by any wilful act causing the destruction of life, whether intended to kill, or displaying such wicked recklessness as to imply a disposition depraved enough to be regardless of consequences."[65]

It can be seen from this that there are two alternative forms of the *mens rea* of murder. A person who causes the death of another is guilty of murder if (i) he intended to kill; or (ii) was "wickedly reckless".

In *Drury v H.M. Advocate*,[66] it was said that Macdonald's definition was incomplete, and that an intention to kill must (like recklessness) also be "wicked" before the actor can be guilty of murder. Quite what the court meant by "wicked" in this context is unclear, but it seems that an intention to kill will always be regarded as "wicked" unless the defences of provocation or diminished responsibility apply.[67] These are partial defences which "reduce" murder to culpable homicide, and are discussed below in that context.[68]

Wicked recklessness was defined by Lord Sutherland in *H.M. Advocate v Hartley* in the following terms:

H.M. Advocate v Hartley

1989 S.L.T. 135

Lord Sutherland: "That ['wicked recklessness'] sounds a bit archaic. If it does, it is not surprising, because it is a definition which has been in existence for hundreds of years, and has stood the test of time. And basically what it means is simply this. If you act in such a way as to show that you don't really care whether the person you are attacking lives or dies, then that can constitute this degree of wicked recklessness which is required to constitute murder. It may, in the end of the day, come as a considerable surprise to you, and indeed a matter of regret too that your victim dies, but that doesn't alter the fact that you have committed murder, if you have, during the course of the attack, displayed such wicked recklessness as to show that you are regardless of the consequences, that you have no particular interest in whether your victim lives or dies."

---

[59] *Jean McCallum* (1858) 3 Irv. 187.

[60] See generally G.H. Gordon, *Criminal Law* (3rd ed., 2001, by M.G.A. Christie), Vol.II, Chap.28.

[61] *cf. McCluskey v H.M. Advocate*, 1988 S.C.C.R. 629.

[62] Criminal Procedure (Scotland) Act 1995, s.205.

[63] See, *e.g. Burns v H.M. Advocate*, 1998 S.C.C.R. 281 (sentence of 240 hours community service).

[64] *Kirkwood v H.M. Advocate*, 1939 J.C. 16.

[65] Macdonald, *Criminal Law* (5th ed., 1948), p.89.

[66] 2001 S.L.T. 1013.

[67] For a criticism of the court's approach, see James Chalmers, "Collapsing the structure of criminal law", 2001 S.L.T. (News) 241.

[68] The terminology of "reducing" murder to culpable homicide was disapproved in *Drury* but rehabilitated in *Galbraith v H.M. Advocate (No.2)*, 2002 J.C. 1.

Culpable homicide

14–15 There are three forms of culpable homicide which are recognised by Scots law:

- voluntary culpable homicide (this covers cases where the actor has the *mens rea* of murder but one of the two partial defences available to murder—provocation or diminished responsibility—applies and "reduces" the crime to culpable homicide);
- unlawful act culpable homicide (this covers cases where the actor has committed another crime which has resulted in death); and
- involuntary culpable homicide (this covers cases where the actor does not have the *mens rea* of murder, but has been grossly negligent).

Each of these categories will now be considered in more detail.

Voluntary culpable homicide

14–16 Where the requirements for the crime of murder have been made out, an accused may nevertheless be convicted of culpable homicide if a "partial defence" applies. There are two such partial defences recognised by Scots law: provocation and diminished responsibility.

Provocation

14–17 The plea of provocation, if successful, will result in the accused being convicted of culpable homicide rather than murder. It is not a complete defence. While evidence of provocation may be considered in mitigation of sentence for any other crime (most commonly assault), it is only in homicide cases that it can have any effect on the offence of which the accused is convicted.

When considering a plea of provocation, a jury must address the following questions.[69]

(1) Was there a recognised provocation? Scots law only recognises two forms of provocation—firstly, provocation by assault (*i.e.* the deceased assaulted the accused) and secondly, provocation by infidelity. For provocation by infidelity to operate, the accused must have been in a relationship of fidelity (not necessarily marriage, or even a heterosexual relationship).[70] The accused must have discovered that his partner was unfaithful, and killed either the partner or their paramour in consequence of that revelation. Although the defence may, historically, only have applied where the accused caught the parties in the act of infidelity, this is no longer the case, and a simple confession of infidelity will suffice.[71]

Under Scots law as it currently stands, words can never be sufficient to found a defence of provocation.[72]

(2) Did the accused lose his self-control? A person is only entitled to plead provocation if he loses his self-control and kills in the heat of the moment. A person who kills for revenge may not plead the defence.

(3) Would an ordinary person, subjected to such provocation, have been liable to react in the same way?

If all of these questions are answered in the affirmative (or, strictly speaking given the burden of proof, if the Crown has failed to prove beyond a reasonable doubt that any one of them should be answered in the negative), the defence will succeed and the accused will be convicted of culpable homicide and not murder.

---

[69] See generally, *Drury v H.M. Advocate*, 2001 S.L.T. 1013.

[70] *McKay v H.M. Advocate*, 1991 J.C. 91; *H.M. Advocate v McKean*, 1996 S.C.C.R. 402.

[71] *H.M. Advocate v Hill*, 1941 J.C. 59.

[72] See Macdonald, *Criminal Law* (5th ed., 1948), p.93. This is not the case in England: Homicide Act 1957, s.3.

Diminished responsibility

This partial defence is generally considered to have originated in the 1867 case of *Alexander Dingwall*.[73] In that case, Dingwall—an alcoholic—killed his wife, with whom he was generally on good terms, after a quarrel. He was mentally ill, but not insane. Lord Deas directed the jury that it was open to them to convict Dingwall of culpable homicide rather than murder on the grounds of the "extenuating circumstances" of the case, which they did. **14–18**

The requirements for the defence are now governed by the decision of five judges in the leading case of *Galbraith v H.M. Advocate (No.2)*,[74] and are as follows:

(1) The accused must have been suffering from an "abnormality of mind" at the time of the killing. This abnormality can take any form, provided that it is one "recognised by the appropriate science". Prior to *Galbraith*, it was thought that only a "mental disease" qualified (and the defence could, therefore, not be based on a personality disorder), but this is no longer the case.[75] Two specific abnormalities of mind are excluded, however. The defence may never be based on self-induced intoxication or psychopathic personality disorder.[76]

(2) The abnormality of mind must have "substantially impaired the ability of the accused, as compared with a normal person, to determine or control his acts."[77]

The accused must prove both of these requirements on the balance of probabilities (*not* beyond reasonable doubt).[78] This is an exception to the general rule that the burden of proof in a criminal case is always on the prosecution.

As with provocation, evidence of diminished responsibility can be taken into account in mitigation of sentence on any charge, but it is only on a charge of murder that it can alter the offence of which the accused is convicted.

Unlawful act culpable homicide

It is thought that any criminal act which results in death is always culpable homicide. The position is clearly settled in relation to assault, and the leading case is the 1952 decision in *Bird v H.M. Advocate*.[79] **14–19**

Bird v H.M. Advocate

1952 J.C. 23

Bird believed that a woman had taken money belonging to him. He followed her for half a mile and forcibly restrained her from boarding a passing car, whereupon she collapsed and died. It was later discovered that she had a diseased heart. Lord Jamieson directed the jury that if it was proved that Bird had assaulted the deceased, and that this had caused her death, this was sufficient for a finding of guilty of culpable homicide. It was therefore unnecessary to show any *mens rea* on Bird's part beyond the *mens rea* which is required for assault. Bird was convicted of culpable homicide, and his conviction was upheld on appeal.

---

[73] (1867) 5 Irv. 466.

[74] 2002 J.C. 1. See generally James Chalmers, "Abnormality and Anglicisation: First Thoughts on *Galbraith v H.M. Advocate (No.2)*" (2002) 6 Edin.L.R. 108.

[75] See *Connelly v H.M. Advocate*, 1990 J.C. 349 and *Williamson v H.M. Advocate*, 1994 J.C. 149, both of which were overruled in *Galbraith*.

[76] *Galbraith v H.M. Advocate (No.2)*, 2002 J.C. 1, *per* the Lord Justice-General (Rodger) at 17.

[77] *Galbraith v H.M. Advocate (No.2)*, 2002 J.C. 1, *per* the Lord Justice-General (Rodger) at 21.

[78] *Lindsay v H.M. Advocate*, 1997 J.C. 19.

[79] 1952 J.C. 23. On unlawful act culpable homicide generally, see Jenifer Ross, "Unlawful Act Culpable Homicide: A Suitable Case for Reappraisal", 1996 S.L.T. (News) p.75.

It is clear that this rule extends to any criminal act which involves a foreseeable risk of personal injury—and so, for example, it was applied in *Mathieson v H.M. Advocate*[80] to find the accused guilty of culpable homicide after he had committed a fireraising which resulted in the deaths of some occupants of a nearby building. It is not clear, however, whether the rule applies to criminal acts which do not involve a foreseeable risk of injury, although for obvious reasons, a charge of unlawful act culpable homicide based on such an offence would be unlikely.[81]

Involuntary culpable homicide

14–20 This crime is committed where the accused causes death through an act which is not unlawful (or at least not a basis for a charge of unlawful act culpable homicide) and does so with the *mens rea* of this form of culpable homicide.

The classic statement of the *mens rea* of this form of culpable homicide can be found in *Paton v H.M. Advocate*, where it was said that the *mens rea* required was "gross, or wicked, or criminal negligence, something amounting, or at any rate analogous, to a criminal indifference to consequences".[82] That is a rather lengthy formulation, and in the more recent case of *McDowall v H.M. Advocate*,[83] Lord Abernethy directed the jury that if the accused had shown "a complete disregard for any potential dangers which might result" from his actions, that was sufficient *mens rea* for the crime. In McDowall's subsequent appeal against conviction, it was accepted that this direction was correct.

Because, as noted above, any unlawful act which results in death is necessarily culpable homicide, without the need to prove this *mens rea*, it has been said that this form of culpable homicide "is almost entirely confined to traffic cases".[84] Driving a car (unlike, for example, assaulting someone) is perfectly lawful in itself—but if it is done with complete disregard for the safety of the public and a death results, the driver will be guilty of culpable homicide.

> **Key Concepts**
>
> **Murder** is committed where a person causes a death while either (a) wickedly intending to kill or (b) acting in a such a way as to display a wicked recklessness of the consequences of his actions.
>
> If a person would otherwise be guilty of murder but successfully pleads either **provocation** or **diminished responsibility**, they will be convicted of **culpable homicide** instead. This form of culpable homicide is referred to as **voluntary culpable homicide**.
>
> **Diminished responsibility** applies where a person, at the time of the killing, suffered from an abnormality of mind which substantially impaired his ability, as compared with a normal person, to determine or control his acts.
>
> **Provocation** applies where a person (a) is subject to a recognised provocation (violence or a revelation of infidelity), which (b) causes him to lose control and kill another person, provided that (c) an ordinary person subjected to such provocation would have been liable to react in the same way.

---

[80] 1981 S.C.C.R. 196. See also *Sutherland v H.M. Advocate*, 1994 S.L.T. 634.
[81] See, however, *Lourie v H.M. Advocate*, 1988 S.C.C.R. 634.
[82] 1936 J.C. 19, *per* the Lord Justice-Clerk (Aitchison) at 22.
[83] 1998 J.C. 194.
[84] G.H. Gordon, *Criminal Law* (3rd ed., 2001, by M.G.A. Christie), Vol.II, p.366.

> A person is guilty of **unlawful act culpable homicide** where he commits an unlawful act which involves a foreseeable risk of physical injury (such as an assault) and this causes a death.
>
> A person is guilty of **involuntary culpable homicide** if he causes a death by acting with a complete disregard for any potential dangers which might result from his actions.

NON-FATAL OFFENCES AGAINST THE PERSON

Assault

Actus reus

The *actus reus* of an assault is simply an "attack upon the person of another".[85] This will normally **14–21** involve force being applied to the victim, often (but not necessarily) resulting in injury. Examples of "attacks" found in the case law include spitting at a person (*James Cairns*),[86] whipping a pony which was being ridden by a boy so that it threw him off its back and injured him (*David Keay*),[87] and setting a dog on a person (*Kay v Allen*).[88] The attack need not, however, involve any actual force being applied to the victim, as the following case illustrates:

> **Atkinson v H.M. Advocate**
> 1987 S.C.C.R. 534
>
> Atkinson was convicted of assaulting a shop assistant by coming into the store wearing a mask and jumping over the counter at the assistant. On appeal, it was held that this was sufficient for assault even although it had not been proven that Atkinson had physically touched the shop assistant: "an assault may be constituted by threatening gestures sufficient to produce alarm."

Essentially, then, there are two forms of "attack"—actions which apply force to the victim, and actions which put the victim in fear of an immediate application of force. (Threatening the use of force at some point in the future may, in certain circumstances, be a criminal offence, but it would not be assault.)

An assault may be regarded as "aggravated" (and usually, therefore, will be more severely punished by the courts) by a number of circumstances, such as the use of a weapon (and the type used), the severity of the injury caused, any danger to life which resulted, or the character of the victim—particularly where the victim is a police officer. There is a specific statutory offence of assaulting, resisting, obstructing, molesting or hindering a constable in the execution of his duty.[89]

---

85 Macdonald, *Criminal Law* (5th ed., 1948), p.115.
86 (1858) 1 Swin. 597.
87 (1837) 1 Swin. 543.
88 (1978) S.C.C.R. Supp. 188. See also *Quinn v Lees*, 1994 S.C.C.R. 159.
89 Police (Scotland) Act 1967, s.41.

Mens rea

14–22 The *mens rea* of assault is "evil intent".[90] To be guilty of assault, therefore, a person must intend either to apply force to the victim or to put them in fear of an attack. The use of the word "evil" might be taken to suggest that a particular type of motive must be proven. This is, however, not the case, as the following decision illustrates:

> **Lord Advocate's Reference (No.2 of 1992)**
>
> 1993 J.C. 43
>
> A man ["X"] entered a shop, presented an imitation firearm at the shop owner and said "Get the money out of the till and lay on the floor." He fled after noticing that another member of staff was present. He was charged with assault and, as a defence, argued that his actions were a joke, that he had never intended to rob the shop, and therefore had no "evil intention". The trial judge directed the jury that if X had in fact been joking, he would have had no evil intention and should therefore be acquitted of assault. The jury acquitted him.
>
> The Lord Advocate referred the point of law involved to the High Court for an opinion. It was held that X's claim that he had been acting as a joke was irrelevant. Macdonald's statement that "evil intention" was the essence of assault meant only "that assault cannot be committed accidentally or recklessly or negligently". The trial judge had therefore misdirected the jury.

It should be made clear that, although it is no "defence" to say "it was a joke", a person who carries out a joke which unintentionally results in injury will not be guilty of assault, because they do not have the intention to attack which is necessary for the crime. The holding in the *Lord Advocate's Reference* means only that a person who intends to attack another person *as a joke* is guilty of an offence despite their supposedly "humourous" motivation.[91]

Although assault cannot be committed recklessly, the intention may be "transferred". So, if A throws a glass intending to hit B, but misses and hits C instead, he can be found guilty of assaulting C. This is because he intended to assault B, even though he had no intention of assaulting C, the actual victim.[92]

Specific defences

14–23 Although the general defences discussed at the end of this chapter apply equally to assault as to other crimes, there are a number of defences specific to assault which should be considered at this point.

Reasonable chastisement of children

14–24 A person who uses force to discipline a child may be entitled to plead the defence of "reasonable chastisement". This defence is available only to parents or to persons *in loco parentis* (*i.e.* having care of a child in place of a parent). In deciding whether the chastisement used was reasonable, the court will take into account the nature of the punishment, the age, health and sex of the child, and

---

[90] Macdonald, *Criminal Law* (5th ed., 1948), p.115; *Smart v H.M. Advocate*, 1975 J.C. 30.

[91] See also *Quinn v Lees*, 1994 S.C.C.R. 159; *Gilmour v McGlennan*, 1993 S.C.C.R. 837.

[92] *Connor v Jessop*, 1988 S.C.C.R. 624; *Roberts v Hamilton*, 1989 S.L.T. 399.

the effect of the punishment on the child.[93] Actions involving a blow to the head, shaking or the use of an implement can never be considered "reasonable".[94]

Consent

It is generally said that consent is not a defence to assault. The leading authority is *Smart v H.M. Advocate*: **14–25**

Smart v H.M. Advocate

1975 J.C. 30

Smart was charged with assaulting another man, Wilkie. He admitted that he had assaulted Wilkie, but claimed that Wilkie had consented to a fight. He was convicted of assault, and appealed against his conviction. In upholding the conviction, it was held that any such consent was irrelevant and that Smart was guilty of assault whether or not Wilkie had consented to the fight.

It appears, however, that consent is a valid justification insofar as socially accepted procedures such as surgery, tattooing and ear-piercing are concerned.[95] Consent may also be a defence to assaults which do not involve injury.[96] It has also been said that "for conduct in a sporting game to be criminal, it would require to be shown to be outwith the normal scope of the sport",[97] which goes some way towards explaining why boxers, etc. are not guilty of assault. The position is more difficult where persons consent to activities which are not "socially accepted" in this way. In the English case of *R v Brown*,[98] it was held that a group of sado-masochists who used "nails and sandpaper… in ways that would make a self-respecting carpenter blush"[99] were guilty of assault notwithstanding that all the parties concerned had consented.

Reasonable restraint

Police officers are entitled to use reasonable force in order to arrest or detain persons. If such force is excessive, however, they will be guilty of an assault. So, in *Marchbank v Annan*,[1] two police officers engaged in a high-speed chase after a boy who had stolen a car. When the car was forced to a halt, one of the officers used his baton to smash the window, hit the boy on the head, then dragged him out and kicked him on the body two or three times. On his appeal against a conviction for assault, the High Court held that he had gone "far beyond the limit of the force which a police officer is entitled to apply when attempting to apprehend a suspect" and upheld his conviction. **14–26**

---

93 Criminal Justice (Scotland) Act 2003, s.51.
94 Criminal Justice (Scotland) Act 2003, s.51(3).
95 See G.H. Gordon, *Criminal Law* (3rd ed., 2001, by M.G.A. Christie), Vol.II, p.415; *R. v Brown* [1994] 1 A.C. 212, *per* Lord Templeman at 231.
96 G.H. Gordon, "Consent in assault" (1976) 21 J.L.S.S. 168.
97 *Lord Advocate's Reference (No.2 of 1992)*, 1993 J.C. 43, *per* the Lord Justice-Clerk (Ross) at 48.
98 [1994] 1 A.C. 212. *cf. Wilson* [1996] 2 Cr.App.R. 241.
99 C. Munro, *Studies in Constitutional Law* (2nd ed., 1999), p.345.
1 1987 S.C.C.R. 718.

Key Concepts

An **assault** is committed by a person who (a) attacks another person and (b) does so with evil intent. An attack can involve either injuring a person or putting them in fear of immediate injury. The term "evil intent" merely emphasises that assault cannot be committed recklessly; it does not mean that a person must have an "evil motive" in order to be found guilty of assault.

There are three specific **defences** to assault, as follows:

Consent to a fight is not a defence to a charge of assault. However, consent does operate as a defence where socially acceptable practices such as surgery, tattooing or ear piercing and sports are concerned.

The defence of **reasonable chastisement of children** is available to parents (or persons acting in the place of parents) who use reasonable force to discipline children.

A police officer who uses reasonable force to arrest or detain a suspect is entitled to the defence of **reasonable restraint**.

Reckless injury

14–27 It is a crime to recklessly cause injury to another person. The *mens rea* required is an "utter disregard" for the consequences of one's actions.[2] It used to be thought that it was necessary to show that the public at large had been endangered by the accused's actions,[3] but this is no longer required.[4] There is in principle no limit to the number of ways in which this crime can be committed. Examples include giving a quarter pint of whisky to a seven-year-old child, which rendered the child permanently liable to convulsions (*Robert Brown and John Lawson*),[5] and throwing a bottle out of the fifteenth floor of a block of flats which struck and seriously injured a passer-by (*RHW v H.M. Advocate*).[6] In the recent case of *H.M. Advocate v Kelly*,[7] Kelly, having tested positive for HIV, had unprotected sexual intercourse with his girlfriend after falsely claiming to her that he was not HIV-positive. She subsequently contracted HIV, and he was convicted on a charge of recklessly injuring her.

Reckless endangerment

14–28 It is a crime to recklessly endanger the safety of the public. The *mens rea* required is, again, an "utter disregard" for the consequences of one's actions.[8] Again, there is in principle no limit to the number of ways in which this crime can be committed. Examples from the law reports include discharging firearms so that bullets might have ricocheted in the direction of a public road (*Cameron v Maguire*),[9] burning straw in a field so as to send smoke over a road, obscuring the

---

[2] *Cameron v Maguire*, 1999 J.C. 63.
[3] *Quinn v Cunningham*, 1956 J.C. 22.
[4] *H.M. Advocate v Harris*, 1993 J.C. 150.
[5] (1842) 1 Broun 415.
[6] 1982 S.L.T. 420.
[7] High Court at Glasgow, unreported, February 13-23, 2001, but see James Chalmers, "Sexually Transmitted Diseases and the Criminal Law", 2001 J.R. 259.
[8] *Cameron v Maguire*, 1999 J.C. 63.
[9] 1999 J.C. 63.

vision of passing drivers (*Macphail v Clark*),[10] and allowing a live puma to roam around an Edinburgh public house (*Reynolds v Lockhart*).[11] Persons who have falsely claimed to police officers, prior to being searched, that they have no sharp objects or needles in their possession have also been found guilty of this offence.[12]

It is not clear whether it is a criminal offence to endanger individuals (as opposed to the public at large), but the authorities (particularly the cases on exposing police officers to a risk of injury from needles) appear to support the proposition that endangering a small number of people, or even a single person, is a criminal offence.

Reckless supply of harmful substances

In *Khaliq v H.M. Advocate*,[13] the accused were charged with having "culpably, wilfully and recklessly" supplied what might be referred to as "glue-sniffing kits" to children between the age of 8 and 15 years. The court held that this was a valid charge, although the nature of the crime involved is not exactly clear. It was treated by the court as a form of "causing real injury", but it had not been alleged by the Crown that the children were in fact injured by their use of the "kits", only that their health had been endangered. This seems almost to be a form of reckless endangerment, in that the supplier is held responsible for the danger to the purchaser's health which is caused by their subsequent use of the substance. In *Ulhaq v H.M. Advocate*,[14] it was held to be sufficient that the accused had supplied substances such as lighter fluid and glue in their normal containers to adults whom he knew intended to use them for the purposes of solvent abuse. The significance of these cases is that they hold that the "victim's" voluntary act does not break the chain of causation where the seller knows of their intentions at the time of supplying the substance (or perhaps even where he is reckless as to their intentions). He can therefore be held responsible for the consequences of their substance abuse in such cases. **14–29**

In *Lord Advocate's Reference (No.1 of 1994)*,[15] the accused supplied amphetamine to a number of persons, one of whom died as a result of taking the drug. It was held that, by an extension of the principle invoked in *Khaliq* and *Ulhaq*, this could amount to the crime of culpable homicide. It seems that this would be "unlawful act" culpable homicide,[16] based on the initial crime of supplying the controlled substance.

Key Concepts

The crime of **reckless injury** is committed where a person causes injury to another person while acting with an "utter disregard" for the consequences of his actions.

The crime of **reckless endangerment** is committed where a person endangers the safety of the public while acting with an "utter disregard" for the consequences of his actions. This crime may—although the law is unclear—also apply to putting specific individuals in danger as opposed to the public at large.

The crime of **reckless supply of harmful substances** is committed where a person supplies harmful substances to a person knowing that the recipient will abuse the substance to the danger of their health. This crime may be viewed as a special form of reckless endangerment.

---

[10] 1983 S.L.T. (Sh. Ct) 37.
[11] 1977 J.Crim.L. 57.
[12] *Donaldson v Normand*, 1997 J.C. 200. *cf. Mallin v Clark*, 2002 S.L.T. 1202.
[13] 1984 J.C. 23.
[14] 1991 S.L.T. 614.
[15] 1996 J.C. 76.
[16] See above, para.14–19.

SEXUAL OFFENCES[17]

Rape[18]

14–30 Rape is generally considered to be the most serious of the sexual offences, although it should be observed that it is narrowly defined (being limited to penile-vaginal penetration of a woman by a man), and that other sexual offences can be equally harmful and degrading to the victim.

Actus reus

14–31 Until recently, the *actus reus* of rape was understood to be sexual intercourse by a man with a woman "against her will, and by force" (or threats of force).[19] The requirement of force meant that a sleeping or unconscious woman could not be raped (although to have sexual intercourse with a sleeping woman was the separate offence of clandestine injury).[20] Where a man plied a woman with drink or drugs in order to render her unconscious so that he could have sexual intercourse with her, that was treated as constructive force and, therefore, was rape despite the absence of direct force.[21]

However, this definition has recently changed. In a trial in March 2001, a student was acquitted of rape on the basis that the Crown had failed to lead sufficient evidence to prove that he had used force to overcome the victim's will. The resultant media outcry led to the Lord Advocate presenting a reference to the High Court for an authoritative ruling on the *actus reus* of rape. In the resultant decision, *Lord Advocate's Reference (No.1 of 2001)*,[22] it was held that the *actus reus* of rape "is constituted by the man having sexual intercourse without her consent".[23] Where the complainer is under the age of 12, or incapable of giving consent, the absence of consent will be presumed. Force is no longer required. This definition may in itself present problems, because the concept of "consent" is somewhat ambiguous. It has been suggested elsewhere that such problems could be addressed by adopting a statutory definition of consent.[24]

For the purposes of the law of rape, "sexual intercourse" is understood as meaning penetration of the vagina by the penis. Any other form of sexual intercourse cannot be rape, but may amount to indecent assault. In England, the crime of rape was extended in 1994 to include penile-anal penetration of either a man or a woman,[25] but no such extension has taken place in Scotland.

A consent to sexual intercourse may be rendered invalid by the fraud of the accused, but the extent of this rule is not clear. It is rape for a man to have sexual intercourse with a woman by impersonating her husband,[26] but it is not clear whether it would be rape if the consent was obtained by the impersonation of a man other than the woman's husband.[27] Although there is no direct Scottish authority, it appears that consent may be rendered invalid by a fraud as to the nature of the act (*e.g.* a claim that it is a medical procedure).[28]

---

17 See generally C.H.W. Gane, *Sexual Offences* (1992).

18 See generally Pamela R. Ferguson, "Controversial Aspects of the Law of Rape: An Anglo-Scottish Comparison" in *Justice and Crime* (R.F. Hunter ed., 1993), p.180.

19 Hume, *Commentaries*, i, p.302.

20 *Charles Sweenie* (1858) 3 Irv. 109.

21 *H.M. Advocate v Logan*, 1936 J.C. 100; *H.M. Advocate v Grainger and Rae*, 1932 J.C. 40.

22 2002 S.L.T. 466. For comment, see James Chalmers, "How (Not) To Reform the Law of Rape" (2002) 6 Edin.L.R. 398.

23 2002 S.L.T. 466, *per* the Lord Justice-General (Cullen) at 476. For an argument against defining rape in such terms, see Victor Tadros, "No Consent: A Historical Critique of the *Actus Reus* of Rape" (1999) 3 Edin.L.R. 317.

24 Home Office, *Setting the Boundaries: Reforming the Law on Sex Offences* (2000), para.2.10 *et seq.*

25 Criminal Justice and Public Order Act 1994, s.142.

26 Criminal Law (Consolidation) (Scotland) Act 1995, s.7(3), a statutory rule which dates from 1885 and which effectively overrules *William Fraser* (1847) Ark. 280.

27 *cf.* the English case of *Elbekkay* [1995] Crim.L.R. 163.

28 See the English cases of *R. v Case* (1850) 4 Cox CC 220; *R. v Flattery* (1877) 13 Cox CC 388.

Until relatively recently, it was thought (both in Scotland and in England) that a man could not be guilty of raping his wife. This is no longer the law.[29]

Mens rea

The *mens rea* of rape has been the subject of considerable controversy in recent years. In *Jamieson v H.M. Advocate*,[30] it was held that a man who has sexual intercourse with a woman in the honest belief that she is consenting is not guilty of rape, however unreasonable his belief may be. This followed the earlier (and highly controversial) English decision in *DPP v Morgan*.[31] **14–32**

Following *Jamieson*, it would appear that the *mens rea* of rape is present where the man (a) knows that the woman is not consenting or (b) is reckless as to whether she is consenting.[32] The "honest belief" rule has been the subject of much criticism,[33] and it may be that it will be reviewed by the courts at some point in the future.[34]

Indecent assault

Indecent assault "is not a specific crime, it is simply an assault accompanied by circumstances of indecency".[35] It is sometimes suggested that there is a distinction between indecent assault and assault, in that consent is specifically recognised as a defence to the former but not the latter.[36] However, an alternative approach is to say that this is simply a practical distinction rather than a technical one: consent may (although the law is not settled) be a defence to all assaults which do not involve injury, indecent or otherwise.[37] Conversely, it is unlikely that the Scottish courts would recognise consent as a defence to an indecent assault which did in fact involve the infliction of injury.[38] **14–33**

Key Concepts

Rape is committed by a man who has sexual intercourse with a woman who does not consent, provided that he (a) knows that she does not consent or (b) is reckless as to whether she is consenting.

A man who has an **honest belief** that the woman is consenting to sexual intercourse cannot be convicted of rape, however unreasonable his belief may be.

In Scots law, rape can only be committed by a man on a woman and is limited to penile-vaginal intercourse. Other forms of non-consensual sexual contact may be prosecuted as **indecent assault**, which is simply any assault in circumstances of indecency.

---

29 *S v H.M. Advocate*, 1989 S.L.T. 469 (also reported as *Stallard v H.M. Advocate*, 1989 S.C.C.R. 248). In England, see *R. v R* [1992] 1 A.C. 599.

30 1994 S.L.T. 537. See also *Meek v H.M. Advocate*, 1983 S.L.T. 280.

31 [1976] A.C. 182.

32 See also *Lord Advocate's Reference (No.1 of 2001)*, 2002 S.L.T. 466, *per* the Lord Justice-General (Cullen) at 476.

33 See C.H.W. Gane, *Sexual Offences* (1992), pp.40–45; Home Office, *Setting the Boundaries: Reforming the Law on Sex Offences* (2000), para.2.13 *et seq.*

34 *cf. Lord Advocate's Reference (No.1 of 2001)*, 2002 S.L.T. 466, *per* the Lord Justice-General (Cullen) at 476.

35 G.H. Gordon, *Criminal Law* (3rd ed., 2001, by M.G.A. Christie), Vol.II, p.406.

36 *Smart v H.M. Advocate*, 1975 J.C. 30.

37 For further discussion of this difficult point, see G.H. Gordon, "Consent in assault" (1976) 21 J.L.S.S. 168.

38 *cf. R. v Brown* [1994] 1 A.C. 212.

Incest and related offences

14–34 The Scots law governing incest and related offences is found in ss.1–3 of the Criminal Law (Consolidation) (Scotland) Act 1995.[39] These provisions create three separate offences, as follows:

- Incest (s.1) is committed by a person who has sexual intercourse with a close relative of the opposite sex. This covers sexual intercourse with ascendants, descendents, aunts, uncles, nieces and nephews. It does not, however, cover cousins or adoptive siblings.
- Intercourse with a step-child (s.2). This section provides that a "step-parent or former step-parent who has sexual intercourse with his or her step-child or former step-child shall be guilty of an offence if that step-child is either under the age of 21 or has at any time before attaining the age of 18 lived in the same household and been treated as a child of his or her family".
- Intercourse with a child under 16 by a person in a position of trust (s.3). This section provides that any person of 16 or over who has sexual intercourse with a child under 16, while being a member of the same household as that child, and who is "in a position of trust and authority in relation to that child" is guilty of an offence.

There are four specific defences, which must be proved by the accused on the balance of probabilities if they are to succeed. These are as follows:

- that he or she did not know and had no reason to suspect that they were related in this way (a defence to the s.1 and 2 offences);
- that he or she believed on reasonable grounds that the person with whom they had intercourse was over the relevant age (a defence to the s.2 or 3 offences);
- that he or she did not consent to have sexual intercourse or to have sexual intercourse with that person (a defence to all of the offences); and
- that he or she was validly married to that person (a defence to all of the offences).

It should be noted that all of these offences are limited to (heterosexual) "sexual intercourse". Although this term is not defined in the statute, it appears to be limited to penile-vaginal penetration. Sexual acts falling short of this between related persons may, however, amount to the common law crime of shameless indecency. See the case of *R v H.M. Advocate*,[40] which is discussed below.

Homosexual offences

14–35 Sexual acts between males were criminal at common law, either as sodomy (a crime which is restricted to anal intercourse), or as shameless indecency. It appears that sexual acts between women are not criminal at common law in Scotland, and the following discussion therefore relates only to male homosexual acts.

Although homosexuality was decriminalised in England and Wales in 1967,[41] following the recommendations of the Wolfenden Committee,[42] decriminalisation did not take place in Scotland until 1980.[43]

Initially, homosexual acts were decriminalised provided that they took place in private between two males over the age of 21 (commonly referred to as the "age of consent"). That age was reduced to 18 in 1994,[44] but was nevertheless two years higher than the age of consent for heterosexual intercourse. In 1997, the European Commission on Human Rights ruled that the

---

[39] These provisions derive from the Incest and Related Offences (Scotland) Act 1986, which repealed the Incest Act 1567. See Scottish Law Commission, *Report on the Law of Incest in Scotland* (Scot. Law. Com. No.69, 1981).

[40] 1988 S.C.C.R. 254.

[41] Sexual Offences Act 1967, s.1.

[42] *Report of the Committee on Homosexual Offences and Prostitution*, Cmnd. 247 (1957).

[43] Criminal Justice (Scotland) Act 1980, s.80.

[44] Criminal Justice and Public Order Act 1994, s.145.

differing ages of consent for heterosexual and homosexual intercourse in the UK violated Arts 8 (the right to privacy) and 14 (non-discrimination in the enjoyment of rights) of the European Convention on Human Rights.[45] The UK Government subsequently legislated to reduce the age of consent for homosexual intercourse to 16.[46]

Shamelessly indecent conduct

The crime of shameless indecency is based on a statement in Macdonald's *Criminal Law* to the effect that "all shamelessly indecent conduct is criminal".[47] That statement was judicially approved in the 1934 case of *McLaughlan v Boyd*,[48] but received relatively little judicial attention either before or after that case until the 1978 decision in *Watt v Annan*,[49] where the High Court relied on Macdonald's statement in order to hold that a man who had shown a "blue movie" to members of a private club in a hotel was guilty of an offence. **14–36**

The years following *Watt v Annan* saw an explosion in the use of shameless indecency charges, primarily against newsagents and others who sold publications which were considered "indecent or obscene".[50] The tide of such prosecutions appears to have been largely halted by the 1981 decision in *Dean v John Menzies (Holdings) Ltd*,[51] where it was held that a company could not be prosecuted for the offence.

In modern practice, the crime appears to be of importance in three contexts.[52] First, it covers what has been described as "corruption of public morals".[53] This can include the supply of indecent materials (although such prosecutions appear to be rare), the staging of indecent displays[54] and showing indecent material to children[55] (although simply failing to prevent them viewing such material will not suffice).[56] It appears that the *mens rea* required is an intention to corrupt or deprave the person(s) to whom the conduct is directed, or a knowledge that the conduct is liable to corrupt or deprave.[57]

The second form of shameless indecency is indecent exposure ("the exposure of those parts of the person that are usually concealed").[58] This form of the offence can be committed recklessly.[59]

Thirdly, it covers certain forms of sexual relations, as indicated by the decision in *R v H.M. Advocate*:

R. v H.M. Advocate

1988 S.L.T. 623

R was charged with shameless indecency. The Crown alleged that he had committed various sexual acts with his 16-year-old daughter, but did not allege either that the acts were non-consensual, or that they involved sexual penetration—which meant that they could not amount to either rape or incest. The sheriff held that the charge was relevant, and the jury convicted R. R appealed against his conviction to the High

---

45 *Sutherland v United Kingdom* [1998] E.H.R.L.R. 117.
46 Sexual Offences (Amendment) Act 2000, s.1(3).
47 Macdonald, *Criminal Law* (5th ed., 1948), p.150 (and the 1st ed., 1866, at p.202). For an extended criticism of this statement, see G.H. Gordon, *Criminal Law* (3rd ed., 2001, by M.G.A. Christie), Vol.II, p.536.
48 1934 J.C. 19.
49 1978 J.C. 84.
50 See, *e.g. Robertson v Smith*, 1980 J.C. 1; *Tudhope v Barlow*, 1981 S.L.T. (Sh. Ct) 94; *Ingram v Macari*, 1982 J.C. 1.
51 1981 J.C. 23.
52 See C.H.W. Gane, *Sexual Offences* (1992), p.143.
53 C.H.W. Gane, *Sexual Offences* (1992), p.146.
54 *Lockhart v Stephen*, 1987 S.C.C.R. 642 (Sh. Ct); *Geddes v Dickson*, 2000 S.C.C.R. 1007.
55 *Carmichael v Ashrif*, 1985 S.C.C.R. 461.
56 *Paterson v Lees*, 1999 J.C. 159.
57 *Geddes v Dickson*, 2001 J.C. 69.
58 G.H. Gordon, *Criminal Law* (3rd ed., 2001, by M.G.A. Christie), p.531.
59 *Usai v Russell*, 2000 S.C.C.R. 57.

Court, which upheld his conviction and approved the following five propositions of law which the sheriff had relied upon:

1. "It is a principle of the law of Scotland that all shamelessly indecent conduct is criminal."
2. "The scope of the offence is quite deliberately imprecise."
3. "The offence may be committed in private."
4. "The person against whom the conduct is directed may participate in or consent to or offer no objection to the conduct."
5. "It is not the indecency of the conduct which makes it criminal, but the quality of shamelessness."

It is not easy, following *R. v H.M. Advocate*, to know how it is to be decided whether certain forms of sexual conduct amount to shameless indecency. The closest that the *R* court comes to formulating a test is when it states that the conduct engaged in by *R* was regarded "at least as repugnant to society".[60] Following *R*, it has been held that it is shameless indecency for a man to have sexual intercourse with his foster daughter (*H.M. Advocate v K*).[61] This is despite the fact that the foster daughter was over 16 and would only have been prevented from marrying K by the law of bigamy. It has also been held to cover intercourse between a schoolteacher and a pupil on the basis that this involved a "breach of trust."[62] In the more recent case of *H.M. Advocate v Roose*,[63] however, Lord Marnoch declined to hold that the crime covered sexual intercourse by a 38-year-old man with a 13-year-old girl. (Normally, this would amount to the statutory offence of unlawful sexual intercourse, but prosecutions for this offence must be brought within a time limit of one year,[64] which had passed—which was why the Crown sought to rely on the offence of shameless indecency).

Key Concept

The offence of **shamelessly indecent conduct** covers three types of behaviour: firstly, "corruption of public morals"; secondly, indecent exposure and thirdly, certain forms of sexual relations which are regarded as repugnant to society.

"Corruption of public morals" covers exposing persons to indecent material. The *mens rea* required for this form of the offence is an intention to corrupt or deprave those persons, or at least knowledge that the material is likely to have that effect.

Miscellaneous sexual offences

14–37 The common law offence of lewd, indecent and libidinous practices criminalises sexual acts with children under the age of puberty (for boys, 14; and for girls, 12). There is also a statutory offence which covers such acts with girls between the ages of 12 and 16.[65] Physical contact with the child is not an essential element of the offence, which can be committed by performing sexual acts in the presence of a child.[66]

[60] *R. v H.M. Advocate*, 1988 S.L.T. 623, at 626.
[61] 1994 S.C.C.R. 499.
[62] *Batty v H.M. Advocate*, 1995 J.C. 160.
[63] 1999 S.C.C.R. 259. See J. Chalmers, "Is Underage Intercourse Shamelessly Indecent?", 2003 S.L.T. (News) 123.
[64] Criminal Law (Consolidation) (Scotland) Act 1995, s.5(4).
[65] Criminal Law (Consolidation) (Scotland) Act 1995, s.6.
[66] See generally G.H. Gordon, *Criminal Law* (3rd ed., 2001, by M.G.A. Christie), Vol.II, p.530.

There are a number of further miscellaneous statutory sexual offences which are consolidated in Pt I of the Criminal Law (Consolidation) (Scotland) Act 1995.[67] These include, first, the offence of sexual intercourse with a girl under 16.[68] It should be noted that there is no statutory offence of having sexual intercourse with a boy under the age of 16, and it appears that heterosexual intercourse with a boy under that age is not a criminal offence (although if the boy is under the age of 14, the offence of lewd, indecent and libidinous practices would be applicable). Secondly, the statute contains various offences relating to prostitution and brothel-keeping.[69] In this context, it should be noted that the actual *act* of prostitution (selling sexual intercourse for money) is not itself criminal. Instead, the statutory offences cover acts such as procuring women to act as prostitutes, running brothels and living off the earnings of prostitution.[70]

PROPERTY OFFENCES

Theft

Actus reus

The *actus reus* of theft may be defined as the "appropriation of property without the consent of the owner or custodier".[71] There are therefore three elements to the *actus reus*: **14–38**

(1) appropriation;
(2) of property which is capable of being stolen; and
(3) without the consent of the owner or custodier.

The concept of appropriation covers more than simply the physical removal of property (which Hume appeared to consider an essential part of the crime).[72] While such physical removal would certainly suffice, appropriation can take place by other means. It has been said that "appropriation involves conduct which without authorisation deprives the owner of one or more of those rights, for example possessory rights, which his ownership of the property in question would in the circumstances entail."[73] See the following case:

Carmichael v Black; Black v Carmichael
1992 S.L.T. 897

Black was charged with having committed theft by using "wheel clamps" to immobilise vehicles which had parked on his property in contravention of a warning notice intimating that he would take such action against anyone who parked there without authorisation (and would charge a fee of £45 for the removal of the clamps).

The High Court held that this was a valid charge of theft. The Lord Justice-General (Hope) said: "It seems to me that the act of depriving the motorist of the use of his motor car by detaining it against his will can accurately be described as stealing

67 See also the Sexual Offences (Amendment) Act 2000, s.3 (abuse of position of trust).
68 Criminal Law (Consolidation) (Scotland) Act 1995, s.5.
69 Criminal Law (Consolidation) (Scotland) Act 1995, ss.7–12.
70 This offence is restricted to male persons, but a female can be guilty art and part: *Reid v H.M. Advocate*, 1999 S.C.C.R. 19. It is thought, however, that a prostitute cannot herself (or himself) be guilty of this offence: see Sheriff Gordon's commentary to the S.C.C.R. report.
71 Macdonald, *Criminal Law* (5th ed., 1958), p.16, as interpreted in *Carmichael v Black; Black v Carmichael*, 1992 S.L.T. 897.
72 Hume, *Commentaries*, i, p.57.
73 G.H. Gordon, *Criminal Law* (3rd ed., 2001, by M.G.A. Christie), Vol.II, p.12. It follows that a non-owner who is lawfully in possession of property can subsequently steal it: see, *e.g. Elizabeth Anderson* (1858) 3 Irv. 65.

> something from him ... the physical element of appropriation is clearly present, in my opinion, since the purpose and effect of the wheel clamp was to immobilise the vehicle and use of it as a motor car."

Only "corporeal" (*i.e.* physical), moveable property can be stolen.[74] "Incorporeal" property (such as a legal right, or intellectual property), or "immoveable" property (land and buildings) cannot be stolen under Scots law.[75] However, if incorporeal property such as information is contained within a physical item (such as a document), that physical item is itself capable of being stolen, and if items which form part of land (such as potatoes in a field)[76] are removed from the land, then such property becomes treated as moveable property and can be stolen. As a matter of practice, Scots law regards electricity as property which is capable of being stolen.[77]

It is not theft if the property is appropriated with the consent of the owner. This probably applies even where the owner's consent has been obtained by fraud (and a charge of fraud, rather than theft, would therefore be appropriate in such a case).[78]

Conversely, if an item of property has *no* owner (as in the unusual case of wild animals), it cannot be the subject of theft.[79] The fact that property has been abandoned or lost, however, does not make it ownerless—Macdonald gives the example of taking property from a lost luggage store, which is clearly theft.[80] A person who appropriates abandoned property may, however, lack the *mens rea* required for theft, which is discussed below.

Mens rea

14–39 The *mens rea* of theft is based around an intention to deprive the owner of his property, but its exact scope is not at present entirely clear. It has always been clear that an intention to deprive the owner *permanently* is sufficient, but it appears that less than this may suffice in certain cases.

First, an intention to deprive *indefinitely* will also suffice—and so, in *Fowler v O'Brien*,[81] where the accused took the complainer's bicycle without his consent and abandoned it in a place where it was only found several days later, it was held that his intention to deprive the complainer "indefinitely" of his property was sufficient *mens rea*.

Secondly, an intention to deprive *temporarily for a nefarious purpose* is also sufficient. For example, it is theft to appropriate property for the purpose of extorting money from the owner. In *Kidston v Annan*,[82] the complainer had given a television set to the accused in order to get an estimate for repair work. The accused then repaired the television set without authorisation and refused to return it until his bill was paid. The court held that the accused was effectively holding the television set to ransom, and was therefore guilty of theft. It is not clear whether "nefarious purpose" is restricted to "criminal purposes" or can include other motives.[83]

Thirdly, it has recently been suggested that an intention to deprive *temporarily* will suffice for the *mens rea* of theft, even in the absence of a nefarious purpose.[84] If that is true, then it would be possible to describe the *mens rea* of theft as simply being an "intention to deprive", regardless of the purpose of the deprivation or whether it was intended as temporary or permanent. However,

---

[74] Under Scots law, property may be classified into corporeal and incorporeal property, and moveable and immovable property.

[75] As regards immoveable property, see G.H. Gordon, *Criminal Law* (3rd ed., 2001, by M.G.A. Christie), Vol.II, p.20. For incorporeal property, see *Grant v Allan*, 1987 J.C. 71.

[76] *Andrew Young*, (1800) Hume, i, p.79.

[77] G.H. Gordon, *Criminal Law* (3rd ed., 2001, by M.G.A. Christie), Vol.II, pp.18–19.

[78] For a review of the complex case law on this point, see G.H. Gordon, *Criminal Law* (3rd ed., 2001, by M.G.A. Christie), Vol.II, pp.38–43.

[79] *Valentine v Kennedy*, 1985 S.C.C.R. 89 (Sh. Ct).

[80] Macdonald, *Criminal Law* (5th ed., 1948), p.17.

[81] 1994 S.C.C.R. 112.

[82] 1984 S.L.T. 279.

[83] See *Milne v Tudhope*, 1981 J.C. 53, *per* the Lord Justice-Clerk (Wheatley) at 57.

[84] See *Carmichael v Black; Black v Carmichael*, 1992 S.L.T. 897, *per* the Lord Justice-General (Hope) at 901–902.

the cases in which this suggestion has been made have all been cases which did in fact involve a nefarious purpose, and it has been suggested that "it is open to doubt whether a bare intention to deprive temporarily will suffice."[85]

It is sometimes suggested that the accused's intention to deprive must be *dishonest*. This is supported by the decision of the High Court in the recent case of *Kane v Friel*,[86] where Kane was convicted of having stolen a quantity of metal piping and a sink unit which he claimed to have found lying behind a local shop. On appeal, it was held that the prosecution had to show that his appropriation of the property had been "dishonest", and because the prosecution had not proved that Kane "must have known that the items were property which someone intended to retain", he should not have been convicted of theft. The court's assumption that dishonesty is part of the *mens rea* of theft is, however, somewhat controversial, because it finds only very limited support in the earlier Scottish decisions.[87]

Key Concepts

The *actus reus* of **theft** is the appropriation of another person's property without their consent.

Appropriation is not limited to physically removing property from another's possession. It covers any act which deprives the owner of any of the rights associated with the ownership of property.

The *mens rea* of theft is an intention to deprive the owner of the property (a) permanently; (b) indefinitely or (c) temporarily for a nefarious purpose. It may be that a simple intention to deprive temporarily is sufficient, but the law is unsettled. From recent authority, it appears also that the intention must be **dishonest**.

Housebreaking

Scots law recognises a crime of "housebreaking with intent to steal". Housebreaking will frequently involve physically damaging the property in order to gain entry (in which case the accused is probably also guilty of the offences of malicious mischief or vandalism),[88] but any case where "the security of the building has been overcome" is considered housebreaking.[89] So, for example, it would be housebreaking to enter a building by using a stolen key, or picking a lock, or even—as in the case of *Rendal Courtney*[90]—coming into a house down the chimney! **14–40**

It should be noted that housebreaking is not in itself a criminal offence unless it is done with an intention to steal. For that reason, a charge of "housebreaking with intent to rape" was held irrelevant in *H.M. Advocate v Forbes*,[91] but the court in that case said that such actions could be charged as a breach of the peace, or possibly attempted rape.

It was observed in *Forbes* that the significance of the crime of housebreaking with intent to steal lies in the fact that attempted theft was not itself an indictable offence until 1887, and the crime therefore partially filled a gap left by the non-availability of a charge of attempted theft. Nowadays, most cases of housebreaking with intent to steal would also be cases of attempted theft, and the question of which charge to use is entirely at the discretion of the prosecutor.

---

85 G.H. Gordon, *Criminal Law* (3rd ed., 2001, by M.G.A. Christie), Vol.II, p.50.
86 1997 S.L.T. 1274.
87 But see *Mackenzie v Maclean*, 1981 S.L.T. (Sh. Ct) 40.
88 See below, paras 14–47 and 14–48.
89 Alison, *Principles of the Criminal Law of Scotland* (1832), p.282.
90 (1743) Hume i, p.99.
91 1994 S.L.T. 861. For comment, see Jenifer Ross, "Housebreaking with intent", 1994 S.L.T. (News) 315.

Embezzlement

14–41 The crime of embezzlement is closely related to theft. Indeed, because it is possible to commit theft of property which is already lawfully in one's possession, it has been said that the distinction between the two crimes is "rather technical than substantial".[92] The distinction between the two offences is not a sharp one and an act may amount to both offences.

If a person is lawfully in possession of the property of another, but is under an obligation to account for that property to the true owner, and he appropriates that property, this will amount to the *actus reus* of embezzlement.[93] Incorporeal property can be the subject of this crime (unlike the crime of theft), and so it was held in *Guild v Lees* that a club treasurer who had used the club cheque book to pay his electricity bill was guilty of embezzlement.[94] The court observed that this could not have been charged as theft, because the property which had been appropriated by the accused was incorporeal (it was technically part of a debt owed by the bank to the club) —but the charge of embezzlement was a valid one.

The *mens rea* of the offence is a dishonest intention to appropriate the property of another.[95]

Robbery

14–42 Robbery may be defined as "theft accomplished by means of personal violence or intimidation."[96] While in the normal case this will involve property being removed from the victim's person by force, this is not an essential element of the crime—and so, for example, it would be robbery to force someone to unlock a safe by threats of violence (assuming property was removed from the safe thereafter).[97]

The violence (or threats of violence) must have been used in order to obtain the property—and so, for example, it is not robbery if violence is used after the property has been appropriated; nor is it robbery if the violence has been used for some other purpose and the appropriation of property thereafter is merely opportunistic.[98] Such cases would be considered as separate offences of assault and theft.

Extortion

14–43 Extortion may be defined as an attempt "to enforce either legal or illegal demands by illegal means."[99] There are therefore two elements to the crime: (a) a demand; and (b) the illegal means which are used to back it up. The demand need not be for the payment of money—in *Rae v Donnelly*,[1] it was a demand that the complainer withdraw her claim for unfair dismissal which she was pursuing before an industrial tribunal.

The more difficult question is this: what constitutes "illegal means" for the purposes of this crime? The issue was explored in the following case:

---

92 *H.M. Advocate v Laing* (1891) 2 White 572, *per* Lord Kincairney at 576.
93 See Macdonald, *Criminal Law* (5th ed., 1948), p.45.
94 1994 S.L.T. 68.
95 *Allenby v H.M. Advocate*, 1938 J.C. 55.
96 *Cromar v H.M. Advocate*, 1987 S.C.C.R. 635, *per* Sheriff Pirie at 635. This statement appears to be a quote from Gordon's *Criminal Law*: see now G.H. Gordon, *Criminal Law* (3rd ed., 2001, by M.G.A. Christie), Vol.II, p.91.
97 See Alison, *Principles of the Criminal Law of Scotland* (1832), p.281.
98 *cf. James Templeton* (1871) 2 Coup. 140.
99 *Alex. F. Crawford* (1850) J. Shaw 309, *per* Lord Moncrieff at 329, cited with approval in *Carmichael v Black; Black v Carmichael*, 1992 S.L.T. 897, *per* the Lord Justice-General (Hope) at 900.
1 1982 S.C.C.R. 148.

Carmichael v Black; Black v Carmichael

1992 S.L.T. 897

Lord Justice-General (Hope): "In my opinion it is extortion to seek to enforce a legitimate debt by means which the law regards as illegitimate, just as it is extortion to seek by such means to obtain money or some other advantage to which the accused has no right at all. Furthermore, the only means which the law regards as legitimate to force a debtor to make payment of his debt are those provided by due legal process. To use due legal process, such as an action in a court of law or a right of lien or retention under contract, or to threaten to do so, is no doubt legitimate. It is not extortion if the debtor pays up as a result. But it is illegitimate to use other means, such as threats which are not related to the use of legal process, or the unauthorised detention of the debtor's person or his property, and it is extortion if the purpose in doing so is to obtain payment of the debt."

Fraud

The *actus reus* of fraud consists of three elements: (1) a false pretence; (2) a definite practical result; and (3) a causal link between the pretence and the result.[2] **14–44**

There is no limit to the type of action which may be a false pretence: obvious examples would include false claims as to one's identity, qualifications or status, or false claims as to the nature or quality of goods. False pretences may take more unusual forms, and so, for example, it was held in *Richards v H.M. Advocate*[3] that a statement of "present intention as to future conduct" could amount to a false pretence if in fact the actor had no such intention, while in *James Paton*[4] the false pretence consisted of puncturing and inflating with air the skins of bulls who were to be entered in a prize exhibition, and attaching artificial horns to their heads in order to give them a "better and more symmetrical appearance" so that their chances of winning prizes in the exhibition would be increased.

The fraud is not complete unless another party is deceived by it and therefore acts in a way which he would not otherwise have done (or refrains from doing something which he would otherwise have done). This represents the second and third elements of the *actus reus* which were identified earlier—the causal link and the definite practical result. It is not necessary that anyone should in fact be prejudiced or suffer loss in order for there to be a definite practical result, as the following case illustrates:

Adcock v Archibald

1925 J.C. 58

Two mine workers were convicted of fraud, in that they had tampered with pins on a coal-mining "hutch" so as to suggest that the coal contained therein had been mined by Adcock (instead of Wilson, another miner) and therefore induce their employers to pay Adcock for having mined the coal. However, the employers operated a minimum wage scheme, and because Adcock and Wilson had both mined less than the relevant amount of coal, they both received the minimum wage—meaning that they were both paid exactly the same amount as if the tampering had not taken place. On appeal, it was held that they had nevertheless been correctly convicted of fraud.

---

[2] *MacDonald v H.M. Advocate*, 1996 S.L.T. 723, *per* the Lord Justice-Clerk (Ross) at 726, approving a statement in Gordon's *Criminal Law*: see now G.H. Gordon, *Criminal Law* (3rd ed., 2001, by M.G.A. Christie), Vol.II, p.129.

[3] 1971 J.C. 29.

[4] (1858) 3 Irv. 208.

The Lord Justice-General (Clyde) observed that it would be "a mistake to suppose that to the commission of a fraud it is necessary to prove an actual gain by the accused, or an actual loss on the part of the person alleged to be defrauded. Any definite practical result achieved by the fraud is enough." The fact that the employers had calculated the miners' pay on the basis of false information seems to have been a sufficient "definite practical result".

It is essential that the definite practical result has been caused by the false pretence. So, in *Mather v H.M. Advocate*,[5] Mather was accused of committing fraud by writing a cheque which he knew would not be honoured in payment for nine cattle. It was held, however, that because Mather had obtained delivery of the cattle (the alleged result) *before* writing the cheque (the pretence), the "result" could not therefore be regarded as having been caused by the pretence, and Mather could not be convicted of fraud.

There are two elements to the *mens rea* of fraud. First, the actor must know that the pretence which he is making is a false one. It seems that recklessness as to the truth of a statement will not suffice for fraud.[6] Secondly, the actor must intend to deceive the victim and thereby achieve the "definite practical result".

Forgery and uttering as genuine

14–45 Under Scots law, a person who forges a document (assuming he does nothing with it) does not commit a criminal offence at common law (although there is a statutory offence of making counterfeit currency).[7] Forgery only becomes a criminal offence when the forgery is "uttered as genuine": that is, where the actor exposes the document to another person with the intention of deceiving that person and prejudicing someone thereby (usually, but not necessarily, the person whose name is forged).[8] The crime is complete when the document is exposed (or placed in the post to be delivered),[9] and it is not necessary to show either that the actor was successful in his deception or that any person was in fact prejudiced.[10]

The crime of uttering was probably of particular significance when attempted fraud was not itself an indictable crime.[11] Now that this is no longer the case, most cases of forgery and uttering will probably be attempted frauds, but there may be exceptional instances where this crime applies but attempted fraud does not.[12]

Reset

14–46 Reset has been defined as "the receiving and keeping of stolen goods, knowing them to be stolen, with the design of feloniously retaining them from the real owner."[13] By virtue of statute, it also applies to property appropriated by embezzlement or fraud,[14] but the following discussion will refer to "stolen goods" for the sake of clarity of expression.

The *actus reus* of the crime consists of "receiving and keeping" stolen goods. It is not essential that the actor receives the goods from the actual thief: they may have passed through the hands of others in the interim.[15] The actual thief cannot himself be guilty of reset.[16] It is not reset to acquire

5 (1914) 7 Adam 525.
6 *Mackenzie v Skeen*, 1971 J.C. 43.
7 Forgery and Counterfeiting Act 1981, s.14.
8 The requirements of the crime are set out in *John Smith* (1871) 2 Coup. 1, *per* the Lord Justice-General (Inglis) at 8–10.
9 *cf. William Jeffrey* (1842) 1 Broun 337.
10 *Macdonald v Tudhope*, 1984 S.L.T. 23.
11 Prior to the Criminal Procedure (Scotland) Act 1887, s.61.
12 See G.H. Gordon, *Criminal Law* (3rd ed., 2001, by M.G.A. Christie), Vol.II, para.18.35.
13 Alison, *Principles of the Criminal Law of Scotland* (1832), p.328.
14 Criminal Law (Consolidation) (Scotland) Act 1995, s.52.
15 Alison, *Principles of the Criminal Law of Scotland* (1832), p.329.

the proceeds of stolen property (so where goods are stolen and then sold for cash, it is not reset for a third party to take possession of the money).[17]

While it will normally be essential that a person takes possession of stolen goods in order to be guilty of reset, it has been that a person may also be guilty of reset by being "privy to the retention" of stolen property,[18] such as by allowing a thief to hide stolen goods in his house,[19] or accepting a ride in a stolen car.[20]

There are two elements to the *mens rea* of the crime: first, knowledge that the goods are stolen and secondly, an intention to keep them from the real owner (so that a person who intends to return the goods to the owner, or the police, cannot be guilty of reset). Where a person has "wilfully blinded" himself to the fact that goods are stolen, this wilful blindness may be regarded as equivalent to knowledge and therefore sufficient *mens rea* for the crime, as the following case demonstrates:

Latta v Herron

(1967) S.C.C.R. Supp. 18

Latta, a criminal lawyer, collected weapons. He was informed that a client had firearms for disposal and met the client in a Glasgow alleyway at 11pm at night to purchase them. They transpired to be stolen and he was charged with reset. He denied having known that they were stolen. It was held that even if his claim were true, he had "wilfully blinded himself to the obvious", and that this was sufficient *mens rea* for reset.

Key Concepts

A person is guilty of **embezzlement** if (a) he is lawfully in possession of property; (b) is under a duty to account to the true owner for that property, and (c) he intentionally appropriates the property.

Robbery is theft accomplished by means of personal violence or intimidation.

Extortion is an attempt to enforce either legal or illegal demands by illegal means.

The *actus reus* of **fraud** has three elements: (1) a false pretence; (2) a definite practical result; and (3) a causal link between the pretence and the result. The *mens rea* required is an intention to deceive the victim (knowing that the pretence is false) in order to achieve the definite practical result.

Forgery is not itself criminal under Scots law, but passing off a forgery as genuine is the offence of **uttering as genuine**.

Reset is the taking possession of (or being privy to the retention of) stolen goods with the intention of keeping them from the true owner.

---

16 *Druce v Friel*, 1994 S.L.T. 1209.

17 *cf. Helen Blair* (1848) Ark. 459.

18 Macdonald, *Criminal Law* (5th ed., 1948), p.67.

19 See *H.M. Advocate v Browne* (1903) 6 F.(J.) 24, *per* the Lord Justice-Clerk (Macdonald) at 26; Hume, *Commentaries*, i, p.113.

20 *McCawley v H.M. Advocate* (1959) S.C.C.R. Supp. 3.

Malicious mischief

14–47 Damaging—or possibly simply interfering with—the property of another person may amount to the offence of malicious mischief. It was formerly thought that the *actus reus* of this offence extended only to damaging or destroying property, but that view was rejected in the following case:

H.M. Advocate v Wilson

1984 S.L.T. 117

Wilson was charged with having committed malicious mischief by pressing an emergency stop button on a power station generator, causing the loss of £147,000 worth of electricity generation. He argued that the charge was irrelevant, in that it did not allege that there had been any physical damage to the property concerned. The High Court rejected the challenge, holding that interference with property which caused financial loss was sufficient for the *actus reus* of malicious mischief, even if there was no physical damage.

Interference with property which does not cause either damage to that property or financial loss is not malicious mischief.[21] Despite the term "malicious", the *mens rea* requirement is satisfied by either an intention to cause damage or financial loss, or recklessness as to the possibility of such damage being caused.[22] Nor is it essential that the accused had any "malicious purpose", provided that this basic *mens rea* requirement of intention or recklessness is met.[23]

Vandalism

14–48 Vandalism is a statutory offence under Scots law. Section 52 of the Criminal Law (Consolidation) (Scotland) Act 1995 provides that, "any person who, without reasonable excuse, wilfully or recklessly destroys or damages any property belonging to another shall be guilty of the offence of vandalism."[24] When this offence was introduced by statute in 1980, it was admitted by the then government that it added nothing new in substance to Scots law—because such acts would already amount to malicious mischief —but it was suggested that it was desirable to have a more specific and readily understood offence covering acts of vandalism.[25]

Fireraising

14–49 There are two separate offences of fireraising in Scotland: "wilful fireraising" and "culpable and reckless fireraising". Until very recently, it was thought that the distinction between the two crimes was that they applied to different types of property, and that the crime of "wilful fireraising" applied only to setting fire to houses, corn, coal workings and woods, all of which had been considered capital offences prior to 1887.[26] This had the curious result that intentionally setting fire to other types of property was occasionally charged as "culpable and reckless fireraising" despite it being quite clear that the accused's actions were deliberate.[27]

---

21 *Bett v Brown*, 1997 S.L.T. 1310.

22 *Ward v Robertson*, 1938 J.C. 32.

23 *Lord Advocate's Reference (No.1 of 2000)*, 2001 J.C. 143.

24 As to "reasonable excuse", see *McDougall v Ho*, 1985 S.C.C.R. 199 and *John v Donnelly*, 1999 J.C. 336.

25 See C.H.W. Gane and C.N. Stoddart, *A Casebook on Scottish Criminal Law* (3rd ed., W. Green, 2001), p.551.

26 Capital punishment for wilful fireraising was abolished by the Criminal Procedure (Scotland) Act 1887, s.56.

27 See *Wither v Adie*, 1986 S.L.T. (Sh. Ct) 32 (setting fire to a man's shoelaces).

This unsatisfactory state of affairs was remedied very recently by the Full Bench decision in *Byrne v H.M. Advocate*.[28] *Byrne* makes it clear that both offences can be committed in respect of any type of property—so the *actus reus* of each offence is simply setting fire to property.

The two offences are distinguished by their different *mens rea*: "wilful fireraising" is fireraising committed intentionally, and "culpable and reckless fireraising" is fireraising committed recklessly. Recklessness, in this context, means a "complete disregard for any dangers" which might result from one's actions.[29]

Key Concepts

The *actus reus* of **malicious mischief** is either (a) damaging the property of another or (b) interfering with the property so as to cause financial loss. The *mens rea* is an intention to cause damage or loss, or recklessness as to the possibility of damage or loss being caused.

A person who "without reasonable excuse, wilfully or recklessly destroys or damages any property belonging to another" is guilty of **vandalism**. There is a considerable overlap between this offence and malicious mischief.

There are two separate offences of fireraising in Scotland. Deliberately setting fire to property belonging to another is **wilful fireraising**; recklessly causing another's property to catch fire is **culpable and reckless fireraising**.

OFFENCES AGAINST PUBLIC ORDER

Breach of the peace[30]

Breach of the peace is a crime of extremely wide scope, and operates as something of a "catch-all" offence in Scots law. It is probably popularly thought to cover the sort of conduct which might be described as "drunk and disorderly". While it certainly does cover such activity, it can cover much more besides this. For example, breach of the peace charges have been held to cover "peeping tom" activities,[31] making indecent remarks to young boys in private,[32] and even inconsiderate driving.[33] **14–50**

Concern has been expressed for some time about the rather vague and wide nature of the offence, and in particular whether this is compatible with the European Convention on Human Rights. The issue was considered by the High Court in the following case:

Smith v Donnelly

2002 J.C. 65

Pamela Smith was convicted of having committed a breach of the peace by lying on the road in front of a naval base and disrupting traffic as a protest against nuclear weapons. She appealed against her conviction, arguing that the definition of the offence was so wide and unclear that "a citizen could not know with reasonable certainty what actions would breach criminal law", and that the offence was therefore

---

[28] 2000 J.C. 155. For comment, see James Chalmers, "Fireraising: from the ashes?" 2000 S.L.T. (News) 57.

[29] *Carr v H.M. Advocate*, 1994 J.C. 203; *Thomson v H.M. Advocate*, 1995 S.L.T. 827.

[30] See generally M.G.A. Christie, *Breach of the Peace* (1990).

[31] *Raffaelli v Heatly*, 1949 J.C. 101; *MacDougall v Dochree*, 1992 J.C. 154; *Bryce v Normand*, 1997 S.L.T. 1351.

[32] *Young v Heatly*, 1959 J.C. 66.

[33] *Horsburgh v Russell*, 1994 S.L.T. 942; *Austin v Fraser*, 1998 S.L.T. 106.

contrary to Art.7 of the European Convention on Human Rights, which prohibits retrospective criminal legislation and requires that the criminal law meets basic standards of clarity.

The court rejected Smith's challenge to her conviction. It was said that breach of the peace "is conduct which does present as genuinely alarming and disturbing, in its context, to any reasonable person." The law was sufficiently clear as to be compatible with the Convention.

The *Smith v Donnelly* court left open the question of whether certain charges of breach of the peace, such as that faced by Smith, might breach the right to freedom of expression which is guaranteed by Art.10 of the European Convention, as that point had not been argued in the appeal.[34]

Although it is clear from *Smith v Donnelly* that the *actus reus* of the crime is "conduct which does present as genuinely alarming and disturbing, in its context, to any reasonable person",[35] it is not clear what *mens rea* is required for the crime. It may be that it is sufficient to show that the actor should have known that his conduct presented a risk of alarm and disturbance.[36] It is difficult to envisage a case where the *actus reus* has been proven and yet it has not been proven that the accused should have known of this risk, which may explain why there has been very little discussion of *mens rea* in the reported cases on breach of the peace.

Mobbing

14–51 Where a group of people assemble for an illegal common purpose which causes public alarm, this may amount to the crime of mobbing.[37] The group must be of a reasonable size, although as few as eight persons has been held sufficient.[38] Charges of mobbing appear to be seldom used nowadays, and in the recent case of *Coleman v H.M. Advocate*, Lord Coulsfield suggested that "far from providing a simple means of dealing with cases of group violence, a charge of mobbing and rioting involves embarking on an area of law which is full of uncertainties and narrow distinctions."[39] For that reason, the prosecution may prefer to bring charges relating to the specific illegal actions of the mob, rather than rely upon the more generalised crime of mobbing.

Key Concepts

Breach of the peace may be defined as "conduct which does present as genuinely alarming and disturbing, in its context, to any reasonable person".

Where a group of people assemble for an illegal common purpose which causes public alarm, this may amount to the crime of **mobbing**.

---

[34] See further, Pamela R. Ferguson, "Breach of the peace and the European Convention on Human Rights" (2001) 5 Edin.L.R. 145.

[35] *Smith v Donnelly*, 2002 J.C. 65, *per* Lord Coulsfield at 71.

[36] *cf. Hughes v Crowe*, 1993 S.C.C.R. 320.

[37] See generally Scottish Law Commission, *Mobbing and Rioting* (Consultative Memorandum 60, 1984).

[38] *Hancock v H.M. Advocate*, 1981 J.C. 74.

[39] 1999 S.L.T. 1261, at 1272.

OFFENCES AGAINST JUSTICE

Attempting to pervert the course of justice

Attempting to pervert the course of justice is arguably simply a catch-all term for a variety of different offences such as perjury, but in recent years it appears to have become recognised as a crime in its own right.[40] It covers such actions as knowingly making a false statement to the police,[41] escaping from lawful custody,[42] and intimidating witnesses.[43] Wasting the time of the police by falsely reporting a crime is also a criminal offence,[44] although this is generally treated as a specific crime in its own right rather than as an attempt to pervert the course of justice. **14–52**

Perjury

A witness in a trial—criminal or civil—who gives false evidence is liable to prosecution for perjury. The *mens rea* required is knowledge of the falsity of the statement. It is sufficient, however, that the witness makes a statement which he does not know to be true, even if he does not actually know that it is false.[45] It is not necessary to show that the false evidence had any effect on the outcome of the trial.[46] A person charged with a crime who gives false evidence in his own defence is guilty of perjury, although a prosecution would be unusual in such a case.[47] Inducing a person to give false evidence amounts to the crime of subornation of perjury.[48] **14–53**

Contempt of court

Contempt of court takes two forms: first, contempt "in the face of the court" and secondly, the publication of material likely to be prejudicial to court proceedings. It is not, strictly speaking, a criminal offence, but because it is punishable as if it were a crime, it has been suggested that it "may be regarded as virtually a crime".[49] **14–54**

Contempt in the face of the court can take various forms, such as a failure to appear in court when required, refusing to answer questions, "prevaricating", which in general terms means being evasive in response to questions, or offensive conduct in court (such as conduct which disrupts proceedings).[50]

Contempt by the publication of prejudicial material is now largely governed by the Contempt of Court Act 1981. It is a contempt to publish material "which creates a substantial risk that the course of justice in the proceedings will be seriously impeded or prejudiced."[51] Liability for this form of contempt is strict: there is no need to prove any intention to interfere with the course of justice.[52]

---

[40] For a full discussion, see G.H. Gordon, *Criminal Law* (3rd ed., 2000, by M.G.A. Christie), Vol.I, pp.29–35.
[41] *Watson v H.M. Advocate*, 1993 S.C.C.R. 875.
[42] *H.M. Advocate v Martin*, 1956 J.C. 1.
[43] *Dalton v H.M. Advocate*, 1951 J.C. 76.
[44] *Kerr v Hill*, 1936 J.C. 71; *Gray v Morrison*, 1954 J.C. 31.
[45] *Simpson v Tudhope*, 1988 S.L.T. 297.
[46] *Lord Advocate's Reference (No.1 of 1985)*, 1986 J.C. 137.
[47] *H.M. Advocate v Cairns*, 1967 J.C. 37; *Milne v H.M. Advocate*, 1996 S.L.T. 775.
[48] See Hume, *Commentaries*, i, pp.381–383.
[49] G.H. Gordon, *Criminal Law* (3rd ed., 2001 by M.G.A. Christie), Vol.II, p.749.
[50] See generally C.H.W. Gane and C.N. Stoddart, *A Casebook on Scottish Criminal Law* (3rd ed., W. Green, 2001) pp.598–606.
[51] Contempt of Court Act 1981, s.2(2).
[52] Contempt of Court Act 1981, s.1.

INCHOATE OFFENCES[53]

14–55 A person—or group of persons—may form a criminal purpose, but not complete it. Such a purpose may remain "inchoate", or "incomplete" for any number of reasons. The actor may, for example, have tried but failed to fulfil the purpose, changed his mind before completing the scheme, or been prevented from doing so by the police or a third party.

In such circumstances, there may be good reasons for holding that the actor is criminally liable even though the offence has not been "completed". It would clearly be absurd if the police were unable to intervene to prevent a person committing a crime, or were able to intervene but unable to charge them with any offence.

Consequently, Scots law recognises three forms of "inchoate offences": incitement, conspiracy and attempt. It should be noted that these are not crimes in themselves, but are perhaps best understood as modified forms of the complete offence. For example, the inchoate forms of murder are "incitement to murder", "conspiracy to murder" and "attempted murder". It would, strictly speaking, be wrong to simply speak of someone as being guilty of "incitement", "attempt" or "conspiracy".

Incitement

14–56 A person will be guilty of incitement if it can be shown that he "reached and sought to influence the mind of [another] person towards the commission of a crime".[54] It is irrelevant whether or not the crime is in fact ever carried out.

Conspiracy

14–57 A conspiracy consists of two or more persons agreeing to commit an act which would be criminal if done by a single individual.[55] The conspiracy is complete when the agreement is made, and it is not necessary to show that any action was taken in furtherance of the conspiracy.[56]

Attempt

14–58 There is explicit statutory provision to the effect that any attempt to commit a crime is itself criminal.[57] Identifying the *actus reus* of an attempted crime may prove difficult. It must be shown that the accused has "got beyond the stage of preparation into the stage of perpetration".[58] This test—the application of which is a question of fact rather than law—can be rather broad in its application. In *H.M. Advocate v Camerons*,[59] a husband and wife planned to defraud insurers by staging a fake robbery. It was proven that they had staged the robbery, and that they had reported the theft to their insurance broker—but it was not proven that they had actually made a claim. Nevertheless, the jury convicted them of attempted fraud.

It is often assumed that "attempt" implies an intention to commit the completed crime—and as a matter of the English language, that may well be correct. However, under Scots law, where a person acts with the *mens rea* which is required for the completed crime, this will provide sufficient *mens rea* for guilt of the attempted crime. The point is illustrated by the following case:

[53] See generally, S. Christie, *Inchoate Crimes* (W. Green, 2001).
[54] *Baxter v H.M. Advocate*, 1998 J.C. 219, *per* the Lord Justice-General (Rodger) at 221.
[55] Macdonald, *Criminal Law* (5th ed., 1948), p.185. See also *Maxwell v H.M. Advocate*, 1980 J.C. 40, *per* Lord Cameron at 43.
[56] See G.H. Gordon, *Criminal Law* (3rd ed., 2000, by M.G.A. Christie), Vol.I, pp.234–235.
[57] Criminal Procedure (Scotland) Act 1995, s.294.
[58] *H.M. Advocate v Camerons*, 1911 S.C.(J) 110, *per* the Lord Justice-General (Dunedin) at 115.
[59] 1911 S.C.(J) 110.

Cawthorne v H.M. Advocate
1968 J.C. 32

Cawthorne was charged with attempted murder, in that he had shot repeatedly at four persons through a locked door. At the trial, Cawthorne's counsel argued that he could only be found guilty of attempted murder if it was proved that he had intended to kill. This argument was rejected by both the trial judge and the appeal court. The Lord Justice-General (Clyde) observed that "attempted murder is just the same as murder in the eyes of our law, but for the one vital distinction, that the killing has not been brought off and the victim of the attack has escaped with his life. But there must be in each case the same *mens rea*, and that *mens rea* in each case can be proved by evidence of a deliberate intention to kill or by such recklessness as to show that the accused was regardless of the consequences of his act whatever they may have been."

Impossibility and inchoate offences

Is it a criminal offence to attempt something which is in fact impossible? There was formerly some confusion in Scots law on this point, because while it had been held in two cases that there could be no crime of attempted abortion where the woman was not actually pregnant,[60] it had been held in another case that it was attempted theft for a man to try and pick an empty pocket.[61] **14–59**

The position was settled by a Full Bench in *Docherty v Brown*.[62] In that case, Docherty was charged with attempting to possess a controlled drug with intent to supply. Although he believed that the tablets in his possession were a controlled drug (MDMA, or "ecstasy"), they were in fact laxatives.[63] The court held that the impossibility of what he was trying to do was no defence to the charge, and that the cases which held that there was no crime of attempted abortion where the woman was not pregnant had been wrongly decided.

Although *factually* impossible attempts are criminal, *legally* impossible attempts are not. So, if Docherty had known that the tablets in his possession were laxatives, but wrongly thought that it was a criminal offence to sell laxatives, he could not have been convicted of any offence.

The courts have taken the same view of impossibility with regard to conspiracy,[64] and it is thought that the same approach would be taken with regard to incitement if the issue were to arise.

Key Concepts

Scots law recognises three **inchoate** (incomplete) forms of offences: **incitement**, **conspiracy** and **attempt**. These are not offences in themselves, but incomplete forms of other offences.

Incitement consists of attempting to influence another person towards the commission of a crime.

Conspiracy is an agreement by two or more persons to commit a crime.

60 *H.M. Advocate v Anderson*, 1928 J.C. 1; *H.M. Advocate v Semple*, 1937 S.L.T. 48.
61 *Lamont v Strathern*, 1933 J.C. 33.
62 1996 J.C. 48. For comment, see David Sheldon, "Impossible attempts and other oxymorons" (1997) 1 Edin.L.R. 250.
63 A fact which does not appear in the law reports, but was reported in the press: "Accused faces jail over rave laxatives", *The Scotsman*, March 21, 1996.
64 *Maxwell and Others v H.M. Advocate*, 1980 J.C. 40.

An **attempt** is committed by a person who has moved from preparation to the stage of perpetrating a crime but does not complete the offence. The *mens rea* requirement is the same as for the completed offence.

It is no defence to a charge of an inchoate offence that the accused was trying to do something which was **impossible**.

ART AND PART LIABILITY

14–60 Where two or more persons participate in carrying out a crime, they are all equally guilty of the offence. (There may, of course, be differences in their culpability or level of involvement, which can be reflected in sentencing). Lord Patrick explained the concept in the following case:

H.M. Advocate v Lappen

1956 S.L.T. 109

Lord Patrick: "To illustrate this doctrine of the law ... if a number of men form a common plan whereby some are to commit the actual seizure of the property, and some according to the plan are to keep watch, and some according to the plan are to help to carry away the loot, and some according to the plan are to help to dispose of the loot, then, although the actual robbery may only have been committed by one or two of them, every one is guilty of the robbery, because they joined together in a common plan to commit the robbery."

Art and part is a doctrine by which persons who participate in a criminal enterprise may be held liable for the complete offence even though they did not personally execute every part of the enterprise. It is not a crime in itself, but simply a doctrine by which persons may be held guilty of existing criminal offences.

Two conditions must be satisfied for a person to be held guilty of a crime art and part. First, a common purpose must be proven. In *H.M. Advocate v Welsh and McLachlan*,[65] two men were charged with theft by housebreaking and murdering the occupant of the house. Because it could not be shown which of the men had killed the occupant, and it could not be shown that the men had agreed to use lethal violence as part of the housebreaking, it followed that neither could be convicted of murder.

Secondly, a person must participate in the criminal enterprise in order to be guilty art and part. In *H.M. Advocate v Kerr*,[66] it was held that an allegation that a man had stood behind a hedge and watched a rape without intervening or calling for assistance could not be sufficient to find him guilty of the rape art and part. The situation would be different where a person was under a legal duty to intervene, such as a policeman who fails to prevent a junior officer assaulting a suspect.[67]

Key Concept

A person may be guilty of a crime **art and part** if, even though he did not carry out every part of the crime himself, he had (a) a **common purpose** with another person or persons and (b) **participated** in the commission of the crime.

[65] (1897) 5 S.L.T. 137.
[66] (1871) 2 Coup. 334.
[67] *Bonar and Hogg v McLeod*, 1983 S.C.C.R. 161.

GENERAL DEFENCES

As was noted earlier, we tend in ordinary language to refer to anything which might result in an accused's acquittal as being a "defence". This would include simple denials of *actus reus* or *mens rea* (*i.e.* claims that the accused did not actually commit the prohibited act, or did not do so with a legally culpable state of mind). This section, however, is concerned with defences in the sense of a justification or excuse which the accused offers for his conduct. Scots law recognises a number of "general defences". These are "general" in the sense that they are not specific to particular crimes. **14–61**

Mental abnormality

Insanity

The concept of insanity figures in Scots criminal law in two different ways which must be carefully distinguished, particularly because "insanity" has a different meaning in each context. **14–62**

First, insanity may be a plea in bar of trial. This is on the basis that it would be inappropriate to subject a person to a criminal trial if they are not able to properly participate in that process. The important question here is a person's condition at the time of the proposed trial—not at the time of the alleged offence. Of course, if their condition subsequently improves, then a trial may take place at a later date. In this context, insanity means a mental disorder which "prevents a man from doing what a truly sane man would do and is entitled to do—maintain in sole sanity his plea of innocence, and instruct those who defend him as a truly sane man would do."[68] If the plea succeeds, an "examination of facts" may be held. The accused cannot be convicted at this hearing—the most that can happen is that the court can make a finding that he "did the act or made the omission constituting the offence"[69]—but he can be acquitted, which would preclude him being tried for the offence at a future date.

Secondly, where a person is fit to stand trial, they may plead as a defence that they were insane at the time the offence is alleged to have been committed.[70] The question of whether the accused was insane is one of fact. It is not a medical decision, but "is to be judged on the ordinary rules on which men act in daily life."[71] In *Brennan v H.M. Advocate*, it was said that "insanity in our law requires proof of total alienation of reason in relation to the act charged as the result of mental illness, mental disease or defect or unsoundness of mind".[72] This is the test which would be applied by the courts today.

Insanity must be proven by the accused on the balance of probabilities, which is an exception to the rule that the burden of proof is normally on the prosecution in a criminal trial.[73] At the time of writing, the possible reform of the defence was under consideration by the Scottish Law Commission.

Automatism

As has been seen, the defence of insanity applies where there is a "total alienation of reason" caused by mental illness. What is the situation where a person suffers a total alienation of reason due to an external factor such as a drug? The leading case is *Ross v H.M. Advocate*: **14–63**

---

68 *H.M. Advocate v Brown* (1907) 5 Adam 312, *per* the Lord Justice-General (Dunedin) at 343.
69 Criminal Procedure (Scotland) Act 1995, s.55.
70 See generally Victor Tadros, "Insanity and the capacity for criminal responsibility" (2001) 5 Edin.L.R. 325.
71 *H.M. Advocate v Kidd*, 1960 J.C. 61, *per* Lord Strachan at 70.
72 1977 J.C. 38 at 45.
73 See *Lindsay v H.M. Advocate*, 1997 J.C. 19.

Ross v H.M. Advocate

1991 J.C. 210

Ross was drinking lager from a can which, unknown to him, had been "spiked" with temazepam and LSD. Within about half an hour, he proceeded to lunge about with a knife, severely stabbing a number of people. He was convicted of a number of counts of assault. On appeal, he argued that he should be acquitted of the charges on the basis that his involuntary intoxication meant that he was not responsible for his actions. The court, in quashing his convictions, held that where an actor has suffered a total alienation of reason—and thus lacks *mens rea*—he should be acquitted, provided that this was the result of an external factor which he was not bound to foresee.

Because a total alienation of reason is required, it is not sufficient for a person to say only that their drink was spiked and that they did something which they would not have done sober. So, in *Cardle v Mulrainey*,[74] the accused had attempted to steal a number of cars after drinking a can of lager spiked with amphetamine. He later admitted that he had known what he was doing but did not know why. It was held that, because he had understood what he was doing, the requirement of a total alienation of reason had not been satisfied and the defence could not apply.

The requirement that the total alienation of reason be caused by an external factor which the accused was not bound to foresee means that a person who takes a drug or other substance knowing that it will or is likely to have this sort of effect is not entitled to plead the defence.[75] Such cases are regarded as examples of voluntary intoxication, which is discussed immediately below.

Voluntary intoxication

14–64 It is commonly said that self-induced intoxication is no defence to a criminal charge in Scots law. The leading case is *Brennan v H.M. Advocate*:

Brennan v H.M. Advocate

1977 J.C. 38

Brennan drank between 20 and 25 pints of beer, a glass of sherry and took a microdot of LSD. Later that day, he had an argument with his father which resulted in him stabbing his father to death. He argued that his extreme intoxication provided a defence, either because (a) he should be regarded as temporarily insane or (b) it showed that he did not have the *mens rea* required for murder. The court rejected this argument, holding that (a) a plea of insanity could not be based upon the transient effects of self-induced intoxication and (b) Brennan's actions in getting wholly intoxicated could demonstrate in themselves the criminal recklessness which is sufficient *mens rea* for the crime of murder.

Brennan appears to leave open the question of crimes which require intention or knowledge as *mens rea*. Should a person who lacks the relevant intention or knowledge for criminal guilt because of their own self-induced intoxication therefore be acquitted? The answer appears to be a clear no. In the subsequent case of *Ross v H.M. Advocate*, the Lord Justice-General (Hope) stated that where a condition "which has resulted in the absence of *mens rea* is self-induced … the accused must be assumed to have intended the natural consequences of his act".[76] Evidence of self-induced intoxication may, therefore, either suffice in itself to show *mens rea*, or—if it excludes

[74] 1992 S.L.T. 1152.
[75] See *Ebsworth v H.M. Advocate*, 1992 S.L.T. 1161; *Finegan v Heywood*, 2000 J.C. 444.
[76] 1991 J.C. 210, at 214. See also *Donaldson v Normand*, 1997 J.C. 200.

mens rea—will result in a presumption of *mens rea* being applied. Either way, it will not result in an acquittal.

Involuntary intoxication, by contrast, may provide the basis for a defence of automatism, as discussed earlier.[77]

> **Key Concepts**
>
> A person is entitled to the defence of **insanity** if, at the time of committing the act, they were suffering from a "total alienation of reason ... as the result of mental illness, mental disease or defect or unsoundness of mind". The test is a legal and not a medical one.
>
> The defence of **automatism** applies where an accused was suffering from a total alienation of reason caused by an external factor which they were not bound to foresee.
>
> **Voluntary intoxication** is not a defence under Scots law.

External threats and compulsion

Self-defence (or private defence)

A person who acts in order to protect themselves (or a third party) from a violent attack may be entitled to plead self-defence. The requirements for the defence are set out in the following case: **14–65**

H.M. Advocate v Doherty

1954 J.C. 1

Lord Keith: "First of all, there must be imminent danger to the life or limb of the accused, to the person putting forward this defence; there must be imminent danger to his life and limb; and, secondly, the retaliation that he uses in the face of this danger must be necessary for his own safety. Those are two fundamental things you will keep in mind, that there is imminent danger to life and limb and that the retaliation used is necessary for the safety of the man threatened ... Again, if the person assaulted has means of escape or retreat, he is bound to use them."

Although Lord Keith refers to "imminent danger to the life or limb of the accused", it is clear that the defence is equally applicable where the accused has acted in defence of a third party.[78] For this reason, some writers prefer to describe the defence as "private defence" rather than "self-defence", but the latter is the term which is normally used in Scots law.

It can be seen from *Doherty* that there are three requirements for the defence, as follows:

(1) There must be imminent danger to life or limb. A mistaken belief as to such danger will suffice to found the defence, but the mistake must be based on reasonable grounds.[79]

---

[77] See above, para.14–63.

[78] *H.M. Advocate v Carson*, 1964 S.L.T. 21; *Moss v Howdle*, 1997 J.C. 123 at 128–129.

[79] *Owens v H.M. Advocate*, 1946 J.C. 119; *Jones v H.M. Advocate*, 1990 J.C. 160. See, however, Fiona Leverick, "Mistake in self-defence after *Drury*" 2002 J.R. 35.

(2) The force used by the actor must be necessary in the circumstances. This means that it is never permissible to use lethal force in response to an attack which does not place the actor at risk of death, with the exception that a woman may use lethal force to prevent a rape.[80] In general terms, the actor's response must be proportionate to the attack, but it is commonly said that this is not a matter which should be "weighed in too fine scales"—allowance must be made for the fact that the accused acted out of fear and in the heat of the moment.[81] A person who kills using excessive force may be entitled to the partial defence of provocation if the requirements of that defence are met.[82]

(3) There must have been no means of escape or retreat available to the actor. Such means of course, must be reasonable.[83] For example, a person cannot be required to opt for a means of escape (such as leaping out of an upstairs window) which would in itself expose him to serious risk of injury.

Coercion

14–66 A person who is forced to commit a criminal offence by threats may plead the defence of coercion.

Thomson v H.M. Advocate

1983 S.L.T. 682

The High Court recognised that a defence of coercion could be available where the following factors were present:

(1) Threats of death or serious injury against the accused or a third party. The threats must be of present and not future injury.

(2) The threats must be "of such a nature as to overcome the resolution of an ordinarily constituted person of the same age and sex as the accused."

The reason for requiring that the threats be of present and not future injury is that a person threatened with injury at some point in the future is expected to seek assistance from the police or other appropriate authorities and not to comply with the demands which the threats accompany.

Coercion is probably not available as a defence to a charge of murder.[84] A person who knowingly exposes himself to the risk of being coerced—such as a person who associates with a gang or similar organisation which is known to carry out violent crime—will not be entitled to plead the defence.[85]

Necessity

14–67 In circumstances of emergency, a person may feel that it is necessary to break the criminal law in order to prevent a "greater evil" occurring. In such a case, that person may be entitled to plead the defence of necessity. For some time, it was not clear whether and to what extent the defence was recognised by Scots law, but doubts on this matter were settled by the 1997 decision in *Moss v Howdle*.[86] From that case and subsequent decisions, it is clear that there are three requirements for the defence to succeed:

---

[80] *cf. McCluskey v H.M. Advocate*, 1959 J.C. 39.
[81] See *H.M. Advocate v Doherty*, 1954 J.C. 1, *per* Lord Keith at 4–5.
[82] See above, para.14–17.
[83] *McBrearty v H.M. Advocate*, 1999 S.L.T. 1333.
[84] See *Collins v H.M. Advocate*, 1991 S.C.C.R. 898, *per* Lord Allanbridge at 902.
[85] See the English case of *R. v Sharp* [1987] 3 W.L.R. 1.
[86] 1997 J.C. 123. For comment, see Michael Christie, "The mother of invention?" (1997) 1 Edin.L.R. 479.

(1) There must be an immediate danger to life or of serious injury. So, in *Ruxton v Lang*,[87] the accused drove off in fear of a knife attack despite having drunk too much alcohol to lawfully drive. She was stopped by the police two miles away. It was held that while her initial actions might have been justified by necessity, the "immediate danger" had passed well before she had driven two miles and that the defence was therefore unavailable.

(2) The circumstances must have constrained the actor to break the law. If there is a "legal way out", it must be taken. In *Moss v Howdle*, the accused argued that he had broken the speed limit out of necessity because his passenger had shouted out in pain and he wanted to get to a service station area quickly. It was held that, because the prudent course of action would have been to pull over to the side of the road and ascertain what the problem was, Moss's actions in breaking the speed limit could not be regarded as justified by necessity.

(3) The actor must have broken the law *because of* the circumstances of necessity. If he would have acted in the same way regardless of those circumstances, the defence will be unavailable.[88]

There is no Scottish authority on whether necessity can ever be a defence to murder, but the English courts have ruled that it is unavailable in such cases.[89]

Key Concepts

A person may plead **self-defence** if, in circumstances of immediate danger, where there is no reasonable means of retreat available, they use reasonable force to defend themselves or a third party.

The defence of **coercion** is available where a person is forced to commit a criminal offence by threats of death or serious injury against that person or a third party, provided that an ordinary person would also have given in to the threats.

The defence of **necessity** is available where a person commits a criminal offence in order to avoid a greater harm occurring, provided that there was immediate danger to life and limb and that there was no "way out" other than committing the offence.

---

[87] 1998 S.C.C.R. 1 (Sh. Ct).

[88] *Dawson v McKay*, 1999 S.L.T. 1328.

[89] *R. v Dudley and Stephens* (1884) 14 QBD 273. But *cf. Re A (Children)* [2001] 2 W.L.R. 480.

Quick Quiz

General principles of criminal liability

- What are the elements of a criminal offence?
- In what circumstances does the law impose criminal liability for an omission to act?

Homicide

- What is the definition of murder?
- What are the various types of culpable homicide recognised by Scots law? How are these defined?
- What partial defences to murder are recognised by Scots law? How are these defined?

Assault

- It is said that "evil intention is of the essence of assault"—but what does this mean?
- Can you assault a person without physically touching them under Scots law?

Sexual offences

- What is the definition of rape?
- What are the other principal sexual offences recognised by Scots law?

Property offences

- How is theft defined?
- What types of property can be stolen under Scots law?
- Can embezzlement be clearly distinguished from theft?
- What is the meaning of a "definite practical result" in the offence of fraud?
- Is forgery a crime under Scots law?
- What criminal offences exist to protect the physical integrity of property?

Inchoate offences

- What inchoate offences are recognised by Scots law?
- Can it be a crime to attempt the impossible?

Defences

- How are the defences of insanity and automatism differentiated from each other?
- Is voluntary intoxication a defence to a criminal charge?
- What are the requirements for the defence of self-defence?
- What are the differences between the defence of necessity and the defence of coercion?

Further Reading

The leading textbook on the criminal law of Scotland is **Gerald H. Gordon's *Criminal Law***, which is now regularly referred to by the courts. The first edition of this book was published in 1967, and a third edition (edited by Michael G.A. Christie) was published in two volumes in 2000 and 2001.

While "Gordon" is a standard—and extremely detailed—reference work, students approaching the subject for the first time would be well advised to consult a more concise introduction, such as **Jones and Christie, *Criminal Law*** (3rd ed., 2003), or **McCall Smith and Sheldon**, ***Scots Criminal Law*** (2nd ed., 1997). **Clare Connelly, *Criminal Law*Basics** (2002) is a very brief introduction to the subject and a useful revision guide.

C.H.W. Gane and C.N. Stoddart, *A Casebook on Scottish Criminal Law* (3rd ed., W. Green, 2001) contains extracts from leading cases and statutory materials, accompanied by detailed commentary. It can be used as a supplement to a more traditional textbook or as a standalone text on the subject.

The Scottish courts will frequently make reference to older works on Scottish criminal law which are considered (to varying degrees) to be authoritative. The leading work here is **(Baron) David Hume's *Commentaries on the Law of Scotland, Respecting Crimes*** (4th ed. with Bell's Notes, 1844). **(Sir) Archibald Alison's *Principles of the Criminal Law of Scotland*** (1832) and **Macdonald's *Criminal Law*** (5th ed., 1948) are also frequently referred to, but do not have the same high standing as Hume.

Appendix 1

STUDY, REVISION AND EXAMINATIONS

James Chalmers[1]

LECTURES AND TUTORIALS

Most undergraduate law courses are taught by a combination of lectures and tutorials. (Advanced, or "honours" courses are often taught by way of seminars, which are broadly similar to tutorials but are often longer and require more in the way of preparation.)

Why bother attending lectures?

Most universities do not enforce attendance at lectures. For that reason, it can often be tempting to skip lectures (particularly those at 9am in the morning!) and to obtain lecture notes from other students later. It is, however, always preferable to attend lectures yourself and take your own notes. Not only is it often difficult to make sense of another student's notes, there is some benefit to be gained simply from listening to the points being made—a benefit which you will not get from photocopying someone else's notes and then frantically trying to decipher them on the eve of the exam. If you do have to miss lectures, it is normally a good idea to write up your own set of notes for the part of the course you missed, based on a combination of another student's notes, the course handout, and a relevant textbook.

Should I read in advance of lectures?

Many course handouts will include suggested reading for the topics which are to be covered in lectures. Sometimes, depending on the size of the class, you may even be questioned on this material. While it can often be difficult to find time to read relevant material in advance of lectures, you may find that this makes the lecture easier to follow and understand.

[1] Lecturer in Law, University of Aberdeen.

What is the purpose of tutorials?

Tutorials generally provide an opportunity to discuss specific legal problems in small groups. You should not treat these as a note-taking exercise; there is nothing more frustrating for a tutor than being surrounded by a group of students who are all scribbling down notes and saying as little as possible. Apart from this, you are unlikely to benefit from taking detailed notes in a tutorial, which is normally much more loosely structured than a lecture. Instead, tutorials provide an opportunity to develop your skills in identifying the issues which arise in legal problems and constructing arguments for and against particular positions—exactly the sort of skills which you will be expected to demonstrate in the exam. The only effective way to develop these skills is by participating.

EXAMINATIONS

Revising for examinations

How should I revise?

There is no single method of revising for law exams, and you will have to try and find a method which works for you personally. One important point is that most (although not all) students find it difficult to revise effectively simply by reading and re-reading their notes and other material.

You may find it helpful to rewrite your lecture notes as a means of revision. If you do this, you should read your notes alongside a relevant textbook and other materials such as case reports in order to add in further relevant material to your notes and to make sure that your notes do not contain any errors. You should not rely solely on your lecture notes when revising, but should treat them as a statement of the bare minimum of knowledge required for the course, and seek out other sources such as textbooks, articles and cases—but make sure you are comfortable that you understand the basics of a subject before grappling with more complex material.

Once you have a complete set of notes, you may find it helpful to condense these into a set of "summary" notes and key points—but again, this is a technique which works for some students and not for others.

When you come to read over your lecture notes, or read textbooks and other material, you may find that you have difficulty in getting to grips with aspects of the course. There is a lot to be said for discussing those points with other students, and you may find it helpful to study in a group, something which works for some students and not for others. Equally, you should not hesitate to approach your lecturers or tutors to ask for clarification where you find yourself in difficulty.

You may find it helpful in your revision to make use of exam papers from previous years, and to practice writing answers to past questions, or simply testing yourself on whether you can identify the relevant issues which would have to be dealt with in an answer.

Why do students fail exams?

The blunt answer is that most students who fail exams do so because they do not know enough about the subject which is being examined. Revision and examination technique plays an important part, however. If you do fail an exam, and you are unsure as to why this has happened, you should not hesitate to ask the examiner for feedback on your exam paper.

Do I have to know all the cases?

Most law courses will cover a considerable number of cases, except sometimes in areas which are largely codified in statute. The idea of remembering over two hundred cases for an exam can, for obvious reasons, be somewhat daunting. For that reason, students commonly ask whether it is really necessary to know *all* the cases that are covered in a course.

The best answer that can be given, unfortunately, is "yes". Few students will ever remember every single relevant case, but that is unlikely to create serious problems in an exam. However, if you only aim to learn (say) half the cases covered in a course, then not only do you have the problem of deciding which half, you will inevitably not remember all of those, and many of them will turn out to be irrelevant to the issues which come up in the exam.

It may help to remember that you are *not* being tested on your ability to remember the facts of cases. Instead, you are being asked to use cases as authority for the legal rules which you will refer to in an exam. Many of the cases which you will learn can be summarised in as little as one sentence for this purpose, and you should concentrate on learning those key points. By contrast, you will not receive any credit for being able to conjure up irrelevant facts from the cases in your exam answer. And contrary to a common myth, you do not need to memorise case citations for exam purposes, nor should you attempt to!

Do I have to know all the course?

In revising, many students select particular parts of the course which they think are likely to come up in the exam and revise only those parts of the course. Such students fail exams with remarkable regularity. "Question-spotting" in this way is often disastrous.

If there is a small part of a course which you have real difficulty with compared to the rest of the course, then there may be something to be said for writing that part off as a "lost cause" and concentrating on revising the rest of the course instead. But even that is only a realistic option if you know that the exam will offer you a choice of questions. If the exam includes compulsory questions, or only has a very limited choice of questions, then this is a very high-risk strategy indeed. You should make absolutely sure that you know *exactly* what format the exam paper will take before you make any decisions of this sort.

Sitting examinations

Make sure that you know the answers to the following questions in advance of the exam:

- When and where is the exam?
- How long does it last?
- What materials (such as statute books), if any, can be taken into the exam?

You should not feel that you have to start writing as soon as the exam starts. Instead, take time to read the exam paper and decide which questions you are going to answer (assuming you have a choice of questions). Many students find it helpful to scribble down notes of key points and important cases—either on the exam paper itself or at the start of the exam book—before starting to write an answer. Before you start to write an answer, you should have a good idea of what issues you intend to cover in your answer and the order in which you intend to address them. Again, you may find it helpful to write these down in note form before starting. Once you have finished writing the answer, go back and look at those notes to check that you have not missed out any of the points you identified.

You should make sure that you have a watch (or perhaps a small clock) with you so that you can keep track of time during the exam. (Do not rely on the clock of a mobile phone, as many universities ban any use of mobile phones during examinations.) Make sure that you know roughly how much time you have for each answer, and try not to overrun in answering the first few questions. If you do run out of time towards the end of the exam, then it is a good idea to use the last few minutes of the exam to make a list of the points (and cases) which you intended to cover if you had not run out of time, and you will at least receive some credit for this (assuming the points are relevant!)

If you have time left at the end of the exam, you should use this to re-read your answers, correcting any errors which you notice and adding in any additional points which occur to you. (You should always make sure that you leave enough space between answers to allow for points to be added later—you will normally be required to start each new answer on a fresh page in any case).

If you make a mistake in an exam and want to correct it, simply score the offending portion of what you have already written. Using correcting fluid is a waste of your time—which, in an exam, is precious—and will not improve your mark.

Questions in law exams tend to take two forms: problem questions and essay questions. The next section of this chapter considers each of these in turn.

Answering problem questions

The following is an example of a problem question, taken from a criminal law examination:

> Archie goes into the Post Office, armed with what is obviously a bright green plastic water-pistol. He expects to find his sister behind the counter, and without looking presents it at the counter-clerk and says: "Hands up – your money or your life". Unfortunately, it is not his sister behind the counter but Benny, a young man of extremely nervous disposition. Benny faints, banging his head on the counter as he falls. Colin, a customer in the post office, taking advantage of what has happened, jumps over the counter, opens the cash-register, and helps himself to £150. As he is running out of the post office, he thrusts two £20 notes into Archie's hands, saying "Thanks mate, I couldn't have managed it better if we had planned it." Archie, realising that there is no-one else around, takes the money and walks out of the post office. He later uses the money to buy flowers for the injured Benny.
>
> Discuss the criminal liability (if any) of Archie and Colin.

In answering this question, like most problem questions, you need to do four things. The first thing is to identify the relevant *issues*. In this example, you would have to identify the crimes which *might* have been committed by Archie and Colin (most obviously, assault, theft and reset). Secondly, you should identify the relevant *rules*: in other words, how are these crimes defined? Thirdly, you should *apply* those rules to the facts you have been given; and fourthly, you should reach a *conclusion*. This structure (Issue, Rule, Application, Conclusion), which is somewhat mechanistically taught in many US law schools, can be referred to as IRAC for short.

Most importantly, you should remember that it is often the conclusion which matters least in answering a problem question. Often, there will be no right answer—perhaps because the law is unclear, or because you simply do not have enough factual information to come to a definite conclusion. The most important thing is to identify the legal rules which apply to the problem with which you are faced. You may well have to say that you are not certain what conclusion would be reached by the courts, or that you would need to know more facts before coming to a conclusion. There is nothing wrong with that (and indeed, you would receive credit for being able to specify the additional facts you would need to know).

You should always provide authority for the rules which you refer to in your answer. Usually that authority will be cases to which you have been referred during the course, or (depending on the subject) your authority may also be a statute, or perhaps an authoritative legal textbook. For example, part of the answer to the question quoted above might read as follows:

> The *actus reus* of an assault is "an attack upon the person of another" (Macdonald's *Criminal Law*), which can include threatening gestures which put a person in fear of injury (*Atkinson v HM Advocate*). The *mens rea* required is "evil intent" (Macdonald; *Smart v HM Advocate*). If the accused had the intention to cause injury or fear of injury, it is no defence that his actions were intended as a "joke" (*Lord Advocate's Reference (No. 2 of 1992)*).

Answering essay questions

Essay questions in law exams may simply ask you to write "short notes" on a number of legal topics. This in itself is fairly straightforward, and will normally require you to summarise a topic in a similar manner to the way in which it was covered in lectures. You must remember, of course, to back up your answers by reference to relevant authority.

In more lengthy essay questions, there is often a temptation simply to "throw back" at the examiner all the material which was covered in lectures on the topic in question. That is, generally, a bad idea. Before you start writing, you should identify the issues which you feel need to be addressed in the essay. The focus of your essay should be on those issues, and you should use cases and statutory material to back them up, rather than jumping immediately into a discussion of the cases and statutes themselves. An essay which has a logical structure to it will read much better than a haphazard listing of all the relevant cases and statutes, and will receive a much better mark.

"Open book" examinations

In some exams, you may be allowed to take in relevant reference material such as statute books. More unusually, you may be allowed to take in your own notes, or even relevant textbooks.

Many students tend to assume that open book exams are easier than their "closed book" counterparts and require less revision. This is a myth. Many lecturers find that the standard of answers produced in open book exams is no better (and sometimes even worse) than the standard of answers produced in closed book exams.

Unless you know your textbook or notes very well indeed, you will simply not have sufficient time to search through them in the exam for the "right answer". If you don't understand the subject in the first place, a two-hour examination is not the best place to start learning it!

- *Make sure you know the structure of the book in advance.* This will minimise the amount of time you spend searching through the book when you refer to it. Of course, the more you have used the book during your revision, the easier this will be.

- *You should not be referring constantly to the book (or books).* In an open book exam, you should normally only be referring to the textbook occasionally to check points that you are unsure of.

- *Don't feel that you **have** to refer to the book.* If you know the subject well enough, there may well be no reason to refer to the book at all during the exam. There is absolutely nothing wrong with this.

- *Don't simply copy out from the book.* Apart from the fact that this is unlikely to produce a relevant answer to the question which you have been asked, this is plagiarism and can have serious consequences. If you do want to quote from the book, make sure that you put the quote in quotation marks and make the source clear.

Multiple choice tests

Multiple choice (or "objective") tests are not commonly used for law courses in United Kingdom universities, although it is not unknown for courses in US law schools to be graded entirely on the basis of such exams. Nevertheless, such tests are used to a limited extent, perhaps contributing up to a quarter of the final mark for a course. Given that they are less time-consuming to mark than "traditional" exams or essays, they may become more common as a way of reducing the inevitable marking load on lecturers which results from increased student numbers.

While you will probably want to revise for a multiple choice test in the same way as you would for a "normal" exam, you should bear the following points in mind when it comes to taking the test:

- *Make sure you know how the exam is graded.* In particular, do marks get *deducted* for wrong answers? If so, you should be careful about guessing where you do not know the answer or have serious doubts, and it may be better to not answer such questions. But if no marks are deducted for wrong answers, there is nothing to be lost by guessing on the answer to questions you are unsure about.

- *Read the questions carefully.* It is very easy to skim through the question, misunderstand it, and select an answer which may be right for the question that you *think* you have been asked, but which is wrong for the question you have *actually* been asked.

- *Consider every possible answer.* There will normally be more than one possible answer which "looks right" for each question. Rather than just picking the first answer you see which looks correct, you should consider each of the answers and be able to satisfy yourself that you are sure they are incorrect. You may find that this makes you revise your first impressions!

- *Don't rush.* Find out in advance how much time you have available in the exam and how many questions you have to answer. Most (but not all) multiple choice tests are not speed tests! You will probably be able to answer some questions very quickly; you may find it easier to leave any questions which you are unsure about and come back to them when you have completed the rest of the paper.

Appendix 2

SAMPLE EXAM QUESTION AND ANSWER

James Chalmers[1]

In her will, Wilhelmina Fergusson left money for a bursary fund for prospective philosophy students at Aberdeen University. Her will directed that the bursaries should be restricted to "young girls of the parish of Clatt". Despite the income of the bursary being sufficient to fund five students annually, only two applications have been received in the past ten years despite extensive advertising. Advise the trustees as to whether they can take any steps to open up the bursary fund to a wider class of applicants.

Suggested answer

Opening up the fund to a wider class of applicants would involve a variation of the trust purposes. The first question, therefore, is whether this trust is public or private, because the legal rules governing variation are different depending on the type of trust.

Here, the trust is for the benefit of a section of the public rather than for specified individuals, and so the trust is a public one. There are therefore two possible means of variation: first, the common law *cy-près* jurisdiction, or variation under s.9(1) of the Law Reform (Miscellaneous Provisions) (Scotland) Act 1990. Each of these routes may be considered in turn.

To consider *cy-près* first of all: it appears that the trust has, at least initially, been given effect to, and therefore it is not necessary to establish a "general charitable intention" on Ms Fergusson's part in order for *cy-près* to operate. It is only necessary to show impossibility. Generally, the courts will not consider a difficulty in giving effect to the trust purposes to amount to impossibility (*Scotstown Moor Children's Camp*), and it would be difficult to argue that the fact that the funds exceed what is currently required for the trust purposes means that it is impossible to give effect to those purposes.

A better approach, therefore, would be to look to the 1990 Act. That statute permits variation where "the purposes of the trust provide a use for only part of the property available under the trust", which seems clearly applicable here. Another attraction of this approach is that if the trust is a small one (with an annual income of under £5,000), the trustees may be able to vary the trust purposes without taking a court action, provided they follow procedures laid down in statute and regulation. This could represent a considerable financial saving to the trust.

It appears, therefore, that grounds for variation are clearly made out. The question then becomes one of what sort of variation should be sought. The varied purposes must be as close as possible to the original purposes (the "principle of approximation"). Widening the class of beneficiaries, as the trustees seem to wish, is acceptable (see, *e.g.*, *Trs of Carnegie Park Orphanage*). There are various possibilities here: perhaps opening the bursary up to a wider range of subjects, to additional universities, to male students, to a wider geographical area, or some combination of those options.

[1] Lecturer in Law, University of Aberdeen.

INDEX